Renaissance Theory

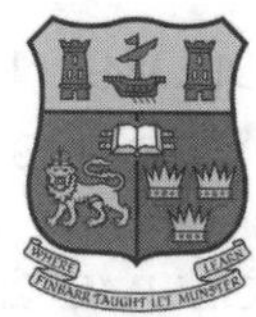

University College Cork
Coláiste na hOllscoile Corcaigh

Volume 5 in The Art Seminar series, *Renaissance Theory* presents an animated conversation among art historians about the optimal ways of conceptualizing Renaissance art, and the links between Renaissance art and contemporary art and theory. This is the first discussion of its kind, involving not only questions within Renaissance scholarship, but issues of concern to art historians and critics in all fields. Organized as a virtual roundtable discussion, the contributors discuss rifts and disagreements about how to understand the Renaissance and debate the principal texts and authors of the last 30 years who have sought to reconceptualize the period. They then turn to the issue of the relation between modern art and the Renaissance: why do modern art historians and critics so seldom refer to the Renaissance? Is the Renaissance our indispensable heritage, or are we cut off from it by the revolution of modernism?

The volume includes an introduction by Rebecca Zorach and two final, synoptic essays, as well as contributions from some of the most prominent thinkers on Renaissance art, including Stephen J. Campbell, Michael Cole, Fredrika Jacobs, Claire Farago, and Ethan Matt Kavaler.

James Elkins is E.C. Chadbourne Chair in the Department of Art History, Theory, and Criticism at the School of the Art Institute of Chicago, and Head of History of Art at the University College Cork, Ireland. His many books include *Pictures and Tears*, *How to Use Your Eyes*, and *What Painting Is*, all published by Routledge.

Robert Williams is Professor of Art History at the University of California, Santa Barbara. His fields of specialty are Italian Renaissance art and the history of art theory. He is the author of *Art, Theory, and Culture in Sixteenth-Century Italy* (Cambridge, 1997) and *Art Theory: An Historical Introduction* (Blackwell, 2004).

The Art Seminar

VOLUME 1
ART HISTORY VERSUS AESTHETICS

VOLUME 2
PHOTOGRAPHY THEORY

VOLUME 3
IS ART HISTORY GLOBAL?

VOLUME 4
THE STATE OF ART CRITICISM

VOLUME 5
RENAISSANCE THEORY

VOLUME 6
LANDSCAPE THEORY

VOLUME 7
RE-ENCHANTMENT

Sponsored by the University College Cork, Ireland; the Burren College of Art, Ballyvaughan, Ireland; and the School of the Art Institute, Chicago.

Renaissance Theory

EDITED BY

JAMES ELKINS and ROBERT WILLIAMS

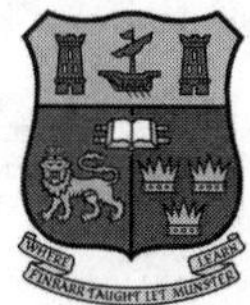

University College Cork
Coláiste na hOllscoile Corcaigh

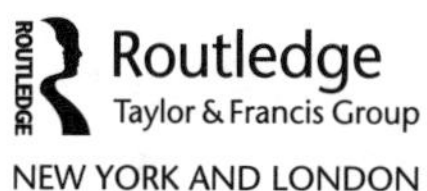

Routledge
Taylor & Francis Group

NEW YORK AND LONDON

First published 2008
by Routledge
270 Madison Ave, New York, NY 10016

Simultaneously published in the UK
by Routledge
2 Park Square, Milton Park, Abingdon, Oxon OX14 4RN

Routledge is an imprint of the Taylor & Francis Group, an informa business

© 2008 Taylor and Francis Group

Typeset in ACaslon-Regular by Swales & Willis Ltd, Exeter, Devon
Printed and bound in the United States of America on acid-free paper by
Edwards Brothers, Inc., Lillington, NC

Library of Congress Cataloging in Publication Data
Renaissance theory / edited by James Elkins and Robert Williams.—1st ed.
    p. cm.   (The art seminar; v. 5)
  Includes bibliographical references and index.
  1. Art, Renaissance.   2. Art—Philosophy.   I. Elkins, James, 1955–   .   II. Williams, Robert, 1955–
N6370.R39 2008
709.02′4—dc22   2007037830

ISBN10: 0–415–96045–2 (hbk)
ISBN10: 0–415–96046–0 (pbk)
ISBN10: 0–203–92986–1 (ebk)

ISBN13: 978–0–415–96045–8 (hbk)
ISBN13: 978–0–415–96046–5 (pbk)
ISBN10: 978–0–203–92986–5 (ebk)

TABLE OF CONTENTS

SERIES PREFACE

James Elkins

It has been said and said that there is too much theorizing in the visual arts. Contemporary writing seems like a trackless thicket, tangled with unanswered questions. Yet it is not a wilderness; in fact it is well-posted with signs and directions. Want to find Lacan? Read him through Macey, Silverman, Borch-Jakobsen, Žižek, Nancy, Leclaire, Derrida, Laplanche, Lecercle, or even Klossowski, but not—so it might be said—through Abraham, Miller, Pontalis, Rosaloto, Safouan, Roudinesco, Schneiderman, or Mounin, and of course never through Dalí.

People who would rather avoid problems of interpretation, at least in their more difficult forms, have sometimes hoped that "theory" would prove to be a passing fad. A simple test shows that is not the case. The table, below, shows the number of art historical essays that have terms like "psychoanalysis" as keywords, according to the *Bibliography of the History of Art*. The increase is steep after 1980, and in three cases—the gaze, psychoanalysis, and feminism—the rise is exponential.

Another sampling shows that citations of some of the more influential art historians of the mid-twentieth century, writers who came before the current proliferation of theories, are waning:

In this second graph there is a slight rise in the number of

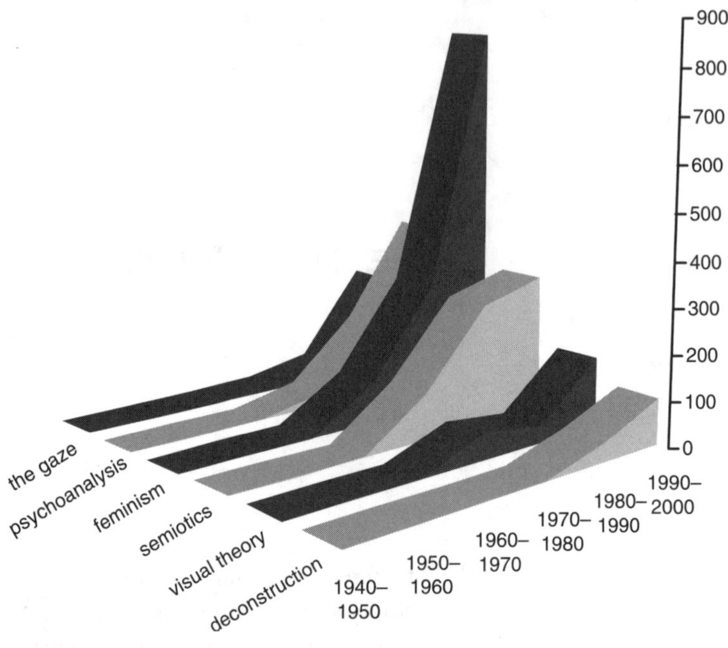

Figure 1   Theory in art history, 1940–2000.

references to Warburg and Riegl, reflecting the interest they have had for the current generation of art historians: but the graph's surprise is the precipitous decline in citations of Panofsky and Gombrich.

Most of art history is not driven by named theories or individual historians, and these graphs are also limited by the terms that can be meaningfully searched in the *Bibliography of the History of Art*. Even so, the graphs suggest that the landscape of interpretive strategies is changing rapidly. Many subjects crucial to the interpretation of art are too new, ill-theorized, or unfocused to be addressed in monographs or textbooks. The purpose of *The Art Seminar* is to address some of the most challenging subjects in current writing on art: those that are not unencompassably large (such as the state of painting), or not yet adequately posed (such as the space between the aesthetic and the anti-aesthetic), or so well known that they can be written up in critical dictionaries (the theory of deconstruction). The subjects

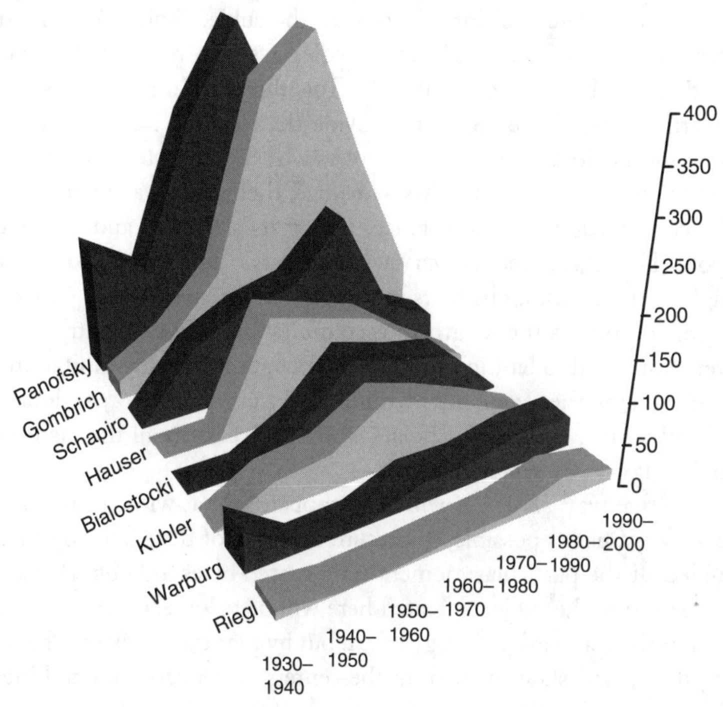

Figure 2 Rise and fall of an older art history, 1930–2000: citations of selected writers.

chosen for *The Art Seminar* are poised, ready to be articulated and argued.

Each volume in the series began as a roundtable conversation, held in front of an audience at one of the three sponsoring institutions—the University College Cork, the Burren College of Art (both in Ireland), and the School of the Art Institute of Chicago. The conversations were then transcribed, and edited by the participants. The idea was to edit in such a way as to minimize the correctable faults of grammar, repetitions, and lapses that mark any conversation, while preserving the momentary disagreements, confusions, and dead-ends that could be attributed to the articulation of the subject itself.

In each volume of *The Art Seminar*, the conversation itself is preceded by a general introduction to the subject and one or more "Starting Points," previously published essays that were distributed to participants before the roundtable. Together the Introductions and "Starting Points" are meant to provide the essential background for the conversation. A number of scholars who did not attend the events were then asked to write "Assessments"; their brief was to consider the conversation from a distance, noting its strengths and its blind spots. The "Assessments" vary widely in style and length: some are highly structured, and others are impressionistic; some are under a page, and others the length of a commissioned essay. Contributors were just asked to let their form fit their content, with no limitations. Each volume then concludes with one or more "Afterwords," longer critical essays written by scholars who had access to all the material including the "Assessments."

In that way *The Art Seminar* attempts to cast as wide, as fine, and as strong a net as possible, to capture the limit of theorizing on each subject at the particular moment represented by each book. Perhaps in the future the subjects treated here will be colonized, and become part of the standard pedagogy of art: but by that time they may be on the downward slide, away from the centers of conversation and into the history of disciplines.

1
Introduction

Renaissance Theory: A Selective Introduction

Rebecca Zorach

Does Renaissance Theory mean anything more than "theories about the Renaissance," on the one hand, or "art theory in the Renaissance" on the other? In this introduction, as is also true of the essays and conversations that follow, I propose to deal to some degree with both. And yet, is there something that connects the Renaissance more deeply to the very notion of "theory"—at least as we mean it today, in the early twenty-first century, following the age of "high theory" in American academia? If I might try to define high theory, I would call it the emergence of the European post-68, post-structuralist critique of the European philosophical tradition in the new context of the United States, a culture both exuberantly capitalistic and anti-intellectual—and one that had partially, but only partially, absorbed that tradition in the first place.

The specificity of Renaissance art history with respect to these issues might derive from the twin facts that in the mid-twentieth century, it was one of the most important sites of the partial absorption of the philosophical tradition; and in the later twentieth century it was one of the sites most resistant to the critique. Resistance, here as elsewhere, came in the form of appeals to tradition, standards, ideals, values, and meaningfulness (against the perceived nihilism and theoretical overdetermination of poststructuralist approaches). It also came in the form of an appeal to the empirical, an insistence that "something really did change"—that is, Art Was Revolutionized—in the Renaissance. Those who embraced the critique did not necessarily argue that nothing had changed in the Renaissance. But was the change a discovery or an ideology, an achivement or an imposition? The origins of naturalism, or of colonial oppression? The origins of the *modern*, pro or con?

In David Lodge's novel *Small World*, the protagonist, in a fit of contrariety—provoked by the suggestion that his work is a purely mechanical mapping of influence—misrepresents his thesis on T. S. Eliot's borrowings from Shakespeare as its reverse: a study of Eliot's *influence on* Shakespeare.[1] In doing so, in a sense, he encapsulates something that is also a problem for Renaissance art history: the Renaissance is a taken-for-granted canonical point of origin, but our understanding of it is deeply colored by modernism. The influence of modernist values upon our understanding of *Renaissance* art, I think, has even outlived their hegemony in the art of the present.

I've posed these issues starkly here, perhaps overdramatically; most of the answers you will find in this volume—in position papers and the Art Seminar round table and responses—are more complex and nuanced. My introduction to these texts and their themes will be admittedly idiosyncratic—an argument for positions of my own, even while I try to do justice to those of others. I will begin by presenting a picture of the place of the Renaissance in the discipline of art history at large, and address major themes in current approaches to the field. I'll then address the influence of modernism on our readings of the Renaissance, suggesting ways in which Renaissance art history might have taken an alternate route. Finally I discuss how we define what "theory" and "art" mean in a Renaissance context, suggesting some alternatives to our current habits.

One thing I must confess: I will use the term Renaissance as if it means something that we all understand. In this respect at least I defer to the discussions that follow; I will not here attempt to establish whether or not there ever was such a thing.

Renaissance art now!

Until recently Renaissance art was the focal point—or the significant counterpoint—of nearly every major art historical methods to arise since the origins of the discipline in the late nineteenth century. When graduate students in art history take classes in methods and/or historiography, most likely they will encounter authors whose primary engagement was with Renaissance art. The historiography class that I took as a student, for example, presented such approaches to the Renaissance as cultural history (Burckhardt), stylistic analysis (Wölfflin), connoisseurship (Morelli, Berenson), Aby Warburg (a methodology unto himself), iconology (Panofsky and other German emigres influenced by Warburg); and social history of art (Michael Baxandall). Some of the most prominent intellects in our field have engaged with the Renaissance. But while many interesting things are still going on in Renaissance art history, and while the Renaissance still has popular appeal (even if it now comes via novels like *The Da Vinci Code*), the center of gravity of art history as a discipline has shifted elsewhere. Perhaps this might be an opportunity for the field—a chance to speak, paradoxically, from the margins.

From a distance, it sometimes seems that the Renaissance carries no other content than an assertion that change happens: the *idea* of the Renaissance often appears as a paradigm for historical change that can be mobilized to support the values (optimistic, pessimistic, or otherwise) any particular writer seeks to propound. Such a picture does not reflect the creative and passionate work one can see in the field on closer inspection. Newer approaches to Renaissance art struggle to be heard, however, because for many in the discipline who *don't* study the Renaissance, the field—when noticed at all—serves the sole function of holding down a traditionalist pole in art history, a place of origins, the canon. Art history departments in colleges and universities have shifted to include more non-western areas—a much-needed shift, but one perhaps not accompanied by a critical enough reflection on the field. Departments have also created positions in twentieth- and, now, twenty-first-century art. Pre-modern western art history, in many cases, has often been pared down to one or two positions per department, even at major universities.[2]

Is the field, then, in disarray—as the discussion in the Seminar suggests—and if so, is that a bad thing? Two of the recent approaches that have had the most impact, as will become clear in the Seminar, drew on both post-structuralism and the social history of art, belonging in different ways to the legacy of "high theory." I'm referring to feminism and post-colonial studies.[3] In this volume they are represented most directly by Fredrika Jacobs and Claire Farago respectively, but their impact is implicit in much of the discussion. Feminist art historians have brought to the fore not only the history of women artists but also issues of the gendered gaze, masculinity, and the gendering of basic cultural and artistic concepts; feminism also in large part opened the way to questions of the erotic, of non-normative gender (the "virile woman"), and of sexual orientation, and served as inspiration to queer approaches to art history. As John Elliott argued of the European encounter with the Americas in the early modern period, postcolonial approaches have, perhaps, had a more "blunted" impact in art history than feminism has had.[4] Perhaps this is simply demographics. To Latin Americanists the need to have a grasp of European art history is obvious; only gradually have Europeanists begun admitting the reverse and allowing for global issues to affect the way we do business. As Lubomír Konečnŷ points out in this volume, attention to the "other" in Western Europe's own back yard, Central and Eastern Europe, may be lagging even further behind. But even as we bear witness to the substantial contributions these approaches have made in the study of Renaissance art, and even as we are grateful for their vital and pervasive contribution to intellectual life in the humanities as a whole, we might still ask the question: in the Renaissance, do these approaches have specifically *art* historical, as opposed to historical, things to say? Can they say them without demolishing the objects they study? Are gender and sexuality on the one hand and colonial encounters and exploration on the other at the heart of Renaissance *art*? Do art historians have as much to say as historians, on the one hand, or artists, on the other, on this score? Witness the artists examined by Mieke Bal in her *Quoting Caravaggio*:[5] in some ways, perhaps, artists might be better positioned to express their ambivalence toward canonical objects in ways that take risks, make strong and passionate statements, and interrogate pleasure without apologizing for it. Charlotte Houghton, in her response in this volume, nonetheless hopes art historians might too.

Many art historians who study the Renaissance are still doing some variation on social history, which in some cases might represent a return to issues and objects that once were of more obvious concern to art historians. For instance, before the middle decades of the twentieth century, media other than painting held a much greater place in the work of art historians, especially scholars in the Germanic world—Riegl, Schlosser, Warburg, and many others. Of late, renewed attention has been given in prominent places to media other than the traditional trio of painting, sculpture and architecture. Prints have received particular attention: as Lisa Pon and Marzia Faietti both point out in their responses here, prints in particular were anything but marginal, whether as objects in their own right or as vehicles for the reception of other art forms. Art historians are also giving renewed attention to furniture, goldsmithery, ceramics, manuscript painting, and other materials.[6] As Maria Ruvoldt writes here, pointing out the extent to which now-canonical Renaissance artists designed in (and were imitated in) all these media, "the traditional hierarchy fails to reflect the reality of Renaissance visual culture." But this is still somewhat controversial, as Fredrika Jacobs suggests in her essay: to some this range of media is not the proper bailiwick of academic art history at all, but rather of visual culture or anthropology or the cataloguing work of museums.

Another approach that might represent a return to the "roots" of Renaissance art history connects art history to intellectual history. In fact, this might be the area of the greatest common ground among the authors and interlocutors represented in this book. The mid-twentieth-century authors who are our disciplinary grandfathers—Erwin Panofsky, Ernst Gombrich, the less well-known Edgar Wind (about whom I will say more later)—were all deeply engaged with both Renaissance and modern philosophy. Their engagement with Renaissance humanism often manifested itself as both a content and a methodology inspired by neoplatonism. For the past thirty years or so, hostility to the use of neoplatonism (and, sometimes, to other philosophically informed approaches) has been palpable in our field, just as intellectual history ebbed during the ascendancy of social historians in that field. There was something more, too—a suspicion of platonism as in some sense totalitarian, via its imposition of abstract ideas on material realities. This was the view of Karl Popper in his *The Open Society and its Enemies*; in some sense this is a hostility to theory *tout court*.[7] Multiple strands, then, also including connoisseurship, militated against bringing philosophical texts (old or new) to bear on images, and it almost seems that for years most art historians simply didn't read them. Robert Williams is perhaps the representative in this book who most overtly practices art history *as* intellectual history, claiming a status for art as knowledge itself, but the other authors and interlocutors all work in this vein to a substantial extent. Intellectual history might mean studying philosophy and art theory and their interconnections; it might also mean relating the visual arts to literary and rhetorical studies. This has a long tradition, most recently maintained by the work of Charles Dempsey, Elizabeth Cropper, and their students (among whom Stephen Campbell, though his approach has its own independent and contrarian character, is the representative here).[8] While religious art has always been a subject of study, recent work on the relationship of art to religious experience, conflict, ideology, and modes of reading has become increasingly theoretically self-conscious and influential.[9]

Another significant force in recent years in the field is an approach that is both old and new. It might be called an internal history of art: one that seeks to free the history of art from subordination to political ideology and social history, considering it as an autonomous sphere with its own history. This is a history that considers primarily (but not only) formal developments, via the responses and engagements by artists with earlier forms of art. In contrast to earlier notions of *Kunstwollen*, this approach, in its current form, generally emphasizes the agency of individual artists. In contrast to the practice of connoisseurship, the act of borrowing, responding, or repeating, is taken to have substantial cultural or individual meaning of its own: it's not merely taken for granted. At its best, this approach produces not a survey as a flat chronological listing but a finer-grained history of call and response, of embedded and flaunted temporalities, of struggle with the "anxiety of influence," of dialectical innovation, of art about art, of a history of highly self-conscious and creative methods of reading images. (One way of thinking a similar set of issues with a critical political edge might be an institutional history that would examine the development of political and social structures that enable or disable such an independent history.[10])

The keyword here is autonomy; Kant's *Critique of Judgment* is the locus classicus for this notion, but perhaps more relevant for twentieth-century art history is Clement Greenberg's "Toward a Newer Laocoon." Greenberg's 1940 essay is often read as a manifesto in favor of formal purism and the autonomy of art, but he quite clearly situates the autonomy of abstract painting as appropriate to its own historical moment and not necessarily to others past or future. He also, importantly, emphasizes art as labor: the "escape from ideas . . . meant a new and greater emphasis on form, and it also involved the assertion of the arts as independent vocations, disciplines and crafts."[11] Associated with the "internal" approach, as might be guessed from the influence of Greenberg, is renewed emphasis on the medium, both materially and conceptually. Whether Greenbergian or not, an interest in the medium in both senses is perhaps most clearly evident in the work of Michael Cole, also a participant in the Art Seminar. In his article, "The Demonic Arts and the Origin of the Medium" he traces the modern notion of the artistic medium to Renaissance ideas about magic (a notion that also resonates in Pamela Smith's essay in this volume).[12] In his book on Benvenuto Cellini, he joins an emphasis on materials with an examination of the sculptor's self-aware artistic (and scientific) labor.

The Renaissance is a favorite foil for modernism,[13] and Greenberg himself, when examined for such prejudices, does not disappoint. "Renaissance space" (the surface of the canvas as a window on the world, the space of the canvas as a three-dimensional, perspectival box), the concealment of craft, the preeminence of subject matter, all place it at an opposite pole from his craft-conscious, medium-specific, modernist abstraction. Yet Renaissance art historians who have adopted something like Greenberg's system of value have sometimes, perhaps paradoxically, found Greenberg's modernist qualities in certain species of Renaissance art. Creighton Gilbert, for instance, in his 1952 "On Subject and Not-Subject in Renaissance Art," argued for a notion of pure painting in the Renaissance. A similar notion emerges in Svetlana Alpers's *Art of Describing*, in which non-narrative painting that engages self-consciously with the act of seeing marks the difference (and, implicitly, superiority) of Dutch art over Italian.[14]

Some of the most vigorous recent debate has been around work that considers the Renaissance as the moment of the "origins of art." Williams addresses this notion in his work, including his essay in this volume, and it is at the heart of debates staged in the *Art Bulletin* via Alexander Nagel and Christopher Wood's essay, "Towards a New Model of Renaissance Anachronism," responses to it, and other work by both Nagel and Wood.[15] This notion of an origin of a concept of art in the Renaissance seems to have a familiar ring to it. New textures are being given to it, new explanations offered, but some might ask: is it purely and simply old-fashioned to *insist on* the invention of art in the period of western culture traditionally thought of as the period of the invention of art? The discipline as a whole has shifted toward something called "visual culture" or "visual studies"—in part because of the impact of work in non-western and premodern cultures, in part because of contemporary new media. One wonders where else the defense of art and its origins will find an audience. This does not mean it's wrong. But from the point of view of more overtly political approaches (social art history, feminism, post-colonial studies etc.) it might look like a repetition of an old and somewhat discredited view. To take the other side for a moment, however, it might also look like approaches driven by social and political issues—social history, feminism, postcolonial studies—are themselves getting a bit long in the tooth. And I sense a certain impatience of late—not only in Renaissance art history but in other academic areas as well—with the political. We might feel irritated by what seems to be an austere moralism in feminist or postcolonial approaches; they might seem to threaten the pleasures we take in art. Or, on the other hand, we might feel exhausted by our own failures to use a politicized art history as a tool for substantive change.

If not social history, what then? Williams argues in his essay here that social-historical approaches, by emphasizing patrons over artists, have been reduced to a form of self-congratulatory bourgeois consumerism. This is not the case in every instance. A critical version of a patron-based approach might be seen in Martin Warnke's *Court Artist*, in which art gained its "modern" prestige not through the heroic individual efforts of the artist, but as the reflected glory of powerful patrons.[16] At its worst, though, the approach reinforces something even worse than bourgeois consumerism: authoritarianism. A patron has an idea, and an artist shows cleverness in successfully carrying it out: artists are reduced to tools by which power successfully exercises itself. This is nothing more sinister, I think, than a kind of unconscious absorption of contemporary political ideology in which power breeds more power—but its effect is potentially to make the work we do all the more trivial. The best social history of art does nothing of the kind (what I have just caricatured cannot even really be called social history of art), but it does sometimes raise the question I noted earlier: is it really about art as much as it is about social history?

The main alternative it seems we have to fall back on—one it sometimes seem our students desperately crave—is hardly progressive: great white men creating great works of art. Although there is a diversity of approaches in museums, many exhibitions reinforce this view of art history. Art history, indeed, is caught between allegiances—to academia on the one hand and to museums on the other. More than many of its sister disciplines, art history is beholden to an institution with different rhythms and capital investments and flows than that of academia. Museum collections, buildings, institutions and installations inevitably affect the work we do. And, despite recent changes, the museum is still a very *modern* (in the sense of modernist) institution, promoting values that we might try to chip away at, with our rebellious versions of art history, but never seem quite able to overturn. "Here, we deal with objects," a curator once said to me. I do not mean to disparage work with objects; as Adrian Randolph hints in this volume, to bridge the gap between curators and academics might mean to gain the potential to ask and answer different types of questions. But the convulsive irritation with political and social-critical approaches often presents itself as a return to the object that's also a more truly historical approach, stripping away the ahistorical baggage of theory.[17] And too often this form of history devolves simplistically into GWMs creating GWAs—a notion that has a history, and is itself predicated on twentieth-century ideas.

As Farago points out in the Seminar, women artists have come and gone in survey texts; rather than a comforting narrative of progress toward greater equity, one finds a repetitive series of erasures, by which women artists are very often treated with more equity by their contemporaries than by later art historians. Biases are always at work as the inevitable paring down of artists and works to a manageable canon takes place. The body of work available for our consideration as Renaissance "art" is still determined by modern institutions (not only the museum collection and installation, but also, to be sure, the art history survey class and textbook). These defining institutional practices, though they have earlier roots, flowered in the context of mid-twentieth-century American modernism, which was not only male-dominated, but dominated by a masculinist ideology.

Not only, of course; the values propounded by Greenberg and others include the primacy of painting, and abstract painting at that; art is secular, formal, not religious but a religion-substitute (it is contemplated in the isolation of a transcendant experience—Michael Fried's presentness as grace[18]). In the mid-twentieth-century American context modernism also stood for American preeminence (understood to spring, historically, from European underpinnings).[19] Modernism drew upon, and yet rejected as unselfconscious, media and objects from other times and places. In this context, historical ornament had to be disparaged because otherwise the very properties thought to be newest with modernism (non-narrativity) might be observed in it; for more on ornament and its untimeliness, see Ethan Matt Kavaler's essay in this volume.[20]

Renaissance art in the age of the modern

In the twentieth century, even as a certain rejection of the Renaissance was canonized, the Renaissance itself loomed large in cultural and educational debates. It is curious how important Renaissance art history became during the apogee of modernism in the mid-twentieth century. To what extent did it adapt itself to the impulses of modernist painterly abstraction (as in Creighton Gilbert's essay, mentioned above)? To what extent did it work against them, with iconology—and its insistence on meaning and subject matter in images—aligned, perhaps, with what would become conceptual art? In 1942, Edgar Wind, a German Jewish émigré art historian and committed iconographer, lectured on symbolism in *modern* art in the belly of the beast, at the Museum of Modern Art. Reviewing the lecture in *Art News*, Alfred Frankfurter opined as follows: "If any one contribution to contemporary aesthetics is wanted today, it is an intelligent restoration of balance to subject-matter in painting. The layman has been fed so long on a monotonous diet of apples when not on undiluted geometry that his sense for the meaning of what he sees has begun to atrophy."[21] Wind's primary scholarly investments were in the Renaissance, and perhaps this ground, more than modern art itself, provided a venue for the defense of subject matter that could in a sense engage obliquely with contemporary ideas like Greenberg's. It would be too simple to suggest that modernist impulses ruled unchallenged even during the heyday of modernism. Iconology, in its own way, argued for something different.

Wind was a devotee of Aby Warburg's ideas and a contemporary and sometime student of Erwin Panofsky, also an émigré and the man most associated with the method of iconology. Though the method had been heralded in a much earlier article by Panofsky, it was in the postwar American context—in which both Panofsky and Wind taught—that iconology became a privileged interpretive tool for the study of Renaissance art.[22] This may be because the educational reforms of that period required teachable, rationalist, methods for large numbers of students (including GIs but not only) who had not, before college, had a classical education. This was a period in which prominent American educational theories stripped the study of *history* away from the study of art and literature, presenting creative works in isolation as studies in form, and emphasizing particularist, inductive method (as opposed to abstract, deductive theory). Method generally meant formal analysis—a way of looking at images that could be made clear to masses of increasingly middle-class students with little historical training.

While iconology offered an alternative to modernist preoccupations with form, it was also (especially in simplified form) a teachable method, one that could, perhaps, be presented as appropriate to the particular achievements of Renaissance art. In this sense it is connected to another kind of appeal the Renaissance had for postwar students and teachers. The very idea of it suggested change and renewal—precisely the atmosphere that educational reformers of the mid-twentieth century hoped to foster. A picture of the Renaissance emerged in which the individual pried himself out from beneath the weight of religious sentiment (with the crowbar of a kind of secularized classicism composed of a collection of formal motifs, rationally applied). It thus prefigured the ascendancy of painting, the autonomy of art and a contemplative but non-religious attitude toward it. In the American context, the Renaissance served a variety of different agendas, in a sense, caught in Cold War paradoxes of competing cultural values. Emison and Randolph, in their essays, both point out specifically Cold War and American agendas at work in the history of our discipline, though the fact that one's Renaissance might serve a contemporary agenda is not restricted to that place and time, as Ingrid Ciulisová points out regarding both Jacob Burckhardt and Jan Białostocki.

The twentieth-century view on Renaissance individualism had its precedents, notably in Jacob Burckhardt's *Civilisation of the Renaissance in Italy*. Like Wind and Panofsky after him, Burckhardt was heir to a long tradition of German philosophy that placed central emphasis on the relation of subject and object. In Burckhardt's view, medieval people slumbered under a veil of ignorance in indistinction from their environs; bourgeois culture in the Italian Renaissance created modern distinctions between subject and object, allowing man to discover *both* himself *and* the world as distinct from one another.[23] Ernst Cassirer extended and refined this notion with a careful study of early Renaissance (largely neoplatonic) philosophical writings on the microcosm and macrocosm. He looked, for instance, at Charles de Bovelles, who claimed that man was the (potentially comprehensive) mirror of the world, separate from it and thus able to reflect on it, to represent it.[24] In art historical terms, in part thanks to Panofsky's *Perspective as Symbolic Form* (though the text was not widely read in Anglophone contexts[25]), this divide was thought to have materialized in the practice of perspective. In the assumptions of twentieth-century art history, the Renaissance picture is a window on the world that distances subject and object and constitutes them separately in so doing. The Renaissance stands for a comforting clarity of subject and object; perspectival practice in art—Leon Battista Alberti's window, which distances the viewer from the object and at the same time produces (a view of) objective space—stands as the sign of that clarity.

Perspective certainly constitutes a distinct and theory-driven feature of Renaissance painting. And yet art history has tended to fetishize it as theory and practice, construing it as the sign of the rational modernity of the Renaissance—ignoring the larger field of geometry in which perspective was categorized at the time. In Elizabeth Holt's *Documentary History of Art*, for instance, Holt footnotes Bartolommeo Fazio's description of Jan van Eyck's skill in geometry thus: "*geometry*: perspective."[26] As Kavaler's essay in this volume shows, geometry could mean a good deal more. It may, as I will suggest later in this essay, have provided much of the foundation for what was understood as "theoretical" (and what was understood as "practical") in those arts that were based on *disegno*. The appeal of perspective goes beyond a historicized account of the values of Renaissance art to embrace the very possibility of doing history at all, the capacity to take a distanced and clear view of the historical object: to gaze at it, that is, from the point of view of *theoria*.

The clarity of vision that erupts in the Renaissance according to Burckhardt is also manifest in Panofsky's iconological method; ambiguity is a problem to be solved by proper identification, and images are to be "nailed down."[27] Wind, who was Panofsky's contemporary and sometime student, insisted rather upon a character of anarchic uncontrollability, even danger, submerged in the image and sometimes rising to the surface.[28] The question of the irrational arises in the Art Seminar, and it is a primary point of conflict between Wind and Panofsky, and one that entered the discipline most concretely with Aby Warburg. What happens to a Warburgian in modernist America? Wind argued, following Warburg, that the residue of the irrational had to be reckoned with in any symbolic image possessing power.[29] He wrote—insisting on the complexity of symbols—that they "may work as a magic force to which one must respond by deeds of a ritual nature, or they may appear as a group of intellectual or aesthetic forms which call for analysis or contemplation. The tension between these opposing functions cannot be reduced to a simple antithesis of mutually exclusive terms, for it makes up the drama of civilization that the same symbols can and will be interpreted in both ways." Nor is enlightenment absolute and irreversible; "enlightened symbols are always in danger of falling back into symbols of superstition, for they remain vivid and significant chiefly by virtue of their oscillation between these two poles, and no theory of symbols can be complete which ignores either the conflict or the correlation between these opposite tendencies."[30] The tension between reason and ritual is not so easily dismissed. Along with this Wind resisted the art historical narrative of secularization—chiding his closest American colleague, the economic historian John Nef, for seeing the Renaissance as "a purely secular movement in art."[31] Wind later became the first Professor of art history at Oxford; but he was, in his own way, an "outlier." Some of his ideas have a familiar ring to us: they might appear in work labeled "visual culture," in the study of art and religion, and in the revival of interest in Warburg as a road not taken in twentieth-century art history as American modernist-influenced approaches prevailed. My point here is not simply to praise Wind's approach as forward-thinking, but to show that alternatives were indeed presented in the mid-twentieth century, that such issues were a matter of active debate.

Theory vs. practice

Modernism is, of course, no longer prevalent in the art world. Painting goes on, but Art means something quite different now than it did in 1942, or 1952. One of the clearest changes to which one can point is the emergence, both inside and outside the institutions of art, of time arts and performance art—and, in general, artists who use theatricality, the situation, the intervention, the happening, the event, the ephemeral action, and other like forms. In this connection Alice Jarrard cites the Situationists and others in her essay in this volume, suggesting that such practices, in calling art objects into question, may have obliquely contributed to the study of the emergence of the category "art" in the Renaissance. If the category has an end, does it have a beginning? Yet we don't think of Renaissance analogues for such practices when we think about the Renaissance "invention of art." This, I suspect, is all about modernism. Our understanding of the Renaissance is still the product of an art history driven to find the sources of modern art in the fifteenth and sixteenth centuries even while understanding modernism at the very same time as the over-coming of the Renaissance. If we are to continue to posit the beginnings of art in the Renaissance, then we might need to reconsider what exactly we mean by art.

As art history defines "art" today, the word cannot be clearly mapped in any meaningful way against a single Renaissance concept. Something *called* "art" that looks anything like our definition is hard to find in the Renaissance. Looking at Latin works published in the Renaissance whose titles include the word *ars*, one finds moral philosophy, devotional exercises, mathematics, astronomy, mysticism, love, medicine, politics, war, logic, dialectic, alchemy, botany, crypt-ography, optics (including the making of telescopes as well as the technique of perspective drawing), preaching, oratory, and poetics. One hardly finds the visual arts at all. "The arts" in the sixteenth century as a collective term still largely referred to the trivium and quadrivium of the medieval university—grammar, rhetoric, logic, arithmetic, geometry, music and astronomy. Art in the singular is human activity (as opposed to nature); it is a *how to*, a practical *way* of doing something, perhaps a "best" way. When cognate words do appear, particularly in the vernaculars, in relation to what we now call the visual or fine arts, they are most commonly meant in exactly this sense—a technique for carrying out some specific practice—not as a broader category of the aesthetic. We might get closer to our notion of art with the word "disegno" (see Williams *infra*) but this too is both *more* and *less* specific than our word "art." More specific because it is about plan, intention, design, as opposed to execution; less spe-cific because it is about those things in many contexts other than that of the visual arts. For Vasari and many of his contemporaries, *disegno* formed the basis of painting, sculpture, and architecture in particular. But in both theory and practice (and even in the work of many of those artists whose biographies he wrote), design also formed the basis for work in other, more portable and "popular" media. The "arts of *disegno*" will not actually get us to the fine arts in a modern sense.

Let me suggest, then, that instead of a single abstract and aesthetic concept of art, the Renaissance had multiple arts, each understood as a specific practice that could be done more or less artfully or well. If we use a true period notion of "art" to elevate us to some level of abstraction, we are left with something much broader than the visual arts, and something quite difficult to reconcile with "theory." But if art was not "art" in the Renaissance, was theory "theory"? Much of what we call Renaissance art theory is not theory at all, but guidance for practice: generalizations about method, the history of the practice, examples, biographies. (This is largely true, too, of the manifold writing on portraits that Joanna Woods-Marsden sketches in her essay, which gives a place back to portraiture in discussions of art "theory.") As Williams argues, much Renaissance writing on art involved a drive toward systematicity. But what sort of systematicity? Theoretical discussions often seem to have been provoked by *difference* and preoccupied with explaining it. This is true whether what is at issue are differences observed between historical periods; among artists within a historical context; or between regions; among stylistic temperaments (as with Lomazzo's use of the planets to understand personality and style).[32] Many of these texts, additionally, have as much to say about literary genres, tropes, and topoi as they do about art.

A certain notion of systematicity with respect to *ars* is perceptible much earlier, but it is in a context the Renaissance art historian would be unlikely to recognize as belonging to art. In the system set out by the *Ars magna* of the thirteenth-century writer Ramon Llull, a set of basic truths could be combined via mathematical methods (presented materially in manuscript diagrams and rotating volvelles) to represent all knowledge available to human minds. Llull understood the physical world, from the microcosm to the macrocosm, as a system that mapped the four elements and their properties according to numerical values as the constituents of all natural things (so, for instance, anise had 1 part heat while cinnamon had 3). With this knowledge one might work with the very elements as one's raw material, recombining hot and cold, wet and dry to therapeutic effect.[33] Though Llull was widely read in the later middle ages and Renaissance, it is hard to say what impact he might have had on art theory. He does, however, remind us that art theory, in the Renaissance, was often established upon a basis not only of the physical world but also of mathematics, and that mathematics did not mean simply (as Holt suggested in her footnote to Fazio) perspectival theory. Renaissance mathematics has much to tell us about Renaissance psychology, and can provide us with useful analogies for thinking about art.

Though art historians have a tendency to ignore this aspect of art theory, in questions of theory vs. practice, one of the most pertinent points of reference, for literate artists, was that of theoretical vs. practical geometry. In the middle ages and Renaissance, theoretical geometry meant Euclid and reasoning by means of proofs concerning the construction of and relations among abstract geometric figures. Practical geometry was about measurement by instruments and "by art"—often involving surveying fields and measuring the heights of buildings. The emphasis on measurement followed the etymology of the name (geo-metry, the measurement of the earth). Both theoretical and practical geometry had relevance to artists, who were charged both with inventing compositions (in their *fantasie*) and with executing them materially. The status of geometric figures—as real, imaginary, abstracted from reality or present in the divine mind—was heavily contested in Renaissance thinking. Classical, medieval and Renaissance authors frequently discuss this topic in terms reminiscent of favorite art historical themes—the status of images, perception, and *disegno*. Are mathematical figures abstract ideas existing in the world of forms (as they were in a certain reading of Platonism), or a concept with no reality derived by the operations of the human mind from empirical observation of the natural world (as they were for Aristotle)? Leon Battista Alberti (who also wrote a text on mathematical "games" that are really exercises in surveying techniques) presents the first book of his *De Pictura*—perhaps the first book on art that most art historians would recognize as theory—as literally a work of mathematics that will show the "roots in nature" of painting. He begins with a brief account of Euclidean theory, but a difference from "pure" mathematics is immediately evident. Mathematicians, he writes, echoing writers on geometry, "measure with their minds [*ingenio*] alone the species and forms of things separated from all matter." We, on the other hand, "who wish the thing to be placed under the gaze, will therefore use in writing, as they say, a fatter Minerva" (a more material form of knowledge).[34]

Alberti's distinction between abstract mathematics and the fatter Minerva of art aligns closely with the distinction between theoretical and practical geometry, and also alludes the debate over the reality or ideality of mathematical figures. This debate had important consequences for knowledge. Alberti's close contemporary Nicholas of Cusa presented an elegant solution to the problem of the knowledge of divine ideas, or forms: we have oblique knowledge of immaterial forms by analogy with mathematical knowledge. We can understand an immaterial figure through our knowledge of its material manifestations (the figure of a triangle conjoined with the material of a wall, for instance). In his *De Possest*, he writes, "If we know something about [divine works], we surmise it by likening a figure to a form. Hence, there is no precise knowledge of any of God's works, except on the part of God, who does all these works. If *we* have any knowledge of them, we derive it from the symbolism and the mirror of [our] mathematical knowledge. E.g., from figure, which gives being in mathematics, [we make an inference about] form, which gives being: just as the figure of a triangle gives being to the triangle, so the human form, or species, gives being to a man. We are acquainted with the figure of a triangle since it is imaginable; but we are not acquainted with the human form, since it is not imaginable and does not have quantity . . ."[35] Charles de Bovelles extended this notion to place mathematical entities squarely between the physical world and the spiritual realm of metaphysics.[36]

In a certain sense, such notions enabled ambitious artists trained in mathematics to consider their practice of *disegno*, by analogy with mathematics, as a form of access to truths both divine and natural. As a form of materialized abstraction, design or "figure" might well correspond to Bovelles's mathematical entities, situated between the physical and the metaphysical. Mathematics ruled the physical world and those who knew the secrets of mathematics should have superior control over it. Yet did they really? Bringing figure under the control of the human mind also subjects it to the troubling vagaries of the imagination. In Llull's writings the insistence on rationalizing all of creation was taken, we might say, to irrational extremes. In Thomas Bradwardine's much-read account of the distinction between practical and theoretical geometry, much cited in later treatises, geometric figures are prone to "passions" (passions that are, however, to be investigated theoretically by reason). Mathematics was not purely and simply rational; in Plotinus and Boethius, fertile angles procreate, a notion that was picked up and extended in the work of Bovelles, where angles give birth to solids, and the mind produces concepts via an analogy, extended over many pages, with sexual intercourse and procreation.[37] We remember that Cassirer saw Bovelles as a primary harbinger of an objective view on the world. But as with the creations of artists, for Bovelles the very concept of concepts is predicated on a fantasy of male birth: that clear, objective mirror of the world suddenly appears as a pregnant body. Investigating the old concept of the "Renaissance subject" (or perspective, or *disegno*) from a slightly different point of view, one that is both theoretical and practical or even technical, sometimes brings us to (surprisingly? or not?) to issues of gender and sexuality. The same may be true, in different ways, for other traditional topics. It has been said before, but it bears repeating, that addressing such questions does not necessarily mean importing in purely twenty-first-century concerns, but it might mean thinking about them in twenty-first-century ways.

Lost objects

If a notion of art as the modern "fine arts" is not a Renaissance concept, it seems there is little to stop us from bringing more recent notions of art to bear on the Renaissance. If we are, now, in a fundamentally different situation as far as the function of art goes, can art *history* go on doing the history of painting, sculpture and architecture alone? Is art history, indeed, the history of something that has no real meaning in the present? What if we were, for instance, to pay more attention to Renaissance "performance art"?[38] While performance art has developed into one of the primary genres of contemporary artistic practice, with its own history, subgenres, styles and intellectual problems, it does not seem to have had much impact on art historians' notion of what counts as art history before modernity. On the other hand, might performance inform our understanding of historical precedents for contemporary works, or our sense of the "beholder's share" (our understanding of viewing and perceiving and of the art object as a form of communication), or our understanding of the art historian's practice?

An awareness of contemporary performance art, at interactive, immersive, or event-based work, might cause us to look to the past for instances of "performance art" that can illuminate and be illuminated by contemporary practices. While it would not be historically appropriate to take the art of our own time as an absolute standard, what if we were to take modernism (for the sake of argument) as a "parenthesis" rather than a rupture, as suggested by the title of a recent colloquium at the Centre Pompidou in Paris?[39] In doing so, we might find ourselves dealing with events, performances, spectacles and celebrations like royal entry ceremonies, in which the literary arts combine with the visual and musical arts—a perfect instance, perhaps, of "interdisciplinarity." Performance certainly seems like a ready conceptual tool for thinking about much of the work produced in the Renaissance, though it also has more troubling associations: the focus on "performance" as opposed to "objects" in contemporary art seems not unrelated to the withering of industrial capitalism in favor of a fast-paced global economy that requires lightning-quick adaptation of bodies and minds to new types and standards of economic performance.

For the early modern period, we have ready case studies in the events, processions, spectacles and celebrations in which the literary arts combine with the visual and musical arts. If art historians have not entirely neglected these events, they have nonetheless tended to cede them to historians and literary scholars. But a consideration of performance art in the present might cause one to look to the past for instances of performance that can illuminate and be illuminated by contemporary practices. And, indeed, recent work in medieval and Renaissance art history has underlined the extent to which artists were "design professionals" in a very broad sense. Those who might be designated as painters or even architects painted furniture and banners and designed luxury objects and tapestries, making objects that were given shape and significance by complex scenes of social and cultural performance. Objects were thus both performed and performing. To account for their complex "lives"—and not only, as Vasari did, for the lives of the artists—would require a methodological orientation that pushes art history to its interdisciplinary limits.

In his essay in this volume, Stephen Campbell addresses Mantegna's *Triumphs of Caesar* as a *summa* of a particular Renaissance sensibility. These canvases, as he argues, represent both an ancient event and a modern metaphor—that of the conquest of a "lost visual and material culture." Yet they also allude to its activation in contemporary ceremony—whether religious procession or triumphal entry. They were used in 1504 as part of a "Theater of Fortune"; the related set of prints or others like them were used half a century later as part of the script for a quasi-imperial triumph, the entry of Henri II and Catherine de' Medici into Rouen in 1550.[40]

This ceremony depended on objects made by artists not only for inspiration, but also for the performance itself. None exist today (except the printed book and manuscript that document the entry). They include costumes and gifts but also floats—chariots, faux-elephants—and carefully crafted automata and other sculptural installations that moved and bore messages as well as presenting wondrous sights for the eye. By any contemporary definition, they had as much to do with "art" as frescoes on the walls of Fontainebleau. Events like this one, presented by cities at the command of the king, have tended to be viewed as expressions of royal ideology. On some basic level, an entry necessarily enacted royal ideology: it worked on the assumption that it was the right and privilege of the king to enter his cities, and that it was the duty of the subjects to welcome him with pomp. Viewed from closer to the "ground," however, the smooth and uninterrupted transmission of royal ideology is harder to see. The entry's performance involved the large-scale efforts of most of Rouen's inhabitants; even if we consider only its authorship, it was a collaborative project. The artistic invention, order, and visual and narrative elements of the entry had to be approved (if not actually conceived) by a committee. Instructions had to be given to each

group within the city—professions, confraternities, guilds, militias—
on its performances. Other desiderata had to be discussed with
artisans; presumably there was some discussion of what, on the
part of the city council, was desired, and what, from the point of view
of the artists, was feasible. Sometimes performances failed mis-
erably: Etienne Jodelle's apology for a failed play (in his *Recueil des
inscriptions*) provides a good example of this.[41]

Rouen was riddled with social conflict, and some of these social
conflicts expressed themselves, more or less clearly, in the documentation of the event. There was resentment of the king's imposition of
taxes and in the protracted wars into which he dragged his subjects.
There was sympathy for Protestant "heretics"—including, perhaps,
those who had been burned in the recent royal entry in Paris as part
of the spectacle. Different accounts of the entry contain disagreements with one another even at the level of the identities of the
theatrical characters who appeared in it. The Rouen entry is a relatively well-documented ceremony, as Renaissance ceremonies go, but
if I set out to study it as an art historian, it is not at all clear what the
actual object of study is—where are the boundaries that might define
it? We often speak of the objects of art history as if material objects
were the same as objects of study, attention, or consciousness. The
distinction is blurred by the dual meaning of the word "object," but
also by art historical practice, in which it has become a convenience
to conflate the material object with the object of consciousness.
Existing objects—particularly those presented in museums—seem to
provide a convenient kind of closure or boundedness; they do not
require an effort to determine what counts as figure and what counts
as ground. Thus, we might take the printed book that documents the
entry as a bounded object of study in its own right. Or we might
attempt to produce the Platonic idea of the entry—whatever the
organizers determined as what they wanted to convey. But convey
to whom? Who constituted the audience and who constituted the
performance? For the Rouennais poor, a royal entry meant being
rounded up and forced to stand on the sidelines as spectators—much
as, on other days, they were rounded up and forced to work dig-
ging ditches for fortifications; were required to wear identifying
marks clearly visible on their clothing; were required to register with

parishes in order to receive alms; were forbidden to beg in public and in particular at certain streets, squares, and city gates. On most days, they were required to be unseen, or visible only as a marked and degraded population. On a ceremonial day, however, they were obliged to be seen as part of the symbolic body of the city; thus, presence at the entry was, in itself, a performance of the integrity of the civic body. Meanwhile Henri II viewed the processions and installation pieces but was also there to be viewed: was he an actor or a spectator? At either end of the social scale, therefore, we confront a version of the same question. On a more global scale, different questions, in the vein of Claire Farago's work, might also be raised. One of the most frequently cited elements of the entry is its "Brazilian" village and battle, which seems to have involved the forced performance of Brazilian captives.[42] The colonial endeavors of early modern Europe are rarely far from the surface of its performances of power. But the distinction between European and non-European does not map easily along lines of power, as we see when we consider the European poor. Thus in this case, a shift in the type of contemporary European phenomena we consider part of art history, combined with the kinds of questions social history asks, also has the power to bring into fuller view the complex intersections in this period between Europe and the non-European world.

Performing paintings

As far as our disciplinary definitions of Renaissance art go, this entry ceremony appears rather unpromising. It took place in northern France and not in Italy; was an event and not an object, collaborative and not individual, driven by royal ideology and therefore not "autonomous." Art historians *do* deal with such events, but what they are doing is then often called visual culture or history and not art history. But what if painting in the Renaissance were more like this processional event than we generally admit? It was collaborative in planning and execution; it extended through time; it was often ambiguous in its positioning of producers and consumers; it was sometimes produced for an event or to frame particular activities or to make a display of political power; it was, as Elizabeth Honig points out, usually site-specific. At this point it might be useful to turn to a different foundational moment in art history, the work of Giovanni Morelli, a founder of the subdiscipline of connoisseurship, on which all art historians, like it or not, rely. Morelli's primary goal was to establish correct attributions: to give objects to their proper subjects.[43]

The novelty of Morelli's approach was that he situated the individuality of authorship not in the central features that received the most attention (by artists and viewers) but in the unintentional, unconscious and overlooked detail—an earlobe or a toenail. In an influential essay Carlo Ginzburg has connected Morelli with Sigmund Freud and Arthur Conan Doyle, suggesting that they exemplify a typically modern (and also medical) emphasis on the seemingly irrelevant detail, the unintentional clue—that is, the unconscious (as, for Freud, the slip of the tongue that speaks volumes). The subject of this creation is a doubled subject, not fully in control of its actions.[44]

This also resonates with the Romantic fragment, with the trope of irony—an aesthetic mode in which what seems least important might turn out to be most important not in spite of but *because* it is grounded in an autonomous individual subject. We might, however, think of this formulation as a bit backwards for the Renaissance, in which the central site of agency, we might argue, is still not the individual but the social or professional group. *Of course* individuality appears in the details—but not because the seemingly insignificant details, by ironic reversal, tell us what's most important. Rather, workshop practice demanded a collective conformity to certain norms, norms that were practiced and performed, synchronically and diachronically, by multiple "contributors." Training was accomplished through repetitive imitation of authoritative models. Individual style, flair, expression, desires, distortions, and idiosyncrasies existed, but tended to be incremental and not dramatic. Thus, they were often confined to less important areas. When too overt, idiosyncrasies might be sharply criticized.[45] And thus, where each case is an amalgam of the intentional/individual and the general/collective, it may have been the general and collective that most viewers noticed and cared most about.

Perhaps Morelli drew the wrong conclusion by finding the individual in the details, because he was primed to accept the overwhelming cultural authority of the individual—in particular that of such figures as Raphael. To critique these assumptions is not to say that Raphael did not possess special talents. For his contemporaries much of Raphael's achievement was to synthesize the best of his contemporaries (as Zeuxis did with his five models). His cultural authority in the late nineteenth century was not the simple product of his genius. It was the result of the long process by which his genius was constructed: by the power of the Popes for whom he worked; by the humanist and antiquarians with whom he conversed; by the many artists who collaborated with him, whether on Vatican frescoes or tapestry cartoons or portraits; by his early death and the later romance of an unfinished career; by the dissemination of the prints of Marcantonio Raimondi and others, which branded "Raphael" as a name; by the academic painters of the seventeenth century onward who took him as their unparalleled model and repetitively copied from him in drawings and prints and paintings; by the visits of northern European collectors to Italy; by the art market and museums in the nineteenth century. Raphael himself, as individual genius artist, is the product of a long, repeated process of construction by artists, academicians, collectors and historians.

But that does not mean—I want to emphasize—that the sixteenth-century artist Raphael was not up to anything interesting. A final residue of modernism I want to mention, and one I find especially puzzling, is the tenacity of the imperative not to commit the "intentional fallacy." This notion, originally put forward by the new criticism as a way to force attention to the text (or image) rather than biography, has, I think, paradoxically come to constitute a kind of crypto-sacred cult of the creator.[46] In addition to the aspects I catalogued earlier, modernism also saw art as the product of ineffable individual expression—something deeply individual and expressive and also non-verbal. The avoidance of comment on an artist's intentions or intellectual ideas has been raised to the level of orthodoxy, and it is extended to the notion not only that one cannot judge the meaning or quality of a work by its author's intentions, but that *one can never know* an artist's intentions. What's odd about this is that we cannot know the intentions of people in all kinds of situations in which we nonetheless have no trouble speculating about them. This makes the viewer, or critic or historian, the locus of meaning, which gives it a certain appeal to critics and historians. Yet I think it has the perverse effect of enforcing a view of artistic creation, from afar, as godlike mystery, one not to be understood by the rest of us. The god-like mystery, within contemporary consumer culture and an increasingly authoritarian political situation, sets up an artificial divide between creative producers—a special quasi-divine type of person—and consumers, the rest of us, who can only look on in wonderment. (For popular culture, the mystery makes of artists like Leonardo a case to be solved by the fortuitous discovery of portentous membership in an auratic cult.)

In contrast to the way in which we usually consider a figure like Raphael, the 1550 entry and more recent forms of performance art are avowedly collaborative. There is less likely to be a distinct individual author, and yet because Raphael is the disciplinary model, our options for accounting for collective creation seem limited: to invoke an individual or to subsume the individual into an undifferentiated collective authorship whose depths are no more plumbable than those of the individual. We tend to collapse multiple authorship into a unitary co-authorship, an author-function, or a master-artist story. In the reverse operation, we might instead disaggregate "Raphael," and consider him not as individual but as collective construction.[47] Thinking of agency as multiple might help us understand "individuals" differently: considering both supra-individual and sub-individual agency, not denying the existence of individuals but displacing them as the crucial (and therefore unanalyzed) site of origins. Though I differ on the question of rationality, here I would align myself with Williams's recent plea for attention to the labor of art. What if we did not fear that in speculating about the motives and intentions of artists at work—the interweaving of their intellectual with their physical work—we might be committing a form of sacrilege?[48]

I return to my curator friend and his objects. A museum's objects are presented as objects of contemplation, framed and set off by white walls in a space designed for that purpose. They provide psychological, even quasi-religious, relief from the boundary confusions of everyday life, in which it is not always clear who or what is the object and what or who is the subject. But the museum state of art is not the *essential* state of art. One might view art as much more (creatively?) disruptive, as threatening and confusing as it is enthralling. Such confusions, as with the productive disarray of our field, might provide an opportunity to examine the constitution of subjectivity in a more deeply historical way.[49]

The danger of objects that affect their viewers powerfully, in a bodily way, is such that those objects—when they belong to the context of popular cult—are more likely to be downgraded as unworthy of the attentions of true art history (see Jacobs's essay, and the discussion in the Art Seminar of David Freedberg's *The Power of Images*). And yet such *sensation* reappears in the most orthodox contexts, as when Filarete describes a feeling of rebirth upon associating with amateurs of the antique or viewing antique objects (see Campbell's essay). Tying these threads together with that of the European encounter with non-European others, Farago suggests here that the question of the idol deserves richer study both synchronically and diachronically: it not only bears upon the definition of art vs. non-art, but also poses questions of subjectivity and historical definitions of the human. Jeannette Peterson points out that the very concept of the Renaissance can be mapped only with great difficulty onto the corresponding period in the Americas. Perhaps we might make greater headway by framing our work with (duly historicized) concepts like idolatry, performance, anachronism and labor, as well as gender, power, and cultural exchange.

If subjects and objects stood in a disorderly relation to one another in the Renaissance, must the same not be said for our relationship to our objects of study? If we jettison the stable, bounded object we seek in history (or in a framed picture on a white museum wall), then do we jettison ourselves as well, becoming like Julia Kristeva's abject? Perhaps we can never fully detach ourselves from the (sentimental?) notion of the Renaissance as origin, revolution, model, and foundation of historical objectivity. But our attachment to *that* Renaissance might be well worth interrogating. If there remains a modernist urge to locate aesthetic autonomy in Renaissance painting, is this anything more than an investment in our own freedom—as it was for anti-totalitarian modernists—or, perhaps, a fantasy thereof? Fantasy is not a bad thing, but it might be worth a good, hard look. We might thereby explore the confusions and boundary-crossings in our own experiences of art and power, the ways in which neither we nor our artworks are, in the end, autonomous.

Notes

1. David Lodge, *Small World* (Harmondsworth: Penguin, 1995), 52.
2. Perhaps even more problematically, it is usually expected that a canonical version of the Renaissance will be taught; the same insistence does not appear in other fields. As Joseph Koerner observed a few years ago, it sometimes seems as if one must work on Michelangelo to get a job in Renaissance art history today—this despite the fact that the (sub)field itself has changed enormously, taking on a wide range of newer methods and ever more diverse objects of study. Tracing the history of the Renaissance to a moment when everything changed forever seems an eternal project—but one bound to help us very little as historians. Comments made in introduction to CAA panel, "Re-mastering the Renaissance," Philadelphia 2002.
3. Feminist art historians have dealt with histories of women artists, relations between gender, sexuality, and artistic creation, and the gendering of vision and visuality. For gender and early modern art, a (still incomplete) selection of major work would include the following: Elizabeth Cropper, "On Beautiful Women: Parmigianino, Petrarchismo and the Vernacular Style." *Art Bulletin* LVIII/3 (Sept 1976): 374–394. Mary Garrard, *Artemisia Gentileschi: The Image of the Female Hero in Italian Baroque Art* (Princeton: Princeton University Press, 1989); *Artemisia Gentileschi Around 1622: The Shaping and Reshaping of an Artistic Identity* (Berkeley: University of California Press, 2001). Rona Goffen, ed., *Titian's "Venus of Urbino"* (Cambridge, New York: Cambridge University Press, 1997), 63–90; "Titian's Sacred and Profane Love: Individuality and Sexuality in a Renaissance Marriage Picture," in *Studies in the History of Art* (Washington, DC) 1993, v. 45, 120–144; *Titian's Women* (New Haven: Yale University Press, 1997). Fredrika Jacobs. *Defining the Renaissance Virtuosa: Women Artists and the Language of Art History and Criticism* (Cambridge, New York: Cambridge University Press, 1997). Mary Pardo, "Artifice as Seduction in Titian," in *Sexuality and Gender in Early Modern Europe: Institutions, Texts, Images*, ed. James Grantham Turner (New York: Cambridge University Press, 1993); "Veiling the Venus of Urbino" in *Titian's Venus of Urbino*, ed. Goffen. Linda Seidel. *Jan Van Eyck's Arnolfini Portrait: Stories of an Icon* (New York, Cambridge: Cambridge UP, 1993). Patricia Simons, "Women in Frames: The Gaze, the Eye, the Profile in Renaissance Portraiture." *The Expanding Discourse: Feminism and Art History*, eds. Norma Broude and Mary Garrard (Boulder: Oxford Westview Press, 1992); "Portraiture, Portrayal and Idealization: Ambiguous Individualization in Representations of Renaissance Women," in *Language*

and Images in Renaissance Italy (Oxford: Clarendon Press, 1995), 263–311.
Work dealing with sexuality (complicating histories of women as objects
and subjects of art) has included Patricia Simons, "Lesbian (In)Visibility in
Italian Renaissance Culture: Diana and Other Cases of Donna con Donna."
Gay and Lesbian Studies in Art History, ed. Whitney Davis (New York:
Haworth Press, 1994), 81–122; Bette Talvacchia, *Taking Positions*; and—as
is mentioned by the seminar participants—Leo Steinberg, *The Sexuality of
Christ in Renaissance Art and Modern Oblivion*. See also the influential
article by Linda Nochlin, "Why Have There Been No Great Women
Artists?" AR*Tnews*. Jan. 1971: 22–39, 67–71. On Renaissance art in
relation to European colonial history, see Gauvin Bailey, *Art on the Jesuit
Missions in Asia and Latin America, 1542–1773* (Toronto: University of
Toronto Press, 2001); Samuel Edgerton, *Theaters of Conversion: Religious
Architecture and Indian Artisans in colonial Mexico* (Albuquerque: University
of New Mexico Press, 2001); and Claire Farago, *Reframing the Renaissance:
Visual Culture in Europe and Latin America, 1450–1650* (New Haven: Yale
University Press, 1995). Claire Farago also lists some notable scholars of the
colonial Americas during the Seminar; see below.

4. John H. Elliott, "Renaissance Europe and America: A Blunted Impact?"
    First Images of America: The Impact of the New World on the Old, ed. Fredi
    Chiappelli (Berkeley: University of California Press, 1976), v. 1, 11–23.

5. Mieke Bal, *Quoting Caravaggio: Contemporary Art, Preposterous History*
    (Chicago: University of Chicago Press, 1999).

6. For prints, see David Areford, "The Image in the Viewer's Hand: The
    Reception of Early Prints in Europe." *Studies in Iconography*, v. 24 (2003),
    5–42. Michael Cole, et al. *The Early Modern Painter-Etcher* (University
    Park, PA: Pennsylvania State University, 2006); Patricia Emison,
    "Prolegomenon to the Study of Italian Renaissance Prints." *Word & Image*,
    v. 11, no. 1 (Jan-Mar 1995), 1–15. David Landau and Peter Parshall.
    The Renaissance Print: 1470–1550 (New Haven: Yale University Press,
    1994). Evelyn Lincoln, *The Invention of the Italian Renaissance Printmaker*
    (New Haven, London: Yale University Press, 2000). Peter Parshall, et al,
    eds. *The Origins of European Printmaking: Fifteenth-Century Woodcuts and
    Their Public* (Washington: National Gallery of Art, in association with Yale
    University Press, 2005). Lisa Pon, *Raphael, Dürer, and Marcantonio
    Raimondi: Copying and the Italian Renaissance Print* (New Haven: Yale
    University Press, 2004). Bronwen Wilson, *The World in Venice: Print, the
    City and Early Modern Identity* (Toronto, Buffalo: Toronto University Press,
    2005). For other media, see Cristelle Baskins, *Cassone Painting, Humanism,
    and Gender in Early Modern Italy* (Cambridge, New York: Cambridge UP,
    1998); Elena Calvillo, *Imitation and Invention in the Service of Rome: Giulio
    Clovio's Works for Cardinals Marino Grimani and Alessandro Farnese*. PhD
    diss., John Hopkins University, 2003; Jacqueline Musaccio, *The Art and
    Ritual of Childbirth in Renaissance Italy* (New Haven: Yale UP, 1999). Hugo
    Van der Velden, *The Donor's Image: Gerard Loyet and the Votive Portraits of
    Charles the Bold* (Turnhout: Brepols Press, 2000); Evelyn Welch, *Shopping
    in the Renaissance: Consumer Cultures in Italy 1400–1600* (New Haven: Yale
    University Press, 2005).

7. Karl Popper, *The Open Society and Its Enemies*. See also Horst Bredekamp, "Götterdämmerung des Neuplatonismus," in *Kritische Berichte* 14:4 (1986).

8. See Francis Ames-Lewis, *The Intellectual Life of the Early Renaissance Artist* (New Haven: Yale UP, 2000); Charles Dempsey, *The Portrayal of Love: Botticelli's "Primavera" and Humanist Culture at the Time of Lorenzo the Magnificent* (Princeton: Princeton UP, 1992); Elizabeth Cropper and Charles Dempsey, *Nicolas Poussin: Friendship and the Love of Painting* (Princeton: Princeton UP, 1996); Stephen Campbell, *Cosmè Tura of Ferrara: Style, Politics, and the Renaissance City, 1450–1495* (New Haven: Yale University Press, 1997).

9. Works dealing with "late medieval" devotional imagery (often contemporary with the Renaissance) and, implicitly or explicitly, with period distinctions made on aesthetic grounds, include Hans Belting, *Likeness and Presence: A History of the Image Before the Era of Art* (Chicago: University of Chicago Press, 1994). Carolyn Walker Bynum, *Fragmentation and Redemption: Essays on Gender and the Human Body in Medieval Religion* (New York: Zone Books, 1991) and Jeffrey Hamburger, *The Visual and the Visionary: Art and Female Spirituality in Late Medieval Germany* (New York: Zone Books, 1998). On images as vehicles for subjective practices of religious meditation, see Walter Melion, "Benedictus Arias Montanus and the Virtual Studio as Meditative Place." *Inventions of the Studio: Renaissance to Romanticism*, ed. Michael Cole and Mary Pardo (Chapel Hill, NC, London: University of North Carolina Press, 2005), 73–107, and *The Meditative Art: Studies in the Northern Devotional Print, 1550–1625* (Philadelphia: Saint Joseph's University Press, forthcoming). On religious conflict, ideology, and the origins of art, see Joseph Koerner, *The Reformation of the Images* (London: Reaktion, 2004).

10. For anxiety of influence, see Harold Bloom, *The Anxiety of Influence* (New York: Oxford University Press, 1973). Within art history I am thinking of Leonard Barkan in *Unearthing the Past: Archeology and Aesthetics in the Making of Renaissance Culture* (New Haven: Yale University Press, 1999); Rona Goffen, *Renaissance Rivals: Michelangelo, Leonardo, Raphael, Titian* (New Haven: Yale University Press, 2002); Alexander Nagel, *Michelangelo and the Reform of Art* (Cambridge, UK: Cambridge University Press, 2000); Joseph Koerner, *The Moment of Self-Portraiture in German Renaissance Art* (Chicago: University of Chicago Press, 1993). See also Stephen Campbell, " 'Fare una cosa morta parer viva': Michelangelo, Rosso, and the (Un) Divinity of Art," *Art Bulletin* Vol. 84, n. 4 (2002), 596–620, on modes of reading and mythology, and *The Cabinet of Eros: The Studiolo of Isabella d'Este and the Rise of Renaissance Mythological Painting* (New Haven: Yale University Press, 2004). Karen-edis Barzman, *The Florentine Academy and the Early Modern State: The Discipline of Disegno*. Cambridge: Cambridge UP, 2000.

11. Clement Greenberg, "Towards a Newer Laocoon," in *Clement Greenberg: The Collected Essays and Criticism*, vol. 1, ed. John O'Brian (Chicago: University of Chicago Press, 1986), 5–37, 28. Originally published in *Partisan Review*, vol. 7, n. 4 (July–August 1940), 296–310.

12. See also Hans Belting, "Image, Medium, Body: A New Approach to Iconology." *Critical Inquiry* v. 31, no. 2 (Winter, 2005): 302–319. As "medium specificity" this derives from modernist criticism (Clement Greenberg, et al.). Michael Cole, "The Demonic Arts and the Origin of the Medium," *Art Bulletin* 84 (2002), 621–640.

13. In her "Giotto's Joy," Julia Kristeva wrote—even as she presented a non-normative Giotto—that her reflections on the late medieval painter should serve to "present the avant-garde with a genetic-dialectical reflection on what produced it and/or that from which it sets itself apart." (In Norman Bryson, ed., *Calligram : Essays in New Art History from France* (Cambridge, UK: Cambridge University Press, 1988), 27–52, 50. The essay "La Joie de Giotto" was first published in 1972 [*Peinture* 2/3 (January 1972), pp. 35–51]; in this sentence, Kristeva appears to identify herself with the avant-garde as she characterizes late-medieval or Renaissance painting as both what the avant-garde came from and what it opposes.

14. Creighton Gilbert, "On Subject and Not-Subject in Italian Renaissance Pictures," *Art Bulletin* 34 (1952): 202–216; Svetlana Alpers, *The Art of Describing* (Chicago: University of Chicago Press, 1983). See also the discussion of Alpers in the Art Seminar.

15. Alexander Nagel and Christopher Wood, "Towards a New Model of Renaissance Anachronism," *Art Bulletin*, 87 (2005): 403–432 and responses by Michael Cole, Charles Dempsey, and Claire Farago. See also Nagel, *Michelangelo and the Reform of Art*, and Wood, *Albrecht Altdorfer and the Origins of Landscape* (University of Chicago Press and Reaktion Books, 1993).

16. Martin Warnke, *The Court Artist: On the Ancestry of the Modern Artist* (Cambridge; New York: Cambridge University Press, 1993). See also responses to Warnke's approach in Stephen Campbell, ed., *Artists at Court* (Boston: Isabella Stewart Gardner Museum, 2004).

17. Admittedly a straw man, but Roger Kimball, in *The Rape of the Masters*, provides a clear statement of this point of view. A more thoughtful version of this view appears on the website of the Association for Art History (an organization founded by Bruce Cole, now head of the NEH, and Andrew Ladis): "It strives to accomplish this through discussion, which is free of jargon, ephemeral ideology and doctrinal rigidity. By fostering openness and diversity of inquiry, the Association creates a forum for art historians from all fields. Furthermore, by asserting the importance of the philological, humanistic, and scholarly aspects of art history as a research discipline and by insisting upon the centrality of the art object itself, the Association nurtures and sustains the venerable but ever-maturing discipline of art history, while promoting an intellectually coherent approach to the comprehension of the object, its image and its meanings." http://www.indiana.edu/~aah/goalslink.html; accessed 1/11/07.

18. Fried, "Art and Objecthood," *Artforum* 5 (June 1967), 12–23.

19. See e.g. Joan Marter, "The Ascendancy of Abstraction for Public Art: The Monument to the Unknown Political Prisoner Competition," *Art Journal* 53 (Winter 1994): 28–36.

20. A self-conscious "intelligence of art" quite different from Italian models

might be found in late Gothic ornament, as Kavaler asserts; for another alternative, earlier in Italy, of self-conscious play in image-making, see Anne Dunlop, *Secular Frescoes and Early-Renaissance Art* (Pennsylvania State University Press, forthcoming).

21. Editorial in *Art News* May 15–31, 1942, vol. XLI, no. 7, p. 7. [Alfred M. Frankfurter, ed.]

22. Erwin Panofsky, "Iconography and Iconology: An Introduction to the Study of Renaissance Art," in *Meaning in the Visual Arts* (Garden City: Doubleday, 1955), originally his introduction to *Studies in Iconology* (Oxford, 1939) and originally based on his "Zum Problem der Beschreibung und Inhaltsdeutung von Werken der bildenden Kunst," *Logos* XXI (1932), 103–119.

23. Jacob Burckhardt, *The Civilization of the Renaissance in Italy*, trans. S. G. C. Middlemore (London: Phaidon, 1945).

24. Cassirer, *Individual and Cosmos in Renaissance Philosophy* (Oxford: Oxford University Press, 1963).

25. Erwin Panofsky, *Perspective as Symbolic Form*, trans. Christopher Wood (New York: Zone Books, 1997).

26. Elizabeth Gilmore Holt, *A Documentary History of Art* (Princeton: Princeton University Press, 1982), vol. 1, 200.

27. Panofsky and Wind did not always see eye to eye. In *Pagan Mysteries in the Renaissance* (New Haven and London: Yale University Press, 1958), Wind writes that given a choice between studying the ordinary and the exceptional, "it would seem that to choose the exceptional for study is, in the long run, the smaller risk. An eminent iconographer who preferred the opposite course"—a not quite fair description of Panofsky—"discovered that 'the symbolical creations of geniuses are unfortunately harder to nail down to a definite subject than the allegorical inventions of minor artists.'" This is a direct quote from Panofsky's "The Neoplatonic Movement and Michelangelo." Wind continued, "If this be so, there is something wrong with the manner of nailing down." (*Mysteries*, 190–191, citing Panofsky, *Studies in Iconography*, 228.)

28. Wind was a student and roughly a contemporary of Panofsky, but more than that he was a disciple of Aby Warburg. Wind worked in the US for 15 years, lecturing widely and teaching at the University of Chicago and Smith College, before spending the rest of his life at Oxford. On the legacy of Warburg, see also Georges Didi-Huberman, *L'image survivante: Histoire de l'art et temps des fantômes selon Aby Warburg* (Paris: Éditions de Minuit, 2002).

29. Warburg had interests in the survival of the "low" (media, genres, feeling) in the "high," the antique in the (Renaissance) modern, and, as Nietzsche had also done in his *Birth of Tragedy*, the wild and irrational in the antique. Neither Warburg nor Wind suggested that the *interpreter* should succumb to the irrational; when later interpreters like Gombrich reacted against an irrationalism they saw in Warburg's work they may in fact have been superimposing their knowledge of his intermittent mental illness on his writings.

30. Wind, Introduction, Bibliothek Warburg, *Kulturwissenschaftliche*

Bibliographie zum Nachleben der Antike, ed. Hans Meier, Richard Newald, and Edgar Wind (Leipzig, Berlin: Teubner, 1934), vi–vii.

31. He continued, "With that I cannot quite agree; and possibly I could convert you?" University Archive, University of Chicago, John U. Nef Jr. papers, Box 46 Folder 17, Wind to Nef 2/23/43.

32. This emphasis on difference runs directly counter to Michel Foucault's view of pre-classical representation, in *The Order of Things,* trans. Alan Sheridan (New York: Pantheon, 1971).

33. See Ramon Llull, *El libro de la "Nova geometria,"* ed. José Ma. Millás Vallicrosa (Barcelona: Asociación para la Historia de la Ciencia Española, 1953).

34. Leon Battista Alberti, *De pictura* (Basel: 1540), 3. "Illi enim solo ingenio omni seiuncta materia, species & formas rerum metiuntur. Nos uero, quod sub aspectu rem esse positam uolumus, pinguiore idcirco, ut aiunt, Minerua scribendo utemur."

35. Nicholas of Cusa, *De Possest* 43, in Jasper Hopkins, *A Concise Introduction to the Philosophy of Nicholas of Cusa* (Minneapolis : A.J. Banning Press, 1986), 936.

36. Bovelles, *Liber de propria ratione* (Paris, 1523), XLVIIIr: "Mathematica entia, inter physicas & metaphysicas substantias, medium locum tenent."

37. Bovelles, *Mathematica Corporum,* in *Que hoc volumine continentur . . .* (Paris, 1511). For more on similar ideas about mathematics, see George Hersey, *Pythagorean Palaces: Magic and Architecture in the Italian Renaissance* (Ithaca and London: Cornell University Press, 1976).

38. For one version of this see Evelyn Welch, "Painting as Performance in the Italian Renaissance Court" in Campbell, ed., *Artists at Court.* On performance from an art historical perspective, see Gertsman, Elina, "Pleyinge and Peyntinge: Performing the Dance of Death" in *Studies in Iconography* 27 (2006), 1–43, and other work; Alice Jarrard, *Architecture as Performance in Seventeenth-Century Europe: Court Ritual in Modena, Rome, and Paris* (Cambridge, UK: Cambridge University Press, 2003); Terry, *Politics on the Cloister Walls: Fra Angelico and his Humanist Observers at San Marco,* Ph.D. diss., University of Chicago, 2005; and a dissertation in progress, Christina Normore, *Eyeing the Feast in Late Medieval Burgundy,* University of Chicago. The literature on "festival" is enormous, but is dominated by scholarship in literary studies, history, and drama, rather than art history. See J.R. Mulryne, et al., eds., *"Europa Triumphans": Court and Civic Festivals in Early Modern Europe* (Aldershot and Burlington VT: Ashgate and the Modern Humanities Research Association, 2004); J.R. Mulryne and Elizabeth Goldring, eds., *Court Festivals of the European Renaissance: Art, Politics and Performance* (Aldershot and Burlington VT: Ashgate, 2002); Roy Strong, *Art and Power: Renaissance Festivals 1450–1650* (Woodbridge: Boydell and Brewer, 1984).

39. *La parenthèse du moderne : Actes du colloque 21–22 mai 2004* (Paris: Éditions Centre Georges Pompidou, 2006). See also Bruno Latour, *We have never been modern,* trans. Catherine Porter (Cambridge, MA: Harvard University Press, 2006).

40. The printed book produced for the entry is available in facsimile, with a

useful introduction by Margaret McGowan. *L'Entrée de Henri II à Rouen, 1550* (Amsterdam: Theatrum Orbis Terrarum; New York : Johnson Reprint Corp., 1970). Most recently, see Michael Wintroub, *A Savage Mirror: Power, Identity, and Knowledge in Early Modern France* (Stanford: Stanford University Press, 2006). On the poor see also *Documents concernant les pauvres de Rouen : extraits des archives de l'Hôtel-de-Ville*, ed G. Panel (Rouen: Lestringant, 1917–1919).

41. See Etienne Jodelle, *Le Recueil des inscriptions*, ed. Victor E. Graham and W. McAllister Johnson (Toronto: University of Toronto Press, 1972).

42. I say "seems" because a majority of the performers were probably French sailors.

43. Giovanni Morelli (Ivan Lermolieff), *Italian painters: Critical Studies of their Work*, trans. Constance Jocelyn Ffoulkes (London: J. Murray, 1892–1893).

44. Carlo Ginzburg, "Clues: Roots of an Evidentiary Paradigm," in *Clues, Myths, and the Historical Method*, trans. John and Anne C. Tedeschi (Baltimore, 1989). Freud also studied artworks, and he used them not to *determine* authorship but to diagnose the author. This is still, in some sense, what the "case in art history" looks like in the popular imagination of paranoid fiction, that is, *The Da Vinci Code*. The question is not that of the identity of the author but the determination of the author's secret.

45. For instance, Vasari's criticisms of Parmigianino, Piero di Cosimo, Uccello, Pontormo, Spinello Aretino, et al.; Vasari connects personal idiosyncracy with artistic failings.

46. William K. Wimsatt and Monroe C. Beardsley. "The Intentional Fallacy." *Sewanee Review*, vol. 54 (1946): 468–488. Bob Williams touches upon this point in his discussion of patronage studies, and Stephen Campbell also finds it curious that Renaissance art historians hesitate to posit self-reflexivity in artistic practice.

47. See Lucian Goldmann, *Marxisme et sciences humaines* (Paris: Gallimard, 1967).

48. Robert Williams, "Repressing the Renaissance," CAA presentation, Boston, Feb. 2006.

49. This is certainly true of several of the scholars represented here, perhaps most recently Stephen Campbell's *Cabinet of Eros*.

2
STARTING POINTS

Introduction to an Abandoned Book

James Elkins

This is the Introduction to a book that I toyed with writing for a number of years. It was going to be called Streams into Sand: Connections between Renaissance and Modern Painting. *After the Introduction, I have added a note with some reasons why I have abandoned the project.*

I once had a student, an artist, who became interested in Tintoretto's *Rape of Lucretia* in the collection of the Art Institute in Chicago. The course was on Renaissance art, so I told her the painting would be an appropriate topic for a paper. I started her off by giving her the major references; she read Ridolfi and several modern monographs. But her project was a real surprise. She produced an artist's book, into which she had pasted pages from the texts I'd recommended, and then smeared gesso over them so they couldn't be read. On every other page she had painted details from Tintoretto's painting. There were only two details in the book, repeated over and over: the contours of Lucretia's knee, enlarged so the bend of her kneecap became an abstract landscape, and her pearl necklace, which Tintoretto depicted just as it broke, scattering pearls over her dress and onto the ground. In my student's book, each pearl was enlarged to the size of a page, and there were strange visual puns between the curves of Lucretia's kneecap and the asymmetrical pearls. That was all that had ever interested my student in the painting, in Tintoretto, and in the Renaissance. She didn't claim to understand Tintoretto: for her, pearls and knees were the only comprehensible parts of Tintoretto and the only useful and meaningful parts of the painting. I showed her the passage in Daniel Arasse's book *The Detail*, about the pillow that Tintoretto also depicted falling in mid-air, but she was not interested in pillows or even in the contemporary literature on details. For her, the Renaissance was comprised of pearly kneecaps and knobby-kneed pearls, and she did not know, or care, about anything beyond them.

That student had a sense of the past that has been repeatedly identified as "appropriation" in the critical literature since the 1970s. The word is right—it conjures a past in ruins, from which an artist can take whatever shards and treasures they find—but it does not do justice to the fact that my student was not uninterested in history, or oblivious of how the past shaped her own practice. For her, the kind of history that mattered, that had to be kept in mind and attended to while working, began sometime around Warhol. Nothing much before Pop art had the continuity, the narrative coherence, of history. She felt no pressure from the more distant past because for her, it was not constituted *as* history.

I do not think art historians are that different. From the perspective of some modernist and postmodernist art history, the rivers of Renaissance traditions seem to have divided into Baroque streams, and then into Enlightenment rivulets. By the time romanticism was waning and modernism was getting underway in the mid-nineteenth century, only a few Renaissance traditions were still in play. There were many revivals but few continuous discourses or shared problems. With twentieth-century modernism and postmodernism, the sparse rivulets soaked into the ground and vanished, leaving what appears to be an entirely new landscape. At least that is how the Renaissance can appear to art historians who do not make it a special object of study.

I don't want to say this generates a sense of loss, as Michael Holly, Hans Belting, and others have argued, because it seems to me that there isn't much mourning except among those few art historians who feel the absence of Renaissance interests. The Renaissance has simply vanished from the work and imagination of any number of scholars and critics who work on modernism and postmodernism. I think, for example, of Rosalind Krauss, whose points of reference rarely go back further than the French Revolution. That is not to say her themes cannot be connected to the premodern past, or that her arguments are weaker because they aren't connected to their plausible origins in the Renaissance: it is to say that the shape of history, as it presents itself to her, undergoes a fundamental change sometime around the French Revolution. The same kind of argument could be made about any number of modernist art historians from Robert Rosenblum (for whom modern begins abruptly with the International Style of 1800) to Michael Fried (the fact that he has been writing about Caravaggio since 1995 is a special case, a problem requiring separate discussion). There are, of course, exceptions: Christopher Wood, Thomas Crow, Hubert Damisch, Keith Moxey, and Michael Holly all write about a range of examples from the middle ages to the present.

Yet in my experience this break in the intuited structure of Western art history can be generalized without too many exceptions. In *Master Narratives and Their Discontents*, I found it was possible to gather the principal theories of modernism proposed over the last half-century without needing to make more than a few passing references to art of the seventeenth century or earlier.[1] Most historians of the modern and the contemporary draw the line somewhere in the nineteenth century—often between David and Manet—and see anything beyond that line only darkly. They are likely not to seek precedents for modernist practices farther back than the mid-nineteenth century. For others, such as Thierry de Duve or Arthur Danto, the turning point is within the twentieth century, so that plausible accounts of modernism and postmodernism do not need to open the question of what happened in the Renaissance.

Yet it is not the case that art historians who specialize in premodern art have solved this problem. Any number of specialists in art made before the late eighteenth century study *only* older art: they have effectively forsworn any living engagement with contemporary visual culture, or any responsibility to trace a broader account of art history. (I hope it is clear that I do not think it is enough to say that it is hard to write outside of one's specialty, or that there is not time to do everything. These questions go to the sense scholars have of art history itself, and they are only superficially limited by training or the constraints of time.) Current scholarship is Janus-faced, with the Janus mask placed somewhere between the French Revolution and the generation of Manet. One face looks only forward, to the project of modernism and postmodernism: and one looks only back, as if there were no present.

In many respects critical thinking on modern art seems to have jettisoned the Renaissance, letting it drift into the isolation of specialized scholarship. In comparison *modernism's* genealogy is an indispensable concern in much of art history, cultural history, and literary criticism. Reading Clark's review of the English translation of Walter Benjamin's *Passagen-Werk*, I find myself in the middle of a dense field of historical meditation. "And of course our return to the past is interested and partial," Clark writes, "and in a sense we make the past we desire. Benjamin's project could not be more up front about that. But why do we desire *this* past specifically?" Benjamin's essential past is the Paris of the arcades, but for Clark, the *Passagen-Werk* is not "sufficiently aware that its arcades were pathetic enclaves of dreaming—reservations of the marvelous—in a great desert of the smart."[2] The two senses of modernity's past are both located in Paris, both tangled in the rise of the bourgeoisie. The one is solitary, camouflaged, and partly petrified; the other is full of promise, clarity, and harshness: but both are bound in a common conversation on central concepts of loss, memory, romanticism, collecting, the place of the bourgeoisie, "dialectical" images, nostalgia, and above all the meaning of modernism. It is a rich and unsettling conversation, but when I read it, I think of the Renaissance. The Renaissance isn't *these* pasts, the ones that generate and energize so much of contemporary art history—but I cannot say why. Is it finally, or merely, because the bourgeoisie and modern capitalism had not yet developed? Or because painting was still attached to other goals, as Michael Fried has argued? The problem with searching for answers in this fashion is that there are so many answers, and they are so easy to find: that in itself is suspicious. The explanations are ready to hand, but they don't seem promising or particularly interesting, and I take that as a sign that a more difficult problem has been covered over by an apparently simple solution. Meanwhile, the literature on *these* pasts—the ones I am exemplifying with Benjamin's visual imaginary and Clark's objections to it—continues to grow, leaving the question of links between Renaissance painting and contemporary art to flounder in a nearly perfect vacuum.

The relative lack of writing on affinities between Renaissance and modern painting is one of the themes of this book, and it is a constraint on the focus and unity of the chapters that follow, which are tentative and experimental. For some readers I imagine the essays in this book may seem a little airless. To a Renaissance specialist some of my comparisons may appear overly large, others too speculative, or inappropriately idiosyncratic. When an artist like Giotto is put in an essay together with an artist like Beckman, some violence is apt to be done to the reception of both. So if the laces of well-disciplined scholarship come a bit loose in the chapters that follow, it is because I am trying to discover what happens to historical sense when Giotto and Beckmann are posited as artists working in the same tradition. I want to know just what kinds of historical understanding need to be broken in order to think of them together. In some cases it's just the customs of the discipline that warn against putting Giotto and Beckmann together—it's gauche, or sloppy. But the oddness of the pairings I experiment with in this book may sometimes also be a sign of the structural depth of the break between Renaissance and modernism.

Renaissance painting is in a perilous, or perhaps I should say a paradoxical, situation: it is at one and the same time the desiccated and nearly lifeless remnant of some inaccessible past, and also the heavy anchor of the entire project of modernism. It is that strange condition that motivates the far-flung comparisons I attempt in these chapters. Either we find some viable links to the past, or we will be compelled to admit that somehow, against any deeper sense of history, the Renaissance has become disconnected from what we now call painting, history, and even art. I want to know if the Renaissance is like one of those desert rivers that slowly disappears into a stream bed, leaving nothing but dry sand. Downstream, where we are, it may seem the land is dry because the water runs so far underground that it is of no use to anyone.

That is the Introduction I wrote first around 1998, and revised in spring 2006. So why is this book never going to appear? Because the chapters I projected now seem like the wrong ones. This was the Table of Contents:

1. *Introduction* ....
2. *Caravaggio, Stella: Abstraction's Sense of History*.....................
3. *Crivelli, Kirchner: On Modern Impatience* ....
4. *Castagno, Dalí: Signs of Religion* ....
5. *Giotto, Balthus: The Impossibility of Narrative*.......................
6. *Piero, Picasso: The Aesthetics of Discontinuity* ....
7. *Uccello, Duchamp: The Ends of Wit*......................................
8. *Il Rosso, Sherrie Levine: The Artistic Temperament* ....
9. *Postscript: Streams into Sand* ....

The majority of the chapters were published in the mid 1990s, so as I write this, in June 2006, the book has been shelved for about ten years.[3] *Some of the chapters might still be worth defending: the notion of "modern impatience," for example, has resonance with current critical concerns. It's still an open question how best to think of the fact that artworks, like Carlo Crivelli's, appear to have required tremendous patience (and therefore to have risked being boring, either for the artist or for his assistants) and those, like Ernst Kirchner's, that seem to have avoided boredom at all costs, and to be structured as ways of getting around patience.*

But as the last rivulets of the Renaissance disappear into the landscape, they shift and change and are hard to see properly. I think Joseph Koerner is probably right to concentrate on the very largest issues, the ones that pertain to our sense of ourselves in history—issues such as the inception of historical consciousness in painting, the origins of the depiction of the present, and the first acknowledgments of the workings of allegory. Chapter 7, on the appearance of the idea that pictures could be witty, is probably the closest to a workable theme. There, I was trying to argue that Uccello is one of the principal places in the Renaissance in which pictures gain the capacity to show wit—to be clever, to be ingenious—and that once started, the machinery of pictorial wit is ultimately self-destructive. Duchamp's apparently endless capacity to make fun of himself is the modern foil in that chapter.

It's not that the theme of the book seems wrong—Streams into Sand *was what first made me think that* Renaissance Theory *might be a good idea—but that the idea of searching for links, or criticizing links that seem poorly conceptualized, isn't quite the right way to go about it. This Table of Contents seems like a list of fossil streambeds, places where the water has already dried. They were living themes in the 1980s, some of them, and others were artificial or especially short-lived. Few people other than Bernard Berenson, for example, really thought that Piero della Francesca looked like a cubist avant la lettre, so the theme of my Chapter 6 was never one that provoked much controversy. And yet these fossils are traces of things that were once real. The Piero-Picasso fallacy is repeated in many places, and even T.J. Clark mentions it, without criticism, in* Farewell to an Idea. *Chapter 4, comparing Castagno's apparently sincere attempts to put religious doubt and conviction into his paintings with Dalí's intentionally over-blown and therefore wholly dubious religiosity, takes on an issue too broad and shallow for one essay. And Chapter 8, comparing Il Rosso's feverish prints with Barbara Kruger, tries to say something about the equally unencompassable topic of the the artistic temperament, and how it is prone to sometimes hyperbolic exaggeration (in Il Rosso's "madness") or overly punctilious critique (in Kruger's pedantic insistence on the end of "genius"). So: too large, too small, too artificial, too late.*

Maybe someday I will come back to this book, but then I imagine this Table of Contents will be transformed beyond recognition.
June 2006

Notes

1. *Master Narratives and Their Discontents*, with an introduction by Anna Arnar (New York: Routledge, 2005).
2. Clark, "Reservations of the Marvelous," *London Review of Books* 22 no. 12 (22 June 2000), 3–9, quotations on pp. 6, 9 respectively.
3. Chapter 2, "Caravaggio, Stella: Abstraction's Sense of History" was published, in an earlier version, as "Abstraction's Sense of History: Frank Stella's *Working Space* Revisited," *American Art* 7 no. 1 (winter 1993), 28–39; Chapter 3, "Crivelli, Kirchner: On Modern Impatience" was

published, in an earlier version, as "On Modern Impatience," *Kritische Berichte* 3 (1991), 19–34; Chapter 4, "Castagno, Dalí: Signs of Religion" was published, in an earlier version, as "A Hagiography of Bugs and Leaves: on the Dishonesty of Pictured Religion," *Journal of Information Ethics* 2 no. 2 (1993), 53–70; Chapter 5, "Giotto, Balthus: The Impossibility of Narrative" was published, in an earlier version, as "On the Impossibility of Stories: The Anti-Narrative and Non-Narrative Impulse in Modern Painting," *Word & Image* 7 no. 4 (1991), 348–364; Chapter 6, "Piero, Picasso: The Aesthetics of Discontinuity" is unpublished; Chapter 7, "Uccello, Duchamp: The Ends of Wit" was published, with minor changes, in *Zeitschrift für Ästhetik und allgemeine Kunstwissenschaft* 36 (1991), 199–224; and Chapter 8, "Il Rosso, Sherrie Levine: The Artistic Temperament" was published in French as "La Persistance du 'tempérament artistique' comme modèle: Rosso Fiorentino, Barbara Kruger, Sherrie Levine," *Ligeia* 17–18 (October 1995/June 1996), 19–28.

Vasari's Renaissance and its Renaissance Alternatives

Stephen J. Campbell

It is possible, and important, to distinguish two broad senses of the term "Renaissance art." One is as a chronological shorthand for a broad range of crafted objects produced in the period ca.1400–ca.1600, which may often—but do not necessarily—share stylistic or formal characteristics. Such production forms part of a phenomenon variously described as an "image explosion" or as a "revolution in consumer culture", founded on a demonstrable increase in demand for painting, sculpture and other visual media alongside other luxury craft objects across a wider spectrum of society, and a greater ubiquity of images in social life, from the late 1300s to the 1600s.[1] This phenomenon, even when no longer conflated with others like the rise of humanism in the same period, is often identified as "the Renaissance", although the supposedly more neutral description "Early Modern" is often preferred.

The other sense of "Renaissance art" is as a kind of ideological investment, a particular polemical designation of what art—chiefly painting, sculpture, architecture—is or might be. Lorenzo Valla, writing around 1440, offers a succinct early formulation. It concerns harnassing these three arts to a notion of revival that Valla and his humanist colleagues saw themselves as bringing about in the world of learning, and of conceding their status as liberal arts—practices founded on a theory, carried out for their own intrinsic dignity and interest, independent of practical or commercial ends: "I do not know why the arts most closely approaching the liberal arts—painting, sculpture in stone and bronze, and architecture—had been in so long and so deep a decline and almost died out together with literature itself; nor why they have come to be aroused and come to life again in this age; nor why there is now such a rich harvest both of good artists and good writers."[2]

Figures closer to the world of practice and the marketplace—Ghiberti, Cennini, Filarete, Piero, Mantegna, Leonardo, Dürer—employed broadly similar terms to characterize what they were doing, and to express a broadly-shared sense of newness about the art of their own time—but they did this with inventive variations in meaning, and (as we will see) not always in verbal form. Their notion of "revival" is often richly metaphoric, since it is used to characterize what art is and what art does to its viewers. For the sculptor/architect Filarete, writing in the mid-fifteenth century, revival or revivification was what happened in the experience of the viewer: "when I associated with those [who work today in the antique manner], they woke me up in such a way that I now could not produce the smallest thing in any manner but the *modo anticho*." And "I seem to see . . . [in these new structures] those noble edifices that existed in Rome in classical times and those that, we read, existed in Egypt. I appear to be reborn [*mi pare rinascere*] when I see these worthy edifices, and to me they seem still more beautiful." For the poet/painter Francesco Lancilotti, writing in 1509, painting is a miraculous power to make dead things come to life: "To make some dead stuff seem quick, living and active: by what kind of science could the feat be surpassed? Oh, happy the man who gains that objective."[3]

Like the various forms of Modernist art practice and polemic, that which called itself the "modern manner" around 1500 elicits recognition and engagement from its audience. Contemporary art history, on the other hand, is often skeptical of the complicity such engagement can involve. Hence the appearance of disarray, a proliferation of sub-specializations that separately seek to address what appears excluded by the ideologies of Renaissance, with an increasingly unwillingness to agree on what is included.

This paper will consider Renaissance art in its programmatic sense, especially with regard to art which presents itself as "practiced theory." It shares certain points of broad agreement with Robert Williams' formulation that "the central achievement of Renaissance art is a theoretical one," but seeks to widen the field of what constitutes art theory.[4] In doing this, I am also seeking to address the problem just alluded to, that invoking a Renaissance at all (in describing myself as a historian of Renaissance art rather than Early Modern art) one is professing open complicity with Vasari, which might not be always a good thing. But it is also not necessarily the case. There are other vantage points from which to describe the phenomenon available within the period itself.

Vasari's history of art adopted the humanist model of the revival of learning, as we saw it employed by Valla (who himself did not invent it) in the early fifteenth century. And this view of *rinascita* or rebirth has dominated subsequent accounts of "Renaissance art," including the most revisionist:

> For having seen in what way [painting], from a small beginning, climbed to the greatest height, and how from a state so noble she fell into utter ruin, and that, in consequence, the nature of this art is similar to that of the others, which, like human bodies, have their birth, their growth, their growing old, and their death; [artists] will now be able to recognize more easily the process of her second birth and of that very perfection whereto she has risen again in our times.[5]

"Renaissance" is a resurrection or a rebirth of something lost: Vasari's *Lives* and its allegorical frontispiece, with a kind of "Last Judgment" presided over by allegories of Painting, Sculpture and Architecture, insinuates that it is his *writing*, his own historiographical project, that secures this resurrection, as much as anything that art itself has achieved. The woodcut is captioned: "This breath [i.e. this book] will proclaim that these men never perished and were never vanquished by death [*Hac sospite nunquam/ Hos periisse viros, victos/ aute morte fatebor*]." As long as we recognize a Renaissance, it seems, we are stuck with some version of an art history shaped by a teleology of artistic progress, male genius, and the "rebirth" of art. Even powerful revisionist accounts from a medievalist perspective which seek to resist the perspective of Vasari—such as Hans Belting's idea of an "era of the image" and an "era of art," fall rather neatly into a Vasarian paradigm.[6]

This will only be the case, however, if we fail to see Vasari's writing as a polemical intervention, a powerful response to other possible formulations, other ways of thinking and theorizing about art, which occurred in his generation and in those preceding it. A large number of artists and writers in the period 1400–1600 shared a commitment to the view that they were making a new art, one that embraced characteristics such as naturalism (in all its different and entangled senses); that naturalism should somehow coexist with *style*, a studied distinctness of rendering form; and that making new art involved a systematic imitation of canonical models from the past and recent present (i.e. laying claim to a particular place in history, an acceptance of the contingency of style). Yet there is nothing monolithic about this: artists and writers may differ from one another in the kinds of meaning they give to these qualities. The goals of naturalism, style, and imitation are deeply fraught—art theory might even be read as demonstrating their fundamental incompatibility—but they are real goals.

If we accept Vasari and other theorists of the late Renaissance (Armenini, Comanini, Lomazzo, Zuccari, Bocchi) as spokesmen, we need to grasp the work of closure pursued by their texts, which is in part a product of their drive to impose an all-encompassing system on disparate and contending positions. We also need to recognize that Italy, and the world, was a very different place in the 1560s, when the definitive edition of the *Lives* appeared, than it was in 1500, and that the historical experience represented by that text is in many respects *discontinuous* from that of the Renaissance as many of us now understand it: art in the period from Brunelleschi to the death of Michelangelo. These remarks thus also proceed from a conviction that confronting theory without a sense of its historical implicatedness is an impoverishment of both history and of theory.

What is perhaps most distinctive about Vasari, in fact, is that history is constituted as the privileged form of theoretical reflection upon art. In modern scholarship this has more often been seen as a loss than as a gain. For Georges Didi-Huberman in *Confronting Images: Questioning the Ends of a Certain History of Art*, both "Renaissance" and "History of Art" acquire their joint formulation or invention in the writings of Vasari, and with a particularly intractable force which still holds sway over all subsequent considerations of both:

> The discipline sought to arrogate to itself the prestige of its object of study; by grounding it intellectually, it sought to regulate it. As for the *knowledge about art* whose field it opened up, it resolved henceforth to envisage or accept only an *art conceived as knowledge*: as reconciliation of the visible and the Idea, denial of its visual powers, and subjection to the theory of *disegno*. Art was acknowledged less as a thinking object—which it had always been—than as an object *of* knowledge, all genitive senses conflated.[7]

Like many critiques of Vasari that hold him responsible for nearly everything wrong with the History of Art, Didi-Huberman both challenges Vasari's centrality and reinscribes it yet more emphatically. His account of the Vasarian moment sees it as effectively a moment of *metatechne*, in Williams' terms, but in very different terms to those provided by Williams himself in his own, far more affirmative account of the achievements of sixteenth-century theorists. Williams has provided a powerful appreciation of just what is *gained* in sixteenth-century art theory. Its central theoretical achievement lies not, after all, in the values of progress, beauty, naturalism (as Didi-Huberman and numerous others would have it), but in that of *systematicity*. Art is describable as having an orderly and systematic character arising from principles such as perspective, style, decorum, and the theory of *disegno*. Some of these principles are also established as central to social life, to what we would now call "culture" itself, while *disegno* links the artist's manual operations with higher principles of philosophical and scientific knowledge: art is founded on a philosopher's knowledge of the world, even as a "superintendency" of all other forms of knowledge. The achievement of Vasari, Lomazzo, Zuccari, then, is that art is established as a form of knowledge.

Through a different route, Didi-Huberman has reached a similar description of Vasari, but his assessment is hardly positive: "There is indeed a system in Vasari, but it is a cracked system."[8] The system is founded on beauty, mimesis and imitation, but "What is [imitation], if not the puppet goddess of a simulacrum of a system . . . A large sack open to all winds, a cornucopia upon which Vasari, like many others, drew generously to pull out whatever he wanted,"[9] and ". . . It is no exaggeration to say that the history of art began, in the sixteenth century, by creating art in its own image, so as to be able to constitute itself as an 'objective' discourse."[10] Art is thus constituted as something more than a menial/manual operation, but at what cost? With such spokesmen, art itself (as opposed to writing about art) is stripped of its own ability to "think" or "speak." That which eludes the terms of the critic or the historian or the philosopher (Vasari, Kant, Panofsky) is consigned to the domain of "not-knowledge." Aesthetics filters out that which is extrinsic to the beautiful; iconology reduces the image to its textual subject matter; the archive based approaches of recent art history make art disappear altogether: "The history of art would have to kill the image so that its object, *art*, might try to escape the extreme dissemination imposed upon us by images—from the ones that haunt our dreams and float by in clouds to the ones, 'popular,' horribly ugly or excessive, before which five thousand of the faithful willingly kneel as one. To kill the image, this was to want to extract from a *subject* that is always rent, contradictory, unconscious, in a sense "stupid," the harmonious, intelligent, conscious, and immortal *humanity* of man."[11]

Didi-Huberman is pursuing his own valorization of the "primitive" and "anti-humanist" tendency in fifteenth- and sixteenth-century painting, centered on his earlier interpretation of Fra Angelico, but he has noticed something valid about Vasari. Using somewhat different terms, I would frame this observation as follows: it is hard to avoid the impression that Vasari's will to order involves a filtering operation, that images themselves are silenced because of an unruliness that resists the order of language because they are fraught with levels of ambivalence and paradox that resist the characterization of art as knowledge, or because they elicit responses from the beholder that codes of decorum in place by the time Vasari wrote would not admit. A paradigmatic case for Didi-Huberman, as it was for Belting, is Vasari's deliberate failure to understand the issues at stake in Ugo da Carpi's altarpiece of the Veronica, "*fata senza penello*", which he dismisses with a joke attributed to Michelangelo[12]; another might be Vasari's professed incomprehension towards the heterodox but hardly unintelligible frescoes by Pontormo in the choir of San Lorenzo, and his (prudent?) misreading of an anti-Medicean Carnival of Death staged by Piero di Cosimo shortly before the reestablishment of the regime in 1512.[13] The work of Michelangelo itself needed very careful handling by Vasari. Michelangelo served the Vasarian view of art to a far more limited degree than might be expected, given the writer's copious adulation of Michelangelo and the length and near hagiographic character of the *Life*; by the second edition of the *Lives*, and in Vasari's own practice and that of the Academy of Design, Raphael is by far the more useful model for Vasarian art theory, since the painter from Urbino is seen to embody principles of perspective, decorum, *disegno*, and—above all—of *imitation*. The "divine" Michelangelo was characterized instead as "beyond" imitation by others, and the emphatic insistence of the piety of the artist and the moral probity of his art is an oblique confrontation of the ongoing scandal around the Sistine *Last Judgement* (1545), widely regarded as an affront to artistic decorum, even as a work of idolatry that placed pagan license over Christian doctrine.[14]

In his more recent essay on "systematicity," Williams pre-empts the anti-humanist/neo-primitivist line of critique typified by Didi-Huberman: "There will be resistance to seeing the Renaissance in the way proposed here. It may be that our fundamental investment in a sentimental—and hypocritical—irrationalism is too deep, that such irrationalism serves a cathartic function too important in contemporary life (331)." Williams takes a bold stand here against the (by now) predictable nature of much Postmodern constructions of the Renaissance and of academic traditions, but the challenge now is to address what makes this view so compelling, to acknowledge where it hits its mark and to answer it.

If theory may be defined not only as a body of general principals abstracted from and prescriptive of practice, but placed under demonstration in practice, then we need to consider the possibility of an art theory without treatises: a theory that can be seen not only

as imposing a consistency on practice, but on which artists themselves might be seen to reflect and examine critically at the level
of practice. Specialists on Medieval art (Herbert Kessler, Michael
Camille), Chinese art (Martin Powers) and Modern/Contemporary
art (most scholars in the field) have no problem positing this
self-reflexive dimension to practice; it less commonly occurs in
Renaissance art history, where practice is discussed largely as an
instantiation or illustration of theory. The acknowledgment of resistance or dialogue between practiced theory and prescribed theory is
rarer still, especially of a practiced theory that raises and questions the
ends of art, or that seeks to broaden or critique available models of
systematicity.[15]

In the case of Michelangelo, as well as Rosso, Pontormo,
Bronzino, Cellini (in fact, much of the Florentine Mannerist art
practice that Vasari disliked), the resistance to a view of art typified
by Raphael and Alberti is not necessarily "irrational," or even anti-
humanist, but can be seen as methodical. Imitation, surely one of the
chief grounds by which an art practice makes a claim for systematicity, appears in their work as agonistically competitive with its models,
sometimes as outrightly parodic of them (the older Michelangelo
employs such a subversive approach to his own earlier work). In place
of perspective, these artists employ decidedly paradoxical modes of
spatial organization, and towards the ends of virtuosity rather than
naturalism. Rather than the *convenevolezza* or "decorum" of the art
treatises, these artists embrace *licenza*, and are attacked for so doing
(Michelangelo's *Last Judgement*, whatever the artist himself may have
intended, was regarded as an offense to decorum, yet it gave rise to
works like Bronzino's *Martyrdom of St. Lawrence* of 1565–69, which
takes the earlier fresco's perceived flouting of decorum as a point of
departure and insists on its internal consistency as a genre[16]); in place
of naturalistic representation, these artists conceive the project of art
as one of *simulation*—the instillation of life into fictitious bodies,
even as the animation of dead matter (the play between composition
and de-composition is particularly marked in the case of Rosso, who
made figures of saints look like living cadavers, and in Pontormo's
manifesto-like *Deluge* and *Resurrection* at San Lorenzo). Above all,
such artists are devoted to the production of *force*—the assertive

engagement of the beholder through wonder, shock (*stupore*) or seduction.

Vasari's account of art (and his own writing) as "resurrection" is an attempt to rein in such hubristic experiments to the more acceptable didactic norms of the academy, to standards of decorum characteristic of the courtesy books and the civilizing process (on another front, Vasari's imperative of imitation is a rebuke to the copying and marketing practices of many Renaissance artists, most notably Perugino). Yet Vasari is only one of several formulations within the period 1400–1550 of the position that something has happened in the arts of painting, sculpture and architecture, in tandem with changing attitudes to these practices, to the extent that it was necessary to formulate the rationale for their existence, the claims that might be made for their importance either in their own terms or in terms of their participation in other social practices and institutions.

For me, the most striking thing about the Vasarian moment is that (like Alberti before him) it displaces a question that clearly preoccupied reflections on "art" written by artists before Vasari—Cennini, Filarete, Leonardo, Hollanda—the question of what was art *for* and of what art could or should do. Such interventions were either responding to or seeking to bring about a critique of new social ideals and values implied in the production and circulation of art objects of various kinds: what did it mean to make art, to buy art, to profess an interest in or love of art? What distinguished the art object from other kinds of object? Why do the "liberal arts" of *disegno* exclude forms of skilled production like wax ex-votos, Sacra Monte tableaux, reliquaries and monstrances, chased and embellished armor?

Vasari writes as if these issues are unproblematic: his writing on art in the *Lives* de-emphasizes the embeddedness of art in, say, politics, religion, civil and domestic life, as if art since Giotto had always been an end in itself: gifted artists are a special kind of human being, motivated by a unique natural disposition (one that impels shepherd boys to sketch on flat stones), and the proprietors of a unique form of knowledge. Questions of what is and is not art are displaced by others: for instance, is painting superior to sculpture? This was a momentous move and it enabled a great deal for Vasari and his fellow *artefici*, but it meant a closing off of a rich array of other possibilities.

I. Mantegna and genealogies of the image: what is a painting?

Andrea Mantegna provides a good example of a theoretically engaged artist active around 1500, one who appears to have been conversant with the principles of texts such as Alberti's *De Pictura*. Unlike the more usual examples of theoretically engaged artists such as Filarete, Piero della Francesca and Leonardo, Mantegna did not himself write art theory; his work cannot be thus reduced to simple instantiations of theoretical precept, his own or others, which is often what happens in familiar art historical accounts of "Alberti's influence on Mantegna." This lack of a neat fit with bodies of precept, however, makes all the more evident a quality of epistemological engagement and self-awareness which draws his enterprise closer to that of "theory" in our contemporary sense of the term.

In my current work on Mantegna, I explore the artist's apparent preoccupation with painting as a category of human production. Through his Paduan heritage, dominated by the legacy of Giotto and by proto-academic models of art education (the *studium* of Squarcione), Mantegna inherited a philosophically momentous concept of "artist" with roots deep in the medieval past. In the 1290s the *artifex* Niccolo left a self-laudatory inscription on the facade reliefs of San Zeno in Verona (which Mantegna studied intently), right over a carving of God creating Adam.[17] The notion of "artist" had long existed (Vasari uses the Italian form of *artifex*) but not a notion of "art" which could secure any special distinction for painting: the products made by an *artifex* constituted a deeply heterogeneous category. It was Alberti who analyzed the activity he called *pictura* and referred to individual instantiations of *pictura* as *historia* (an image, whether painted or in relief). But the notion of what characterized *a painting*, of painting as an art that demonstrated its defining theoretical principals, required further elaboration. Mantegna's own explorations of the principals of painting thus parallel but are not reducible to Alberti's *De Pictura*, which may have appeared rudimentary and obvious by the 1460s.

Mantegna explored the nature of painting as a medium through a close emulation of the effects of sculpture and sculptural relief, above all in his late grisailles which appear to assert the superiority of pictorial *relievo* with regard to the production of atmospheric and spatial effects. He also sought to establish painting as a practice that could assimilate other and especially older dispensations of painting and sculpture, even while recognizing fundamental distinctions between his own *pictura* on one hand and a whole antique and Medieval heritage of *signa* and *imagines* on the other.

His work thus measures the properties of painting against three other broad categories of image-practice, whose relation to each other lacked systematic definition: the *signa* or *statuae* of classical antiquity; the *imagines* of Christian devotional and liturgical tradition; the modern practice of Giotto and his followers in painting and Donatello in sculpture. The relation between these three broad designations was by no means clear; certainly it lacked the kind of systematicity that a disciplinary "History of Art" would later give it: Golden Age (antiquity), decline (Medieval art), and revival (the modern manner and its early Renaissance antecedents). In general, it would appear that icons, idols and *istorie* were understood not only (or not primarily) as historically successive, but as having discrete and separate functions and natures—different but imprecisely distinguished "systems" of images. But all three were in their own way deeply prestigious, and not only prestigious but powerful.

That power can lie in their authority and their authorship: in the case of icons, those that were attributed to St. Luke or St. Gregory; in the case of ancient art, examples inscribed with the (spurious) signatures of Phidias, Praxiteles or Vitruvius; in the case of modern work, as one humanist theorist of imitation explained it "One should do what the painters of our own age do, who though they may look with attention at famous paintings by other artists, yet follow the models of Giotto alone."[18] Or, that force can be located in a particular potency of the image—a supernatural potency in the case of some Christian images, a risky power of fascination in the case of a beautiful and alluring ancient sculptures, a power to "move the soul" in the case of ancient and modern works.

Mantegna's project of imitation is about an emulation by *pictura* of these different possibilities of force in images. Force is not just about painting's power to move: it concerns the enlivening of painting itself, a vitality which entails the production or extension of itself in time, its generation of an afterlife, its ability to bring other objects like itself into being. Force or energy, here, is not directed only at the beholder, but at the traditions of image-making in which his work intervenes.

A distinction is necessary here between *imitation* and *transmission*, two different ways in which artistic tradition (the relation of images to previous images) might be constituted. A medieval artist could claim, in copying an icon, to transmit the force it constituted; Giusto de'Menabuoi (c. 1320–1391), a painter carefully studied by Mantegna, painted a Virgin and Child based on a much venerated icon in the cathedral of Padua, and his stylistically up-to-date version itself acquired a legendary reputation based on its association with the iconic original.[19] By imitating works believed to possess this kind of efficacy, Mantegna, however, is no longer claiming to transmit their miraculous force: through inscriptions and signing practices, and through the simultaneous allusion to different models, they make an issue of mediation as representation, of their non-identity with their models. He rather creates surrogates for the pictorial *force* possessed by some venerated images through new pictorial technologies of illusion and expressive address. A small distemper painting of the Blessing Christ Child in Washington is modeled on the same miraculous icon in the cathedral of Padua, but its hold on the viewer lies largely in its emotional impact and its emphatic sculptural presence, which it achieves in a simultaneous emulation of a work by Donatello—the frowning and urgently gesturing Christ child of the Santo altar in Padua.

The transmission of originals preserves the authority of the original, but imitation, understood in the strong sense as "emulation," might be better understood as displacement or substitution.[20] Aligned with the evocation of tradition here is also the desire to *become* tradition, to imprint his mark indelibly on subsequent practice. This objective was served most effectively by his pioneering use of reproductive engraving, resulting in a canonical series of compositional exemplars for sacred and profane imagery that left their mark on generations of artists from Durer to Rubens and Poussin.[21]

Art history has had a problem coming up with the terms to characterize the monumental series of nine canvases that Mantegna executed at the conclusion of his career, between 1487 and 1505, and known as the *Triumphs of Caesar*. I would like to consider the *Triumphs* as a pictorial *summa* of a category of artistic representation coming into existence over the previous century or more, and one which Vasari (whose own grudging admiration of Mantegna amounted effectively to a disavowal of his place in history[22]) will proceed to define and delimit in a written form.[23] In its unprecedented evocation of the world of things, the *Triumphs* offer a programmatic pictorial characterization of what we now call "Renaissance art," engaging its stylistic desiderata, its technical accomplishments—and, in ways that excede any theory committed to writing—its ideological implicatedness.

1. The myth of rebirth

The lost arts of antiquity become visible once more, re-constituted through and as a form of knowledge proper to artists like Mantegna. Something has been put together that has been lost or fragmented, to the extent that it can be seen to be born again; the painting of the ancients, which also subsumes its sculpture and other arts. The very processional motion of the Triumphs is also programmatically about this "bringing back" of the riches of a lost world: Mantegna has visualized a whole world of lost visual and material culture: statues, paintings, vases, coins, buildings (carried as miniature trophies), and precious metalwork. The processional movement across open countryside implies that this rebirth is also a relocation or *translatio* (in this case, from Rome to Mantua).

2. Imitation

The series of paintings solicits recognition as a declaration of authority on the part of the artist who made it, a testimony to his unequaled acquaintance with the arts of antiquity. Yet there is hardly a single, direct reference to a recognizable ancient source: Mantegna's imitation of antiquity entails its thorough assimilation, and its replacement by a surrogate antiquity of his own invention. The work is conceived as a "classic" or canonical model for imitation by others, and its

subsequent fortune in reproductive media and in the imitative practice of others shows that in large measure it succeeded in being this.[24]

3. (Renaissance) art or (early modern) objecthood?

Mantegna invites us to consider an array of objects (paintings, sculptures, objects in precious metals, even architectural models) in two
ways—on one hand, in terms of the *pathos* of their displacement,
bearing traces of a lost culture, as objects which need to be read or
interpreted—and on the other, in terms of the leveling effect produced by the triumphal display of plundered riches. In the former
case, the objects possess semiotic virtuosity as bearers of knowledge;
in the latter, they are mere objects, interchangeable for one another.
This is precisely the tension that besets the history of collecting in
the 1400s and 1500s. However manifold in their origin or purpose,
weapons, coins, and other artifacts may be subject to the leveling
category of the trophy, of luxury objects at the disposal of the elite,
which might be sold or exchanged or salvaged for their materials.
Mantegna painted in 1506 what can be seen as a kind of addendum
to the *Triumphs*: in *The Introduction of the Cult of Cybele to Rome*,
painted for the *studiolo* of a Venetian collector, the relocation of an
object obtained through conquest is given a more determinate significance: a work of sculpture here is more than a work of sculpture,
but a bearer of force which constitutes a civilizing process and a
moment of civic foundation (It is no accident that this work was
destined for a *studiolo*, for it is in this kind of space that the value of
objects—especially the more than material value of objects—was
specially at stake in the late fifteenth and early sixteenth centuries).
In the *Triumphs*, the "real" medium of the spectacle itself—painting—acquires a particular distinction in its capacity to encompass the
form and quality of so many other items of human manufacture.
Here perhaps there is some anticipation of Vasari's insistence that
there are three arts of *disegno*: painting, sculpture, architecture—but
the *Triumphs* does allow the confrontation of other possibilities,
some of them less optimistic, and other media.

4. Naturalism or simulation?

As reflections on art, the paintings both instantiate and reflect upon the principles of the *maniera moderna*. Through color, perspective and chiaroscuro (affording a rich sense of *rilievo* in the later canvasses) the paintings unfold an understanding of art as *mimesis* approaching illusion. Mantegna's enterprise here speaks of other deep preoccupations that undergird the early ideology of "Renaissance" or "Renaissance art," anxieties that were finally dispelled by Vasari in that they related directly to controversies about the art of Michelangelo in particular, and to a climate of censorship at mid-century: to the discourse of imitation and representation, we need to add that of art-as-simulation, of spurious animation and phantasmatic illusion. The resurrection or everlasting life promised by art is specious and illusory. The representation of images within images, of suits of armor that evoke the ghostlike bodies of warriors, the presence of faces in the clouds, entails a reflection on the falsehood of appearances which takes it beyond the usually more celebratory purview of Renaissance art theory.

5. Classical revival and imperial ideology

Mantegna's *Triumphs* is, in part, a kind of *vanitas* that shows empire to be no more than a mere effect of images and spectacle, a *topos* of humanist meditation on the vestiges of antiquity. It was, after all, produced at a time when the reach of Imperial power in Italy was extremely weak, and in 1504 was used as part of a "Theater of Fortune" to teach the instability of all earthly glory. Yet the ironic converse of this would also have been appealing to Mantegna's patrons, the Gonzaga: if Empire is no more than a system of objects, a theater-state that can be taken apart and re-assembled elsewhere, then the Gonzaga can appropriate Empire. All of this could be said to have changed by the mid-century when Vasari was writing. The imperial domination of Italy was then a fact; Vasari's patrons, the Medici rulers of Florence, held power through the concession of the new Caesar, Charles V, whose troops had sacked Rome itself in 1527. There is hardly a page in those devoted by Vasari to the recent past that does not speak of this, but largely through tactful allusion or omission. It was his own murals in the courtyard of the Palazzo Vecchio, views of imperial cities painted on the occasion of the marriage of Francesco de'Medici to Joanna of Austria in 1565, that designated the Medici residence as a Hapsburg palace.

II. Art in Renaissance collections: a system of objects or a system of images?[25]

We can locate further reflection on the category "art" in particular uses or displays of art: in the era after Vasari, the rise of the gallery testifies to a view of art very much in accordance with the *Lives of the Artists*. Devotional images, portraits and didactic paintings disembedded from churches and other context-specific installations are presented alongside "works of art," the primary purpose of which is to exemplify "art" according to the newly emerging academic and theoretical principles through which art is organized as a form of knowledge: as the work of a particular artist, as the work of a particular regional school, and for a *spectator* who peruses the series in a specified order. But contrast this use of images, where they are used to constitute a systemic "history of art," with the pre-existing paradigm of the *studiolo* or the overlapping one of the *kunstkammer*, in which paintings and sculptures do not exemplify a form of knowledge in themselves, but form a system with other bodies of knowledge— through what they represent, through the analogy they provide of the dynamic creativity of the natural world, through the interpretative acumen they exact from viewers (which implicates them in the activity of reading and writing associated with the *studiolo*), through their amenability to philosophical *contemplatio*.[26]

Or at least that is their rationale. Paintings and sculptures formed an apparatus with books and antiquities and objects from the natural world; the authorship of the paintings and sculptures, along with the virtue and cultivation of their maker, is often of extreme importance, yet they are not yet detached—as specimens of the art of *disegno*—from mechanical arts or indeed other liberal arts, as they would be in the era of the academies which is ushered in with Vasari's *Vite*.

There is no apparent principle of decorum at work here, and even less any sense of an emerging autonomy of art. The systematicity at work here, if any, is entirely due to the creativity of the viewer, who is here better defined as a "reader" rather than as a spectator. As the critic Giovan Battista Strozzi wrote at the end of the sixteenth century, in demonstrating the principle of unity: "when in some study or chamber there are paintings, statues, minerals, petrified things, and other objects of this kind, if they are not organized among themselves, the mind organizes and arranges them on its own, and if they are organized, it is pleased by this, and however different they may be, the mind considers them as similar and assembled to make the unity that it desires, and it includes them under the category decoration and marvels."[27]

In the 1500s the *studiolo* is the culmination of a process already underway in the early quattrocento through which an interest in art is legitimated, and not yet as an end in itself. The claim implicit in the *studiolo*—that man made images could constitute part of an apparatus of knowledge, and of therapeutic "technologies of the self"—is an ideological one: it served to legitimate collecting by associating it with reading, self-cultivation and the pursuit of virtuous knowledge (which included knowledge of the self). Painting and sculpture manage to distinguish themselves from other luxury goods, and profess to be more than trophies of status acquired through material display, but not because "art" was a transcendent category that could justify its own existence. Works produced for the collecting milieu, such as Giorgione's *Tempest* and Lotto's *Portrait of Andrea Odoni*, can be seen to stage such an argument about themselves, linking the ownership and enjoyment of art to knowledge of nature and knowledge of the self. They thus answer charges (already broached in Mantegna's *Triumphs*) that collecting might be a wasteful pursuit of the goods of fortune, a pretense of cultivation and distinction befitting the new rich, and that the secular cult of objects is vain curiosity bordering on idolatry.

III. Conclusion: Vasari's painted encyclopedia of painting

In the 1560s, while Vasari was bringing the second edition of the *Lives* to its completion, he was engaged in another epic project which might be seen as a supplement to the *Lives*: the *Sala Grande* program in the Palazzo Vecchio is an attempt to paint the image of the Tuscan state, in terms of its history and manifest destiny, its traditional Republican constitution and the Medici overlordship which is its inevitable outcome.[28] Yet it should also be seen as an attempt to reveal the principles of art (or in this case, primarily the art of painting), as well as a demonstration of the capacity and utility of the knowledge constituted in art. The images of the Sala constitute an encyclopedia of painting, a demonstration of its properties and the diversity of its kinds: history, landscape (incorporating topographical surveying), portraiture (including numerous attested likenesses of the illustrious dead), allegory or poetic invention; the panoramic landscape views of the Flemish with the relief-like clustering of bodies to evoke Michelangelo and the ancients. In effect it seeks to be a kind of super-painting, void of the idiosyncracies of personal style of the team of artists who worked on it. Emulating the Sistine Chapel in its scale, it asks to be considered as an archetype of the modern manner. Yet in attempting to be a pictorial *summa*, the *Sala Grande* project set the scene for its own obsolesence. In later histories of art, from the nineteenth and twentieth centuries, it appears as a servile capitulation of art to the ends of propaganda, barely conceivable as art at all. The precarious subtleties of its dialectical operation were all but lost: the power of art (through its constitutive knowledge) can demonstrate itself in serving the power of the state, but in so doing it always has to show itself as more than a mere operation or effect of state power. Instead of being the painted realization of the vision of art in the *Lives*, it is undermined by the very criteria for recognizing "art" set forth in the *Lives*, against which the *Sala* paintings could only speak of artistic autonomy compromised by absolutism. Vasari had here participated in the tradition of self-demonstrating images, of practiced theory, but it was the *Lives* that would have the last word.

Notes

1. For a sociological explanation of the rise of visual culture see Bram Kempers, *Painting, Power and Patronage. The Rise of the Professional Artists in Renaissance Italy* (London, 1987); for the perspective of an economic historian, and a neo-Burckhardtian view which celebrates the invention of

"Renaissance Man" as a consumer, see Richard Goldthwaite, *Wealth and the Demand for Art in Italy 1300–1600* (Baltimore, 1993). On the role of economic and social catastrophe in shaping the demand for art (identified as an enterprise of memorialization) see Samuel Cohen, *The Cult of Remembrance and the Black Death* (Baltimore, 1992). For the culture of luxury goods and a characterization of Renaissance cultural style, see Luke Syson and Dora Thornton, *Objects of Virtue: Art in Renaissance Italy* (London, 2001). Goldthwaite's highly influential view is challenged by Evelyn Welch, *Shopping in the Renaissance* (New Haven and London, 2005) which, despite its title, argues for a *longue durée* of consumer culture in Italy that exceeds the normal chronological limits of the Renaissance (1350–1600).

2. Lorenzo Valla, *Elegantiae linguae latinae* (c.1440); quoted in H. Weisinger, "Renaissance Theories of Revival in the Fine Arts," *Italica* 20 (1943), 164. On ideas of "Renaissance" current in the Renaissance see also Weisinger, "The Renaissance Theory of the Reaction Against the Middle Ages as a Cause of the Renaissance," *Speculum* 20 (1945), 461- and Erwin Panofsky, " 'Renaissance'—Self-Definition or Self-Deception?" in *Renaissance and Renascences in Western Art* (New York, 1960, 1969), 1–42.

3. For discussion of Lancilotti see Michael Baxandall, *Words for Pictures* (New Haven and London, 2003), 1–5, from which the passage is quoted.

4. A position developed at length in Robert Williams, *Art, Theory, and Culture in Sixteenth Century Italy: from Techne to Metatechne* (Cambridge, 1997); the present essay is mainly engaged with the more recent article "Italian Renaissance Art and the Systematicity of Representation," *Rinascimento* 43 (2004), 309–331.

5. Vasari, *Lives of the Painters, Sculptors, and Architects* trans. Gaston du C. De Vere with Introduction and notes by David Ekserdjian 2 vols. (London, 1927, 1996), I, 46.

6. Hans Belting, *Likeness and Presence. A History of the Image before the Era of Art* trans. Edward Jephcott (Chicago, 1994).

7. English version of *Devant l'image: Question posée aux fin d'une histoire de l'art* (Paris, 1990); trans. John Goodman (University Park, PA, 2005), 82.

8. *Ibid*, p.69.

9. *Ibid*, p.74.

10. *Ibid*, p.87.

11. *Ibid*, p.219.

12. *Confronting Images* 195–199; Hans Belting, *Likeness and Presence* 221–224.

13. The frescoes were destroyed in the eighteenth century, but can be reconstructed using Pontormo's drawings for the project, topographical views of the choir, Pontormo's own diary and, no less importantly, Vasari's own description. On the case for heterodoxy and intelligibility, arguing that the frescoes expound the doctrine of *sola fides* which had been proscribed by the Council of Trent, see Massimo Firpo, *Gli affreschi di Pontormo a San Lorenzo. Eresia, politica e cultura nella Firenze di Cosimo I* (Turin, 1997). Without going as far as Firpo, it might be said that the frescoes manifest an experimental approach to religious iconography grounded in Dante and poetic theory, which Vasari found it prudent not to be seen as endorsing by

the 1560s, notwithstanding the fact that his own earlier religious allegories manifest a similar approach. For Vasari's attitude to the Pontormo circle, albeit one that tends to emphasize professional rivalry over attitudes to art, see Elizabeth Pilliod, *Pontormo, Bronzino, Allori: A Genealogy of Florentine Art* (New Haven and London, 2001).

14. See Campbell, "*Fare una cosa morta parer viva*: Michelangelo, Rosso, and the (Un) Divinity of Art." *Art Bulletin* LXXXIV (2002), 596–620. The most useful account of the scandal is Bernardine Barnes, *Michelangelo's Last Judgement. The Renaissance Response* (Berkeley and Los Angeles, 1998).

15. But see, for example, Leo Steinberg, "Leon Battista Alberti e Andrea Mantegna," in *Leon Battista Alberti* ed. Joseph Rykwert and Anne Engel (Milan, 1994), 330–336. Charles Dempsey *Annibale Carracci and the Beginnings of Baroque Style* second edition (Fiesole, 2000), 50–73, has argued that the art practice of the Carracci should also be understood in terms of a theoretically-informed resistance to Vasari, both as a writer and as a painter. For the critical annotations to Vasari by the Carracci see Mario Fanti, "Le postille carraccesche alle Vite del Vasari: il testo originale," *Il Carrobbio* 5 (1979), 148–164.

16. Campbell, "Bronzino's *Martyrdom of St. Lawrence*. Counter Reformation Polemic and Mannerist Counter Aesthetics." *RES 46: Polemical Objects* (2004), 99–121.

17. For discussion and photographs see Giovanni Lorenzoni and Giovanna Valenzano, *Il Duomo di Modena e la basilica di San Zeno* (Verona and Modena).

18. Pier Paolo Vergerio, discussed in Michael Baxandall, *Giotto and the Orators. Humanist Observers of Painting in Italy and the Discovery of Pictorial Composition, 1350–1450* (Oxford, 1971), 43–44.

19. On Giusto's image and its model, see *Luca Evangelista. Parola e Immagine tra Oriente e Occidente* exh. cat. (Padua, 2000), 408 (catalogue entry by Giordana Canova Mariani).

20. On emulation see Thomas Greene, *The Light in Troy. Imitation and Discovery in Renaissance Poetry* (New Haven and London, 1982), 58–59, 172–179, and Thomas Crow, *Emulation: Making Artists in Revolutionary France* (New Haven, 1995).

21. For a recent discussion that questions Mantegna's role as engraver, that demonstrates his concern to control the circulation of his inventions, see Andrea Canova, "Gian Marco Cavalli incisore per Andrea Mantegna e altre notizie sull'oreficieria e la tipografia a Mantova nel XV secolo." *Italia medioevale e umanistica* 42 (2001); 149–179. See also Evelyn Lincoln, *The Invention of the Italian Renaissance Printmaker* (New Haven and London, 2000).

22. For a critical analysis of Vasari's Life of Mantegna, see Giovanni Agosti, "Su Mantegna, 5 (Intorno a Vasari), *Prospettiva*, 80 (1995), 61–89.

23. This will expand upon my earlier discussion in "Mantegna's Triumph: The Cultural Politics of Imitation all'antica at the court of Mantua, 1490–1530" in *Artists at Court: Image Making and Identity 100–1550*, ed. Stephen J. Campbell (Boston, Isabella Stewart Gardner Museum, 2004), 91–106.

24. On the reception of the Triumphs in the sixteenth century, see Giovanni

Agosti, "Su Mantegna, 4 (A Mantova, nel Cinquecento), *Prospettiva* 77 (1995), 58–83, especially 72 and note 129.

25. The phrase comes from Jean Baudrillard, *The System of Objects* trans. James Benedict (New York, 1996).

26. On the Renaissance *studiolo* see Dora Thornton, *The Scholar in his Study. Ownership and Experience in Renaissance Italy* (New Haven and London, 1997), and the classic account by Wolfgang Liebenwein, *Studiolo: Die Enstehung eines Raumtyps und seine Entwicklung bis um 1600* (Berlin, 1977). On the kunstkammer and museum see Horst Bredekamp, *The Lure of Antiquity and the Cult of the Machine* trans. Allison Brown (Princeton, 1995), and Paula Findlen, *Possessing Nature: Museums, Collecting, and Scientific Culture in Early Modern Italy* (Berkeley, London and Los Angeles, University of California Press, 1994). On the *galleria*, see Cristina De Benedictis, *Per la Storia del Collezionismo Italiano: Fonti e Documenti* 2nd edition (Milan, 1998), 56–87. For a historical and theoretical perspective on the history of collecting see Krzysztof Pomian, *Des saintes reliques à l'art moderne. Venise-Chicago XIIIe–XXe siècle* (Paris, 2003).

27. Giovanbattista Strozzi, from *Dell'unità della favola*, a lecture on Ariosto delivered before the Florentine Accademia degli Alterati in 1599, quoted in Lina Bolzoni, *The Gallery of Memory*, trans. Jeremy Parzen (Toronto, 2001), 211

28. On the political argument see Robert Williams, "The Sala Grande in the Palazzo Vecchio and the Precedence Controversy between Florence and Ferrara," in *Vasari's Florence. Artists and Literati at the Medicean Court* ed. Philip Jacks (Cambridge and New York, 1998), 163–182, and Henk Van Veen, " 'Republicanism' not 'Triumphalism': On the Political Message of Cosimo I's Sala Grande," *Mitteilungen des Kunsthistorischen Instituts in Florenz* 27 (1993), 475–480.

THE CONCEPT OF THE RENAISSANCE TODAY: WHAT IS AT STAKE?

Claire Farago

… in the years 1940 to 1944, the German occupying power in Europe designated all resistance movements, in France and elsewhere, as terrorists. Almost every state defends its claim to hold a monopoly of organized violence, in the name of peace and security, by defining the violence of its adversaries—those who do not equate legality with legitimacy—as terrorist.

Sam Weber, "War, Terrorism, and Spectacle: On Towers and Caves," 2002[1]

Preamble: a provocation

I have been thinking and writing about the limits of conceptualizing the Renaissance for a long time, and for this reason I am delighted to be included in the present discussion, but at the same time I am wary: Jim Elkins describes our collaboration as a joint interest in "optimal and competing ways of representing the Renaissance. . . . the question is now to theorize the Renaissance, especially given the history of previous conceptualizations, and given our current position. . . ."[2] My wariness stems from the conviction that our current position behooves us for a number of political reasons to reframe the concept

69

"Renaissance" in light of historical interactions between the nation-states and their precedent collective entities that gave us the retrospective term "Renaissance" in the first place. Revisiting the "Renaissance Problem" in 1995, I urged the subbfield of Renaissance art history to consider how much more is involved in reassessing the history of Renaissance art than trading one modern category for another, less restrictive one that includes a wider range of cultural activities, such as rituals and popular images, with regard to a wider range of purposes than the category usually implied by "work of art."[3] The aesthetic system of classification that gradually emerged over several hundred years grounded Jacob Buckhardt's writings in a humanist model of culture, despite his inclusion of popular culture to characterize the "Italian national spirit" in the early modern period. The problem that Burckhardt did not consider is that of circumscribing "Renaissance" within the limits of European art whereas "Renaissance art" was exported from various locations on the Italic peninsula and circulated globally during the early modern period, and meanwhile works of art and other cultural products from all parts of the world were imported into Europe, where they formed prize specimens in early modern collections and made an impact on European ideas of art and on the practices of European artists. Much less is known about these processes.

Nor can "Renaissance" the concept or the period be hermetically sealed, separated from the space in which we historians write about the past. In the words of Serge Gruzinski, anthropologist of Meso-american culture:

> If we knew the sixteenth century better—the century of Iberian expansion—we would no longer discuss globalization as though it were a new, recent situation. Nor are the phenomena of hybridization and rejection that we now see on a worldwide scale the novelty they are often claimed to be.[4]

Our understanding of Renaissance culture, fundamentally shaped by Burckhardt's study of Italy, has been changed and enriched by generations of debate over his characterization of historical periods, of individuality, of the Middle Ages, and of his treatment of gender. Yet we still need integrated accounts that allow the disparate voices that have contributed to European conceptions of art to be heard. Parallel accounts that represent the same events from mutually exclusive points of view do not offer this perspective. Why have Renaissance art historians remained largely isolated to this day from debates regarding the questions of intercultural exchange? Modern national identity, colonialism, and capitalism did not emerge fully grown in the nineteenth century. Yet there seems to be even less interest now than there was a decade ago, when I first raised the preceding questions and made the arguments to support them in *Reframing the Renaissance*, in undercutting anachronistic cultural and aesthetic boundaries that interfere with our ability to see the complexity of artistic interactions during the time we identify with the term "Renaissance." Part of the challenge of defining "Renaissance" in terms that address broad issues relevant to contemporary intellectual needs, stems from the circumstance that the geographical, cultural, chronological, and conceptual boundaries of the Renaissance as it is usually defined need to be redrawn. In fact, the term "Renaissance" itself may be so fundamentally part of the problem that the term cannot be part of the solution.

There is a pressing need to revise disciplinary practices at an epistemological level. The fundamental lesson for historians today is the responsibility to recognize the undigested projections of past generations in our present-day theoretical extensions of existing scholarship. Connections between what is still viable and what is no longer tenable need to be considered fully if our heritage is to be truly relevant today. The central premise of the category "Renaissance" suffers from *metalepsis*, or chronological reversal, meaning that the object of study seems to justify its presence on the basis of a preexisting historical context, whereas "Renaissance" is the construction of a context based on the historian's prior understanding of history's significance. The question for us today is the extent to which contemporary theoretical projects can follow the alternatives of the past.

In the social network of contemporary society, individuals play specialized roles that discourage (although they do not prevent) reflection on the broad social effects of the information/knowledge they produce. Cultural historian bell hooks addresses the crucial issue of self-reflexivity to the field of cultural studies in the following blunt way: "Participants in contemporary discussions of culture highlighting difference and otherness who have not interrogated their perspective, the location from which they write in a culture of domination," create "a field of study where old practices are simultaneously critiqued, re-enacted, and sustained."[5]

To what extent is it our responsibility as scholars operating in today's social networks to feel responsibility for the effects of the knowledge we produce? What is the relationship of ideology to commerce within the frame of academic practices? Historians commonly argue that scholarly publications are not driven by profit motives in theory or fact. From the standpoint of the intellectual's ethical responsibilities to society, however, it matters not at all whether the profit is going directly into the pockets of publishers or scholars. To what extent are the historical circumstances in which the category "Renaissance" originated and the manner in which these circumstances are reproduced in current cultural relations not our responsibility today? Today, the entertainment industry and the mass media perpetuate the racial stereotypes on which the modern discipline of art history was founded in the nineteenth century. The common presence of dated ideas in popular culture may partly explain why art history the discipline and Renaissance art history the subdiscipline continue to rely on categories rooted in theories of cultural evolutionism, but it would be a serious short circuit of logic to blame the current situation on individuals operating in a vast network of diffused power/knowledge relations.

By analyzing the connections among individuals structurally, on the other hand, we can try to understand the ways in which contemporary discriminatory practices are grounded in historical circumstances in order to change them, not justify them. Mieke Bal's analysis of collecting as a form of narration is relevant to the current status of the concept "Renaissance": when the object collected is re-contextualized in a new syntegmatic field of relations, the status of the object as a thing remains the same, but the object as a sign becomes radically different. The narratives entailed at "the intersection of psychic and capitalist fetishism," as Bal puts it, where signs have exchange value, turn collecting into a "tale of social struggle."[6]

Let us consider our current practices as art historians, at this un-negotiated intersection of conflicting vested interests. A historical artifact of human manufacture—a work of art in the most generic sense of the word—is one of those peculiar objects of historical inquiry that, in seeming defiance of time itself, is still with us today. As Michael Ann Holly articulated the conundrum at the core of the art historical enterprise, "works of art are both lost and found, both present and past, at the same time."[7] We understand works of art as objects whose significance transcends the historical circumstances of their making. Precisely—paradoxically—it is the materiality of the object that is at once affected and unaffected by time. Unless we comprehensively attend to the epistemological underpinnings of our intellectual heritage, rather than selecting what seems personally most compelling to study, that which is indefensible will continue to haunt contemporary history writing in precisely the sense that Michel de Certeau defined the mnemic trace as "the return of what was forgotten, in other words, an action by a past that is now forced to disguise itself."[8]

But can one draw the line between individual and collective responsibility? The subdisciplinary boundaries that divide the study of Italian Renaissance art from English Renaissance art from Spanish Colonial art from Native American art—the list of compartmentalizations goes on and on—renders the complicities of historians with nation-state ideology (to name but one pernicious alliance of knowledge/power relations) invisible to the individual scholars working in the specialized subfields in which academic practice is encouraged and to which it is largely confined. We may tend, therefore, to discount the sorry history of imperialism or make it out to be trivial or disconnected to us by hindsight, but it is certainly not invisible, trivial or a *fait accompli* on all sides of the social equation.

As the first part of my contribution to the Cork roundtable, I circulated my response to Alexander Nagel and Christopher Wood's "Interventions: Toward a New Model of Renaissance Anachronism" (*Art Bulletin*, September 2005), to which the authors responded that "they concur with virtually everything" I had to say about disciplinary responsibility and self awareness and about the ideological force of the discourse of chronological reason, but they "do not actually feel addressed" by my critique regarding the disengagement of Renaissance art historians from politics and society at large. Why? In their own words, because they "explicitly signaled" the connection of their discussion to Benjamin's reception of Surrealism and to a body of "highly creative prewar thinking about the temporality of the figure," and because their own effort is consequently "by its nature a challenge to enlightened [*sic*] historical models."

Why are we still circling the same geographically and figuratively circumscribed destinations as our historical predecessors who served imperialistic nation-states by writing histories of their "national cultures"? Why does there seem to be no way for most art historians to connect the political present—signaled in Sam Weber's discussion of terror, excerpted at the beginning of this essay—with the shape of the past cast in nineteenth-century terms as "The Renaissance"? Why must we still work IN the Renaissance to be "Renaissance art historians"? Shouldn't part of the responsibility be to question relentlessly what being "in the Renaissance" entails? (Why should I feel like a terrorist for questioning this status quo?) Is not the most fundamental problem at hand for conceptualizing the discipline as an ethical practice the notion of identity itself? Art historians assume the role of "managers of consciousness" who fabricate, maintain, and naturalize the individual and collective identities of modern subjects. Adequate solutions must substantively rethink the polity of practice as such. The problem, in other words, is no longer simply one of "adequate" representation, but of "representation" itself imagined as being unproblematic. In the present era of transnational mega-corporate capitalism and neo-colonial labor practices, certain very different accounts of the formation of the modern subject offer productive directions for rethinking the ethical practice of intellectual work in the global community of citizenship. "In the post-cold war period of 'globalization' and transnational capitalism," Sam Weber writes in the same essay on terrorism I just cited, "a new 'enemy' seems to be needed to consolidate the role and to reinforce the legitimacy of nation-states that are ever more openly dependent on, and agents of, transnational corporate interests."[9]

The issues I am discussing in terms of the category "Renaissance" in the field of art history have been the preoccupation of philosophers and critical historians such as Giorgio Agamben and Judith Butler who insist upon "acknowledging our complicity in the law that we oppose": "there is in effect something that humans are and have to be, but this is not an essence or properly a thing: It is the simple fact of one's own existence as possibility or potentiality."[10]

A case study: the body of/in this paper[11]

Discussions of idolatry and art emerged in the context of European colonization, based on the same inherited theories of human cognition as their counterpart arguments in Europe. The Scottish theologian John Major was one of the principal authors of the neo-Aristotelian theory of the "natural slave," described in Books I and 3 of the *Politics* as lacking in the higher faculties of the human soul, and elaborated in the sixteenth century to discuss the Amerindians' mental capacity.[12] Although the famous debates on the issue held in Valladolid, Spain, in 1550–51, left the legal status of Amerindians unresolved, these records and discussions of the humanity of the indigenous peoples of the Americas that preceded them established the conceptual framework for modern pseudo-scientific theories of "race" two centuries later.[13] The mental capacity to recollect—that is, to draw a series of inferences, as Aristotle and his commentators defined the distinction between the human faculty of memory and the retentive memory of animals—was both directly cited and indirectly implied throughout sixteenth-century discussions of the Amerindians' mental capacities. By 1539, the terms on which the Indians' mental capacities were judged were part of an international discourse in which the culturally dispossessed also participated—at least to the limited extent of a few assimilated members of the Amerindian elite.[14]

Consider in this context of historical debates on what constitutes humanness that the fifteenth-century Dominican Archbishop of Florence Saint Antonine's *Summa theologica* was among the earliest books recorded in New Spain.[15] Archbishop Antonine urged his readers to learn the art of projecting sacred concepts into memory figures. Drawing on the same Aristotelian concept of recollection, and conceivably on this exact text, the Flemish Franciscan lay brother Pedro de Gante established innovative methods for teaching

Christian doctrine to Amerindian neophytes at his school in Mexico City San José de los Naturales, in operation as early as 1526.[16] De Gante and other missionaries used visual images extensively during the early years of the Conquest when language was an extreme barrier to communication, as is known from numerous sources, including the Italian publication of an important pedagogical text in Latin, *De Rhetorica Christiana* (Perugia, 1579), written and illustrated by de Gante's pupil Diego Valadés, a Christianized, assimilated Aztec nobleman.[17] Valadés, like Antonine, focused on the role played by the art of memory in teaching sacred doctrine to neophytes. Valadés provided engraved illustrations of catechism classes being taught in the open-air atrium of the Franciscan mother church at San José using rebus-like visual signs in this manner. He also introduced a sort of pictographic syllabry of his own, involving signs with connotations on both European and Mexican sides of the cultural and linguistic divide. Some of Valadés's heart signs include recognizable elements from Nahuatl pictograms. Although their exact meaning has never been deciphered, the manner in which they function in his text makes the important point that they are a culturally hybrid means of communication among fully human creatures capable of recollection, that is, of drawing a series of inferences.

This bare armature of philosophical issues in relation to political events is necessary in order to understand why and how questions of idolatry arose simultaneously in New Spain and Europe. In studying the discourse about art and idolatry in a transcultural context, it is important to bear in mind that the same neo-Aristotelian theory of human cognition that justified the use of images also justified their condemnation. The sixteenth-century condemnation of costly religious art is not novel—in the twelfth century, when St. Bernard of Clairvaux condemned elaborate displays of carved monstrosities for attracting and distracting pilgrims, he cited the needs of the poor as a more legitimate expense.[18] In the sixteenth century, Ulrich Zwingli and others identified the *Abgott* in the patron's soul as the source of idolatry that finds its external, monstrous expression in/as works of art. As reductive as it may be in terms of content to connect arguments made by writers such as Leonardo da Vinci on the discursive powers of the painter's *ingegno* or Vasari's praise of Michelangelo's "divino intelletto," with Protestant charges about idolatry arising first in the mind, all of these writings are variants in a longstanding literature about the nature of images made by art.[19]

Both the Protestant theological arguments against images and the Italian defenses of the arts appear to be unprecedented in one significant respect: they re-directed the connections traditionally made between the image made by art and its divine referent. Renaissance art historians are more accustomed to considering as novel the claims made for and against the inventive powers of the artist to determine the appearance of the work, yet in both cases, theoretical interest shifted in the early modern period from the referent *in* the image (the holy person represented) to the maker *of* the image (the artist or patron).[20]

Let's consider what is at stake in refocusing theories of images to a concern with the mentality of image-maker, beginning with the orthodox account. Briefly stated, the difficulty on both sides of the controversy over images since the inception of the discussion in sixth-century Byzantium consisted in grasping the *hypothetical* nature of duplicating the powers of the original that are signified in art. Decisive here, writes Agamben about the manner in which the problem was articulated in Scholastic texts, is the idea of an *inessential* commonality.[21] This relationship, which Agamben aptly calls "taking-place," is not conceived as the persistence of an identical essence in single individuals (which might otherwise be described as a chip-off-the-old-block theory). Rather, in the passage from the idea to the common human form [that is, in the transfer of power from the original], what belongs to common nature and what is proper become absolutely indifferent. In the passage from potentiality to act, one is contained wholly by the other. This difficult notion can be illustrated by the image of the line of writing in which the *ductus* of the hand passes continually from the generic form of the letters to the individual marks—so too in a face, human nature continually passes into existence and this incessant emergence constitutes the dynamic expressivity of the face.[22]

To explain how divine immanence plays out in the concrete work of art in devotional practice, Byzantinist Robert Nelson has articulated the exchange between a Greek Orthodox icon and a worshiper in modern semiotic terms as being governed by an existential relation to what is signified. The "code" in the icon is only comprehensible in the present-oriented, spatially and temporally coextensive relation that the "speaker" and "listener" maintains with the work of art.[23] Like their grammatical counterparts in the pronoun relationship of "I/you," visual "shifters" such as the figure of Christ that faces and looks directly at the beholder, create and are created by an event— their referents are dependent upon that situation.[24] The frontal gaze visually establishes an internal dialogue directed from the beholder to the image that is articulated in the Orthodox theology of the icon. As the human face and the icon face one another, what belongs to common nature and what is proper are considered "absolutely indifferent." According to Nelson, Greek Orthodox doctrinal theory, as this practiced system of communication demonstrates, is "performative" in simultaneously animating and personalizing the cultural message contained in material form. The icon, then, is a mediator—a way for the believer to comprehend God existentially through an interactive medium.

To return to what is at stake in refocusing theories of images to a concern with the mentality of image-maker, sixteenth-century arguments against idolatry and writings on the artist's powers of invention introduced what might be called "meta-signifiers" of the work of art as a sign: that is, the person responsible for fabricating the image, whether this is the patron-as-artist or the artisan who fabricated the object. Imagining, for the sake of the present argument, that the work of art functions as a screen onto which interpretations can be projected, sixteenth-century theoretical writings on images offer new trajectories in an existing chain of semiosis that runs between the sign and its signified(s). Locating the new discourses on idolatry and artistic invention in a larger discursive formation in this manner, the relationship between signifier and signified can be seen as offering numerous possibilities. As new concerns entered the debate on theories of images, a confusing range of new possibilities emerged. What we want to focus on in the present context of discussion is the unprecedented relation being worked out in early modern texts between subjects and objects.

The following analysis of Mexican painted manuscripts indicates that the frame of reference for discussing the relationship of the work of art (the sign) to its contents (the signified) underwent a similar destabilization and opening up of new possibilities for the role of art in New Spain as it did in Europe. In focusing on the signifying chain of idolatry in its Spanish colonial context, it is nonetheless important to bear in mind the European discourse on the grotesque and monstrous. Zwingli's condemnation of idolatry as an inner monstrosity leading to outward manifestations is one extreme position in the critical spectrum. Other, mostly Italian, writers discussed the artist's inventive powers in positive terms using the same metaphors connoting the difference between the rational intellect and the sub-rational powers of the imagination. For example, Paolo Giovanni Lomazzo, writing in the 1580s, considered *grotteschi* synonymous with invention and the highest test of the painter's powers: "because in the invention of *grotteschi* more than in anything else, there runs a certain furor and a natural *bizarria*, and being without it they are unable to make anything, for all their art."[25]

Most of Lomazzo's contemporaries were more cautious in their assessment of the artist's productive imagination following the Council of Trent's 1563 decree on images. Invoking the same contrast between reasoned imagination and the capricious fantasy, Cardinal Gabriele Paleotti, author of an influential treatise on painting (1582; Latin edition of 1594), introduced extensive new qualifications drawn from the standard authorities. He constructed a theory of style that, in effect, favored the scientific embellishments of optical naturalism, but retained the artist's right to depict *grotteschi* as long as these vivid representations were not capricious figments of the imagination. Paleotti developed his position in consultation with his lifelong friend Ulisse Aldrovandi, the renowned naturalist and collector of New World materials, as documented in their correspondence.[26] He seems to have taken to heart Aldrovandi's advice concerning the proper principles guiding artistic illustration when, for example, he admitted that painters should be allowed to represent novel things that seem to lie outside the order of nature (*se bene fuori dell'ordine suo*), as long as they actually do exist. These include "monsters of the sea and land and other places."[27] The difference is that embellishments that have counterparts in nature are "proportioned to reason" (*proporzionati alla ragione*) while *grotteschi* refer to fantasms, things "that have never been, that could not exist in the manner in which they are represented." These condemned forms of artifice are [contra Lomazzo] the *capricci* of painters, products of their irrational imaginations (*irragionevoli imaginationi*).[28]

The central point in Paleotti's considerations of *grotteschi*, and similar considerations of the time by Federico Borromeo, Carlo Borromeo, Lomazzo, Pirro Ligorio, and other Italian writers, is the distinction between the delusions of a dissolute person and the true visions of a prophet.[29] This distinction is also the pivotal point in a wide variety of sixteenth-century discussions of art and idolatry by Protestants and by Catholic missionaries. Thomas Aquinas provided the terms of discussion when he differentiated the eternal substance of an object from its accidental, external appearance: the mutation in appearance was external to the visionary's eyes, but the imagination of the dissolute person caused him to mistake the image for the thing itself, thus he was captivated by demonic illusions (*Summa theologica* 3.76.8).[30] Writing in 1582, Paleotti condemned the representation of monstrous races, of infernal rites and demonic gods, idol worship and human sacrifice for the same reasons: they are evidence of the imagination of a dissolute person. The significant difference in the sixteenth-century text is that the grotesque sign refers to the maker of the image.

Bartolomé de Las Casas, the most famous European apologist for the Americans in the sixteenth century, was acutely aware of the problem of classifying his converts and potential converts as lacking in the higher faculties of the human soul. Though he believed that Amerindians possessed the full potential for civility, he still imposed Christianized norms. The faint but distinct echo of ideas recorded by Vincenzo Borghini, Benedetto Varchi, Vasari, and others who contributed to the rising status of painting, sculpture, and architecture as liberal arts in Europe, can be heard when Las Casas writes that the Indians possessed skill in the mechanical arts which were a function of the rational soul (*habitus est intellectus operativus*).[31] Yet with the same words, Las Casas helped to construct an inferior collective identity for the indigenous cultures of the "New World" when he argued that the Indians were capable of assimilating European culture under European guidance.[32]

Nearly all the Mexican painted manuscripts known today are located in European collections, where they were originally valued as trophies, gifts, souvenirs—exotic items sought by European collectors. These colonial productions derived from pre-contact screenfold books, a format known in a few copies, none of which are indisputably pre-Columbian in date. Recent scholarship has stressed that the body of Mexican pictorial manuscripts document a process of transculturation, not simply acculturation.[33] This process is readily seen in the evidence internal to the manuscripts, which are based on a combination of Nahuatl and European models. These hybrid compilations document the operations by which "idolatrous" content unacceptable to Christian compilers was isolated from "scientific" content admired by the same missionary audience and their European patrons. In the process of reframing the indigenous material, not only was the "idolatry" singled out and objectified, it was gradually eliminated entirely from the reader's consciousness.

The discourse on idolatry preserved in Mexican pictorial manuscripts is complex. Figures alone could pass unnoticed by the censors as mere curiosities. Verbal descriptions of idolatrous practices overlay indigenous knowledge provided by informants whose own memories and knowledge were compromised by distance from the pre-conquest culture they described. Reframed as phobic projections of European fears, native information was not returned to its pure state by successive generations of copying and editing. Native knowledge became increasingly attenuated and divorced from its cultural context as it was successively reformatted in conformity with European modes of knowledge production. As Walter Mignolo has suggested using other examples, indigenous, pictorial forms of record keeping gradually lost their authority to European forms of textual documentation.[34] The otherness of Nahuatl beliefs is neutralized in the mediated process of passing from a native artifact to its European imitation to a thoroughly Europeanized format. Otherness is domesticated, the grotesque "idol" is transformed into an intriguing exotic decoration. One could even venture further to postulate a certain fear of contagion, as if the very representation of the idolatry of other peoples, either verbal or visual, were enough to make the same monstrosity spring up spontaneously in Europe.

The process of successive copying and editing of Mexican painted manuscripts provides a clear case of the manner in which Europeans misrepresented Mexica cultura by reframing it within a western system of beliefs. Gruzinski argues that the category of "the grotesque" enables indigenous pictorial traditions to coexist comfortably with ancient European mythological signs.[35] It is important to bear in mind that this "coexistence" positions indigenous truth values in a subaltern relationship to European knowledge. The same hierarchical, two-way process of cultural interaction can be discerned in the hybrid style of all Mexican painted manuscripts. They are all culturally hybrid documents, compilations of ideas, statements, and representations functioning in an "enunciative network," to borrow Foucault's formulation, driven by the political importance of defining Amerindians.[36] The Mexica regarded the figures of their ritual calendar as sacred, while the Spanish inscribed them as false. An inquiry into the categories of representation and language indicates that they are governed by identifiable structures of knowledge and power. While the style may be hybrid, the order, structure, and message of the ritual calendar are not. The use of the category "grotesque" has traditionally served to label cultural differences. This is an ethnocentric approach to the pursuit of knowledge because it imposes the ideology of the European observer and thus occludes other cultural meanings.

The earliest European viewers of Mexican pictorial manuscripts would have projected their imaginary, symbolic, and real fears onto their images: imaginary insofar as the depictions corresponded to the preexisting and current European vocabulary of the fantastic and monstrous; symbolic insofar as the practices described in the accompanying texts fed their programmed fears of "false gods" in both appearance and behavior (such as demanding human sacrifice); and "real" insofar as that which was excluded because it did not fit into the Eurocentric categories of description was gradually erased from view—the violence of cultural projection was masked, its effects supposedly neutralized by the means that generations of copyists (from the sixteenth-century Dominican missionary Bernardino da Sahagun to the eighteenth-century Creole nobleman Mariano Fernandez Veytia) practiced to eliminate obvious signs of idolatry while embedding the discourse of idolatry at a deeper level, continuing the same process of objectification and fetishization that they claim to eschew.

Staking a claim: implications for the framing of Renaissance art

All three conditions—the imaginary, the symbolic, and the real—are simultaneously at work in art history's institutional history. The "cause" or origin of Mexican painted manuscripts as the record of idolatry is erased through editing. What is left in the material record reveals both the compiler's desire to understand Mexica religious practices and his need to disavow them. Mexican painted manuscripts of the early contact period are an excellent case of the manner in which hybrid cultural products in which "Renaissance" art combines with the representational system of a previously unrelated culture serves as a site of cultural translation: two types of semiotic systems, one native American and the other European, are combined. Central to the compiler's ambivalent attitude is the multivalent, shifting presence of the grotesque figured in its various familiar guises of the ridiculous, the laughable, the monstrous, the abhorrent, the repulsive, the fabulous, and the fantastic. Far from providing insight into cultural differences, projections of conflicting European ideas of the monstrous or grotesque co-exist with the subjectivity of the compiler in the ethnographic record. The coupling of semiotic systems with different cultural origins under these conditions creates complex tensions within the text. The superimposition of different representational practices is difficult to interpret, not just for the modern scholar but probably for each attentive reader since it was compiled. We can safely infer that the contestation of signs that constitutes the material object bears traces of the power struggle that produced it. These are the complex circumstances of production and reception that defeat any attempt to distinguish among the vested interests of authors/producers in binary terms of colonizer and colonized.

Critical understanding of the institutional history of the discipline of art history calls for integrated attempts to define the issues that produced the narratives of our current disciplinary formations.

Idolatry is one such problematic, with the potential to integrate art historical studies around significant questions involving the formation of modern individual and collective identities. Idolatry is also a topic of major historical and theoretical consequence that bears on significant contemporary preoccupations elsewhere with the criteria for what it means to be human and, ultimately, what it means not to be human.[37] The history of these contemporary preoccupations deserves to be better understood. At present, however, when we study the theology of idolatry, we segregate the primary texts and their historical contexts. Although David Freedberg's *Power of Images* (1989), written for a broad intellectual audience, is a notable exception, it remains an isolated occurrence. As for interactions across longer times and distances, art historians isolate the peripatetic histories of objects and texts from deeper levels of historical relatedness such as those that have been the focus of the foregoing discussion. In keeping with entrenched routines, despite extensive critical interest in the institutional history of art history for the past three decades, the profession treats theories of images as if the historical discussion of art somehow did not belong to the same sphere as the objects themselves.

Yet the questions: Why maintain this disconnection today? Who benefits from it? Who doesn't? remain important. They are legitimate, but as long as our disciplinary formations remain undisturbed at the institutional level, the primary lessons that institutional critiques offer go unheeded. The contours of research continue to evolve within the set parameters of categories such as "Northern" and "Southern Renaissance," "Italy," "France," and so on. These formations have been maintained in various institutional settings to define the expertise of scholars, the latter playing a significant role in determining how and what subjects of inquiry are framed and investigated. What is lacking, perhaps, is a clear correspondence between historical entities and the categories by which we understand them. Contemporaneous events in northern and southern Europe and in the Americas (and elsewhere for that matter) did not take place in separate universes during the sixteenth century. Artifacts circulated in trading networks of immense scale. The products of intensive contact between previously unrelated societies constitute under-utilized forms of historical evidence, especially when they fall outside the range of modern categories of art or do not correspond to the recognized "styles" and "periods" associated with the European "fine arts."[38]

Studies of cultural interaction lead to questions of whether and how the historical complexities of collective identity formation and dissolution might re-organize research protocols at the institutional level. Consider in this context the statement by Walter Benjamin, excerpted from a letter to Max Horkheimer in which Benjamin offered a corrective to his colleague's view of the closure of the past: "History is not simply a science but also and not least a form of remembrance [*Eindenken*]."[39] For Benjamin, the manner in which art and cultural history were to be integrated was the subject of investigation rather than its methodological premise.[40] Benjamin's attempts to reject the humanist notion of periods of decline and progress—his admiration for Aloïs Riegl's success in this regard is well known to art historians—were in part catalyzed by the symptomatic difficulties that the experience of art poses.

Unlike the position of the humanist Aby Warburg, who viewed works of art as privileged sites for the harmonious reconciliation of psychological tensions in society, Benjamin understood cultural production in more explicitly Marxist terms as the document of economic oppression: "art and science owe their existence not only to the great geniuses who created them, but also, in one degree or another, to the anonymous toil of their contemporaries."[41] Benjamin developed his ideas regarding the work of art's social relevance beyond the lifetime of its original producers in a Marxian framework as a foil to the commodity, the foundational concept in Marx's economic theory. The "surplus value" of what Marx called the commodity-fetish is the inverse of the "surplus value" of the work of art. In his recent reading of Marx, Jacques Derrida summed up the dialectical relationship between these two kinds of objects in the terms that Benjamin had recognized: "if a work of art can become a commodity, and if this process seems fated to occur, it is also because the commodity began [historically] by putting to work, in one way or another, the principle of art itself."[42] The early modern work of art, because of the extraordinary value attached to it, anticipates Marx's concept of surplus value in the industrialized mass production of commodities, the source of both the capitalist's profit and the worker's exploitation. However, because the work of art is too complex to be explained in terms of base and superstructure alone, it provides a test case for developing a theoretical model sufficiently complex to explain the political economy.

Art, as Benjamin recognized in 1937, is not a timeless, universal category. On the basis that the category "art" emerged in specific cultural and historical circumstances, he challenged the separation of specialized fields of history. He put into question the integrity of a discipline that decides in advance on the nature of objects and practices as "art." He further argued that the work of art is never complete because it is by virtue of its after-history that the work of art's fore-history is recognizable. Since the process of embodying and distinguishing itself from the world is continued in the interpretations of the work, the work of art is never completely present. Consequently, objects of the past cannot be fully possessed and they will always disrupt the efforts of the present to contain them within its categories or forms of narrative. For Derrida, the play of infinite substitutions is similarly inexhaustible because the "field" is missing a center that grounds it. This is the movement that Derrida refers to as "supplementarity," the inability of the "meaning" of any work of art to be complete in the present, or ever for that matter.[43]

It is in this sense of history's unavoidable incompleteness that the experience of the past exceeds both individual and collective remembrance [*Eindenken*]: "history is not simply a science but also and not least a form of remembrance."[44] This condition of the artwork's dynamic ongoing production makes the work of art an exemplary case of the impossibility of ever possessing the past. As such, Benjamin's critique is also addressed to the empiricist methodology of art history practiced as a "science" of objects. For Benjamin, the possibility of a dialectical cultural history depends on utilizing the "destructive element" of the past's effect on the present. The "reserve of the past" enables the past to destroy aspects of the present and open it to the future.[45]

In the final analysis, the movement of "supplementarity" includes not only the "objects" we write about, but also our writing about them. The critique of art first mounted by Protestant Reformation writers noted that inanimate material objects might replace human understanding of the world rather than enhance it. The same fear was invoked by Marx's immediate predecessors and contemporaries. In the Romanticist reading of fetishism, clearly audible in Marx's arguments, when "the mind ceases to realize that it has itself created the outward images or things to which it subsequently posits itself as in some sort of subservient relation," it lapses into passivity, "seeing a world of dead relations rather than living images."[46] Marx's explanation of value is based on the essential contradiction between "variable capital," i.e., labor-power, which adds more than it costs in the production process, and "constant capital" which refers to the objective factors (such as the machinery needed to produce more commodities at a faster rate in order to compete successfully in the marketplace). Viewing profit in these terms, writes Teresa Brennan in an analysis of the role of time in Marx's theory of the political economy, ultimately "depends on the difference a living subject makes to a dead object."[47] By definition, art historians are the labor-power in the production process of art history, just as artists are the labor-power in the production of art. If we forget that the discipline is our own creation, we not only exploit ourselves, we produce a world of dead relations instead of the living conditions that made our objects of study possible in the first place.

The study of what art was considered idolatrous, and why, and to whom it pertained, highlights the arbitrary and transitory nature of established disciplinary and sub-disciplinary formations. While Protestant Reformation theologians denounced lavish religious displays and material aids as idolatrous, their ecclesiastic counterparts in New Spain levied charges of idolatry against their newly colonized subjects.[48] How often are these contemporaneous events involving the discourse of idolatry and art considered within the same frame of reference? The relationships of power that materialized in such complex exchanges simultaneously taking place at close range and over long distances are ignored as long as historians maintain models of scholarly specialization such as those based on modern nation-state identities that—in fact—only fully materialized some three centuries later.[49] Left with a magnificent but inert treasury of inherited objects, art historians who do not stray from their inherited categories are consequently unlikely to articulate complex questions of self-other relationships that produced these storehouses in the first place. Nor are they likely to develop an interest in the marginal position of the culturally dispossessed and the politically disempowered who leave no provenances of ownership or even their names in the historical record.

For writing to be "a writing," Derrida maintains, it must continue to "act" and to be readable even when the author is absent in all senses of the word.[50] What is our responsibility to our students and to future generations of students of "Renaissance" art? A lot more is at stake than might appear to the naked eye. Jim Elkins argues, in his own contribution to this Roundtable, that "critical thinking on modern art seems to have jettisoned the Renaissance, letting it drift into the isolation of specialized scholarship." Further, he adds, that, as lifeless a remnant of some inaccessible past the Renaissance seems, it is also "the heavy anchor of the entire project of modernism." I agree, but as I hope I have argued effectively, a lot more is at stake in remembering the Renaissance than connecting Giotto to Beckmann and other artists "working in the same tradition." Whose tradition are we talking about?

Notes

1. Sam Weber, "War, Terrorism, and Spectacle: On Towers and Caves," *South Atlantic Quarterly* 101/3 (Summer 2002): 449–458, citing p. 451.
2. Jim Elkins, email to Roundtable participants, December 8, 2005.
3. Claire Farago, "Editor's Introduction : Reframing the Renaissance," in *Reframing the Renaissance: Visual Culture in Europe and Latin America 1450 to 1650* (London-New Haven: Yale University Press, 1995), 1–20, especially 3–6.
4. Serge Gruzinski, *The Mestizo Mind: The Intellectual Dynamics of Colonization and Globalization*, trans. Deke Dusinerre (New York-London: Routledge, 2002), 4.
5. bell hooks, *Yearning: Race, Gender, and Cultural Politics* (Boston: South End Press, 1990), 125.
6. Mieke Bal. "Telling Objects: A Narrative Perspective on Collecting," in *The Cultures of Collecting*, eds. John Elsner and Roger Cardinal (Cambridge, Mass.; Harvard University Press, 1994), 97–115; citing pp. 111 and 114.

7. Michael Ann Holly, "Mourning and Method," in *Compelling Visuality: The Work of Art in and Out of History*, ed. Claire Farago and Robert Zwijnenberg, (Minneapolis: University of Minnesota Press, 2003), 159.

8. Michele De Certeau, "Psychoanalysis and its History," *Heterologies: Discourse on the Other*, trans. Brian Massumi (Minneapolis and London: University of Minnesota Press, 1986), 3.

9. Weber, "War, Terrorism, and Spectacle," 452, citing Echelon, a worldwide system of surveillance.

10. Judith Butler, *Psychic Life of Power: Theories in Subjection* (Stanford: Stanford University Press, 1997), 130–132, citing Giorgio Agamben, *The Coming Community*, trans. Michael Hardt (Minneapolis: University of Minnesota Press, 1993), 43.

11. The following section of this paper is adapted from an article I have co-authored with Carol Komandina Parenteau, "The Grotesque Idol: Imaginary, Symbolic, and Real," forthcoming in *The Idols in the Ages of Art: Objects and Devotions in the Early Modern World*, ed. Rebecca Zorach and Michael Cole (Aldershot: Ashgate, 2008).

12. Aristotle distinguished between two types of enslavement: through capture and through being born "slaves by nature," constitutionally incapable of fully human powers of reasoning. See Lewis Hanke, "Pope Paul III and the American Indians," *Harvard Theological Review* 30 (1937), 65–102; Robert Schaifer, "Greek Theories of Slavery from Homer to Aristotle," *Harvard Studies in Classical Philology* 47 (1936), 165–204; Anthony Pagden, *Spanish Imperialism and the Political Imagination: Studies in European and Spanish-American Social and Political Theory 1513–1830* (New Haven-London: Yale University Press, 1990), 16–33; and *The Fall of Natural Man: The Amerindian and the Origins of Comparative Ethnology*, 2nd ed. (Cambridge: Cambridge University Press, 1986), 27–56.

13. A central issue was whether Amerindians had the ability to maintain dominion over their own property. I have discussed this history further in relation to the evaluation of Indian forms of society and artistic products according to European categories, in "The Classification of the Visual Arts in the Renaissance," in *The Shapes of Knowledge from the Renaissance to the Enlightenment*, ed. Donald R. Kelley and Richard H. Popkin, 23–48 (Dordrecht-London: Kluwer Academic Publishers, 1991). For additional historical examples, see Gruzinski, *The Mestizo Mind*.

14. See Elena De Gerlero, Donna Pierce, and Claire Farago, "The Mass of St. Gregory," in *Painting a New World*, exh. cat., ed. Donna Pierce, Denver Art Museum (Austin: University of Texas Press, 2004), 98–102.

15. See Samuel E. Edgerton, *Theaters of Conversion: Religious Architecture and Indian Artisans in Colonial Mexico* (Albuquerque: University of New Mexico Press, 2001), 111–113.

16. The Franciscan trade school adjacent to the monastery of San Francisco in Mexico City was functioning as early as 1526; on its organization, curriculum, and relationship to other mission schools, see Jeanette A Peterson, *The Paradise Garden Murals of Malinalco: Utopia and Empire in Sixteenth-Cemtury Mexico* (Austin: University of Texas Press, 1993), 50–65; Edgerton, *Theaters of Conversion*, 111–127.

17. Diego Valadés, *Rhetorica christiana* (Perugia: Petrumiacobum Petrutium, 1579). See the excellent discussion in Edgerton, *Theaters of Conversion*, 237–246.

18. St. Bernard of Clairvaux, " 'Apologia' to William, Abbot of St.-Thierry," excerpted in *A Documentary History of Art, Vol. 1: The Middle Ages and the Renaissance*, ed. Elizabeth Gilmore Holt, 1: 18–22 (Princeton: Princeton University Press, 1947).

19. Michelangelo's sonnet "Giunto é già corso della vita mia" expresses the artist's concerns about art becoming his "idol and Monarch," terms that resonate with Zwingli's attack on art as excess driven by greed. *The Poetry of Michelangelo*, ed. and trans. James M. Saslow (New Haven-London: Yale University Press, 1991) n. 285, 476. Thanks to Michael Cole and Mary Pardo for this reference.

20. The Pauline doctrine that Christ is made in the image (*eikon*) of God provided the terms in which the Iconophile defense of images was expressed; see discussion in David Freedberg, *The Power of Images: Studies in the History and Theory of Responses*, (Chicago: University of Chicago Press, 1989), 393–395.

21. Giorgio Agamben, *The Coming Community*, trans. Michael Hardt (Minneapolis-London: University of Minnesota Press, 1993), 18.9.

22. Agamben, *The Coming Community*, 18.9: explaining the passage from potentiality to act, from language to the word, "as a shuttling in both directions along a line of sparkling alternation." In the words of Peter of Abelard's teacher Guillaume de Champeure, "the idea is present in single individuals non *essentialiter, sed indifferenter*." Agamben rephrases this to say that "the communication of singularities in the attribute of extension does not unite them in essence, but scatters them in existence."

23. Robert Nelson, "The Discourse of Icons Then and Now," *Art History* 12 (1989), 144–157.

24. Nelson, "The Discourse of Icons," 148, citing E. Benveniste, "The Nature of Pronouns," *Problems in General Linguistics*, trans. Mary Elizabeth Meek (Coral Gables, FL University of Miami Press, 1971), 217–220; and R. Jakobsen, "Shifters, Verbal Categories, and the Russian Verb," in Roman Jakobson, *Selected Writings* (The Hague-Paris: Mouton, 1971), 130–133.

25. G. P. Lomazzo, *Trattato dell'arte de la pittura* (Milan: Paolo Gottordo Pontio, 1584), 424, cited with further discussion in David Summers, *Michelangelo and the Language of Art* (Princeton: Princeton University Press, 1981), 62. On *grotteschi* as emblematic of artistic license to invent, see further David Summers, "Michelangelo on Architecture," *Art Bulletin* 54 (1972): 146–157; and "The Archaeology of the Modern Grotesque," in *Modern Art and the Grotesque*, ed. Frances S. Connelly (Cambridge; Cambridge University Press, 2003), 20–46.

26. Aldrovandi's correspondence with Paleotti extends over many years. His 1582 letter about *grotteschi* is published in *Trattati d'arte del cinquecento*, ed. Paola Barocchi, 3 vols. (Bari: Giuseppe Laterza e Figli, 1961), II, 512–517.

27. *Trattati d'arte*, II: 425 (Book 2, chapter 37); see also 382–389.

28. *Trattati d'arte*, II: 425 (Book 2, chapter 37); see also 382–389.

29. In the 1570s, Pirro Ligorio wrote at great length about *grotteschi*, arguing

for their allegorical significance, yet he also condemned "errors against nature." See David Coffin, "Pirro Ligorio on the Nobility of the Arts," *Journal of the Warburg and Courtauld Institutes* 27 (1964), 191–210.

30. The same arguments and sources were used in Spanish America; see Sabine MacCormack, "*Calderás La Aurora en Copacabana*: The conversion of the Incas in Light of Seventeenth-century Spanish Theology, Culture, and Political Theory," *Journal of Theological Studies* 33 (1982): 448–480.

31. Bartdomé Las Casas, *Apologetica historia sumaria*, ed. Edmundo O'Gorman (Mexico: UNAM, 1967) chapters 61–65, citing the Italian humanist Paolo Giovio, a personal friend of Vasari's and advisor to Pope Paul III, on the products manufactured by laborers and artisans and comparing the arts of the Old and New Worlds to prove the rationality of Amerindian peoples. By contrast, according to Francisco de Vitoria (*Obras*, ed. Téofilo Urdanot, Madrid: Editorial Católica, 1960, 723–725), Indians possessed no knowledge of the liberal arts, no proper agriculture, and produced no true artisans: cited by Pagden, *Spanish Imperialism and the Political Imagination*, 20.

32. *Argumentum apologiae adversus Genesium Sepulvedam theologum cordubensem*, 1550, facsimile reproduced in *Apologia*, ed. Angel Losada (Madrid: Editoria Nacional, 1975) fol. 24r-25r. See Pagden, *The Fall of Natural Man*, 136.

33. I follow the terminology introduced by Louise M. Burkhart, *The Slippery Earth: Nahua-Christian Moral Dialogue in Sixteenth-Century Mexico* (Tucson: University of Arizona Press, 1989).

34. Walter Mignolo, "Literacy and Colonization: The New World Experience," in *1492–1992: Re/Discovering Colonial Writing*, ed. René Jara and Nicholas Spadaccini (Minneapolis: Prisma Institute, 1989), 510–596.

35. Serge Gruzinski, *El Pensiamiento Mestizo*, trans. Enriqe Folch Gonzálex (Buenos Aires: Paidós, 2000), 206–208.

36. Michel Foucault, *The Archaeology of Knowledge and the Discourse of Language* (New York: Pantheon Books, 1972), 91.

37. Although the connections of his arguments to the discourse of fetishism have disappeared from view, the same arguments and distinctions form the implicit ground of Heidegger's widely influential discussion of the origin of the world as picture, a text contemporary with Benjamin's urgent questioning of cultural history, both of which constitute responses to an acute crisis in the history of defining what constitutes the humanity of human beings. Another crisis is being forged on the same anvil of race and aesthetics now. Martin Heidegger, "The Origin of the Work of Art," (1935–36), in *Poetry, Language, and Thought*, trans. and intro. Albert Hofstadter (New York–London: Harper Colophon Books, 1971), 15–88. On the current situation evolving out of prison torture in Abu Graib, Guantanamo Bay, Afghanistan, and elsewhere, see Giorgio Agamben, *The Open: Man and Animal*, trans. Kevin Attell (Stanford: Stanford University Press, 2004) and Judith Butler, *Precarious Life: The Powers of Mourning and Violence* (New York–London: Verso, 2004).

38. A point well made by Spanish Colonial specialists such as Marcus Burke (see his essay in *Art and Faith in Mexico: the Nineteenth-Century Retablo Tradition*, ed. E. Zarur and C. Lovell (Albuquerque: University of New

Mexico Press, 2002); and Edward Sullivan, "European Painting and the Art of the New World Colonies," in *Converging Cultures: Art and Identity in Spanish America*, ed. Diana Fane, exh. cat. Brooklyn Museum, March 1—July 14, 1996 (New York: Harry N. Abrams, 1996), 28–41.

39. Cited in Howard Caygill, "Walter Benjmain's Concept of Cultural History," in *The Cambridge Companion to Walter Benjamin*, ed. David S. Ferris, 73–96 (Cambridge: Cambridge University Press, 2004) citing 76–78.

40. Caygill, "Benjamin's Concept of Cultural History," 79, as the basis of Benjamin's critique of the leading Marxist cultural historian of the time Eduard Fuchs, from which essay the epigram is cited.

41. Walter Benjamin, "Eduard Fuchs, Collector and Historian," (1937), *Selected Writings Volume 3, 1935–1938*, ed. Howard Eiland and Michael W. Jennings, trans. Edmund Jephcott et al. (Cambridge–London: The Belknap Press of Harvard University Press, 2002), 267, cited by Caygill, "Benjamin's Concept of Cultural History," 92, who notes that the unacknowledged labor implicit in objects of culture is the context for Benjamin's famous claim, following in the text, that "there is no document of culture which is not at the same time a document of barbarism." I have discussed Warburg's problematic ideas on primitive religious imagery in "Letting Objects Rot," in *Artwork through the Market*, ed. Jan Bakos (Bratislava, Slovakia: Komenius University Press, 2005), 239–262; and "Re(f)using Art: Warburg and the Ethics of Scholarship," in Claire Farago, Donna Pierce, et al., *Transforming Images: New Mexican Santos in-between Worlds* (University Park, Pa.: Pennsylvania State University Press, 2006), 259–274.

42. Jacques Derrida, *Specters of Marx: The State of the Debt, the Work of Mourning, & the New International*, trans. Peggy Kamuf, intro. Bernd Magnus and Stephen Cullenberg (New York-London: Routledge, 1994), citing p. 162.

43. Jacques Derrida, *Writing and Difference*, trans. and intro. Alan Bass (Chicago: University of Chicago Press, 1978), 289–292. The sign which replaced the center's place in its absence occurs as a surplus, a supplement— which results in the fact that there is always more (p. 290).

44. Walter Benjamin, *Arcades Project*, trans. Howard Eiland and Kevin McLaughlin (Cambridge, MA: Belknap Press of Harvard University, 1999), 471, cited in Caygill, "Benjamin's Concept of Cultural History," 94.

45. Benjamin, "Fuchs," 268.

46. David Simpson, *Fetishism and Imagination: Dickens, Melville, and Conrad* (Baltimore: Johns Hopkins University, 1982), xiii.

47. Teresa Brennan, "Why the Time Is Out of Joint: Marx's Political Economy without the Subject," in *Strategies for Theory from Marx to Madonna*, ed. R. L. Rutsky and Bradley J. Macdonald (Albany: State University of New York Press, 2003), 23–38

48. On the synchronistic Catholic religion of the later colonial period regarded as idolatrous practices in Spanish America, see Carmen Bernard and Serge Gruzinski, *De la idolatrya: Una arqueología de las ciencias religiosas* (Mexico: Fondo de cultura económica, 1992).

49. In the last quarter century, a new generation of scholars has significantly altered the concept of nationalism on which disciplinary paradigm of art

history was fashioned. Ernst Gellner, Eric Hobsbawm, Benedict Anderson, and others restrict the modern concept of a nation to the large-scale political units that emerged in the nineteenth century. See my discussion in " 'Vision Itself Has Its History': 'Race,' Nation, and Renaissance Art History," in *Reframing the Renaissance*, 67–88, especially 70–72, with further references.

50. Jacques Derrida, "Signature Event Context" (1977), *Limited, Inc.*, trans. Samuel Weber, ed. Gerald Graff (Evanston, IL: Northwestern University Press, 1988) developed the discussion of the ways that the work of art is never entirely present nor complete on the basis of its "iterability."

RETHINKING THE DIVIDE: CULT IMAGES AND THE CULT OF IMAGES

Fredrika Jacobs

To articulate a narrative account of the history of art is to authorize a relational experience that is, ultimately, strategically situational.[1] It is an act of historical self-consciousness which, as Robert Armstrong has argued, is at its most fundamental level an attempt to come to grips with "that highly generalized order of phenomena" that arises when "one asks the question, 'What is it that is Romantic in the arts of the Romantic period of European civilization?' or 'In what respect are *classical* arts *classical*?"[2] Expanding these queries, we can ask two others. First, accepting the term "Renaissance art" as a "chronological shorthand for a broad range of crafted objects produced in the period ca. 1400–1600," what intrinsic patterns of signification allow these objects to be categorized as "Renaissance"?[3] In other words, what is uniquely revealed and coherently displayed in the procedures and productions of this period that constitute a marked variation from those art historical eras preceding and succeeding it, and perhaps more significantly, do our perceptions of these revelations divulge prevailing cultural conditions and values of that time or do they instead disclose putative—or subsequently constructed—"truths"? The second query is posed in light of the first. Does (or should) the history of Renaissance art accommodate systemic relationships beyond the canonical to include a broad range of aesthetic productions, including those labeled "popular," categorized as "low," and not infrequently segregated from "art" by the rubric "visual imagery"? These questions are important ones given the destabilization of value that results from an erasure of long-standing distinctions as well as the fact that once answers are proffered the culture runs the risk of "forever thereafter . . . exist[ing] in its total statement as a portion of reality."[4]

Among the "realities" art history has articulated as defining the Renaissance is the paradigm shift "from cult images to the cult of images," the transformation of the image from something that "formerly had been assigned a special reality and taken literally as a visible manifestation of the sacred person" into "the work of the artist and a manifestation of art" evincing "the growing internalization of images, in the sense . . . that the image might both press on and flow from the [individual] imagination."[5] Early critical texts provide ample evidence to support this thesis—one need cite only Giorgio Vasari's *Lives of the Most Eminent Painters, Sculptors and Architects*, second edition 1568, which bears the unmistakable stamp of hagiography and establishes a chronology privileging perceptions of originality in concept (*invenzione*) and evidence of a learned authorial hand coupled with powers of imagination (*ingegno*). As Vasari's brief description of Mantegna's *Madonna della Vittoria*, 1496, makes clear, his interest in the miraculous was principally concerned with what the artist achieved and the patron's satisfaction with that achievement.[6] He says nothing about the transformation of Mantegna's altarpiece into a miraculous image capable of protecting the threatened and healing the ill even though, as Francesco Gonzaga's secretary Antimaco observed, its perceived efficacy was attracting an ever-increasing "throng" of devotees bearing offerings of gratitude within hours of its installation in a new chapel next to the church of San Simeon, Mantua.[7] Yet what Vasari, guided by his announced desire to investigate and evaluate the methods and means of making, opted to ignore, others have in recent years acknowledged.[8] As David Freedberg notes, correspondence between Federico and Isabella d'Este disclose "the full array of the complex relations between artistic skill and perceived efficacy, between orchestrated devotion and local popularity."[9]

Although expanded to include interpretive methods such as

Petrarchism, Renaissance art history has tended to follow Vasari's lead, focusing on style and the impress of humanism and classical antiquity. This is not to say that the discipline has failed to challenge the master narrative of *The Lives*.[10] However, "the 'rise' of the artist from craftsman to intellectual, a development that is . . . one of the principal themes in any traditional account of Renaissance art" remains, as Robert Williams argues, in need of interrogation. For him, even the "array of new approaches" to the field, including the social-historical, have "simply supplant[ed] the traditional artist-centered account with a patron—or consumer—centered one" that is no less, albeit perhaps more subtly, limited. Although the contribution of studies of this kind has been "enormous," they "ignore the still deeper way in which, in Renaissance Italy, art was discovered to work, and thus fall short of offering an adequate account of the period's distinctive art-historical achievement." In response to this short-coming, Williams suggests that with its "theoretical emphasis on knowledge" the art of the Italian Renaissance can be viewed as "structured by the assumption that what is properly artistic is a concern with the specifically systematic features of representation," such as style, which "can be understood as something determined by a set of objective formulae," or decorum, which "permits art to engage social codes systematically and thus to enter into sophisticated social discourse." In the final analysis, Williams sees Renaissance artists' preoccupation with the "systematicity" of representation as "an indication of their sophistication and ambition, their sense that a more complex time called for art of a more complex kind."[11] His arguments are compelling yet they are also rife with the kind of ideological investment that perpetuates the divide between cult images and the cult of images, the "high" and the "low," "art" and "image."

In light of sixteenth-century theoretical texts, it can be argued that Robert Williams has rightly placed obstacles in the way of Postmodernism's in-roads to and impositions on the history of Renaissance art. Indeed, he is not wrong in viewing an unfortunate number of social-historical studies as "an apology for the modern bourgeois mode of engagement with art." Yet is it imperative, as Claire Farago has questioned, to embrace the established "intellectual horizons of our investigations at the expense of other issues that are just as much a part of the history of aesthetics"?[12] Is aesthetic appreciation at odds with an emotional recognition of worth or, as suggested by the letters exchanged between Federico Gonzaga and Isabella d'Este concerning the reception of Mantegna's *Madonna della Vittoria*, is a viewer's expectation and satisfaction of each co-existent and relational? If both are kept in play, if they are placed in dialectical relationship with one another is something meaningful gained? Do we learn something about the nature of visual experience and how representation constitutes culture? I would venture to say "yes." The difficulty is determining how this is to be done. The exacting nature of the challenge is perhaps best demonstrated by the counter-positioning and implications of two of the terms we employ to describe the objects we study: "art" and "imagery." The difference between the two can be rather startling given the fact that the latter is sometimes rejected from the purview of art history.

David Freedberg introduced his often cited *Power of Images*, 1989, with an attention grabbing statement. "This book is not about the history of art. It is about the relations between images and people in history. . . . It is the product of a long-standing commitment to ideas which traditional forms of the history of art—as well as most current ones—seem either to have neglected or to have left inadequately articulated."[13] Fifteen years later, Erik Thunø and Gerhard Wolf prefaced a collection of essays clearly indebted to Freedberg's book, *The Miraculous Image in the Late Middle Ages and Renaissance*, 2004, with a sentence suggesting that little had changed. "In recent years the miraculous image has been recognized as an important phenomenon of medieval visual culture, but its place and significance in the visual culture of the early modern period has been widely overlooked by art historians."[14] It is not so much the on-going state of neglect that has left miraculous images and ex-votos marginalized in art historical scholarship that is notable in these statements but rather the disclaimers, which are both explicitly stated—this is "not about the history of art"—and implicitly acknowledged—this is about "visual culture." Where does this leave the literally hundreds of miracle-working images, particularly those of the Virgin Mary, as well as the thousands of painted panels and modeled figures offered to them in thanks for grace received? As the sub-title and chapter headings of David Morgan's *Visual Piety: A History and Theory of Popular Religious Images*, 1998, suggests, we are left in the realm of "material things" and the "aesthetics of everyday life." Offering a "justification" for this he concludes his preface by noting that "popular religious images contribute to the construction of reality," that "people use images to make and maintain their worlds."[15] The same can be said of "art." Indeed, "popular religious imagery," not unlike the paintings and sculptures assembled in the Renaissance *studiolo*, had its own systematicity.[16] Visual prototypes were acknowledged, narratives of efficacy were formulaic, meditational practices prescribed, experiential states anticipated, and knowledge, albeit concerned with immanent presence rather than worldly endeavor, was acquired.

Tackling the problem

Miraculous images, particularly those of the Virgin Mary, not only thrived during the Renaissance, they proliferated, prompting the staging of popular processions and festivals, the institution of rules and regulations ordering these and other acts of adoration, and the construction of pilgrimage complexes to provide sanctuary for the venerated image, shelter its visitors, house the attendant clergy, and accommodate the commercial manufacture and sale of votive images and effigies as well as souvenirs.[17]

Any attempt to come to some understanding of these cultic images as well as the ex-votos accompanying them, including *boti*, or wax effigies, and *tavolette*, or small devotional paintings depicting scenes of distress in which the Madonna intervened on the sufferer's behalf, is fraught with difficulties. Despite the fact that in the fifteenth and sixteenth centuries there were hundreds of miracle-working Madonnas, scores of *boti* populating holy places like SS. Annunziata in Florence and S. Maria delle Grazie, Milan, and literally thousands of *tavolette* covering virtually every inch of a church's interior walls, votive images have been relegated to the "marginal place" of the "popular."[18] There are several explanations for this. Survival is a principal one. Votive images [*imagini*] were, in essence, ephemeral. They were subject to the effects of political reversals, economic needs, and current assessments of value. Thus, for example, wax effigies of the Medici in SS. Annunziata were destroyed in the wake of the family's expulsion from Florence in 1494 and again in 1527. Those fabricated in precious metals, such as the silver portrait bust of Lorenzo de' Medici in Florence's baptistery, were frequently melted down, the inherent value of the material judged to far outweigh the prestige of the portrayed person.[19] An absence of political turmoil did nothing to preserve and protect these offerings. In 1673, Pietro Paolo Raffaelli recorded the house-cleaning that took place at Loreto. All "useless monuments and superfluous testimonies to the holiness of the place" were removed. Those objects made of gold and silver, which included models of cities delivered from natural or military crises, crowns offered to the Madonna di Loreto, and miscellaneous votive tablets that numbered more than sixty at the end of the cinquecento, were quite simply "converted . . . to a more useful purpose."[20] Similar objects in other locations, such as Trapani in Sicily, fared only slightly better.

In contrast to politically charged *boti* or materially valuable ex-votos crafted of gold and silver, sixteenth-century *tavolette* continue to exist in large numbers. At the shrine dedicated to the Madonna dell' Arco on the outskirts of Naples alone more than 750 painted panels dating to the period between 1499 and 1600 can still be seen affixed to the walls of the church's north transept. These images are plagued by a different problem, one that is frequently shared by the image of the miracle-working Madonna herself. Often rather crude in style, unimaginative in conception, and lacking known authorship, *tavolette* have been characterized as "naïve" and, if considered at all, relegated to the distant periphery of art history. Because they are viewed as decidedly incompatible with contemporaneous canonical works of art and therefore resistant to the genre practices of the discipline, they are handed over to anthropologists and social historians. It can admittedly be argued that the variety of votive gifts, which can range from silver portrait busts, gold crowns with or without the addition of precious stones, painted panels, representations of body parts fashioned in wax, and even candles, makes it impossible to study cultic images and votive offerings within a theoretical framework, although some, like Lenz Kriss-Rettenbeck, have tried.[21] Success has come when the scope of study has been focused on one type of ex-voto or a particular theoretical issue, as is the case with Hugo van der Velden's work on *boti* and Jane Garnett's and Gervase Rosser's study of the representation and replication of cult images in Liguria. In the case of the latter this can be attributed to the authors' engagement with theories of reproduction, derivatives, and sites of display.[22] In the former case this might be explained by several factors. First, votive effigies can be placed within the established discourse of Renaissance portraiture. Second, in addition to general observations and information found in diaries and inventories, *boti* found a place in texts on art, including Giorgio Vasari's *Lives*. Third, at least in some cases the hands of the *ceraiuoli* or *fallimagini* are known. Whether or not, or at least to what extent, should these factors be affected by a lack of physical evidence is not a point I wish to address here. Nonetheless, the available amount of visual evidence coupled with textual descriptions demands that attention now be turned to this long-dismissed group of images.

The question at hand is how is this to be done? Clearly, casting an inquiry within the parameters of periodization is of little help. Because the practice of exchange between an image that bestows a blessing and a recipient who returns thanks for the benefaction has deep medieval roots, devotional images cannot be seen as either enlightened or clouded by the nascent "era of art."[23] An alternative approach is to consider the intrusion of the profane into a sacred context. Although Aby Warburg employed this strategy with provocative results in his study of *boti*, it is difficult to extend the critical approach beyond this specific type of votive offering. The related tactic of analyzing personal expressions within the public sphere is similarly limited, proffering a view of the practice that is, one can argue, one-dimensional. It might be more constructive to consider these works in the context of what Marcel Mauss calls the social phenomenon of gift exchange.[24] This should not be restricted to diplomatic gifts, such as the gifting of copies of Santa Maria Maggiore's so-called *Salus Populi Romani* to Caterina of Portugal, Philip II of Spain, and other sovereigns. Although Mauss's *The Gift* has been described as essential reading for students of social anthropology and sociology, it has in recent years been used by art historians to discuss masterworks by master artists, such as Michelangelo's *Rebellious* and

Dying Slaves and Baccio Bandinelli's *Laocoön*. This system of analysis can be applied to the "popular." Situating miraculous images and ex-votos within a system of reciprocity that has bearing on every item of status, spiritual, or material meaning offers a constructive way to cross the divide between cult images and the cult of images.

The problems confronted when dealing with votive images inheres in popular piety itself. As Van der Velden so aptly put it in his analysis of *boti*, it is the "popular" aspect of *imagini* that has caused cultic and votive images to be classified as "imagery rather than art." Is it then even possible to bring the term "Renaissance" and all that it implies as a stylistic and cultural designator with heuristic value to bear on a class of works that seem so dissimilar to those that form our understanding of that era? The manner in which the history of art has in recent years turned attention to cultic images has implicitly suggested ways this question might be resolved. Focusing principally on acheiropoietic items, such as the Veronica or icons attributed to the hand of St. Luke, it has fore-grounded a work's origins. This has prompted an exploration of, among other things, the relationship of "image and art, original and copy, trace and representation," issues that have relevance for discussions of works by Michelangelo and Raphael as well as for those not made by human hands.[25] Yet evaluating the presence of the "divine" hand, whether it is St. Luke's or that of Michelangelo—"Il Divino"—omits the vast majority of cultic images, to say nothing of *tavolette*, from the discourse. Not all cultic images were recognized as divine in origin. Many were quite humble. Indeed, the names of the artists and the dates of the majority remain unknown. For example, the Madonna dell'Arco, Naples, and the Madonna della Corte, Ferrara, in contrast to the Virgin Annunciates of Trapani in Sicily and SS. Annunziata in Florence, both of which claim the intervention of an apostolic or angelic hand, were acknowledged as wholly human productions.[26] Their venerated status, like that of the Madonna del Monte di Cesena, the Virgin of Monte Berico in Vicenza, and the Madonna at Savona on Italy's Ligurian coast, resulted from a demonstrated ability to perform "rescue" miracles and thaumaturgic cures. These miracle-working Madonnas were (and are) recognized as possessing the power to make the blind see, the crippled to walk, the mute to speak, the infertile to bear children, and generally heal just about any and all ills. Accordingly, these Madonnas have much to do with what an image does rather than what the artist did. This is underscored by the fact that many of these cultic images, which are frequently related to visionary experience, are essentially "found objects." In some cases, the report of a vision lends credence to the miraculous nature of the long neglected image, as happened when, on July 6, 1484, an eight year old boy playing among the ruins of a prison in Prato witnessed the metamorphosis of paint into apparitional substance as the Virgin stepped away from her image and proceeded to descend into the prison vaults.[27] In other instances, the image is "taken as proof of the reality of the apparition."[28]

Regardless of the spin placed on these rediscovered images, their acquisition of revered status and a belief in their agency results in the recognition of them as *vera effigie* and this, in turn, frequently led to characterizing them with terms that were also employed in the celebration of authored masterpieces. They are "*miracoli*" and they possess an aura of being alive by reason of their vivid and vibrant presence. Not surprisingly, this quality of *vivacità* extends to wax effigies, one need remember only Benedetto Varchi's account of the "slaughtering" of Medici *boti*, which is coupled with the attempted "killing" "in fact" of the Medici by the Pazzi conspirators.[29] Obviously, the texts in which this descriptive language appears, and therefore the implications and nuance of meaning, is of critical importance. Vasari's praise of Raphael's *St. Cecilia* as a living and miraculous painting cannot be understood in the same way as Arcangelo Domenici's veneration of like qualities in the fresco of the Madonna dell'Arco. A critic-*cum*-historian is motivated by interests other than those inciting a Dominican friar to put pen to paper. At the very least, qualities distinguishing a cultic image from one belonging to that class of pictures acknowledged as giving rise to the cult of images, like Raphael's *St. Cecilia*, need to be examined first within this context.

The perceived divide between cultic images and the cult of images is great, marked by differentiating adjectives like "low" and "high," "simple" and "complex." When the two are discussed in relationship to one another it is in the context of adaptation, the manner in which an icon like the *Salus Populi Romani* informs an image like the Madonna del Pozzo, which hundreds of years later is said to have miraculously surfaced from the depths of a well located by a stable next to the church of Santa Maria in Via, Rome. Although, as David Freedberg has noted, "simple images can . . . generate higher ones. . . . the opposite of this, the downward transformation of canonical prototypes, happens even more frequently."[30] Despite the opening disclaimer that *The Power of Images* "is not about art history," Freedberg's consideration of prototypes and the process of repetition and modification from high to low and/or low to high fits within the discipline's investigative modes. It is a study that goes beyond the descriptive recording of what cult images and the ex-votos made in response to their efficacy look like to examine how they might be categorized.[31] In doing so it destabilizes what is historically taken as "high" and "low" by suggesting a rethinking of exchange value. Recent studies on *boti* have done this as well, successfully grappling with the likeness and difference of high and low within the theoretical framework of conventions of portraiture, social prominence, and conspicuous display.[32] Although *tavolette* often depict in a more narratival form incidents clearly referenced in *boti*, such as a person's survival of the tortuous *strappo* used by criminal interrogators, portraiture cannot be used to relate votive panels to conventions in portraiture, as is the case with effigies, or, for that matter, *istorie*. Is it, therefore, either constructive or even necessary to maintain the qualitative categories of "imagery" and "art" and perpetuate a discourse that traces the transliteration of the religious into the artistic?[33] Besides the rituals and obligations of gift-giving is there a way of thinking about all of this in a way that allows for an erasure of distinctions? Clearly cultic images, no less than those belonging to the cult of images, can be said to possess the efficacy of effect, something which is, arguably, equally present in what Armstrong in the context of African art calls "works-in-invocation" and "works-in-virtuosity."[34]

It would be foolish to deny that the vigorous theoretical debates concerning the nature of profession, which began in earnest with the Latin humanists in the mid-fourteenth century, failed to have an effect on the visual arts.[35] By the same token, it is misguided to assume that the prevailing cultural conditions of the Italian Renaissance should be explained within the framework of academic debate without the consideration of more popular and long-standing forms of expression. The insistent disciplinary practice of championing the intellectual assumptions of a classicizing and canonizing history of craft skews perspective. The cultural landscape of Renaissance Italy was marked by hills and valleys that are quite simply flattened when viewed from this vantage point alone. This is not to deny the emergence of the cult of the image, which developed with the cult of the artist and is celebrated in contemporaneous texts, but rather to admit that it coexisted with an on-going recognition of and ardent devotion to cultic images that were obscure in origin and votive works that have been marginalized as naïve. How, then, is the recognized "reality" of a shift from cultic images to the cult of images to be discussed? Indeed, what is uniquely revealed and coherently displayed in the procedures and productions located in this time and place that disclose prevailing cultural conditions and communicate values endemic to both cults? Philip Wheelwright has suggested a way. We might explore the possibilities offered by "the juxtaposition of previously unjoined words and images" and consider how "new qualities and new meanings can emerge . . . out of some hitherto ungrouped combination of elements."[36] It is with this in mind that I propose considering the following.

In 1533, Michelangelo sent Tommaso Cavalieri a gift of drawings. Writing to the artist, the young nobleman reported that "everyone" in Rome was flocking to his home to see it, including Pope Clement VII and Cardinal Ippolito de' Medici.[37] The admiring Cardinal requested to have two of the images—the *Fall of Phaeton* and the *Tityus*—in order that he might have them reproduced in crystal. At least one artist visiting the Cavalieri home made a replica of one of the drawings, probably a tracing of the *Tityus*. As happened with other drawings by the master's touted "divine" hand, re-presentations in a variety of mediums followed, some of which maintained the autonomy of the original composition, others which adapted borrowed figural motives to new arrangements.[38] A very different yet strangely familiar series of events took place around an image in Naples nearly six decades later. In 1591, Pope Gregory XIV received a letter informing him that all of Naples, including "the major part of the nobility," was "devoted" to a painting of the Madonna and Christ Child which had been anonymously frescoed under an archway sometime during the previous century. Albeit for different reasons and with more broad-based appeal, this anonymously painted fresco attracted a parade of viewers just as Michelangelo's drawings had done years earlier in Rome. In fact and as was the case with Mantegna's *Madonna della Vittoria*, the image, known as the Madonna dell'Arco, was reportedly being visited "every hour" by infinite numbers ("*infinita gente*").[39] Moreover, it had already been—and continues to be—reproduced in different materials and contexts. As noted, approximately 750 sixteenth- century small wood panel paintings illustrating the Virgin's immanent presence during times of accident and hardship have survived.[40] And, just as Michelangelo's *Tityus, Fall of Phaeton*, and other similar works, as well as the many prints, drawings, and paintings made in response to them, are preserved in institutions designed to safeguard the sanctity of fine art, so is the Madonna dell'Arco and the thousands of *tavolette*, minted medals, and other objects produced in gratitude for grace received enshrined in a pilgrimage church and its adjacent museum.

The history of art has not been inclined to speak of cultic images of the type of the Madonna dell'Arco and the cult of images arising from the deification of artists of Michelangelo's stature in the same breath. The reasons are obvious, ranging from differences in medium, distinctions in authorship, and dissimilarity in function and, hence, viewer expectation. As the latter difference suggests, audience is a factor of significance. Although the Madonna dell'Arco attracted "*la maggior parte della nobilità*," the inverse does not hold for Michelangelo's drawings. The master's drawings did not move the masses to acts of homage. If Wheelwright's advice is followed and this pair of previously unjoined images is juxtaposed, is there some fundamental social language revealed that defines both as culturally, if not stylistically, "Renaissance" works? Because in this particular case the divine hand, be it that of "Il Divino" or St. Luke, does not come into play as a point of nexus, common ground must be sought elsewhere. This odd pairing is perhaps best considered in terms of "presence."

Images "bearing presence," according to Armstrong, fall into two basic but not exclusive groups. A "work-in-invocation" embodies "who-ness" or "what-ness." Like an individual, the work has an identity. It is "who or what the work is said to be."[41] In the case of the Madonna dell' Arco, the "who" is the Virgin Mary, or more accurately this specific Madonna as opposed, for example, to the Madonna del Monte di Cesena or the Madonna dei Bagni. In this respect, the painting is "alive." Here, it is worth referencing Hans Belting's statement concerning the use of the term "living painting" (*empsychos graphe*) by the eleventh-century writer Michael Psellus. "The term first serves to defend painting against the old charge of being dead matter that in vain pretends to provide the illusion of life. In addition, the term equates painting, which is not mute but capable of speech, with poetry, which touches the feelings by arousing persons and events to life. That which has a soul can speak to the soul."[42] A "living painting," which is a "work-in-invocation," thus "tends to exist in an ambient of time" and through "performance."[43] Works of this kind are valued for what they do; the miracles they perform and the prayers they answer. Value is strategically situational. By contrast, a work by Michelangelo has presence in what Armstrong calls "the aesthetic of virtuosity." What garners attention is "how-ness," the excellence of conception and execution. Efficacy does not exist in some sort of transactional relationship between the viewer and the image as the former negotiates with the latter to perform some action. Nonetheless, and as is the case with "works-in-invocation," a viewer's conscious affirmation of presence is a critical component of validation.

Although Armstrong contends that a "work-in-virtuosity," in contrast to a "work-in-invocation," has autonomy in as much as presence is the result of internal qualities and significances, it too depends upon viewer acknowledgement. Presence exists as long as there is a culture attending to it. During the Renaissance, as in other periods, prestige accrued in accordance with the acknowledgment of presence, which in turn aroused a viewer's possessive desires. Cardinal de' Medici's expressed wish to borrow Michelangelo's drawings from Cavalieri in order to own them in the form of a crystal reproduction, Cardinal Reginald Pole's prideful ownership of a version of the *Pietà* drawing gifted to Vittoria Colonna by the master, or the fact that a number of Michelangelo drawings exist in multiple versions—some made by Michelangelo, others not—speaks for itself. As for cultic images, they too were reproduced for individual ownership as well as communal use. In 1580, for example, Girolamo Angelitta reported a brisk business in the sale of images of the Madonna di Loreto stamped onto tin, silver, and gold plates that took place in the vast courtyard in front of the church in which the Holy House and its Madonna were enshrined.[44] A decade earlier, in 1569, the Jesuit General Francis Borgia had ordered copies of the *Salus Populi Romani* to not only be distributed to the order's institutions throughout Europe and as far away as Brazil but that special chapels be built to house each of these replications.[45] In the following century the novices of San Andrea al Quirinale gathered twice a day to venerate their copy. In some sense then cultic value is both possession-*cum*-exhibition value and vice-versa.

In Renaissance texts one of the most common ways of conveying presence was the designation of a work as a living image, one that advanced the illusion of life from an arrangement of inert matter that *appears* to breathe, speak, or move. The critical texts of Vasari, Lodovico Dolce, Giambattista Armenini, to name but a few, are filled with acknowledgments of this sort, complete with descriptions of works like Michelangelo's *David* and Raphael's *St. Cecilia*, which are praised for being "more alive than lively" and can even be said to be "truly alive."[46] In detailing the Virgin of the Annunciate in SS. Annunziata, a collaborative work begun by a mortal but completed by an angel, Francesco Bocchi relies on similar language.[47] While it can be argued that here the accompanying designation of the work as something that is "*miracoloso*" reflects on the origin of the image, the term does not function as a stylistic designator as it does when applied to the masterful *miracoli* made by Michelangelo and Raphael. On the experiential level a "work-in-invocation" clearly responds to a different set of viewer expectations and taps into a well of different sensibilities than those anticipated from and aroused by a "work-in-virtuosity." The two can nonetheless co-exist with one aspect enriching the other and both shedding light on how the object constitutes its subjects.[48] In framing discussions of "works-in-invocation" and "works-in-virtuosity" it is worth looking for points of nexus as well as divergence. Indeed, one often serves to highlight the other thereby allowing for insights into the usages of critical vocabulary that may or may not substantiate or modify some of the long established notions of the art historical discourse. The paradigm shift from cultic images to the cult of images, for example, can by no means be denied but neither can it be viewed as marking a decisive break from one art historical period to another. Indeed, while it is accurate to say that Renaissance writers were critical in establishing the cult of the image by advancing the work of art as a product that both pressed on and flowed from the artist's imagination, it is also true, as Vasari's discussion of the miraculous survival of Raphael's *Lo Spasimo* demonstrates, that these same Renaissance writers drew on the established narratives of cultic images in order to enhance further the reverential aura they were busy constructing around the cult of the image.

The way we see and discuss works of art are no less situational than the ways in which they were experienced in their time and place of making. Considered in the context of the interplay of the acheiropoietic and ex-votos, thamaturgic images can be understood in one way. Viewing the latter as images within images (here the votive panel in the lower right corner of Titian's *Pietà*, 1576, or the interior church walls laden with *tavolette* in a predella panel illustrating a scene from the life of St. Vincent Ferrer in the Accademia, Florence, can stand as two examples) broadens that understanding. Examining the stories surrounding miraculous images, whether the miracle-working Madonna of Trapani or Raphael's *Lo Spasimo*, against folkloric traditions and strategies of narrative-appropriation, offers different insights.[49] So, too, does a consideration of the efficacy of effect and the affective aspects of a viewer's response. Anonymously painted miracle-working Madonnas can heal. Conversely, Raphael's *St Cecilia* so stunned Francesco Francia, says Vasari, that the Bolognese painter fell faint and soon thereafter died as he reflected on his mortal abilities compared to Raphael's godlike, creative capacities.[50]

My point has not been to argue that the standing processes of validation—and evaluation—must be revised. It has been to query if "imagery" and "art" are so distinctive that the relegation of the former to the aesthetic judgments devised in consideration of the latter have to stymie efforts to see both as expressions of the prevailing cultural conditions of the Renaissance. Hobbled by the designations "low" and "popular," votive images are persistently viewed as artifacts—and here I must admit that I use the term "artifact" quite consciously given its recent application to such "high" works of art like Carpaccio's *Vision of St. Jerome*.[51] Determining whether or not Armstrong's explication of a "work-in-virtuosity" and a "work-in-invocation" has application to Renaissance "artifacts" (in the expanded sense of the word) is a worthwhile endeavor. As Claire Farago has so ably demonstrated, "viewing 'high art' through the lens of participatory material culture is [not only] justified," it also mitigates against perpetuating aesthetic myopia.[52] Coupled with Philip Wheelwright's suggestion that "the juxtaposition of previously unjoined words and images" affords the possibility that "new qualities and new meanings can emerge . . . out of some hitherto ungrouped combination of elements," we might possibly have a way to start the conversation. Destabilizing what is historically taken as "high" art can allow for a broader range of aesthetic productions to inform our understanding of Renaissance culture.

Notes

1. See Hayden White, "The Value of Narrativity in the Representation of Reality," *Critical Inquiry*, 7 (1980), 5–27. I am grateful to Bernard L. Herman for discussing with me aspects of this paper and directing me to sources in material culture that have broadened my perspective.
2. Robert Plant Armstrong, *The Affecting Presence: An Essay in Humanistic Anthropolgy* (Urbana, IL: University of Illinois Press, 1971), xiii.
3. In his essay for this volume, "Vasari's Renaissance and its Renaissance Alternatives," Stephen J. Campbell notes two broad senses of the term. This one and "Renaissance art . . . as a kind of ideological investment . . . of what art is or might be."
4. Armstrong., xiv.
5. Sylvia Perino Pagden, "From Cult Images to the Cult of Images: The Case of Raphael's Altarpieces" in *The Altarpiece in the Renaissance*, ed. Peter Humphrey and Martin Kemp (Cambridge: Cambridge University Press, 1990), 165–189; Hans Belting, *Likeness and Presence: A History of the Image before the Era of Art*, trans. Edmund Jephcott (Chicago: University of Chicago Press, 1994), 471. The final quote comes from Michael Cole's

reflections on Belting and Gerhard Wolf, *Schleier und Spiegel: Traditionem des Christusbildes und die Bildkonzepte der Renaissance* (Munich: Wilhelm Fink, 2002), in *"Nihil Sub Sole Novum," Art Bulletin* 87 (2005): 422. Although these and other scholars recognize a paradigm shift, they do not agree on the forces affecting it.

6. Giorgio Vasari, *Le vite de' più eccellenti pittori, scultori ed architettori* in *Le opere di Giorgio Vasari*, ed. Gaetano Milanesi (Florence: G.C. Sansoni, 1906), vol. 3, 402–404.

7. David Freedberg, *The Power of Images: Studies in the History and Theory of Response* (Chicago: University of Chicago Press, 1989), 145–146; Dana E. Katz, "Painting and the Politics of Persecution: Representing the Jew in Fifteenth-Century Mantua," *Art History* 23 (2000): 474–495.

8. Vasari, as in note 6, preface to part 2, vol. 2, 93–94.

9. Freedberg, as in note 7, 468, note 20. The letters are in Paul Oskar Kristeller, *Renaissance Concepts of Man and Other Essays* (New York: Harper & Row, 1972), 558–562.

10. The recent exchange between Alexander Nagel, Christopher S. Wood, Charles Dempsey, Michael Cole, and Claire Farago on anachronism in *Art Bulletin* 87 (2005), 403–432, is a case in point. So too is the work of Georges Didi-Huberman.

11. Robert Williams, "Italian Renaissance Art and the Systematicity of Representation," *Rinascimento* 43 (2004): 309–331.

12. Claire Farago, "Aesthetics before Art: Leonardo through the Looking Glass" in *Compelling Visuality: The Work of Art In and Out of History* (Minneapolis: University of Minnesota Press, 2003), 51.

13. Freedberg, as in note 7, xix.

14. Erik Thunø and Gerhard Wolf, eds., *The Miraculous Image in the Late Middle Ages and Renaissance* (Rome: Bretschneider, 2004), 7.

15. David Morgan, *Visual Piety: A History and Theory of Popular Religious Images* (Berkeley: University of California Press, 1998), xv.

16. Stephen J. Campbell, "Vasari's Renaissance and its Renaissance Alternatives" in this volume.

17. Perhaps the best example of this is the complex at Loreto. See, for example, Horatio Torsellini, *De L'Historia della Santissima Casa della B. V. Maria di Loreto, Libri cinque* (Venice: Domenico Imberti, 1601); Kathleen Weil-Garris, "Cloister Court and City Square," *Gesta* 12 (1973): 123–132; Floriano Grimaldi, *La chiesa di Santa Maria di Loreto nei documenti dei secoli XII–XV* (Ancona: Archivio di Stato, 1984; and Floriano Grimaldi, *Historia della chiesa di Santa Maria di Loreto* (Loreto: Cassa di risparmio di Loreto, 1993). Saints' relics also hold an important place in the phenomenon of the miraculous and, indeed, many of the ceremonial/processional aspects of miracle-working Madonna images are practiced in the context of relics. They are not part of this discussion for obvious reasons. A skull, scapula, or other kind of bone cannot be mistaken as a work of art!

18. Hugo van der Velden, "Medici Votive Images and the Scope and Limits of Likeness" in *The Image of the Individual: Portraits in the Renaissance*, eds. Nicholas Mann and Luke Syson (London: British Museum Press, 1998), 126.

19. Luca Landucci, *Diario Fiorentino dal 1450 al 1516*, ed. I. del Badia (Florence: G. C. Sansoni, 1883), 330.

20. Oratio Torsellino, *Laurentanae historia libri quinque*, as cited in R.W. Lightbrown, "Ex-votos in gold and silver: a forgotten art," *Burlington Magazine* 121 (June, 1979): 352.

21. Lenz Kriss-Rettenbeck, *Ex Voto*. Zeichen, Bild und Abbild in Christlichen Votivbrauchtum (Zürich: Atlantis, 1972).

22. Jane Garnett and Gervase Rosser, "Translations of the Miraculous Cult Images and their Representations in Early Modern Liguria" in *The Miraculous Image in the Late Middle Ages and Renaissance*, Erik Thunø and Gerhard Wolf, eds. (Rome: Bretschneider, 2004), 205–222.

23. For the continuum, see Richard Trexler, "Florentine Religious Experience: The Sacred Image," *Studies in the Renaissance* 19 (1972): 7. As Nagel has noted, "socio-historical and anthropological approaches to the Renaissance have only confirmed the pervasive presence of religious traditions and institutions in the life of the period." See Alexander Nagel's review of Jörg Traeger, *Renaissance und Religion: Die Kunst des Glaubens im Zeitalter Raphaels* in *Art Bulletin* 82 (2000): 773.

24. Marcel Mauss, *The Gift: The Form and Reason for Exchange in Archaic Societies*, trans. W.D. Hall (New York: W.W. Norton, 1990).

25. A particularly rich corpus of studies is found in *The Holy Face and the Paradox of Representation, Papers from a Colloquium Held at the Bibliotheca Herziana, Rome and the Villa Spelman, Florence, 1996*, ed. Herbert L. Kessler and Gerhard Wolf (Bologna: Nuova Alfa Editoriale, 1998).

26. See H.W. Kruft, "Die Madonna von Trapani und ihren Kopien. Studien zur Madonnamythologie und zum Begriff der Kopi in der sizilianischen Skulptur des Quattrocento," *Mitteilungen des Kunsthistorischen Institus in Florenz* 14 (1970): 297–322; Francesco Bocchi, *Le bellezze della citta di Fiorenza, Dove à pieno di Pittura, di Scultura, di sacri Tempii di Palazzi I più notabili artifizii, & più preziosi si contengono* (Florence: no publisher, 1591), 217–218. Also see Gisela Kraut, *Lukas malt die Madonna. Zeugnisse zum künstlerischen Selbstverständnis in der Malerei* (Worms: Wernersche Verlagsgesellschaft, 1986).

27. Giuliano di Francesco Guizzelmi, *Miracoli della Madonna delle Carceri di Prato* [1505], Biblioteca Roncioniana, Prato, MS 87: 8v–9r; and Andrea del Germanino, *Miracoli et Gratie della Gloriosa Madre Vergine Maria delle Charceri di Prato, l'anno 1484*, Biblioteca Roncioniana MS 86: 37r. See Robert Maniura, "The Images and Miracles of Santa Maria delle Carceri," in *The Miraculous Image in the Late Middle Ages and Renaissance*, eds. Erik Thunø and Gerhard Wolf (Rome: L'Erma di Bretschneider, 2004), 81–95; Robert Maniura, "Image and Relic in the Cult of Our Lady of Prato," in *Images, Relics, and Devotional Practices in Medieval and Renaissance Italy*, eds. Sally J. Cornelison and Scott B. Montgomery (Tempe, AZ: Arizona Center for Medieval and Renaissance Studies, 2006), 193–212.

28. Mary Lee Nolan and Sidney Nolan, *Christian Pilgrimage in Modern Western Europe* (Chapel Hill and London: The University of North Carolina Press, 1989), 270.

29. Varchi, as cited in Richard C. Trexler, *Public Life in Renaissance Florence* (Ithaca: Cornell University Press, 1980), 123.

30. Freedberg, as in note 7, 141–143, discusses this using the *Schöne Maria* at Regensberg as the example. There is in addition the "middle level, where good images—not to refine our qualitative usage any more at this stage— adapted from miraculous archetypes, are transformed first into high art, and then, because of the power of the latter, are infinitely modified down."

31. Far more typical are texts like Paolo Toschi and Renato Penna, *Le Tavolette Votive della Madonna dell'Arco* (Naples: Di Mauro, 1971), and L. Novelli and M. Massaccesi, *Ex Voto del Santuario della Madonna del Monte di Cesena* (Forli: Società Tipografica Florivese, 1961).

32. Van der Velden, as in note 18, 126–137, notes 221–227. Also see Georges Didi-Huberman, "Ressemblance mythifiée et ressemblance oubliée chez Vasari: La légende du portrait 'sur le vif,' " *Mélanges de l'Ecole Française de Rome, Italie et Méditerranée*, 106, no. 2 (1994): 383–432. Aby Warburg, "Bildniskunst und florentinisches Bürgertum," *Gesammelte Schriften* (Leipzig, 1932), I, 89–126 and 340–352; Julius von Schlosser, "Geschichte der Porträitbildnerei in Wachs. Ein Versuch," *Jahrbuch der kunsthistorischen Sammlungen des allerhöchsten Kaiserhauses*, 29 (1910–1911): 171–258.

33. It must be noted that this route has been followed to good effect by Sylvia Perino-Pagden, "From cult images to the cult of images: the case of Raphael's altarpieces" in *The Altarpiece in the Renaissance*, ed. Peter Humphrey and Martin Kemp (Cambridge: Cambridge University Press, 1990), 165–189.

34. Robert Plant Armstrong, *The Powers of Presence: Consciousness, Myth, and Affecting Presence* (Philadelphia: University of Pennsylvania Press, 1981), 10–13.

35. See, for example, George W. McClure, *The Culture of Profession in Late Renaissance Italy* (Toronto: The University of Toronto Press, 2004).

36. Philip Wheelwright, *Metaphor and Reality* (Bloomington: Indiana University Press, 1962), 85–86.

37. For Cavaliere's letter dated September 6, 1533, see *Il Carteggio di Michelangelo*, 5 volumes, ed. Paola Barocchi and Renzo Ristori (Florence: S.P.E.S., 1979), vol.4, 49.

38. See, for example, *Il Mito di Ganimede, Prima e Dopo Michelangelo*, ed. Marcella Marongiu (Florence: Mandragora, 2002).

39. Michele Miele, *Le origini della Madonna dell'Arco: Il "Compendio" di Arcangelo Domenici, Introduzione, testo, note e illustrazioni* (Naples-Bari, Domenicana Italiana, 1995), 7.

40. Toschi and Penna, as in note 31, and Antonio Ermanno Giardino and Michele Rak, *Le Tavolette dipinte ex voto per la Madonna dell'Arco, Il Cinquecento* (Pompei: ci.esse.ti, 1983).

41. Armstrong, as in note 34, 10.

42. Belting, as in note 5, 261.

43. Ibid., 11.

44. Girolamo Angelitta, *L'Historia della Translatione della Santa Casa della Madonna a Loreto* (Marche: Sebastiano Martellini, 1580), 74–75.

45. Kirstin Noreen, "The Icon of Santa Maria Maggiore, Rome: An Image and its Afterlife," *Renaissance Studies* 19 (2005): 664.

46. Fredrika Jacobs, *The Living Image in the Renaissance* (Cambridge: Cambridge University Press, 2005).

47. Francesco Bocchi, *Le bellezze della citta di Firenza, Dove à pieno di Pittura, di Scultura, di sacri Templii, di Palazzi I più notabili artifizii, & più preziosi si contengono* (Florence, 1591), 217–218.

48. Farago, as in note 12, has done this in her study of Leonardo's *Virgin of the Rocks*, 45–92.

49. For Raphael's *Lo Spasimo*, see Vasari-Milanesi, 1906, 4: 357–358. For See, for example,Charles M. Radding, "Il riconoscimento del miracolo nella società medievale: cultura ecclesiastica e cultura folklorica" in *Miracoli dai segni alla storia*, ed. Sofia Boesch Gajano and Marilena Modica (Rome: Viella, 1999), 91–107.

50. Vasari, as in note 6, vol. 4, 357–358.

51. Alexander Nagel and Christopher S. Wood, "Interventions: Toward a New Model of Renaissance Anachronism," *Art Bulletin* 87 (2005): 403–415.

52. Farago, as in note 12.

Gothic as Renaissance: Ornament, Excess, and Identity, Circa 1500

Ethan Matt Kavaler

How should we conceive of a Renaissance in Northern Europe?[1] Does it open with the visually seductive paintings of Jan van Eyck and his contemporaries? Or should we hold to a more traditional emphasis on the critical reception of the legacy of antiquity, directly and through the mediation of Italian art? Indeed, many would insist that northern art achieves its Renaissance only after 1500, when artists, patrons, and critics were forced to contend with ideas and artefacts originating south of the alps.[2]

What, then, is to be made of sixteenth-century Gothic? More than fashionably late, it is often regarded as a lithic manifestation of the Middle Ages exceeding its bounds. Until at least 1530, however, Gothic remained the leading architectural mode throughout Northern Europe, where it was nurtured by the most talented artists and prominent patrons.[3] Gothic architecture, in fact, witnessed a burst of creative development at the end of the fifteenth century, a dramatic renewal of an authoritative manner of design.[4] Yet a sense of trespass on Renaissance territory has long made it difficult to accept these Late Gothic creations as legitimate products of their own culture; they are frequently disowned by paradigms of artistic progress that privilege the adoption of Italianate forms.[5] Many *seiz-ièmistes* still have difficulty finding a place for the transept façades of

Senlis Cathedral, the looping-rib vaults at Annaberg in Saxony, or the whole of Segovia Cathedral—Gothic structures that all slightly postdate Michelangelo's frescoes for the Sistine ceiling.

This is partly the consequence of a Burckhardtian enshrinement of the Italian Renaissance as birthplace of the modern world, a phenomenon with a legitimizing force for other cultures.[6] When imported as a reference for northern lands, the Renaissance is often conceived as a utopian expression of order, simplicity and harmony, an ideal manifest in few if any actual works that can nonetheless validate the achievements of nearly all northern European countries.[7] Issues of national identity[8] and cultural heritage are often registered in a rhetoric of purity. Historians of Netherlandish art, for instance, speak of "a pure Renaissance figure",[9] "a purer Renaissance style",[10] "a more or less pure Renaissance designer",[11] "the pure interpretation ... of classical principles".[12] François Bucher conceives of the very Late Gothic in Germany as a "defensive phase ... directed against the planar purity of Renaissance architecture".[13] For those in search of modernity and national character, a Renaissance must signal rebirth and rejection of the past. It does not vouchsafe authenticity to surviving Gothic sensibilities. And it does not allow for gradual transformation. The term "hybrid" obliquely invalidates works that combine northern and Italianate features—two recognized species that have produced mongrel offspring.[14]

An alternate emphasis on "realism" or "naturalism", as the true mark of a Northern Renaissance has done little to foster recognition of these "Renaissance Gothic" structures. The historical discourse on realism was equally tied to issues of nationalist identity and expressed in terms of competitive claims to the genesis of the modernity.[15] Central to this concern was the evaluation of the painting of the Netherlandish "Primitives", not the contemporary architecture of their land.[16]

Such a preoccupation with notions of realism has actually inhibited appreciation of the abstract principles of geometric composition in Late Gothic creations—regardless of the epoch to which we assign them. Joseph de Borchgrave d'Altena's popular study of Brabantine carved altarpieces, published in 1943, makes almost no mention of their elaborate Gothic frames. The two reproductions of the spectacular Lombeek Altarpiece from around 1525, for example, present delicately carved figural groups showing exquisite detailing of costumes and facial expressions—all without any indication of their highly original and complex architectural casing.[17]

Of course disfavor is frequently meted out to so-called late stages of period styles.[18] Dominant models of periodization privilege a conveniently linear progression, an orderly sequence of artistic manners, each of which rises phoenix-like from the ashes of its predecessor and is implicitly held to embody a distinct worldview.[19] Although stylistic pluralism is recognized, it rarely challenges this governing schema.

The lack of attention paid to Late Gothic architecture is not simply an issue of exclusion from the conventional canon. Rather, it impedes our ability to deal with questions of artistic mode or language at a time when conscious choice replaced inevitable recourse. And to ignore Gothic design at the beginning of the sixteenth century is to ignore a principal field of aesthetic expression in Northern Europe.[20] Gothic ornament, on the facades, vaults, gables, and furnishing of churches and secular halls—as on painting—became a significant register of the imagination or *fantasia* of leading artists. It was also an important means of equipping monuments and framing spaces for religious service. Tilman Riemenschneider's carved wood altarpieces are unthinkable without their towering Gothic cases. And Jan Gossaert's *Malvagna Triptych* would have been neither possible nor meaningful without the contemporary esteem for this mode of design.

Gothic design was indeed haunted in these years by the antique manner. The Fugger Chapel, begun about 1509 in Augsburg, indelibly marked the imported Antique or *Welsch* mode on German soil. Italians and Italian art had been welcomed even earlier at French Courts.[21] And in the Netherlands, Margaret of Austria first considered designing her church at Brou in the manner of "antique things" that her court painter, Jean Perréal, had seen in Italy.[22] Nonetheless, Margaret opted instead for a virtuoso late Gothic manner.[23]

By the second decade of the century Gothic and Italianate inventions might appear side by side as indices of the multiple stylistic solutions then possible, a situation that pertains to most capitals of

Northern Europe.[24] Well-known artists such as Jan Gossaert and Bernart van Orley in the Netherlands, Pierre Chambiges in the Paris region, Roland Le Roux in Normandy, Bernard Nonnenmacher in Alsace, Erhard Heydenreich in Bavaria, and Benedikt Ried in Bohemia worked concurrently in both manners. Yet a certain self-consciousness about design practices had existed for some time. François Bucher, Paul Crossley, and Hubertus Günther have contended that ever since German architects were called down to work on Milan Cathedral at the end of the fourteenth century, an awareness of alternative Italian practice had spread through the German lands.[25] The elite Gothic of the sixteenth century was, in part, a system under siege. No longer unproblematic, it had become a deliberated option, a preference over alternative Italianate manners. Although custom and decorum might dictate the use of the Gothic for certain projects, an awareness of other possibilities impaired the perception of these structures as signs of universal authority.

Ornament and excess

In many of the most famous examples of Late Gothic architecture, ornament overwhelms its putative carrier and dictates aesthetic response. The Church of Our Lady at Louviers in Normandy presents itself on its market side through a remarkable filigree screen that forms its extensive porch. The massive buttresses seem to dissolve under the myriad diminutive tabernacles that sheath their surface, fragmenting light and dispelling any sense of stable monumental form. This porch, this attachment to the building proper, comes to characterize the entire edifice. It can stand as a metaphor for celestial architecture, unfettered by the requirements of mundane engineering—but in any event, it commands attention. In the southern and eastern German lands, church vaults are cloaked by complex geometric nets of straight and looping ribs that meander across the webbing. At times they hang in free air, miraculously suspended beneath the shell. In both cases, these elaborate vaults displace the fabric of the church in the eye of the beholder.

Opulence and material richness were essential to the appeal of these buildings. Even Albrecht Dürer, no trained architect himself, made several studies of sophisticated vault designs and illustrated one in his treatise of 1525, the *Unterweysung der Messung*. His stated goal was to describe columns and piers, but he included the intricate vault as a tribute to the taste for magnificent display. He concedes: "because there are many who have a great love for incorporating unusual richness in vaults, due to their opulence, I shall draw an example below".[26] Dürer's words testify to the pleasurable sensory experience afforded by even the most abstract geometric configurations and their obligatory presence in elite structures.

There were, of course, many aspects to this revitalization of Gothic architecture. But the imaginative and novel use of ornament was often an essential enterprise for architects of the later fifteenth and sixteenth century. In fact, the term "flamboyant", which now refers generally to a late Gothic stage in French architecture, derives from a particular ornamental feature: the flame-like tracery forms found in certain French churches around 1500—classic examples decorate the gables, rose window, and façade of the Church of the Trinity at Vendôme, built around the beginning of the new century.[27] In Germany, the architect Lorenz Lecher referred to Late Gothic forms as *Zippernwerkh*, a term likewise related to irregular tracery figures.[28] Throughout Northern Europe, ornamental fields displaying idiosyncratic geometric forms were an inescapable feature of the church interior.

The relatively little attention that has been paid these issues is due partly to a long-standing dismissal of Gothic ornament as extraneous to the essential properties of architecture and to a prejudice against replete decoration as a sign of decadence and decline. Even such a sympathetic critic of Late Gothic as François Bucher categorizes as "overrich" the porches at Louviers, Albi, and Strasbourg.[29] And he refers to the florid vaults in the western chapels at Ingolstadt as "the last stand of a dying style . . . based on a disciplined geometric grid which explodes into fireworks of incredible technical and design sophistry".[30] This is, of course, symptomatic of a pervasive modernist aesthetic that conceives of ornament as necessarily opposed to structure and inevitably antithetical to the functional elements of buildings.[31] Recent attention to ornament as a system, however—from Islamic carving to twentieth-century architecture—has shown how it can actively engage the viewer and serve as an effective agent of self-representation and cultural change.[32]

In bearing the brunt of the responsibility for immediate visual response, these species of ornament expose a perceived insufficiency in the essential structure of the building. Ornament, the supplement, comes to supplant the work itself. It is the sensory counterpart to the abstract, intellectual understanding of the building. This idea of ornament as accessory or *parergon*, "augmenting the delight of taste", is embedded in Kant's *Critique of Judgment* and constitutes an important aspect of Enlightenment aesthetics. Derrida's reading of Kant is important for our project, for it conceives of the work as inevitably manifesting a lack, which can only be remedied by its supplement.[33]

The notion of ornament as requisite accessory is already present in Alberti's treatise on architecture, *De re edificatoria*, first published at Florence in 1486. Alberti distinguishes between beauty and ornament but judges both necessary to the creation of "graceful and pleasant appearance".[34] For Alberti, "beauty is some inherent property, . . . that reasoned harmony of all the parts within a body, so that nothing may be added, taken away, or altered, but for the worse".[35] Ornament, on the other hand, "has the character of something attached or additional".[36] And yet Alberti is not wholly resigned to beauty's self-sufficiency, for he considers ornament a desirable enhancement, "a form of auxiliary light and complement to beauty".[37] As Rykwert, Leach, and Tavernor state, beauty is ultimately "the overall intellectual and primary framework—the essential idea—while ornament is the phenomenon—the individual expression and embellishment of this frame".[38] This latter part largely generates the aesthetic and registers the personality of the artist.[39]

It is worth noting that Alberti's treatise may well have impressed learned and professional circles in Germany and the north, offering them some intellectual basis for a consideration of their own architecture. Copies of the first edition were owned by the prominent humanists Conrad Peutinger in Augsburg and Hartman Schedel in Nuremberg—the latter with notable professional ties to Albrecht Dürer.[40] A manuscript edition of Alberti's treatise rested in Mathias Corvinus's library at Buda, where the great Late Gothic architect

Benedikt Ried refined his practice.[41] In the last decade, Paul Crossley and Hubertus Günther have argued for a theoretical awareness on the part of Late Gothic architects in the German lands, especially with regard to their development of vegetal ornament.[42] Crossley and Günther aver that a knowledge of Italian theory and practice were taken up in southern Germany and used to modify German architecture and microarchitecture in this distinctive manner. Vitruvius, stating that architecture had sprung from trees bent together in the forest, offered the justification for a radical imitation of natural forms. The two authors point to the year 1486, when Vitruvius and Alberti's *De re aedificatoria* were first published. That year the Regensburg master mason Matthäus Roriczer published a short treatise on the proper way to make finials and pinnacles. Such a work, however modest in comparison, was to be read as a reposte, they argue, a statement of German theory and an intellectual defense of their architecture.

Picturing geometry

By the end of the fifteenth century, the invention of complex, self-contained geometric figures had become a conspicuous feature of architectural design. This amounted almost to a process of drawing on architecture, of creative inscription on available surfaces. The shells of vaults, the gables of guild houses, the balustrades to galleries and pulpits, the fames of altarpieces, the backs of choir stalls and other areas came to bear distinctive geometric configurations. These elaborate designs, which occupied significant sites, became emblems of artistic achievement. At times they might serve as tokens of the identity of their creator, an elaborate and imaginative signature of sorts. They also became independent studies, objects of beauty in themselves.[43]

We might view these configurations as *pictures* of geometry. They are contained by railings, moldings, and arches that act as frames, defining an image and isolating it for regard. This is not a matter of geometric planning, a process common to architecture of nearly all cultures. It is not the same use of geometry that contributed to the plotting of a Gothic choir. These designs are discontinuous with the rest of the structure. They stand apart as illustrations of basic geometric figures that have undergone a series of operations. Such attached patterns can signify the science of geometry itself, or more specifically, geometric construction, which conveys the role of creative intelligence.

These compositions, ever more intricate, soon became an independent field of endeavour in lodge practice, as Bucher has observed. The numerous exercises in geometric construction that have survived attest, among other things, to the availability of paper as a support, which enabled this kind of competitive enterprise—most Gothic drawings, date from the later fifteenth and sixteenth century.[44] We find growing prestige attached to the design itself apart from its service as blueprint for construction. The appreciation of two-dimensional notation for three-dimensional projects signals a greater recognition of the role of the individual in contrast to the often communal enterprise of large-scale building. Accomplished conceits were readily adapted to works of widely differing scale, from the monumental towers of churches to the carved tabernacles above statues or the miniature spires of gold reliquaries. A concomitant interest in private experience of artworks and in the subjective nature of perception is likewise related to a taste for ambiguous ornamental patterns, which the attentive viewer is challenged to comprehend and resolve.

These geometric configurations were most impressive when displayed on church vaults that extend like canopies over entire chapels, choirs, and naves. The art of vault construction progressed dramatically during the fifteenth century and assumed ever greater importance in church design, especially in Southern Germany, Spain, and Bohemia. There is continually less emphasis placed on wall articulation; many German churches built around 1500 exhibit flat, unbroken mural surfaces. Simple cylindrical or octagonal piers replace the earlier compound piers with multiple shafts that slowly chan-nelled the eye upward.[45] Attention is now directed immediately to the decorative pattern of ribs in spectacular figured vaults, which become increasingly divorced from basic structural requirements.[46]

The design of intricate rib patterns became an art in itself. In the churches at Annaberg, Kutná Hora, and Most, for instance, a series of looping ribs inscribe lyrical, six-petaled floral designs across the shallow shells of the nave vaults. This schema had been largely devised by the architect Benedikt Ried, active in Prague at the turn of the sixteenth century. Ried had first employed the plan for the capacious Vladislav Hall in the Royal Palace and then for the churches he helped construct at Kutná Hora and Louny. His assistants brought related designs to other edifices in Saxony, Austria, and Bohemia. To an extent, the flower-like composition of ribs continued to be associated with Ried's flourishing concern.[47]

Numerous distinct rib configurations appeared in churches throughout southern Germany, Austria, and Bohemia. Another remarkable vault exhibiting the most delicate tracery is found in the choir of the parish church at Freistadt in Upper Austria. The elongated ovals that appear along the centre are filled with lobed diamonds that contain four-pointed stars, while intersecting rings of curved ribs radiate from the piers. The Freistadt vault is the only example of this genre for which we possess a document indicating the wishes of the consistory. We are told that the church was "to be vaulted and fitted with a bold structure" (*ein tapfer pau*). The German word *tapfer*, meaning "bold" or "daring" would seem to imply some extraordinary feat of engineering. Yet although the Freistadt vault employs the latest double-curved ribs, it is not particularly advanced from a technical point of view. Its distinguishing feature is its ornamental elaboration, its geometrical invention, and its pictorial quality. It is significant that the prototype for the choir vault is an extant architectural drawing, a two-dimensional record of geometrical design. Drawing no. 17003 in the Akademie der bildenden Künste in Vienna was soon adapted to a number of actual construction sites, most notably the choir at Freistadt and the Spulir chapel at Jindřichův Hradec (southern Bohemia), both of which preserve the graphic qualities of the *Riss*.[48]

The fashionable figured vault designs of around 1500 seem to have been exceedingly well known throughout the German lands.[49] Their popularity was so great that they spread to the smallest village churches; in some cases inexpensive ribs made of stucco were used to imprint geometric designs on otherwise spare surfaces. At Weigersdorf in Lower Austria, for example, plaster moldings of intersecting squares, semicircles and quarter-circles are attached to the shell above the nave. Although individual motifs are easily recognized within the space of the church, the orderly arrangement of perfect geometrical shapes is visible only on the ground plan.[50]

The pictorial aspect of these late figured vaults is central to their creation and reception.[51] There remains an inevitable dialectic between the design on paper and the projection of the vault over three dimensions, but the drawing is often prime, a discrete area of activity and competition. A drawing in the Akademie der bildenden Künste in Vienna (no. 16981), for example, shows a vault design of simple intersecting circles. It is quite close to the ground plan of the Gothic passageway in the Niederösterreichisches Landhaus in Vienna of about 1513, yet its ideal properties are distorted in the construction. The actual vault is a dynamic, undulating surface, exhibiting little of the regularity and transparent proportions seen in the two-dimensional transcription.[52] The drawing is in certain ways the principal expression, to which the building refers.[53]

Complementing their vaults, church interiors were frequently appointed with balustrades and railings containing geometric tracery. We find these carved fields in France and the Netherlands as well as in the German lands.[54] In all regions, the designs from around 1500 differ from earlier decoration in their greater prominence and complexity, their predilection for incomplete and interpenetrating forms. These framed geometric compositions are often characterized by fragmented, interlacing circles, ordered around a latticework of foci. While individual elements are recognizable, the logic of the entire design remains hidden, a perceptual puzzle. The Church of St. George at Nördlingen was one of many to contain striking examples of such tracery. Stephen Weyrer, the author of the ornamental vaulting, contributed his own composition for the balustrade on the west Gallery.[55] This decoration was complemented by open-work fronting the winding stair to the pulpit, likewise a composition of broken arcs and circles that impresses itself upon the viewer.[56]

Burckhard Engelberg, Weyrer's teacher at Augsburg, was an acknowledged master of this manner of design, supplying distinctive examples of openwork and blind tracery to several major building sites in the German lands. A prominent instance of this genre is the wall and closure about the west choir of Augsburg Cathedral, an imposing barrier that greets visitors entering through the building's principal portal.[57] The formidable choir wall is fully dressed with friezes of curving geometric patterns: a series of concentric circles with interlocking fish tails with a register approximating sine curves above.

Older august structures were fitted with galleries in the new style; in the cathedral of Strasbourg, Hans Hammer's intricate geometric balustrade rests opposite the famous Angels' Pillar in the south transept. Significantly, the carver has included a limestone bust of a man who appears to look out over this barrier—likely a portrait of Hammer himself.[58] This class of ornament soon spread to the corners of the Hapsburg Empire. In the parish church at Niederlana in the Tyrol, designed by Hans Hueber, the extensive west gallery is adorned with a balustrade containing open tracery in the form of three-quarter circles filled with lobed triangles and other geometric motifs.[59] The distinctive composition is continued along the sides of the nave in a frieze of blind tracery.

Brazenly nonfunctional, these carvings could convey the very idea of geometry. They could engage the beholder in acts of puzzle-solving, encouraging attempts to discover the operations used to generate the design. Much in this manner, Jügen Julier has detected perspectival games or riddles in the complex geometric construction of works of Late Gothic microarchitecture such as the baptismal font in Strasbourg Cathedral. He considers the designers of these objects to be expressing a form of architectural humor or irony, deliberately defying the expectations of the observer.[60] Playing with habits of perception also became an important preoccupation for Netherlandish Gothic designers at this time. There are puzzle-like aspects to many of the complex frames for Netherlandish carved altarpieces, such as the one at Lombeek, which seem intentionally confusing and disorienting in its irregular subdivision. These works encourage the viewer to discover the underlying system of proportions in order to restore a sense of order.[61]

Ornament and identity

The importance placed on sophisticated geometric patterns allowed particularly inventive compositions to point to the designers as a sort of imaginative signature. Such a use went hand-in-hand with a new sense of self-awareness on the parts of designers and a heightened sense of their social status. Indeed, several writers consider the mark of a new epoch in the north typified by a self-consciousness on the part of artists toward their creations and the recognition by their society of the equivalent of artistic genius, a socially and perhaps spiritually elevating talent or gift.[62]

This was the age of the self-portrait, in Italy and the north.[63] But there were also less conventional means of representing the artist. Michael Baxandall has observed that the German limewood sculptors of this period developed drapery patterns into signature devices. The abstract linear pattern of garment folds would be recognized as a personal creation of the artist, much the way that a distinctive melody, or *Ton*, would be acknowledged as the intellectual property of the contemporary *Meistersinger*.[64] German painters, following Dürer, likewise began to cast their pictures as expressions of their individuality. They inserted monograms or initials, with or without pictograms, like Cranach's snake or Herri met de Bles's owl.[65] These are truly accessories or attachments. More interestingly, painters and engravers adopted a distinctive graphic style, a characteristic *"ductus* or linear mannerism"*, in the words of Christopher Wood.[66] In this way, their individuality became integral to the work itself.

Inventive Gothic ornament might offer a similar claim to personal authority in the architectural design of the time. In Nuremberg, Adam Kraft presents a spectacular example of complex tracery for the balustrade to his tabernacle in the church of St. Lawrence; this virtuoso openwork is placed directly above a kneeling figure of the artist himself and stands as a supplementary sign of authorship.[67] It seems to emerge from his head as the product of his *ingenium* and takes its place between the coats of arms of the patron on the dais.[68]

Jan Gossaert's idiosyncratic baldachins in the *Malvagna Triptych* seem to have served the same supplementary function.[69] Only twenty inches wide, the triptych opens to reveal a miraculous world in miniature. The Virgin and Child enthroned among angels appear on the central panel with Saints Catherine and Barbara on the wings, while above them hover massive canopies of intricate and finely crafted Gothic tracery, a seeming forest of pendants and diminutive spires that are joined and supported by compound piers and flying arches. The middle baldachin contains a number of individual tracery figures that are essential to its design. At the center, above the Virgin's head, is a striking motif that resembles a butterfly, an ornamental detail that was received as a signature device. Gossaert's geometric motifs were adopted individually by other artists. The famous *Grimani Breviary*, for instance, includes a number of Gossaert's decorative inventions taken singly from the *Malvagna Triptych*—among them, the notable butterfly-like tracery figure.[70] The painters of the *Grimani Breviary* acknowledge Gossaert as author of virtuoso architectural ornament. In fact, we find the name "Gosart" or "Cosart" inscribed in one of the images, appearing on the entablature to one of the buildings depicted in the manuscript.[71]

The quality of ornamental invention in this Late Gothic manner was an accepted gauge of an artist's proficiency and thus closely linked to his professional image. It is no accident that when Bernart van Orley painted his *Altarpiece of the Apostles Thomas and Matthias*, he signed his name on the fictive Gothic frame that divides two of the scenes. Set within stone borders is a field of fictive virtuoso gold work in geometric and floral patterns, an unusual and complex tracery figure, which resembles an inverted heart. At the bottom of this composition the painter recorded his authorship in a more customary manner: "BERNART VAN ORLEI". The placement of the signature is remarkable since the two narrative scenes are set in conspicuously Italianate structures.[72] Despite the obvious interest in these inventions, they take a back seat to the carefully crafted Gothic frame.[73]

These idiosyncratic designs betray a certain kinship with older masons' marks, the simpler geometric figures cut in quarried blocks that insured credit and accountability for less prestigious labour. During the fifteenth century masons' marks were placed on coats of arms, divorced from practical concerns, and transformed into emblems of identity. Jörg von Halspach, the architect of the Church of Our Lady in Munich, is typical of many elevated craftsmen in this respect. His epitaph, which stands against the west entrance of this church, prominently displays his mark as the charge on his escutcheon.[74] Adam Kraft's inventive tracery could likewise be associated with the artist beneath and function as a sort of trademark or badge of identity.

In the Netherlands, the more elaborate geometric figures often occupy sites that traditionally held individual or corporate insignia. They frequently serve as frames or cartouches for coats of arms, personal devices, or statues of patron saints venerated by religious institutions. When notable tracery motifs appear alone in these privileged locations, however, they can usurp the role of conventional markers, serving in their place as a distinguishing sign, an indicator of the singular nature of the structure.[75]

The potential service of inventive decorative motifs as personal or institutional devises owed much to a gradual abatement in the use of heraldic imagery under Burgundian and Hapsburg rulers and to a general proliferation of signs of identity in European society. As Emmanuel Bourassin and others have related, traditional coats of arms depended on prohibitively complex rules and were inconveniently inflexible. Although heraldry remained a critical language of honour and territorial alliance for royalty and the high nobility, it slowly ceded place to more fluid *imprese*, mottos and other emblematic devices, signs more readily adaptable to the changing role of the elite during this dynamic period and more easily tailored to individual needs.[76] Often these supplementary insignia accompanied coats of arms; at other times they replaced them. On the tomb of Margaret of Bourbon at Brou, for example, an angel supports a shield that carries merely the initials of Margaret of Austria and her late husband, Philibert of Savoy, joined by a love knot. With the atrophy of stable heraldic display, improvisation became more accepted, and tracery figures might be charged informally with associations of personal identity, office, status and possession.

The inscription of transcendence: geometry as sacred sign

We might say that the presence of these geometric fields was over-determined, for they address several different needs and desires.

Once the invention of geometric patterns became securely embedded in lodge practice as an area of competition and achievement, it was applied to religious and secular edifices alike. Yet when located in churches, these ornamental projects might help convey the sacred character of the encompassing building. Given a consonant frame of mind, the beholder might intuit such inscriptions as a sign or index of the celestial realm of pure ideas that existed above the world of human experience. Geometric symbolism, of course, is nothing new to the literature on Gothic architecture.[77] Otto von Simson, Nigel Hiscock and others have detected cosmological significance in the use of geometry to plan certain medieval churches. I am less interested here, however, in such a procedural application of geometry, largely hidden from view in the actual building, than in the presentation of geometry as a visible symbol. Further, in many cases ornamental forms undergo a kind of development within the space of the church that allows for a narrative reading.

The tradition for associating geometry and geometric figures with the divine spans more than a millennium; Augustine and Boethius had famously praised geometry as a means of cognition, as an instrument for understanding God's creation.[78] A major strain of this writing was clearly platonic,[79] based above all on the *Timaeus*, the dialogue best known to medieval authors, which describes the creation of the world in terms of geometric figures.[80] The belief in the metaphysical nature of geometry, number, and proportion continued to resonate in the late Middle Ages.[81] Alan of Lille, the twelfth-century theologian who enjoyed considerable popularity in the fifteenth century, reveals his debt to this tradition when he claims that "Every mathematical name is less improperly said of God than is a concrete name".[82]

Currents in late medieval culture encouraged a reading of geometric figures as archetypal identities, as perfect and essential forms. Reducing objects to mathematical properties purged them of the specifics of their material manifestation and approached the divine blueprint. Nicholas of Cusa, for example, speaks of ideal forms descending to enjoy a limited existence in matter.[83] Because tracery compositions were studies in the system of mathematical proportions that was considered a gift of God, they might be received as a register of forms in the perfection of their idea before their materialization in the world. When presented in fragmentary state as tracery, as broken or incomplete circles, these figures could convey a departure or descent from this highest state. They signal the notion of becoming, the *process* of corruption that necessarily accompanied material embodiment.[84]

These concepts, platonic and otherwise, found their way into popular devotional texts, a measure of their broad currency. Exemplary is Guillaume de Deguileville's *Pilgrimage of Human Life*, which, although composed shortly before 1350, continued to enjoy a significant vogue in the fifteenth and sixteenth century.[85] In the first book, a geometric figure is introduced as an image of divine legacy Christ's "testament of peace" is illustrated by a right-angle "carpenter's square"—"a jewel formed and shaped by my father". A diagram is provided in the text, and the reader is instructed to label its parts. Geometric properties, critical to the design, guarantee its truth and authority.[86]

The general tendency to seek analogy to divine concepts in geometric terms is far more important than specific allusion. It is a habit of thought, deeply entrenched, that is revealed in both learned and popular texts. A belief in the cosmic significance of numerical relationships, and of music and geometry as their embodiment, was so widely held and resonant that it remained a constant potential reference.[87]

Hierarchy and anagogical relations

Artistic representations of divided terrestrial and celestial worlds are common in the fifteenth and sixteenth century. Although the two regions are sometimes shown as contiguous, they signified discontinuous realms, related to each other mystically or anagogically.[88] Significantly the arrangement and placement of geometric decoration was hierarchic. In retables, the baldachins, those complex assemblies of linear geometric parts, rest above the range of human figures. On buildings, geometric patterns are usually set above areas occupied by viewers or inhabitants of the architectural space; they occur most frequently in triforia, window tracery, tympana, gables and crests to porches.

The understanding of a universe split between material form and idea is implicit in a number of figural reliefs and altarpieces from this period. A lower area is occupied by carvings of humans or divine beings, while an upper register is given over to a presentation of geometric shapes. One example of this format is the Epitaph for Wolfgang and Sigmund von Keutschach, appended to the exterior wall of the pilgrimage church at Maria Saal in Carinthia.[89] In the large lower field, Christ and God the Father crown the Virgin Mary, while the dove of the Holy Spirit hovers with outstretched wings at the top. A thin layer of clouds divides this figural relief from an upper field displaying three intersecting semicircles and a series of reverse arcs. A moment's observation discloses a correspondence between the two halves of the relief, since the three semi-circles agree in number and place with the three actors in the figural field below. The semi-circles in the relief can be seen as inscriptions of mathematical ideas and, as such, represent a higher plane than the material representation of the figures, even given their divine status.

This is not to suggest that Gothic tracery had some stable, conscious and verbally articulated significance. Rather, in its present application, it signals that a certain manner of understanding was relevant. It suggests to the viewer a particular way of relating visual appearance to conceptual structure. Under proper conditions, formal configurations that were homologous with a division between earth and heaven might be intuited as embodiments of this paradigm. The stone offered a physical structure, a matrix upon which similarly ordered ideas could be projected. Seeking God, pursuing signs of the celestial realm, was a probable activity for a visitor to a church, and carvings of geometric shapes offered a ready reminder of established notions of the divine and its register in the world.

Architecture, real or represented, could thus refer to metaphysical relationships through homology. It offered material confirmation of ordering systems and consequently privileged certain types of relationships over others; in the words of Theodor Adorno, it permitted "that which [was] about to slip away to be objectified and cited to permanence".[90] The viewer identifies the screen or altarpiece as an object of experience while simultaneously recognizing agreement with a significant conceptual structure. Art can thus give presence to vague and transitory impressions in the form of a stable sensory phenomenon; its aesthetic truth would be its potential for disclosing an accepted truth.[91]

Narratives of ornament

The ornamental articulation of these Late Gothic buildings and furnishings often encourages a narrative reading that imposes a sense of order on geometrical figures. As one scans the elevation of certain church facades, the arrangement of baldachins in Gothic altarpieces, and the vault patterns in successive bays of a nave or choir, decorative motifs may seem to undergo gradual change.[92] In place of human characters there are geometric shapes that become objects of protracted regard.[93] If conventional plots are lacking, these figures may undergo sequential transformations that lead toward an ultimate state. Archetypal forms are identified and differences reconciled, often by combining properties of two different motifs in subsequent figures.[94] This kind of mathematical story-telling may come to seem natural enough. Indeed, Hayden White has argued that narrative is the privileged mode of understanding in western civilization; historians tend to organize their data into narrative patterns when giving them meaning.[95] But the tendency is not of recent vintage, for medieval writers like John of Garland (thirteenth century) had already classified most narrative as hermeneutic (*ermeneticon*).[96]

Vertical progression is one of the privileged dynamics in this model of interpretation, though it can be complemented by other axes of reading.[97] As saints rise to heaven so religious edifices ascend toward a metaphorically higher and more blessed state. This is the standard arrangement of tabernacles, such as those at Ulm, Nuremberg, and Louvain.[98] The lower ranges commonly encase statues or figural groups which advance in scriptural order from level to level, culminating in Eucharistic images of Christ. Looking up, the viewer notes that structural members are gradually reduced to a single pinnacle: unity out of multiplicity or chaos.

Aspects of twentieth-century narrative theory may be useful in raising to full awareness what would have been a pre-conscious mode of understanding for sixteenth-century viewers. It is essential to recognize that geometric transformations are performances of mathematical operations on a given figure. Each resulting new shape is as much a register of such an operation, an act, as it is a distinctive entity in itself. Such a process is articulated in the writings on narrative by Vladimir Propp and A. J. Greimas. In his fundamental study of Russian folklore, Propp classifies fairy tales not according to specific characters but according to the generic acts that advance the plot. Characters provide agency but are classified in terms of the functions they perform, the essential components of the tale. Propp observes that stories begin with a situation establishing norms, followed by the introduction of a conflict which is gradually resolved.[99] Greimas, too, considers characters as registers of narrative transformation rather than as significant entities; he terms them *actants* rather than *acteurs*. He further discusses the way in which a series of plot actions can be read as a single argument, a sentence directed toward a specific point or goal. "A story", he maintains, "is a discursive unit which ought to be considered as an algorithm, that is, as a succession of state-actions oriented toward an end. . . . In order to have meaning, a story must be a significant whole; it manifests itself, therefore, as a simple semantic structure".[100] This teleological aspect of narrative is also applicable to our understanding of Gothic ornament, which can progress toward a resolution of oppositions apparent in the juxtaposition of forms.[101]

Narrative understanding is invited, for example, by the great tabernacle in Ulm Münster, completed by 1471, the largest work of microarchitecture in the Late Gothic world. Achim Timmerman refers to the structure as a "complex geometrical argument", and indeed there is something almost rhetorical about it.[102] A program of Old Testament prophets is encased in the tabernacle, offering a scriptural basis. But its enormous impact is greatly enhanced by its intricate architectural articulation, its multiplicity of tubes and struts that are winnowed and simplified as the tabernacle rises. A series of intersecting arches provides connections between the shafts and pinnacles, leading the eye along numerous paths from the outset. The vertical elements are linked at various points by inverted ogival arches which unite pairs, reducing them to a single upward extension. Buttresses, struts, bell shapes, and arches create intersections, detours, and proper channels to the culmination of the tabernacle, the solitary pinnacle at the top.

The ascent of the Ulm tabernacle is given a ready theological gloss, for it is set against a painting of the Last Judgment painted on the wall to the choir.[103] The top of the structure stands opposite the palace of the Heavenly Jerusalem in the fresco, associating a narrative of salvation with its course. The Ulm tabernacle can be read like an intricate sentence with oppositional clauses and a predicate. Doubleness is unified, oppositions are resolved, and a conclusion is ultimately reached. The eye is led along the lines of the tabernacle, noting true and false pathways. Geometric figures—the intersecting arches and bell figures—transform the plot, addressing states of absence or abundance. They might loosely be compared to the *actants* in the narrative theory of Greimas, figures of change in the story line.

Church façades of the Late Gothic are sometimes designed to be read in similar ways. Here a vertical orientation is essential to the ascription of meaning. An instance of this manner of composition is the north transept façade of Évreux Cathedral, designed by Jean Cosart and completed by 1517.[104] The façade is organized around three large triangular gables. The lowest surmounts the portal, the middle gable tops the rose window, and the final member of the trio crowns the gallery between the two towers. All three gables are paired with circles or semi-circles in different ways. Directly above the portal, a (semi)circle is entirely enclosed in the lowest gable. In the centre of the façade, the rose window transforms the gable, expanding and curving its sides while making the top ogival. At the highest gable between the towers, circular contours have broken through and now frame the triangle. The façade seems to demonstrate the escalating importance of the circle over the triangle. The direction is again upward, from the ground to heaven.

And certain vaults of the period also allow of a narrative reading. At the pilgrimage church at Krenstetten in Lower Austria, curved and straight ribs form a series of distinct and self-contained figures on the vaults. In the bays over the crossing, the vault displays three pairs of elongated ovals.[105] This pattern changes over the choir: first, the paired ovals contract to circles in the choir's western-most bay.

Next the doubled forms are replaced by a central cross with curving arms, a recognizable shape, but one that eliminates the closed figures that precede it. Finally, a few fragmented and indistinct shapes fill the remaining space to the choir wall. This eastern zone, nonetheless, conveys the impression of geometric order. Arc and straight line are still the building elements, though the overall pattern is enigmatic. This use of geometry resembles a sort of writing that one recognizes as language but cannot read—perhaps a bit like the Islamic inscriptions in certain mosques that are progressively stylized until they are no longer legible but continue to signify as a holy utterance.[106] Throughout the vaulting at Krenstetten there is a perceptible progression from double ovals to double circles to the elimination of all doubleness and, finally, to opacity at the east end of the choir.[107]

In the case of Krenstetten, the geometric rib configurations might be perceived as a type of metalanguage, or rather, as a material register of one. In the choir, the most sacred part of the church, the language is too complicated to be comprehensibly recorded in stone. It is not possible to give a definite reading of the Krenstetten vaults, only a likely path of inquiry and reflection. The designs at Krenstetten imply notions of difference, development, hierarchy, and the limits of comprehension.

Much of what we see involves the erasure of disparity or divergence as registered in geometric forms. It is worth observing that the elimination of difference, a reconciliation of opposites, is a common goal in late medieval and early modern culture. There are many parallels in the literature of the period. Here, the eradication or suppression of difference can signal a program of ideological legitimation in the subtext, which depends on narrative for its realization.[108] Chrétien de Troyes's *Erec et Enide*, for instance, presents the unknown knight as a threat, less on account of his belligerence than for his refusal to divulge his identity; he is difference as much as potential evil. Forced to reveal his name and status, the knight is reintegrated into the common aristocratic social structure and loses his malevolent character.[109]

Oneness consistently represents ethical and practical ideals. In the English translation of Froissart from the early sixteenth century, the clear and distinct speech of English diplomats contrasts with Burgundian *"double of understandige"*.[110] That *"parfyt vnyoun"* of opposing forces is also the ideal in John Lydgate's verse. In the *Troy Book*, war insures that "*Yngeland and Fraunce / May be al oon, withoute variaunce*".[111] The essential unity and integrity of Henry V becomes his identifying marker. Praised as "*ay in oon withoute chaunge*" in John Pages' *Siege of Rouen*, the king is free of all French "*doblynesse*".[112]

Innovation and reaction

The Gothic of circa 1500 was in many ways a Gothic reinvented for the new age. A fascination with ornament has come to characterize this period of design, and although there were many other aspects to the architecture, the conventional view holds an essential truth. Many architects devoted considerable energy to ornamental display. Circles, triangles, crosses, and rhomboids became the heroes of church interiors. Distinctive patterns might stand for the most imaginative designers, a signature and synecdoche of their art.

It is likely that the printing press heightened sensitivity to geometric configurations. Publishing not only spread knowledge of alternate traditions but also encouraged a change in the way that the act of thinking was understood and expressed. Scanning became an essential skill as the quantity of information available increased dramatically, and greater attention was paid to the visual presentation of texts that facilitated their assimilation.[113] Academics were more inclined to use diagrams when explaining the interrelationships between logical propositions. The complexity of these matrices and the technical skill required to pen them legibly restricted their benefit in manuscript, whereas printing nurtured the use and reuse of geometric designs, as are found in the work of the first generation of post-Gutenberg writers. Spatial organization across two-dimensional fields became an ever more prevalent manner of conceptualization.[114]

The question of the individual, of creation and authority, inevitably relate to this issue. Writing, composing, adapting, copying in scriptoria, publishing and editing, all helped determine the idea of the text, the process of reading, and the model of knowledge.[115] Spatial and specifically geometric paradigms became increasingly common and facilitated the reading of architectural fields as texts with similar semiotic properties.

As geometric designs appeared in easily visible, bounded, and less conventional sites, they were able to reinforce an immediate and sensory intuition of transcendent authority. This development partly coincides with a period of self-reflection on the part of Gothic designers, as Bucher, Crossley, and Günther have defined it. And it comes at a time when numerous political and religious institutions were undergoing radical change, and when the knowledge of possible alternatives to many unquestioned matters was quickly disseminated through print.

By the second decade of the sixteenth century, the Late Gothic had become a mode, a preference over an alternate Italianate manner. Ornament thrived as the necessary supplement to the edifice, the accessory that channelled regard and clothed the buildings in a sensible sign of beauty and order. It is arguable that the increasingly conspicuous presentation of geometric forms was in part a polemical assertion of local practice, a response to the waning power of a traditional symbolic language. At any rate, the carved tracery and rib configurations of sixteenth-century Gothic assisted in interpreting larger and far more complicated structures, in mediating the experience of architecture.

Notes

1. Aspects of this essay are drawn from my article, "Renaissance Gothic: Pictures of Geometry and Narratives of Ornament," *Art History* 29 (2006), 1–46, in which many of the illustrations will be found.
2. In his recent consideration of the Renaissance, Peter Burke, for instance, retains this emphasis on the reception of antiquity by Italian artists and thinkers, though he rejects associations with the rise of modernity. See Burke, *The European Renaissance: Centres and Peripheries*, The Making of Europe (London: Blackwell/Munich: Beck/Barcelona: Critica/ Paris: Éditions du Seuil/Rome: Bari, 1998).
3. For a discussion of the adoption of Late Gothic forms in Italy, see Jürgen Wiener, " 'Flamboyant' in der italienischen Architektur", in: *Italienische Frührenaissance und nordeuropäisches Spätmittelalter: Kunst der frühen Neuzeit im europäischen Zusammenhang*, ed. Joachim Poeschke (Munich: Hirmer, 1993), 41–65.
4. There is little analysis of specifically sixteenth-century traits of Gothic architecture. For a critical and historiographical consideration of the Late Gothic, see Jan Białostocki's review article, now four decades old but still useful when supplemented by more recent studies: Jan Białastocki, "Late Gothic: Disagreements about the Concept", *Journal of the British*

Archaeological Association, 3rd series, 29 (1966), 76–105; Ulrich Coenen, *Die spätgotischen Werkmeisterbücher in Deutschland als Beitrag zur mittelälterlichen Architekturtheorie* (Aachen: G. Mainz, 1989); Ute Germund, *Konstruktion und Dekoration als Gestaltungsprinzipien im spätgotischen Kirchenbau Untersuchungen zur mittelrheinischen Sakralbaukunst*, Manuskripte zur Kunstwissenschaft in der Wernerschen Verlagsgesellschaft, 53 (Worms: Wernerschen Verlagsgesellschaft, 1997); Franz-Josef Sladeczek, "Was ist spät an der Spätgotik? Von der Problematik der kunstgeschichtlichen Stilbegriffe", *Unsere Kunstdenkmäler* 42 (1991), 3–23.

5. François Bucher, "Fifteenth-Century German Architecture, Architects in Transition", in *Artistes, artisans et production artistique au moyen age*, Colloque international, ed. Xavier Barral I Altet, 3 vols (Paris: Picard, 1987), vol. 2, 416. Bucher, for example, insists that "the Gothic style began to lose its patronage around 1500", a situation that would not arise for several decades.

6. On Burckhardt's project and the consequences of his work, see Wessel Krul, "Realism, Renaissance and Nationalism", in *Early Netherlandish Paintings: Rediscovery, Reception and Research*, ed Bernhard Ridderbos, Anne van Buren and Henk van Veen, trans. Andrew McCormick and Anne van Buren (1995; English ed., Amsterdam: Amsterdam University Press, 2005), 254–256; John Roderick Hinde, *Jacob Burckhardt and the crisis of modernity* (Montreal and Ithaca: McGill-Queen's University Press, 2000), 9–13; Hayden White, "Burckhardt: Historical Realism as Satire", in *Metahistory* (Baltimore: Johns Hopkins University Press, 1975), 230–264; Robert Klein, "Burckhardt's Civilization of the Renaissance Today", in *Form and Meaning: Essays on the Renaissance and Modern Art*, trans. by Madeline Jay and Leon Wieseltier (New York: Viking Press, 1979), 25–42. Donald R. Kelley insists: "The 'French Renaissance' represents the intersection between two complex traditions which are also at least partly mythical constructs. One is French nationality, which can be perceived over some nine or ten centuries, but which has been vastly exaggerated by historians and has never been fully realized even in a political sense. . . . Without the old and even larger myths of human progress and modernity, neither French nationality nor the European Renaissance carry much meaning. . . ." See Kelly, "France", in *The Renaissance in national context*, ed. Roy Porter and Mikuláš Teich (Cambridge: Cambridge University Press, 1992), 123.

7. It has been noted that Panofsky valued the Renaissance Dürer, fresh from his Italian travels, above the Gothic Dürer of the *Apocalypse*. Panofsky's esteem for the artist's rationality has been related to the author's political situation in Germany. See Keith Moxey, "Panofsky's Melancolia", in: *The Practice of Theory: Poststructuralism, Cultural Politics, and Art History* (Ithaca: Cornell University Press, 1994), 65–78.

8. On the role of national identity in the historiography of the Renaissance, see Peter Burke, "The uses of Italy", in Porter and Teich, 13–18; Claire Farago, " 'Vision Itself Has Its History': 'Race', Nation, and Renaissance Art History", in *Reframing the Renaissance: Visual Culture in Europe and*

Latin America 1450–1650, ed. Claire Farago (New Haven and London: Yale University Press, 1995), 67–72.

9. J. Gabriels, "De beeldhouwkunst en het ornament in de tweede helft der xvi^e eeuw. De nationale beweging", in: Stan Leurs, ed., *Geschiedenis der vlaamsche kunst* (Antwerp: De Sikkel, 1936), 565: "Onder den drang van den tijd welke de groteske fantazie terugdrong voor de klaarheid van een architectonische ordonnantie, waarin alle elementen logisch moeten worden aangebracht, ontpopt zich nu de barok-gotische meester als zuiver Renaissance figuur".

10. M. D. Ozinga, "De strenge Renaissance-stijl van onze tegenwoordige kennis", *Bulletin & nieuwsbulletin Koninklijke Nederlandse oudheidkundige Bond*, 6th series, 15 (1962), 14: "Het tijdstip an overlijden van de land-vooges Margaretha einde 1530 lijkt wel het punt, waarop het getij begon te keren ten gunste van een zuiverder renaissance-stijl in architectuur en decoratie . . .".

11. Ibid.: "Dit is in ons geval speciaal te betreuren, omdat wij in [Jacques Du Broeucq] een min of meer zuiver renaissance-ontwerper mogen vermoeden".

12. M. W. Stenchlak, *Bouwkunst in de Nederlanden: de renaissance. Architektuur in de zuidelijke en noordelijke Nederlanden in de zestiende eeuw* (Rijswijk: Elmar, 1985), 73: "Maar de zuivere interpretatie (uitlegging en toepassing) van de klassieke principes won in de Nederlanden steeds meer terein".

13. F. Bucher, "Medieval Architectural Design Methods, 800–1560", *Gesta* 11: 2 (1972), 44.

14. See, for instance, the discussion of the Hackeney Jubé, built in Mechelen around 1517: Jean Mogin, *Les jubés de la Renaissance* (Brussels: Éditions du cercle d'art, 1946), 8; Jan Steppe, *Het Koordoksaal in de Nederlanden*, Verhandelingen van de Koninklijke Vlaamse Academie voor Wetenschappen, Letteren en Schone Kunsten van België, klasse der schone kunsten, 7 (Brussels: Paleis der Academiën, 1952), 214; Robert Wellens, *Jacques Du Broeucq, sculpteur et architecte de la Renaissance (1505–1584)* (Brussels: La Renaissance du Livre, 1962), 54; H. R. Hitchcock, *Netherlandish scolled gables of the sixteenth and early seventeenth centuries* (New York: New York University Press for the College Art Association of America, 1978), 22. John Shearman likewise uses the term "hybrid" in his discussion of the early accommodation of Italian principles in northern lands. See *Mannerism* (1967: London: Penguin, 1990), 25. On the term "hybrid" and biological models of artistic development, see J. A. Schmoll, "Stilpluralismus statt Einheitszwang—Zur Kritik der Stilepochen-Kunstgeschichte", in: M. Gosebruch and L. Dittmann, eds., *Argo. Festschrift für Kurt Badt zu seinem 80. Geburtstag* (Cologne: Dumont, 1970), 85–86.

15. Keith Moxey, "Art History' Hegelian Unconscious: Naturalism as Nationalism in the Study of Early Netherlandish Painting', in: *The Subjects of Art History: Historical Objects in Contemporary Perspective*, ed. Mark A. Cheetham, M. A. Holly, and K. Moxey (Cambridge: Cambridge University Press, 1998), 25–51; Krul, 252–289; Erwin Panofsky, *The Life and Art of Albrecht Dürer* (1943; Princeton: Princeton University Press, 1971), 3. Panofsky opens his classic monograph with a paean to artistic achievement

as national property: "The evolution of high and post-medieval art in Western Europe might be compared to a great fugue in which the leading theme was taken up, with variations, by different countries. The Gothic style was created in France; the Renaissance and Baroque originated in Italy and were perfected in cooperation with the Netherlands; rococo and nineteenth-century Impressionism are French; and eighteenth-century Classicism and Romanticism are basically English".

16. Krul, 252–253. Others judged Early Netherlandish painting to be wedded to Gothic forms of figure and frame. Without any interest in secular subjects so typical of the new age, they were best relegated to the latest stage of medieval art rather than to a new epoch of a Renaissance.

17. Comte J. de Borchgrave d'Altena, *Les retables brabançons 1450–1550*, L'art en Belgique (Brussels: Éditions du cercles d'art, 1943), pls. 15–16.

18. The most prominent formulation of the organic growth of artistic style is Henri Focillon's notion of the "vie des formes". Focillon distinguishes four "ages" in the development of a style. The ultimate "baroque" state evinces a final efflorescence of possibilities inherent in the style; forms "vivent pour elles-mêmes avec intensité, [qu']elles se répandent sans frein, [qu']elles prolifèrent comme un monstre végétal". Henri Focillon, *Vie des formes* (Paris: Ernst Leroux, 1934), 25. On Focillon's developmental theory of style, see Daniel Arasse, "Lire 'Vie des Formes,' " in *Henri Focillon*, ed. Jacques Bonnet (Paris: Centre Georges Pompidou, 1986), 153–169, especially 158–159; Jacques Thuillier, "La Vie des formes: une théorie de l'histoire de l'art" in *Relire Focillon: Principes et théories de l'histoire de l'art* (Paris, Musée du Louvre et École nationale supérieure de Beaux-Arts, 1998), 75–96. The notion of "aesthetic fatigue" as a mechanism for stylistic change, first introduced by Adolf Göller, is discussed by George Kubler. See Kubler, *The Shape of Time: Remarks on the History of Things* (New Haven: Yale University Press, 1962), 80–82.

19. On the issue of period style see Lawrence Besserman, "The Challenge of Periodization: Old Paradigms and New Perspectives", in *The Challenge of Periodization: Old Paradigms and New Perspectives*, ed. Lawrence Besserman (New York and London: Garland, 1996), 3–27; Hans Blumenberg, *The Legitimacy of the Modern Age*, trans. Robert Wallace (Cambridge, Ma.: MIT Press, 1983), 457–480; Karl-Georg Faber, "Epoche und Epochengrenzen in der Geschichtsschreibung", *Zeitschrift für Kunstgeschichte* 44 (1981), 105–113; Martin Gosebruch, "Epochenstile—historische Tatsächlichkeit und Wandel des wissenschaftlichen Begriffs", *Zeitschrift für Kunstgeschichte* 44 (1981), 9–14; F. Schalk, "Über Epoche und Historie", in: *Studien zur Periodisierung und zum Epochen begriff*, ed. H. Diller and F. Schalk, Akademie der Wissenschaft und deutschen Literatur in Mainz, Abhandlung der Geistes- und Sozialwissenschaften, no. 4 (Mainz: Verlag der Akademie der Wissenschaften und der Literatur, 1972), 12–38; Robert Suckale, "Die Unbrauchbarkeit der gängigen Stilbegriffe und Entwicklungsvorstellungen. Am Beispiel der französischen gotischen Architektur des 12. und 13. Jahrhunderts", in: *Stil und Epoche Periodisierungsfragen*, ed. Friedrich Möbius and Helga Sciurie (Dresden: Verlag der Kunst, 1989), 231–250; Götz Pochat, "Der Epochenbegriff und

die Kunstgeschichte", in: *Kategorien und Methoden der deutschen Kunstgeschichte 1900–1930*, ed. Lorenz Dittmann (Stuttgart and Wiesbaden: F. Steiner, 1985), 129–167.

20. The notion of aesthetics is problematic for the middle ages, as Joseph Margolis usefully notes. The term normally applies to a post-Kantian understanding of disinterested regard or contemplation of beauty. Rather than rely on late medieval texts for their account of self-conscious, highly intellectual theories of beauty in the Pythagoran tradition, it may be more useful to explore expressions that indirectly suggest incipient stirrings of a peculiarly modern aesthetic attitude. Such indications must be read between the lines of existent texts, since no concept had yet emerged to account for these interests. Notions of craft and its satisfactions, and especially of "curiosity" or *curiositas* seem especially rewarding. "Curiosity" was often used to describe the purposeless wanderings of attention dictated by the object of regard. Ethically suspect during the high Middle Ages, it gradually became a neutral and then a positive term, ultimately signaling an acceptance of the art object as subject. See Jospeh Margolis, "Medieval Aesthetics", in *The Routledge Companion to Aesthetics*, ed. Berys Gaut and Dominic McIver Lopes (London and New York: Routledge, 2001), 27–36; Christopher S. Wood, " 'Curious Pictures' and the art of description", *Word and Image* 11 (1995), 333–343. For the more traditional literature on medieval aesthetics, see Edgar de Bruyne, *Études d'esthétique médiévale*, 3 vols (Bruges: De Tempel, 1946); Władysław Tatarkiewicz, *History of Aesthetics*, 3 vols (The Hague and Paris: Mouton, 1970–74), vol. 2, 47–303, vol. 3, 1–110.

21. The Modenese Guido Mazzoni had come to France in 1495 at the behest of Charles VIII, who had invaded Lombardy the year before. Mazzoni, in turn, was followed by the Giusti, a family of Italian sculptors who settled in Tours around 1505. The Giusti created most notably the Tomb of Louis XII at Saint-Denis, which provides a rough imitation of Andrea Sansovino's manner in the figures of the apostles and virtues that surround the central classicizing aedicule. See Anthony Blunt, *Art and Architecture in France 1500–1700* (1953; Harmondsworth: The Pelican History of Art, 1973), 36–40. In Picardy, Raoul de Lannoy, formerly the French governor of Genoa, ordered the gisants for his tomb at Folleville from the Genoese sculptors Antonio della Porta and Pace Gagini. Du Broeucq's first-known sculptural commission was for the Tomb of Philippe de Sainte-Aldegonde, who was married to Bonne de Lannoy. The sculptor may consequently have been particularly attentive to French patronage of Italian art. See J. Lestocquoy, "Jacques Du Broeucq en Artois", *Revue Belge d'Archéologie et d'Histoire de l'Art* 11 (1941), 237.

22. Margaret first approached the French court painter Jean Perréal, who assured his patron that his plans were conceived in the spirit of *choses antiques* that he had seen in Italy. Max Bruchet, *Marguerite d'Autriche, Duchesse de Savoie* (Lille: L. Danel, 1927), 192, n. 11.

23. Margaret eventually replaced the French painter Perréal with Jan van Rome and Loys van Boghem, highly esteemed Netherlanders. See Ethan Matt Kavaler, "Margaret of Austria, Ornament, and the Court Style at Brou", in:

Artists at Cour: Image-Making and Identity 1300–1550, edited by Stephen J.
Campbell (Boston: Isabella Steward Gardner Museum, 2004), 124–137.

24. In Prague, Hungary and Poland, the juxtaposition of modes occurred
earlier. Benedikt Ried's Italianate windows of 1493 decorate the exterior of
the Vladislav Hall in the Castle of Prague, contemporary with the
innovative Gothic vaulting inside. See Białostocki, *The Art of the
Renaissance in Eastern Europe* (Ithaca: Cornell University Press, 1976),
15–16.

25. Bucher, "Fifteenth-Century German Architecture", 409–419; Paul Crossley,
"The Return to the Forest: Natural Architecture and the German Past in
the Age of Dürer", in *Künstlerischer Austausch: Artistic exchange*, Akten des
XXVIII. Internationalen Kongresses für Kunstgeschichte, 3 vols (Berlin:
Akademie Verlag, 1993), vol. 2, 71–80; Hubertus Günther, "Die ersten
Schritte in die Neuzeit,", in *Wege zur Renaissance: Beobachtungen zu den
Anfängen neuzeitlicher Kunstauffassung im Rheinland und den
Nachbargebieten um 1500*, ed. Norbert Nussbaum, Claudia Euskirchen, and
Stephan Hoppe (Cologne: SH-Verlag, 2003), 31–87.

26. For Dürer's drawings of vault patterns, see Walter L. Strauss, The complete
Drawings of Albrecht Dürer (New York: Abaris Books, 1974), vol. 1,
1506/5–1506/8; Albrecht Dürer, *Vnderweysung der Messung, mit dem
Zirckel vnnd Richtscheyt, in Linien ebnen vnnd gantzen Corporen / durch
Albrecht Dürer zu samen getzogen, zu Nutz allen Kunstlieb habenden mit zu
gehörigen Figuren in Truck gebracht* (Nuremberg: Hieronymus Andreae,
1525), G3v: "Nach dem aber vil sind die grosse lieb haben zů selzamen
rychungen in den gwelben zůschliessen / von wolstandes wegen / so will ich
unden eine aufreissenn / ob die ymant gefelt der mag sich ier gebrauchen.
Auch will ich etlich grund zů den pfeileren machen und aufreysen".

27. François Cali, *L'ordre flamboyant et son temps: Essai sur le style gothique du
XIVe au XVIe siècle* (Paris, Arthaud, 1967), 12–15, 154, illus. 27. The term
"flamboyant" and its association with flames date from the seventeenth
century. The façade of Vendôme was designed by Jean Texier, the author of
the spire of the north tower of Chartres Cathedral.

28. Gerstenberg, *Deutsche Sondergotik*, 18–19. And in the Netherlands, architects
such as Rombout II Keldermans and Loys van Boghem designed a
comprehensive ornamental system of distinctive tracery motifs that
imparted a sense of unity to the larger structures while signalling important
features or moments in the ensemble. See Kavaler, "Renaissance Gothic in
the Netherlands", 233–239.

29. Bucher, "The Medieval Architectural Module: Generating and Ornamental
Concept", in *World Art: Themes of Unity in Diversity*, Acts of the 25th
International Congress of the History of Art, edited by Irving Lavin, 3
vols (University Park and London: Pennsylvania State University, 1989),
vol. 1, 225.

30. Bucher, "Medieval Architectural Design Methods", 48.

31. Bucher concludes his dismissal of sixteenth-century German vaults with
the comment: "The Renaissance was to reject these games with a
vengeance, very much as the Bauhaus was to obliterate Art Nouveau".
Bucher, "Medieval Architectural Design Methods", 48. For a discussion of

attitudes toward ornament versus structure in architecture, see Anne-Marie Sankovitch, "Structure/Ornament and the Modern Figuration of Architecture", *The Art Bulletin* 80 (1998), 687–717.

32. One of the more notable indications of renewed interest in ornament is the English translation of Alois Riegl's fundamental study *Problems of Style: Foundations for a History of Ornament*, transl. E. Kain, annotated by David Castriota (Princeton, Princeton University Press, 1992). For a discussion of this issue see P. Crowther, "More than Ornament: The Significance of Riegl", *Art History* 17 (1994), 482–494. See also Oleg Grabar, *The Mediation of Ornament*, (Princeton: Princeton University Press, 1992); Güru Necipoğlu, *The Topkapi Scroll—Geometry and Ornament in Islamic Architecture* (Santa Monica: The Getty Center for the History of Art and the Humanities, 1995), especially 217–223; Lambert Schneider, "Les signes du Pouvoir: Structure du langage iconique des Thrâces," *Revue Archéologique* 2 (1989): 227–251; Barbara Grunbaum, "Interlace Patterns in Islamic and Moorish Art," *Leonardo* 25 (1992): 331–339; Jean-Charles Depaule, "Improbables détachements: L'architecture et les arts dans la culture islamique," *Cahiers da Musée National d'Art Moderne* 39 (Spring 1992): 26–41; and Joseph Nevadomsky, "The Clothing of Political Identity: Costume and the Scarification in the Beam Kingdom," *African Arts* 28 (Winter 1995): 62–73.

33. See *Kant's Critique of Aesthetic Judgment*, trans. James Creed Meredith (Oxford: Clarendon Press, 1911), paragraph 14: "even what is called ornamentation [Parerga], that is, what is only an adjunct, and not an intrinsic constituent in the complete representation of the object, in augmenting the delight of taste does so only by means of its form". In Derrida's reading of Kant, the work itself inevitably exhibits a lack that can only be remedied by its supplement. See Jacques Derrida, *The Truth in Painting*, translated by Geoff Bennington and Ian McLeod (1978; English ed., Chicago and London: University of Chicago Press, 1987), 37–147, especially 53–54, 92–93. Derrida's argument has provided art historians like Christopher Wood with a ground against which to judge several "supplemental" aspects of Renaissance art. See Wood, *Albrecht Altdorfer and the Origins of Landscape* (London: Reaktion Books, 1993), 54–65. Derrida's notion of the supplement is also taken up by Rebecca Zorach, who concentrates on the notion of ornament as frame. Her understanding of the autoreferential aspect of ornament depends on its opposition to the representational nature of the subject framed; it is consequently less relevant for a consideration of the non-representational forms of Gothic architecture. See Zorach, *Blood, Milk, Ink, Gold: Abundance and Excess in the French Renaissance* (Chicago: University of Chicago Press, 2005), 151–154.

34. Leon Battista Alberti, On the Art of Building in Ten Books, translated by Joseph Rykwert, Neil Leach, Robert Tavernor (1988; Cambridge, MA; MIT Press, 1991), book 6, chapter 1, 155: "Now graceful and pleasant appearance, so it is thought, derives from beauty and ornament alone, since there can be no one, however surly or slow, rough or boorish, who would not be attracted to what is most beautiful, seek the finest ornament at the expense

of all else, be offended by what is unsightly, shun all that is inelegant or shabby, and feel that any shortcomings an object may have in its ornament will detract equally from its grace and from its dignity".

35. Alberti, book 6, chapter 2, 156.

36. On Alberti's ambivalence toward ornament, see Veronica Biermann, *Ornamentus: Studien zum Traktas "De re aedificatoria" des Leon Battista Alberti* (Hildesheim: Georg Olms, 1997), 134–150; Joseph Rykwert, "Inheritance or Tradition", *Architectural Design* 49 (1979), 3. Biermann translates *afficti et compacti*, the modifiers of *ornamentum*, as "attached form-giving" rather than "attached and additional" the more conservative rendering chosen by Rykwert, Leach, and Tavernor. See Alberti, book 6, chapter 2, 156: "From this it follows, I believe, that beauty is some inherent property, to be found suffused all through the body of that which may be called beautiful; whereas ornament, rather than being inherent, has the character of something attached or additional". For the original Latin text, see Alberti, *L'Architettura [De re aedificatoria]*, transl. Giovanni Orlandi, introduction and notes by Paolo Portoguese (Milan: Edizioni Il Polifilo, 1966), vol. 2, 449: "Ex his patere arbitror, pulchritudinem quasi suum atque innatum toto esse perfusum corpore, quod pulchrum sit; ornamentum autem afficti et compacti naturam sapere magis quam innati".

37. Alberti, *On the Art of Building in Ten Books*, book 6, chapter 2, 156: "If this is conceded, ornament may be defined as a form of auxiliary light and complement to beauty". Again, for the Latin text, see Alberti, *L'Architettura [De re aedificatoria]*, vol. 2, 449: 'Illis, ni fallor, adhibita ornamenta hoc contulissent, fucando operiendoque siqua extabant deformia, aut comendo expoliendoque venustiora, ut ingrata minus offenderent et amoena magis delectarent. Id si ita persuadetur, erit quidem ornamentum quasi subsidiaria quaedam lux pulchritudinis atque veluti complementum. I thank Giancarlo Fiorenza for directing me to this passage.

38. Alberti, *On the Art of Building in Ten Books*, 420.

39. Alberti insists on the satisfactions of both conceptual design and expert craftsmanship, of the object and its supplement, a tandem that is equally applicable to Late Gothic architectitecture. See Alberti, *On the Art of Building in Ten Books*, book 6, chapter 4, 159: "The pleasure to be found in objects of great beauty and ornament is produced either by invention and the working of the intellect, or by the hand of the craftsman, or it is imbued naturally in the objects themselves. The intellect is responsible for choice, distribution, arrangement, and so on, which give the work dignity; the hand is responsible for laying, joining, cutting, trimming, polishing, and such like, which give the work grace; the properties derived from Nature are weight, lightness, density, purity, durability, and the like, which bring the work admiration. These three must be applied to each part of the building, according to its respective use and role . . ."

40. Bayrische Staatsbibliothek, Sig. 2° Inc.c.a. 1540 m; Bayrische Staatsbibliothek, Sig. 2° Inc.c.a. 1541. Peutinger studied at the universities of Bologna and Padua before returning to his home town of Augsburg, where he served as town clerk and advisor to the emperor. His enormous library was famous in its day. On Peutinger's antiquarian activities and his

relationship with the Emperor Maximilian, see Wood, "Maximilian I as Archeologist", *Renaissance Quarterly* 58 (2005), 1130–1138.

41. Bialostocki, *The Art of the Renaissance in Eastern Europe*, 7, 15–17; Fehr, *Benedikt Ried*, 16–19.

42. Paul Crossley, "The Return to the Forest", 71–80; Günther, "Das Astwerk und die Theorie der Renaissance von der Entstehung der Architektur", in *Théorie des arts et création artistique dans l'Europe du Nort du XVIe au début du XVIIIe siècle*. Actes du colloque international organize les 14 à 16 décembre 2000 à l'Université Charles-de-Gaule—Lille (Lille: Université Charles-de-Gaule, 2002), 13–32. See also by Günther, "Die deutsche Spätgotik und die Wende vom Mittelalter zur Neuzeit", *Kunsthistorische Arbeitsblätter* 7/8 (2000), 49–68.

43. Studies in geometry inevitably recalled an earlier medieval aesthetics of proportion, of the beauty of number extended over space, long supported by thinkers like St. Augustine and Boethius with their platonic interpretations of mathematical form. On this tradition, see below.

44. Werner Müller, *Grundlagen gotischer Bautechnik: Ars sine scientia nihil* (Munich: Deutscher Kunstverlag, 1990), 18–19. On the development and distribution of paper in the fifteenth century, see Lucien Febvre and Henri-Jean Martin, *The Coming of the Book: The Impact of Printing 1450–1800* (1958; London: Verso, 1984), 37–43.

45. In certain churches in Lower Austria such as Sankt Valentin and Krenstetten, the vaults appear to make a clean break with their supports. Box-like "capitals" that connect with the shell grip the cylindrical piers like a carpenter's vice, obstructing any sense of visual continuity. See Günter Brucher, *Gotische Baukunst in Österreich* (Salzburg and Vienna: Residenz Verlag, 1990), 200–203, 230–231.

46. On the structural function of ribs and the development of figured vaults, see Nussbaum and Lepsky, *Das gotische Gewölbe* (Munich: Deutsche Kunstverlag, 1999), 60–68, 234–270; Nussbaum, *German Gothic Church Architecture*, 150–151, 180–184, 195–216; James Acland, *Medieval Structure: The Gothic Vault* (Toronto: University or Toronto Press, 1972), 142–144. Star- and simple net vaults had been in use since the fourteenth century, but complex figured vaults, often using curvilinear ribs, were developed during the later fifteenth and sixteenth century.

47. "Floral" patterns were developed elsewhere, too—in the Salvatorkirche at Passau, for example. A drawing in the Akademie der bildenden Künste in Vienna attests to the popularity of Ried's designs, even though Austria developed its own genre of vaults with double curved ribs. See Johann Josef Böker, *Architektur der Gotik: Bestandskatalog der weltgrössten Sammlung an gotischen Baurissen der Akademie der bildenden Künste Wien* (Salzburg: Anton Pustet, 2005), 317–318, no. 17007.

48. Brucher, *Gotische Baukunst in Österreich*, 204–209; Brucher, "Architektur von 1430 vis um 1530", in *Geschichte der bildenden Kunst in Österreich: Spätmittelalter und Renaissance*, ed. Artur Rosenauer (Munich: Prestel, 2003), 204–206, 238–239; Böker, 313–314: Walther Buchowiecki, *Die gotischen Kirchen Österreichs* (Vienna: F. Deuticke, 1952), 395: ". . . willens die pfarrkirchen, die widerumb bedeckt war, gwelben zu lassen und etwas

ein tapfer pau daran zu verpringen". I thank Kathy van Driel for calling the Freistadt document to my attention.

49. The designs of vaults erected throughout the German lands are recorded in drawings preserved in numerous collections and sketchbooks. See, for instance, Böker, Koepf, Müller, "Einflüsse der österreichischen und der böhmisch-sächsischen Spätgotik in den Gewölbemustern des Jacob Facht von Andernach", *Wiener Jahrbuch für Kunstgeschichte* 27 (1974), 65–82. The Strasbourg architect Hans Hammer was presumably one of many who traveled widely; he is documented as having journeyed to Hungary and seems to have visited additional sites, for he records the designs of vaults from Erfurt and other locations in his sketch book. Some of these drawings show vaults with double-curved ribs, testimony to the early knowledge of these designs in Alsace. See François Joseph Fuchs, "Introduction au 'Musterbuch' de Hans Hammer", *Bulletin de la Cathédrale de Strasbourg* 20 (1992), 12, 52–53.

50. Brucher, 211; Buchowiecki, 303. The vaulting scheme comprises two parallel grids of circles and squares. The choir, which is vaulted in stone and reveals a less elaborate geometric figure, dates from the end of the fifteenth century. The parish church at Walmersdorf has a thick latticework of ribs made of wood and plaster affixed to its shell. See Brucher, 199.

51. For a discussion of the relative decorative and structural aspects of figured vaults, of pictorial qualities, and of geometry as a generating system of forms, see Müller, "Über die Grenzen der Interpretierbarkeit spätgotischer Gewölbe durch die traditionelle Kunstwissenschaft. Ein Beitrag zum Thema 'Unmittelbarkeit und Reflektion,'" *Jahrbuch des Zentralinstituts für Kunstgeschichte* 2 (1986), 47–69; Müller, *Grundlagen gotischer Bautechnik*, 151–197, 233–240, 247, 257–277; Müller, "An Application of Generative Aesthetics to German Late Gothic Rib Vaulting", *Leonardo* 11: 2 (Spring, 1978), 107–110.

52. Böker, 292–293; Brucher, 203–205. Once conceived on the drafting board, geometric compositions were applied to many types of architectural ornament. There are even close connections between tracery designs and rib configurations, despite practical considerations of engineering that regulated vault construction. Drawing no. 17091 in the collection of the Akademie der Bildenden Künste in Vienna shows a geometric pattern often used for the openwork of balustrades as found on German, French, Austrian, and Czech structures. The draftsman, however, has signalled the new venue by indicating the joins of the rib sections. The design clearly appealed as a two-dimensional image, since actual construction would have obscured the regularity of the geometric configuration. Not surprisingly, certain drawings are framed in ways that suggest their self-sufficiency as objects of study rather than their function as aids in further stages of production. See Böker, 402–405; Koepf, no. 17091; Hans Körner, 75–76; Nussbaum and Lepsky, 177–178; Bucher, *Architector, The Lodge Books and Sketchbooks of Medieval Architects*, vol. 1 (New York: Abaris Books, 1979), 197–199.

53. A perfectly flat wooden ceiling, such as that of the church of SS. Peter and Paul at Lavant in the Tyrol, offered the perfect opportunity to translate

drawing into building without distortion. Fixed to the ceiling, which is dated 1516, are rows of intersecting ogival arches, which are superimposed over a grid of crossing diagonal bars that form large squares. Lavant shows the priority placed on geometric patterning divorced from any technical function and hypostatizes tendencies that are less fully realized at countless other sites. See E. Schubert, L. Madersbacher, et al, *Die Gotik*, Tiroler Ausstellungsstrassen (Milan: Charta, 1994), 128–129.

54. For France, see Henri Zerner, *Renaissance Art in France: The Invention of Classicism*, trans. Deke Dusinberre, Scott Wilson, and Rachel Zerner (1996; Paris: Flammarion, 2003), 27–49.

55. Schmid, 75–77, Bischoff, 317. The West gallery was built between 1511 and 1519.

56. Schmid, 73–74; Dehio, *Handbuch der Deutschen Kunstdenkmäler, Bayern III: Schwaben*, ed. Bruno Bushart and Georg Paula (Munich: Deutscher Kunstverlag, 1989), 773. The pulpit was executed by Augsburg craftsmen in 1499.

57. An openwork balustrade crowns a frieze carved with rows of contiguous half-circles. Order and proportionality are conveniently read, even if precise numerical relationships are obscured by the tight, repetitive pattern. The structure comes from Burckhard Engelberg's workshop and was completed about 1501. See Bischoff, 294–297. Bischoff attributes the enclosure to Engelberg himself.

58. In Strasbourg, the gallery, designed by Hans Hammer, facing the Angels' Pillar probably dates from about 1486. Hans Reinhardt, *La Cathédrale de Strasbourg* (Paris: Arthaud, 1972), 143. For Hammer's drawings for the balustrade, see Fuchs, "Introduction au 'Musterbuch' ", 61–63. A similar balustrade of geometric openwork once faced the organ tribune. In the Cathedral of Freiburg, up-to-date galleries decorate the interior of the west façade. On the refitting of older French churches with Late Gothic ornamental patterns, see Peter Kurmann, "À propos des restaurations effectuées sur les cathedrals gothiques à la fin du moyen âge", *Annales d'Historie de 'Art et d'Archeologie* 25 (2003), 19, 26–29.

59. C. Gufler, *Die Pfarrkirche Maria Himmelfahrt in Niederlana*, Laurin Kunstführer, no. 108, (Bozen: Verlaganstalt Athesia, 1997), 14–21. The church in Niederlana was built principally between 1483 and 1492, most probably by Hans Hueber. The parish was wealthy enough to purchase in 1502 an extraordinary carved retable from Hans Schnatterpeck of Meran, for which Leonhard Schäuffelein painted the outer wings. See Herbert Schindler, *Der Schnitzaltar: Meisterwerke und Meister in Süddeutschland, Österreich und Südtirol* (Regensburg: Friedrich Pustet, 1978), 125–133.

60. Julier, *Studien zur spätgotischen Baukunst am Oberrhein* (Heidelberg, Carl Winter, 1978), 190–191, and criticism by Müller, "Über die Grenzen der Interpretierbarkeit spätgotischer Gewölbe", 49–51.

61. Kavaler, "Renaissance Gothic in the Netherlands", 240–241. These formal *jeux* develop as puzzles the ambiguities inherent in geometric construction. In the music of the time there seem to be associated developments, for John Tucke lists in his contemporary musical treatise the term *ambigua*, which is defined as the substitution of a longer tone for a shorter one or vice versa

with consequent rhythmic ambiguity. Although the technique is observable in a number of compositions, the word is not known in other music treatises, suggesting its recent coinage and an incipient self-conscious attention to its principles. See Ronald Woodley, *John Tucke: A Case Study in Early Tudor Music Theory* (Oxford, Clarendon Press, 1993), 98–99.

62. Joseph Leo Koerner, *The Moment of Self-Portraiture in German Renaissance Art* (Chicago: University of Chicago Press, 1993); Keith Moxey, "Making 'Genius' ", in: *The Practice of Theory: Poststructuralism, Cultural Politics, and Art History* (Ithaca: Cornell University Press, 1994), 111–147; Jeffrey Chipps Smith, *The Northern Renaissance*, Art & Ideas, (London and New York: Phaidon, 2004). 12–15. Koerner (p. 8) traces historical attention to this tendency to the romantic/nationalist writing of the early twentieth century, notably in Hugo Kehrer's commentary of 1934 on Dürer's self-portraits: "This representation of the I is at once a spiritual self-analysis and self-dissection. One could say, in that hour of Dürerian self-observation the German Renaissance awoke". See Kehrer, *Dürers Selbstbildnisse und die Dürer Bildnisse* (Berlin: Mann, 1934), 31.

63. See, for instance, Gunter Schweikhart, "Das Selbstbildnis im 15. Jahrhundert", in *Italienische Frührenaissance und nordeuropäisches Spätmittelalter: Kunst der frühen Neuzeit im europäischen Zusammenhang*, ed. Joachim Peoschke (Munich: Hirmer, 1993), 11–39. For a discussion of the historical situation and reception of self-portraiture and self-representation in the arts, see Joseph Leo Koerner, 3–59.

64. Michael Baxandall, *The Limewood Sculptors of Renaissance Germany* (New Haven: Yale University Press, 1980), 121–127.

65. On Dürer's monogram as supplement and its pictorial equivalents, see Friedrich Teja Bach, "Albrecht Dürer: Figures of the Marginal", *RES* 36 (1999), 80–99.

66. Christopher S. Wood, *Albrecht Altdorfer and the Origins of Landscape* (London: Reaktion Books, 1993), 62.

67. On Kraft's tabernacle, see Corine Schleif, *Donatio et Memoria Stifter, Stiftungen und Motivationen an Beispielen aus der Lorenzkirche in Nürnberg* (Munich, Deutscher Kunstverlag, 1990), 16–75; Johann-Christian Klamt, "Artist and Patron: The Self-Portrait of Adam Kraft in the Sacrament-House of St. Lorenz in Nuremberg", *Showing Status: Representation of Social Positions in the Late Middle Ages*, ed. Wim Blockmans and Antheum Janse, Medieval Texts and Cultures of Northern Europe 2 (Turnhout: Brepols, 1999), 415–443; Herbert Bauer and Georg Stolz, *Engelsgruß und Sakramenthaus in St. Lorenz zu Nürnberg* (Königstein im Taunus: Karl Robert Langewiesche Nachfolger Hans Köster, 1989), 8–12.

68. On the self-portraits of Adam Kraft and Tilman Riemenschneider and the notion of artistic self-consciousness, see Corine Schleif, "Nicodemus and Sculptors: Self-Reflexivity in Works by Adam Kraft and Tilman Riemenschneider". *The Art Bulletin* 75 (1993), 599–626, especially 614–624.

69. Jan Gossaert, eminent artist to the high nobility and well-heeled commoners, is primarily known for his *Neptune and Amphitrite* of 1516, a large picture of mythological figures standing unclothed in an archaeologically precise setting. The image reflects the antiquarian interests

of his patron, Philip of Burgundy, and the fruits of Gossaert's own trip to Rome. Indeed, Lodovico Guicciardini and Karel van Mander would hail the artist for naturalizing the monumental nude in the Netherlands. Yet contemporary with these humanist *poesie* are paintings by Gossaert that depict spectacular Late Gothic constructions, of which the *Malvagna Triptych* is one of the most exuberant. On Gossaert's patronage and development, see Ariane Mensger, *Jan Gossaert: Die niederländische Kunst zu Beginn der Neuzeit* (Berlin: Reimer, 2002).

70. It is found on the page that depicts Joseph as viceroy of Egypt, at the lower right corner, slightly truncated, where it supports a marginal narrative scene in grisaille. Another page representing David Anointed by Samuel reproduces one of the spires in Gossaert's painting, copied precisely, which serves in its new setting as a golden baldachin for a secondary miniature of David and Goliath. Elsewhere in the Grimani Breviary Gossaert's ogival-tear shape and other figures appear in the embellished frames around the principal subject, details excerpted from Gossaert's larger composition. See *The Grimani Breviary, Venice*, Biblioteca Marciana ms. lat. XI 67 (7531). References are to *The Grimaldi Breviary*, ed. Mario Salmi and Gian Lorenzo Mellini, facsimile ed, (Woodstock, N.Y.: Overlook, 1974), pls. 39, 47, 70, 72, fols. 192r, 289r.

71. The name is inscribed on the entablature of a vaguely Italianate building that stands adjacent to an exceptional Gothic porch, fitted with a decorative gable, prominent openwork, pendentives, and a hanging keystone. Salmi and Mellini, pl. 106, fol. 284v. As Gian Lorenzo Mellini suggests, the recording of Gossaert's name is most likely a tribute rather than a putative signature or acknowledgment of direct authorship.

72. Van Orley's Italianate forms are certainly fantastic and indicative of the relatively recent vogue for design *à l'antique*. The friezes, capitals, pediments, and pedestals suggest a synthesis of Lombard forms, French adaptations, and architectural ephemera from the recent Joyous Entries of King Charles, later Charles V—all of which helps date the painting to the years 1516–18.

73. Klaus Demus, Friderike Klauner, and Karl Schütz, eds., Flämische Malerei von Jan van Eyck bis Pieter Bruegel d. Ä.: Katalog der Gemäldegalerie (Vienna: Kunsthistorisches Museum, 1981), 261–262. In a devotional context, the delicate forms of gold work might be likened to celestial architecture; van Orley seems to be playing on this association, as had many artists before him. This frame with its stone base is situated outside the world of the figure, which it supports and contains, separating in space and time the events from the lives of Saints Thomas and Matthias.

74. P. Pfister and H. Ramisch, *Der Dom zu Unserer Lieben Frau in München* (Munich: Erich Wewel, 1994), 8, 22–24.

75. Note, for instance the tracery figures that form spectacular frames for coats of arms on the choir screen in the church of St. Bavo in Haarlem. The splendid partition was designed around 1509 by the local artist *"Steven die beeldsnyder"* (Steven the sculptor), who carved the elaborate oak frame and prepared wooden patterns for the uprights, which were cast in bronze by the eminent Jan Fierens of Mechelen; the assembly was standing in place by

1517. See F. Allan et al., *Geschiedenis en beschrijving van Haarlem van de vroegste tijden tot op onze dagen*, vol. 3 (Haarlem: Van Brederode, 1883), 141–147; Bierens de Haan, *Het Houtsnijwerk in Nederland* (1921; reprint, The Hague: Nijhoff, 1977), 64–66, pls. 60–61; and Jeremy Dupertuis Bangs, *Church Art and Architecture in the Low Countries before 1566*, Sixteenth Century Essays and Studies, vol. 16 (Kirksville, Mo.: Sixteenth Century Journal Publishers, 1996), 45–46.

76. E. Bourassin, "La hérauderie au XXVe siècle: Rois et hérauts d'armes", in *Jeanne d'Arc: Une époque, un rayonnement*, Colloque d'Histoire Médiévale, Orléans, Octobre 1979 (Paris: Éditions du CNRS, 1981), 107–111; Pichel Pasatoureau, "Aux origines de l'emblème", in *L'hermine et le sinople: Études d'héraudique médiévale* (Paris: Léopard d'or), 1982, 327–333; Jacques Lemaire, "L'intérét pour l'héraldique dans les prologues des chroniques Bourguignonnes", in *Sources de l' héraldique en Europe occidentale: Actes du 4e Colloque International d'Héraldique* (Brussels: Archives Générales du Royaume, 1985), 78–80; M. Pastoureau, "Aux origines de l'emblème: la crise de l'héraldique européenne aus XIVe et XVIe siècles", in *Emblèmes et devises au temps de la Renaissance*, ed. M. T. Jones-Davies (Paris: J. Touzot, 1981), 129–139. The development of *devises* and badges seems to begin in the late fourteenth century. See Werner Paravicini, "Gruppe und Person: Repräsentation durch Wappen im späteren Mittelalter", in *Die Repräsentation der Gruppen: Texte—Bilder—Objekte*, ed. Otto Gerhard Oexle and Andrea von Hülsen-Esch (Göttingen: Vandenhoeck & Ruprecht), 1998, 366–368.

77. See Nigel Hiscock, *The Wise Master Builder: Platonic Geometry in Plans of Medieval Abbeys and Cathedrals* (Aldershot: Ashgate, 2000); Gordon Strachan, Chartres: *Sacred Geometry, Sacred Space* (Edinburgh: Floris, 2003); George Lesser, *Gothic Cathedrals and Sacred Geometry*, 3 vols. (London: A. Tiranti, 1957), 1964; Otto von Simson, *The Gothic Cathedral: Origins of Gothic Architecture and the Medieval Concept of Order* (1956; Princeton: Princeton University Press, 1974), 13–42.

78. Origen and Cassiodorus were also prominent among writers who interpreted geometry as a divinely ordained cognitive instrument. See Hiscock, 114; Eugeny A. Zaitsev, "The Meaning of Early Medieval Geometry From Euclid and Surveyors' Manuals to Christian Philosophy", *Isis* 90, 1999, 530.

79. On art history's preoccupation with neoplatonism and its close connection with the practice of iconology, see Horst Bredekamp, "Götterdämmerung des Neuplatonismus", *Kritische Berichte* 14 (1986), 39–48. I thank Christopher Wood for this reference. Nonetheless, platonic notions of number seem to have been critical to the reception of geometric forms in the later Middle Ages. The Greek platonists had judged the universe to be divided into three levels. The upper region contained solely eternal ideas, whereas the lower held the changeable matter of the natural world. The middle level, however, comprised mathematical and especially geometric forms, a register of communication between perfect concepts and imperfect natural objects. Zaitsev, 522–523; 530–531. In the *De opiticio mundi*, Philo discusses how God first made a world of perfect ideas, which he used as a

pattern for the imperfect material world. See John Block Freedman, "The Architect's Compass in Creation Miniatures of the Later Middle Ages", *Traditio* 30 (1974), 424–425; Philo, translated by F. H. Colson and G. H. Whitaker (Cambridge, Mass.: Harvard University Press, 1949), I.iv.17–20: "[God] brought to completion a world discernible only by the mind, and, with that for a pattern, the world which our senses can perceive".

80. It was probably through other texts, however, that the idea reached the later Middle Ages. The passage in the *Timaeus* describing the generation of the four elements through regular triangles was not taken up in Calcidius's translation, the principal version of Plato's text available until the late fifteenth century. Calcidius's commentary did treat in distinctly geometric terms Plato's notion of the *chora*, a preexistent place for things to be created that allowed the embodiment of ideas. The platonic interpretation of geometry is fully present, however, in Proclus's commentary on Euclid, *In primum Euclidis*, definitions 26–29, 166–167. Even better known was Aristotle's reference to Platonic theory in *De caelo*, whereas Cassiodorus explicitly presents geometry as a divine instrument of creation in his *Institutiones*. See Aristotle, *De caelo* 279 B 33; Cassiodorus, *Introduction to Divine and Human Readings*, trans. Leslie Webber Jones (New York, 1946), 197; Zaitsev, 540–541; Hiscock, 115–116. On the survival of platonism in the Middle Ages, see M. T. Gibson, "The Study of the *Timaeus* in the Eleventh and Twelfth Centuries", *Pensamiento* 25 (1969), 183–194; R. Klibansky, *The Continuity of the Platonic Tradition during the Middle Ages*, Supplement, *Plato's Parmenides in the Middle Ages and the Renaissance: A Chapter in the History of Platonic Studies* (Millwood, New York: Krauss Reprints, 1981); P. G. Ruggiers, "Platonic Forms in Chaucer", *Chaucer Review* 17 (1983), 366–381. Well into the sixteenth century, treatises on geometry continued to extol regular two-dimensional figures and polyhedrons as the essential forms of the universe. Wenzel Jamnitzer's *Perspectiva Corporum Regularium* of 1568, for instance, mentions the *Timaeus* in its complete title. See Wenzel Jamnizer, *Perspective corporum regularium das is ein fleissige fürweisung wie di fünff Regulirten Cörper, darvon Plato in Timaeo und Euclides inn sein Elementis schribt*, Nuremberg, 1568; Martin J. Kemp, "Geometrical Bodies as Exemplary Forms in Renaissance Space", in *World Art: Themes of Unity in Diversity*, vol. 1, 238–239.

81. Several writers of the fifteenth century considered geometric terms and shapes characteristic of the ideal, abstracted language of divine thought and mechanism of creation. Among the most prominent was Nicholas of Cusa, for whom the curve and the straight line were indicative of the dual nature of the universe; the circle was the "perfect figure of unity and simplicity". In *De docta ignorantia*, Nicholas follows the platonic tradition in describing how God fashioned the world using geometry along with arithmetic, music, and astronomy. His notion of the divine and infinite "absolute maximum" is likened to the interaction of geometric forms: "just as the sphere is the act of the line, triangle and circle, so the Maximum is the act of all things". In fact, Nicholas expresses God's relationship to created matter in geometric terms: "[God], therefore, is the final cause of all. But since beings are finite their attraction to Him as their end necessarily differs from one to another. Some

are attracted through the intermediary of others, in much the same way as the line is to the sphere through the triangle and circle, the triangle to the sphere through the circle, and the circle directly to the sphere". We find a similar strain in the writing of Charles de Bovelles, for whom geometry was a guide in measuring the qualities of the Trinity. See Nicholas Cusanus, *Of Learned Ignorance*, trans. Germain Heron (New York: Routledge, 1954), bk. 1, ch. 21, 46; bk. 1, ch. 23, 51–53; bk. 2, ch. 13, 118–119. Nicholas's works were published in a reliable edition by Martin Flach at Strasbourg in 1488. See also Charles de Bovelles, *Le Livre du sage*, ed. and trans. Pierre Magnard (Paris: Librairie Philosophique J. Vrin, 1982), 198.

82.   Alan of Lille, *Theologicae regulae*, no. 31. Several of Alan's works were published in many editions before and slightly after 1500; the *Regulae* appeared in 1492 at Basel from the press of Jacob Wolff of Pforzheim. See E. J. Butterworth, "Form and Significance of the Sphere in Nicholas of Cusa's *De ludo globi*", in *Nicholas of Cusa: In Search of God and Wisdom*, Essays in Honor of Morimichi Watanabe by the American Cusanus Society, ed Gerald Christianson and Thomas Mizbicki (Leiden: Brill, 1991), 89–90; Françoise Hudry, "Introduction", in: Alain de Lille, *Règles de théologie suivi de Sermon sur la sphère intelligible* (Paris: Cerf, 1995), 7–80; Jean Jolivet, "Remarques sur les Regulae Theologicae d'Alain de Lille", in *Alain de Lille, Gautier de Châtillon, Jakemart Giélée et leur temps*, ed. H. Roussel and F. Suard (Lille: Presses universitaires de Lille, 1980), 83–99. Alan of Lille strongly influenced Chaucer, who refers explicitly to Alan's *Anticlaudianus* in *The House of Fame* (II.985–990).

83.   Cusanus is clearest on this point in the dialogue *De ludo globi*, in which one speaker asserts: "Thus materialized, no form is true, but rather only an image of the truth of true form, since the truth of form is separated from all material". Nicholas of Cusa, *De ludo globi*, in Nikolaus von Kues, *Philosophisch-theologische Schriften*, ed. Leo Gabriel, transl. Dietlind and Wilhelm Dupré, 3 vols (Vienna: Herder, 1964), vol. 3, 231.
This use of geometry as a concentrated sign of the higher realm of divine thought is in keeping with the views of earlier writers such as the popular Dionysius the Pseudo-Areopagite, whose works were extensively published with commentaries in the late fifteenth and sixteenth century. In *De ecclesiastica hierarchia* (2.III.2) Dionysius typically insists that "sacred symbols are actually the perceptible tokens of the conceptual things". In *De coelesti hierarchia* (1.3) he explains, "He revealed all this to us in the sacred pictures of the scriptures so that he might lift us in spirit up through the perceptible to the conceptual, from sacred shapes and symbols to the simple peaks of the hierarchies of heaven". See Hiscock, 123. *De caelesti hierarchia* and *De ecclesiastica hierarchia* were published separately at Paris (1498 and 1515) and Strasbourg (1502). Editions of collected works containing these treatises were published at Bruges (c.1478); Paris (1498 and 1515), Strasbourg (1502 and 1503), and Basel (1539). A similar notion of the division between material objects and divine ideas is expressed by Charles de Bovelles, who writes of "the perceptable signs that make known the divine and most high trinity". See Charles de Bovelles, *Le Livre du sage*, 191.

84. An intimation of this transformation is found in Michael Pacher's St. Wolfgang Altarpiece, completed in 1481. Above the scene of the Coronation of the Virgin floats the dove of the Holy Spirit. The form of this bird, with its wing outstretched, clearly mimics the crossing lines of tracery immediately behind and above it. The gently curving ogival arches of the baldachin seem to comprise a geometric matrix from which the material form of the dove is generated. In allowing itself to be represented as a dove, the Holy Spirit condescends to assume the mantle of perceptible form. See Michael Baxandall, *The Limewood Sculptors of Renaissance Germany* (New Haven and London: Yale University Press, 1980), 252–254, plate 13.

85. There exist several fifteenth-century manuscript editions of this work. See, for instance, ms. germ. fol. 624, Berlin, Staatsbibliothek zu Berlin, Preußischer Kulturbesitz. The text was published repeatedly in the fifteenth and early sixteenth century. A Spanish translation, *El pelegrino dela vida humana*, was printed at Toulouse in 1490 by Heinrich Mayer. In addition, French editions were issued at Paris by Bertold Rembolt and Jean Petit (1500 and 1515) and Antoine Vérard (1511). On the popularity of Guillaume de Deguileville's *pélerinages* in England in the fifteenth century, see Emily Steiner, *Documentary Culture and the Making of Medieval English Literature* (Cambridge: Cambridge University Press, 2003), 20.

86. De Deguileville, *The Pilgrimage of Human Life* (New York: Garland, 1992), 34–35, v. 2512–2579.

87. H. Junecke, *Die wohlbemessene Ordnung, Pathagorieische Proportionen in der Historischen Architektur*, Berlin, 1982; Hallyn, *The Poetic Structure of the World*, 21, 57, 173. Plato's understanding of cosmological harmony in music in the *Timaeus* was important for Augustine, who posits a similar interpretation in book six of *De musica*. Boethius likewise conceived of music as a measure of divine order in his own treatise, *De musica*, which endured as an authoritative text until the Renaissance. See Hiscock, 65, 77–78. For Nicholas of Cusa's reference to music as a measure of divine harmony, see *Of Learned Ignorance*, bk. 2, ch. 1, 68. It is worth recalling, by the way, that the well-known image of God as a geometer using a compass to create the world survived into the late Middle Ages. Several miniatures from the fourteenth and fifteenth century demonstrate the continuing relevance of this notion for the late Middle Ages. Again, the *Timaeus* underlies much of this imagery in suggesting the picture of God imposing form on inchoate matter. But there were also biblical passages that would have strengthened this notion in the mind of medieval readers, such as the well-known verse from the Wisdom of Solomon (11:21) that relates God's creative process in the following terms: "Thou hath disposed everything according to measure, number, and weight". See Freedman, 419–424; John E. Murdoch, *Antiquity and the Middle Ages*, (New York: Scribner, 1984), 330; Erwin Panofsky and Fritz Saxl, Dürer's *"Melancholia I": Eine quellen- und typengeschichtliche Untersuchung* (Leipzig and Berlin: B. G. Teubner, 1923), 67–70; Zaitsev, 536.

88. Charles de Bovelles nicely describes this bifurcated model in stating, "the intelligible world is double: one of substance and the other of reason; one

above the afirmament and the other below". And again, for Nicholas of
Cusa, "the visible universe [was] a faithful reflection of the invisible". Such
anagogical relationships were hierarchal and vertical, "leading to higher
things" (*ad superiora ducens*). See Charles de Bovelles, *Le Livre du sage*, 5,
155; Nicholas of Cusa, *Of Learned Ignorance*, ch. 11, 25.

89. L. Schultes in *Geschichte der Bildende Kunst in Österreich Spätmittelalter und
Renaissance*, ed. by Artur Rosenhauer (Munich: Prestel, 2003), 341, no. 123.
The epitaph, of Salzburg provenance, has been attributed to Hans
Valkenauer and was originally in the interior of the church. The relief is
dated *circa* 1511.

90. T. W. Adorno, *Ästhetische Theorie* (Frankfurt: Suhrkamp, 1993), 114: "Denn
in Kunst wird das Entgleitende objecktiviert und zur Dauer zitiert".

91. For Adorno, art allows us to seize the significant insight, that truth that
would otherwise be lost among the multitude of references evoked. Artistic
truth must encompass both the acknowledgment of irreconcilable
antagonism in the world and the paradoxical tendency toward a utopian
reconciliation. This is a potential that is realized by the viewer. Albrecht
Wellmer, attempting to demystify Adorno's writing, focuses on truth in art
as a perceptual effect rather than an intrinsic quality. For Wellmer, aesthetic
truth can only be metaphorical. It arises from the simultaneous reception of
the art work as a symbolic construct with internal criteria of aesthetic
validity, *and* as an object of experience that is judged according to non-
metaphorical categories of truth. According to this model, the observer
must perceive some essence of reality in the work of art while
simultaneously viewing the work as reality showing itself through this
medium. Yet since the revelation is part recognition, it must confirm
something previously known. As Wellmer argues, "We can only recognize
the 'essence' which 'appears' in the apparition if we already *know* the essence
as something which does not appear". A perceived structural similarity
between the known idea and its manifestation as art work, a like
relationship between parts and the whole, would account for this identity,
despite the radically different ways in which the two are expressed. See
Adorno, 182–187, 251; Albrecht Wellmer, "Adorno's Aesthetic
Redemption of Modernity", *Telos* 62 (1984–5), 92, 105–109; Thomas
Huhn, "Adorno's Aesthetics of Illusion", *Journal of Aesthetics and Art
Criticism* 44 (1985–6), 181–189; Lambert Zuidervaart, *Adorno's Aesthetic
Theory. The Redemption of Illusion* (Cambridge, Mass.: MIT Press, 1991),
288–289; Immanuel Kant, *Critique of Judgment*, trans. J. H. Bernard (New
York: Hafner, 1951), 25–34, 48–58 (paragraphs 8, 9); Christopher Norris,
"Utopian Deconstruction: Ernst Bloch, Paul de Man and the politics of
music", in *Music and the Politics of Culture*, ed. Christopher Norris (New
York: St. Martin's Press, 1989), 333–334.

92. Narrative readings are not limited to religious edifices; the running
decoration on secular buildings such as the Ghent Town Hall is
transformed at significant sites; the progress of passersby establishes
expectations of continuity that are either met or denied In this respect, there
is a relationship with the temporal appreciation of musical melody See
Leonard Meyer, *Emotion and Meaning in Music* (Chicago: University of

Chicago Press, 1956), 88–127; Kavaler, "Renaissance Gothic in the Netherlands", 234–237.

93. See Michael Fried's discussion of the abstract sculpture of Anthony Caro, which despite its nonrepresentational nature conveys something of the human body, movement, and language of gesture through its "syntax". Michael Fried, *Art and Objecthood* (Chicago and London: University of Chicago Press, 1998), 28–30, 161–162.

94. The fundamental studies on narrative by Propp, Lévi-Strauss and Greimas have been helpful in suggesting patterns of response to non-representational carving, as have investigations into the semiotics and ideology of music by Jean-Jacques Nattiez, Françoise Escal, Christopher Norris and others. See Jean-Jacques Nattiez, *Music and Discourse. Toward a Semiology of Music*, trans. Carolyn Abbate (Princeton: Princeton University Press, 1990); Françoise Escal, *Espaces sociaux, espaces musicaux* (Paris: Payot, 1979); Célestin Deliège, *Invention musicale et idéologies* (Paris: C. Bourgois, 1986); Norris, "Utopian Deconstruction", 305–337; Alastair Williams, "Music as Immanent Critique: Stasis and Development in the Music of Ligeti", in *Music and the Politics of Culture*, 187–225. On the history of interpretation of Gothic Architecture, see Paul Crossley, "Medieval architecture and meaning: the limits of iconography", *Burlington Magazine* 130 (1988), 116–121.

95. Hayden White, *Metahistory: The Historical Imagination in Nineteenth-Century Europe* (Baltimore: Johns Hopkins Press, 1973), 1–42.

96. Jean Pépin, "L'Herméneutique ancienne", *Poétique* 23 (1975), 291–300; Eugene Vance, "Pas de Trois", in *Interpretation of Narrative*, ed. Mario J. Valdés and Owen J. Miller (Toronto: University of Toronto Press, 1978), 122–134; *The Parisiana Poetria of John of Garland*, ed. and trans. Traugott Lawler, Yale Studies in English, vol. 182 (New Haven: Yale University Press, 1974), 101.

97. Many carved altarpieces from Antwerp and Brussels, for instance, are commonly bi-axial. Here the hierarchic order is displayed vertically, while the narrative sequence is shown horizontally.

98. This is also true for other potentially narrative arrangements. At Beauvais, for example, Martin Chambiges designed bells, trefoils and groups of *mouchettes* and *souflets* to be steadily transformed as they ascend the façade. See Murray, *Beauvais Cathedral*, 135–6; Christopher Wilson, *The Gothic Cathedral*, 252–256.

99. Vladimir Propp, *Morphology of the Folktale*, trans. L. Scott (Austin: University of Texas Press, 1990), 25–28, 35–36, 42–52, 84–86, 92. The conflict can take the form of an absence, interdiction, or violation of an interdiction, for instance. Lack or desire and transference by means of a donor are among the "moves" that perpetuate the narrative, which concludes with an act of conciliation or transcendence.

100. A. J. Greimas, *Du Sens: essais sémiotiques* (Paris: Editions du Seuil, 1970), 187. I borrow from Eugene Vance's translation of this passage; see Vance, "Pas de Trois", 132.

101. Contrasting geometric figures can appear in conflict, resolved by subsequent conflations of their differing properties. This achievement of

unity out of difference also has strong ideological connotations. In this regard, it is interesting to note Claude Lévi-Strauss's treatment of narrative, which is seen as bringing about a poetic or creative resolution of active social conflict by symbolically reconciling difference. See Claude Lévi-Strauss, *Structural Anthropology*, trans. C. Jacobson and B. G. Schoepf (New York: Basic Books, 1963), 206–231; Lévi-Strauss, *Tristes tropiques*, translated by John Russell, New York, 1963, 176–80; Fredric Jameson, *The Political Unconscious: Narrative as a Socially Symbolic Ac*, (Ithaca: Cornell University Press, 1981), 77–79.

102. Achim Timmermann, "Staging the Eucharist: late Gothic sacrament houses in Swabia and the Upper Rhine: architecture and iconography", 2 vols, diss., University of London, Courtauld Institute of Art, 1996, 94–98.

103. Timmermann, 94.

104. A. Gosse-Kischinewski and F. Gatouillat, *La cathédrale d'Évreux* (Évreux: Fromont-Glatigny, 1997), 25, 65–66.

105. Such a clear pattern of shapes, immediately readable, is unusual. The marked emphasis on basic squares and circles as templates of design suggests some familiarity with ratios common in Italy. See P. Benedikt Wagner, *Pfarr- und Wallfahrtskirche zu Unserer Lieben Frauen Himmelfahrt in Krenstetten—Niederösterreich* (Salzburg: Verlag St. Peter, 1997), 12.

106. See Grabar, 48–50, 88–89. Grabar cites the tenth-century writer al-Thaʿalibi as claiming that "the worst of writing is the writing of angels because it must be illegible to humans".

107. The vaults in the nearby church at Sankt Valentin in Lower Austria represent a different manner of narrative development. The vaults over the nave show a regular progression of bands bearing distinctive geometrical motifs—lobed lozenges within squares—alternating with bays of thick net vaults. The vaulting over the choir, by contrast, portrays a bewildering array of incomplete figures, paired rows of strange shapes composed of various arcs over a diamond grid. The final bay resolves this doubleness and fragmented quality in a single, central radiating star with seven curving rays. See Brucher, 202–203.

108. Jameson, 82–83. Jameson discusses the subtext as the place both of social conflict and ideological opposition. Social dissonance may be expressed through contradiction, whereas ideological opposition is expressed in antinomy or paradox, which appeals to the narrative of the text for resolution.

109. Jameson, 118–119; *Eric et Enide*, 1042: "Sire, Yidiers, li filz Nut, ai non". See also Jean Lemaire, *Oeuvres de Jean Lemaire de Belges*, edited by J. Stecher, 3 vols (Louvain: J. Lefever, 1883), vol. 3, 98–134. In his *Concorde des deux langages*, Jean Lemaire undertakes to marry the two vernaculars of poetic renown. In triplets customary of Italian verse he constructs a "Temple de Venus", whereas a French "Temple de Minerve" is fashioned in Alexandrines. On this latter site he hopes for an "amoureuse concordance".

110. *The Chronicle of Froissart*, translated by John Bourchier, 8 vols (London: J. M. Dent, 1906), vol. 6, 113–114; Froissart, *Oeuvres*, edited by A. Kervyn de Lettenhove, 25 vols (Brussels: V. Devoe et cie, 1867+), vol. 15,

114–115; Lee Patterson, "Making identities: Henry V and Lydgate", in *New Historical Literary Study*, ed. Jeffrey N. Cox and Larry J. Reynolds (Princeton: Princeton University Press, 1993), 83. The passage deals with problems at the negotiations between John of Gaunt and Richard, Duke of York with Philip of Burgundy and Jean, Duke of Berry in 1394.

111. John Lydgate, *Lydgate's Troy Book*, ed. Henry Bergen (1906; Millwood, New York: Krauss Repring, 1975), vol. 3, 870; Patterson, 80.

112. *The Brut, or the Chronicles of England*, Early English Text Society, OS 136, ed. Friedrich W. D. Brie, London: Kegan Paul, Trench, Trubner, 1908), part 2, 410; Patterson, 85.

113. Elisabeth Eisenstein, *The Printing Press as an Agent of Change*, 2 vols (Cambridge and New York: Cambridge University Press, 1979), vol. 1, 33, 88.

114. W. J. Ong, *Ramus, Method and the Decay of Dialogue* (1958, Cambridge, Mass. and London: Harvard University Press, 1983), 92–101, 112–114.

115. Roger Chartier, *The Order of Books: Readers, Authors and Libraries in Europe between the Fourteenth and Eighteenth Centuries*, trans. L. Cochrane (Stanford: Stanford University Press, 1994), N3–1.

Italian Renaissance Art and the Systematicity of Representation[*]

Robert Williams

What would be the best possible way to organize an account of Italian Renaissance art? The question seems both presumptuous and irrelevant: presumptuous in that it suggests a dissatisfaction with all the accounts that already exist; irrelevant in that current research seems to have rejected the kind of preoccupation with master narratives that such a question implies. On the one hand, the achievement of the Renaissance would seem to have been so thoroughly and authoritatively defined by generations of great scholars that its fundamentals are no longer in question; on the other, an array of new approaches has yielded a new set of themes for investigation that do not so much challenge those old definitions as move beyond them altogether into new conceptual terrain.

These new approaches have made valuable contributions to the field, and are often said to have revitalized it, yet the study of Italian Renaissance art actually finds itself in something of a backwater within the discipline of art history, so that one wonders whether their effect has been as positive as is claimed. Despite all the new sources of interest they have disclosed, many linked to themes also being explored by literary and social historians, they avoid—or suppress—others that are perhaps even more significant. They seem unconcerned or unable to define the achievement of

Italian Renaissance art in such a way as to expose its distinctive historical importance and thus its distinctive interest. And though they dispense with some of the limitations and false assumptions of the older scholarship, they also leave others—deeper, more crippling ones—untouched. Indeed, they often reinforce what most needs to be questioned; they often seem more like symptoms of the older scholarship than effective remedies against its shortcomings. The critical project they began seems to have lost direction and to have stalled far short of its goal.

Traditional attempts to describe the distinctive character of Renaissance art almost always evoke the concept of naturalism. The belief that Renaissance art is fundamentally more naturalistic than the art of the Middle Ages is already fully developed in Vasari, and Burckhardt easily adapted it to his interpretation of the Renaissance as the "rediscovery of the world and of man". In more recent times, the emphasis on naturalism has been explicitly associated with the scientific ambition to understand and dominate nature, most insistently—that is, adapted to a dogmatic neo-positivism—by E.H. Gombrich,[1] but also by others such as Martin Kemp[2] and David Summers.[3] One of its familiar features, for instance, is the emphasis on the scientific study of optical experience evident in the development of perspective.

The modern investment in this naturalistic or scientific point of view obviously depends upon the prestige enjoyed by science in modern times, on the assumption that our own scientific outlook on the world is the natural and correct one. Yet our thinking about art has also been shaped by the idea, which emerged in the Enlightenment and with special strength in the Romantic period, that art is unlike science and even in some fundamental way opposed to it. By the end of the nineteenth century, a strong reaction to positivism was underway in those areas of culture closest to the arts; this development affected the way art history was studied, leading to an emphasis on the non-rational that still pervades most modern scholarship. We no longer expect modern art to have any relation to nature, but we seem to need to believe all the more strongly that Renaissance art is defined in some essential way by its relation to nature. The Renaissance is thus made to serve both as an anticipation of our own time and as a foil for it; we have locked it in a kind of choke-hold with which we force it to support a certain image of ourselves. Despite the pervasiveness of anti-positivism in contemporary scholarship, naturalistic and even scientific assumptions continue to circulate, and have even been revived in recent work on the relation between art and technology.[4]

Also central to traditional accounts of Renaissance art is the theme of beauty. For Vasari, Renaissance art was not just more naturalistic than medieval art, it was more beautiful in a way that related it to the art of classical antiquity, on the one hand, and to idealistic philosophy, on the other. The complementarity of naturalism and idealism was what, for Heinrich Wölfflin, made High Renaissance art "classic".[5] Erwin Panofsky and some of his contemporaries associated the cultivation of beauty with Neo-Platonism,[6] a move that did not sit well with positivists such as Gombrich, for whom all forms of idealism are anti-scientific and thus intellectually regressive.[7] Elizabeth Cropper seems to have found a way out of this dilemma by relating the pursuit of beauty in art to vernacular traditions of courtly love poetry, especially Petrarchism.[8] She has thus reclaimed the importance of beauty precisely by detaching it from idealism, and in so doing she can be said to have given a kind of indirect support to the naturalistic view of the Renaissance. Her efforts to ground the pursuit of beauty in erotic motivations have helped open the way to gender-based approaches.

Another way of defining the achievement of Renaissance art has been to emphasize the relation of art to literature, an idea expressed in the phrase *ut pictura poesis*. The significance of this idea has been differently assessed by different scholars: Rensselaer Lee saw it as essentially dependent upon the values of Renaissance humanism and as constituting something like the backbone of European artistic theory and practice in the early modern period;[9] Charles Dempsey, a student of Lee, has seen it as deeply significant for the aims of Renaissance art and values of Renaissance culture as a whole.[10] Michael Baxandall, while not denying its importance, has taken care to show that there might be a significant discrepancy between the theoretical insistence on the principle and its actual application in practice.[11] In the work of younger scholars this range of attitudes has only widened: on the one hand, there are those who minimize the significance of *ut pictura poesis* or see it only in the narrowest terms, motivated, one senses, by the desire to sever art from humanism in the same way that Cropper severed beauty from idealism.[12] On the other, there are those who insist that the idea of *ut pictura poesis* points beyond the specific relation between painting and poetry, or painting and rhetoric, to the relation between the visual and verbal arts generally, to the relation between art and language, and even to an ideal of total cultural integration.[13]

The notion that painting is like poetry is not necessarily incompatible with the belief that it is closely related to science. Renaissance artists and theorists clearly assumed that the deeper relation of art to language implied in the notion of *ut pictura poesis* could also be made to associate art with discursive thought, reason, and thus also with science or philosophy. For us, the hiers to Romanticism, however, poetry and art are fundamentally non-rational, and we thus tend to dismiss Renaissance claims for the rationality of art as misguided. Many art historians are attracted to the idea that visual art is somehow fundamentally unlike verbal or discursive modes of expression, and is thus at an even further remove from reason than poetry; some believe that the whole interest of the discipline lies in the ways in which images seem to exceed language.[14]

Both the emphasis on art as science and on art as poetry can be seen as aspects of the "rise" of the artist from craftsman to intellectual, a development that is also one of the principal themes in any traditional account of Renaissance art, surely because it is so crucial to our modern conception of what an artist is.[15] While the rise of the artist has been used to support the cult of artistic personality, of "genius"—a recurrent feature of the older scholarship that we now find especially indicative of its limitations—it can also be seen as documenting a change in the nature of the *work* an artist does, and thus in the *social function* of art. It reflects an awareness that art plays an important, even essential role in social life, that while artists may be lowly servants of power, they also fashion and refashion the signs on which power depends. The rise of the artist thus forces us to recognize the emergence of a new conception of what art is or can be, and to acknowledge it, in turn, as a fact of social history.

The most explicit indication of the redefinition of the function of art is the emergence of an *idea of art* in the theoretical writings of the period. Just what kind of weight is to be given to the exalted claims made in theory is also a matter of debate: this issue, too, has its minimalists, who tend to see theory as a sterile and pedantic super-fluity, as something essentially false. One scholar who acknowledges the importance of the claims made in theory, Hans Belting, nonethe-less sees the idea of art that emerges in the Renaissance as suppressing an older, more instinctive way of relating to images. In the nineteenth and twentieth centuries this rationalistic superimposition has been overthrown, permitting us a more liberated, more natural mode of engagement with objects. For Belting, Renaissance art is only of interest insofar as it retains vestiges of a more archaic visual culture, and modernism actually involves a return to pre-Renaissance values.[16]

Belting's desire to get around or behind or beneath the idea of art and the rationalistic values associated with it is shared by many younger scholars. Georges Didi-Huberman seeks to describe a radi-cally anti-humanistic enterprise, motivated by mystical scholasticism, at work in Fra Angelico;[17] Paolo Berdini a similarly anti-humanistic one, motivated by Counter-reformation piety, in Jacopo Bassano.[18] Alexander Nagel has sought to explain Michelangelo's innovations as a religiously motivated "reform" of art that in fact looks back to medieval images and is deeply at odds with the rationalistic principles of Alberti.[19] In an especially fine and elegantly-crafted book, Stephen Campbell makes the case that the Ferrarese painter Cosmè Tura also worked in conscious opposition to Alberti's ideas.[20] Michael Cole's outstanding study of Cellini emphasizes the relation between art and occult lore of different kinds, using Vasari's theor-etical rationalism as a foil.[21] The only way to make the Renaissance interesting, it seems, is to discount the testimony of its leading spokesmen. We reject Alberti and Vasari, and persuade ourselves that we are being original and critical when we do so, yet the Renaissance we end up with is one to which our commonplace modernist assumptions have disposed us all along.

Although the emergence of an idea of art documents a trans-formation in the social function of art and thus an important social-historical event, most social-historical approaches to art have treated it even more dismissively than have Belting and his followers. The concern to show how social and economic conditions directly affect the production and consumption of art has led to an emphasis on patronage,[22] material culture,[23] and gender.[24] These avenues of research began as critical efforts to remove art from the pedestal of traditional aesthetic interest and return it to the ebb and flow of political, social, and economic life. Their contribution has been enormous but, at the same time, subtly limited: they excel at showing how specific works of art make reference to specific social circumstances, they even show how art contributes to social life in a deeper, more indirect way, by engaging the system of signs and values we call "ideology", but they ignore the still deeper way in which, in Renaissance Italy, art was discovered to work, and thus fall short of offering an adequate account of the period's distinctive art-historical achievement.

Indeed, social-historical approaches have in some ways betrayed their original critical purpose: patronage and material culture studies, for instance, have wound up simply supplanting the traditional artist-centered account with a patron- or consumer-centered one. They turn out to have functioned as a stand-in for—a kind of inoculation against—more probing forms of social-historical analysis. Like positivism and Romantic irrationalism, they are not so much a mode of inquiry as of self-justification; specifically, they are an apology for the modern bourgeios mode of engagement with art. Gender studies too, while having helped to "enlarge the canon", have lost much of their critical edge: they often seem to fight shy of a deeper, more comprehensive approach to issues such as the ways in which art contributes to the constitution of subjectivity; they thus often seem like a stand-in for a more serious mode of inquiry.[25]

Some social-historical approaches go further still, impugning the value of the very category "art". Again, this trend may originally have had a laudable critical intention—to question the distinction between "high" art and visual imagery or craft activity of a less exalted kind,[26] to interrogate the traditional standards of value that privileged, say, central Italian art over the art of northern Italy,[27] or Italian art generally over the art of Northern Europe,[28] or even European art over non-European art[29]—but it has also gone from being critical to being formulaic. The enlargement of the canon has not been matched by a corresponding development in analytical depth. Among other things, it has suppressed the process by which certain representational strategies were explored, only to be discarded or relegated to subordinate status in favor of others: this process is an important part of the historicity of art, central to the *critical* work art does, and essential to the achievement of the Italian Renaissance. We should not be surprised that the tendency to suppress the category "art" has had a particularly debilitating effect on the study of Italian Renaissance art: it only demonstrates how essentially our notion of art is bound up with an idea developed in the Renaissance, how deeply the category "art" is linked to the achievement of this specific time and place.

This criticism of social-historical approaches is not intended to imply that the history of art can be anything other than social-historical, only that the time has come for a social history that does not oversimplify, that makes room for the full range and depth of the ways in which art works, and that is capable of accepting the fact that the idea of art, rarified as it might seem, is a profoundly important social-historical achievement. Something more—something deeper—is going on in Italian Renaissance art than either the older tradition of scholarship was disposed to articulate or that much of the most recent work is disposed to address. To define that something more clearly is to set the study of Renaissance art back on a critical track more appropriate to the critical sophistication of its object.

* * *

If the development of an idea of art documents a transformation in art's social function, then it is essential to the historical development of Renaissance art and must play an important role in any account of it we might want to fashion, particularly that best possible account to which we aspire. This idea of art is most explicitly documented in the theoretical writings of the period, but only documented: that is, theory articulates it—and in a variety of ways—but does not offer a necessarily accurate, still less, complete, description of all the ways it manifests itself in practice. Theory can thus be said to represent the idea of art in idealized form: it does not necessarily explain practice, but reveals something about what was felt to be at stake in practice.

Renaissance theory defines art as a form of knowledge. At the simplest level, art is said to involve a mastery of various specific techniques and skills, but at the most ambitious, it is described as a superintendency of all techniques and skills, an implicit comprehensive grasp of all modes of knowing.[30] Renaissance theorists tend to emphasize the relation of art to speculative knowledge, the highest type of knowledge, but it is important to note that any attempt to connect making to knowing necessarily implies doing: the absolute knowledge envisioned by the theorists thus also involves the principles of action, of human conduct, and implies an ideal disposition toward the world, an ideal mode of being; indeed, in ideal form it comprehends all modes of being in their ideal interrelation. We modern readers balk at such knowledge claims, especially when pushed to grandiose extremes, and tend to dismiss them entirely, but we should also recognize them as idealized expressions of something deeper: the relation of art to action can be said to express a sense of its relation to labor; its relation to knowledge a sense that in order to fulfill its real potential, its real social function, art must engage complex mental processes, the kind of abstract, discursive processes that life in complex culture requires. We might say that the theoretical emphasis on knowledge and, specifically, the superintendency of knowledge, is an idealized expression of the conviction that art is a means of engaging, integrating, and critically relating all possible representations, that the function of art is to superintend the fundamental faculty of representation.

Representation might be defined as the capacity of the mind to form what we commonly call ideas: these can be eidetic perceptions of the external world, but also abstract thoughts of all kinds, and all possible imaginings. While suggesting a single label for these different things may seem to court confusion, their interdependence is a fact of lived experience; to insist upon it is to insist upon a crucial aspect of their historical reality. At the same time, representation can be seen in a whole series of practices: in language, but also in things like social behavior or dress, as well as in collective activities such as rituals. Again, the superimposition of these various categories corresponds to the way they are lived, and to insist on the fluidity, the interpenetrability of the mental and the social enables us to relate "inner" and "outer", "private" and "public", "subjective" and "object-ive" experience to one another in a way that is necessary for the work of historical interpretation. To insist that representation should be understood as a principle that connects the individual imagination to social practice, the "subjective" to the "objective" world, is thus not an arbitrary gesture, but one that enables us to grasp a real historical phenomenon.

In the Renaissance, internal forms of representation—ideas—were generally understood to precede and then to impose themselves upon the external world. This model may strike us as too simple or idealistic, but again, we should recognize it as revealing something deeper: a sensitivity to the strict interdependence of internal and external, to the way in which representation creates a reciprocal rela-tionship between subject and object, self and society. We might say that representation is thus recognized to constitute culture: not that culture cannot be defined in other ways, or that it did not exist prior to the Renaissance, but that it now involved both a distinctive sense of the self as a social construct and the objective order of society as responsible to the needs of individuals. The real disposition of power is thus overlaid with an ideal reciprocity and made subject to poten-tial reconfiguration. Representation harnesses the internal resources of individuals to the larger order of society but it also enables indi-viduals to conceive alternatives to that order. The Renaissance recog-nition of this mechanism anticipates modern conceptions of the workings of ideology even as it saves a place for the liberatory power of ideas.

The new conception of art that emerges in the Renaissance is directly related to this new sense of the significance of representation: art is redefined as a principle that superintends representation, both as a mental faculty and a social practice. Art can involve more than representation, of course—a building shelters its inhabitants in add-ition to representing the idea of shelter, or solidity, or nobility, or any of the other things a building might represent—but because repre-sentation is understood to play such an important social role, an urgent need develops to explore its properties and possibilities and to assess their relative value: art absorbs this task, comes to be identified with it, and is eventually redefined by it; art is thus reconstituted as a *critical* superintendency of representation. The idea of art is not an idealistic superfluity, but a critical tool forged in urgent response to powerful social pressures.

In proceeding to clarify the significance of this hypothesis, we should remember that the social dimension of representation has already been abundantly recognized in contemporary cultural-historical scholarship, especially in the body of work—devoted mostly to English literature of the Elizabethan period—commonly called "new historicism". These studies have shown how crucial a matter representation was, how the complex forms encountered in literature and art are direct extensions of social practices necessary to survival and advancement in a complex culture. Perhaps the best attempt to develop a new historicist orientation in connection with Italian art is Campbell's study of Tura, already mentioned.[31] Campbell sees Tura's peculiar style as a highly self-conscious construct that the artist uses to position himself intellectually and socially. At the same time, this strategy is riddled with a sense of the inadequate, "ambiguous", or "fallen" quality of pictorial artifice, an ambivalence that will subsequently be lost in the High Renaissance.[32]

While such subtlety and complexity are certainly possible in the art of the period, and constitute innovative explorations of the limits of expression, the case that needs to be made is that Italian Renaissance art is motivated by an even deeper, more self-conscious representational strategy than new historicism recognizes. Italian art does not just employ opportunistic forms of representation, but is guided by a comprehensive effort to determine the best possible form of representation, that is, to survey all possible forms and to deduce from within that array the best possible options. That art should take on such responsibility is an indication of the awareness that any individual representation exists in relation to other representations and works within a system of representations, that *systematicity* is one of the crucial conditions of representation. Anticipating the modern insight that there is no necessary or natural relation between signs and things, Renaissance artists and thinkers understood the relation between signs and things to be potentially infinite; they realized that any attempt to determine the best possible relation must involve an engagement with the systematicity of representation.

To insist upon this point is to say something significantly different about the social function of art than is said by new historicism. Instead of emphasizing the casual, improvisational quality of art, its direct relation to everyday representational practices—an emphasis that ultimately plays back into the traditional naturalistic account of the Renaissance—the interpretation advanced here suggests that Italian Renaissance art is structured by the assumption that *what is properly artistic is a concern with the specifically systematic features of representation*. This emphasis could be said to reflect a sense that representation sets human beings in a distinctively, complexly attenuated relation to nature: the deepest impulse at work in Renaissance art is thus not so much a reverence for nature as an emerging sense of our independence of nature, and a need to reckon with the implications—both liberating and frightening—of that condition. This engagement with the particular challenge posed by the systematicity of representation is crucial to the distinctive historical achievement of Italian Renaissance art, and thus crucial to the kind of historical account it requires.

While the word "systematicity" is abstract and awkward-sounding, its great virtue is that it allows us to defer the question of whether or to what degree representation actually *is* systematic and to leave it to linguists, semioticians, or philosophers of mind. The order or structure or inner logic to which the idea of systematicity refers may reveal itself in many ways; it may be present in different, superimposed ways even within the same work of art. It is something we respond to intuitively when we experience particular works of art, manifest in our sense of "rightness", our feeling that a consistent principle of some kind governs the treatment of details, that the appearance of all the parts has been shaped, as it were, by a consistent sort of pressure. Such a feeling depends upon an awareness, however unconscious, of something having been withheld or suppressed: much as a self-evident visual abundance may seem to be what most affects us, what is *not* represented is also essential to our experience. What is absent is present, and the meaning of the whole resides as much in what we cannot see as in what we can.

One way in which the sense of the systematicity of representation reveals itself in practice is in the importance attached to perspective from the beginning of the fifteenth-century. Perspective offered artists a means of creating plausible illusions of three dimensional space on two dimensional surfaces; its appeal lay not only in its apparent fidelity to natural appearances and optical experience, but in its consistency. Perspective establishes a system, a pictorial economy in which every detail is dependent upon the overall structure, in which the representation of any individual thing is responsible to, conditioned by, the structure as a whole. No detail exists in isolation and the ability to represent any one thing correctly depends upon the ability to represent everything else correctly. Perspective emphasizes the radically contingent or conditional nature of visual perception and representation, yet, at the same time, as a means of organizing any possible contingency, it comprehends all contingency within a larger order.

For Leonardo, perspective is simply one aspect of the systematicity of painting: it provides a conceptual armature onto which one can add an understanding of light and shade, atmosphere, anatomy, human expression, indeed, all one's knowledge of the world. As perspective is to painting, so is painting to the world as a whole: the perfect integrative instrument for all knowledge, a means for expressing a comprehensive—systematic—understanding of nature. The demands of consistency are even greater than for Alberti: all aspects of a picture, including the treatment of color, are as deeply interdependent as those elements governed by perspective. Painting thus becomes an even more comprehensive, and, as a result, more self-reflexive, more critical activity.

The importance attached to style is another way in which art registers the systematicity of representation. Style can be understood as something determined by a set of objective formulae—as in the low, middle, and high styles of ancient rhetoric—or as particular to an individual artist and indicative of a unique subjective disposition. Either way, it involves a consistency of treatment, a principle or set of principles governing the various features of a work, and it can be as rigorous in its own way as perspective or any of the scientific requirements so important to Leonardo. Style can also be understood as a principle which shapes individual details in obedience to an overarching order; our responsiveness to it and our recognition of it as a positive quality have to do with our awareness of the selectivity it involves, our sense that the choice of what to represent and what not to represent has been governed by a principled, even if intuitive, process.

Since styles vary, style too involves radical contingency. Consciousness of the diversity of possible styles leads to efforts to combine the best features of different ones, even to see them in systematic relation to one another, as collectively mapping some larger field of representational possibilities. An important part of Raphael's achievement was the way in which he seemed to fuse the outstanding features of the styles of his older contemporaries,[33] and his example was followed in more systematic fashion by the Carracci and all later academic painters.[34] When Paolo Pino says that the ideal picture would be an Adam and Eve in which the Adam was painted by Michelangelo and the Eve by Titian,[35] and when Lomazzo then goes further to say that his ideal picture would feature an Adam drawn by Michelangelo but painted by Titian, and an Eve drawn by Raphael but painted by Correggio,[36] they are documenting a deepening awareness of the systematicity of representation. Consciousness of the diversity of individual and regional styles, and of stylistic change over time leads to a sense of historical development: Vasari's organization of stylistic diversity accomplishes much the same mapping of possibilities—the same articulation of systematicity—as does Lomazzo's schematic one.

The systematicity of representation is revealed in another, perhaps deeper, more significant way, in the preoccupation with decorum, a principle that operates on a number of different levels and that becomes more important as the sensitivity to the social function of art becomes more widespread and profound. We moderns have a hard time thinking of decorum as anything but a noxious constraint on artistic freedom, the principle which requires art to follow social norms, to reinforce myths, the principle of censorship; yet Renaissance artists and theorists seem to have regarded it in largely positive terms: decorum is what enabled an artist to clothe his or her ideas with greater apparent correctness, and thus to give them greater authority and efficacy. It is what permits art to engage social codes systematically and thus to enter into sophisticated social discourse; it is as much a source of power as a constraint.

The most conspicuous manifestation of decorum is the characterization of figure types: following the principles of ancient rhetoric and poetics, theorists beginning with Alberti insisted that figures conform to the historical personalities they represent or the stories they illustrate, and that they also be consistent with the general "laws" of human nature. Decorum is thus the principle that governs the relation of objects in an image to objects in the world, but because it extends to the way in which a work as a whole relates to its setting and functional context, it also governs the order of the image as a whole to the order of the world as a whole. Decorum establishes a consistent—systematic—relation between representation and reality: it is what allows the order of the world and the order of art to enter into each other in a process of reciprocal correction.

Decorum acknowledges the radically contingent or conditional nature of representation, the fact that the way any object in a picture or any picture as a whole appears will depend on an array of specific factors. Yet it too sets that contingency within a larger systematicity, an order within which the accidental is made to seem inevitable, the particular made to seem universal. In this respect it is also like perspective: the appearance of objects in a picture is conditioned by social codes in the same way that perspective conditions them according to optical rules. Decorum, we might say, is cultural perspective. As viewers, our understanding of the larger order may not be explicit, but our apparently instinctive sense of "rightness" or "wrongness" could be said to "prove" the existence of a larger order, the larger systematicity of representation. Our sense, when we look at an image, that the key has been found, not only to representing a particular thing the right way in a particular context, but of relating representation as a whole to reality as a whole in the best possible way, is an effect that art must now strive to achieve, that is essential to the work it now sets itself to do.

One of the most revealing manifestations of the systematicity of representation, closely related to style and decorum, is the idea of the hierarchy of the genres. Also derived from ancient literary theory, it emerges in connection with the visual arts in fifteenth- and sixteenth-century Italy and achieves more hieratic formulation in French academic theory of the seventeenth century. It is already evident in Alberti's treatise on architecture, where certain types of pictures are said to be appropriate to certain settings.[37] Leonardo distinguishes between artists who excel at portraits and those who excel at history painting,[38] a distinction that would be elaborated by a later theorist, Vincenzo Danti, in terms or *ritrarre* and *imitare*.[39] G.B. Armenini and Federico Zuccaro discuss complementary modes of decoration.[40] Counter-reformation writers—Gilio, Paleotti, Molanus, Comanini—were also concerned to distinguish pictorial modes.[41] Lomazzo provides an ambitious inventory of pictures types.[42] All these theories, different as they are, testify to the systematicity of representation, to the sense that representation is structured in depth, so to speak, as well as in breadth.

The theoretical ideal of a hierarchal order among the genres may seem to exist in unclear relation to the facts of their historical development and proliferation. Portraiture, for instance, emerged independently of any explicit theoretical system, and its continued practice was surely not dependent on any theoretical rationalization. The proliferation of genres in the sixteenth and seventeenth centuries seems to have been driven by the market, by fashions and the desires of patrons rather than by theoretical necessity. Yet just because a genre like portraiture might have an independent historical origin does not mean that its subsequent development is not conditioned by its absorption into a theoretical system, and that as the self-consciousness of artists and patrons grows, it becomes necessary to rethink the aims and nature of portraiture with respect to the possibilities of representation as a whole. Such a process in fact explains many of the innovations in Italian portraiture in the decades around 1500. The ramification and proliferation of the various genres in the subsequent generations, governed by a similar self-consciousness, might thus be said to document a real-life—"organic" —rationalization parallel to that found in theory.

Because the subordinate genres were cultivated with particular skill by Northern European artists, and those genres emerged in the nineteenth century as instruments of the great transformation of art-istic values associated with modernism, there has been a tendency to see Northern art as more progressive, as possessed not only of a distinctive visual poetics, but of a distinctly more modern approach to the world.[43] An implication of the hypothesis being advanced here, however, is that the development of the genres in Northern Europe takes place within the larger systematicity of representation already excavated, as it were, by Italian art. What is modern is not the proliferation of the genres but the system within which or in relation to which they work, not the apparent freedom but the hidden order.

The concept of *disegno* is yet another expression of the systematicity of representation. Elaborating upon older ideas, Vasari defined it as a principle that unites the visual arts of painting, sculpture, and architecture and establishes their relation, as a group, to other crafts, professions, and fields of knowledge. Later theorists defined it in even more comprehensive and exalted terms. The idea that all forms of visual expression are manifestations of a single principle reveals something of the rationalism implicit in the concern with systematicity, yet it also suggests how that rationalism is motivated by a sense of the dynamic quality of representation. Systematicity is not just manifest in static arrangements or hierarchies, but in a faculty or power that operates in an organized way: the important thing is not the necessity or truth content of particular signs, but the force that makes signs, remakes them, and unmakes them. The significance attached to *disegno* documents the awareness that the faculty of representation—understood as a dynamic force—is what actively creates and sustains the order of things. And because it is never entirely present in a single work of art, yet evident in every detail, *disegno* offers another expression of the sense that the meaning of images is fundamentally dependent upon what they do not contain. In pointing beyond individual images, so to speak, it thus indicates the larger systematicity in which images participate.

The idea of art developed in Renaissance Italy is thus not an idle theoretical dream, but manifest in all sorts of ways in practice, in the details of individual works and the overarching developmental trajectory of art as a whole. It emerged in response both to a new sense of the social importance of representation and to a deepening awareness of how representation works. That artists were preoccupied with the systematicity of representation in particular is an indication of their intellectual sophistication and ambition, their sense that a more complex time called for art of a more complex kind. We need not assume that their motives were especially high-minded: their principal concern, after all, was to make better, more effective illusions. They realized, however, that within the knowledge necessary to create the best possible illusions is also the capacity to recognize and express the truth. In defining their task the way they did, they defined art as a critical activity; they can thus be said to have invented a distinctly modern idea of art. Despite all the ways things have changed in the intervening centuries, that idea still conditions our expectations of what art should do.

*   *   *

If an engagement with the systematicity of representation is what makes Renaissance art modern, then what of that systematicity survives in artistic modernism? At first sight, modernism would seem to have rejected the idea of systematicity: during the nineteenth century, it slowly dismantled the theoretical edifice so carefully refined by the academies, playing havoc with decorum and overturning the hierarchy of the genres. In place of a system of art expressible in codifiable rules, it seemed to want to liberate art from rule.

The answer is that modern art, though apparently a rejection of systematicity, in fact involves another form of systematicity: it does not represent the liberation of art so much as its subordination to a new, more complex set of rules. We might not want to define art in terms of knowledge as was done in the Renaissance, but art still requires knowledge, and of a comprehensive kind not altogether different from what was described in Renassiance theory. Instead of the formulae characteristic of older academic teaching, it engages unwritten, newly-emergent, and powerfully-sensed codes governing all the forces at work in our culture, from the function of images in particular to the general conditions of existence. Its choices are determined by a comprehensive, if often intuitively-directed awareness of available strategies and their viability in particular contexts; its critique of system involves a meta-systematicity that can be understood as an extension, rather than a rejection, of Renaissance ideas regarding the conditions of representation and the role of art.

When Emile Zola undertook to defend and explain the work of Manet, for instance, he claimed that the painter had sought to liberate himself from traditional representational conventions, "to forget everything he had learned in the museums".[44] Yet Manet never forgot older pictorial conventions and engaged them with extraordinary sophistication: his pictures deploy codes in order to undermine them; they critique earlier painting by insisting that even the aspiration to pure realism is dependent on codes; they thus expose the fact that all representation consists of codes. Manet violates traditional expectations, including old notions of decorum, but exposes a new decorum, built on the new terms and conditions of representation and its place in modern life. He adheres to a logic as rigorously as any academic painter, even if it is not a codified logic. The systematicity of his work lies partly in its capacity to serve as a model for subsequent artistic practice.

Early twentieth-century modernism is also much engaged with systematicity: Cubism involves a further rigorous exploration of the conditions governing representation; it too exposes the arbitrary and conventional nature of old devices, redeploying them within a larger array of representational strategies, discovering new possibilities and proposing structural relations among them. D.H. Kahnweiler's claim that the Cubists discovered the resemblance of pictorial representation to "script"—that is, the relation of painting to writing, of art to language[45]—emphasizes their concern with a theme of great importance in the Renaissance, as well as the way in which they anticipated the insights of modern linguistic theory and semiotics. Though famously averse to rationalism of the common kind, Picasso gave striking expression to his sense of the underlying logic of his own practice when he said that he thought of a picture as "a sum of destructions."[46] His remark distills into pure form the Renaissance sense of images being crucially constituted by what they exclude.

Some early twentieth-century modernists were motivated by theoretical principles that explicitly engage the idea of systematicity. Kandinsky conceived of painting as a universal language of expression, and sought, by careful, systematic research to determine the conditions of the best—most direct, most powerful, most articulate—form of expression.[47] Mondrian understood artistic modernism as an historical process that led from the representation of particular forms to the representation of relations between forms and finally to the representation of pure relations, to the dissolution—or as he preferred, like Picasso, to say, "destruction"—of particular form, the revelation of a deeper truth beyond the reach of particular utterances.[48] For Mondrian, the movement toward increasing abstraction, itself driven by an internal logic, is indicative of our increasingly attenuated relation to nature, of the way in which art must step up to assume the regulatory function that nature, on its own, can no longer provide.

Dada might be said to empty the art object of its transcendental value, of its claim to special status by virtue of its specific properties as an object, and to demand from the viewer an even greater attentiveness to the network of conceptual, institutional, and cultural factors that define art: it displaces the interest of art onto the system lying invisibly around it, insisting that art-making is not an innocent act, but conditioned by the cultural context in which it occurs.[49] Surrealism sought nothing less than to break down the separation between art and life, to redefine the aims and methods of art in the most ambitious imaginable terms, and thus to become a comprehensive liberatory practice. While its cultivation of the irrational might seem to repudiate the idea of systematicity, the irrational is made to serve a calculated therapeutic function, to purge reason and thus help to restore the lost fullness of human life.[50]

Some forms of conceptual art are intensively concerned with systematicity: among the artists whose work comes immediately to mind are Sol Lewitt, Joseph Kosuth, and the Art and Language group.[51] Even if conceptualism empties system of its authority, its pretence to embody order, it indicates the ubiquity of system. Much of the artistic postmodernism of the years around 1980 contends with representation in its reified forms, that is, with mass-culture imagery; it seeks to expose the ways in which images are implicated in an invisible system—social, economic, semiotic—and thus to illuminate critically the preconditions of representation.[52]

Such an overview is hardly a comprehensive account of artistic modernism; its purpose is merely to suggest the need for a serious consideration of the ways in which the systematicity of representation continues to concern us.[53] This is not to say that the differences between Renaissance and modern art are unimportant, only that there is a continuity of enterprise beneath the apparent dissimilarities. The Renaissance preoccupation with systematicity turns out to have been a first and crucial step toward artistic modernism; engaging the systematicity of representation was a way of confronting a critical challenge that art must still address. Like all those approaches inventoried at the beginning of this essay, the interpretation proposed here is thus resolutely modernist, but it attempts to undo some of the modernist misconceptions that prevent us from seeing the past more clearly. In reclaiming the modernity of Renaissance art in a new way, it challenges us to see our own modernity in a new way. To break our choke-hold on the Renaissance is also to liberate ourselves.

There will be resistance to seeing the Renaissance in the way proposed here. It may be that our fundamental investment in a sentimental—and hypocritical—irrationalism is too deep, that such irrationalism serves a cathartic function too important in contemporary life. It may be that the object-oriented nature of most art historical scholarship—which is largely a disguised form of bourgeios consumerism—is also too pervasive and deeply ingrained. The need to continue with business as usual may be too strong. Indeed, it may be that we are no longer able to reckon with the intellectual ambition, depth, and concentration of Italian Renaissance art, and can only adopt approaches that on some level refuse to address it, that can only ever yield incidental insights. The best possible approach, on the other hand, the approach which the Renaissance demands, must risk disturbing our preconceptions and unacknowledged investments; it must be critical in the way that Renaissance art itself is critical.

Notes

*   This essay has been slightly modified since its original appearance in *Rinascimento* 43 (2004) 309–31

1.   See, for example, his *Art and Illusion: A Study in the Psychology of Pictorial Representation* (Princeton, 1972; orig. ed. 1960); the essays on Leonardo and "The Leaven of Criticism in Renaissance Art: Texts and Episodes," in *The Heritage of Apelles: Studies in the Art of the Renaissance* (Ithaca, 1976).

2.   *Leonardo da Vinci: The Marvellous Works of Nature and Man* (Cambridge, MA, 1981); *The Science of Art: Optical Themes in Western Art from Brunelleschi to Seurat* (New Haven, 1990).

3. *The Judgment of Sense: Renaissance Naturalism and the Rise of Aesthetics* (Cambridge, 1987); *Real Spaces: World Art History and the Rise of Western Modernism* (London, 2003).

4. This trend has been stimulated by the rapid growth of the history of science as an academic discipline. An influential study of scientific thought in Italy is P. Findlen, *Possessing Nature: Museums, Collecting, and Scientific Culture in Early Modern Italy* (Berkeley, 1994). Studies that set early modern art in relation to scientific developments include: H. Bredekamp, *The Lure of Antiquity and the Cult of the Machine: The Kunstkammer and the Evolution of Nature, Art, and Technology*, A. Brown, trans. (Princeton, 1995); D. Freedberg, *The Eye of the Lynx: Galileo, His Friends, and the Beginnings of Modern Natural History* (Chicago, 2002); and the exhibition catalogue *Iconoclash: Beyond the Image Wars in Science, Religion, and Art*, B. Latour & P. Weibel, eds. (Cambridge, MA, 2002).

5. *Classic Art: An Introduction to the Italian Renaissance* (London, 1952; orig. ed. 1899).

6. Exemplary instances of Panofsky's emphasis on Neoplatonism include *Idea: A Concept in Art Theory*, J. Peake, trans. (New York, 1968; orig. ed., 1924), and the concluding essays in *Studies in Iconology: Humanistic Themes in the Art of the Renaissance* (New York, 1972; orig. ed. 1939).

7. For Gombrich's attack on idealism, see especially the opening pages of *Art and Illusion* (as in n. 1), a position modified in his later *In Search of Cultural History* (Oxford, 1969), and *Tributes: Interpreters of Our Cultural Tradition* (Ithaca, 1985) esp. pp. 51–69. Especially revealing of the limitations of his approach is the essay "Ideal and Type in Italian Renaissance Painting", *New Light on Old Masters: Studies in the Art of the Renaissance IV* (Chicago, 1986) 89–124, in which he argues that idealism in art is simply a reversion to pre-existent schemata.

8. "On Beautiful Women: Parmigianino, Petrarchismo, and the Vernacular Style," *Art Bulletin* 58 (1976) 374–94; "The Beauty of Woman: Problems in the Rhetoric of Renaissance Portraiture," *Rewriting the Renaissance: Discourses of Sexual Difference in Early Modern Europe*, M.W. Ferguson, et al., eds. (Chicago, 1986) 175–90; and esp. "The Place of Beauty in High Renaissance Art and its Displacement in the History of Art", *Place and Displacement in the Renaissance*, A. Vos, ed. (Binghamton, 1995) 159–205.

9. *Ut Pictura Poesis: The Humanistic Theory of Painting* (New York, 1967; orig. ed. 1940).

10. *Annibale Carracci and the Beginnings of Baroque Style* (Glückstadt, 1977); *The Portrayal of Love: Botticelli's "Primavera" and Humanistic Culture at the Time of Lorenzo the Magnificent* (Princeton, 1992).

11. *Giotto and the Orators: Humanistic Observers of Painting in Italy and the Discovery of Pictorial Composition, 1350–1450* (Oxford, 1971).

12. The leading advocate of this position has been C. Hope. See, for example, his "Artists, Patrons, and Advisers in the Italian Renaissance," *Patronage in the Renaissance*, G.F. Lytle & S. Orgel, eds. (Princeton, 1982) 293–343; "Aspects of Criticism in Art and Literature in Sixteenth-Century Italy", *Word and Image* 4 (1988) 1–10; and, with E. McGrath, "Artists and

Humanists", *Cambridge Companion to Renaissance Humanism*, J. Kraye, ed. (Cambridge, 1996) 161–88.

13. See, for instance, C. Hulse, *The Rule of Art: Literature and Painting in the Renaissance* (Chicago, 1990) esp. p. 19: "Each gesture, each act of linkage between the arts, or between artistic theory and practice, is also a gesture from within toward cultural totality. Hence each local and individual union of artistic products, social practice, and conceptual modes . . . has hidden somewhere within it a dream of cultural synthesis that is paradigmatic for the totalizing impulses within Renaissance culture generally."

14. See, for instance, W.J.T. Mitchell, *Picture Theory: Essays on Verbal and Visual Representation* (Chicago, 1994); M.A. Holly, *Past Looking: Historical Imagination and the Rhetoric of the Image* (Ithaca, 1996); J. Elkins, *On Pictures and the Words that Fail Them* (Cambridge, 1998). For a critique of this position, see the review of Elkins in *Oxford Art Journal* 25 (2002) 97–102.

15. Recent treatments of this theme include E. Barker, et al., *The Changing Status of the Artist* (New Haven, 1999); and F. Ames-Lewis, *The Intellectual Life of the Early Renaissance Artist* (New Haven, 2000). An account that stresses the importance of gender is F. Jacobs, *Defining the Renaissance "Virtuosa"* (Cambridge, 1997).

16. *Likeness and Presence: A History of the Image before the Era of Art*, E. Jephcott, trans., Chicago, 1994; *The Invisible Masterpiece*, H. Atkins., trans. (Chicago, 2001).

17. *Fra Angelico: Dissemblance and Figuration*, J.M. Todd, trans. (Chicago, 1995).

18. *The Religious Art of Jacopo Bassano: Painting as Visual Exegesis* (Cambridge, 1997).

19. *Michelangelo and the Reform of Art* (Cambridge, 2001).

20. *Cosmè Tura of Ferrara: Style, Politics, and the Renaissance City, 1450–1495* (New Haven, 1997) esp. pp. 13–14, 70.

21. *Cellini and the Principles of Sculpture* (Cambridge, 2002). Hostility toward Vasari is even more pervasive these days than hostility toward Alberti, and is found at all levels of sophistication, from serious scholarly attempts to reckon with his limitations, as in E. Pilliod, *Pontormo, Bronzino, and Allori: A Genealogy of Florentine Art* (New Haven, 2001); to simpleminded dogmatism, as in N. Solomon, "The Art Historical Canon: Sins of Omission," *The Art of Art History: A Critical Anthology*, D. Preziosi, ed. (Oxford, 1998) 344–55.

22. Influential early studies of patronage include E.H. Gombrich, "The Early Medici as Patrons of the Arts," *Norm and Form: Studies in the Art of the Renaissance* (London, 1966; orig. ed. of essay 1960); and F. Haskell, *Patrons and Paintings: A Study in the Relation between Italian Art and Society in the Age of the Baroque* (New Haven, 1980; orig. ed., 1963). Later overviews include B. Kempers, *Painting, Power, and Patronage: The Rise of the Professional Artist in the Italian Renaissance*, B. Jackson, trans. (London, 1994); M. Hollingsworth, *Patronage in Renaissance Italy from 1400 to the Early Sixteenth Century* (London, 1994); and the same author's *Patronage in Sixteenth-Century Italy* (London, 1996). See also C. King, *Renaissance*

Women Patrons: Wives and Widows in Italy, c. 1300–1500 (Manchester, 1998).

23. Important for this trend has been the work of the economic historian R. Goldthwaite, such as *Wealth and the Demand for Art in Italy, 1300–1600* (Baltimore, 1993). L. Jardine, *Wordly Goods: A New History of the Renaissance* (New York, 1997) gives a memorable indication of the motives behind it when she describes Carlo Crivelli's *Annunciation* in the National Gallery, London, as "a celebration of conspicuous consumption" and likens it to "a modern mail order catalogue" (p. 9). An outstanding attempt to present an overview of Renaisance art from the perspective of material culture studies is E. Welch, *Art in Renaissance Italy, 1350–1500* (Oxford, 1997).

24. A study influential in the promotion of this trend was J. Kelly-Gadol, "Did Women Have a Renaissance?" *Becoming Visible: Women in European History*, R. Bridenthal & C. Koone, eds. (Boston, 1977) 137–64. Among the most important studies by art historians are: P. Simons, "Women in Frames: The Gaze, the Eye, the Profile in Renaissance Portraiture," *The Expanding Discourse: Feminism ad Art History*, N. Broude & M. Garrard, eds. (New York, 1992; orig. ed. of essay 1988) 59–86; "Portraiture, Portrayal, and Idealization: Ambiguous Individualism in Representations of Renaissance Women," *Languages and Images of Renaissance Italy*, A. Brown, ed. (Oxford, 1995) 263–312; Cropper (as in n. 8); Jacobs (as in n. 15); P. Tinagli, *Women in Italian Renaissance Art: Gender, Representation, Identity* (New York, 1997); R. Goffen, *Titian's Women* (New Haven, 1997); King (as in n. 22). Representative anthologies include *Picturing Women in Renaissance and Baroque Italy*, G. Johnson & S. Grieco, eds. (Cambridge, 1997); and *Women in Italian Renaissance Culture and Society* (Oxford, 2000).

25. Perhaps the most sophisticated and ambitious thesis about the role of gender in Renaissance art has been advanced by Cropper in "The Place of Beauty" (as in n. 8). Her idea is that beauty was what—even in the minds of Renaissance observers like Vasari—distinguished High Renaissance achievements from earlier art; that it was gendered, and that art itself was thus gendered. This argument comes close to the claim found in modern feminist theory dependent on Lacan that gender is fundamental to representation, that the category "woman" is an essential effect or "symptom" of representation. Yet while Cropper's essay contains an important insight, it is not persuasive as a comprehensive explanation of High Renaissance art: there is plenty of evidence against the specific kind of gendering she emphasizes, so that what she takes to be the principal motive can only be secondary, an effect rather than a cause. In a recent book, A. Randolph, *Engaging Symbols: Gender, Politics, and Public Art in Fifteenth-Century Florence* (New Haven, 2002) argues that gender figured centrally in fifteenth-century Florentine viewers' responses to art, but also avoids the kinds of evidence that would set the phenomenon in a larger context. Interesting and valuable as these studies are, they thus also expose the limits of current gender-based approaches.

26. Evident, for example, in recent work on the "minor" art of printmaking:

P. Emison, "Prolegomenon to the Study of Italian Renaissance Prints", *Word and Image* 11 (1995) 1–15; also her *Low and High Style in Italian Renaissance Art* (New York, 1997); B. Talvacchia, *Taking Positions: On the Erotic in Renaissance Culture* (Princeton, 1999); E. Lincoln, *The Invention of the Italian Renaissance Printmaker* (New Haven, 2000).

27. Evident—again, at a very sophisticated level—in Campbell (as in n. 20), who discusses the "symbolic domination" of central Italian art in the scholarly tradition (p. 3). The concept of symbolic domination is borrowed from E. Castelnuovo & C. Ginzburg, "Centro e periferia," *Storia dell'arte italiana*, G. Previtali, ed. (Torino, 1979) vol. 1, 285–352.

28. S. Alpers, *The Art of Describing: Dutch Art of the Seventeenth Century* (Chicago, 1983) has claimed that traditional art history, dependent on paradigms derived from the study of Italian art, failed to appreciate the real significance of Northern European art. The influence of this argument on the study of Italian art is evident in Emison, *Low and High Style* (as in n. 26), where an effort is made to rehabilitate Italian art essentially by demonstrating its resemblance to Northern European art as described by Alpers and her followers. For a more detailed critique of Emison's position, see the review in *Art Bulletin* 82 (2000) 356–7.

29. For a discussion of this development, see the introduction to C. Farago, ed., *Reframing the Renaissance: Visual Culture in Europe and Latin America* (New Haven, 1995).

30. R. Williams, *Art, Theory, and Culture in Sixteenth-Century Italy: From Techne to Metatechne* (Cambridge, 1997).

31. Most attempts to apply new historicist techniques to the study of art have dealt with Northern European art. See, for example, the reading of Holbein's *Ambassadors* in the opening pages of S. Greenblatt, *Renaissance Self-Fashioning: From More to Shakespeare* (Chicago, 1980); and the study of Dürer and Baldung presented in J. Koerner, *The Moment of Self-Portraiture in German Renaissance Art* (Chicago, 1993).

32. Campbell (as in n. 20), esp. pp. 4, 12, 24, 38, 56, 93, 126, 129, 151, 158.

33. *Le Opere di Giorgio Vasari*, G. Milanesi, ed. (Florence, 1906) vol. 4, esp. pp. 373–9.

34. For a discussion of this issue in relation to the Carracci, see C. Dempsey (as in n. 10); also the same author's introduction to *Gli Scritti dei Carracci*, G. Perini, ed. (Bologna, 1990).

35. *Dialogo di pittura*, in *Trattati d'arte del Cinquecento*, P. Barocchi, ed. (Bari, 1960) vol. 1, 126–7.

36. *Idea del tempio della pittura*, R. Klein, ed. (Florence, 1974) vol. 1, p. 153.

37. *On the Art of Building in Ten Books*, J. Rykwert, et al., trans. (Cambridge MA, 1983) esp. pp. 244, 294, 299–300.

38. *The Literary Works of Leonardo da Vinci*, J.P. Richter, ed. (London, 1970; orig. ed. 1888) vol. 1, esp. pp. 94, 308.

39. *Trattato delle perfette proporzioni*, *Trattati d'arte del Cinquecento*, P. Barocchi, ed. (Bari, 1960) vol. 1, esp. p. 241.

40. *I Veri Precetti della pittura*, M. Gorreri, ed. (Turin, 1988), esp. pp. 169–70, 196–212; *Scritti d'arte di Federico Zuccaro*, D. Heikamp, ed. (Florence, 1961), esp. pp. 239–40. For a discussion of Armenini's ideas, see

R. Williams, "The Vocation of the Artist as seen by Giovanni Battista Armenini," *Art History* (1995) 518–36.

41. For Gilio, Paleotti, and Comanini, see *Trattati d'arte* (as in n. 35) vols. 2 & 3; see also Molanus, *Traité des saintes images*, F. Boespflug, et al., trans. (Paris, 1996). On the representational modes discussed by the theorists, see C. Dempsey, "Mythic Inventions in Counter-Reformation Painting", *Rome in the Renaissance: The City and the Myth*, P. Ramsey, ed. (Binghamton, 1982) 55–75. P. Jones, *Federico Borromeo and the Accademia: Art and Patronage in Seventeenth-Century Milan* (Cambridge, 1993); "Art Theory as Ideology: Gabriele Paleotti's Hierarchical Notion of Painting's Universality and Reception," *Reframing the Renaissance* (as in n. 29) 127–39.

42. *Trattato dell'arte de la pittura*, Milan, 1584 (repr. Hildesheim, 1968), book 6, 338–403.

43. This argument, which is in fact a recurrent motif in Northern European art-scholarship since the nineteenth century, has been revived in recent times by S. Alpers (as in. 28), and has been carried further by V. Stoichita, *The Self-Aware Image: An Insight into early Modern Meta-Painting*, A.-M. Gasheen, trans. (Cambridge, 1997); for whom a decisive break with Renaissance painting, and the emergence of a modern pictorial "self-awareness" occurs in the genre scenes of Aertsen and Beuckelaer. Leaving aside the fact that the reversal of foreground and background that Stoichita believes so epoch-making is found in earlier Italian painting—in Piero's *Flagellation*, for instance, even in Raphael's *Transfiguration*—the deeper objection to his thesis is that pictorial self-awareness can manifest itself in all sorts of other ways. How is the *School of Athens*, say, *not* a self-aware image? Leonardo's *Last Supper*? Masaccio's *Trinity*?

44. This passage from Zola's essay on Manet is cited in: C. Harrison, et al., eds., *Art in Theory, 1815–1900* (Malden, MA, 1998) 557. Authoritative studies of Manet's modernism include: T.J. Clark, *The Painting of Modern Life: Paris in the Art of Manet and his Friends* (Princeton, 1986); and M. Fried, *Manet's Modernism, or, The Face of Painting in the 1860's* (Chicago, 1996).

45. Cited and discussed in Y.-A. Bois, "Kahnweiler's Lesson", *Painting as Model* (Cambridge, MA, 1990) 65–97. See also R. Krauss. *The Picasso Papers* (New York, 1998).

46. Quoted in *Art in Theory: 1900–1990*, C. Harrison & P. Wood, eds. (Cambridge, MA 1992) 499.

47. W. Kandinsky, *The Complete Writings on Art*, K. Lindsay & P. Vergo, eds. (Boston, 1982).

48. *The New Art—The New Life: The Collected Writings of Piet Mondrian*, H. Holtzman & M. James, trans. & eds. (Boston, 1986); Y.-A. Bois, "The Iconoclast", *Piet Mondrian*, Y.-A. Bois, et al. (Boston, 1995) 313–72.

49. A recent consideration of dada's implications for traditional esthetics is T. De Duve, *Kant after Duchamp* (Cambridge, MA, 1996). Another perspective is offered by A. Danto, whose encounter with Warhol's work in the 1960's can be seen as a belated recognition by analytic philosophy of the implications of dada: "The Artworld," *Journal of Philosophy* 61 (1964) 571–84; also "Pop Art and Past Pictures," *Art After the End of Art: Contemporary Art and the Pale of History* (Princeton, 1995) 117–33.

50. Evidence of the Surrealists' concern with systematic procedure, with "research", is their establishment of the Bureau de Recherches Surréalistes at the very moment of their consolidation as a movement in 1924. The relation of Surrealism to ethnographic and sociological thought has been the focus of much recent study: *The College of Sociology (1937–39)*, D. Hollier, ed., D. Wing, trans. (Minneapolis, 1988); J. Clifford, *The Predicament of Culture: Twentieth-Century Ethnography, Literature, and Art* (Cambridge, MA 1988); H. Foster, *Compulsive Beauty* (Cambridge, MA 1993).

51. S. Lewitt, *Critical Texts*, A. Zevi, ed. (Rome, 1999); J. Kosuth, *Art after Philosophy and After: Collected Writings, 1966–1990*, G. Guercio, ed. (Cambridge, MA, 1991; C. Harrison, *Essays on Art and Language* (Oxford, 1991).

52. V. Burgin, *The End of Art Theory* (Atlantic Highlands, NJ, 1986).

53. Contemporary sociology has offered some indications of the ways such an inquiry might proceed. The most suggestive works include: P. Bourdieu, The Rules of Art: *Structure and Genesis of the Literary Field*, S. Emanuel, trans. (Stanford, 1996; orig. ed. 1992); N. Luhmann, *Art as a Social System*, E. Knodt. trans. (Stanford, 2000; orig. ed. 1995); A. Wellmer, *The Persistence of Modernity: Essays on Aesthetics, Ethics, and Postmodernism*, D. Midgley, trans. (Cambrdige MA, 1991), and, by the same author, *Endgames: The Irreconcilable Nature of Modernity*, D. Midgley, trans. (Cambridge MA, 1998).

THE ART SEMINAR 3

This conversation was held April 3, 2006, at the University College Cork, Ireland. The participants were: Stephen Campbell (The Johns Hopkins University), Michael Cole (University of Pennsylvania), James Elkins (University College Cork / School of the Art Institute of Chicago), Claire Farago (University of Colorado), Fredrika Jacobs (Virginia Commonwealth University), Ethan Matt Kavaler (University of Toronto), and Robert Williams (University of California at Santa Barbara).

James Elkins: Bob and I thought we would divide today's conversation into two topics. In this morning's session, we will be talking about sources of coherence or disarray within Renaissance studies; and in the afternoon we'll address the apparently larger topic of relations between Renaissance studies and studies of modernism and postmodernism—and especially the strange fact that the Renaissance seems at once tremendously important, pivotal, or indispensable in art history as a whole, and at the same time sunken into a kind of neglect or "oblivion," to use Leo Steinberg's term.

1

To start, then, with the apparently smaller—but in some ways much more difficult—issue of what might count as optimal ways of conceptualizing the Renaissance. I have an interest in observing, as an outsider, various specialties within art history, and I will risk conjuring some in order to suggest that specialties have their own "cultures," by which I mean their own *kinds* of disagreement, their own sources of harmony.

For example, fifteen or twenty years ago, seventeenth-century Dutch studies was riven by a controversy when Svetlana Alpers's *Art of Describing* challenged the field and the state of scholarship in an interesting way.[1] That book caused a division that was widely watched within art history—the question being, Should there be a new paradigm for ways of looking at seventeenth-century Dutch art, or should it follow the studies of emblemata and literary sources that were prevalent in Dutch scholarship?

Nineteenth-century French studies is another specialty that people tend to watch in order to see the state of art history in general; it is more or less filled with people who do social art history (for example Tim Clark and Tom Crow), but there are interesting exceptions to that. There is a new interest in gender studies (for example Darcy Grigsby's work), and there is also work that follows on from books written by Michael Fried; that work is more or less engaged with phenomenology, and so more or less opposed to social art histories.

I'll just mention two other specialties, which are perhaps closer to home in terms of their internal structures. In Chinese art history, there are very interesting divisions that still run in some measure down national lines, between scholars who work in China and Taiwan and do a kind of aesthetics mixed with art history, and scholars who work in Western universities and practice a number of interpretive methods including postcolonial theory. That division is a known issue in the field, but it runs so deep that it is not always even noticed as a division *within* a single field.[2]

Last, I'll mention modernism, which will form part of our conversation this afternoon. Modernism is a very interesting case: it is deeply divided in many ways, and there are scholars who differ widely from one another. On the other hand the book *Art Since 1900* will, I think, more or less set the standard for conversations on pedagogy; it more or less represents what has become a consensus view in North American and western European scholarship of modernism.[3] Despite the many complaints and criticisms it has already gotten, I think the book will unify the field in ways that may be less than fortunate—I see Donald Preziosi in the audience, shaking his head!—but there doesn't seem to be an alternate on the horizon.

So I am conjuring these specialties briefly, to open the question of the state of Renaissance scholarship, and the mainstreams and divisions within it.

Robert Williams: When we were talking yesterday, there seemed to me to be a shared sense of Renaissance art studies having lost not only the privileged position they once occupied in art history as a whole, but even their fundamental identity and coherence; at very least, there was a sense of that identity being subject to radical contestation. It is tempting to use the negative word "crisis" to describe this situation, and there certainly are negative aspects to it: we spent a good deal of time yesterday complaining about the downsizing of humanities faculties at

American universities and the kinds of gratuitous disciplinary anxiety it tends to generate. On the other hand, this sense of disarray or fragmentation might also signal a wholly positive process of redefinition, a moment of unusual fecundity, of a productive proliferation of new possibilities.

In either case, the current situation calls for—seems to me to demand—an especially energetic, searching, substantive dialogue among scholars in the field, no matter how awkward such exchange may be to initiate. I noticed yesterday that we were traversing common points of interest but from different directions and on different trajectories, so to speak, crossing each other's path in passing; perhaps that characterization might serve as a starting point for discussion.

Stephen Campbell: One question to consider might be: What is wrong with disarray? Is our job to impose order and tidiness on a very multi-centered field of study? I think the Italian Renaissance field never went through a kind of polemical phase, like seventeenth-century Dutch, or northern European art did, twenty years ago. It's a very non-polemical field, and in some ways a collaborative field. People don't polemicize against each other, at least not overtly, and this is not necessarily a good thing.[4] This lack of dissent or polemic is also manifest in a tendency to repress dissident or challenging ideas rather than to engage with them. A routine and cursory citation takes the place of real debate.

Michael Cole: That's true, though in some ways the situation is not that different from the one Jim associated with the study of Chinese art, if you compare what's happening in Italian scholarship with what's happening elsewhere. I note that all of the panelists here work in North American institutions—that suggests something about who could even participate in the kind of conversation we're expected to have today. I'm not sure that is because there was once a moment of coherence that has subsequently been lost. I can't imagine Roberto Longhi and Erwin Panofsky, fifty years ago, having a more productive discussion of

"Renaissance Theory" than we might have with our Italian counterparts today. The questions are different.

Claire Farago: I think we could enlarge that a thousand-fold if we consider the Renaissance as a global phenomenon of exchange, entry, and re-entry into Europe during the early modern period. So it is relevant to ask: Do we mean "Renaissance" as a concept? A time period? A place? A subset of stylistic situations? In each case, the answer can't be provided by any three or four people from any one place. Part of the collaborative nature that Stephen just brought up is that we need to understand what an enormous topic we are dealing with.

Fredrika Jacobs: I see the disarray Stephen mentioned as a positive. While we all recognize certain canonical works as representative of the Renaissance, the "disarray" has attempted—with varying degrees of success—to revisit the canon without displacing it. Even if we don't go as far as Claire, and study the global Renaissance—even if we stay within the geographical confines of the Italian peninsula—we find "disarray" in a variety of voices and perspectives and in an assortment of styles and media that reflect myriad influences and interests. Recent scholarship has dealt with some of this in constructive ways. One can argue that the result has enabled us to better situate masterworks within the culture.

The problem is that if you're going to consider the Renaissance as a field, if you are going to attempt to teach it, write about it, grasp it, or otherwise define it, some sort of *system* needs to be in place. Bob's paper on systematicity offers a viable approach.[5] Nonetheless, "systems" are problematic: Do we use style? Do we use periods? Do we use phases? To what extent do we follow the models established by Renaissance authors like Vasari? And how do we proceed beyond Italy's borders? How do we, for example, include Matt Kavaler's study on the representations of constructed errors and other forms of ornament in northern Renaissance architecture?[6] His work points to some of the obstacles we need to overcome if we are to understand what constitutes the discipline.

Ethan Matt Kavaler: As the token northern Renaissance person, I notice quite a difference in the way the subject is handled here, and among my colleagues. Disarray, or rather polemical opposition, is nothing new to the study of northern European art, particularly since Alpers's book. There are a number of differences between Italian and northern Renaissance art. One of them is that northern art is bereft of the plethora of texts dealing with art in the sixteenth century, at least texts dealing with painting. The first major statement regarding northern art is Karel Van Mander's *Schilder-Boeck*, published in 1604. So there isn't the tradition of writers discussing painting in the North, as there is in the South. Hence there are few models for the relation between art and rhetoric. There is also a divide between European and North American scholars, as Jim has implied. North American scholars tend to focus on a few conceptual issues and tend to do so with reference to the art of different periods. These concerns are, in particular, issues of realism and naturalism, and the epistemological force of painting. European scholars tend not to refer to as many theoretical debates; they generally have a wider sense of the monuments of the period. They refer not only to what we might think of as the canonical paintings of the northern Renaissance, but to sculpture, architecture, and stained glass—objects we might think of as charting the national patrimony of each scholar's region. Thus, they are not as restricted to collectable artifacts preserved in modern museums. These are some of the differences I see between my agenda, that normally stipulated to be that of my colleagues in Europe, and that of the other panelists here today.

SC: I would say that Matt's comments apply equally well to the study of Renaissance art in Italy. Given the sheer quantity of material and primary sources to work on, the notion of "Renaissance" seems very tangible and self-evident there—it's apparently not something that gives rise to methodological debates about periodization; Renaissance art appears as something real that requires to be mapped out and described in all its complexity. Another observation about Matt though: it is ironic that our token northern Renaissance person is also the only person here working on architecture. That has become a kind of sect unto itself.

MC: Stephen, what do you mean by that? I find that architectural historians tend to have much broader interests than, say, historians of painting. That Matt is also working on sculpture comes as less of a surprise than it would if someone else at this table announced that his or her next book was going to be on, say, Bramante.

SC: I agree. Some of the most important and intellectually challenging work in the Renaissance is by architectural historians: Manfredo Tafuri, Marvin Trachtenberg, Christine Smith, and this panel does not represent that fact. Historians of painting seem increasingly to have less training or intellectual investment in history of architecture (of course there are exceptions) and I wonder if that's not because architectural historians have their own conferences and publications, and you tend to encounter them in architecture programs rather than in history of art.

MC: Maybe it has to do as well with the mobility of most paintings, and even—getting back to what Matt was saying—with the experience of the modern museum. Historians of painting imagine their objects to be autonomous, removable from the settings for which they were made and studiable as independent works, while historians of architecture can't but be sensitive to the fact that every important Renaissance building also included works in different media, probably as part of its fabric. And in many cases, of course, the major architects came to the practice from painting or sculpture or goldsmithery or some other figurative art.

JE: I am a little wary of worrying too directly about what we mean by "the Renaissance," even though it's proper and inevitable. I'm wary mainly because the various possible definitions always appear entangled with one another. Some years ago there was a conference on the inception of perspective, at the Dibner

Center at MIT, organized by Jehane Kuhn. Sam Edgerton gave a paper there, with some of his material about sixteenth-century paintings in Latin American churches, which were done under the direction of Spanish priests, but executed by indigenous artists. It was understood that all the papers in that conference would be published, but Jehane told Sam his wasn't appropriate because it wasn't Italian, and perspective started in Italy.[7] Jehane's criterion was geographical and political, but it was also entangled with questions of chronology (his work was slightly later than what she wanted to focus on), and with question of style (it didn't exemplify the styles she wanted), and with questions of theory (it didn't have the right theoretical apparatus, because there weren't texts to be adduced). That's why I wonder how far you get if you address the question of what "the Renaissance" is too directly.

CF: Well, Sam Edgerton's work was excluded for all of the wrong reasons.

JE: Yes.

CF: I wonder how my colleagues here would feel about my saying that.

JE: And I didn't mean the criteria were all potentially apposite; I meant they were all wrong, all together.

CF: I'll go further and say they were all wrong in their entanglement. If we judge what counts as Renaissance as Jehane Kuhn did, in geographical, political, and chronological terms that exclude the production of art and architecture in "Renaissance styles" because they occur at the wrong place, time, or in the wrong political circumstances, we then repeat and reproduce existing biases—taking what is "Renaissance" as a premise whereas it is the subject to be investigated—without being aware of the fact that we're controlling the field by doing so. I am talking about the necessarily, unavoidably empirical nature of historical investigation. I think we should look at all the processes that answer to the name "Renaissance." Maybe the question of disarray should be theorized further: a disarray assumes there is an array, and if there was never an array, then who is to put themselves in the position of being the judge to decide what is excluded and what isn't?

JE: I thought that a way of not having to be too specific about *one* center, or to try to think through "the Renaissance," would be to make an informal survey of some of the scholars who are taken to be somehow off to one side of the field. Claire, I hope you won't mind if we talk a little about your work in that context.

One of my favorite metaphors for the idea of being "inside" or "outside" a field is what statisticians call an *outlier:* a point that is somewhere off on the thin tail of the bell curve, outside normative cut-off points. ("Standard distributions," in statistics.) In that model, Claire, your work could be imagined as being *way* out there: it would have very radical consequences for the field of Renaissance studies if it were taken seriously by the majority of, say, pedagogic practices. In other words there are practices that are not only on the slopes of the bell curve, and contribute to or enrich the center, but also practices that belong to other configurations, and could do without the center altogether.

CF: I would say my work could be a test case for the center. Any outlying work could be examined, and perhaps excluded. But the question is, Do we want to exclude that kind of work, or is it exactly where we want to pay attention? I think of chaos theory, which grew out of paying attention to anomalies, and led to new insights that strengthened what was at the center.

JE: There is also the question of how anxious people at the center are to police that exclusion. Sometimes the center massively ignores the margins, and other times it shows its anxiety by looking to the margins and wondering about them, which is part of what we're doing here.

SC: The center being people who work in a kind of mainstream?

JE: Yes—it's a delicate question, what the center is. You're not going to get anyone to say they're in the center—certainly not any of us! Just for conversation's sake, and politely avoiding the present company, I'll put a few names on the table: Charles Dempsey, Elizabeth Cropper, Chris Wood, Alex Nagel. They are central in terms of scholarship in ways I will refuse to define, and they also work in central institutions.

MC: I'm not sure those four would understand themselves to represent the same mainstream—except perhaps in the sense that all are very conscious of a substantial early twentieth-century literature on the Renaissance which helps establish a kind of "state of the question."

JE: Yes, I didn't mean there is a single, unified center, but there is a clustered center—I wanted to avoid implying there is nothing but a more-or-less collegial aggregate of scholars orbited by some outlying voices.

MC: I just meant that your list brought to mind another thing that sets Renaissance studies apart from nineteenth-century studies, or even from studies of seventeenth-century Dutch painting: that those other fields lack that largely German canon of writing that underlies what we do, challenging us to think about a much longer historiographic arc as we pose our questions.

SC: I wonder if it wouldn't make more sense to think about "the center" in terms of certain enshrined or canonical topics: say, Florence, Michelangelo, Dürer etc. rather than in terms of who may or may not be more central in the profession. It also happens that the people Jim mentions have worked on canonical artists, although often working to change the state of the questions about those artists. And then you have a figure like Joseph Leo Koerner who might be unorthodox in terms of the kind of intellectual profile he brings to the field, but he wrote a book on Dürer which is "central" in the sense that everyone else in the field now has to deal with it, even if they'd rather not.

Scholarship in Italy has its own way of conceptualizing the center in terms of a dialectic of domination and resistance between "center" and "periphery"—I refer here to the well-known article by Carlo Ginzburg and Enrico Castelnuovo, which argues that local or provincial artistic cultures need not be seen as passively reflecting the influences trickling from the center, but as resisting or critiquing or transforming the art of the center.[8] That kind of approach is called to mind by Claire's work as well. When myself and Stephen Milner undertook our edited volume *Artistic Exchange and Cultural Translation in the Italian Renaissance City*, we were responding to Ginzburg and Castelnuovo, and to Claire's edited collection *Reframing the Renaissance*. The central argument is that you don't have to cross the globe to find the critical dialogue with the center. Italy is not the nation state it tried to become in the nineteenth century: it was and is a mosaic of local dialects and allegiances, sometimes highly contentious in their interaction. Morten Steen Hansen showed that for a painter in sixteenth-century Ancona or Bologna, you can respond to Michelangelo with an ironic distance that might be less possible in Rome.[9] And I have been trying to demonstrate for a long time that dealing seriously with the art of a small center like Ferrara utterly transforms the questions we ask when looking again at a major center like Florence. Perhaps what is different in Claire's analysis is the colonial dimension, the operation of power.

MC: But isn't a similar kind of critical dialogue possible even for those who work on the traditional centers? The writing on Florence, for example, has been so dominated by the study of Medici patronage that even recovering different voices—those of academic poets, for example, whose interests were sometimes at odds with their rulers'—transforms the questions.[10] Tracking the way that disempowered viewers or "minor" artists responded to or ignored the big public commissions can constitute its own challenge to the center. It undermines the idea that art is explained by describing the programmatic intentions of its sponsors, and ultimately, it points to the limits of a certain variety of iconographical method. There are also scholars who, likewise staying in major centers, nevertheless look at works that the literature on the people in power has ignored, or who complicate our understanding of what power looks like in the Renaissance, or who even focus on conflict as such—I think, for example, of Helen Hills's book on conventual architecture in Naples.[11]

SC: We have to attend to the differences within Florence as well as between Florence and other centers. Both Bronzino and Cellini, as you well know, are good representatives of an artistic program that consciously does not align with the academic and official one of Vasari. But what is different in Claire's analysis is that the colonial dimension means that we have to think differently about the operations of power.

CF: In my own research, I am simultaneously working on things central to the field as traditionally defined—I have been publishing on Leonardo da Vinci for fifteen years and my current Leonardo project studies the historical reception of his Treatise on Painting in a cross-cultural setting in which the political dimensions of this influential text's reception can be charted concretely. I would say that such a project—which is a collaborative effort involving over twenty scholars—is also testing what constitutes that traditionally centered field. So it's not a matter of choosing the baby or the bathwater (I think I used that terrible analogy yesterday), but of trying to keep both in play, of considering "Renaissance" an open-ended system always under investigation. Power operates everywhere. I am moreover concerned with the ethical dimensions of what we produce as scholars: what do we pass on to future generations? What kinds of political implications are there to the knowledge we produce? Our work can seem a-political when we produce it, but at the same time it excludes other work from taking place, or relegates that work to the margins.

Maybe that's more where I feel the field of early modern art should be: it should include everything—Chinese Renaissance art, Bolivian, Japanese, anything. Objects made in the Renaissance style were exported all over the planet, as were artists working in that style. Why should the fate of these objects and artists *not* be the concern of Renaissance art historians? And why not think about every micro-study as something that can engage with the same issues of what constitutes the Renaissance or the center of a field of studies defined in whatever traditional manner? What happens to Renaissance style and humanist ideas in Latin America? Gauvin Bailey, for example, is writing about the Jesuits in Latin America and China.[12] Jeanette Peterson a Mesoamericanist as well as Sam Edgerton have written about the hybrid artistic productions of colonial artists working under the direction of missionaries during the early contact period.[13] Such studies, sensitive to both sides of the cultural and political interaction, should be encouraged. After all, there is no pure "Renaissance" identity, and once we start thinking of things from this broader perspective, we can see the inherited paradigms structuring our contemporary practices in fresh ways. The most fundamentally flawed aspect of our inherited practices, which we're still trying to come to terms with, is the legacy of a progressive or evolutionist theory of art in its vast and multiple ramifications. Sometimes we avoid noticing those ramifications by doing micro-studies.

SC: Where do you see this evolutionary virus operating? I can see that to teach freshman classes, you might have to order things schematically and diachronically—

CF: Stephen, let me interrupt you here for just a minute. Do we have to teach freshman classes schematically and diachronically? What if freshman were taught the history of the concept of the Renaissance along with the monuments? Or what if the initial survey of Italian Renaissance introduced monuments from around the world? If the course is a world survey, why should Chinese art exclude colonial building built in the Renaissance style, for example. As Bailey's research, for one, makes absolutely clear, there are major artistic and architectural monuments constructed in hybrids of Italianate Renaissance and local, indigenous styles pretty much all over the world during the period we identify as the Renaissance. We could talk about the clash, export, interaction of cultures in an entirely different manner, and it would be historically valid, more valid in fact than using vague astrological terms like the "influence." And I am not too sure that chronology at the introductory survey level should be treated as unproblematic either. Of course, these objections are not new. What Jim referred to as the culture of a specialty, with its own kinds of disagreements and harmony, is somehow at work when we as a discipline can go through years of debate over the best way to organize the introductory survey, and then go on with basically the same old survey of monuments drawn from canonical, ethnocentric texts that change only a few monuments every few years to force everyone to buy the latest edition of the textbook. I don't think we do have to teach freshman classes quite as schematically and diachronically as these textbooks would like us to.

SC: But to turn to scholarship, where do we see the legacy of a progressive or evolutionist theory of art manifesting itself? The evolutionary logic you critique in your work would certainly be part of the scholarship we inherit, and the foundation of art history, and of the Renaissance (Wölfflin, Riegl, this kind of thing, going back to Vasari), but where is that now? It seems to me there are any number of practices under the umbrella of Renaissance studies that are in a certain way realizing the kind of study you're calling for. The study of print culture, for instance, has led historians of the Renaissance around the world, following the Jesuits' didactic and propagandistic uses of prints.

CF: You're absolutely right. And although I'm not going to start naming names, I can think of a number of other topics, not organized in terms of individual artistic identities, that put into practice the kinds of work I was calling for a decade ago. Studies of collecting practices are another case in point, as your own most current work exemplifies. Case studies, strategically defined, are less numerous among Renaissance specialists, but excellent work is coming out of Latin Americanist scholarship—here I must mention a few names—Carolyn Dean, Dana Leibsohn, Barbara Mundy, Serge Gruzinski, Cecelia Klein, Tom Cummins—the list goes on. Most of us here, on this panel, do multi-evidentiary kinds of studies, and we don't rely just on texts. We're putting things together in different ways, so as to undercut the force of progressive or evolutionary theories. That also deserves to be mentioned.

But when we get six of us together, and none of us is a Latin Americanist, per se (I'm an ersatz, stretching out into unknown regions), then that's how the evolutionary logic gets reproduced.

MC: I took Stephen's point to be in part that we should be cautious about defining "centers" exclusively in terms of geography. There are a number of scholars who work primarily on Italian material—not just on prints but on domestic arts, or on cult images—who could certainly argue that what they do has political dimensions, and even a polemical edge, going against the mainstream of the field.

SC: Of course often that polemical edge is not theorized, and it becomes part of a museum-like taxonomy of objects without any real critical purchase.

EMK: Although there is a strain in northern Renaissance studies that emphasizes ties with the Middle Ages, another one of those problematic periods, most of us who study the Renaissance have an idea of Italy as central, and that is one of the subversive things about Claire's works, and her statements this morning. Also, Italian culture is usually considered to have initiated many of the traditions of the modern world, and that is one of the reasons why the substitution of "early Modern" for "Renaissance" doesn't really revise the situation; "early Modern" denotes even more forcefully the earliest stages of modernity. This alternate expression continues the tradition of Burckhardt, with Renaissance Italy as the birthplace of the modern world. That's really a heritage that we have not successfully come to terms with.

MC: Of course, many people who favor the term "early Modern" don't intend it to carry so much weight. They just want to include fourteenth- or seventeenth-century material in their discussions, or to assume that the cultures of Renaissance Italy are continuous with those in other places, and they find the traditional boundaries implied by the term "Renaissance" too constrictive.

CF: One thing to do is not just settle on one term, but keep the alternates in play.

JE: This metaphor that you were half-recalling from yesterday, about the baby and the bathwater—what you actually said yesterday was that we can keep the baby *and* its dirty bathwater. That suggests that a critique of the field might result in a slightly unpleasant chaos. I'd like to mark the difference between a critique that works "from the outside," and addresses and retains what it identifies as the "center"; and a critique that creates a new configuration. If your work were to become, magically, 80% of the work that is done in the field, not only would curricula completely change, but the center would be radically disrupted. It would not just be interrogated, diminished, or unpredictably altered. Your critique, I think, is not just a matter of adding from the outside, but undermining from the outside—

CF: Or maybe undermining from the inside.

JE: Okay, but with the potential of creating a wholly different cartography from what would result if any of the rest of us on this panel would produce if we were to be magically given 80% of the discipline.

CF: I think about the issues that interest me, working on the formation of new collective identities in different places. Perhaps one of the things that could come out of this would be a sense of what unifies our practice right now, that has nothing to do with periodization per se, or even with style, but rather with the complexity of the work of art and its ability to be a communicative tool. How does visual culture signify? A number of people I think we will be discussing—Georges Didi-Huberman, Aby Warburg—have been fundamentally concerned with the complexity of being faced with a work of art from another time. How do you understand it? There is always going to be a gap, and just thinking about that brings together a number of possible common points in contemporary approaches.

JE: So, Claire, another person whose work has been considered as an outlier is David Freedberg, whose *Power of Images* appeared sometime in the late 1980's . . .

CF, FJ, EMK: 1989.

JE: In that book, Freedberg was addressing what he saw as a limitation of Renaissance studies, and by implication art history in general—its debt to Kantian aesthetics, and its exclusion of images that have sexual, political, or religious power.[14] I find that *Power of Images* is being cited more and more often, but often in the same context: people say, Here's a really interesting thing that could really shake up the field, but it didn't quite fit, so let's hope someone writes something better. Several of us are engaged in projects that seek to undermine that same Kantian wall between aesthetic appreciation and the wider powers and uses of images. That's especially true, I suppose, of your work, Fredrika, because your work on *boti* concerns images that have power in Freedberg's sense: and yet it seems hard to speak about them in the same way, in the same voice, as you can speak about aesthetic objects.[15]

FJ: Of the "Starting Points" essays, I think everyone's except mine can relate to Bob's essay on systematicity. When I first noticed that, I wondered what it meant. My project got started, in part, thanks to Freedberg's book; he has a chapter on the power of votive offerings. But the objects I study do not fit into the "center," whatever that might be; these objects cannot be assessed in the usual ways; many of them were painted or fabricated anonymously—

JE: They're not masterpieces.

FJ: Yes, and so they are shunted aside. The challenge for me has been to try and find a way to talk about these objects *within* the discipline. I am beginning to develop some ideas but I have yet to find a solution that would effectively challenge the tendency to discard these works as "popular" or "low." Some recent studies, and here I'm thinking of Jane Garnett's and Gervase Rosser's essay on miraculous cult images in Liguria, have moved in very interesting theoretical directions with respect to issues of copies, the translatability of the miraculous image, and efforts by both church and state to legislate control of reproduction.[16]

JE: You're like an asteroid, feeling the pull of two different planets. One would be art history, and the other anthropology. If you fell into that orbit you'd become a distant object, as Freedberg's book sometimes seems to be.

SC: Fredrika, does art history have something to contribute here that anthropology does not?

FJ: That's the big question, but I think it might if we consider these images in ways that may have their basis in anthropological studies yet have been applied to canonical works. One of the sessions at the most recent meeting of the Renaissance Society of America was "Gifting Art and Artful Gifts." Each of the papers delivered in that session was informed by Marcel Mauss's *The Gift*, which is as the author states an anthropological study. Because the practice of votive images is one of giving a gift for grace received this might be one way to cross the divide between disciplines.[17]

RW: The first sentence of Freedberg's book was: "This book is not about the history of art." That is, he emphatically distinguished his enterprise from what he understood to be art history, and he did so in order to advance an alternative study of "images." That gesture was typical of its moment, but also very consequential: it contributed to a division of the art historical community between those who saw their primary object of inquiry as art, and those who see their primary object of inquiry as images.

EMK: Or objects.

RW: Right, art on the one hand and images or objects on the other. They are often assumed to denote the same thing, but they don't. Freedberg's gesture was part of a larger trend in the 1980's, a displacement, even a suppression, of the category "art," motivated by a desire to get around all the value-loaded assumptions associated with that word. Even what we've been saying here about center and periphery has to do with an implicit distinction between art and other kinds of visual production or visual interest. Fredrika, I think you follow Freedberg—and Jim, too, and the majority of progressively-inclined scholars—in insisting on the primacy of the image, while I would hold out for the primacy of art.

FJ: You're right, I would like to insist on "images" even though I am quite probably in the minority. As Hugo van der Velden so aptly noted in his study on Medici votive *boti* and *imagini*, the "popular" aspect of these works have prompted their classification as "imagery rather than art."[18]

One of the texts crucial to me at the beginning of my career was Vasari. It's hard to be more in the center than that. I've also written on Michelangelo: that too is in the center. But I also try to keep in mind the name of our discipline; *art history*. It has two components; art and history. If you read the expression *art history* in one way, it should include all sorts of things that are now peripheral; but if you read those two words as Vasari did, then you need to keep to a narrative that leads to a pinnacle of perfection, to fine art. Should we limit the history of art to Vasari's model, complete with all the biases that inhere within it?[19]

RW: But to concentrate on art and what makes it different from other kinds of productive activity—even to distinguish it from the production of other kinds of images or objects—is not necessarily to accept Vasari and all his biases. The emergence of art as an idea is an historical phenomenon of the greatest importance, yet its significance is still far from being fully appreciated or understood.

EMK: I think that's one of the subjects, not just the object, of our discussion. Or rather, we're interested in what it became in the Renaissance. In our period, art migrated to a distinct class of object and activity, and became the practice of a specific type of performer. The degree to which we are able to look back reflectively and appropriately apply post-Kantian ideas of aesthetics to the Renaissance is one of the themes we're all dealing with.

MC: I wonder whether your reminder that Renaissance art so frequently has to do with different kinds of performance doesn't help get us past the sense that we have to choose between images and objects. What if we talked about "artifacts" or "artworks"—that is, objects that have been worked, usually so as to embody or mediate images—instead of simply pictures or things?[20] Of course, this still puts us in territory quite different from Freedberg's, whose book is not primarily about objects or images or artifacts, but rather about responses to them.

SC: True, but then art historians already interested in response —especially the erotic dimensions of beholder engagement and its mediation through historically specific codes, such as Petrarchism—might have found those areas of *Power of Images* to be disappointing; Freedberg's book was thus not something that they felt the need to engage with in their subsequent work.[21]

The notion of art is fundamental to what you're talking about, Fredrika. You're studying late examples of miraculous Madonnas, not the Or' San Michele, Black Death, thirteenth- and fourteenth-century examples. The works you study arose in part in response to the category called *art*; at that time the sacred image, the devotional image, was in a way no longer functioning, so it was necessary to have an enlarged image practice. It was about getting *around* the privilege associated with, say, Guido Reni altarpieces in churches. We need something more than metonymic associations, something closer to us, something not provided by the stately donor images.

RW: "We" being modern art historians.

SC: Actually, I meant to refer to sixteenth- and seventeenth-century Christian beholders and their specific needs, but I can see that "we" might also apply to historians and their own needs as well.

CF: The Getty theme for 2007 is "Religion and Ritual," so it's not only "we art historians" but also something at the institutional level that is reshaping the field, and in that sense the field is in a moment of enlargement.

JE: Possibly: I hope so.[22] But it is also a ritual concern *of* art history: there's a lot of talk about religious and ritual meanings, first after Freedberg's book, and again, I think, beginning at the *fin-de-millennium*, but it remains an outlying subject.

CF: Yes; I think the institutional critique we'll address in the afternoon session will be helpful here, because this sense of what subjects are valid and important to investigate and what subjects are optional or outlying (to use your good terminology) happens at the level of institutions.

FJ: This discussion of "art" and "history" has to go back, at least for us, to Vasari. (Matt, you might say Vasari and Van Mander.) Who was he writing for? Who were his collaborators, and whom were they associated with in the Medici court? What was the program, the motivation, that we've all now adopted? We might question Vasari's intent and point out the inaccuracies in his text, but it seems to remain in place. This goes to your question, Jim, about what counts as the *art* in art history. The votive images I study are ignored in Vasari's *Lives*, except in one place where he notes some ex-votos that were made as effigies;

but his only interest in them is their technology, not their potential status as art. There are *other* texts, however, that we can use—Bocchi, for example.

JE: As you can tell, I'm pessimistic about this.

FJ: I can tell.

JE: Every field has its Others, its outliers, that it needs to have out there, and to keep at arm's length. Every field makes welcoming gestures to its outliers, and then rejects them.

FJ: Well, you know, I did the same thing with women artists in the Renaissance. When I went to college, at an all-women's institution, not a single female artist was talked about in any of my art history classes with the sole exception of Angelica Kaufmann. That is certainly not the case any longer; I have written on Renaissance women artists, and I could have said, "I am pessimistic about this having any sort of effect." Well, guess what? It wasn't a *great* effect, but now there is some representation of women artists in the basic art history Renaissance textbooks. When I embarked on that project I had to go into, and practically *underneath*, the bowels of storage in museums in Italy. Now they hang on the walls of museums like the Brera. More to the point, my objective was not to argue that sixteenth-century women artists produced paintings and sculptures comparable to those of the "masters" but rather to draw attention to the critical language that was used to characterize their works as distinctly "feminine". The way language operates in art criticism and art history needs to be attended to. Indeed, it goes back to the issue I noted earlier concerning the distinction between imagery and art.

JE: That's a weird metaphor, "underneath the bowels of storage."

FJ: It is odd, but it gets across the essence of the challenge I faced at that time.

JE: I'd be happy to say my skepticism about this *is* bottomless. I don't see there was a huge difference made by the inclusion of women artists in Renaissance studies. The new works and artists aren't tokenism: it's not that kind of problem. It's that the fundamental narratives that structure and motivate the field itself remain completely intact. I find these kinds of inclusion to be superficial: not always, but often.

FJ: That would be quite discouraging.

MC: But Fredrika, is it any less discouraging to see the marginally larger number of pictures by women artists that now hang in Renaissance galleries as the real success story? It seems to me that the fundamental narratives, to use Jim's expression, have changed, and that writings motivated by feminist interests have been a major reason for this, but that the changes have less to do with the practices of women artists than with other things. This is to say, of course, that your own work on the virtuosa is somewhat exceptional, if only because there's just not that much material to study. Even where the canon is concerned, I would say that the biggest recent transformations have to do with the new and truly widespread attention to women patrons, to "gendered" spaces, and to the so-called "minor arts," rather than with the identification of underappreciated women painters. On the other hand, these kinds of contributions, many of which come from men, don't always present themselves as "feminist"—maybe the assumption is that this is implicit.

What do you think: Is the feminist history of Renaissance art as vibrant as it was in the 1990s, and if so, what does it look like today? One might think about your own trajectory as a case in point.

CF: Let's talk for a moment about what it means to theorize or not theorize a subject of study. I think Steve and now Matt's point is crucial to our discussion of how a specialization maintains its stranglehold on interpretation: Joan Kelly's famous question, did women have a Renaissance? (which she answered with an emphatic no), like Linda Nochlin's famous question a few years earlier, why have there been no great women artists?, were important for their theoretical contributions to a patriarchal discourse. Here, by theoretical, I only mean that these two feminist scholars analyzed the structure of society to come up with their questions, and their answers. They did not limit their investigations to the study of women, as most scholars do today who add positive knowledge to the field—what Steve termed a "museumlike taxonomy"—by enlarging the canon of women artists or of women patrons or of the so-called decorative arts. Studying women does not necessarily make you a feminist.

The debate on this is now quite dated: you can't in fact understand how society is gendered without studying the context in which women lived. And that includes our histories about them. Whitney Chadwick, writing in an excellent undergrad survey text on women artists and society, notes that over the centuries since Vasari, women's names have been added and dropped from the lives of the artists literature with what she calls "astonishing arbitrariness," thus maintaining a patriarchal status quo.[23] Jim, you mentioned this textbook, *Art Since 1900:* there's another example of a group of art historians who started by questioning the status quo; but what they seem to have done is overturn the status quo, and then they have assumed the position of a new canonical authority. Their book offers an extremely narrow perspective on art since 1900. If you give it that credence, and say that it will achieve a canonical status, then it will: but let me quickly add: this book has already received a number of negative reviews.

JE: That's right. It was also received more or less negatively at two of its launches, in Bristol and at the Tate Modern. (The latter is archived on the Internet.[24])

RW: Maybe it's the Vasari of the twenty-first century!

CF: But Vasari was the Vasari of the nineteenth century, in a way.

JE: Yes. That's nicely said.

CF: The preeminence that we accord Vasari in the field found its institutional form only with the professionalization of the discipline in the nineteenth century. It didn't have that status when it was a new book.

RW: I'm not sure I agree with that. It was in the nineteenth century that Vasari's authority, which had been solid for several centuries, began to collapse. Only with Ruskin is Vasari's account of Renaissance art finally overthrown, replaced with one which privileges the fourteenth and fifteenth centuries over the sixteenth.

CF: But that didn't start in 1550. Vasari's *Lives* as the foundation of art history, like the term Renaissance itself, is a foundational myth that depended on art history becoming a subject studied in schools as universities, as Wallace Ferguson argued with extensive evidence many years ago.[25] It took many generations for Vasari's *Lives* to achieve canonical status—although we could discuss the exact chronology.

SC: Earlier, the resistances are striking. The Carracci write all over it, saying things like "Vile liar Vasari!" "This is not the case!"[26]

MC: El Greco, too.[27] And Alessandro Lamo, writing his own set of artists' lives in Cremona around the same time, attacks Vasari as an uninformed chauvinist.

EMK: The fact that people have to inscribe their opposition on the text of Vasari is significant in itself.

MC: It shows how seductive the book was, even where it was opposed.

RW: There certainly were resistances—rather predictable objections to his regional bias, as in Dolce and the Carracci, and a more interesting objection to his whole notion of the progress of art in Armenini—but the immediate reaction was overwhelmingly positive. Van Mander offers perhaps the most impressive indication of the authority Vasari's model had acquired within a generation, and he was a Northerner, someone from whom one might have expected even stronger resistance than from among the Italians!

MC: But there's debate about that, too, isn't there? Walter Melion takes Van Mander to have recognized Vasari's hegemonic motives and to have consequently reframed the Italian *Lives* in his own text in a way that qualifies their authority: running them up against historical schemes that compete with Vasari's framework, inflecting Vasari's conception of artistic virtuosity, and generally establishing Vasari's "contingency."[28]

RW: Melion was a student of Alpers, and his book was obviously intended to support the idea of a distinctive Northern orientation toward art advanced in her work. His argument is over-drawn, and suppresses the fact that Van Mander's orientation is overwhelmingly Italianate.

EMK: The two editions of Vasari's book were widely dissemi-nated, distributed among many northern European humanists. It became a model for discussions of art history before the nineteenth century. It circumscribed what art was, and it gave primacy to painting. It had a profound effect.[29]

CF: I agree; I was saying it wasn't instant.

MK: It developed over centuries.

CF: And nuancing that development is a legitimate object of study, rather than just assuming it is canonical from the start.

EMK: I think the professionalized discipline of art history took the textual tradition that was based on Vasari, and gave it a kind of university credence that it had not had before.

CF: And I hope it's worth noting that Vasari does not have that authority now. Who wrote Vasari's *Lives* has been the subject of investigation since the beginning of the twentieth century, and the current hypothesis that several humanists collaborated and framed his authorial identity is not just a matter of accuracy in source criticism, but a matter of how we deal now with the cult of personality taking shape in and through his very influen-tial text.

JE: I wonder if we can continue our discussion of outliers—after Claire and David Freedberg, although it's interesting how Vasari got in there as the original outlier—by bringing back a person whose name always elicits sighs, and that is Svetlana Alpers. There is a sense in which *The Art of Describing* is an asked-and-answered question in art history. But I was surprised yesterday when one of us said that the effect of that book was to *narrow* Renaissance art history; I had never thought of it that way. But the book, *Art of Describing*, was written with the intention of creating an opposing voice, of being an outlier: she wanted to construct an alternate discourse to set alongside the one that, from that moment, became the "dominant" one. That was the initial gambit of the book. It has worked in ways she couldn't have expected, but it is interesting that it now seems like something from the discipline's past, even though it continues to have reverberations in present practice. I wonder if that is partly because it is not just a strong alternate model, an independent critical voice not beholden to the "center," but because it has in fact operated according to the logic of Orientalism: as an entrancing and suggestive Other, offering an apparently unlimited freedom, but ultimately ineffective and beholden to the center itself.

SC: It had its moment. It was a powerful innovation in the 1980s and 1990s, and it sustained a lot of interesting work. Now, I think we have come to the moment where scholars want to keep the book as a model of how we might work between the history of science and the history of art, but where its most problematic claims have to be revised. The way it reifies differences between North and South as "description" and "narration" (and a whole set of other oppositions) has been critiqued for a long time. They are dangerously easy to assimilate, especially in the classroom.[30]

EMK: Instead of paradigms of Italian artists as textually engaged, and northern artists textually detached, it vastly opened up the discussion of northern Art, and removed it, as Jim said, from a suffocating association with emblem literature, which had become a fashion in the late 1970s and 1980s.

But it was restrictive in another way. It emphasized a so-called indigenous aspect of northern art as opposed to an indigenous aspect of Italian art. In so doing, it reified late nineteenth-century ethnicist studies by Hippolyte Taine and others, who had written, almost racially, of qualities that lay in the "blood and soil" of different countries.[31] Alpers tends, for different reasons, to endorse that tradition, and it has been picked up by many of her pupils: Walter Melion, Celeste Brusati, Mark Meadow. It has become one of the unfortunate consequences of a book that otherwise opened up the field.

CF: I think that is very important: it shows the effect of the evolutionary model even today, of not having understood the structure of the paradigm enough to understand how this structure keeps getting reproduced in other forms in our writing of history. One of the most productive critiques that postcolonial theorists made of Edward Said's *Orientalism* is that it maintains a binary opposition, a base-superstructure opposition, where the actual historical situation can only be explained in much more complex terms. Postcolonial theory elucidates processes like mimicry[32]—trying to take on the semblance of the dominant member of the binary opposition—and that is exactly what Svetlana Alpers did, at the metacritical level. She took on the position of the dominant voice, in order to write a subaltern study.

RW: But I don't think it is a subaltern study; it masquerades as one. The values she associates with Italian art had long been in eclipse; the qualities of Dutch art that she emphasizes had been well-established features of modernism since at least the time of Courbet. I think she set up Italian art as a straw target so that she could appropriate for the support of Dutch art a whole array of long-accepted, thoroughly institutionalized modernist values.

JE: One reason I wanted to bring Svetlana's book into the discussion is because it's a different *kind* of outlier than Freedberg's book, or than your own work, Claire. A lot of Freedberg's book, for example, can be assigned to anthropology, or religious studies if you'd rather, but this is different. The hope was that the best way to shake up a field was to create an independent voice starting from the elements of the field itself, which of course creates an unequal dichotomy, from which it seems the author can't escape. Some of Alpers's rhetorical moves—announcing a change of subject, proposing new terms, trying for discursive independence—also occur in different forms in your essay, Matt.

MC: It's these features you're describing that gave Alpers's book its magnetism. But they also contributed to what we were talking about yesterday, the way the book ended up narrowing Renaissance art history, in part simply by making the study of Northern Europe seem exciting, and the Italian Renaissance seem stale. Surely we can't link a single publication to the shrinking representation of Italian art history at universities across the U.S., but *The Art of Describing* did reinforce the impression, growing through the 80s, that the action was elsewhere. Thinking about the reshaping of the field in this period, I wonder whether it's useful to expand the discussion of "outliers" to encompass institutions as well as individuals. I'm tempted to suggest that there was, in the 1980s and 90s, a "Berkeley school," one that included not just Alpers but also Michael Baxandall (in his *Limewood Sculptors* days) and perhaps Joseph Koerner, not to mention the journal *Representations*. It was at Berkeley that Stephen Greenblatt wrote *Renaissance Self-Fashioning*, a book that's had at least as big an impact on Renaissance art history than any other one we've mentioned. What the Italianists were doing there was also groundbreaking—think of the two books that Loren Partridge and Randolph Starn co-authored—but I can only imagine that, if this panel were taking place fifteen years ago, it would have had to include more northern Renaissance scholars, and more Californians.

RW: I think that the most important reason Alpers's book had the effect it did was that it made Northern art seem like a direct anticipation of modern art. Italian art, based on literary, humanistic, rationalistic ideas, is old-fashioned; Northern art, based on direct encounters with the real, is somehow closer to the truth of things. Dutch art is linked to the emergence of the new natural sciences—to Enlightenment science, essentially—while at the same time the suggestion is advanced that the displacement of narrative and other literary structures—the pursuit of a kind of immediacy—anticipates modern phenomenology.

CF: It's unavoidable that we write history backwards, retrospectively. One of the healthiest trends in current discussions of historical methodology concerns anachronistic forms of telling time. Of course, interwar critical theorists like Walter Benjamin and French Annales School historians like Marc Bloch framed the discussion along ago, but I think that their experimental and politically engaged forms of history writing are highly relevant now. I think you could say the same about the vibrancy of colonial studies: they have the possibility of producing new knowledge through the study of new sources and new configurations in the historical record. Postcolonial studies could seed the field of Renaissance art with new students, looking at new objects in new ways. This is something different from using the past to anticipate the present, as Bob says Alpers did to reconfigure seventeenth-century Dutch art history. I'm not sure where I am going with this, except to open up our discussion of methodology.

MC: I find it ironic that our last two examples of outliers—*The Art of Describing* and *The Power of Images*—are two of the most widely-read books in the field.

RW: Exactly. Jim has said that he thinks all this experimentation in the last twenty years has not had its intended effect—

JE: I didn't say *all* the experimentation: I was talking about women artists, and about anthropology.

RW: Okay, much of it hasn't had the effect its advocates would like to see; it hasn't moved the mountain, so to speak. And yet, Michael is right: this is precisely the kind of work that students and younger scholars read, admire, and try to emulate. On the one hand, it seems not have accomplished what it set out to do; on the other, it has succeeded too well, become a kind of orthodoxy of its own. To me that suggests that something is still missing, that the strategies on which it is based need to be rethought and revised. Much of what passes for progressive in fact plays back into and serves to perpetuate wholly conventional assumptions and values.

JE: This is what is so interesting: the field is transforming, but when you look a individual models, it's hard to know how that happens. I don't want to make Claire a representative of something she might not want to represent, so take our other two models, Freedberg and Alpers: they both function as attractive but problematic models, ones that are by now almost traditionally inassimilable.

SC: But *The Art of Describing* worked. You could make that kind of intervention in northern art; I am not sure Italian Renaissance art is organized that way. It is interesting that David Freedberg has written one of the strongest implicit contestations of Alpers, in his latest book *The Eye of the Lynx*, which deals with the visual culture of art and science in Rome in the 1600s.[33] That book might stir things up as a response to *The Art of Describing*, but it will not be seen as controversial in Italian Renaissance and Baroque studies.

MC: So far, we also seem to be suggesting that the most transformative books in our field have been written in other places.

SC: Medieval studies.

MC: I was thinking especially of Hans Belting, but also of Michael Fried—certainly it was his work, as much as anything written by Renaissance scholars, that compelled many of us to reflect on the act of artmaking, and about the beholder of the image. But I was more curious about the broader phenomenon. It's hard to imagine a panel of modernists agreeing the most transformative books for their field have been written by art historians working on other periods.

JE: That's interesting. Hans Belting was going to be my next example, but I wasn't thinking of mentioning Michael Fried in this context. Let's consider Belting: there is someone who was at the center of medieval studies, and now, since he's been writing about modernism, he has become an outlier of a particular sort, different from our first three examples.

For Renaissance studies, the important distinction would be the one he makes between *Bild* (art, in the Renaissance and later the Kantian sense) and *Kult* (objects meant for devotion, which have a wider range of meanings and uses).[34] I'm not clear what kind of reception that has within Renaissance studies: we can talk about that. Within modernism, our subject for this afternoon, it has had a somewhat negative effect; Belting has been negatively reviewed for example by Charles Harrison, and it does not seem to me that his interventions are having an effect, at least not yet. People are skeptical of his claim that the wider uses objects had before the Renaissance can be seen as returning in recent art.

RW: And yet Belting has been influential, both in Germany —one thinks of Gerhard Wolf and Klaus Krueger—and in America: Alex Nagel and Chris Wood, for instance, both studied with him.

CF: Within the field, it's always more complex. We know that the processes he names *Bild* and *Kult* both continue during the Renaissance. Fredrika's work deals with that split, not just with cultic practices, and so do I in a book I have coming out.[35] So *Bild und Kult* is like Alpers's book in a way: it makes a big claim, and shakes the field up, and then along come the historians who try to make it more accurate, to revise it and resist it, without rejecting it. (A rejection would just put the same values in place, but inverted.)

JE: Would Belting's book then be an outlier *mainly* because it makes a strong distinction?

SC: It would have to be that, in its problematic distinction between the "era of the image" and the "era of art." Because otherwise I find Belting's two books on "the image" to be ubiquitous in Renaissance studies, which is not really what one would expect from an outlier. It has shaped the work of so many of us: Alex Nagel, Chris Wood, Klaus Krueger, Victor Stoichita, Megan Holmes, Jeffrey Hamburger, Peter Parshall, even as these scholars dissent from some of Belting's views.

RW: Again, like Freedberg, he sees himself as studying images rather than art. He calls his practice *Bild-Anthropologie*—"Image Anthropology."[36]

JE: Well, I think *Athropologie* there means something very different from what it means to Freedberg: it's more a Continental sense of philosophic anthropology that's at stake. I agree with you, but I would not compare the two books.

RW: Yet they are widely perceived as similar and mutually supporting. The original version of *Bild und Kult* came out in 1990, at the same moment as Freedberg's: I still remember how excited some people were about the way the two overlapped and seemed to map out a new kind of art history.

JE: *Bild und Kult* and *The Power of Images*, yes: I meant that *Bild-Anthropologie* is a different project, and relies on a different sense of anthropology.

MC: Coming back to Claire's remark about what Renaissance scholars have resisted and revised in Belting: It's not that we don't have a sense that something called "art" is invented in the Renaissance—Bob has tracked what happens to that idea.[37] What seems incorrect about Belting's account is the idea that at the moment of the Renaissance, artworks suddenly cease to have cult value, that Raphael's altarpieces are no longer altarpieces. That is the more controversial claim.

RW: What bothers me most about it is the implication that the invention of art as an idea, including its elaboration in theoretical writing, is simply a kind of rationalistic overlay that works to suppress deeper, more instinctive, more interesting responses to images. Again, the modernist prejudice behind this point of view emerges clearly in his writings on modern art; in modernism, he says, the rationalistic tradition is overthrown, returning us to a more direct, more authentic mode of engagement with images, one that in essential ways resembles that of the Middle Ages. He creates a genealogy of modernism that circumvents the Renaissance altogether.

JE: Bob, thanks: you've very usefully introduced yourself as another outlier. I have a kind of covert agenda here, exploring different kinds of outliers. Claire, your work is definitely one, and we've talked a bit about Freedberg, Alpers, and Belting (with an odd detour into Vasari—but we can reopen that can of worms anytime). Bob and I were thinking of a fifth model, which could be exemplified in your work, and now I think is a good time to bring it in. It would be a distinction between scholars who are mainly interested in the rational structures of Renaissance art (and that would include your work), and those who are interested in what I'll provisionally call irrational qualities or properties of Renaissance art.

SC: I would qualify that a little by saying that *humanism* has become an outlier in Renaissance studies. It has been stigmatized by Panofsky's formulation of iconology as a humanist project, entailing a subordination of the work of art to literary traditions, a position to which few of us (including those who work on art and literature) would want to revert.[38] Another problem that has beset the fortunes of Renaissance Latin humanism is the rise of nationalist ideologies in the nineteenth century, which Claire addresses as a problem in conceiving the Renaissance as a whole. In his recent book *The Lost Italian Renaissance* Chris Celenza has done an excavation of how national cultures excluded the humanists from their canons of national literatures.[39] The Italian humanists wrote in Latin rather than Italian: they didn't fit with models of nationalism. And this is itself a recognition of the fact that humanism is an interesting example of a vibrant trans-national culture. Erasmus is more important in Italy in the sixteenth century than any corresponding Italian.

CF: And Erasmus was certainly known in the Spanish Americas among the governing state officials and ecclesiastics who have never have been considered a subject of study for Renaissance art historians. Like Stephen, I am talking about studying humanism as a historical phenomenon that has the potential to revise our understanding of both the past and the present.

SC: There is a sense of humanism as elitist, as a betrayal—

RW: Right. And much of modern thought—the whole tradition of Nietzsche, Heidegger, Foucault—is emphatically, militantly anti-humanistic.

SC: I agree, but those thinkers were targeting a different version of humanism.

RW: Yet this intellectual climate conditions the way in which we approach the subject: it exerts tremendous pull on all work being done in the fields of cultural history and makes it almost impossible to approach humanism or rationalism in any positive way. I think that is another indication of how our investment in certain modernist values blinds us to the reality of the past —even, I would say, to the modernity of the past.

I should add, by the way, that there is also an emphatic anti-humanism at work in some mainstream empirical scholarship: I'm thinking of Charles Hope and Elizabeth McGrath, for example, who consistently minimize the connections between art and humanism.[40] Humanism is under attack from both sides.

SC: Exactly. We have to *alienate* humanism, and cut it off from the later baggage it had accumulated by the time Heidegger was doing his critique of humanism. That was a different model, centered in the rationalism of the Enlightenment, and characterized also for better or worse in Foucault's account of the "human sciences." Earlier humanism is not defined by any concern it might have with "the human" or the "Nature of Man," although Burckhardt, Kristeller and their followers have tried to make it be about that. In the fifteenth century, humanism was a project of intellectual self-definition centered on the study of language and on rhetoric. It was an epistemological project, but I think that aspect trails off in the sixteenth century.

RW: I don't know if it trails off, exactly: it gets institutionalized in the later sixteenth century; it survives the collapse of the city-state culture that nurtured it and could be said to thrive under absolutism—though whether one understands that process as one of evolution and fulfilment or as a denaturing and betrayal will depend on one's point of view. It would be an interesting thing to discuss here, not at all irrelevant to our theme, but perhaps the more urgent point, the point I feel it is most important to make, is that the notion that humanism somehow contaminated art with rationalism—and that we have to undo the process—is a pervasive, almost irresistible force in modern scholarship: it's the shared assumption underlying Alpers, Freedberg, and Belting. It's a straightforward projection of modernist values, yet as an interpretative strategy it is incomplete —I would say flawed—which is perhaps why it hasn't proved entirely effective.

JE: This does seem to me to be one of the most interesting ways of dividing the field of Renaissance studies right now. It is treacherous because of these words "rationality," "rationalism," "irrationality," and "irrationalism," but I would like to keep using them for a while, and not fret about them too much. They are serviceable, as tags.

Bob, I think your brave listing of people in the "irrational" camp, in your essay, is very apposite. (Brave because it includes two people at this table, Michael and Stephen!)

RW: Well, but let me say that both Michael and Stephen address humanism and the rational content of art with truly exquisite subtlety in their work; indeed, their engagement with it seems to me to pick up in the most productive way from where Baxandall left off in *Giotto and the Orators*.

JE: An initial problem I would have with your position, Bob, is the genealogy *of* the irrationalism. The claim is that twentieth-century scholars have become interested in recovering non-rational elements in artworks, but I wonder where those interests come from. For my part, I'd like to assign them to Fichte and Schelling: I'd like to go back to first- and second-generation Romantics. I know you have mentioned they can be assigned to Symbolism, though I think that among recent precedents the interest in the irrational owes more to Surrealism. There would be a link between the "irrationalist" Renaissance scholars you mention and the *October* circle.

These are important choices, but at the moment I want just to note that the desire to explore sources other than rational ones is clear, but the intellectual indebtedness is not.

RW: You're absolutely right about Romanticism, though I think we could even go back beyond the Romantics to Kant, to the notion of the aesthetic as "conceptless." That is the point of departure for Romantic speculation about the arts, which in turn became the point of reference for the Symbolists and Surrealists. Perhaps that's the basic problem: we have to recover the idea of art—and the modernity of that idea—without having recourse to the idea of the aesthetic.

CF: One of the richest aspects of Renaissance humanist discussions of art concerns the ways that sub-rational processes some into play. I think we all share in that interest; I am not sure how that fits into the trajectory you want to pose, Jim, or into the polemical pair of rationalism and irrationalism. Humanist texts that discuss the sub-rational processes involved in artmaking—primarily the *fantasia* and the productive imagination—and religious texts that discuss the viewer's response, are very similar in a fundamental respect: they are both grounded in the same neo-Aristotelian theory of cognition. By neo-Aristotelian I mean that the language derives from Aristotle, but the ideas themselves incorporate additional ideas—including Platonist ideas about images, for example. Current discussions of *Bild und Kult* would benefit greatly from recognizing these continuities. To the extent that they don't rcognize these deeper continuities, I think it supports Bob's claim that modernist values are projected unconsciously on the historical material.

JE: I think the polarity is dangerously seductive, or to put it optimistically, potentially very fruitful. It could include people like Freedberg as outliers, but also even Alpers, because the terms she chooses—like the idea that the world "stains" the canvas instead of being optically projected onto it—are deliberately distinct from rational Italian models.

SC: It's seductive because of the allure of what might be called magical thinking, when words and things become the same, when the represented can be controlled through its representation. And that's what we *love*—some of us. Not always including me. The magical or "irrational" is also part of the appeal of Belting's work on "the image." Didi-Huberman and others resurrect this dimension to subvert an alleged hegemony of humanist rationalism.

But in the terms of sixteenth-century humanism, the possibility of links between sign and referent, while not held by everybody, may not be so irrational after all. You don't subvert anything by appealing to a distinction between rationalists and irrationalists, because the distinction is fairly hard to sustain in the intellectual history of the sixteenth century. Reason in the sixteenth century is not the reason of the Enlightenment.

RW: I would agree that the distinction creates problems when applied to the historical material; my point is that modern scholarship has created the distinction, that the emphasis on the irrational to the exclusion of the rational has led to a situation in which we must now work with such terms to correct the balance.

JE: Bob, I think it's important to say that you are in a tiny minority in taking seriously the rational component of Italian Renaissance artmaking. Most of the rest of us at this table, and also in the discipline, are less convinced of it—

SC: Although we take it seriously. Others, I think, resist it.

JE:—and "irrationalism," under whatever name, is pervasive in historical research in general. It is usually assigned to a revival of what are understood as medieval values (as you say about Belting, Bob), or to a rejection of Enlightenment values. What I think matters much more than what is ostensibly being revived is the proximate sources of people's interest—Romanticism, Surrealism. One problem with the tag "irrationalism" is that it misses those nuances; it sounds transhistorical.

I think that to make any headway on this issue we need to acknowledge, as a starting point, that this problem, under whatever name (irrationalism, return to the premodern, rejection of the Enlightenment) is a larger, deeper question than art history.[41] We are just a tributary of wide currents of thought— Blumenberg, Habermas, Gadamer—and so if *art history* or even just *Renaissance art history* are going to be places where this issue is rethought, it will have to be by virtue of the exemplarity of the visual.

RW: I like your use of the term "exemplarity": it seems to me to open onto the way in which the visual works in relation to the non-visual, in which it models knowledge, for instance, but perhaps that's another discussion altogether. As for being in the minority, I'm happy to be there—for the time being—yet I see myself as part of the larger critical project in which we're all engaged; I see myself as trying to move the mountain too, trying to get beyond a set of deeply embedded assumptions that hold us all back.

But to return to something that was said a minute ago: Claire, when you describe the ways in which Renaissance theory makes a place for irrationality, you're right, but it seems to me that that place is carefully circumscribed, confined pretty much to the ways in which visual perceptions lead to abstract thought, that it is limited to what might be called the mechanics of sense perception. What happens later, perhaps in the eighteenth century or with the Romantics, is that art comes to be understood as irrational in a far deeper, more comprehensive way. Renaissance accounts of either the rationality or irrationality of art are unlikely to satisfy post-Enlightenment readers.

CF: "Irrationalism" is not an early modern word, and it doesn't make sense in a Renaissance context. The mental processes of cognition, and the series of events that leads to a rational thought, is seen as a continuum, not an opposition.

RW: In Aristoteleanism, right. But even if leading theorists—Leonardo or Zuccaro—subscribe to it, wouldn't we be mistaken to assume that Aristotelian perceptual theory offers an adequate description of what is going on in Renaissance art? There are so many things it does not explain: all that is implied, I would say, by the idea of *ut pictura poesis*—signification, engagement with literary and abstract philosophical content, the mobilization of social codes. And more importantly, Aristotle is ultimately a rigorous rationalist: for him, art is "a state of capacity to make that reasons truly", and a logos—an "order"—in the working process. The question for modernists is whether Renaissance art theory isn't fundamentally misguided, or even dishonest. That's how Didi-Huberman sees it, for example, but it seems to me that many modernists are committed to an orientation that makes it impossible for them to take Renaissance thought about art seriously—except as a symptom of repression.

CF: It is in this period that projection of irrationality on to *other people* begins to appear as a discourse.

RW: As you have shown in your own work.

CF: Discussions of *grotteschi*, for example, document emerging racist views about people expressed in terms of the kinds of art, or styles of art, they make.[42] The implication is that those who depict things according to the imagination, without correspondence to things in the actual world and without proper proportions, are deluded and lacking rationality. Four hundred years later, the Surrealists embraced this association of the irrational with the abject.

MC: I'm still thinking about your remark that "irrationalism" doesn't make sense in a Renaissance context. For myself, I can't say that I find the polarity "rationalist / irrationalist" a terribly helpful way to divide the field. Where does that leave the work of, say, Charles Dempsey, who writes on love and nightmares and other seemingly Romantic, seemingly non-rational experiences, but who is especially interested in the way these experiences were conceived, even invented, by the most systematic and modern philologists and artists? And what should we make of the fact that topics like alchemy and astrology have primarily attracted scholars who are looking for the proto-scientific aspects of the Renaissance? I wonder whether we can be true rationalists and really be interested in the Renaissance at all.

JE: Well, I would see this as a matter of desire. Just in relation to Renaissance alchemy: the scholars attracted to it tend to be either strictly "rational" historians of chemistry, or indulgently "irrational" practitioners. In Freudian terms, the choice is cathected for twentieth-century scholarship: both poles are intensified, even fetishized. That's an overly metaphoric way of saying I think the fundamental phenomenon here is a deep attraction to the "irrational."[43]

MC: Okay, the point about the history of alchemy is well taken. Maybe the study of Renaissance astrology is a better illustration of what I'm getting at: most of the people who write on this are really trying to understand the "system," whether that system is ultimately a cosmology or a way of ordering mythological knowledge or a regimen of propaganda or something else. To slightly rephrase Stephen, the distinction between the rational and the irrational is fairly hard to sustain.

EMK: A word that we might consider along with "rationality" is "self-reflection" or "self-awareness." "Rationality" is used by certain German historians to talk about the early Modern period; what they seem to be talking about is what we would call self-awareness, the artist's sense of himself or herself, and in the mental processes, together with a *deliberateness* in the choices of materials and references.[44]

JE: Would this be a useful place to bring Vasari back into the discussion? There is a way to think of Vasari as a precipitation of ideas about art, self-reflexivity, and rational historical structures. And can I also bring in Michael Baxandall's now-famous line about Vasari, that everything in art history is already in Vasari? In a sense it's a throwaway line, and when I've seen it cited I have the impression it is very hard to elaborate; but it implies something crucial for our conversation, namely that there is something systematic and rationalizing in Vasari that is carried on in what we now recognize as art history. We would all be necessarily partly on the side of that structure—despite whatever anti-rationalist uses we may be trying to put that structure to.

MC: It's interesting, from this point of view, that Baxandall's line is a variation on the famous remark by the logician Alfred North Whitehead, that the history of Western philosophy consists of a series of footnotes to Plato. The interventionist Vasari a number of us were talking about earlier would not seem so all-encompassing.

RW: Of course Didi-Huberman thinks that Vasari's rationalism is the original sin of art history: it is precisely what must be overthrown if we are ever to get at the real complexity of images. But I think Vasari's investment in the rational has a lot to do with the fact that Renaissance artists in general were invested in the rational: it is not an idiosyncratic projection on his part but an insight of great documentary value into the real workings of history. And I should add—since we skipped quickly from rationalism to humanism earlier—that this investment does not just come from humanism: even from a narrowly technical, artisanal point of view, materials and processes might be thought to imply, require, or exemplify a kind of reason.

FJ: What about the way that Vasari talks about the irrational elements in drawings, *schizzi?* And his ideas about the artist being divine?

RW: But he also says that drawing is the direct projection of the mind, the most immediate manifestation of the artist's idea.

MC: One can also trace the migration of terms like *concetto* and *modello* from designating drawings to designating ideas.

FJ: But when he talks about splotches, how it's hard to tell one thing from another, and when he juxtaposes that to the more rational process of translating the splotches into art.

RW: He actually begins by saying drawing is the union of the three arts—

FJ: But it's a paradox—

RW: This is typical of our difference of approach: you emphasize the disorderly, the chaotic—

JE: You see, Fredrika, you're a typical twenty-first-century art historian, excavating the rational for traces of the irrational. It is exactly what Bob once accused me of doing.[45]

FJ: What about the "epidemic of paradox," which runs through all of sixteenth-century writing, including Leonardo's discussion of the point? I recently heard a lecture by Frank Fehrenbach in which he addressed this topic, arguing that Leonardo viewed the point as something that is simultaneously nothing and a thing, as both absent and present.[46] Perhaps the penchant for masking can fit here as well. In much of this the appearance of irrationality is in play. The intent is to confuse, confound, and perplex. In sixteenth-century literature this takes the form of masquerading and problematizing identity. A perfect example is

Castiglione's tale of a goatherd masquerading as a courtier, who then masquerades as a goatherd. The paradox here, it seems to me, is that the behavior is at once rational and irrational. There are instances where Vasari characterizes artists and/or the creative process in equally complex ways. Raphael, for example, is so susceptible to human sexual urges that it causes his demise yet because he is also blessed with creative divinity he rise above his mortality.[47]

RW: Vasari's book is extremely complex, full of errors, contradictions, unresolved tensions; still, it is one of the greatest books ever written about art, arguably the greatest, certainly the most influential: I think that's what Baxandall meant. Vasari is certainly mindful of the messiness of the creative process, but he also insists on its susceptibility to rational instrumentalization.

FJ: In favor of your argument, of course, is Vasari's account of Piero di Cosimo's life, and how he walks the streets looking at stains in the sidewalk—

RW: That comes straight out of Leonardo, of course.

SC: Vasari systematizes madness and eccentricity. He wants to put order on the whole of artistic behavior. He is trying to contain a tradition of writing about artists.

RW: Or perhaps trying to fashion a better way to write about artists, one which does a better job of addressing what he thinks is most important—even if it results in an exclusivity that we find objectionable. He certainly was trying to fashion a master narrative—unabashedly!—yet in doing so he was trying to excavate, to illuminate and preserve in written form something he thought was implicit in the historical phenomena he was surveying, something he thought desperately precious and important to articulate, a confluence of motives and interests that led to a series of transformative events, an ongoing dialogue, a common work. Why would it have been so important for him to insist on what we consider the rationalistic aspects of art in doing so?

JE: Or for you? Why is it important for you to insist on these aspects of Vasari?

RW: I'm just trying to recover what's at stake in the intellectual investments we no longer share (or seem to share) in what we have chosen to ignore, in what, for one reason or another, we need to ignore. As far as *disegno* is concerned, for instance, it seems to me to involve a more complex process than our notions of irrationality allow. Didi-Huberman says some perceptive things about Vasari's concept of *disegno*, but in the end he uses it as a foil to set up his own post-rationalist, Freudian approach to images: he characterizes *disegno* as both mimetic and idealistic, and contrasts it to the dream-work, yet I would say that the kinds of transformative, even negative powers attributed to the dream-work are implicit in *disegno*.

Vasari's rationalism also extends to other authors—to Lomazzo and Zuccaro, for example—so that it must be indicative of larger historical forces. We mentioned the idea of progress a minute ago—certainly one of Vasari's most problematic ideas, from our point of view. Yet I think that that the idea of progress was his way of making more fundamental points: that art involves a critical process, first of all. Indeed, the argument for the rational nature of art, pervasive in Renaissance theory, is ultimately an argument for the critical nature of art. The emphasis on progress, too, is a way of saying something else, expressing a deeper insight: that art has a history, and that its historicity—its embeddedness in time and its development over time—is essential to what makes it interesting, meaningful, important. That he had recourse to a simple biological metaphor—infancy, youth, maturity—is an almost reflexively rhetorical way of thinking, typical of humanism.

I should say that I don't think the rationalism of these writers is ultimately motivated by an investment in rationalism per se—that they were instinctively more rationalistic or idealistic than we are, even though their language often suggests that they were—so much as by a deeper sense that life in a complex culture demands some form of rationality, that there is no avoiding it, and that engaging the pressures created by such a situation is the specific and urgent challenge of a modern art. To put it in other words, the modern world was felt to require an art in which reason was thematized in some important, even essential way.

JE: See, Bob, to me what's interesting in this project of yours is that you're speaking against the grain of vast amounts of philosophy and scholarship in the twentieth and twenty-first century by openly admitting that you're interested in the rational. That seems to me an exemplary polemics, and can have all sorts of consequences in ordinary inquiries that require adjustment to various mixtures and complexities.

But at the same time I wonder how far the discipline as a whole can get from Vasari. I'm saying this now because of the way you've just characterized Vasari: that his work is driven by ideas of structures of history, that historical unfolding is part of what demonstrates art's importance as an activity. Is there any distance between those formulations and the unavoidable self-description of any activity that could be recognizable as art history?

RW: Well, if we can recognize the specifically critical element in Vasari's rationalism, if we can detach his insight about historicity from his idea of progress, we have already begun to establish a certain distance: we begin to glimpse an account of Renaissance art that salvages the strengths of Vasari's account without committing us to sharing them completely or reproducing them as stated.

JE: But can you return to something that is already constitutive of the discipline?

RW: Well, to go back to the distinction between art and images that I brought up at the beginning: perhaps art is not a kind of object, but rather a kind of work, a particularly complex, highly-structured, demanding kind of work. In that case, Vasari's book might be seen as an attempt to describe how that work—the work of being an artist—had evolved over the three hundred years leading up to his own time. That's why the biographical format is so essential: it isn't a celebration of "genius"—which is how modernist critics always dismiss it—so much as an affirmation of the meaning of human productivity. His book is about a process of redefining art as a culturally significant kind of labor. To think of art as labor might provide a point of contact between Fredrika's orientation and mine, between a concern with images or objects usually thought of as marginal to the history of art, and a preoccupation with high art and theory.

I should say that other theoretical texts of the period can also be read this way and be seen to stress slightly different aspects of the labor involved; aspects of this redefinition are also visible in practice. Michael's book on Cellini, for instance, with its emphasis on sculpture as an act, makes this point beautifully.

MC: This is one instance where you can get pretty far even without Vasari. Vasari, perhaps, situates ideas about performance into a historical scheme, but the notion that art is, as you put it, a culturally significant kind of labor is widely shared. One need only look at the ways that Venetian writers on painting link *sprezzatura* to technique; or at Michelangelo's poems on marble carving.

CF: To make things a little schematic for the sake of bringing these ideas into play with contemporary ideas of the irrational: it seems we need to interject an awareness of how art as a form of knowledge was then historically imposed on other people, in other cultures. It was the interplay of rational and sub-rational processes that made art a form of knowledge for Vasari, Leonardo, and others. The problems began when other cultures were thought to have only sub-rational or irrational practices: that is when the dichotomy emerged. Twentieth-century theorists such as feminists and Surrealists embraced *that* irrationality, but still retained a critical, rational system in place. That is one area where Renaissance scholarship can contribute to the discussion, because there is an amazing amnesia about anything that happened before Kant or before the late nineteenth century.

JE: You could also connect that with the beginning of our conversation this morning, because those missing art historians on this panel—the ones from Italy, for example—might also have different ways of drawing the distinction. I imagine the tide of this irrationalism doesn't sweep evenly over all of Europe!

CF: This distinction we're talking about is rooted in Renaissance humanism and its debt to classical sources. So you *have* to have an understanding of that history of see how it was skewed, reworked, and imposed in other places.

RW: The effects of rationality—since that's what you're dealing with in Aristotle—are also evident in the system of the genres developed in the West, and that then get extended and adapted to classify non-Western art.

SC: The hierarchy of the genres reveals an ideological dimension to the rationality of art that many scholars you are addressing might want to resist. The portrait of the King is at the top of the hierarchy, and it legitimizes and rationalizes all other forms. I would add there's another side, too: the competing models of artistic reason, ones that are made by artists themselves in practice. We lose sight of that if we stress Vasari too much. His book is a competitive intervention, positioned against a series of art practices, many of them non-Florentine, that he wants to close down on. He wants to have the last word. It is verbal: it's a logocentric endeavor. Artists, sometimes taking on a subaltern role, could speak for art, and that is not irrational: we can see such artists as being rational themselves, in their own ways.

MC: Yes, and what those ways are, and what's distinctive about them, is still a real question.[48] The topic is starting to interest historians of science as well—there's that recent book by Pamela Smith, *The Body of the Artisan*.[49]

CF: I think Matt's material is just right for this theme. The forms you study are geometry, and that's rational, but it can be reconfigured as flowery organic growth that may, or may not, speak to the rational power of art as defined in sixteenth-century logocentric terms. And Steve, it's more than logocentric, because it also privileges proportion and anatomy, and so the rational is defined according to a kind of Euclidean geometry, because that's at the height of human knowledge.

Number, geometry is where metaphysics meets human knowledge, and the *same* ideas in different form are embodied in so-called Gothic traceries and building patterns that your work, Matt, is concerned with.

EMK: It is interesting that geometry becomes a reference for a number of projects. On the one hand, it can lead to the inscription of transcendence in religious building. On the other hand, it can serve as a self-conscious enterprise, an emblem of identity, or a kind of signature. Ornamental devices, which are basically configured geometric shapes, serve as a kind of supplementary signature of the designer in the early sixteenth century.

A related issue is the relation between craft and art in our period. These ornamental devices can serve as signatures through their relation to older mason's marks, geometric designs used to identify those responsible for stone cutting, a far less prestigious labor. Mason's marks then became the charge on escutcheons: they were placed as a new-fangled kind of armorial device. When architecture becomes a more noble occupation, the geometric designs migrate from charges on coats of arms to freestanding signs of identity. That has to be read in conjunction with the rise in status of the architect or designer, from anonymous craftsman to publicly acknowledged identity as artist. I think that figures much of our discussion today, when we talk about identity and self-reflexivity in the arts.

JE: So: luckily there is no way to complete a catalog of dissensions within the field, and I am not going to add any more names. Actually, I think that given the usual fumbly way people have when they try to speak extemporaneously, and given the limitations of time and space, we made quite a good survey of differing approaches in the field. It is strange how seldom art history tends to do this to itself.

One last comment, which I'd like to leave hanging in the air: it was a direct and simple matter to address Claire's work, David Freedberg's, Svetlana Alpers's, Hans Beltings's, and Bob's, as different kinds of "outliers": but I notice no one wanted to go near my little list of people at the "center." If the margins are politically sensitive, the center is exquisitely so.

This may be a good place to break for questions.

Clare Guest [*question from the audience*]: An observation and two questions.

First, on the question of ornament: it would seem to possess both geometric configuration and, in its physiognomy, have the character of metaphoric embodiment.

Then, concerning discussion of Vasari, I wonder to what degree the question is one of Vasari's text and to what extent it concerns the ontology of form—the metaphysics, part Platonic, part Thomistic-Aristotelian—that constitutes a description of reality in Vasari's period.

Finally, regarding the opening point, about the fecundity of approaches: I wonder to what extent that reflects the material that has been studied in the period? Given the proliferation of texts in the sixteenth century, the immense preoccupation with a non-systematic encyclopedism, is it not inevitable that one ends up with a fecundity of approaches, or something that may be seen as a disarray? I find it hard to see how one manages to escape that.

JE: If by "one" you mean art history, it did manage to escape it for a long time! I think I might be unhappy with that line of reasoning because methods have seldom been determined by the historical material. We've been talking about late twentieth-century interests, not approaches governed by the material. We have been seeing what we have desired to see, not what has desired to see us. The disarray doesn't model the terrain, it models our interests.

MC: I would go back to Stephen's comment from the beginning, about whether we should *try* to escape it.

CF: Is disarray a bad thing?

CG: No; in humanist writing, it is almost celebrated at certain points.

CF: The genre of dialogue, as Michael said yesterday, allows for multiple points of view, without subsuming them, as they are in a treatise, to a conclusion.

MC: And the dialogue, more than the treatise, is the preferred form for writing about the arts, at least through the sixteenth century.

CG: And one could go much further in the dialogic model, as in for example Rabelaisian discussions of *copia*.

JE: Hmm, I wonder if we aren't flattering ourselves a bit by assuming our disarray is the result of an increasing sensitivity to the material. I think I'd see what goes on in Renaissance scholarship as more a matter of concerns that don't always go back more than a hundred years or so. That's not an argument about their truth value, but it's a reason to wonder if we see what we expect to find at least as often as we're surprised by what we find. For me, the disarrays (in the plural) in Renaissance scholarship, are often assignable to people from Burckhardt onward, and they'd be there even if the material were stubbornly unified.

John Paul McMahon [*question from the audience*]: This is a question for Bob Williams, about the functionality of your concept of systematicity. I wonder if you can speak a bit about how you see it working. I see it as so all-encompassing that it ends up doing nothing. So I just question the functionality of that concept. Do you see it as a grand narrative that conditions the period of the Renaissance? Also, how is it different from other approaches to the Renaissance? The way I read it, I see it as encircling previous accounts of the Renaissance, but not doing much more than that. Also your denigration of social art history's role in Renaissance studies in your paper makes the concept of systematicity doubly flawed.

RW: Well, I certainly don't denigrate social art history; I attempt to critique it. I say quite explicitly at the end of the first section of the essay that the history of art cannot *not* be social historical. Yet I also think that social historical approaches have tended to deflect attention away from a whole array of crucial issues, specifically—as I said earlier this morning—to displace and suppress the category "art."

As far as systematicity being simply an encircling of other accounts: it certainly does attempt to assimilate what is most valuable about other accounts (it wouldn't be worth much if it didn't), but it also significantly re-orders them and restructures our understanding of the various phenomena they address. When I say, for instance, that decorum is cultural perspective, I'm pretty sure I'm saying something no one else has said; I'm making what I think is an historically accurate and critically useful point about the ways in which categories overlap. Because art was redefinied so comprehensively and profoundly in the Renaissance, I think it's essential to try to understand such overlapping and the kinds of analogies or correspondences between things that strike us as different. If that makes systematicity useless for you—

JPM: I didn't say it was useless altogether, but at the end of your paper, when you started talking about modern systematicities, I began to wonder. I thought if you had contained it in the Renaissance, it would have worked—

RW: Well, okay, that's another issue. I do suggest, rather casually, at the end of the article, that modern art, while apparently a reaction against systematicity, in fact perpetuates it in certain ways. That's obviously not an idea that could be proved without writing a very extensive book about modern art, yet it does seem to me to be necessary to suggest. In the book I am writing now, on Raphael, I go a little further and propose that systematicity anticipates the modern category of the aesthetic, that since, for the Renaissance, what is distinctive and proper to art is a concern with the specifically systematic features of representation, systematicity is the specifically "aesthetic" feature of representation.

Catherine Campbell [*question from the audience*]: Prior to this conversation, my perception of the Renaissance would have been Italian-based; Claire's work opened that up for me, and made me think of the Renaissance in Latin America, and so forth. My question is whether the panel has inadvertently fallen into the same trap: all the experts here come from a similar geographic location.

JE: Let me just say something as co-organizer, and then we can all talk about it. It's a very interesting, but very sensitive, question. Volume 3 in this series, called *Is Art History Global?*, involved people from nearly forty countries, and we had a similar openness in mind here; but when Bob and I sat down to think about people with whom we might have the kind of conversation *we* thought would be interesting, we couldn't think of many outside North American institutions.

RW: And we knew Claire could represent her position very ably.

CF: I have tried my best to deflect any presumption that I am speaking for others, above all those who are not represented here! I am advocating that others be here with us.

JE: It's a good feature of the dialogic nature of these books that what we say here will be followed by thirty or so Assessments. I want to make a prediction about what may happen, based on what happened in volumes 3 and 4: some of the people writing Assessments will want to change the subjects of the conversation. The terms will change, and our voices may be lost in a larger conversation.

All right: we meet back here this afternoon to discuss whether we're relevant at all.

2

JE: Welcome back everyone. The topic this afternoon is the possibly larger question of the relation between writing on the Renaissance and writing on modernism. There are some interesting paradoxes in the air regarding the relation of Renaissance studies and art history as a whole. One would be that the Renaissance is foundational to the discipline, even in a very deep sense, that it provides the discipline with its sense of history and of history's structure. The Renaissance was the time when ideas such as art, criticism, and history, were articulated, and that it continues to perform that foundational role. Some people, like Steve Melville, would say that the Renaissance's sense of perspective and history encompass or comprise our own thoughts on it.[50] That would be an extreme way of putting something that is, I think, commonly acknowledged in more muted forms.

On the other hand, and the reason I say this is a paradox, it is also commonly acknowledged that the Renaissance is sunken into a kind of second-, third-, or fourth-rate status, when it comes to such things as competing for students or jobs, but also conceptually: we have gone beyond some important break in Western art history, and we are now in a different realm. If this view were taken to its extreme, it would entail the notion that the Renaissance is not relevant, in some, many, or perhaps even all ways. This paradoxical choice, between the potential overvaluation of the Renaissance and its perhaps precipitous undervaluation, is structural to art history: it's the way that people talk about Western art. Because it is structural, I don't expect to make any headway on it at all, but I'd like to talk around and about it this afternoon.

Bob and I had a couple of things planned. I thought to get the conversation started, I would mention something I think is a curious litmus test of this paradox, and that is by counting citations—by which I mean how frequently art historians who are modernists cite artworks or texts from the Renaissance. I could make a long list of prominent modernist art historians who basically never think to connect their observations with Renaissance studies: Rosalind Krauss, Benjamin Buchloh, Yve-Alain Bois, Pamela Lee, Joan Copjec, Anne Wagner . . . I could go on and on. This is not, obviously!, a way of finding fault: it is a way of noticing a fault line in our common understanding of Western art history. If only busy scholars, or younger scholars, didn't cite the Renaissance, that would be down to the pressures of the job market or institutional configurations: but virtually no modernists cite Renaissance precedents, and to me that points to the existence of a shared understanding of historical structure.

The big question is where the cut-off point is. If you're talking about someone like Tim Clark, that moment is emblematized by the year Jacques-Louis David painted the *Death of Marat*, crystallizing the idea he calls *contingency* and changing the terms in which painting could be discussed.[51] If you talk to Michael Fried, the cut-off point is the late eighteenth century, and has to do with a nexus of problems that arose in painting and, again, changed the terms under which is was understood. (Even though Tim Clark is now writing about Poussin and Michael Fried is writing about Caravaggio—in the latter case, Michael has adjusted his genealogy somewhat.) Someone like Barbara Stafford would locate such a point in the seventeenth and eighteenth centuries, around issues of natural history, the emergence of the sciences, and ideographic art. The clearest example, I think, is Robert Rosenblum, whose PhD dissertation was on the International Style in 1800, and he has almost never said anything about the sometimes obvious parallels between post-1800 art and art made before that point.

My distinct, unquantifiable sense of this is that Renaissance art historians tend to know more about modernism than modernists know about the Renaissance, and that the inequality points to a structural problem in the discipline.

SC: I think it's true that for someone like myself, in graduate school in the 1980s, the nineteenth century, and the work done by T.J. Clark and others, seemed like the main viable model for how you did the social history of art. I read Richard Shiff to learn about semiotics, and Michael Fried for many others things, such as ways of conceiving the author-function in painting, and the question of the beholder. This was all happening around nineteenth-century scholarship then. I think nineteenth-century scholarship since is not as vital; it had its moment in an interesting way.

EMK: In terms of method, I agree, but I think it's natural that Renaissance art historians should be engaged with modern art: it's the art of our time and easily engages our interests. It is also understandable that modern art historians would *not* be interested in the Renaissance; they don't have the same purchase on the Renaissance that we have on the modern period.

There are many ways of dealing with modern art that do not require Renaissance art as a point of reference. I don't find it as obligatory an enterprise. I think it's perhaps surprising that there aren't more people who do it. But I don't see it as necessary for people who study twentieth-century art.

JE: For me, the reason modernists don't cite the Renaissance is due to more than our institutional habits—or to put it the other way around, our institutions would have grown up around those fault lines. The phenomenon also raises the possibility that Renaissance and modernism trade unequally. From modernism, Renaissance scholars may take critical discourse and methods (as Stephen mentioned), but modernist historians may take something much broader from the Renaissance: they make take their idea of what Western art and art history were. That makes it even odder that they don't cite Renaissance scholarship or works.

CF: The lack of citation seems unacknowledged, so it is undigested, and that is where the space of discussion comes in. The foundational concepts of art history, based on the centrality of the Renaissance as developed by Burckhardt, still underpin the field, and they are the reason why modernist art historians don't feel the Renaissance is relevant.

Periodization, very simply put, keeps people thinking that they can just divide history up into chronological periods, and that there is no strategy of time involved in doing that. Some of the most interesting discussions going on now about the writing of history have to do with thinking things through using something other than a chronological structure. Hayden White famously wrote in the 1970s about the strategies involved in constructing history as chronological sequences, as if that were objective; I think the problematic of how historians structure time is only now being taken up by art historians. Whether modernists will ever recognize that problematic in their own amnesiac constructions of time as the exclusive present remains to be seen.

JE: There are certainly any number of concepts at work in modernist art history that are easily, demonstrably dependent on concepts articulated in and for the Renaissance. And yet there is a lack of feeling of responsibility for addressing them.

CF: Yes. It is a little hard to get Renaissance experts to talk about this, because we're dealing with a different period of history in our research, and because when we're critiquing this modernist construct, we're using it to rethink our own field, not modernism.

JE: As if it's their problem, not ours.

CF: Yes, but I feel it is my problem, too. The work I am doing now is increasingly diachronic in its structure, as a way of encompassing the present. My own position as an historian is part of the same continuum, so I feel increasingly aware of the need to place myself in that continuum, and not separate from my area of study as if I could narrate it from the outside.

RW: Jim is right about the simultaneous dependence of modernist art history on concepts developed for the Renaissance and the unwillingness to interrogate that dependence. The Renaissance is made to serve both as a starting point for the modern and as something against which modernism reacts: in my essay on systematicity, I describe this construction as a "choke-hold." What seems to me to be at stake in the whole chronology issue is genealogy, hence, legitimation: the aim is to help us explain how we got to where we are. Modernism needs that legitimation, yet it also seems to require repressing some aspects of how we got to where we are.

JE: There are a couple of things at stake, aren't there? There's the repression; there are institutional habits, which I do not think are a particularly interesting way of looking at it; there is a sense of the structure of the intervening centuries (if those centuries harbor an abyss, then there is no point in trying to cross it); and then there are ways people conventionally write, so that those historians who try to cross the abyss, like Hans Belting or Mieke Bal, almost *necessarily* begin to appear as outliers.

SC: I am thinking, Bob, about what you said about the project of legitimation. I wonder if the various recent texts on Caravaggio function as a kind of legitimation. That is not necessarily what is going on in Frank Stella, because he sees something in Caravaggio that may elude the rest of us[52]—

JE: I hope it does!

SC: It began with his book, and now it's Mieke Bal, Michael Fried . . . who else?[53]

MC: Leo Bersani—and then there's Derek Jarman, whose film came out the same year as Stella's book.[54]

JE: Yes, and that's the strangest list of people we have had all day long.

SC: Many of us find it exasperating to hear that Western representation is about the Albertian window, which came into being in the fifteenth century. That is how a great deal of modernism constructs the Renaissance.

At the same time it is worth reflecting that there is something about prominent interventions in the field in the last twenty years that lets down other art historians who might be interested. The drive to the social history of art, which I mentioned earlier, has led to a turn to the archive, and also to a tremendous effort directed at works of art that did not survive. In that way the visual and material component slips away. Many Renaissance art historians—including some of the most able and interesting people in the field—do not write about art.[55]

RW: But just because one isn't writing about images doesn't mean that one isn't writing about art.

JE: You know, this disappointment that may be felt by some modernist art historians, whether it's due to the turn from images to archives, or to an unexpected encounter with methodologies that a modernist might recognize as coming from their own field, may be the obverse of the problem that modernists *need* the Renaissance to exist, in order to imagine that something has happened against which they reacted. And because that something is now invisible, the paradox I opened with is even bigger. The need of modernism for the Renaissance is greater, and it is no longer answered by anything.

CF: So if we're writing about the Renaissance, we are functioning the way the medieval period functioned for the Renaissance humanists who wanted to bury *it*, and we are reproducing that structure. That would be another way that a structure which began in the Renaissance continues to drive writing on contemporary art and practice.

It is interesting to talk about this, because when we're doing our micro-studies we're not thinking about this at all.

JE: It is very tempting to elaborate on that, and risk going off into a flight of fancy . . . but it does strike me that it is the modernist moment that would have perceived a structure in the past analogous to the one that the Renaissance perceived in its past. In Joseph Koerner's account, for example, the modernist sense of the past is a perpetual belatedness, and an irretrievable distance from a fragmented and incomplete inheritance, while the

Renaissance sense of the past was of an ideal not limited by historical context. But in this model, both modernists and people in the Renaissance felt the past as a founding moment, one that places demands on the present but is divided from it by a fault-line or rupture, so that the past stands in need of a *quieting* or even a represssion. The *postmodern* moment would be something different: it would be some recalibration, or denial, of that—

CF: —of that rupture. But even the postmodernists in practice do not feel they have to go back to the past.

JE: Or they do, but as appropriation, as apparently random forays into equally distant "pasts."

In this context, that list of contemporary scholars who refer back to Caravaggio is even more bizarre. Stella's book reads Caravaggio, Bronzino, and Rubens, but only for their "negative spaces" (and I can never resist mentioning that no one knows the history of that term, but I think it is no older than the 1880s).[56] Stella's book serves his own artistic project, but it is psychologically beholden to art history—it is very careful about its sources and assertions. Michael Fried's book hasn't appeared yet, even though it was begun around 1995; but at the least it's a surprising extension of ideas that had been applied explicitly to the period after the mid-eighteenth century. Mieke Bal's book is open to a reading that would deny the possibility of art history, as that activity is understood by a large number of art historians (although she has written since then about how she did not intend it in quite that way).[57]

SC: Odd in the sense that they are not part of a modernist mainstream, or that modernism is not part of their project?

JE: I meant odd in the sense that they do not form a coherent group, as in the revivals of Vermeer, or Ter Borch, or Piero. At those moments there were consistent aesthetics and politics.

SC: There is a relation to psychoanalysis in at least two of them. There is also phenomenology.

CF: They are united by models of time that are not based on chronology, but on notions of repression. The work of Walter Benjamin is also relevant here . . .

JE: Yes. This may—or may not be—the time to bring in the last of the outliers we did not get a chance to talk about this morning, Georges Didi-Huberman, because his is also a psychoanalytic reading of history that seeks to disrupt chronology for many reasons. If it were taken on board, it would involve a radical reorganization of chronological art history in the name of certain psychic processes: so it's an equally outlying project.

Maybe what we're looking at here is that these strange bridges (I mean Stella's, Bal's, and Bersani's, but also Didi-Huberman's), which seem impassable, are a sign that the terrain itself is broken.

CF: Or maybe we're becoming more aware of ruptures that are always present. There is no other way to proceed to the Otherness. It is probably an important aspect of why people become historians: they become fascinated with the Otherness of past times.

JE: It's true that there would have had to be a kind of naïveté to say, with Berenson, that Picasso is like Piero.

CF: Maybe, or he was just trying to see what Piero was like. We start from what we know. I think that's where Mieke Bal's work takes off from—that kind of thinking about the Otherness of history, and ways of configuring time other than sequence. Why is it that certain things are appealing to us now? And why was Piero appealing at the end of the nineteenth century, and not before?

JE: Exactly.

CF: It's always like that, but we lose sight of it.

JE: The sense of history that you are inside of is the one that is hardest to see. If what we were calling "irrationalism" is an indirect borrowing from Romanticism, but a direct borrowing from Surrealism, existentialism, psychoanalysis, phenomenology, and other currents of thought around the 1920s and 1930s, then what we're doing now, in 2006, is really following ideas from the 1920s. And those of us, like Bob, who want to work in some measure against that irrationalism have yet to ask themselves what (other than the Renaissance!) they are following, and how "lost" in time they might be.

RW: Not "lost" in time, perhaps just "untimely." If what I've said about the Renaissance is true, then I have succeeded as a historian whether I fit into current trends or not, but also, and just as importantly, I think that insights which challenge modern assumptions have a critical value.

CF: Some ideas about the irrational come from the 1920s, but before them were the 1910s, and so forth: there is a long history of the irrational and the subrational. What we are talking about is a radical act of recuperation by the Surrealists; but it is also a responsible act of recuperation by historians, to be thinking in these terms.

JE: I worry about Georges Didi-Huberman, because there is interesting material there that is *almost* unusable by, in, or as art history. Aside from problems that arise from particular claims he makes, or from the rhetorical and narrative forms he chooses, there is also the question of the structure that would be left— that would be recognizable by art historians—if we were to take everything that he says seriously.

MC: Jim, you started the discussion by tracking whom modernists cite (or, more often, don't cite). Another way to look at this question would be to consider who writes on the Renaissance but aims to reach an audience of modernists. This is probably more common in Europe than in the United States, but one prominent example is Leo Steinberg, who may or may not be an "outlier," but who has published on Renaissance topics in *Art in America, October*, and *Critical Inquiry*. That's unusual; one doesn't really imagine the editors of those journals welcoming submissions from others in our field.

JE: "The Sexuality of Christ" was in *October* in 1983, and *Leonardo's Incessant Last Supper* was Jonathan Crary's choice as editor of the Zone Books imprint in 2001.

SC: His book was published, as you point out, Jim, by MIT Press—an unusual venue for Renaissance art, and essentially in with the *October* people.

JE: To me this is very interesting: why has Steinberg been their choice, intermittently but consistently, for almost twenty years? What was he doing for them that other Renaissance scholars couldn't?

RW: It had a lot to do with his activity as a critic in the 1960s and 1970s; he was one of the critics who helped bring an end to Greenbergian orthodoxy and usher in postmodernism.

JE: Yes, that could be it. I would hope there is something else involved, though.

RW: I think he was an important influence on Rosalind Krauss. What he did with Renaissance art was in some ways an extension of his criticism, so could be seen as both establishing the modernity or—post-modernity—of Renaissance art and a genealogy of contemporary art.

JE: I don't think those reasons are the whole story. I would still want to know why the *October* circle took an interest in having *any* representative of the Renaissance at that point.

SC: It is hard to see what he gave them. *The Sexuality of Christ?* A straightforward, even conservative iconographical project, insisting on a traditional historicist basis: "Here are the texts, and I will only see in the images what the texts tell me to see."

JE: Stephen, that's a strange thing to say. It's true, but surely the texts didn't lead him to those ideas. He saw in ways no one had, and *then* he let the iconographic régime dictate his exposition— but it's only a façade, a kind of travesty of old text-based icon- ography, and maybe that perversion also had something to do with *October's* interest.

SC: Not only is it a strange thing to say, it's also unfair, especially since I admire that book very much. However, I don't think it's a travesty of iconography at all. He's not trying to be out- rageous, and his arguments are verifiable and convincing. But there are wild things happening in those images. The book's title promises a study of sexuality—and we might expect a dis- cussion of highly eroticized images of Christ like that by Rosso at the MFA in Boston. But instead the book was about the iconography of male genitals in Christian imagery.

JE: So maybe the book was of interest to *October* because of things it *didn't* have. It wasn't parroting back various theories that the editors in question may have felt they knew better. But it must have answered to some need to have a new, unexpected *form* of the Renaissance, which in turn would seem to indicate that the Renaissance as it was presented was buried even more deeply than I was thinking.

RW: Only superficially unexpected, though. The argument about the *Last Supper* not being not a narrative painting, not being assimilable to an Albertian approach, but something more complex, charged with symbolic significance and multivalent, does fit the modernist pattern, even the kind of anti-rationalism we discussed earlier.

JE: Well, it's an odd candidate for anti-rationalism. I'd rather see it as hypertrophied rationalism: it is far more dense in rational argument than any book any of us has written, or is likely to write.[58]

RW: True. Yet he dismisses the picture's links to established forms of Renaissance rationalism in order to insist on his own. He shows no interest at all in Leonardo's theoretical writings;

indeed, he implies that they are simplistic, written for unintelligent students, and of no use whatever in understanding the pictures.

CF: It's a very modernist reading in a postmodern framework, and for someone who is actually an historian, it's like the borrowings Stephen was mentioning, which take the Albertian window and central-point perspective to represent the Renaissance. Not that Leo Steinberg is that simple-minded; but there's such a theatricality to the reading, such showmanship, that it becomes interesting to a contemporary public. People would think, "Oh, now I can become interested in this historical issue."

SC: I would also mention Whitney Davis, who is working on representations of the Apocalypse in medieval and Renaissance images. That is again about problems of time and space.

RW: He has been working on perspective and perspectivism in Western thinking.

MC: Steinberg is also interested in the undecidable, where to interpret the work one way is already to misunderstand it.

JE: And the *way* he does that in the *Last Supper* book, out-Empsoning Empson, and at the same time sounding like Thomas Aquinas! I can see how it was refreshing, but what was it refreshing *from*? What was the writing on offer that *Zone* wouldn't have wanted?

These examples point to an interesting misapprehension, a miscognition about the Renaissance. All of us at this table are buried deeper than I had thought twenty minutes ago. There doesn't seem to be a single normative or acceptable account that addresses both Renaissance and modernism: maybe Michael Baxandall would be the exception that proves that rule.

CF: But see, that's exactly what happens: someone who is not trained in Renaissance art goes to Baxandall, reads his conclusion, doesn't hear the background, abstracts from it, puts it into a Lacanian analysis, let's say, of perspective—there you have it, you're off and running. But it creates so much dissonance in the field that no one else picks it up. Yet that's not true of Didi-Huberman's reading of the Fra Angelico frescoes. That was a really wonderful opening up of the field, by thinking very deeply about the non-representational fictive marble panels as harboring the figuration of the formless. That insight into the cultural history of formlessness has been the basis for Didi-Huberman's subsequent theorizing, some of which, lacking the same solid historical foundation as his study of the theology of mystical knowledge regarding the frescoes, seems rather thin.

JE: The Fra Angelico book is also a precedent for the practice, which I think is now standard art historical practice, of citing Didi-Huberman and then putting him in a footnote.[59] The reliance of some of his more recent writing on the *Fra Angelico* book is a blessing for people who want to put him in a footnote. But the tradition of citing-but-not-arguing continues in other instances: for example, in the book *Formless* he gets to be in a footnote, even though he had written an entire book on the subject, because his concept of representation is said to be too naturalistic.[60]

CF: And so the same process of flirting with, but ultimately rejecting, innovation continues.

JE: We have been talking about how the Renaissance appears to modernists. I thought it might be good to change perspectives on this question by talking about institutions, before we return to return to the problem of citation from the other side, and look at how modernism appears to Renaissance specialists.

I think the subject of institutions is at one and the same time completely foundational—you can't make foundational critiques without taking into account politics, institutions, and forms of knowledge—and, on the other hand, too crowded with incidental detail about what happens to take place in particular institutions. Those local stories tend to obscure institutional configurations that have real purchase on knowledge.

I wonder, Claire, if you'd like to open the question of institution . . .

CF: Yes, thanks. Jim asked me, after the morning session, if I could make my differences more clear. I am committed to not setting up oppositional camps; but on the other hand I do not want to blend into the crowd. So the kind of art historical practice I would like to see in Renaissance studies goes all over the world, and deals with all kinds of practices, representational systems, cultural conditions; not at the level of social history, but at deeper epistemological levels, studying what happens when new identities are formed, when new communication occurs, when representational practices that have never been in contact before are suddenly in collision and contention, when the readability of the art changes because of contact, when people's ability to live changes because of their altered material culture.

If those kinds of questions came to be of overriding importance in the field, if they were encouraged at the institutional level, we could have an entirely different kind of art history. It would look genuinely different. We would not just be looking at the canon of old masters in Europe. We would be looking at colonial productions. We would be looking at print culture. We would be looking at things made by artists without training. And we wouldn't be spending our time on taxonomies of that material. We would be examining the interesting processes that occur, maybe in terms of the Renaissance definition of art as work, as process: maybe that would be part of what we would be doing.

A number of people are working on these issues, but mostly outside of the areas that are familiar to us. I think it is important for people with Europeanist training to be engaged, and not just people we brand as colonialists or Latin American specialists. But it depends on institutions to support this. There's the question of the individual, and what kind of work she does, and then there's the question of the institution, and what kind of historian is hired, and what you put together at the level of undergraduate education . . . In many cases, we would be collaborating more. I would love to collaborate with a Byzantin-ist, and collaborate on mixtures of Renaissance styles in the Mediterranean—

JE: How would you describe in political terms the resistance that an imaginary "typical" art historian might feel to this? By that question I mean: Would you imagine the resistance would be finally a matter of nationalism or regionalism, or would you imagine it would be mainly a matter of entrenched habits? Or fear of losing jobs, or students?

CF: Here's how I imagine it. People are trained in a set of texts and images, and a body of historiography, and as they work they learn how much more there is. With every book and article you discover how little you know, and you become an expert in a micro-field. So I think a lot of the resistance is against being in uncharted territory.

SC: But you need a wide range of cultural literacy: you're an Italian-ist, then you learn Spanish, then Nahuatl, other languages, hieroglyphs . . . it does require becoming a multidisciplinarist. There is a tremendous anxiety now about the loss of disciplinar-ity, which is being watered down as administrators issue calls for watering down departments.

CF: I think about that quite a lot. Bill Readings, Sam Weber, and others have thought about exactly what you've brought up.[61] On the one hand, looking at our nineteenth-century foundations and trying to critique them drives us toward a more inter-disciplinary practice. But on the other hand, we play into the downsizing "opportunities" that corporate administrators offer to the humanities, in order to get rid of specific disciplines and replace them with vague things like cultural studies that are not grounded anywhere. So in trying to fix it, we make it worse.

JE: So one aspect of the resistance of a hypothetical "typical" art historian would be the potential loss of disciplinarity. But wouldn't another be a form of nationalism? Take a country at random, say Romania, and its art historians. If you were to try to make changes of the sort you've described, in a country which has no tradition of it, wouldn't most of the resistance come from the conviction that Romanian art historical research and teaching should properly remain central to the discipline?

MC: Isn't the opposite happening in North America? Most universities and even most departments, I suspect, would welcome an expansion or reconfiguration of Renaissance Studies to include Latin America.

JE: I think that describes the situation mainly in relatively large North American and UK universities. I don't see that kind of reasoning in smaller countries. I might even go as far as to say that we are open, in the US, to the study of other cultures: we can be generous because we *own* those cultures, or we will.

MC: Well, administrators—and faculty members, too—are also responding to the presence of Latino students in the community and in the university. It's not just that we own those cultures but that we *are* those cultures. It's not accidental that Claire, our strongest advocate for this ideal, teaches in the Southwestern United States.

JE: Yes, in the case of Latino students in the US. But again I think that is a limited example. I don't find that rhetoric in other places. Here in Ireland, for example, the western European tradition and Irish art history are taken to be the proper focus *regardless* of student demographics. I am just trying to find a reason other than lack of specialization to explain why people resist the kind of expanded Renaissance studies Claire is advocating.

MC: Couldn't it also have to do with the questions that seem productive or unproductive in relation to certain kinds of material? If a scholar is drawn to study the Renaissance not just because he or she loves working in Italy, or Europe, but rather because he or she is interested in particular kinds of topics— humanism, say, or artists' biographies—what's the responsibility of this scholar to dwell on a geographical area where the material to pursue those topics doesn't seem as rich? Now, maybe my hypothetical scholar would find, if he or she looked, that the Latin American material relating to these topics just hasn't been examined. But the suggestion that a scholar should work on a particular region can also be a way of saying that that scholar should be doing a certain kind of art history, should be asking certain kinds of questions. Can't the decision not to engage in a geographically expanded Renaissance reflect commitment as much as resistance?

CF: I agree with Michael that circumscribing a historian's field of investigation geographically may not make any sense and, furthermore, that commitment and resistance are not exactly the same thing. However, I resist the idea of hiring a Latin Americanist to address the commitment to a global vision of the Renaissance because Latin Americanists have to be grounded in something like national identity. A Renaissance specialist has to be grounded in the culture of Italy or France; similarly, a Latin Americanist has to be grounded in language and place. It's not necessarily the kind of cross-disciplinary work that I am suggesting, which goes beyond nation-state identities to interrogate the categories and identities we impose on the historical material as such. To implement the model I have in mind may well mean doing more collaborative work, a model that is under-developed in the humanities for reasons I don't really understand. And yes, of course, some the most culturally chauvinistic practices are among art historians, and not just in Romania—

JE: Thanks for adding that!

CF: So it's a matter of deeply rethinking our identities. We are talking about resisting a change that would involve reworking one's identity: but what a wonderful challenge it would be, to rethink the world in terms that privilege interaction and the unknown over national culture and pride in the familiar.

JE: When we were talking about Renaissance and modern Western art history, there was already enough of a problem for people who tried to bridge the gap. But here, where we're talking about something that is literally global, it seems as if the evaporation of specialties, identities, and national senses of identity might cause more euphoria than trouble.

Let's go back to the narrower, actually existing case, with the institutional status as it is now. In North America, Europe, and parts of South America, in average universities, there is always going to be someone doing Italian Renaissance. It is not dispensable. It can't be integrated or dispersed, because it has to be there. It has an anchoring function.

MC: That's true. In the last fifteen years, Italian Baroque has been rapidly disappearing from American art history departments, but most larger universities still have a Renaissance specialist.

CF: But the misconception is that the anchor-function has to look like Leonardo, Michelangelo, and Raphael, or Petrarch and Boccaccio. Why can't it look like a world of cultural interactions?

JE: Like Matt's work, or like Fredrika's.

FJ: My university has started a Mediterranean studies program, done in consortium with the university of Messina, and the university of Cordova, but it takes in the Balkans. The School of the Arts also has a campus in Doha, Qatar. Pennsylvania State also has a program like that, very well situated. Maybe this is how it starts. It was required by EU laws that Messina had to have a non-EU partner, so it could be that initiatives are already in place, where we won't need to think of the Renaissance in the traditionally defined way but rather as an era rich in the exchange of ideas and the meeting of cultures. Rosamond Mack's *Bazaar to Piazza* illustrates this in interesting ways that include, among other things, the appropriation of eastern forms like kufic script and the patterns of Anatolian prayer rugs into western art and architecture.[62]

JE: I feel like putting on my pessimist's cap again.

JF: Not again!

JE: I think there's a parallel to be made between Renaissance studies and Classics. In the seventeenth and eighteenth centuries,
Latin was known by everyone in educated circles. Now Classics
is still felt to be needed in many universities, but only as a
background, something against which you can define your cultural identity without having to know too much about it.
Renaissance studies may be like that.

FJ: The initiative in our university is not just art history, but literature, theater, performance, film, history, communication and
graphic design—they're looking at what's happening now.

EMK: I think the conservative drag that institutions exert on discourses is often a good thing. It allows creative impulses to react
against a tradition, while still having the tradition present: it
gives the rebellion a structure. I think that is the problem with
renaming art history departments visual or cultural studies
departments, which as Claire says have only very uncertain
traditions to react with or against.

Speaking of classics, there is a tendency of departments to
divest themselves of what were previously considered essentials.
At the University of Toronto, we were considering not hiring
art historians specializing in ancient art, divesting ourselves of
these fields. Regardless of one's personal interest in ancient art,
it seemed to many of us a strange proposal.

JE: You still have a classics department, at least?

EMK: Yes, but to allow ancient art to go to the classics department,
away from art history, and not be included in the institutional
discussions, seemed strange. Similarly, a number of history
departments (not art history departments) are not re-hiring
Italian Renaissance historians. As Claire says, the notion of
the Renaissance should be broadened; but Italian Renaissance
history is one of the bedrocks of traditional history, and it is
hard to see an entire department operating without someone in
this area.

CF: But even beyond providing the whipping post for more contemporary disciplines, our sub-discipline deserves to be rethought and not treated as something static. The downsizing in universities that think they can do away with ancient art, or medieval art, or even pre-modern art (a number of institutions are doing away with pre-modern art), completely misunderstands the dynamics of the field. Sam Weber writes that the episteme that informs these decisions is based on an Enlightenment model in which the value of the new is decided by comparison with the pre-existing, which is the same kind of ethnocentric attitude that got us into the problem in the first place—the idea of looking at other cultures using the barometer of Europe.

JE: We are developing two fairly depressing models of the Renaissance. In one, it is the anchor that needs to be there, but doesn't need to be lifted off the ocean floor (you don't need to know much about it). In the other, which is even more depressing, universities can get rid of the Renaissance altogether, because it is decathected: we don't even worry about it. We think about the Renaissance the way Epicurus worried about the gods, which is we don't. We don't even care.

FJ: That assumes we let the Renaissance continue to appear static.

SC: And it also assumes that the model is to be defined in terms of the apathy of other art historians and the "innovations" of university administrators. One major problem has been that the Renaissance cannot obviously be defended according to the same moral and liberal imperatives that are used to mandate the increasing inclusion of some non-Western or non-European fields. But we could make the argument that the Renaissance is an "other" culture, that it is remote from the present and from twenty-first-century concerns, and that it requires the same kind of empathy with difference as areas of study called for by proponents of multiculturalism. That would also mean taking a stand against the essentialism of identity politics in university education, where students are expected to identify with certain specializations as being more "about themselves," especially when those areas of specialization are non-European.

JE: Or it assumes that innovations can be made to appear *as* innovations. From a modernist art historian's standpoint, what happens in Renaissance scholarship can appear as the return of familiar methods and concerns, or their reappearance in new contexts. That only strengthens the hunch that the Renaissance is the same under its new theory veneer. My dissertation supervisor, Earl Rosenthal, once said that the Renaissance was like a close-cropped field. From his point of view, nearly everything possible had been done. He wasn't thinking of the new methods and objects we've been talking about, but I can see now, twenty years later, that modernist historians might still see that same field when they look past the new methods and objects. (And by the way, I always loved the implicit comparison of art historians and sheep.)

RW: Claire, I agree with you about the importance of encouraging work from non-European perspectives, yet I also think that interest in such perspectives has become fashionable now, and that the effects of that fashion are not entirely positive. On the one hand, its advocates create the impression that any work not done from such a perspective cannot be truly progressive, truly critical. On the other, not all work done from that perspective is necessarily critical: I know people who claim to be doing postcolonial art history, yet whose work simply extends all sorts of commonplace art-historical strategies to new material and is thus just colonialism by other means. So emphasizing the "non-Western" can also function as a kind of evasion—a repressive desublimation. There still seems to me to be plenty of room within the study of European art for significantly—urgently—critical intervention: even the kinds of issues that interest you— the ways in which, say, slavery, structures of domination, and so forth are legible in art—are also present in European art, and need to be addressed there with perhaps even greater energy and acuity.

MC: Yes—Carl Strehkle recently gave a talk on slavery in Renaissance painters' workshops, and along the way noted that the scholars who have been studying "domestic arts" have not really paid attention to this. A few of those people were in his audience, and they took him to task because slaves—though the most valuable property a person could own—do not appear in inventories. I think they felt he was accusing them of not doing their homework, but what he was demonstrating that the kind of relationships we automatically look for when studying colonial interactions remain to be explored in the major Italian centers.

CF: I think you need both. One only needs to look at the studies mentioned before, such as Stephen's co-edited anthology, that have been published in the last decade to see that the cultural interactions that are taking place in Ferrara, across the street as it were, can be quite radical if they are looked at the right way, if their implications are fully analyzed. However, extra-European studies have lagged far behind, despite the obvious fact that cultural inequalities that exist today are often the result of imperialistic practices that developed in the period we study. So by continuing to work within the nationalistic, subdisciplinary formations we have inherited from the heyday of nation-sate formation, we reproduce the same hegemonic schemes, don't we? The irony is that in today's world of weakened nation-states, the study of national culture is worth less and less—and that is ultimately why art history departments are not held in higher prestige at our universities. This goes for all of the humanities. What is my responsibility as an intellectual to society? This question deserves to be driving our research agendas. We'd be doing everyone a big favor by attending to such questions as the history of cultural interactions or slavery or racial thinking on a global scale. There are so many projects waiting to happen.

JE: There is a parallel to be drawn here with visual studies, which also wants to do something with existing art history; visual studies would fragment existing practice, or disperse it and let it find itself in new places. In order to work with visual studies, you have to take its founding assumption on board: that in contemporary culture there is no longer any critical force to the distinction between fine art and mass or popular art. Once you do that, you are free to study the range of images. The price you pay, from the point of view of people who don't like visual studies, is that you lose the ability to talk about fine art in the ways that have been developed for it.[63]

In the same way, an internationalist, multicultural view of the Renaissance could be seen to be risking that. It would not just be an expansion of the Renaissance, but an activity made possible by a kind of revaluation of values—a devaluation of some, in particular.

Now your project, Claire, is a minority in Renaissance studies, so I don't know if it would make sense to apply this to what you do. But visual studies is not a rare thing in comparison to modernist art history, so I can say with confidence that despite many people's wishes, it does not co-exist with modernist art history as an organic extension or expansion. It depends, fundamentally, on overwriting certain values of the pre-existing discipline, especially including its "canon."

It's hard to speak against visual studies in this context, because you don't want to sound like a reactionary: in Renaissance terms, you wouldn't want to be caught saying, "No, I need to have my Michelangelo the way Charles De Tolnay gave him to me!"

CF: I think so much of what keeps more exciting work from happening is really at the level of institutional power, and not at the level of personal choice. When institutions hire their subdisciplinary specialist, they are hiring for certain purposes. Maybe it happens more at the most elite institutions; maybe those are the ones most resistant to change. The exciting initiative that Fredrika describes is being developed at a public institution, so we could get into a more concentrated discussion of which institutions keep the status quo in place more, without getting ourselves to ad hominem arguments. We could ask how traditional disciplinary constructs and problematic values are passed on by administrators who are not trained to be thinking the kinds of thoughts that we're exploring here today.

MC: This institutional question also bears on where we do our research. The libraries and archives alone make it so much more convenient to work in Venice, Florence, and Rome than elsewhere. That shows in the literature, in the difference between what is produced in Turin, say, as opposed to Florence.

CF: It is also easier to do research where some has already been done, so there are pockets of research to draw upon, and familiar objects.

JE: This is why it's good to talk about prominent scholars, because then such restrictions shouldn't matter. For someone like Hans Belting, there is no limitation on the range of scholarship he could do if he wanted: hence his choices are more likely to be indicative of issues in the discipline itself. I'm more interested in cases like that, than in institutions. I agree institutions hamper many people in many ways, but the most active scholars are not so limited, and the fact that only few of them work outside the traditionally conceived Renaissance is important.

CF: Belting speaks in an institutionally sanctioned voice: they picked him, he makes them. He has research funding, students, time to work, while art historians outside the few elite private and state research institutions are teaching more, receiving less support for their research, and therefore generally competing less successfully for a voice in the field through their publications and papers. And if you factor in gender and race, you will see that the conservative force of educational institutions is even more visible: very few women occupy important positions in art history at leading research universities and there are practically no people of color working in Renaissance art history studies at all. I don't know how anyone could claim that institutions are irrelevant to the question of making the field of Renaissance art history more open and diverse.

EMK: Institutions in all fields tend to attract authority to themselves, and respect authority, and authority is a very conservative force. It is not only a problem of administrators, but of colleagues too, in judging and appreciating their fellow colleagues outside their field. This makes it more difficult to engage in subversive conversations. For example, I first wrote on Pieter Bruegel, who stands at the center of the canon; now, with tenure, I feel I can engage in a project like the one sampled in the "Starting Points" essay, that does not immediately elicit recognition among my colleagues.

JE: Or even come to events like this.

EMK: Yes, even events like this. A fellow scholar of Gothic architecture, Peter Murray, told me that he had first considered working on the very late French Gothic around the year 1500 but was uniformly advised not to do so, because he would not readily find an audience. In fact he chose to work on the High Gothic of Beauvais, Troyes, and Amiens. I don't think this is restricted to academia; we all have to contend with the conservative drag of institutions. One thing academia does allow, once one is placed, is expanding the margins of discourse. That is one of the benefits of tenure.

SC: It's also a question of research money. We can't fund our students to do field work for more than two years. The pool of money for graduate PhD preparation is evaporating.

JE: And that is from the position of a large North American university. Here, in a medium-sized university in a smaller European country, we're lucky to fund the very small fees that EU students have to pay (about €3,000 per year). Departments in Ireland usually can't fund non-EU students at all (even though they only have about €8,000 in fees), and no one expects to fund field work. Obviously funding of any sort at all is out of the question in most of the rest of the world.

EMK: I think it is always easier to win approval if one works in the center of any field. But academia allows for survival outside the center, and many fields do not.

SC: For the moment.

CF: Yes, for the moment. The state legislature where I work, in Colorado, is discussing getting rid of tenure.

JE: Well, again, too keep the world outside US academia in view, I'll just say that History of Art at this university is not quite an independent department, and may well shrink back into the History department. Many universities are lucky to have art history, let alone art history—but just to bring the discussion back to the question at hand, I have yet to see an art history department of more than three people where the Italian Renaissance is not taught at all. (This is aside from whether or not there is a Renaissance specialist: that's a luxury of affluent departments, universities, and countries.) On the other hand there are many places where modernism isn't taught.

Let's try to complete the circle of this afternoon's conversation by returning to the place we started, looking at the fault lines between Renaissance and modernism. This time, however, let's look from the other side, and consider Renaissance scholars who do not look forward, for various reasons.

Some of the foundational names in Renaissance studies would place the decisive break or abyss in history *before* their period; that is different from all the modernists I mentioned at the beginning, whose relative lack of citations of Renaissance art points to a sense that the abyss is *between* them and the Renaissance. I think for example of Panofsky and the idea of the expanded Renaissance, an idea that puts his own field of study at the beginning of a sequence that leads onward to modernism—and such things as motion pictures and Rolls-Royce grilles. More contentiously, there is Hans Belting, who puts most of what we study (excepting Matt's material) *after* the divide between *Kult* and *Bild*.

To the extent that this is the case, and Renaissance specialists write as if from the inception of a tradition, there is *even less* excuse not to cite twentieth-century examples than there is for the modernists, for whom the break is somewhere between their field of study and the Renaissance.

MC: That's right: scholars of the "Renaissance" and of the "early modern" both assume the kind of divide you're pointing to; it's one thing we all tend to take for granted, regardless of what we call our period. Do we, then, use the middle ages much the way you're saying that modernists use the Renaissance? I was struck, for example, how insistent Alexander Nagel and Christopher Wood were in their recent *Art Bulletin* piece that there is a Renaissance conception of time that is fundamentally distinct from what one would find in the late middle ages. They close Belting's divide then insist on retaining it. And this from two scholars who know a great deal about medieval art: it's probably even more common among Renaissance scholars not to think much about the middle ages at all. Our ignorance of what happened before Giotto is not that much different from the modernist's ignorance of what we study. We're drawn to look for beginnings rather than for endings.

CF: Burckhardt was less driven by the disciplinary divisions we now practice under. We might, after tenure, study a range of objects from the medieval to the contemporary period; but Burckhardt could look at modernity because its fabric wasn't as institutionalized as the one we now experience.

JE: Who would be contemporary Renaissance specialists whose work might imply the idea of a break *after* the Renaissance? Or is theorizing the renascence a condition of conceiving of the Renaissance?

MC: Well, such a break is certainly structural in our teaching, if not in our writing. There's still a widely assumed distinction between Renaissance and Baroque, at least where the Italian material is concerned. It's reflected in textbooks, in individual specializations, and in the curricula at most universities.

JE: If you take up Panofsky's model, you end up being the custodian of a very broad swath of history.

EMK: Panofsky defines the Renaissance awfully broadly. At the beginning of *Renaissance and Renascences*, he starts by talking about the Renaissance as a limited cultural phenomenon. After a coda, he continues with the words, "From the fourteenth through the sixteenth century, then, and from one end of Europe to the other, the men of the Renaissance were convinced that the period in which they lived was a 'new age' as sharply different from the mediaeval past as the mediaeval past had been from classical antiquity and marked by a concerted effort to revive the culture of the latter." Panofsky thus homogenizes all of Europe over a period of three centuries. That's as extensive as the period between 1600 and 1900! What remarkable, dramatic events don't occur over a span of three hundred years? In order to make his point, he ultimately expands the domain of the Renaissance until it's much less useful a concept.

SC: Arnold Hauser as well, when Mannerism gets expanded, colossally, to last four hundred years.

EMK: The cyclical interpretations of Mannerism are a similar case.[64]

SC: He didn't reach the postmodern moment himself, but he was predicting it, in a certain way. And he influenced some of the critical work from the 1980s that attempted to characterize Postmodernism in terms of Mannerism.[65]

CF: Or there is Ernst Curtius's "long middle ages," which would also weaken periodization.

JE: Broadening, or weakening, might be different from what happens with the modernists. All those I named identify more or less explicit beginning points for modernism. Belting, among historians who write about the Renaissance, may be the closest analogy.

SC: I think maybe people are thinking more in political categories, like absolutism, pre-absolutism, post-absolutism, pre-nation-state, post-nation-state. That has become the dominant form of historical thought, rather than stylistic or Wölfflinian models of Renaissance and Baroque.

RW: Right, and that relates to the issue we raised this morning about what happens to humanism in the course of the sixteenth century.

JE: So your construal of the histories of colonialism, or imperialism, would determine whether or not you felt obligated to be connected to another period such as modernism.

MC: There are also the periodizations that track religious formations. For Northern Europe, "Reformation" has long seemed a more useful category than "Renaissance," and scholars are increasingly testing this against the Italian material as well.

CF: I suspect that the pre-modern period, with its large dynastic formations and religious institutions, is becoming much more interesting to look at in this period of the decline of the nation state and the rise of transnational corporate capitalism. The kinds of loyalties and identity formations have analogs in that period. They may be driving our interest in rethinking periods.

RW: Of course, there is the whole tendency to identify the crucial break as occurring between the Renaissance and the Enlightenment. Some older historians saw the Renaissance coming to an end in the trial and suppression of Galileo; Foucault—unlike the older historians as he was—still argued for the emergence of a radically new episteme at exactly the same moment, in the writings of Descartes.

JE: There is at least one other sense in which the decisive break has been said to come after the Renaissance, and that is the old chestnut of the North-South division, and how northern European art can be figured as modern, as more like our cultural situation.

RW: There have been attempts to relate the modernism of northern Renaissance art to the emergence of certain capitalistic structures, such as the stock market.

EMK: And the market as a whole, in fact.

RW: I'm thinking of Matt's own book on Bruegel, also the work of people like Elizabeth Honig and Charlotte Houghton.[66]

MC: Some Italianists, meanwhile, are now trying to qualify the idea that it's the role of the market that most usefully distinguishes the North from the South. There was a big conference five or six years ago on the art market in Renaissance Italy, and the topic is a significant part of the "Material Renaissance" project on which Sussex and other universities are collaborating.

EMK: The markets in the North are really in vogue now. I am thinking of Filip Vermeylen's work on Antwerp market in the sixteenth century, and Hans Van Migroet's work on seventeenth-century aspects, in particular.[67]

JE: Well, I think this may be a good time to stop, considering that these are all imponderable questions. At least it's good that we aired large-scale questions regarding the Renaissance, which, possibly for important reasons, don't usually get discussed. It may seem to other people that there are ways forward with this. I think that the more we subtract away contingencies, the more we end up with pervasive structures of our understanding of history. It may be impossible to understand them, but it's also impossible to evade them.

John Paul McMahon [*question from the audience*]: Again, to the fact that there are no Italian scholars present. I want to ask the panel: Why do you think *normative* Renaissance historians have a fear of critical theory, postcolonial theory, poststructuralism? I see it as a fear; as a student, I encountered that. There's an opposition to any critical theory; if you put it into an essay on the Renaissance, you'll be marked off for it.

EMK: One answer is that theory subverts the centrality that they enjoy, and feel they should enjoy, and which is already under challenge.

SC: If it's a kind of historian who has done very hard-won, empirical research, they often feel that people who bring in critical strategies are just going for short cuts. "You haven't really done your homework," they'll think, or "You haven't really paid your dues."

EMK: It also has to do with institutional traditions; there are different ways of doing Renaissance studies. At many universities in Europe—the University of Ghent is famous for this—archival studies are a major part of writing a history dissertation. Now, to do archival studies in the Renaissance you have to invest a tremendous amount of time in learning the archive, learning to read the handwriting of the period, learning the language. It's not that these people are somehow lazy: they have just invested their intellectual activity in a very different enterprise, which requires a great deal of training and understanding. Younger scholars can feel quite put-upon with the need to learn a new discipline, a new set of ideas.

JPM: I think critical theory has its own archive as well.

EMK: That is exactly what I am saying.

JPM: There are archives in modernism, but they're different: the archive is the privileged possession of the Renaissance, and I think that's problematic.

SC: I don't think anyone would say that, do you?

MC: I suspect that most scholars who work in archives believe that what they are doing has an enduring value, and fear that theoretically-informed research will inevitably be ephemeral: as if questions will change but the facts will not. And as Stephen says, if you've paid your dues and learned to write things that people will read in thirty years, you don't want to give it up.

EMK: At least there's the illusion that people will. But I think it also has to do with a sense of empowerment. Critical theory tends to relativize, to call into question, many of the empowering concepts. You tend to find this resentment or reluctance to engage in critical theory mostly among people who are active in the center of a discipline. In a way critical theory subverts the centrality of their work.

MC: You could say that scholars who choose one or the other path are pursuing different kinds of power. Critical theory is empowering, but so is knowing information that other people don't. The archive also lets you undermine other scholars' assumptions and conclusions.

JE: I notice all these things we're saying are true of other fields within art history, but one of the things more particular to Renaissance studies, although not unique to it, is the absence on this panel of people from the countries of origin of the works under study. None of us—Matt and Claire included—comes from the part of the world that we study.

EMK: I referred to that obliquely when I said there was a kind of national interest in charting one's regional patrimony. North American scholars have very little of that to deal with.

JE: How disappointing. But really, of course, it's the hunger of the US for cultural patrimony, together with its economic capacity to find that patrimony (I mean that as a euphemism for imperialism), that accounts for the level of scholarship in the US. (We owe our good scholarship to imperialism.)

CF: At the base of this, there's a kind of either-or thinking: *either* I do archival work, *or* I engage in critical theory.

JPM: That's sad, that they can't work together.

CF: I agree; there should be more engagement so there's more openness and less fear.

JE: Stephen, you were saying something?

SC: Fredrika and I were just saying we think that it does happen.

FJ: It does, but not always, and it's not usually as bleak as the situation you're in. I can't imagine someone would mark you down for that.

JPM: I just think this is something that needs to be addressed in the book as a whole: there should be people who do only archival work, and people who mix it with critical interpretations, and people who work in museums. Those people have to be in the book if it's to be seen as a document that *does* question the Renaissance.

JE: It will. I'll just add that the composition of our panel today is to some degree luck, since it changed according to who could come and who couldn't. I hope that, as in other books in this series, we can be wholly inclusive. It's the shape of the whole field that interests me, not any one part.

Clare Guest [*question from the audience*]: There is also the question of the degree to which the question about the role and function of tradition in art history arises from questions about the role and function of tradition in the humanities in general. I would like to add that another possible reason for the antipathy to theory is that many of the questions identified with critical theory have appeared at other times in history, from the Sophists onward, or in late Scholaticism, and there is an awareness—or suspicion—that this historical awareness within some critical theory may be somewhat shallow.

JE: May I mention an acquaintance of mine, who died, as a great example? Michael Camille—his last book, *Master of Death*, has epigraphs that set medieval scholastic writers alongside Derrida and Blanchot. He was a wonderful person, and I should have mentioned him with Michael Baxandall as someone who bridged the gap without seeming—at least to many readers—to be an outlier.

CF: The question addresses very thoughtfully the question you raised, Jim, at the beginning of the afternoon, about the amnesia among historians of contemporary art. It should be taken up by people like Michael Camille as part of the tradition, as epistemological continuities.

JE: I think we may have reached a good place to end: a moment of reasonable optimism, open to the future, and also remembering someone from the past.

Notes

1. Alpers, *The Art of Describing: Dutch Art in the Seventeenth Century* (Chicago: University of Chicago Press, 1983).

2. Needless to say this is just to telegraph a complex issue. See *Discovering Chinese Painting: Dialogues with Art Historians*, edited by Jason Kuo, with an Afterword by James Elkins (Dubuque IO: Kendall/Hunt, 2006). (First edition, 2000.)

3. Rosalind Krauss, Benjamin Buchloh, Yve-Alain Bois, and Hal Foster, *Art Since 1900: Modernism, Antimodernism, Postmodernism* (London: Thames and Hudson, 2004).

4. One example of a polemical figure in the field of Italian Renaissance would be Charles Hope, who is sometimes taken (especially by historians as distinct from art historians) as an example of a skeptical positivist challenge to received (or "Vasarian") ideas as well as to the claims of theory and interpretation. Hope's challenges tend to be limited to matters of fact (archival data, philology, and the technical analysis of works of art), and he generally refuses to engage with the philosophical grounding of much recent work in art history, the product of more than thirty years of intense reexamination of the status of interpretation in the humanities and social sciences which have closed down the possibility of a simple "appeal to the facts." As a result Hope could be said to have marginalized himself as a critical voice, even while his scholarship (on Venetian painting, Mantegna, and Vasari) is exemplary, and central.

5. Reprinted in this volume as one of the "Starting Points" essays.

6. See Kavaler's "Starting Points" essay in this volume.

7. The material was eventually published as Edgerton, *Theaters of Conversion: Religious Architecture and Indian Artisans in Colonial Mexico* (Albuquerque NM: University of New Mexico Press, 2001).

8. For an English edition, see Enrico Castelnuovo and Carlo Ginzburg, "Centre and Periphery," in *History of Italian Art*, edited by E. Bianchini and C. Dorey, translated by E. Bianchini, 2 vols. (Cambridge: Cambridge University Press, 1994), II, 29–113.

9. Morton Steen Hansen, *Artistic Exchange and Cultural Translation in the Italian Renaissance City* (Stephen Campbell, ed., Cambridge: Cambridge University Press, 2004).

10. See, for example, Michael Cole, "Cellini's Blood," *Art Bulletin* 81 (1999): 216–35, and Stephen J. Campbell, "Bronzino's *Martyrdom of St. Lawrence*: Counter Reformation Polemic and Mannerist Counter-Aesthetics," *RES* 46 (2004): 99–121.

11. Helen Hills, *Invisible City: The Architecture of Aristocratic Convents in Baroque Naples*, (Oxford: Oxford University Press, 2004).

12. Gauvin Bailey, *Art on the Jesuit Missions in Asia and Latin America* (Toronto- Buffalo: University of Toronto Press, 1999); and more recently,

his textbook, *Art of Colonial Latin America* (London-New York: Phaidon, 2005).

13. Jeanette Peterson, *The Garden Paradise Murals of Malinalco: Utopia and Empire in Sixteenth-Century Mexico* (Austin: University of Texas Press, 1993); Samuel Y. Edgerton, *Theaters of Conversion: Religious Architecture and Indian Artisans in Colonial Mexico* (Albuquerque: University of New Mexico Press, 2001).

14. Freedberg, *The Power of Images: Studies in the History and Theory of Response* (Chicago: University of Chicago Press, 1989).

15. The essay is included in the "Starting Points" section in this volume.

16. Garnett and Rosser, "Translations of the Miraculous: Cult Images and their Representations in Early Modern Liguria," in *The Miraculous Image in the Late Middle Ages and Renaissance*, edited by Erik Thuno and Gerhard Wolf (Rome: L'Erma di Bretschneider, 2004), 205–22.

17. Marcel Mauss, *The Gift: The Form and Reason for Exchange in Archaic Society*, trans. W.D. Halls (London: Routledge, 1990).

18. Hugo van der Velden, "Medici Votive Images and the Scope and Limits of Likeness" in *The Image of the Individual: Portraits in the Renaissance*, eds. Nicholas Mann and Luke Syson (London: British Museum Press, 1998), 126–37.

19. The establishment of the Accademia del Disegno and the stylistic perfection it sought to develop is obviously tied to this. See Karen-edis Barzman, *The Florentine Academy and the Early Modern State: The Discipline of Disegno* (Cambridge: Cambridge University Press, 2000).

20. For arguments to the effect that Renaissance thinkers understood even some of the most immaterial of images to have a "medium," see Michael Cole, "The Demonic Arts and the Origin of the Medium," *Art Bulletin* 84 (2002): 621–40.

21. I am thinking of Elizabeth Cropper, and her account of erotic response in "The Place of Beauty in the High Renaissance and its Displacement in the History of Art," *in Place and Displacement in the Renaissance*, edited by A. Vos (Binghamton NY: State University of New York Press, 1995), which discusses an important area of "modern oblivion" that very much expands on what Freedberg (or indeed Steinberg) give us with regard to formations of sexuality and the erotic in works of art.

22. Elkins, *The Strange Place of Religion in Contemporary Art* (New York: Routledge, 2005).

23. Whitney Chadwick, *Women, Art and Society*, third edition (London: Thames and Hudson, 2002), 37.

24. www.tate.org.uk/onlineevents/archive/artsince1900/.

25. Wallace Ferguson, *The Renaissance in Historical Thought: Five Centuries of Interpretation* (Cambridge: Harvard University Press, 1948).

26. Mario Fanti, "Le postille carraccesche alle Vite del Vasari: il testo originale," *Il Carrobbio* 5 (1979): 148–64.

27. Xavier de Salas and Fernando Marias, *El Greco y el arte de su tiempo: las notas de El Greco a Vasari* (Madrid: Iberdrola, 1992).

28. See Walter S. Melion, *Shaping the Netherlandish Canon: Karel van Mander's Schilder-Boeck* (Chicago: Chicago University Press, 1991), esp. xxi and

95–125. This reading of Van Mander was not uncontroversial: see the rather bitter review of Melion by Hessel Miedema in *Oud Holland* 107 (1993): 152–59.

29. See Walter S. Melion, *Shaping the Netherlandish Canon: Karel van Mander's Schilder-Boeck* (Chicago: Chicago University Press, 1991, 95–134, 143–59.

30. For some early revisionist responses, see *Documentary Culture: Florence and Rome from Grand-Duke Ferdinand I to Pope Alexander VII*; papers from a colloquium held at the Villa Spelman, Florence, 1990, edited by Elizabeth Cropper, Giovanna Perini, and Francesco Solinas (Bologna, 1992).

31. On this trend, see Thomas DaCosta Kaufmann, *Toward a Geography of Art* (Chicago: University of Chicago Press, 2004), especially 52–57, 68–88. The reference is to the German phrase, *Blut und Boden*, coined by Oswald Spengler.

32. Homi Bhabha, *The Location of Culture* (London and New York: Routledge, 1994). For a recent critique, see Gayatri Chakravorti Spivak, *A Critique of Postcolonial Reason: Toward a History of the Vanishing Present* (Cambridge-London: Harvard University Press, 1999).

33. *Eye of the Lynx: Galileo, His Friends, and the Beginnings of Modern Natural History* (Chicago: University of Chicago Press, 2002).

34. Belting, *Bild und Kult: eine Geschichte des Bildes vor dem Zeitalter der Kunst* (Munich: C.H. Beck, 1990), translated as *Likeness and Presence: A History of the Image Before the Era of Art* (Chicago: University of Chicago Press, 1994).

35. Claire Farago and Donna Pierce, with additional contributions, *Transforming Images: New Mexican Santos in Between Worlds* (University Park: Pennsylvania State University Press, 2006).

36. Belting, *Bild-Anthropologie: Entwürfe für eine Bildwissenschaft*, second edition (Munich: W. Fink, 2002 [2001]).

37. Robert Williams, *Art, Theory, and Culture in Sixteenth-century Italy: From Techne to Metatechne* (New York: Cambridge University Press, 1997).

38. Shortly after this roundtable, my book *The Cabinet of Eros* received a review (*Times Literary Supplement*, April 28, 2006) in which I was congratulated by a fellow art historian for reading through "heroic" quantities of "turgid Renaissance humanism." The humanism being referred to was the work of Angelo Poliziano, Gian Gioviano Pontano and Baptista Mantuanus. If I were working in another field, and the review had applied the adjective "turgid" to, say, nineteenth-century salon criticism, or to medieval theologians, or to any form of non western writing whatsover, there would have been open warfare in the pages of the *TLS*. Latin humanism is still perceived as so institutionally enfranchised that we can openly vent our prejudices against it and expect broad agreement.

39. Celenza, *The Lost Italian Renaissance: Humanists, Historians, and Latin's Legacy* (Baltimore: Johns Hopkins University Press, 2004).

40. Charles Hope and Elizabeth McGrath, "Artists and Humanists," *The Cambridge Companion to Renaissance Humanism* (J. Kraye, ed., Cambridge: Cambridge University Press, 1996) 161–88.

41. Bruce Holsinger, *The Premodern Condition* (Chicago: University of Chicago Press, 2005), argues that French poststructuralism is indebted to medieval

studies and medieval ideas. A review by Bettina Bildhauer (*Times Literary Supplement*, April 14, 2006, p. 26), stresses the fact that Bataille in particular was influenced by Angela of Foligno as well as Aquinas.

42. See my brief discussion in my Introduction, "Reframing the Renaissance," in *Reframing the Renaissance*, 9–12; and an excellent book that deserves to be better known, by Frances S. Connelly, *The Sleep of Reason: Primitivism in Modern European Art and Aesthetics, 1725–1900* (University Park: Pennsylvania State University Press, 1997).

43. Plenty on both sides in my *What Painting Is* (New York: Routledge, 1998), and "Four Ways of Measuring the Distance Between Alchemy and Contemporary Art," *Hyle* 9 no. 1 (2003): 105–18.

44. See, for instance, Hubertus Günther, "Die ersten Schritte in die Neuzeit: Gedanken zum Beginn der Renaissance nördlich der Alpen," in *Wege zur Renaissance: Beobachtungen zu den Anfängen neuzeitlicher Kunstauffassung im Rheinland und den Nachbargebieten um 1500*, edited by Norbert Nussbaum, Claudia Euskirchen, and Stephan Hoppe (Cologne: SH-Verlag, 2003), 31–87, especially 49–60.

45. Williams, "Sticky Goo," *Oxford Art Journal* 25 no. 1 (2002): 102.

46. Frank Fehrenbach, "Leonardo's Point," a lecture at the University of Virginia, Charlottesville, Virginia, May 28, 2006.

47. For a general discussion of paradox in the Renaissance, see Rosalie L. Colie, *"Paradoxia Epidemica": The Renaissance Tradition of Paradox* (Princeton NJ: Princeton University Press, 1966).

48. For a sampling of ways recent writers have approached the topic, see Michael Baxandall, *Patterns of Intention: On the Historical Explanation of Pictures* (New Haven: Yale University Press, 1985); Svetlana Alpers and Michael Baxandall, *Tiepolo and the Pictorial Intelligence* (New Haven: Yale University Press, 1994); Thomas Crow, *The Intelligence of Art* (Chapel Hill: University of North Carolina Press, 1999); James Elkins, *What Painting Is: How to Think about Oil Painting, Using the Language of Alchemy* (New York : Routledge, 1999); and Michael Cole, "Salt, Composition and the Goldsmith's Intelligence," in *Cellini and the Principles of Sculpture* (New York: Cambridge University Press, 2002), 15–42.

49. Pamela H. Smith, *The Body of the Artisan: Art and Experience in the Scientific Revolution* (Chicago: University of Chicago Press, 2004); see also the interesting book by Pamela O. Long, *Openness, Secrecy, Authorship: Technical Arts and the Culture of Knowledge from Antiquity to the Renaissance* (Baltimore: Johns Hopkins University Press, 2001).

50. Melville, "The Temptation of New Perspectives," *October* 52 (spring 1990): 3–15.

51. Clark, *Farewell to An Idea: Episodes from a History of Modernism* (New Haven: Yale University Press, 1999). This and the following examples are discussed at length in my *Master Narratives and Their Discontents*, vol. 1 of *Theories of Modernism and Postmodernism in the Visual Arts* (New York: Routledge, 2005).

52. Stella, *Working Space* (Cambridge MA: Harvard University Press, 1986).

53. Bal, *Quoting Caravaggio: Contemporary Art, Preposterous History* (Chicago: University of Chicago Press, 1999).

54. Bersani and Ulysse Dutoit, *Caravaggio's Secrets* (Cambridge MA: MIT Press, 1998).

55. On a "Renaissance art history without images," here's a list of significant books on Renaissance art from the past twenty years in which surviving works of art are not (or, are only very peripherally) discussed; and some of these books are not illustrated. In terms of authors this also could be described as a strange list of people: Karin-edis Barzman, *The Florentine Academy and the Early Modern State. The Discipline of Disegno* (Cambridge, 2000); Richard Goldthwaite, *Wealth and the Demand for Art in Italy 1300–1600* (Baltimore, 1993); Catherine Soussloff, *The Absolute Artist: The Historiography of a Concept* (Minneapolis, 1997); David Summers, *The Judgement of Sense. Renaissance Naturalism and the Rise of Aesthetics* (Cambridge, 1987); Thomas Tuohy, *Herculean Ferrara. Ercole d'Este (1471–1505) and the Invention of a Ducal Capital* (Cambridge, 1996); Robert Williams, *Art, Theory and Culture in Sixteenth Century Italy. From Techne to Metatechne* (Cambridge, 1997); Louis A. Waldmann, *Baccio Bandinelli and Art at the Medici Court: A Corpus of Early Modern Sources* (Philadelphia, 2004); Evelyn S. Welch, *Art and Authority in Renaissance Milan* (New Haven and London, 1995). The disappearance of Renaissance art in scholarship ironically coincides with its disappearance from the public sphere, or rather its eclipsing by the ever more marketable figures of Leonardo, Michelangelo and Caravaggio. For instance, the Brooklyn Museum of Art owns an important collection of Renaissance paintings, but you will be lucky to see them if you go there. The new Gemäldegalerie in Berlin—a collection of Renaissance and baroque art equal in importance with the Louvre and the National gallery, London—is threatened with a very short life span. Currently more than 2,000 works are on display, but plans are afoot to put all but 200 "masterpieces" in storage, and to move these 200 to an area with more high density tourist traffic.

56. Stella's book is discussed in my "Abstraction's Sense of History: Frank Stella's *Working Space* Revisited," *American Art* 7 no. 1 (winter 1993): 28–39.

57. Bal, "Visual essentialism and the object of visual culture," *Journal of Visual Culture* 2 no. 2 (2003) 5–31.

58. I claim this in my *Why Art Our Pictures Puzzles? On the Modern Origins of Pictorial Complexity* (New York: Routledge, 1999).

59. Stephen's paper in this book is one of the rare exceptions, although what Stephen goes on to do does not at all follow on from Didi-Huberman.

60. Yve-Alain Bois and Rosalind Krauss, *Formless: A User's Guide* (New York: Zone Books, 1997). On Didi-Huberman see my "Einige Gedanken über der Unbestimmtheit der Darstellung," in *Das unendliche Kunstwerk: Von der Bestimmtheit des Unbestimmten in der ästhetischen Erfahrung*, edited by Gerhard Gramm and Eva Schürmann, forthcoming (2007).

61. Bill Readings, *The University in Ruins* (Cambridge: Harvard University Press, 1996); Sam Weber, *Institution and Interpretation*, expanded ed. (Stanford: Stanford University Press, 2001).

62. Rosamond E. Mack, *Bazaar to Piazza: Islamic Trade and Italian Art, 1300–1600* (Berkeley: University of California Press, 2002).

63. My *Visual Studies: A Skeptical Introduction* (New York: Routledge, 2003).
64. See, for instance, Gustav Réné Hocke, *Die Welt als Labyrinth: Manier und Manie in der europäische Kunst von 1520–1650 und der Gegenwart* (Hamburg : Rohwolt, 1968).
65. See, for example, Philip Drew, *The Architecture of Arata Isozaki* (New York, 1982).
66. Kavaler, *Pieter Bruegel: Parables of Order and Enterprise* (Cambridge; Cambridge University Press, 1999); Honig, *Painting and the Market in Early Modern Antwerp* (New Haven CT: Yale University Press, 1998); Houghton, "This was Tomorrow: Pieter Aertsen's Meat Stall as Contemporary Art," *Art Bulletin* 86 (2004): 277–300.
67. Filip Vermeylen, *Painting for the Market: Comercialization of Art in Antwerp's Golden Age*, Studies in European Urban History (1100–1800) 2 (Turnhout: Brepols, 2003); Neil de Marchi and Hans J. van Miegroet, "Art, Value, and Market Practices in the Netherlands in the Seventeenth Century," *The Art Bulletin* 76 (1994), 451–64.

4
ASSESSMENTS

Jan von Bonsdorff

The Inertia of the Canon: Nationalist Projections onto the Works of Hans
Brüggemann and Bernt Notke

At the end of 2004 the Danish minister of culture, Brian Mikkelsen, commissioned panels of experts from different spheres of cultural life to formulate an official "Canon of Danish Art and Culture". The canon was to contain "the greatest, most important works of Denmark's cultural heritage".[1] Each panel, consisting of five members, was instructed to choose twelve works from different categories, including literature, music, and the visual arts. From nine areas, a total of 108 works were thus selected, and the resulting canon was published as a book and on the net in the autumn of 2006. The books were distributed free of charge to most Danish schools and other educational establishments—"as a yardstick for quality—a yardstick that will obviously be constantly challenged and discussed". Of course, this kind of centrally orchestrated, politically engineered, and painfully reductive simplification of a cultural past could not and did not pass unchallenged. The project has been the subject of intense debate in Scandinavia: among other artists, for example, the filmmaker Lars von Trier protested vehemently against his own inclusion in the canon. And yet some political parties in the other Scandinavian countries have placed the establishment of similar canons on their agendas.

In connection with the roundtable's discussion of the invisibility of the Renaissance, it is interesting to see how the different epochs are represented in the Danish Cultural Canon: seventy-five percent of the works of art from all areas date from after 1900, and could be called "modernist" or "contemporary". Only seven works rank as "indispensable" to the definition of Danish culture date from before 1700. One looks in vain for the castle Kronborg at Elsinore (already canonized by the UNESCO as World Heritage property), Tycho Brahe's Uraniborg, or the large building projects of Christian IV, King of Denmark and Norway, in the seventeenth century.

The only work from the sixteenth century included in the Canon is not preserved within the contemporary borders of Denmark: the "Bordesholmer Altar" by Hans Brüggemann from 1521 in the

Cathedral of Schleswig (Danish Slesvig).[2] This altarpiece could be called one of the last dinosaurs of the Middle Ages in Northern Europe, even though it also exhibits Renaissance traits: the Passion scenes are indeed inspired by Dürer's engravings of the Passion, but the Late Gothic style dominates in the profuse, organic decorative carving and the open tracery, mounting to a height of forty feet. Border regions, like the former Duchies of Schleswig and Holstein, with their mixed languages and complex histories of political affiliation, often contain works of art subject to multiple claims of ownership. Thus, the formerly Danish Cathedral of Lund in Scania, now in Sweden, might have been just as appropriate a choice. For the Canon. The question is why one suddenly reverts to historical borders in a canon otherwise founded on ahistorical thinking and the requirements of a perpetual "now".

Sad to say, the Danish canon is the populistic construction of a supposed current "Period Eye". I am reminded of the famous *New Yorker* cover by Saul Steinberg, "View of the World from 9th Avenue", in which Steinberg suggests a radical foreshortening of geographical areas outside New York. The perspective of the Danish Cultural Canon is, however, projected backwards in time. The hubris of "now" is evident: modernity is like Manhattan and preponderant to the Period Eye; premodern time—like the American mid-West or Asia—is an indistinct Other.

There are aspects of this process that correspond to Claire Farago's concerns about the interconnectedness of the Renaissance and present times. Clearly, the Bordesholmer Altar has been mobilized by recontextualization: it is now fraught with more meaning than before. At first sight, this is it should be: the work of art collects interpretations through the ages; it embraces rather than excludes meaning. A work of art cannot politely decline to mean something, once that meaning has become attached; it has no inherent power of negation. Only the forgetfulness of beholders over time can eradicate former contextualizations. Other conceptual models can be used to explain this process, of course: the viewing subject may be thought of as actively projecting its own meanings onto the works, or as being enmeshed in the discursive formations that circulate through the object, but the result is the same. Another example of the process: the works of Caspar David Friedrich and Hans Thoma will probably never be entirely free of the political contextualization created for them by the Nazis to serve ideological ends. Each succeeding interpretation must wrestle with its precedents, taking them into consideration; every interpretation forms part of a collective cultural memory.

It is not quite clear why the Bordesholmer Altar was so readily embraced by the Danish canon committee responsible for the Visual Arts. Frederick, the Duke of Schleswig and Holstein who later became King Frederick I of Denmark and Norway (1471–1533), donated the altarpiece to the Augustinian monastery Bordesholm. When he died, he was buried in the Cathedral of Schleswig, and when the monastery in Bordesholm was closed down in 1666, the altarpiece was moved to the cathedral. One of the members of the canon committee is reported to have said that there is no equal to this altarpiece in Denmark[3]. No mention was made of the altarpiece by Claus Berg in the church of St. Canute in Odense from the beginning of the sixteenth century, or to the enormous Aarhus altarpiece by Bernt Notke from 1479. There are even other wooden sculptures by Hans Brüggemann in Danish collections, which would have been natural choices, such as the large *St. George* in the National Museum and the exquisite *Madonna* owned by Queen Margrethe II (now kept at her residence in Southern France).[4]

I suspect that there is no other explanation for the inclusion of the Bordesholmer Altar than its function as a token for its presumed degree of "Danishness". This is an essence as elusive as Nicolaus Pevsner's "Englishness", Paul Pieper's "das Westfälische" or any other of the similar conceptual short-circuits that surfaced in attempts to territorialize large quantities of art during the first two-thirds of the twentieth century.[5] The projection of this vague quality onto the monument is due to nothing else than its relation to King Frederick I and the fact that the former Duchy of Schleswig was once politically connected to Denmark. The altarpiece is thus arbitrarily made to serve as a nostalgic metonymy for lost territory: its inclusion in the Danish canon is, deliberately or not, blatant colonialism.

In this way, the political present is indeed connected to the past, but certainly not in the way Claire Farago intends. If I understand her correctly, she longs to break the seal of the hermetically closed epoch of the Renaissance and to move beyond an art history that is nothing more than the humble servant of nation-states. In the Danish cultural canon, the nation-state is reinforced again and again—with perfectly circular reasoning—by the superimposition of some vague national essence onto works of art in different media.

Art history today is not yet really global, even if it is moving in that direction, and there are promising signs everywhere, as at the last CIHA congress in Montreal 2004 ("Sites and Territories of Art History") and the forthcoming one in Melbourne 2008 ("Crossing Cultures"). In this larger development, the Western nation-state and its imprint on art can only be interesting as a historical phenomenon. Mostly, the more interpretations a work of art accumulates through time, the greater its chance of survival: having proved its interest, it grows more interesting. Contemporary "banal nationalism"[6] does not enhance this process but stifles it. Such nationalism is monocausal; it tends to petrify interpretation, to overload the History of Art with the History of the Nation. Works of art that have been charged with nationalistic investments become difficult to handle, they become inert and unwieldy.

Of course, art historians themselves contribute to some aspects of this process. In Northern Europe, especially in the smaller countries, there have existed since the end of the nineteenth century an abundance of handbooks and surveys of national art. The conceptual roots of this phenomenon reach back to Hegel; the nation states of the nineteenth century demanded formalized historical accounts of the nation's distinctive spiritual tradition as manifested in its literature, music, and art. Early Scandinavian art historians followed the example of scholars such as Franz Theodor Kugler and Carl Schnaase. In more recent times, the production of such texts has been given impetus by the fact that the large anglophone Western handbooks on art—ubiquitous at Scandinavian universities—are completely devoid of art and architecture from Northern and Eastern Europe. Personally, I have never understood why extraordinary monuments like the great wooden equestrian statue of *St. George* in Storkyrkan, Stockholm, or the fortress of Malbork, Poland, do not appear in the many editions of the leading American textbooks, Janson, Stokstad, and Gardner.[7] The exclusion is not malevolent, of course, just one of those blind spots in the Western Period Eye lamented by many, not only Scandinavians. Depending on the country, Scandinavian handbooks are steadily renewed at a rate of about every ten or twenty years. The newest handbook on Swedish art will be published at the beginning of 2007.[8] In the preface, the editor, Lena Johannesson, lists all precursors and says that the ten-year republication period is perfectly natural, since it allows for the inclusion of new research.[9] It might be added that Scandinavian handbooks are widely read within the Scandinavian countries, including Finland and Iceland. The newest Norwegian survey by Gunnar Danbolt, for instance, is on the art history undergraduate curriculum of most Swedish universities.[10]

Interestingly enough, the canon does *not* remain stable. Let us take a closer look at the aforementioned statue of *St. George* by Bernt Notke in the Storkyrkan church in Stockholm, a work of 1489. This monumental work has been celebrated thoughout its history: the Swedish historian Johannes Messenius (1579–1636) mentioned the work in his chronicle; the monarch Gustavus Adolphus II counts it as one of his favourite works of art; and the nationalistically-oriented author Verner von Heidenstam fabulates freely about mastership and models. The history of its reception reaches a climax on a suitably grey February morning in 1880, when a trainee at the Royal Library in Stockholm—none other than the young August Strindberg—locates the long-forgotten relics that belonged to the statue.[11]

In 1944, Andreas Lindblom attempted the experiment of writing a truly *Swedish* art history handbook. He focussed on the native artists and excluded all art having the least sign of foreignness.[12] In this way, he categorically separated "Immigrant Artists" from "Passage Artists"[13]. The Immigrant Artists were barely tolerated, since they were able to assimilate and achieve a spirit of community [*gemenskapskänsla*] with the Swedish people, but the Passage Artists found no pardon in Lindblom's eyes. Thus, Notke, a citizen of Lubeck who probably lived a decade in Stockholm, is firmly excluded, together with his "de-canonized" statue of *St. George*.

In spite of this exclusion, the Stockholm *St. George* has gathered a wealth of interpretations throughout its history. The most common connect it to the battle of Brunkeberg the 10th of October 1471.[14] This battle was the consequence of noblemen exploiting the old dream of a Nordic union, on the one hand, and, on the other, nationalistic and separatistic ambitions. Christian I of Denmark aspired to continue the union, while the Regent (*riksföreståndare*) of Sweden, Sten Sture the Elder, wanted a separate Swedish state. Sten Sture led an army of peasants and knights from the provinces of Väster- and Östergötland, Småland, Dalecarlia and from the city proper against Christian I, who had the Swedish province of Uppland on his side. The "Danish" host was defeated and Sten Sture claimed victory. The winning party, it was said, had seen the holy sword of the national saint, St. Erik, in the sky; the army of Lord Sten was supposed to have entered into battle singing the old medieval lay of St. George (*Örjansvisan*); and, according to the chronicles, there was a widespread belief that St. George himself had intervened to the favour of the Regent's men.[15]

Johannes Messenius, the seventeenth-century historian mentioned above, is the first to maintain a connection between the victory of the Swedish separatist movement at Brunkeberg and the donation of the statue by Sten Sture. The *St. George* is interpreted as a national monument, as a symbol of Sten Sture's principal political ambition, national unification.[16] This traditional is endorsed by Jan Svanberg in his splendid monograph on the monument, arguing that Sten Sture used the battle at Brunkeberg and the cult of St. George as a "unifying national symbol".[17] But Svanberg also emphasizes the personal dimension in Lord Sture's purchase of the monument: the donations of Sten Sture and other members of leading Swedish families are confirmed through documents preserved in the Vatican Library.

Others maintain a critical attitude toward the nationalistic interpretation. Gerhard Eimer calls it simply "the Brunkeberg myth". He chooses instead to emphasize the numerous coats-of-arms placed on the monument. These belong in part to various families whose members had been part of the State Council (*riksråd*) of the old union between Denmark, Sweden and Norway. As a result, Eimer interprets the *St. George* as a monument to the old Scandinavian union (*Unionsmonument*), a kind of "appeal to the State Council families for concerted action". The desired action would have been a consolidation of the Scandinavian countries in an empire on the model of the Kalmar Union. According to Eimer—here echoing the words of D. Feldmann[18]—the statue of St. George simply could not have served as a "historical retrospect" of the battle of Brunkeberg in 1471, eighteen years earlier. Eimer further denies that the *St. George* had anything to do with the person of Sten Sture the Elder. He chooses to ignore the coats-of-arms of the Sture family—the three water-lily leaves—that are found in several places on the monument, in one case as a kind of painted brand on the loins of the horse. Documents dating from shortly after Sten Sture's death mention one of his horses carrying his mark burnt on its legs.[19] This mark on the sculpture, somewhat hidden though it is, still suggests an effort to establish a relation between the horse of the *St. George* and Sture's own horse. But Eimer interprets the statue as an official monument, not one that makes personal reference to a particular patron. The only personal aspect Eimer takes into consideration is the fact that Sten Sture originally planned the statue to be the final resting-place for himself and his wife, Ingeborg Tott.[20]

Johnny Roosval, pointing out that many contemporary equestrian statues in Italy also functioned as tombs, tried to reconstruct the pedestal with reliefs found scattered in Storkyrkan in Stockholm.[21] These reliefs, depicting scenes from the martyrdom of St. George, originally had openings between the upper rim of the relief and the roof of the base. These openings offered a view into the base structure, and since the roof was painted blue and adorned with gold stars, it must have been intended to be seen.[22] The Sture chronicle tells us clearly that on his death 1503, the body of Lord Sten was laid out in the altar of St. George in Storkyrkan.[23] Soon afterwards, it was moved to the monastery of Mariefred.

So we have three different interpretations: a "unifying national monument", a "political monument for the old Scandinavian union" and, lastly, a tomb. Nor are these the only options. Indeed, I would follow M.J. Liebmann in interpreting the statue as a *memoria*, a monument signifying victory over death and oblivion.[24] The serene, transfigured look on the face of the knight, and especially his gesture, eternally holding aloft his drawn sword, presage the final victory of life over death and good over evil.[25] But fame, *fama*, is closely connected to *memoria*: the heroic deeds of the knight will not be forgotten and will serve as an example for others to emulate. Thus, the personal fame of Sten Sture and his regency is superimposed onto the widespread cult of St. George, with all that it signifies. This quality of memorial (in Swedish, *minnesmärke*) has been recognized by earlier historians: Hildebrand, Anjou, Roosval etc.[26] Anjou, for instance, reads the monument as a political allegory according to which the young knight courageously throws himself over the Danish dragon so as to be able to free the Swedish princess, for whom he assumes a God-given responsibility.[27] My own feeling is that it would be wrong to see the monument as having been intended as a political allegory at the time of its production. The *memoria* of eternal salvation foreshadowed by St. George's victory is clear enough; the *memoria* of a particular historical personality and the military victories associated with him is less explicit, but suggested. While the dignity and heroic virtue of the knight are emphasized, the *memoria* of the nation and political unity can only be the interpretation of later generations—the constructed projection of the nation-state. Liebmann argues that the sculptor Notke, "grazes, but does not transgress, the border to a humanistic understanding of the world".[28] I would go one step further, however, and rather than stay on the verge of the Renaissance, ask whether the personal commemorative function of the *St. George* might not represent a Renaissance idea clothed in the Late Gothic form?

Inclusion, exclusion, re-interpretation: this is the open structure of semiosis, the endless chain of meanings with which we enrich that particular aspect of material culture we call art. We must make allowances for the handbooks: they cannot work without the canon, but they certainly should point out their more or less hidden agendas of inclusion and omission. Interestingly, Lindblom—writing in 1944—did a better job of doing so than many more recent writers. Of course, choices should not be made on the basis of any kind of "essence" supposedly inherent in the work itself, and in this respect Lindblom fails, relying as he does on the essence of "Swedishness". Objects should rather be chosen as a matter of didactic efficacy, as *exempla* fitting an argument that is transparently acknowledged. If the interpretative agenda is properly accounted for, the canon feels much less oppressive, and we can move on to evolve new conceptual frameworks for old art.

Una Roman D'Elia

Popular Elitism: Renaissance Art as a Secret Code

Elitism is—properly, I think—a central concern for the scholars in our field. The panel discussion circled back time and again to perceptions and political polemics about how our objects of study and the ways in which we study them could be considered elitist or popularist. I would like to add to the debate a truly popular form of Renaissance Art History at the moment, *The Da Vinci Code*.[29] I can understand why my colleagues did not mention this international phenomenon. The painfully badly-written book certainly does not merit consideration as fiction or history, and it is alarming to imagine the discussion gliding from Jacques Derrida and Hans Belting to Dan Brown. Nevertheless, if we want to think about how economics, politics, and institutions shape and are shaped by our discipline, the immense popularity of this book and its spin-offs is worth discussing. The Louvre offers *Da Vinci Code* audio tours!

I will first confess that I have read the book, but not seen the movie or taken the audio tour. I did so because students kept asking me about it. When surveyed, only two students out of a lecture class of over one hundred had not read it. The students were probably inspired to take my course (and your courses) by reading the book. My students are not stupid—quite the contrary. So what is it that makes this book so broadly appealing, even to an intelligent, engaged readership?

The interpretations of individual paintings are not worth dignifying with a response. The novel (which the author hints is partially non-fiction) has a fundamentally elitist premise. The not-so-new revelation is that Mary Magdalene was the Holy Grail—that she was married to Christ and bore his child, thus initiating a bloodline of geniuses, including Leonardo da Vinci, which survives to the present day. I find it particularly repulsive that Brown uses a thin veneer of feminism to market the ancient sexist notion of woman as vessel. It is also, of course, fundamentally a racist theory.

In the book, the "true" meaning of Leonardo's paintings is only comprehensible to an elect few, in this case a male Harvard (of course) symbologist (?!?) and his somewhat slow female sidekick. The paintings are a code, so that once the code has been cracked, they are left behind, useless once they have conveyed their banal "truths." The book then offers an extremely popular form of elitism. Perhaps because much of modern art is the province of the few and famously incomprehensible to a broader audience, Renaissance art is thought to be even more elite, even more coded. The book lets you belong to the club, to laugh at those who were so simple as to think that a circle is just a circle, by revealing the interpretation of each clue so excruciatingly slowly that the reader feels smarter even than the Harvard professor!

This way of seeing art as a code is a particularly distorted way of viewing the works of Leonardo, who wrote of how painting is greater than literature because it can show the dust and blood of the battlefield and make you fall in love with a beautiful woman.[30] Leonardo claims that painting can virtually fulfill Pygmalion's dream, become suddenly magically warm and yielding to the touch, alive. Writers and artists of the time hailed Leonardo's paintings precisely because they were wonderfully alive, newly full of energy and blood. Leonardo painted his works for a privileged, private audience, but also for a refectory, for government buildings, and for church altars—public spaces that demand comprehensible, even rhetorically convincing images.

I hesitate when moving from the fun of eviscerating a detective novel to the serious, potentially self-implicating, task of considering whether Renaissance art historians are guilty of similar crimes. Erwin Panofsky's ideas about iconography and disguised symbolism are still foundational for our discipline, and many studies appear today of the complex, hidden symbolism of Renaissance art. Whether you agree with his individual arguments or not, most scholars would have to admit that Charles Hope has been particularly effective and merciless in attacking such attempts to read Renaissance art as a symbolic code. He, understandably, focuses some of his most trenchant criticisms on those who interpret altarpieces—which were seen by broad audiences as a part of the ceremony of the mass—as carriers of erudite theological meaning.[31] Panofsky, however, was not for the most part talking about esoterica. His image, in his famous article on the iconographic method, of a man tipping his hat is revealing.[32] Tipping your hat is a form of gestural language, broadly comprehensible, only enigmatic to those who are from an alien culture (such as our own, in which the gesture is so outmoded that it could easily be misconstrued). That said, as Panofsky was well aware, such forms of communication are not exactly classless or gender-neutral—obviously the person tipping the hat is not a poor woman, or if so, the gesture takes on new meaning. Likewise, you do not have to be a Harvard symbologist to understand the imagery in most Netherlandish paintings (Panofsky's prime examples of disguised symbolism), such as clear water and lilies as images of purity and virginity.[33]

To turn to the state of the field now, I was heartened and excited by the panel discussion and position papers, which implied that Renaissance art was—far from Dan Brown's flat symbols—a living "force" (to borrow Stephen Campbell's felicitous term) in and of the textured, multifarious social and cultural life of the past and present. Perhaps the elitist interpretation of art in the *Da Vinci Code* reflects a particular form of iconographic study that has been long superceded (just as the *Agony and the Ecstasy* conveys an almost nineteenth-century view of the artist as rebellious hero).[34] It would make sense for the popular view of art to lag behind art historical scholarship, even if we hope that through teaching and publication, our ideas will eventually have a broader currency. Nevertheless, the position papers and discussion suggest that the problem of how art communicated in the Renaissance is one of the major fault lines in our field. The panelists debated whether viewers responded to Renaissance art in a rational or irrational manner, and whether this distinction applies to the Renaissance. In the caricatured world of the *Da Vinci Code*, art is a fully systematic, rational language, a code that needs to be cracked, and perhaps secondarily a beautiful objet, but not something that can provoke desire, fear, or belief—not something that magically moves and speaks. Renaissance writers who discuss the communicative function of art, focus not on symbolism, but on decorum. Decorum is a rational system ("cultural perspective," as Williams terms it) by which artists attempt to evoke and control—never fully successfully—what were often powerful emotional and sometimes irrational responses to art.

Hans Belting, another foundational thinker whose work is invoked repeatedly by the panelists, made an influential distinction between cult objects and self-conscious works of art, which has been widely used to define the difference between Medieval and Renaissance art.[35] Belting's theory suggests that Renaissance art is more lifelike but less magically alive than earlier cult objects.[36] Fredrika Jacobs pays tribute to the seminal importance of this idea, but also offers important qualifications, by giving particular examples of paintings that were both cult images and a part of the new self-conscious cult of images. She also discusses how the most prominent patrons, the Medici, commissioned wax-works to sit in the churches on their behalf. Jacobs paid tribute to David Freedberg's *The Power of Images*, a book that like Belting's focuses on the functions of images (rather than the aesthetics of art).[37] Freedberg's account is explicitly ahistorical—he is not concerned with describing the sort of broad historical changes that would help us define the Renaissance and that make Belting's work so compelling and problematic. Freedberg does cite, as examples of the "power of images," along with cult statues and popular photographs, canonical works of Renaissance art. As other historians focusing on response have noted, new-found Renaissance illusionism could be seen as an artful device, an admission that art is mere fiction, but it could also be seductively, even dangerously convincing, a way to make art come vividly alive.[38] Stephen Campbell writes of Vasari's repression of these dangers of illusionism, the potent living energy of Renaissance art.

Art was certainly discussed in the literature of the time as magically alive. Symbolism is scarcely if ever mentioned. (So we are told that we can smell the lilies, but not what they mean.[39]) The tropes of Renaissance ekphrasis are conventional and could be simply literary tradition, not reacting in any meaningful way to innovations in art. For example, in one tender poem, Castiglione's wife talks to and even almost hears a response from Raphael's famous portrait in her husband's absence. John Shearman discussed this poem as an example of the lively communicative nature of Cinquecento portraiture.[40] But, as Shearman noted, it was not Castiglione's wife, but the writer himself who wrote the poem, which is an artful variation on a whole genre of poetry about portraits. Shearman and others (most notably Elizabeth Cropper[41]) have not seen the conventional nature of period writing about art as an impediment, but instead as revealing of period attitudes.

Of course, not all Renaissance works of art offer living, breathing illusions, and many of them are elitist in medium, message, and the enigmatic way in which that message is conveyed. Architecture (the study of which, as mentioned by the panelists, has become almost a separate discipline) is obviously a special case in terms of symbolism and illusion. Likewise, some Renaissance paintings and sculptures are symbolic, rather than realistic—some even offer the viewer cryptic puzzles. Take, for example, Mannerist allegories, which contain enough hermetic wisdom, animal symbolism, and ancient Egyptian lore to be a scriptwriter's treasure trove.[42] Even these elite, self-conscious, coded works, though, were thought to "ravish the soul with marvel and inflame it with ardor."[43]

Perhaps this is another way to begin to define what is particular to the Renaissance, a point of view suggested by some of the position papers. Renaissance art is newly, breathtakingly living, a magical fulfillment of Pygmalion's dream. At the same time, as the panelists discussed, Renaissance art was a part of a theoretical culture, a hothouse environment of the literate elite. Renaissance artists wrote histories, not only of Antiquity, but also of their own times, and evinced therefore an odd historical distance and even nostalgia about their own art, art that left them, and leaves us, both self-conscious and seduced.

Lisa Pon
Do Art Historians in the Twenty-first Century Have a Renaissance?

It is fitting, I think, to begin my essay by reframing Joan Kelly-Gadol's seminal question, "Did Women Have a Renaissance?".[44] In some ways, her own answer to the question that gave her essay of 1977 its title paralleled the response of Denys Hays, who had, a decade and a half earlier, claimed that women's lives did not change much in the Renaissance. But, unlike Hays, who held that "the domestic behaviour of men and women . . . is not history,"[45] Kelly-Gadol's questioning opened up the Renaissance as a field of historical study in a manner that even her own emphatic no would not foreclose. In the decades since her essay appeared, historians, especially art historians, have reconsidered Kelly-Gadol's question in many different ways: by re-examining Renaissance women artists, exploring the figure of the courtesan and the Venetian dogaressa, describing the gendered domestic and public spaces of the period, looking to that singular female patron, Isabella d'Este, and well beyond her. These studies, and many others, have invigorated the field by bringing scholarly attention to these previously marginal or excluded subjects.

And yet my question persists: do we art historians in the twenty-first century have a Renaissance to study? Or have the studies stimulated by Kelly-Gadol's essay fragmented a now-lost unified sense of what was central to the Renaissance? I think the nostalgia for a lost golden age that has settled over some parts of Renaissance studies is less about the new subjects opened up by feminism. Even more fundamentally, it is about how the study of Renaissance art, once not just dominant in the field but (as a department chair once said) "domineering," has slid to a more tenuous position within art history as a whole. As Bob Williams vividly stated, the Renaissance is now in a "chokehold," "made to serve both as an anticipation of our own time and as a foil for it."[46] It has become seen as both an origin for modern art, and the outdated norm against which modern art reacts. How can we study a Renaissance cast as the father of modernism's Oedipus?

I have no set answer, nor should I; it will take more than even one full career's efforts to sketch a response. But I feel privileged to have the chance to think about a few of the many stimulating ideas raised at the Cork Renaissance Roundtable. The theme of center and periphery seems to have been especially resonant, and for a number of good reasons: as Williams and Elkins both noted, the call for the roundtable was to discuss Renaissance art history's current uncomfortable position as both central and peripheral to the discipline; Stephen Campbell pointed to a long-standing interest in the interactions between center and periphery in Italian scholarship; the question of central or outlying scholarly positions was repeatedly engaged and parried. Though I was not present to hear the unrecorded original comment about the baby and the bath water that was alluded to at the round table, that too is a trope about center and periphery.[47] I would like to point out parenthetically that bath water can be invaluable in cleansing, soothing, or reinvigorating a baby, but the more pressing issue is that one has to decide what gets to be the baby and what gets to be the bathwater. The trope naturalizes the relationship between the terms so that one is unquestionably vital and full of potential, and the other (especially when figured as "dirty bathwater") is not only subservient but inevitably discarded.

A more incisive trope was used already a decade ago in Claire Farago's call for "reframing the Renaissance," since framing as active, strategic, always asking what the object of study is, and what is at stake by attending to it.[48] The trope also demands that we consciously consider why we are placing something at the center or margins of our chosen frame, rather than allowing us to assume a fixed and certain value to any subject. Needless to say, the Renaissance is full of canonical places, works, and figures that have long been seen as holding universal and enduring value, and some scholars will insist that these are unequivocally the baby, while others might argue it is time they became the bath water. But is there truly nothing left of interest to say about these canonical places/works/figures? Is this "closely cropped field" in fact completely shorn? Or isn't it important to ask why the art historical sheep have been so avidly grazing there? Why can't re-examining the historical reasons for their centrality be part of the project of reframing the Renaissance?

I very much like the argument Farago put forth at the round-table, that a periphery can come around to reshape a center, that we can and should aspire to a panoramic framing that keeps center and periphery, however defined, in play. This idea also grounds Fredrika Jacobs's suggestion that we bring together familiar and unfamiliar things, in order to see both more completely, or, if I may use an anthropological term, more thickly.[49] Stephen Campbell and Michael Cole, both authors of thought-provoking studies of canonical Florentines, brought up the question of how critical dialogue can be possible even for those working on traditional centers like Florence.[50] In a recent conference paper, Roger Crum beautifully articulated another possibility.[51] He pointed out that the Florentine Republic from the fourteenth century through the mid-fifteenth century was blatantly expansionist in terms of its international economic empire, which reached from London to Constantinople, from Bruges to North Africa. Florence was also expansionist in terms of its political domains, adding a series of Tuscan "new towns" that David Friedman had characterized as its "colonies." In his book, Friedman had commented, "Building a unified community with strong ties to Florence was a more delicate task than the military and political effort that led up to the founding of a town, but the Florentines were not without resources."[52] Art and artists were part of those resources, but Crum asked us not only to consider unfamiliar works of art from Florence's far-flung social, political and economic network outside the city's walls, but also to ask how those works might reshape our understanding of the heart of the canon of Florentine Renaissance art. This type of reevaluation of canonical works has already begun for Venice. I was able to demonstrate that Titian's woodcut of St. Roch was made, not for Venetians, but for pilgrims headed to the Holy Land.[53] Deborah Howard's book, *Venice and the East*, explored the practices of Venetian traders headed across the Mediterranean, and attended to the buildings and building types these Venetians would have seen on their travels, thereby reframing how we can look at and understand monuments no less "central" than the Fondaco dei Tedeschi or the Doge's Palace.

Given my own scholarly interests, I found the roundtable's discussion about Vasari fascinating. Was Giorgio Vasari the "original outlier"? I was bemused to see the discussion circling around the issue of whether he was right or wrong or immediately praised or damned. Following Matt Kavaler's comment that Vasari's books were widely circulated and discussed among northern European humanists,[54] as they certainly were in Italy, I would suggest that we can construe Vasari as a central figure because his text was available for so many people to discuss and agree with or disagree with—what Bruno Latour would call an "immutable mobile."[55] In other words, its material manifestation as a book printed in hundreds of copies that could be—and was—read by hundreds and thousands of people across the world and across the centuries made it, in Kavaler's words, "a model for discussions of art history." Surely this can be the basis for a claim for some sort of centrality.

But the periphery is not always only geographic. One of my advisors, John Shearman, asked me years ago (and I do not think I paraphrase because some days I can still hear his question), "Do you know what departments look for when they hire a Renaissance person? Someone who studies painting or sculpture or architecture." Nonetheless I willfully clung to my topic "on prints," because I believed, as I still do, that the rise of printmaking in the sixteenth century had profound effects on the then emerging idea of a work of art, and, indeed on High Renaissance culture as it was developed and understood for centuries. I hope I have convinced others, as I eventually convinced Professor Shearman, but I know that there are readers of my first book who see my discussions of Raphael drawings, for example, as extraneous or digressive. In fact I intended a main argument to be that Raphael's habits of thinking about drawing, what I called his graphic intelligence, led him to embrace the new technology of print. So separating the study of drawings and the study of prints would be counterproductive.

In proposing my dissertation topic to Shearman, I had argued that my project was on Raphael as much as on prints, and he replied that I could think whatever I pleased, and others would think whatever *they* pleased as well (his response proving his claim to be "a part-time receptionist"). The same statement might be made for the prospective readers of my first book, whose title, chosen by my publisher, was designed to suggest a focus on Raphael, Dürer and Marcantonio Raimondi. Yet I suspect that, though my book may be read by scholars of Marcantonio, it is less often read by those studying Raphael or Dürer unless they are looking for something "on prints." The system of the library catalogue enforces this: those whose favorite way of doing research is still to sit before shelves in a great library (and I am one of these peripatetic scholars) will not find my book when parked in front of the Raphael monographs. My book speaks of Raphael in a manner not comfortably recognized by the structure of the library's cataloguing system.

It is perhaps unsurprising if in this book and the ones to come, I speak in a different voice. There are other scholarly voices in the twenty-first century that will also not fit into neat pre-existing categories. While it is true that Renaissance art history may have lost an arrayed, orderly, monolithic tone, it is my hope and belief that the current state is not one of cacophony but of productive dialogue. A devoted reader of Bakhtin might say that Renaissance art history has lost the dominant voice that disciplines and orders the heteroglossia of its subalterns. But let's not forget that a dialogic imagination is not just Bakhtinian; it is also deeply Renaissance, and Castiglione's great dialogue was structured around the absence of the dominant political figure, the Duke of Urbino.[56] Having begun by invoking a question from a canonical twentieth-century text, I'd like to close by reshaping a formative question from the sixteenth century: What makes an ideal Renaissance art historian in the twenty-first century? The roundtable convened by Williams and Elkins have given us the answers voiced in one gathering's conversation. I look forward to the continuing dialogue.

Charlotte M. Houghton

Polemics, Politics, and Pleasure in Renaissance Studies

". . . the object-oriented nature of most art-historical scholarship . . . is largely a disguised form of bourgeois consumerism . . ."

Robert Williams

Against *politesse*

The final paragraph of Robert Williams's essay for this volume left me simultaneously incensed and invigorated—incensed because the fundamental nature of my intellectual enterprise had been impugned; invigorated because a fellow Renaissance art historian had abandoned the scholarly politesse that so often impedes our saying what we really have to say. I find much to argue with in Williams's paper, but only one thing to criticize: his stirring challenge to business-as-usual was fully stated only on the last page. Bob, you buried the lead.

In reading the proceedings of the Cork seminar, I was particularly struck by two interrelated themes: a sense of malaise that our work's signal on wider disciplinary radar is dimming, and a corresponding acknowledgment that displacement of the Renaissance's once-automatic entitlement as Art History's center is justified. In capitalist terms (*pace* Bob Williams), we are now forced to compete, stripped of our former advantage, in the marketplace of art historical ideas; but we want to do conduct our business honestly, with a social conscience. One way to enlarge our audience without compromising either the quality of our craft or our political values is by producing a livelier product. In our line of work, this means offering bold ideas boldly, relating them to broader concerns within the discipline and/or the world at large, and embracing the consequences. This in no way entails practicing less meticulous scholarship. It does suggest having the courage and the sense of permission to hypothesize more freely from, and beyond, what we can absolutely "prove."

One demonstration of such scholarship is Christopher Wood's and Alexander Nagel's recent article in *Art Bulletin*, in which they proposed that historical artifacts functioned "substitutionally" rather than "performatively" in the Renaissance imagination—that they "stitched through time," allowing "the past to participate in the present" in a way quite foreign to the modern mind. This reconceptualization of the perception of historical time and of how it can change over the centuries does not merely offer new ways of thinking about the early modern period, but posits an alternative way of human thinking altogether. It is therefore fascinating to contemplate on its own terms. I happen not to agree with Wood and Nagel; for one thing, *quattrocento* art contains too many canny, ironic references to earlier artifacts which make sense only if they functioned significantly (performatively) rather than substitutionally in the given image.

Wood's and Nagel's alternate historical universe also prepared me to appreciate Claire Farago's response to them, both in *Art Bulletin* and in her essay for this volume. Processing their argument encouraged me further to relativize my own ideas about how fifteenth-century Italians perceived time; then, reading Farago's response with heightened mental flexibility, I could easily accept her contention that the very notion of a concept of history has been key in privileging certain groups of humans and oppressing others. At the same time, Wood and Nagel's reply to her demonstrates the tenacity of the disciplinary problem she faces; they wrote that they "[did] not feel addressed" by her remarks, while she wonders, understandably, how they possibly could not. Both the *Art Bulletin* forum and the current volume offer welcome opportunities for early modern scholars to disagree publicly on important issues.

I do not presume to prescribe scholarly methamphetamine across our discipline. Not everyone has a taste for provocation, nor do sweeping implications invariably arise from one's research. When inspiration does strike, however, I think we should cultivate it in ourselves and in each other, and encourage publication of work that challenges received wisdom—particularly when that wisdom is our own. When our convictions or disagreements are passionate, rather than repressing that passion we should employ it as a divining rod to lead us to what lies, in Farago's words, so deeply at stake.

I endorse Stephen Campbell's opening observation at Cork that repression of polemic and dissent in our scholarly interactions has done disservice to our field. It makes our work less interesting, and prevents us from learning from one another. Argument need not lead to animosity, nor disagreement to acrimony. We can be at once respectful of and honest with each other; in fact, honest disagreement without malice or condescension is a hallmark of respect. We can trade in ideas—even in occasional epithets—with grace and a sense of humor. Call me a bourgeois consumerist art historian, but when you do it, smile.

The politics of our practice

Our canon is our capital. We should tend it with care, because it finances our forays into underexplored territory. Most of us have our jobs because we superintend "the Renaissance" for a society which (I am grateful to say) still values the concepts "Michelangelo" and "Leonardo," and even "Bruegel" and "Dürer," sufficiently to pay us to teach and to question them. As we all know, "the Renaissance" fills the seats. My hasty survey of course listings in art history departments across the U.S.—even those with exceptionally progressive and adamantly "early modern" scholars—reveals that virtually all maintain

"Renaissance" in course names. Even as we discuss among ourselves whether the term, with all its baggage, should be retired, we understand that no matter how we may intend to reshape or reject it in our teaching, it initially works to our advantage. First, get their attention. I, too, feel a moral imperative to challenge "business as usual," as Claire Farago puts it, but I want an audience to hear me do it.

More profoundly, our canon remains valuable as an archaeological site for material of great disruptive power. As Eve Sedgwick observes:

> Canonicity itself . . . seems the necessary wadding of pious obliviousness that allows for the transmission from one generation to another of [works] that have the potential to dismantle the impacted foundations upon which a given culture rests.

To the frustration of many (for a variety of reasons), our canon was founded by Giorgio Vasari, who enshrined the ethnic art of a narrow tribal cohort of European males from Florence as the standard against which all visual representation should henceforth be judged. We all understand and teach that Vasari had an agenda that included defining the parameters of "art" and elevating the status of the "artist." But as both Stephen Campbell and Fredrika Jacobs have insinuated in these pages, the richest material to excavate in Vasari may be what he so effectively represses.

Jacobs raises intriguing prosopographical questions about exactly with and for whom Vasari was writing, and what their personal motivations may have been. Campbell calls Vasari's a "filtering operation," silencing the "unruliness," "ambivalence" and "paradox" of images. Like Campbell, I want to know the ways images functioned outside of, even to subvert, codes of decorum, for these are central to my own agenda. In many ways, the repressive codes of decorum Vasari and his compatriots promoted inform our own. When released, the subversive potential in Renaissance images that Vasari buried so well, and that generations of art historical enterprise have impacted, becomes available again for use in our own time.

I understand and share Farago's dissatisfaction with the fact that:

> There is less interest today than a decade ago in undercutting

anachronistic cultural and aesthetic boundaries that interfere with understanding the complexity of artistic interactions in "the Renaissance."

It would be difficult to overstate the importance of her project and that of our other colleagues working today to expand the geographical and cultural horizons of our field. But expanding early modern global and ethnic boundaries is not the only progressive initiative in our discipline that has lost momentum and a sense of priority. At the 2006 CAA conference in Boston, Jonathan Weinberg, Richard Meyer and others participated in a session recounting the obstacles that are reemerging to undermine scholarship based in queer studies. I have seldom felt as angry as I did there, listening to tales of archival access and image reproduction rights that, the moment the words "queer" or "gay" arose in relation to the scholar's inquiry, were suddenly, without further explanation, withdrawn or denied. Yet for exploring issues of homoeroticism in visual representation—and just as importantly, exposing our disciplinary complicity in suppressing these issues—there are few bodies of artwork more ripe for discussion, more potentially powerful as agents for change, than those of Leonardo and Michelangelo.

Many of the essays in this volume have identified central problems in our sub-discipline as revolving around a set of binary concepts and the balance (or not) between them that might be best for its future: low/high, images/art, periphery/center, rationalist/irrationalist, empirical/theoretical, humanist-friendly/humanist-mistrusting, object-centered/logocentric. But a sub-discipline doesn't practice art history, only individual scholars do. The sense of appropriate balance between and among these conceptual poles is as unique in each of us as is our DNA. Where we stand in relation to rationalist or irrationalist models of human motivation is largely a matter of experience and conviction, not of abstract decision-making. Whether we choose to engage the high and/or low, the empirical and/or theoretical, is similarly individual.

I hold my own strong positions along most of these spectra, and these inform every aspect of my practice. I hope that my readings of the past prove helpful to other historians, and I would be happy if some decided to adopt aspects of my approach in their own practice. Still, I would not propose some single, most proper area of study (and especially not a single "Renaissance") for us collectively. On the one hand, our topics spring from and involve such personal commitments; on the other, the subject matter of our field cannot but change in response to processes continually occurring around us in both private and public spheres. I share in Stephen Campbell's query: "What's wrong with disarray?"

For all the differences among us, we are co-workers in this vast amorphous project, the disputed, imprecise shorthand descriptor for which is the Renaissance. What is important, politically, is that—as we make all these so individual choices—we carefully consider the broader implications of our work to ensure that they comport with our values. Earlier, I urged us to be honest with ourselves and with each other, and I will try to be so. Bob Williams thinks that the art history most of us practice supports bourgeois consumerism. I fear that his, by privileging Renaissance art theory (largely on its own terms) as the central subject for Renaissance art history, reinforces the claim to superiority of European male values that such theory entails—including preference for the abstract over the concrete, the universal over the particular, and the intellect over the senses. Still, I want to hear more, not less, from Williams. I would like him to unpack his charge, to explain how social history lends support to suspect enterprises. If we both are right about each other's work, then we should further discuss whether consumerism or patriarchy is the more dangerous vice (he could argue, for instance, that consumerism oppresses three-quarters of the world's population, while patriarchy oppresses only half; I could argue that patriarchy oppresses the oppressor as well). We could also try to assess whether other, positive aspects of our scholarship outweigh any collateral damage. In 1989 Kobena Mercer publicly revised his earlier (1986) critique of Robert Mapplethorpe's photography as racist, upon learning his remarks had become a weapon in the hands of homophobes. He sets a powerful example. I like to think that I—and all of us—remain open to changing our practice. We all, I think, want our scholarship not only to be, but also to do, good; we need to offer and to listen to each other's honest criticism as we sort out the implications of our own ideas.

Scholarship as if we enjoyed it

As a profession, we art historians seem not to find much pleasure in our work. How absurd that sentence sounds. Day in and day out, we look at, are privileged to touch, think about, talk about, turn people on to, astonish audiences with insights about art (however we individually define or even reject it). Which of us has not been, at some critical moment, seduced by a passage of paint or a sculptural curve, astonished when an object produced by a different culture suddenly illuminated or subverted ideas about our own, or intrigued by noticing something newly inexplicable in a work we thought we understood? Which of us has not found that these experiences set in motion processes that changed the course of our lives? Even as we learn the treacheries of images, most of us only crave them more. How many of us, in our teaching, do not try to convey the sensual rewards of our subject, or the joy of intellectual discovery? What is all this interpretive activity except a complex, and itself aesthetic, form of play? Yet there is so little impression of this in most of our scholarly writing.

The combined typescripts of the Cork discussion papers and seminar, the product of seven diverse art experts (and, presumably, art lovers), contain 63,572 words. Not one of them is "sensual." The word "sense," as in those receptive capabilities of which we have five or maybe six, occurs exactly twice—once in a quotation of Philo, and again, rather clinically, in the phrase "mechanics of sense perception." Fredrika Jacobs's suggestion that we interrogate an object's "presence" is a very useful one, not least because among the many qualities that may inform this presence she includes its capacity to "arouse possessive desire." Matt Kavaler, who studies in chilly, rainy Belgium, is the one author who repeatedly addresses the delights, both sensory and intellectual, of the artworks he studies—for both Renaissance viewers and himself. He suggests that the concept of a Northern Renaissance could "open with the visually seductive paintings of Jan van Eyck and his contemporaries," and recognizes that Dürer's writings "testify to the pleasurable sensory experience afforded by even the most abstract geometric configurations." He reminds us of Alberti's opinion that "there can be no one, however surly or slow,

rough or boorish, who would not be attracted to what is most beautiful. . . ." (Had Alberti participated at Cork, he may well have revised
this statement.)

Two of this volume's central essayists seem to reject pleasure—
both, in their own reckoning, toward constructive political ends.
Williams's parting admonition about "object-oriented" art historical
scholarship seems like a call to asceticism, which may be aimed partly
at himself. Objects are dangerously alluring and distracting; too
much involvement with them compromises the viewer's better judgment. Overloaded with signals, they jam the intellect and coopt the
art historian to the consumerist machine. Renounce them. I acknowledge a powerful line of (seeming) reason here. I even admit to a
twinge of apprehension and guilt. Am I siding with the serpent? Or
am I trying to really know the animal?

But the allure of objects and the urge toward representation—as
well as the fear of it—long predate the class structures of capitalism.
At Cork, James Elkins referred to art history and anthropology as
"two different planets." Yet I, as an academician studying visual artifice, do consider myself to be engaged in anthropological inquiry.
Two fundamental questions drive my work: first, how is it that we
cede inanimate objects power over us; second, across cultures and
times, how are people(s) more different or alike? These are questions
about being human. I happen to search for answers in a highly specialized way, by examining (primarily visual) representation, of which
one amorphous and maddening subset is, sometimes, in some places,
called "art." I am drawn to objects because I am human, and I explore
and analyze the experience in myself and others. Just as earlier I
suggested we use passion as an analytic instrument, here I urge us to
use our own attractions, in comparison and contrast with those of early
modern viewers, to better understand the nature of this allure itself.

The other call to self-denial appears in an essay with which I
am otherwise in much agreement, Claire Farago's. I begin with a
statement of hers that I endorse:

> Unless we comprehensively attend to the epistemological under-
> pinnings of our intellectual heritage, . . . that which is indefensible
> will continue to haunt contemporary history writing.

So far, so good. It is the phrase I have removed in ellipsis with which I quarrel. The sentence reads, in full:

> Unless we comprehensively attend to the epistemological under-pinnings of our intellectual heritage, *rather than selecting what seems personally most compelling to study*, that which is indefensible will continue to haunt contemporary history writing. (emphasis added)

The conviction—the passion—of Farago's voice throughout her writings leads me to suspect that she *is* studying what she finds most compelling, and not painfully foregoing a connoisseurial career for the greater good. In response I ask: what better place is there to start interrogating the epistemological underpinnings of our practice than by deconstructing, "comprehensively" and honestly, the forces that have shaped our own desire for knowledge? Indeed, at Cork, Farago herself observed "We start from what we know." I hope that she was not simply being polite when, in response to Stephen Campbell's work, she says in the seminar:

> Cultural interactions taking place in Ferrara (right across the street as it were) can be quite radical if they are looked at the right way—if their implications are fully analyzed.

Surely, Campbell's paradigm-challenging scholarship followed upon a visceral attraction to Cosmè Tura's paintings which compelled him to wrestle out an explanation for their glorious weirdness. The kind of commitment that yields such insightful scholarship requires the skills of a professional, but draws its energy from the obsession of an amateur.

On the matter of scholarly pleasure and its broader disciplinary rewards, I think we still have a good deal to learn from Leo Steinberg. Much of the afternoon session at Cork was devoted to him, since Steinberg is perhaps the only Renaissance scholar whom modernists consistently read. A number of questions were raised about how he achieved such—clearly, to the panel members—enviable status. Robert Williams correctly noted his contemporary criticism of the 60s and 70s, and his position of influence with a generation of art historians including Rosalind Krauss. James Elkins also correctly pointed out that in *The Sexuality of Christ* Steinberg saw—or acknowledged seeing—something no art historian had spoken of before. Claire Farago, however, came closest to identifying what I think explains Steinberg's appeal—in her words: "such showmanship." Perhaps I misperceive a tone of disapproval in her voice. In any case, whatever this quality is—I will describe it differently—I think we need more of it.

Steinberg writes with abundant relish, unapologetically delighting in his own prowess. He writes in a personal voice, with which he announces directly to his readers why he thinks his objects of study matter. For Steinberg, these are methodological principles: he set them forth early in his career in "Objectivity and the Shrinking Self," where he called on all of us to "let the ground of our subjectivity show." Farago is right—this is "theatricality." Stephen Campbell is right—Steinberg never actually got around to the sexuality of Christ. Certainly those whose hypocrisies he takes such glee in lancing have grounds for thinking him arrogant. It doesn't matter. We keep coming back for more. To read him is to step into a liberation zone; Steinberg is having so much fun.

So I call upon us to incorporate the pleasure in our work more fully and visibly in our writing, rendering it consequently livelier and more enjoyable. And because one of the most captivating spectator sports is watching people and other animals at play, I suspect we will attract, and affect, more readers if we do.

Lubomír Konečný

The State of Renaissance Art History: Tradition in Distress

When Bob Williams sent me the materials (four "Starting Points" and a written record of "The Art Seminar") from the Renaissance roundtable which took place at the beginning of April 2006 in Cork, my first reaction was that it was indeed "a thrilling read". Right at the beginning of the debate, James Elkins formulated what it would cover. Firstly the participants would talk about the "sources of coherence or disarray within Renaissance studies", and then the discussion would move on to "the apparently larger topic of relations between Renaissance studies and studies of modernism and postmodernism". The deeper meaning of the workshop and its true *raison d'être* was only revealed by Elkins's subsequent dissatisfaction at "the strange fact that the Renaissance seems at once tremendously important, pivotal, or indispensable in art history as a whole, and the same time sunken into a kind of neglect . . .". Throughout all these materials, like a *tema con variazioni*, runs a sense of disillusionment with the current state of Renaissance art studies: "the study of Italian Renaissance art actually finds itself in something of a backwater within the discipline of art history". According to Jim Elkins, as quoted by Claire Farago, "critical thinking on modern art jettisoned the Renaissance, letting it drift into the isolation of specialized scholarship". And, again in Elkins's view, "the Renaissance is foundational to the discipline (of art history)", but paradoxically, "it is also commonly acknowledged that . . . the Renaissance is not relevant in some, many, or perhaps even all ways".

Immediately on the first reading, and even more so after subsequent re-readings, my printout started to turn red, with dozens, if not hundreds, of phrases or entire passages that I had underlined or highlighted in other ways, not to mention question marks, exclamation marks and notes I had made in the margin. For my written assessment, however, I had to make a selection. The commentary that follows will therefore have three parts. The first one is purely "academic" and its aim is to point out what I consider to be by no means unimportant issues that have been passed over in the arguments presented about the present state of Renaissance art history. The second part may appear to bypass the subject under debate, but in my view in spite of this—or perhaps precisely because of it—it is directed right to the heart of it. The third commentary is to a considerable extent a subjective one, for it attempts to describe and define the position of an art historian who spent a substantial part of his professional career in a situation that was very different from that of academics working to the west of his country, and who had to somehow come to terms with this not only before the fall of the communist regime in November 1989, but especially—which was in fact more difficult—after 1989.

Straight away in the introduction, Elkins points out the interesting fact that various specialities within art history have their own "cultures", and that adopting a position with regard to them is then a source of either harmony or else discord in the relevant segments of our discipline. It is revealing that he does not mention any work from the field of Renaissance art history that has put forward a new interpretative paradigm for this speciality, as Svetlana Alpers did for the study of seventeenth-century Dutch art.[57] Implicitly it follows from this that the Italian Renaissance field—in contrast to research on Dutch or northern European art—is "very non-polemical". According to Stephen Campbell, "This lack of dissent or polemic is also manifest in a tendency to repress dissident or challenging ideas rather than to engage with them. A routine and cursory citation takes the place of real debate." Nevertheless, it is my view that Renaissance research, both Italian and non-Italian, also has its polemic "cultures" (or at least "sub-cultures"), in which opinions differ and methodological positions are refined. One of these sub-cultures is the issue of the interpretation of Titian's mythological paintings, or more specifically the painter's female nudes. Erwin Panofsky interpreted them in 1939 in the light of the Neo-Platonic philosophy of love and beauty, and a whole series of art historians followed him in this interpretative strategy.[58] By contrast, Charles Hope sees in them nothing more than a kind of Renaissance "pin-up", and has thus opened up the possibility of other interpretations than the Neo-Platonic ones, without however drawing any more substantial theoretical conclusions from his approach.[59] The target of Hope's criticism of Panofsky & Co. involves just one aspect of the work of a single artist, but nevertheless this issue has a broader implications: it undermines the value of Neo-Platonism as the key instrument for the interpretation of Italian Renaissance art. And it was the Neo-Platonism of Marsilio Ficino and others that was seen by many scholars as the philosophical underpinning for some of the most important Renaissance pictures and sculptures, and became part of what Christopher Wood calls "normative Renaissance".[60] A similar revision of another interpretative model, which was also proposed by Panofsky, but this time for fifteenth-century Dutch art, and the key notion of which is "disguised symbolism", is still taking place today and determines the methodological position of art historians who are working in this field.[61]

My second reaction to the material from Cork was: Why was it the Renaissance and Renaissance art that was the subject of this roundtable? Why not for example the Middle Ages or the Baroque? After all, there is no doubt that medievalists or Baroque scholars also ask themselves questions about the state of studies in their area of interest and its relationship to the art of today. The answer could be: Most likely because it was Renaissance art history that formed the basis for the discipline of art history in general; that it is on this basis that the foundational strategies of the discipline are constructed; that it was in this field that some of the most remarkable and most influential achievements of twentieth-century art history were harvested. And above all because a number of critically oriented scholars feel a sense of disillusionment both with the current state of Renaissance scholarship and with the fact that Renaissance art seems to be separated from what is going on in the art world today. This however does not apply to the art of the Baroque period. Attempts have been made to demonstrate the relationship between Baroque and modern art at more than one recent exhibition, and also for example by Mieke Bal.[62] In contrast to Renaissance studies, the criticism can hardly be levelled at recent Baroque art history that "*normative* . . . historians have a fear of critical theory, postcolonial theory, poststructuralism . . .". A number of new critical approaches to the Baroque and Baroque art have been put forward—from Deleuze's "fold" as "baroqueness's synecdoche", as Mieke Bal calls it, to (most recently) Bal's own "ecstatic aesthetics".[63] These interpretative approaches are motivated by the attempt to avoid both traditional connotations of the term Baroque and standard formalistic categories, previously negative but today simply banal, and to try to approach this phenomenon by means of "the philosophy of art history". This philosophy, concludes Mieke Bal, "is a discourse in the present that—unlike historical thinking— engages past thought in the present but does not 'reconstruct' or causally explain it."[64] If we ask why this difference exists today between the reception of Renaissance art and that of Baroque art, an answer is provided by Bob Williams, although he probably will not agree with me. This is because, according to him, "the best possible way to organize an account of Italian Renaissance art" is by making use of the idea of "systematicity", expressed most clearly in theory writings and in certain aspects of visual representation. Williams claims that "modern art, though apparently a rejection of systematicity, in fact involves another form of systematicity: it does not represent the liberation of art so much as its subordination to a new, more complex set of rules". So far as the Baroque is concerned, however, with the exception of seventeenth- and eighteenth-century academic theory (especially in France), the degree of systematicity in the discourse and artistic practice of the time is considerably less than in fifteenth- and sixteenth-century Italy. It is probably precisely for this reason that Baroque art is closer to contemporary art than is Renaissance art.

3. In the materials of the Cork Renaissance Roundtable the call was made several times for a geographical extension of the field, and for questions of intercultural exchange to be addressed more aggressively. The need to include Latin America, in particular, is perfectly legitimate and timely in view of the long history of artistic contacts between Latin American countries and Spain: it is also a practicable one in view of the more widespread use of the Spanish language in the United States. From my viewpoint, however, there is a region in the very heart of Europe whose Renaissance art has not yet been sufficiently researched and evaluated: I have in mind the territory that is today Hungary, Poland and the Czech Republic (the historical area of Bohemia and Moravia). Anyone familiar with this area, cannot fail to be aware that Renaissance art in this region takes something of a back seat, like a sparsely populated valley between the massive mountain ranges of Gothic and Baroque which determine the shape of this *Kunstlandschaft*. It is true that there is a fairly extensive literature on Renaissance art in these countries, but it consists mostly of basic research, the aim of which is to form corpuses, catalogues and inventories of artistic works and monuments, and to establish which artists made them and the date they were created.[65] Such work is necessary and commendable, of course, but research into Central and Eastern Renaissance art suffers from two major ailments: (1) issues of intercultural exchange are mostly neglected, and (2), they do not receive the appropriate kind of theoretical articulation, and thus tend to "float" outside any kind of theoretical framework. Can we speak of "acculturation" or "transculturation", as Claire Farago does in the case of South America?[66] What parameters should

the protocols of Central European Renaissance art have? The parameters of "normative Renaissance" with its Neo-Platonic agenda definitely do not help us here, and contemporaneous texts that might help us to propose new parameters are few and far between.

Ingrid Ciulisová
*Against Hegemony: Jacob Burckhardt, Jan Bialostocki and the Renaissance**

In 1860, the forty-two year old professor of history at Basel University, Jacob Burckhardt (1818–1867), published *The Civilization of the Renaissance in Italy (Die Kultur der Renaissance in Italien)*. The book is universally recognized as one of the most outstanding contributions to the study of the Renaissance culture and art and one of the most influential texts in the entire history of world art historiography. Less well-known, however, is the fact that its first edition did not meet with much success at a time when the future of German national identity was being sought in the Middle Ages. The disappointing response contributed significantly to Burckhardt's withdrawal into seclusion; after 1867 he stopped publishing altogether.[67] Another book devoted to the Renaissance, *The Art of the Renaissance in Eastern Europe: Hungary, Bohemia, Poland*, appeared in 1976. For its author, Jan Bialostocki (1921–1988), a professor of art history at Warsaw University, the aim was ". . . to bring an important chapter of the history of art in my part of Europe to the closer attention . . . of a world-wide public . . ." An outgrowth of the Wrightsman Lectures delivered by Bialostocki in autumn 1972 at the Metropolitan Museum of Art in New York, the book was actually the first comprehensive account of Renaissance art in the territory of the satellite states of the former Soviet Union to be written in English. Bialostocki's work was successful, and was welcomed especially by art historians working behind the Iron Curtain.[68]

These two, apparently dissimilar examples of pioneering works, are in fact joined by at least one common factor apart from their theme. Both Burckhardt and Bialostocki chose the Renaissance period for concrete, genuinely personal, and essentially similar reasons: it enabled them to address themselves to contemporary political circumstances. The fact that the two authors were separated by more than a century has surprisingly little role. As his correspondence shows, Burckhardt was deeply disillusioned with the political trends of his time. He did not participate in the notorious *Kulturkampf* that led up to—and would continue after—the unification of Germany, and being a persistent and far-sighted critic of the state's aspiration to power he certainly was not enthusiastic about the prospect of unification. The pressures that shaped his vision of the Renaissance have been tellingly described by the French historian Jacques Le Goff. Describing how Burckhardt is responsible for "inventing the Renaissance with a capital R" and identifying it with modernity, le Goff complains that it has had the effect of consigning the Middle Ages to obscurity:

> I do not wish to challenge Burckhardt's intellectual stature, his erudition or the soundness of his methods. His success was, however, a catastrophe. Not only did he reinforce the idea of a dark Middle Ages, he accorded one region special importance. Italy was indeed a brilliant example, often, culturally in the vanguard, but its political evolution lagged well behind . . . His thesis can be challenged in a number of respects. Yet the idea persists in people's minds that there was an "advanced" region and "backward" regions, that a balance had bee achieved and that a certain ideal could not be bettered. Burckhardt's vision of history did of course fit in with German cultural expectations in the nineteenth century. The genius of a divided Greece and a fragmented Italy heralded the genius of a German state extending from Prussia to Austria, which would overcome its divisions and be the new Rome, the new Athens . . . This mixture of neoclassical eclecticism and essentially Italian models was all the rage in the years 1860–1880.[69]

Burckhardt was certainly not the first writer to emphasize the relationship between the Greeks and the Germans: Johann Winckelmann had already "discovered" the similarity around the middle of the eighteenth century. Wilhelm von Humboldt also pointed to it in his *The History of the Decline and Fall of the Greek Republics (Geschichte des Verfalls und Untergangs der griechischen Freistaaten)*. I will not attempt to analyse Le Goff's interpretation in more detail here, although it would undoubtedly be interesting and rewarding in the wider historical context of French-German relations. What is important in this context, and I think that Le Goff would probably agree, is the fact that Burckhardt's book about Renaissance Italy was the work of a scholar who identified with his German cultural background but whose vision of the political future of Germany was at odds with the actual political trends of the time.

Perhaps it is not necessary to emphasize that Burckhardt's concept of Renaissance culture and art in Italy still plays an extraordinarily important role in the field of art history, despite all the critical reactions and alternative paradigms that have developed since his time. As Claire Farago has argued, however, it has survived in modified form, detached from the political circumstances which gave rise to it and from the specific political position which Burckhardt articulated through it.[70] As a result of the dominance of the national political model of European history and standardized ideas about national history, Burckhardt's concept of Renaissance culture in Italy, based on the concept of an "Italy" without centralize government, was gradually transformed or "nationalized", and only then widely accepted. Its triumph meant that in European historiography, the Renaissance art of "Italy" is a determining qualitative norm, set against the art of the Middle Ages; it represents progress, perfection, and modernity. As Bruce Boucher has aptly commented, the evaluation of Renaissance art north of the Alps also derived to a large extent from Burckhardt's views. For Burckhardt, Northern European art is only "so-called" Renaissance art and is only ever judged in relation to Italian models and standards. For example, in a description of the Episcopal Palace in Liège included in his Belgian Cicerone, Burckhardt wrote: "... the so-called Renaissance in the north is nothing more than the gradual spreading of fantastic decorative elements, something innate to the Germanic peoples but which had lain fast-bound by the strict forms of gothic art ..."[71]

Jan Bialostocki was also one of the art historians, who applied the "nationalized" version of Burckhardt's concept in research on Renaissance art. Since Bialostocki spent almost all his life in communist Poland, his approach was marked by certain specific features imposed by the political situation there. Not only was he an iconologist, for whom the Renaissance and its humanist tradition represented an important field of his personal research,[72] the Renaissance had an especially important place in Polish national history. It was associated with the glorious age of Wladyslaw Jagiello and the so-called Imperium Jagiellonicum, a period around 1500 when members of the Jagiello dynasty ruled a great part of Bohemia, Poland, Lithuania and Hungary.[73] Yet the terms "nation" and "national" had very different connotations in the context of Marxist historiography: with the often violent suppression of "national" cultural expression in the so-called Eastern Bloc, the communist regimes pretended that they had overcome nationalism and were working to achieve the future merging of nations into a single, united society. In Marxist theory, the word "nationalism" had a purely negative meaning: it was understood to mean "bourgeois nationalism", opposed to the ideal of "proletarian internationalism". For this reason, the nationalist approach to Eastern European art formulated by Bialostocki, with its emphasis on the historic kingdoms of Hungary, Bohemia and Poland, should be seen as an attempt to interrogate and relativize official dogma; it opened space for a new understanding of the Renaissance and for research into Renaissance art as a "national" dynastic art. Bialostocki's interest in and sensitivity to matters of style and form gave his approach intellectual richness, but also an authoritatively modern quality. This approach enabled Bialostocki to construct a persuasive account of Renaissance art in the limited territorial area of so-called Eastern Europe primarily around the artistic milieu of the royal court, the character of which—owing to the fact that so many of the artists involved were Italian—was seen by him as both progressive and cosmopolitan.[74] As Christopher Wood has stated:" . . . the idea of synthetic, integrated Renaissance culture . . . took on completely different political meanings at different times, depending on what one thought about modernity . . ."[75]

Bialostocki's approach to Renaissance art in so-called Eastern Europe as a national and, at the same time, dynastic art, can thus be seen as the personal manifesto of an art historian opposed to the dominant ideology of his time and place. While Burckhardt chose Renaissance "Italy" as the subject of his attention, so that in the atmosphere of anticipation leading up to the unification of Germany he could express his deep disapproval, Bialostocki researched the national and dynastic character of Renaissance art in the territories of Poland, Lithuania, Hungary, Bohemia, Moravia, Slovakia, and part of Romania under the domination of the former Soviet Union, so that he could express his patriotic and anti-soviet position in a veiled manner. The cultural and political values that both Burckhardt and Bialostocki professed, were both a powerful stimulus to their work and an enduringly significant part of its content.

Frédéric Elsig

The Categories of Renaissance Art and their Impact on Art History

The very existence of a history of art is dependent on the force of categories formulated in the Renaissance. In what follows I will analyze some of these categories, and then evaluate their impact on our discipline, finally discussing their methodological implications for the actual practice of the history of art.[76]

1. The rebirth of antique categories

The categories used by classical authors such as Vitruvius or Plinius the Elder and adopted by Renaissance humanists generated a demand which a new kind of art market supplied.[77] Based on speculation, this new market coexisted with older forms of the art trade (commissions, gifts or exchanges) and gradually developed in three successive stages, which can be represented by the economic success of three distinguished artists: Giotto in the *trecento* Florence and other Italian cities; Jan van Eyck in Bruges (but also influential in the Mediterranean ports in the mid-fifteenth century); Hieronymus Bosch in the Antwerp market during the sixteenth century. The combined effect of humanist categories with the changing forms of an entrepreneurial art market contributed to the phenomena that distinguish Renaissance art: the illusionistic representation of the world, the autonomy of the *tableau* and the recognition of the artistic invention.[78]

Determined by the taste of the Renaissance for rhetoric, the notion of artistic invention added a new dimension to the evaluation of the *artefact*, including the assessment of its devotional value.

Associated with the categories of *dispositio* and *elocutio*, invention defines the singularity of an individual style—that is to say the notion of artistic persona—as illustrated by Bosch's well-known drawing *The Wood has ears, the field has eyes* (Berlin, Kupferstichkabinett) which, conceived as a visual rebus and an emblematic signature, is accompanied by a claim of originality, borrowed from a humanistic adage: *Miserrimi quippe est ingenii semper uti inventis et numquam inveniendis.*[79] The notion of a recognizable artistic personality is determined by the proliferation of artists, and by the necessity of making distinctions between genuine and fake, and the need to assess the economical value of a work of art: the latter came largely to be determined by the authorship of the work. If the term "connoiseurship" appeared only during the eighteenth century, the connoisseurial attitude, assumed by the artists themselves or by learned men such as Marcantonio Michiel (ca. 1520), cannot be dissociated from the rise of the art market.[80] On the basis of the antique model, it also served to classify artistic production into categories. In his *Vite*, Giorgio Vasari linked the individual styles with temperament types, which provided him with a readymade rhetoric (love for Filippo Lippi, melancholy for Pontormo and so on), and ordered them into collective styles as chronological (notions of "period") and geographical (notions of "school") categories.

The notion of "period" was well known during Antiquity. It served to subdivide not only individual but also collective styles into three phases which, determined by an organic or biological model, would correspond to youth, maturity (*acmè*) and decline. It was generally linked to the preexistent chronological frame used by classical and Renaissance historians. Vasari recovered this model and emphasized the evolutionary perception of artistic production which, precisely subdivided into three periods, would culminate in the "modern style". But his originality really consisted in creating a consistent conceptual frame based on style alone. The notion of "period" is thus constituted by stylistic traditions which, generated and perfected by the power of individual invention, are also important for the notion of "school".

If the term seems to appear only at the beginning of the seventeenth century (notably in the writings of Giulio Mancini), the notion of "school" was also used in Antiquity in order to characterize

the cultural identities of Greek cities. With the rebirth of a speculative art market during the fourteenth century, it was manifested
at first in artistic practice, in particular in the stylistic tradition
generated by the inventions of Giotto and consciously associated
with a Florentine identity by painters such as Cennino Cennini, who
claimed his belonging to this artistic genealogy in his *Libro dell'arte*.
The notion was taken up in sixteenth-century art theory which itself
had no small impact on practice. In his dialog *L'Aretino* (1557),
Lodovico Dolce defended the Venetian tradition, represented by
Titian and his sensual use of color, which was opposed to the Florentine and Roman tradition of drawing, personified by Michelangelo
and defended by Vasari.[81] He certainly contributed to the stylistic
evolution of Titian who from the 1550s foregrounded what was
perceived as a distinctive Venetian identity. The opposition between
two urban traditions can be extended to wider cultural identities,
such as that between Italy and the North. In Italian art theory,
the term "gothic" was then intended to disqualify an older type of
architecture, assigned to "Germany" (in a wide sense). In the field
of painting, it could be replaced by the "*maniera tedesca*" which was
synonymous with the "*maniera fiamminga*".[82]

The opposition between "Italia" and "Fiandra" is central for
the rebirth of another fundamental category: the notion of "genre".
Nurtured by classical texts, the humanists progressively manifested
an interest in the secondary elements of a work of art, that is to say the
parerga celebrated by the antique authors. In a famous letter written
around 1530, Paolo Giovio seems to use for the first time the term
genus to describe a kind of subject, in this case the landscape background of a painting by Dosso Dossi.[83] This new interest, which probably existed long before its explicitation, again generated a demand
which two related developments would supply. First, around 1500,
distinguished artistic personalities created new types of painting for
a cultivated elite, as illustrated by the *poesie* of Giorgione and Titian
for Venetian collectors, the landscapes of Altdorfer for the Bavarian
court, or the "drolleries" of Bosch for the Habsburg court in Brussels.
Second, these singular and diversified subjects were reproduced in
copies (based on the composition) and pastiches (based rather on
the invention). For instance in the Antwerp market Netherlandish

painters, adopting the criteria of Italian theory (Giorgio Vasari, Francisco de Hollanda) yet insisting on a "nationalist" dimension (reference to local traditions and proverbs; representation of the countryside and scenes of peasant life), considered themselves specialists in *parerga*.[84]

These two phenomena allow us to define the notion of "genre" as the multiplication of a singularity. The first development—new and original subjects—has primarily been addressed in art history by Erwin Panofsky's iconological method, which principally consists in deciphering a singular and enigmatic subject. The second development—the culture of copying and adapting, which transforms the singularity into a type—seems to reveal a loss or a transfer of the original meaning, where subject matter might be no more than a pretext to display the art of describing, as emphasized by Svetlana Alpers.[85] This has obvious methodological implications for art historians: the paradigm formulated by Alpers about Dutch painters of the seventeenth century does not replace the one associated with Panofsky and his disciples, insofar as both refer to different levels of practice and cannot be transposed. On the other hand, we might wonder whether a third paradigm can be found precisely in the way images determine an ambivalence in their reception, through a stratification of the meanings, as analyzed by Stephen Campbell in his exemplary book on Isabella d'Este.[86] Interpreted by Marcantonio Michiel as a landscape with a gipsy girl and a soldier, that is to say as a genre scene (a *poesia*), Giorgione's *Tempest* has engaged numerous interpreters looking for a precise meaning, but it could originally have been conceived as an ambiguous subject with subtle allusions to a shared culture.[87] However, we have to note an evolution during the sixteenth century from an aesthetics of the *symbol*, addressed to a cultivated elite and defined by a taste for ambiguity, enigma and magical thought, to an aesthetics of *allegory*, addressed to a wider public and characterized by an academic normalization.

2. Transformations of the critical frame

These different categories constitute what we could call a "critical frame", which constantly evolves and assimilates successive ideologies, and whose dynamism is produced by the interaction of two levels. The first one—the empirical level—is determined by the proliferation of works of art; the second level—the theoretical—consists in classifying production and provides in turn the presuppositions of the empirical level. Beginning in the middle of the eighteenth century, the history of art entered a phase of dissociation and specialization. On one hand, art criticism, represented by writers such as Diderot and focused on modern art, distinguished itself from connoisseuship, which concerned itself with older art and was linked with the still growing art market and the emergence of museums. On the other hand, aesthetic philosophy, which gave a more spiritual dimension to the notion of "art", tended to appropriate the theoretical level, which became the scientific justification of the History of Art as a university discipline during the nineteenth century, deeply transforming the categories of the Renaissance.[88]

The notion of "period" then became a particular subject of reflection. Applied to the phases of classical style by Winckelmann, it was theorized by formalists such as Heinrich Wölfflin who, influenced by a diffused taste in the art market and in the contemporary production, chose the Renaissance as his normative point of reference and opposed it to the Baroque. The notion was progressively refined, divided into sub-categories or enriched by new categories. Contemporary production often had an impact on the interests of the art historians: under the influence of Expressionism, the discussion of Mannerism as a transitional phase between Renaissance and Baroque was particularly intense during the 1920s and the 1930s, putting emphasis on artists such as Giulio Romano, who would exemplify the unity of a style across different technical fields.[89] In this context, architecture often serves as a point of reference for characterizing a collective style, insofar it provides a more precise vocabulary and more generalizable forms. It is the case for the notion of "Renaissance Gothic" which, recently forged by Ethan Matt Kavaler to define a collective style in Northern architecture around 1500, concerns questions of identities and can be seen as a parallel to "Gothic Mannerism", intended to characterize a sophisticated type of Antwerp painting resisting the European diffusion of Italianism around 1520.[90] We can also evoke in this context the notion of *"ars nova"*, transposed by Panofsky from the musical renewal of the fourteenth century to the Flemish pictorial revolution of the fifteenth century, and which he saw as progressing independently alongside developments in Italy. The validity and coherence of this stylistic label as established by Panofsky have been upheld by numerous art historians.[91]

Elaborated and refined from the middle of the eighteenth century in the classifications of the museums, the notion of "school" was adapted to the political exigencies and ideologies of the time, such as the determinism of place and climate. Luigi Lanzi's *Storia pittorica della Italia*, for instance, took account of the different regions of Italy. During the second half of the nineteenth century and the first half of the twentieth, the idea of local or national school was contamined by racist ideologies, as exemplified by numerous exhibitions emphasizing the genius of the nation.[92] In more recent times, a new approach—theorized in an influential article by Enrico Castelnuovo and Carlo Ginzburg—combines the reconstruction of the successive movements of an object and the stratification of a cultural territory, on the one hand, and, on the other, the reconstextualization of the object in the artistic exchanges of its time. This "art geography" aims to understand the "symbolic domination" by a center of its periphery and gives particular attention to border zones (called "double peripheries" by Calstelnuovo and Ginzburg), where a cultural identity can be expressed by assimilation, combination, resistance or some alternative strategy.[93] In reaction to the static notion of "school" and influenced by the notion of "artistic landscape" (explored in Germany during the 1920s and then purged of its racist connotations), it proposes a more dynamic and intercultural model of artistic production. It is exemplified in recent exhibitions that have attempted to reconstitute the cultural identity of geographical areas affected by political division, such as the Mediterranean or the Alps.[94] Given impetus by recent developments like the European community or the emergence of a global communication network, it strives to preserve our awareness of the local and regional identities which played such an important role in Renaissance life.[95]

3. The limits of relativism

Since the critical frame constantly evolves, we cannot help but question the pertinence of traditional categories, stuck, as they seem to be, between the second half of the nineteenth century and the first half of the twentieth. If we accept them simply as conventions, however, these categories remain useful not only for the classification of artistic production in museums, libraries, and documentation centers, but also for teaching and reseach, even if academic practice must be especially senstive to the methodological evolution of the discipline. The apparent *stasis* of the categories does not really hinder the updating of the critical frame or the extension of the field of research, especially since the latter is also dependent on indepedent economic and political forces. We can have, say, both the creation of new academic chairs in response to local interests and the development of ambitious interdisciplinary and cross-cultural programs, particularly visible in Renaissance Studies in the form of congresses and specialized journals.

In recent decades, the history of art has been considerably enriched by new approaches which, influenced by the relativism pervasive in other branches of the human sciences, have brought to it a self-reflexive critical dimension as well as an openness to the methods of other disciplines. Fruitful as it has been, this relativism has its limits; it poses three dangers. The first consists in projecting modern preoccupations and values onto the past. The second, which may seem paradoxical, is the compartmentalization of the History of Art into specialized approaches which often seem more in competition for power within the academy than productively addressed to genuinely scholarly issues. The third danger involves forgetting that the initial subject of our discipline is the material object: connoisseurship has suffered, though it is worth remembering that even this process is not without historical precedent. At the end of the nineteenth century, connoisseurship was considered too subjective by many exponents of positivist methods, archival research, and theory; it was progressively and wrongly reduced to a purely empirical practice, identified with the market and the museums, and displaced from the University. Italy was something of an exception: there the rich cultural patrimony required the maintenance of a university tradition of connoisseurship, subject as it was to regional variations and power struggles of its own.

Our aim must be to integrate the different approaches available to us—historiography, social history, taste history, theory, artistic literature and so on—and practice them in knowledgable engagement with connoissuership. Historiography should allow us to work back from our actual encounter with the material object in the here and now to an understanding of its position in an original social context. That context needs to be considered with respect to factors influencing production (technique but also the organization of artistic practice and professional associations such as guilds and academies) as well as those conditioning reception (function, critical response, and the history of collecting and display), all of which presupposes an attentiveness to archival documents and contemporary texts, as is demonstrated in such exemplary manner by the work of Michael Baxandall.[96] Art historians should bring to bear all interpretative resources available for the understanding of their chosen objects; in so doing they will model a form of inquiry resembling the integrated form of learned endeavor pioneered by Renaissance humanists.

Conclusion

This interdisciplinary ideal, which is not the same as the multidisciplinary juxtaposition of discrete competencies, gives a purpose to the history of art which, according to the well-known words of Panofsky, has to be conceived as a "humanistic discipline" or, if we prefer, as a branch of anthropology, one devoted to understanding artifacts of the past.[97] As developed by Jacob Burckhardt and Aby Warburg and then by art historians such as André Chastel, this approach exposes the central, exemplary position of Renaissance art and scholarship in the History of Art as a whole. In such an approach, the material object contitutes a pivot between the past and the present; it also structures the ethical brief of the art historian, whose mission consists not only in refining the critical frame and the understanding of the past, but also in ensuring the conservation of the artifacts of that past and their transmission to future generations. This mission requires a fluid collaboration between university, museum, and art market. In Europe, where university museums do not exist, we have to work especially hard at creating personal links between institutions in order to guarantee such collaboration, the intellectual richness of approach that it fosters, and perhaps most importantly, the sense of the scholar's responsibility.

Jeanette Favrot Peterson
*Renaissance: A Kaleidoscopic View from the Spanish Americas**

As a Latin American art historian, I was, of course, interested to learn from the Roundtable discussion that I am an "outlier" with regards to Renaissance art history. Years ago I moved away from the Italian Renaissance, where I began my scholarly pursuits, to the study of the arts in the Spanish Americas, a shift prompted by both auto-biography and academia. I responded with passion to the visual culture of a place enlivened by family ties and was challenged intellectually by the raw opportunities offered in this emergent field. In contemporary departments of history of art, the once marginalized subfield of Latin American arts subsequently has found a canonical niche in curricula; faculty positions are growing in North American institutions and a remarkable number of exhibitions have been organized in the last decade that feature the colonial arts of the Americas. This shift takes into account the realities of demographic shifts, an ever contracting geo-political world, and an increased awareness—both popular and institutional—of the artistic wealth of an area of the Americas that has impacted significant parts of the United States and that historically has engendered intercultural exchange worldwide from the early modern period forward.

But from an outlier's perspective, I welcome the opportunity to participate in this salutary conversation on the meaning and relevance of the Renaissance to the history of art, however elusive that definition has become even among Europeanists, as the Roundtable discloses. I here focus on a few of the pitfalls that arise in trying to overlay Renaissance, as period and concept, onto the arts of the Spanish Americas. I examine first the implications of applying the rubric Renaissance to cultural expressions outside of its continental birthplace. Two major questions in the parsing and deconstruction of the term are not only how Renaissance can be understood to operate on a more global scale but also whether the concept itself, when evaluated by its many permutations and hybrid end-products, can withstand such scrutiny to have any applicability at all. What does it mean to say that certain artworks far removed from the European models bear Renaissance traits and in what sense is this process "global"? I also turn briefly to questioning assumptions about the impact of Renaissance upon three aspects of New Spanish art: iconography, style and the ontology of sacred artworks. How does the concept of the Renaissance change when understood from the New World? Why do some of its concepts, strategies and social practices endure while others are appropriated and altered beyond recognition? Needless to say, this is a substantial undertaking. It can only be partially treated in this brief discussion that draws primarily from the visual culture of sixteenth-century New Spain or viceregal Mexico.

What's in a name?

While recognizing their inadequate and problematic nature, names tethered to European models, such as Renaissance, Mannerist, Baroque and Ultra-baroque (or Rococo), continue to be used by Latin American scholars of the colonial period (ca. 1520–1820) but in most cases, self-consciously and often reluctantly.[98] This reliance on "foreign" terminology privileges European modes, styles and iconography, thus rehearsing the colonizer/colonized dyad. More importantly, we need to ask whether, in addition to the skewing of interpretative strategies, the use of the term Renaissance substantially advances or impedes our ability to analyze and understand visual culture from the viceregal period? The remainder of my response addresses this central question, but the reality is that the field itself is still young and evolving and it has not yet frontally addressed the problem of appropriate terminology (colonial Mexican art, for example, was only recognized as a "field" with the work of the pioneer colonial scholar, Manuel Toussaint, in the 1920s).

To begin with, early modern Spain itself, the primary conduit for colonial American art theories and styles, was characterized by an eclectic mélange of Islamic, medieval, and Flemish artistic modes at the moment of the overseas conquests. The Italian Renaissance arrived in crates on the Iberian peninsula intended almost exclusively for the decoration of the monastery/palace, El Escorial (1563–82) under the patronage of Philip II. As a late entry to the Iberian cultural mix, "the Renaissance" was fragmentary and inconsistent in its manifestation within a still undefined Spanish style. Italian Renaissance features, particularly portable through architectural copy books, illustrated devotionals and single-sheet graphics, were only one component in the fertile grab bag of pictorial and literary traditions that made the transatlantic passage from Spain to the Americas. Once overseas, these European models were met with the transformative impact of indigenous, Asian and African traditions.

Renaissance influences, nonetheless, are legible in the production of Spanish American visual culture. Given that wholesale importation of European artworks accompanied the colonization of the Americas, their impact is undeniable and immense. Humanist images and ideas were grafted onto a Catholic program of evangelization that formed the powerful right arm of the Spanish imperial project. Literacy in classical literature was surprisingly high and impacted the shaping of a new visual culture.[99] Sir Thomas More's utopian concepts were built into the architecture and planning of idealized indigenous communities. The works of Plato, Aristotle and Seneca were found in many monastic libraries and their portraits were painted on the walls of sixteenth-century monasteries in the company of biblical scenes and indigenous design motives, as in the murals at Atotonilco, Hidalgo. In spite of their undeniable linkages to Renaissance images and ideas, however, these themes were adopted and modified by non-European craftsmen for a multi-ethnic constituency in a different context, a process that inevitably recorded and enacted change. Throughout the early colonial period, even after European artists working in the Americas began to make a measurable impact on the artistic scene, most art was produced by talented Amerindian artists under the supervision of mendicant friars and civil authorities. The very act of transcribing texts or selectively hybridizing images was transformative; the ultimate product necessarily became an "inherently dialogical gamble" or a document recording a plurality of voices.[100] Take, for example, the design template that Vitruvius (through Sebastiano Serlio) provided for friar-architects and indigenous stonemasons; the expertly reproduced classical arcades and columned façades worked hand-in-glove with Gothic tracery, Islamic alfiz doorways and native-style patterns and glyphs. Or, consider the emulation of Renaissance themes copied from texts and prints onto large-scale frescoes, as is the case of Petrarch's *Triumphs* and a Sibylline procession painted in two rooms of the Casa del Deán, Puebla (1580s), or Ovid's *Metamorphases* in the battlescene on Ixmiquilpan's nave walls in Hidalgo. Their orthodoxy was compromised by the insertion of monkeys sporting earrings, hallucinogenic plants and warrior-centaurs, that simultaneously Indianized and Christianized the resultant mestizo imagery, as Serge Gruzinski has noted.[101]

However mimetic the intent, the end result was in every case imbued with a difference that requires we qualify and limit the traditional use of the term Renaissance. But how does one indicate an artwork's genealogy and simultaneously the several degrees of separation of the new creation that must be evaluated on its own terms? I would argue that however indissoluble the mixture that welds indigenous and European features into an organically new interpretation, the degree of hybridity can only be appreciated by untangling, wherever possible, the discrete sources. This transculturative process is evident in the paradise garden murals of the Augustinian monastery of Malinalco, Mexico (ca. 1570s), where artists manipulated both indigenous traditions and the newly imported Euro-Christian features; understanding their bicultural sources enhances our ability to discern the multivalence of the cloister murals in the interpretative space between these divergent modes of representation.[102] It is useful to trace the dolphins in the Malinalco murals back to Italian Renaissance grotesques in illustrated books in order to appreciate their intended function as both ornament and Christological symbols. Likewise, the overall paradise theme of the frescoes is reinforced by correlating the painted conjunction of fruiting tree (Tree of Life), stag at its base, and paired monkeys in the tree branches with a very similar composition in a woodcut by Erhard Altdorfer (1482–1561) of Adam and Eve. Yet, in a startling departure from the European print, the arboreal Malinalco monkeys are depicted holding a unique Mesoamerican plant, cacao pods (chocolate). Both fruit and animals carried positive connotations for a native audience in contradistinction to the Christian signification of monkey as symbol of lust and sin, an interpretation that both corrupts and enriches their doubled meaning for a bicultural audience. In the end, I would not discard the use of "Renaissance" as a descriptor when tracking, through intermediary literary or pictorial sources, the genealogy of colonial artworks but would apply the name judiciously and explicitly. Broader qualifying terms, such as classical or Italianate, have come to have greater currency as they can be applied to recognize specific Greco-Roman motifs and narratives, compositional formats, and idealizing figural types.

There is, however, increasing resistance to using Renaissance (or Mexican Renaissance) to demarcate the entire range of sixteenth-century New Spanish culture, as it cannot begin to embrace the divergent and complex imported and domestic styles and iconographies.[103] Many scholars emphasize the more focused influences on the European artists who settled in New Spain, such as the conservative Romanist tradition that traveled from Sevilla to Mexico in the late sixteenth century and was firmly implanted there by mid-seventeenth century.[104] Others foreground the formation of an independent national school in Mexico as one way of embracing the plurality of styles and as a corrective to the Eurocentric bias.[105] The most neutral periodizations are based on the temporal markers of viceregal rule (ca. 1520–1820) by century, or generic designations of Early, Mature and Late Colonial art; more recently and largely successfully, visual culture across the colonial Americas has been treated thematically and quasi-chronologically.[106] None are tidy or complete, but that is the tedious nature of all nomenclature and classificatory systems. However useful Renaissance may be to track specific features and motifs, the polemic surrounding period names in Spanish America remains unresolved.

The limits of exported Renaissance: the iconography, style, and ontology of sacred images

Although charting how colonial production differs from its European prototypes is still a basic interpretative strategy, it slides too easily into creating a judgmental hierarchy, whether on a vertical descendant scale or working from center to periphery. The culture of copying was, of course, standard practice in the Americas, felt neither to be demeaning, derivative nor exclusive of invention. The intense preoccupation with surreptitious sacrilege made vigilant supervision of artistic practices all the more intense. Be that as it may, within the great preponderance of Europeanizations, creative artistic solutions arose to meet new demands by patron, audience and local contingencies. Artists tweaked or altered dramatically standard iconographic patterns by adding symbolic paraphernalia or novel interpretations. For example, images of Sts. Anne and Joachim, Mary's parents, prospered in colonial Mexico, privileging depictions of St. Anne at the very time her cult was being suppressed in Spain.[107] The frequent inclusion of St. Anne in Mexican compositions of the Holy Family also reflected the matriarchal nature of the extended family in indigenous society.

Moreover, entirely new genres developed independent of Europe. The lack of even one example of a European black Christ is in surprising contrast with the multitudes found in the Americas, from the Señor de los Temblores in Cuzco, Peru, to el Cristo Negro de Portobelo, Panama, and the much duplicated Cristo de Esquipulas of Guatemala, whose satellite shrines stretch northward as far as the Chimayo shrine in New Mexico. By contrast, of the hundreds of black madonnas in Europe, only a handful of American images of the Virgin Mary are *moreno* or dark. Novel iconographic types are also evident in the oft-cited Andean archangels with muskets (harquebusiers), a unique synthesis that conflates two discrete kinds of Renaissance print sources, one of archangels and the other of secular militia figures. Also in the eighteenth century but in Mexico, casta paintings representing racial typologies were invented *sui generis*.

Well documented is the colonizing strategy that relied heavily on visual signs and narratives to teach new doctrinal concepts and Christian values.[108] The ideological power of art was not lost on the colonizers in their ambitions to impose Euro-Christian knowledge systems, and by its very imposition, subjugate and denigrate indigenous visual signs as barbaric, irrational and above all, non-Christian. As mentioned above, decorative programs in the hundreds of monastic establishments, parish churches and private devotional spaces, used images, both horrifying and comforting, to communicate new tenets and model behavior. Didactic images were to function dynamically; what was seen was intended to be affective. But for an Amerindian viewing public for whom Christian images were often only negligibly embedded in a familiar matrix, how can we access what they were "seeing"? And what role did the artwork's imported style features have in their reception?

First, we need to ask how central style was in evaluating and categorizing artistic production in Spanish America, particularly in the initial colonizing period? Some art historians single out the artists' self-conscious usage of recognizable stylistic elements as one of the defining ingredients of Renaissance art, as proposed by Bob Williams in his essay in this volume. When translocated, however, these style traits no longer constituted a coherent whole, nor were they constitutive of any one identifiable style, Renaissance or otherwise. Within precontact Amerindian cultures, the term "art" did not exist, but rather was deflected onto works describing a wide gamut of objects, almost uniformly anonymous and of uncommon artisanship, from featherworking and polychrome ceramics to non-figurative stoneworking.[109] Thus Prehispanic "styles" crossed media and, while useful in identifying cultural production, then as now, are embedded as much in the object's materiality and making (often a ritualized process) as in the appearance of the final product. An awareness of style perse was also of less import in the early colonial period (sixteenth century) certainly for the native artist, as well as due to the bewildering array of artistic traditions. Style as a defining, reflexive trait developed only slowly with the arrival of European artists (and their egos) and the evolution of Mexican schools of art; even then, I suggest, any self-aware adherence to a particular stylistic school was secondary to a clear and moving articulation of the narrative content.

To help elucidate the possible relationship of stylistic features and viewing practices in the Americas we have only indirect evidence, although there is a growing scholarship on the indigenous sensory responses to both the natural and built environment. Recorded reactions of native Americans to sacred art works are, in fact, rare and almost exclusively written by European chroniclers or missionaries whose assessments are less than trustworthy. The Jesuit Andrés Pérez de Ribas, for example, captures the putative reaction to a late sixteenth-century *retablo* or altarpiece, fashioned in Mexico City and sent to a Northern mission [of Torim] among the Yaqui peoples.[110] The Last Judgment scene is described as having Christ and Mary in Glory, and below "the people whom the angels take to heaven as well as the condemned that the demons drag off to hell." Pérez de Ribas goes on to say that, "When they [the Yaqui] saw it painted on the retablo it made a great impression on them. [As their earlier priest wrote] . . ., the retablo struck such *fear and panic* in them that its memory has been powerful enough to deliver them from many temptations and close calls with sin, especially sins of the flesh and adultery [emphasis mine] . . ."[111] However hyperbolic the Jesuit's reconstruction of the Yaquis' "fear and panic" to the Last Judgment images, indigenous peoples were sensitized to the dire implications of the apocalyptic story, grounded as it was in sermons, biblical lessons and a system of rewards and punishment. We can thus assume that their visual literacy was embedded in their ability to recognize the story line and to link it to real life consequences. Can we, however, also attribute their visceral "shock and awe" response to the impact of the newly introduced Renaissance style, as Samuel Edgerton argues? The formal elements of optical naturalism, he asserts, were critical and seductive components of the conversion process. Edgerton claims that "The friars were . . . convinced that perspective and chiaroscuro were powerful tools for Christian proselytization and must have been struck by the manifest amazement of non-Europeans experiencing for the first time the novelty of Renaissance illusionism."[112] Not only were the friars persuaded, in Edgerton's words that, "indigenous 'idols' were rejected in heaven by the divine power of spiritual geometry," but for native Americans, this style of optical naturalism "successfully evoked [in the Indians] a profound and sincere feeling of 'divine presence' . . . just as numinous as their own traditional language of forms."[113]

Unarguably native American artists had extraordinary mimetic skills, with the capacity to fully assimilate the mathematically based system of linear perspective, one of the principles or "codifiable rules" fundamental to the Renaissance (Williams essay in this volume).

However, early colonial art displays a great range of styles, some medieval and anti-perspectival and others more Italianate and illusionistic. Moreover, reminded by Baxandall and others that Western perspective (and all representation) is "conventional and contingent,"[114] it is unlikely that the application of optical rules on a two-dimensional surface, even if read as an extension of visual reality, had the power to persuade and excite an uninitiated viewer.[115] In fact, relief sculpture in the colonial period often moved in the opposite direction, producing designs of abstract, planar and hieratic patterning with power in their own right. Although for native Americans the application of Renaissance optical illusionism and naturalistic figures may have provoked emotive or compelling psychic power as manifestations of the divine (a contention that can never be proven), I would argue that the image's legibility, its physical location, often in traditionally numinous space, and the artwork's ritual armature, trumped a naturalistic style. We cannot privilege style over place in the construction of meaning, as in a colonial setting, the context—physical, symbolic and performative—was critical for the interpretation and reception of all cultural expressions. The plurality of visual codes in circulation in colonial Mexico converged and competed with, but was never entirely subsumed by, European (or Renaissance) iconography and style.

It is important to note that in pre-Hispanic Mesoamerica, sight was also privileged as central to human cognition, but contrary to Albertian ideals, the visual was not dependent on a fixed perspectival vantage point but was sweeping, taking in the totality of objects within view.[116] Moreover, sight was never restricted to a passive cognitive act, but was procreative and multi-sensorial. Stephen Houston and Karl Taube's recent study on the senses concludes that, in pre-Hispanic times, they were linked in a synaesthetic fashion, sight triggering hearing and smell.[117] Accompanied by music, song, movement and the burning of incense, the ritual praxis that developed postcontact around Christian images intensified in the colonial Americas, responding to the long-standing tradition that encouraged active interface with charged images. Effigies were venerated with offerings and libations, fed, processed and sometimes literally consumed, practices that converged with the popular response to sacred images in Catholic Europe.

This leads me to a final query into the inadequacies of the Renaissance notion of "art" for fully understanding much devotional art of the colonial Americas, a concern eloquently voiced in Fredricka Jacobs' essay in this on the artificial divide between cultic images and the cult of images. Here again we need to consider persistent native beliefs on the ontological of preconquest deities that were reinforced by long-standing Catholic attitudes about devotional images; neither tradition, in practice if not in theory, made a clear distinction between the physical image or representation (sign) and the holy personage (referent), as distinguished by Claire Farago in her essay. The blurred boundaries between the real and the unreal, the visible and invisible, are noted in the colonial Mexican concept that the installation of a new Marian figure was thought of as the Virgin herself entering her home.[118] The tendency to vivify the fabricated images, and then to worship them rather than their celestial prototypes, was among the most pressing dilemmas for a Counter Reformation Church working with an extensive non-Christian, or only nominally Christian, population.

Although preconquest deity images were often recognizably figurative, as *teixiptla* or surrogates of the supernatural, the aura of deity representations also resided in costume, accoutrements and body paint designs. When isolated and abstracted, these markers of the sacred could act as synecdochal symbols for the entire spirit being. Representations of the numinous were not entirely, nor even primarily, human-centered, but could just as easily be focused on springs and trees, natural phenomena in the landscape. Some of the greatest potency emanated from aniconic bundles, cult effigies that contained sacred relics and were dependent for their efficacy on mythical and ritual associations. In this aspect, fundamental differences with Catholic holy figures belie the assertion that "divine presence" was augmented by being located in more naturalistic figures who occupied more logical spaces. Thus we need to ask just how meaningful were stylistic modes of naturalism—and for whom? This is not to suggest that aesthetics did not enter into a cult object's appeal. In New Spain, as in sixteenth-century Italy, viewers appreciated what Jacobs in her essay has characterized as the co-existence of the virtuosity of the Renaissance image as well as the living presence (work-in-invocation) evoked by cultic images and votive works.

Globalizing the Renaissance

One of the rationales for stretching the limits of the Renaissance is the exportation and dissemination of cultural products beyond Europe, to places and cultures not traditionally considered within its rubric. The circulation of artworks, some of which emanated from Renaissance workshops in Italy, is frequently termed "global."[119] But is the term "global" appropriate and how does it mean when we apply it to the early modern period of expansion and colonization? We are cautioned to avoid imposing modern assumptions about globalization, with its tendency to homogenize and flatten cultures, onto earlier networks of exchange.[120] In the early modern period the complex trajectories traveled by both goods and ideas emanated from differential nodes of power and the degree of standardization was less complete. Both Walter Mignolo and Frederick Cooper also emphasize the role of the imaginary on earlier world systems, particularly important in the Spanish empire for which "Christianity became the first global design."[121] Thus, supply and demand were driven by a variety of motivations within these networks entailing a mix of mercantile, commercial, political and religious interests, the latter leading to the most potent historical conceit, that of the Spanish monarchy's universalist agenda to spread Christianity worldwide.[122] Given this diversity of sometimes conflicting motives as well as the unevenness (or "lumpiness" as Cooper puts it) of less integrated systems, can we assume that a widespread circulation of goods would implant uniform Renaissance themes, styles and values that carried similar meanings in distant territories?

For example, a flourishing trade in ivories existed that began with the procurement of the raw material in Africa or India but was converted into fine art in East Asian workshops, often using European models, for markets on the other side of the globe. What might it mean to categorize as "Renaissance" or "Baroque" an early seventeenth-century ivory figure of the Mexican Virgin of Guadalupe, made by Chinese carvers working in the Philippines, transported across the Pacific in the Manila galleon fleet bound for Acapulco, and ultimately destined for American and European consumers?[123] Although the ivory Guadalupe sculpture is imminently recognizable by her clothing and pose as a blend of traditional Immaculate and apocalyptic iconography typical of many Renaissance Marian cult images, her makers imprinted her with their own stamp by working in rare ivory and by substituting a distinctly Asian physiognomy for the classically Mediterranean face of the titular image.[124] Given these interventions, how would the familiar Mexican icon be read several generations and ethnicities removed from the originary model and is she still Renaissance? The extraordinary mobility of such objects of value contributed to their mutability, as they accrued layers of signification from place of production to outlying destinations. The ivory Guadalupe evades easy classification (Chinese? Hispano-Philippine?) and destabilizes the dualities of metropole/colony, donor/recipient, self/other. These oppositions, entangled and artificial to begin with, collapse in the face of the inventiveness of colonial artistic output. The differences that arise from partial or imprecise translatability, as visual cultures circulate and collide, need to be acknowledged, indeed celebrated.

New Spanish art on a global scale demands alternate modes of interpretation in which Renaissance features are only one, often minor, part of the story. If establishing the parameters for the Renaissance is problematic within a European context, the task is ever more complicated when that loose assemblage of stylistic, iconographic and intellectual traits is exported. The relationship is also a conflicted one; European styles and models are both "indispensable and inadequate" to our analysis and understanding of "outlier" arts in the same time period.[125] Nevertheless, our acknowledgment of that which can be traced to Renaissance roots enhances our appreciation for the complex internationalization of art from the late fifteenth century forward. I would argue that when evaluated from the margins, from a non-European perspective, the view of the Renaissance is kaleidoscopic—fractured and variegated—but renewed.

Thomas Puttfarken
Thoughts on Vasari and the Canon

Thomas Puttfarken died on 5 October 2006. The text presented here was transmitted by his colleague, Dr. Neil Cox. To judge from internal indications, it represents only about half of what Prof. Puttfarken intended to write, but the editors have chosen to include it both for its intrinsic interest and in regard for the memory of a highly-respected colleague.

In this response I shall concentrate on two issues that surface with some regularity throughout the talks and discussions. Initially they may appear relatively unconnected, yet I think they are intimately linked, and not only with each other but with many of the other issues raised. Those are the issues of the "canon" of Renaissance art and that of its "systematicity". I want to look at the "canon" first as it seems to bring about attacks of anxiety and resentment among the participants. It is clearly something that is regarded as related to "mainstream", as stifling, as holding back progress, as something to be overcome.

By "canon" we mean the sum of works of art of the past which are generally accepted as great art. The issue of the "canon" is thus intimately linked with the questions surrounding the distinction between "great" or "high art" and "low" or "popular art" which surface in several contributions. The paradoxical reference to the "marginal popular arts" makes sense only by reference to the "canon" which defines what is marginal and what is central by assuming its own centrality.

One level down in terms of generality, as far the general public is concerned and those art historians who believe in "high art", most countries or periods seem have their "canon". There are "canonical" "great masters" and "masterpieces", who or which are generally accepted to represent the pinnacle of achievement of a given period or country. These may be Rembrandt and Vermeer, plus a few others, in Dutch seventeenth-century art; or perhaps Chartres, Rheims and Amiens in French Gothic architecture. In the public eye, these "canons", taken together, constitute what is greatest and most admirable in European art history. At another, more specific level, we speak of Rembrandt's "canonical works", meaning those that are generally accepted by the experts and/or regarded as the most typical/best/ most famous by the general public. In an ideal world I would not see much wrong with any of this; to have a "canonical" list of great masters and works should not stop us studying lesser figures, minor works or altogether different problems (but I'll come back to that).

There has been much soul searching about the "canon" of art history in recent decades. In order for there to be a canon of great art there has to be consensus about what constitutes great art. And that consensus no longer seems to hold. It is not my task here to analyse in detail the reasons why that should be so. Suffice it to say that the combined onslaught of psychoanalysis, deconstruction, feminism and some other aspects of contemporary critical discourse seem to have dislodged the stable self, the assured and normal subject which would recognize (since the Abbé Dubos, Hume and Kant), as part of its normal human nature great art when it saw it; the same discourse has denounced the "canon" of great art and the very notion of artistic greatness as political, a means of domination and repression (since Clark), and, of course, as male (since Nochlin).

I shall come back to the question of "great" versus "minor" art, but what interests me in the first place is the observation, confirmed here in the discussions at Cork, that concern about the "canon" tends to be particularly strong among experts working on Italian Renaissance art. (Medievalists do not seem to worry too much about the "canon", nor do experts in nineteenth-century art.) One simple explanation must be that for several centuries of academic training the great masters of the High Renaissance in Italy were regarded as "canonical" not only in respect of their own period and country but in respect of art in general. There is a much stronger tradition of the canon, and it is harder to dismiss out of hand; working in a field that includes, say, Michelangelo and Titian, we remain aware of their "pulling-power" even if, as modern and critical art historians, we no longer believe in the "canon". It is hard to work on so-called minor arts or artists without paying attention to the huge shadows cast by the "great" masters.

And while we, as experts, trained in the ins and outs of critical theory and discourse, may know what to think of the one and the other, there is little doubt that in the eyes of the general public the "canon" still rules supreme, and the Italian one in particular. Other countries may have had their rich crops of great artists (like Germany with Schongauer, Dürer, Grünewald, Altdorfer and the Holbeins), yet these never quite attracted the same degree of adulation in the academies and subsequently public acclaim. The "super-canonical" status of the Italians may no longer be entirely unchallenged, but in the public mind there are even today only very few masters, Caravaggio and Rembrandt come to mind, and Cezanne and van Gogh and a few others, who would seem to be in the same league as Leonardo, Raphael, Titian and Michelangelo. The *Da Vinci Code* would not have been the success it has been if it had been the *Ghirlandaio Code*.

This state of affairs presents some obvious problems for academic researchers. Some are largely practical. Even if one is not opposed to the "canon" and all it is supposed to stand for, one may feel that it could be extremely difficult to say something new about the great masters; perhaps too much has been written on them already. On the other hand, there may be the suspicion (right or wrong) that many students, and perhaps overseas students in particular, want to hear about them, in particular at the point of admission, i.e. before we have had a chance to introduce them to our critical discourse. And as they contribute substantially to the income of universities, there may well be senior administrators who would rather appoint staff willing to engage in great master hagiography than in critical theory. As my own department at Essex has been teaching theory since the early seventies (and even included theory in its name) I may perhaps be allowed to utter a heresy: since critical theory has taken on a dominant role (canonical even?) in the study of art history the discipline may have lost some of its attraction for the average, normal student. If there was buoyant demand for what we are doing, administrators wouldn't worry in the least about whether or not we are teaching the canon.

Yet there is clearly something more profound in the disquiet expressed by many art historians of the Italian Renaissance. What makes the "canon" problematic for them is not just the awkward problem that there seem to have been more great masters in Italy in the sixteenth century than in any other period (a fact which the social historians almost by definition are unable to explain)—and arguably some of the greatest—and that these used to be regarded as role models by most later artists and critics, and that they are still regarded by the wider public (and many students) as the incarnations of supreme artistic achievement. There is the additional problem that these masters have come down to us mediated by a highly persuasive narrative and evaluative account with a similarly "canonical" authority, accepted and sanctioned by centuries of academic approval, that of Vasari's *Vite*. The "canon" of the Italian Renaissance is not only that of the great masters; it is that of the great masters as presented by Vasari. It thereby becomes "Vasari's canon" and as such it seems to impose upon us not only a "canonical" list of great masters but also a supposedly "canonical" way of writing art history.

I happen not to share this disquiet, and it is worthwhile to look briefly at Vasari's *Vite*. For a start, the point needs to be made that the *Vite* are not just about the canonical great masters, although they are the end, the *telos* of Vasari's developmental plan. The *Vite* are also the richest source of information we have, painstakingly (if not always honestly) collected and written up by the Aretine, about a vast number of very minor figures, including Northern engravers.

There are several interrelated themes in "Vasari's canon". One is his account of the progress of naturalism from Giotto to Leonardo, Raphael and Michelangelo; this seems to me largely a matter of historical fact. There is no doubt that a *Madonna* by Raphael is more lifelike than one by Giotto. There is also no doubt that artists, patrons and critics (the "turgid humanists") were aware of this progress at the time and encouraged it. Yet Vasari himself makes it clear that even perfect naturalism is not identical with the greatest art, that of his third period. The technical means of imitating nature are perfected by the end of the second period. The great masters of the third period add further qualities to their work, like licence, judgement, grace etc. The main means by which naturalism, lifelikeness, was to be achieved was *disegno*, and *disegno* was also the central means by which to overcome mere naturalism. It is through constant drawing that the artist creates in his mind idealized forms, which he can then use in his works without having to rely on a deficient particular model in front of his eyes.[126]

Yet as general rules neither the pursuit of naturalism nor its transcendence by idealizing design can explain the emergence, in more or less the same generation, of a series of the greatest masters. And this is where Vasari's third theme comes into play, the divine nature of the greatest artists. They bring to their art a personal quality which is their own, given to them as a divine gift; Raphael's grace, Michelangelo's *terribilitá*. The divine nature of the artist is a typical term of the times, and apart from possibly influencing later romantic ideas about artistic genius, may have had a rather limited lifespan. I am not aware that any French artist, from Poussin to David, was deemed to be "divine".

It is the combination of these three aspects of the *Vite*—the perfection of the means of naturalism, the divine nature of the top practitioners, and the foundation of their art in *disegno*—on which is based Vasari's claim for the superiority of the Italian Renaissance, and the Florentine Renaissance in particular, over all other art, and its presentation as the model for all great art. And it is this claim which seems to me to be very much at the heart of the modern aversion to "Vasari's canon". It is true that the academic tradition fully adopted this claim, adding, for a time, Correggio and Carracci to the Tuscan masters of the High Renaissance, alongside—increasingly—the works of classical antiquity (something which—strangely—figures hardly at all in the Cork talks).

But why should this cause disquiet in the twenty-first century, why should it be regarded as more than merely historical matter, to be analysed and investigated by those who have an interest in it? After all, if this is what we mean by (and dislike about) the canon, then we have to say that it was under attack right from the start, in practice with Titian and the other Venetian masters (who seem to be largely absent from the Cork discussions—why?) and then Caravaggio, but also in Florence itself with Pontormo. In writing Vasari's claims were attacked by all non-Tuscan writers, including again Carracci and El Greco. Virtually no later writer was in a position to adopt his developmental schema for an account of a later period; and in serious theory most of his claims were dismissed by de Piles and Perrault. And when Goethe wrote on Strasbourg Cathedral, and the Romantics and the Nazarenes rediscovered the middle-ages, "Vasari's canon" lost much of what was left of its prestige. Ruskin is rather a late-comer in this development.

We could leave "Vasari's canon" there, depleted and discredited but kept alive for much of the nineteenth century in the academies of Europe—an important but limited chapter of European history and theory of art. However, in its recent usage the term has acquired yet another sense, and that is as a supposed model, the blueprint, as it were, for the emerging academic discipline of art history. The underlying claim is that from its dominant role in the art academies, the "Vasarian canon" simply extended its domination to the emerging academic discipline of the history of art, that it was there from the start and helped to define the discipline in a way which is still affecting our practices and our thinking today in a restrictive way. This is implied several times in the Cork discussions, and it is a claim with which I disagree completely.

It does not really matter where and when we date the beginnings of our academic discipline. For the sake of convenience we may start with Burckhardt. It is true that Burckhardt, who visited Raphael's *stanze* almost at the same time, in 1853, when Ruskin gave a lecture in Edinburgh condemning Raphael's "canonical" masterpiece, had a completely different and entirely positive experience. Where Ruskin saw the ultimate moral decline of religious art in the juxtaposition of *Parnassus* and *School of Athens* on the one hand with the *Disputà* on the other, Burckhardt would have liked to have joined the erudite company in the *School of Athens* and felt entirely comfortable with it. But that does not mean that he embraced a Vasarian view of Renaissance art. Apart from the *Cicerone* he wrote surprisingly little on Italian Renaissance painting and sculpture. He clearly appreciated great art, and in particular that of the High Renaissance, Florentine as well as Venetian, yet what he was aiming at was a history of art according to its tasks and functions (*eine Kunstgeschichte nach ihren Aufgaben*), and according to its pre-conditions, its widest historical context. He himself liked to express his preference for a synchronic view of history over a diachronic one.

And it would be even more difficult to find significant traces of Vasari's supposedly canonical account of art and history in Burckhardt's immediate successors. To claim, as is done here, a direct (presumably canonical) tradition of writing art history linking Wölfflin and Riegl to Vasari seriously misrepresents the work of early *Kunstwissenschaft* in the generation following Burckhardt. Wickhoff in his *Vienna Genesis* of 1895 and Riegl in his *Late Roman Art Industry* of 1901 set out to investigate (and appraise positively) periods of art which, according to Vasari and the academic tradition, should be regarded as in decline, as artistically inferior, perhaps even as non-art. Neither of them would have had any truck with a Vasarian canon. And the same is also the case, if less obviously so, with Wölfflin. It is true that in his various comparisons between classical (Renaissance) and Baroque art, the Renaissance seems to assume a primary role, in the sense that the principal terms with which he describes Baroque art appear to be negations of those evoked by Renaissance works. Yet this, he would have argued, was simply because the Renaissance came first. And his claim that there was an inherent logic in his proposed development of one set of morphological traits into another bears no comparison with Vasari at all. Finally, while he may be seen as the founding father of a now discredited formalism (although there are now signs of a revival in the context of visual culture studies), it is often forgotten that he himself described his account of the change of style as only one of two roots responsible for it, the other being the social history of art. And not many people seem to know that Wackernagel was his pupil.

The attempts of all these early historians to establish systems of periodization of visual styles are profoundly affected by the nineteenth-century historicism of the Hegelian variety. They should not be linked to Vasari, in part because Vasari would not have recognized what they called period styles, but mainly because his distinction of birth, growth and maturity—while looking deceptively similar—is fundamentally different from the typical division of modern period styles into early, high and late. His definition of great art was absolute, and while he acknowledges the risk of decline, he sincerely hoped that his book would help to prevent exactly that and to keep art at the level of perfection it had reached with his great masters— with Raphael's perfection in particular, since Michelangelo's was held to be inimitable. Only in so far as some historicists may mistakenly have been tempted to force Vasari's three phases of Renaissance art into an overarching Hegelian history of continuous development is Claire Farago right when she says that the Vasari of the canon is that of the nineteenth century. The more important founding fathers of our discipline would not have recognized him as such. The emerging academic discipline of art history set out, quite openly, to liberate itself from the narrow focus on the Italian Renaissance perpetuated in the academies of art. In the case of Wickhoff and Riegl it is worth noting that their interest in non-classical art of the past was linked to a keen interest in contemporary non-classical and non-academic art, in Riegl's case Impressionism, in Wickhoff's the art of Klimt.

If we can hold Wölfflin and others responsible for having put the Baroque on the map as a legitimate and (supposedly) equal successor to the Renaissance, then later writers complicated matters further by introducing Mannerism (and then dividing it up into different phases). It is hard to see how either the Baroque or Mannerism could be seen as fitting into or extending a "Vasarian canon". And that has become even truer as most of us have come to either dismiss such terms altogether or use them as shorthand for a given time-span, as convenient labels without much meaning. Calling the whole period "early modern" does away with almost any semblance with Vasari, except that it brings with it the risk of denying or neglecting continuities with earlier medieval art.

If this analysis is true, if the supposed hold of "Vasari's canon" over much of early art history as a discipline was indeed negligible, where then does today's disquiet come from? It seems to me that British art history, of which there was not much in institutional terms before the late 30s, clung much longer than its continental relatives to the supremacy of the Italian Renaissance. One main reason was probably that both Mannerism and the Baroque were too closely allied with the Catholic Church. And a second, I suspect, was that they could both be more erotic than the British pre-sixties were comfortable with. I do not know whether the story is true, but I was told by a well-placed source that Wittkower left London for the States because his students at the Courtauld would not stop sniggering when he showed slides of Bernini's *Apollo and Daphne* and *The Rape of Proserpina*. Giotto and above all Piero, on the other hand, were entirely safe and pure, apparently devoid of both erotic and religious emotions. Then again, neither with Kenneth Clark nor with Anthony Blunt can I find any adherence to a Vasarian canon.[127]

I first heard the term "canon" being used in the seventies. And this makes me wonder whether "Vasari's canon" is really what we are talking about or whether it isn't in fact "Ernst Gombrich's canon". His writings seem to imply that he shared Vasari's view that progress in naturalism was artistic progress, that a better imitator of nature was *ipso facto* a better artist. I don't think that that is what he thought (which is why I have put his canon in inverted commas, too), but that is how he has often been read. If this is correct, then we can assume that "Vasari's/Gombrich's canon" was set up as a dummy, a bogeyman, endowed with as much importance as possible and blown up beyond all recognition, with the aim of knocking it over—the final aim being to undermine the traditional centrality accorded to the Italian Renaissance in British academic teaching and research and to make space and time for new ventures, like Haskell's studies of nineteenth-century art or T.J. Clark's social history of art and above all to introduce to art history exciting new ways of thinking brought along by critical theory.

Perhaps this was just a polite British way for a younger generation to attack an older one, similar to the much stronger and ruder battles fought by young colleagues in Germany against their authoritarian and mostly ex-Nazi superiors in the late sixties and early seventies. Yet while the case for rebellion in Germany was certainly stronger I am not aware that the dummy of "Vasari's canon" played any great role in it. Even the worst authoritarian ex-Nazis among the German professoriate, for reasons good or bad, had a much wider notion of what constituted art history.

In my years as a student in Germany and Austria I did not attend a single lecture or seminar series dedicated to Italian Renaissance painting or sculpture (and one seminar on Brunelleschi); not because I did not want to or had no interest in it, but because there was nothing on offer. The same professor would, in successive semesters, hold forth on Carolingian art and architecture, on medieval illuminated manuscripts, on Caravaggio, on Rubens, and on Rembrandt. It was said that he had once given a series of lectures on Raphael. Of course, this did not stop me studying the Italian Renaissance; every summer vacation was spent in Italy, while spring vacations had me touring Germany, France, Belgium and the Netherlands.

Looking at the early exponents of German *Kunstwissenschaft* another few points deserve a mention. Not only did they attempt to explain historical developments in terms quite different from Vasari's basic birth, rise and maturity, they also opened up the field of art historical studies to artefacts other than those of the supposed "canon" of great art. Wölfflin's principles were meant to apply to all art of a period, not just to the best, on the assumption that the principles were universally of the period, not of specifically high or low art. And Riegl expressly studied "low" or "popular" forms, of *Kunstindustrie* in the belief that these works would provide access to the *Kunstwollen* of the period even in the absence of "high art". While we may no longer share their Hegelian approach to history, we cannot very well blame them alongside Vasari for what we may perceive as inhibitions to the study of "popular" or "low" art.

Patricia Emison

Developing a Twenty-First-Century Perspective on the Renaissance

The period 1300–1600 hasn't changed since those heady days when Wallace Ferguson and Erwin Panofsky held a symposium on the Renaissance and celebrated its vibrancy.[128] We have though. Academics and curators alike are inundated with books and articles and reviews, ones newly published, let alone the previous five hundred years' worth of writing; the level of education among the general public may have risen in terms of degrees and certifications, but basic familiarity with history and literature from before the twentieth century has eroded; world news now is less centered on events in Europe, and Americans are less uniformly emigrants at one remove or another from the Old World. Renaissance works of art, favored when museums were forming and collecting became the avocation of immensely rich industrialists, are seldom up for sale any more. In the twenty-first century in the United States it is possible to know nothing about the Renaissance and not to feel any lack on account of it. For that matter, it is possible to know nothing about art and not feel deficient.

Not all of this is cause for concern. The complacency which

used to reign about the superiority of Renaissance art has become embarrassing even to its supporters (one might, not entirely coincidentally, say the same of American democracy). Once ancient art was the undisputed criterion of excellence; once France was the arbiter of civilized discourse. *Ubi sunt?* Perhaps the time has come for Renaissance art history gracefully to concede its place of primacy; perhaps the time is already past.

On the other hand, those of us who study the period want our work to matter. Here we come to one of the difficulties: the generation of Erwin Panofsky wrote for a public which included many lay persons, whereas now the population of faculty, students, and museum curators is itself a small fiefdom, able at least feebly to support a small industry of reified publication. As this fiefdom has grown sufficiently to splinter into the factions mentioned in the papers from Cork, the respective circulations have sunk threateningly low. "United we stand . . ." and all that. At present, members of the same department often do not keep up with one another's publications; specialists do not, perhaps can not, keep up with everything potentially relevant to their fields; those fields with shorter bibliographies (and Renaissance Studies is definitely not one of them) tend to flourish.

When I began to study the Renaissance, I was instructed more than once to read Jacob Burckhardt—not in a spirit of discipleship but of critical distance. Now there is no such unifying text in the field, nor any unifying conception of what it is we study or what problems we hope to solve. We can't assert definitive boundaries to the period on either side, as once was done; we can't assume the absolute genius of Michelangelo or even Leonardo, as once went without saying; we can't claim an analogy between American bourgeois capitalism and Florentine, as once seemed reasonable.

Now I, for one, didn't study the Renaissance because I found Burckhardt's "melting of a common veil" particularly exhilarating or because I thought Florence was like America, or even because I thought no other art could ever measure up to that of Michelangelo and Leonardo. Insofar as I can excavate that distant decision at all, I wanted to study the Renaissance because it was presented to me as a locus of fundamental intellectual concerns: both concerns contemporary to the period and concerns that filled in the distance between the Renaissance and the present. In other words, studying the Renaissance made me feel connected to many works of visual art, literature, and philosophy from many periods. I was introduced to the Renaissance via R.G. Collingwood and Nietzsche, which I mention not because I think it is necessarily the most estimable route, but simply because it demonstrates that one need not study the Renaissance in a way which excludes the cultures on which it was itself based and which in turn based themselves on it. Exhaustion is of course a complication if one takes on studying the Renaissance as a piece of the whole of western culture, but better exhaustion than a boring liturgy which expounds on the Renaissance as essentially this or that. What we study is a piece of mercury that breaks and shatters as we try to contain it, but also a piece of carbon that manifests itself in many places in many ways. Moreover, like those elements, it simply is what it is, without valence, at least before it is worked on. To like or dislike the Renaissance is not the point; we want to know something about it, or rather about the objects it has left us, like flotsam on a beach the specificities of whose wave will never be known. We accomplish this by attempting to refine the knowledge we have inherited, either by revising the most egregious flaws of omission or those of commission.

That there are no set open problems facing Renaissance art history and thus no potential for triumphal results isn't cause for shame. It simply is the nature of our field that defining the questions takes a large part of our ingenuity, not because the questions themselves are necessarily so ingenious, but because asking questions which both are genuine and have some prayer of being answered reliably is tricky. Soon both the questions and the answers will be inflected by the insinuation of digital images and all their accessories.

Whatever the Renaissance may have been, life then was very unlike life in the first decade of the twenty-first century; the two artistic cultures can be considered only the most distant of cousins. To impose the issues of our day on the period we study is, in my opinion, to reverse the proper flow; it is our studies of an alien place and time which ought to offer insights about the potential for change in our status quo—both a celebration of some of the change that has happened and a recuperation of the odd loss, accidental or deliberate, we may find we regret. We need both to avoid nostalgia and to excavate for valuable insights from the past. This is one of our richest resources for advancing the present. But what about the issues raised in Cork having to do with modernism as dynamically related to certain constructions of the Renaissance?

If the nineteenth century had a myth of the Renaissance,[129] the twentieth century had a debunking of that myth. High Renaissance works formed the core of the Old Master art collections favored by the industrial magnates of the late nineteenth century, works often left to museums for the public good. The Futurists, on the other hand, led the cry that art museums, like pasta, enervated and depleted the needed forward momentum. For them there was something wrong with those arch capitalists' idea of the public good. We likewise might wonder what was so exemplary about the bloody, tyrannical, mercenary, corrupt, oppressive and intolerant time we have dubbed the Renaissance? Even more, what was so good about a period that revived classicism, especially in the eyes of a century in which the Nazis had appropriated classicism?

For Michelet and Burckhardt the tie to classicism had been a rebel's cry against the authority of the church; by contrast, in order to save culture *all'antica* as republican and bourgeois, Frederick Hartt attempted the rather more problematic claim that Florence resembled ancient Athens. Erwin Panofsky, before him, had used humanism as the lever whereby Albrecht Dürer could be rescued from his appropriation by the Nazis and become the artist of rational proto-enlightenment, an artist who avoided the narrowmindedness of both state and church authorities, who—together with Michelangelo and with a good deal of help in both cases from Plato—discovered the concept of artistic freedom. Humanism, for Panofsky, was the key to rescuing classicism from the Nazis.

But whereas the nineteenth century had been happy to admire the period that gave birth to the notion of artistic genius, it was harder for Americans in the twentieth century, brought up to believe that all men are created equal, to accept the notion of divine inspiration for painters and sculptors. Abraham Lincoln might have been helped by God, but Daniel Chester French? The nineteenth century had been much more like the Renaissance than the twentieth century was, from the radical flourishing of commerce and industry to familiarity with Latin. And so, when modernism rejected the nineteenth century, it also, in large part, rejected what had been the intellectual significance of the Renaissance, and reduced it to the stuff of a burgeoning tourism. Mary Shelley knew fourteenth-century Italy the way we tend to know Europe under the Nazis, quasi-obsessively and with a taste for what little was admirable, highlighted as it was against a general brutality. But since then, we have tended to forget the brutality of the Renaissance—despite Burckhardt's good efforts to help us keep it in mind—in favor of a coffee table book perspective according to which whatever makes good photographs is admirable and the rest is forgotten.

Blind idolatry toward the period characterizes Frederick Hartt's influential textbook on Italian Renaissance Art—perhaps not without some spillage from an unstated analogy between the Kennedys and the Medici. Earlier in the history of the discipline, a stern and grudging connoisseurship had reined in art historical gushing by insisting that even Renaissance artistic production ranged from superb to lamentable. But when connoisseurship was pushed aside as the central art historical function, both by the fashion for iconography and the needs of classroom teaching, the heroization of the makers of a heroic and perspectival figural art was unstinting, a kind of polar opposite to Clement Greenberg and his heroes of the flat picture plane.

By comparison with the German, the American Florentine Renaissance was a relatively tame phenomenon. Antiquity played a lesser role in the American version of the Renaissance than it had for Warburg, for instance, and banking a greater one. In the American ambient, characterized by its particular tension with a less internationalist modernism during the post-war period, the glorification of Florence became a patriotic cause. If we compare, for instance, the American response to flooding in Dresden and Prague several summers ago to that in Florence in the autumn of 1966, even factoring in the greater severity of the latter, the disparity reinforces the idea of a special status for Florence in the eyes of Americans. The popularity here of Millard Meiss' rather provincial and even chauvinistic defense of bourgeois, capitalistic Florence ensured that Friedrich Antal's pioneering social art history, a Marxist voice unwelcome in 1950s America, was never really heard. An opportunity was lost then, and the damage didn't begin to mend until Michael Baxandall's book, *Painting and Experience in 15th-Century Italy* (1972) relayed some of the sophistication of Antal's Viennese model to American readers. Nevertheless, the notion that the Florentine Renaissance was a value in itself, as it had been for Voltaire, was deeply engrained. To admire early capitalism was even easier than to admire artistic genius, and in this case, the two conveniently synergized. Meiss had made the point explicitly: capitalism fostered genius.

Sigmund Freud, another Viennese, spanned that transitional period between the Romantics' espousal of the Renaissance and the modernists' rejection. Almost singlehandedly he replaced connoisseurship with interpretation.[130] He refused to worship the artist; instead, he stood aloof watching the artist worshiping his own personal father (or mother) figure. Self-referentiality, the buzzword of the later twentieth century, was as nearly his invention as artistic freedom was the Romantics'.

Freud re-characterized Michelangelo's supposed freedom as a constriction within the web of his own psychic culture. Not for him that Renaissance described by Burckhardt, that melting of the veil of superstition and symbolism to look life in the face, nor Michelet's Renaissance, with its discovery of the poetry of existence, full of sensuality and mystery, albeit rather superficial versions of each. For Freud, as for Warburg, the real object of admiration was pagan antiquity with its unbridled carnality, of which the Renaissance offered but a poor shadow. This had also been the attitude of J.J. Winckelmann long before. He had explicitly stipulated that Michelangelo lacked the distinctively Greek "gentle feeling of pure beauty,"[131] partly due, it is worth noting, to differences between the Tuscan and the Greek climates.

For Michelet and Burckhardt, the Renaissance opened the way to modernity; whereas for Freud, Hegel's great machine of history had stilled, leaving only the essential tendencies of the mind to weave and knot variously. Freud's sense of the limitations of the Renaissance as a case of mere revivalism was highly consequential. The period has never recovered from Freud's depriving it of the role of historical hinge. Foucault reinstated the notion of epoch to historical thought, but moved modernity forward, leaving the Renaissance behind, high and dry without even classicism to call its own. There it sits presently, becalmed, neither medieval nor modern, populated by individuals who have more recently been "self-fashioned" into types, social climbers as a rule. Seen as such, the Renaissance has relatively little to offer. The Renaissance that has subsequently focussed on issues of patronage, consumption, and status is arguably too much like us in capitalist America, as, in turn, the highly humanistic Renaissance was always suspiciously in the image of the classical scholars of the German university tradition.

There was no viable refutation of modernists' rejection of the Old Master tradition, and of the Renaissance as its fountainhead, because those who championed the Renaissance tended not to advocate the internationalist and socialist causes associated with early modernism. They were, therefore, content with that rejection. Yet during Freud's lifetime, while the Renaissance was increasingly functioning as the straw man to modernity, a new art form was developing which had much in common with the Renaissance *istoria*: namely film. Its storytelling, often via the appropriation of a book, provided both delight and instruction. Often, as in the case of Carl Theodore Dreyer's *Passion of St. Joan* (1928), Jean Renoir's *Grand Illusion* (1937), or in a seemingly unending number of films about the Nazi era, it digested and preserved momentous events of history, including the slow events of the *longue durée*. Or, as in David Lean's versions of Dickens, or myriad Shakespearian renditions, it promoted great texts. Documentary realism and unapologetic artificiality existed side by side, just as *mimesis* and *fantasia* co-existed in Renaissance works. The American post-war musical extravaganza was as brashly chauvinistic as any Renaissance project done for the greater glory of the city. The not uncommon movie scene which portrays singers and dancers in rehearsal provides a twentieth-century parallel to the Renaissance development of the collectable sketch and bravura brushwork, as does a film venture in 1964 directed by John Gielgud which uses film to preserve a Broadway production of *Hamlet* starring Richard Burton, the whole thing intended to capture the informality and liveliness of the last rehearsals. The point is not the Renaissance was the necessary and sufficient cause for movie-making, but that more sense of connection could easily have been developed, if that had been a desideratum.[132]

The social and economic aspirations of the stars of film were not so unlike those of Renaissance artists, either. In real life, film actresses occasionally married princes; certainly actors moved in high social circles, though delicately, as had Leonardo and Raphael. Moreover, movie actresses pushed the boundaries of decorum in ways quite comparable to Renaissance paintings of Venus. The contrast between *Little Women* (1933) and *Some Like it Hot* (1959) offers a modern-day parallel to that between Botticelli and Titian. The status of the art form both precipitated and reflected the audacity (to borrow a word from Pliny) of the art.

The fascination of Italy as a land of beauty, style, and sensuality permeated Hollywood's imagination; and as film makers strove to establish their artistic credentials, they may well have looked occasionally to Italian art as something to emulate. Certainly Italian settings had a certain glamor, e.g., *Roman Holiday* (1953). The parallel with Renaissance printmaking is particularly appropriate. Like prints in the Renaissance, movies were multiples; they existed outside of the established culture of church, palace, or museum. Simply by virtue of their medium, they were automatically so novel that their whole relationship to tradition differed from that of the major arts of their time. Movies could espouse tradition as painters could not, since they could take their modernity for granted. Similarly, early Renaissance prints could never match the work of antiquity and so scarcely tried to, instead celebrating contemporary life to a degree quite distinctive from the staider major media.

Not only the *istoria* but Renaissance portraiture, too, might easily have been integrated into the understanding of contemporary developments. Andy Warhol's celebrities, a category he extended to himself, remind us without undue strain of Raphael's crypto-portraits in the *Parnassus* and *School of Athens*. On the other end of the range, Chuck Close's monumentalization of ordinary folk, himself included, suggests Dürer's portrayal of self and peasant, or Bellini's array of ordinary faces made into art with the aid of his new technology, oil paint. The quantity of non-aristocratic, non-bohemian portrayals in Chuck Close is paralleled only in the fifteenth century, and perhaps in Coptic funerary portraits.

Movie directors need not have been thinking of Renaissance *istorie*; photographers need not have been thinking of the birth of portraiture. My point here is not to assert stylistic sources but to suggest that it was purely as a matter of choice that twentieth-century modernism was typically defined in antagonistic relation to Renaissance art. The writers of manifestos did not want to find resemblance, and so they succeeded in defining modern art as rebellious—all the more so since the professors of art history generally wanted to put as much distance as possible between themselves and the non-representational, flat paintings produced by angry young men of dubious social and political credentials, at least until Abstract Expressionism was co-opted as typically American.

Twentieth-century versions of the Renaissance, even the sympathetic ones, made it a very serious and sober matter,[133] again in contrast to modernism, which was often playful. Engravings of a satyr family were typically understood relative to the cult of antiquity, and so made quite serious. A naked girl picking fleas off her dog could just be ignored (despite Van Mander's mention of Lucas van Leyden's engraving); Giulio Campagnola's toddler playing with a cat could be too, or else worked into the theme of secularization. There was very little room in the post-war version of the Italian Renaissance for pictorial fun, very little room, at least initially, for extravagance, material or conceptual. Renaissance art was held to be good because it was so high-toned and so unlike the casual and capricious works of contemporary artists. It was inspired and inspiring; that is why it deserved to be in those museums whose atmosphere was quite church-like.

Such determination to find truth and beauty in the history of art, that very traditional objective held by such luminaries as Winckelmann and Ruskin, tended to slight the lyric and burlesque cultures of love. Yet even if the Renaissance analogue to Charlie Chaplin lies in the performance art of the buffoons rather than in any visual representations, nevertheless, delight was a Renaissance artistic value, one heavily associated with amorous recreation. Clive Bell had memorably described the self-indulgent Renaissance lord, hidden away with his luscious oil paintings of nudes, drooling. Panofsky tried to tuck whatever had to do with love neatly away under the rubric of Neo-Platonism, and thereby make it all into quasi-religion. But, at times at least, the cult of the beloved was no religion. It newly legitimated some degree of respect for human irrationality and beyond that, it introduced some crucial ambiguity into the conceptualization of weakness and strength. The war of the sexes didn't work quite the same way as that other kind of war, which itself was evolving under the pressure of the new technology of cannon. In neither realm could traditional estimations of valor remain unrevised.

The lover was the most powerful type in the Renaissance imagination, but was barely acknowledged in the twentieth-century version of the Renaissance, insofar as that was constructed to make bourgeois, capitalist Americans proud and to free classicists from the Nazi taint. The lover was seldom pictured, and so was easily ignored by art historians. So intent were we on David as a type for republicanism that we barely saw Orlando, or all the Romeos of Boccaccio and Bandello —though they might well have been reminiscent of Hollywood heartthrobs.

The Renaissance version of courtly and Petrarchan love provided, once slightly allegorized, a theory of creativity—and as such, it provided something quite new. Admittedly, God the creator was a familiar trope which offered something along the lines of a theory of creativity, but only inadequately so. It more nearly made god into an artist, a not terribly successful artist, than the artist into god. By contrast, the poetry about loving either beauty, or natural simplicity, tapped an effusiveness that, in good time, would grow into the raptures of Romanticism. At this juncture, it sufficed to take the mode of prayer and to invert, at least potentially, the structures of grace-giving. The key to the poetry of love, what made it more important than epic to an era all set to promote epic, was the sense that the person on his knees was actually dominant over the vision on the pedestal. The poet sensed his strength relative to his beloved, and took her procreativity as type for his artistic creativity. Michelangelo famously said of Francia that his children were better works than his paintings. The same basic metaphor was still in use when Carl

Theodore Dreyer described himself as midwife for his actress in his *Passion of St. Joan* (1928).[134]

This inversion of giver and granter of prayers potentially had broad social, political, and theological repercussions. Lorenzo de' Medici surely wrote sonnets in order to meditate upon his own power as much as he did to express his admiration for the female object. The one-time suppliant had been reinterpreted as conqueror. In that trope lay the modernity of the Renaissance, the decisive upsetting of the careful hierarchies of medieval thought and the conceptual germ of revolutions to come. Who could be more distinctively Renaissance than Caterina Sforza, Mona Lisa, or Ariosto's Angelica? But it has taken our own changes in gender politics for us to be able to recognize how greatly enhanced were the roles for women in Renaissance literature, art, and politics. Paradoxically, this courtly and earthly love seemed to the post-war historians too medieval to countenance as important to the golden age of the Renaissance.

Has the conceptualization of men ever swung as radically as what we see in the disparity between Griselda and Lucretia Borgia? Admittedly, the latter is not only a creature of legend, but the point remains. Not only has it been hard to see the historical and literary women, but even the ones laid out on canvas. Art historians writing in the sixties, during our own sexual revolution, now sound incredibly prudish when confronting Renaissance oil paintings of luscious female nudes. What Mark Twain could see as extremely lusty, or Tolstoy as decadent, was allegorized by Brendel or Panofsky into effete moral philosophy, according to which those lords of the Renaissance were as pure as Thomas Aquinas. If the Renaissance is a time of change, it is so fundamentally in the conceptualization of women. From our perspective, the changing attitudes toward sexuality between the time of Petrarch and the time of Pietro Bembo prefigure the new licentiousness of the sixties, aided and abetted by the color movie. Yet in 1947, a distinguished art historian wrote that luscious nudes by Titian were conceived of as an allegory of sight, hearing, and touch, glossable by reference to Ficino:

the question is not ... how well suited the senses are for the pleasures of love; but how apt are they for the cognition of beauty which is not a sensation but a categorical concept[135]

—one, moreover which "affects vital interests of the Italian Renaissance, which so much insists on exploiting to the limit the natural faculties of man."[136] And finally, "there is no reason to assume that beauty, as the proper object of vision, be limited to the human face"—this of the Madrid version of Titian's *Venus and the Musician* in which the musician's gaze is most impudent.[137]

Neo-Platonism in post-war Renaissance art history rescued the Old Master works of female nudes from seeming thoroughly modern in the wrong sense. Even Bartolomeo Veneto's Frankfurt portrait was taken as a wedding picture by Panofsky, a "young bride in the guise of Flora"—not Flora the courtesan but Flora the happy wife of Zephyr, despite what he sees as "a provocative glance" and "provocative ringlets."[138] In his account *all'antica* voluptuousness signifies chastity. Anything beautiful signifies the ascent of the soul. Indeed, anything does.

Like Winckelmann exalting the Greeks as a means to correct the excesses of Bernini, Frederick Hartt held up Michelangelo's *David* as a moral and cultural exemplar, in implicit contrast, perhaps, to Elvis Presley. Lord Clark was quite explicit about his discomfort with contemporary art; others were less straightforward but no less influenced by their contemporary concerns. The purified Renaissance served as a bulwark against modern licentiousness. The Renaissance could not have done this had its own interest in love poetry and license been more fully explored. We are, I think, still in the process of realizing the degree to which academic art history in America was molded by implicit ideologies about twentieth-century democratic capitalism, in particular the degree to which what was then the core subject, the Florentine Renaissance, functioned as a kind of alter ego for America, a bourgeoisie recuperating from the effects of Romantic disdain, and a formerly provincial culture newly revelling in its own center of gravity. Lorenzo il Magnifico was a name everyone knew, but how many of his admirers had heard about the Sack of Volterra?[139]

The barebreasted women Michelangelo drew, his *Leda* and *Venus*, the nude Mona Lisa knock-offs, all athletes not ones of virtue (in Colin Eisler's phrase), were shunted off to the side. The Italian Renaissance was co-opted, as it had been earlier by Vasari himself. He turned the rather brash art of the nouveau riche Florentines into an emblem of cultural longevity and an attribute of the Ducal regime; we Americans created an Italian Renaissance whose most important artistic contribution was its cultural imperialism over the subsequent centuries. The art of the Italian Renaissance, like the art of ancient Greece, was supposed to provide a standard of excellence which was not culturally relative, and which provided support for the idea that American culture, too, might be exported and become permanent in an age haunted by impermanence. But in order to seem so cardinal, the Renaissance was made into an object of religious devotion itself: its protagonists superhuman, its idealism unadulterated, its art a cluster of masterpieces—rather like the maidens of Crotona, each most lovely, and yet the combination lovelier still.

In general, we have focussed on what was instrumental in Renaissance art, serving the interests of church and/or state, rather than on what made Renaissance art a success in its own time. That it was esteemed because its quality was so great, or because it promised forgiveness for usury, seems to have been the premise. But what made it possible to sell cheap printed images which promised nothing to the viewer in terms of personal salvation? The Romantics would have answered that everyone was celebrating human genius and that artists were the mascots of the age—that ultimately the significance of all the culture of love, poetical and visual, was the exultation of the artist into quasi-divine status. Their mistake was to lose the sense of inversion which this had involved in the original, Renaissance scenario. It was not the object of divine inspiration who assimilated attributes of divinity, but the base suppliant who usurped the place of the quasi-divinity. Panofsky, who was in some ways inescapably a Romantic, missed this distinction and saw the Renaissance artist as god-like with very little complication from the figure of the beloved.

As for the aggressive modernists, their answer to the question of why Renaissance art succeeded hinged on the (for them, suspect) aura of a newly proficient technique, an aura owed both to a rediscovered naturalism and to the splendor of oil paint. As Renaissance theorists had disdained *colore* as glamor devoid of truth, so modernists decried the deceit implicit in systematic linear perspective and in any "realism."

Both accounts, the Romantic and the modern, give precious little weight to the possibility that Renaissance art was sometimes just fun, and that artists weren't always plotting the path to knighthood and other forms of social success. The twenty-first-century understanding of the Renaissance needs not only to balance the traditional high-mindedness with occasional low-mindedness and even smuttiness, but also to allow the possibility that a good chunk of the visual culture fell somewhere in between. Beauty wasn't always about Truth; art wasn't always about Beauty; it wasn't always either base or inspirational. Moreover, Renaissance art was far from unitary on a purely stylistic axis, as those who resist the label "Renaissance" acknowledge. The north knew the art of the south, and vice versa, and that relationship of difference was highly catalytic. The one fostered a degree of abstraction; the other was ever hungry for more data. No artist after the era of printmaking began could ignore the respect due to both traditions, and few artists managed to meld them more plausibly than Dürer in his 1504 engraving of *Adam and Eve*—though many tried.

The things we don't think about are often the things we tend not to see. The Villa La Gallina with Pollaiuolo's dancing nudes, while they have something to do with Etruscan vase painting, have very little to do with athletes of virtue. But they are hard to get to see. To step slightly outside the Italian ambient, but only slightly, Lucas van Leyden's engravings of couples provide plenty of food for thought about the culture of love. What makes them minor and the admittedly marvellous *Dance of the Magdalen* major, except that we associate narrative texts with the project of Renaissance art? It doesn't hurt that the larger *Magdalen* print is worth more on the market. Mantegna's mythological engravings offer an outstanding example of works which are fun, regardless of the details of their interpretation. Here is a man the art historical literature presents as an intense proto-archaeologist, scowling and obsessive, a votary to the greatness of antiquity. Doubtless, to try to understand Mantegna's work without due reference to the reverence inspired by antiquity would be wrongheaded. But the business of art, even for him, wasn't all humanist advisors and seriousness. He built a house that made a moving picture of the sky, in the circular courtyard, and reduced human life to relatively static images against the wall. He was genuinely clever and innovative, and too often he is thought of now as merely programmed. Michelangelo's strange *Children's Bacchanal* needs some rethinking too. I was raised on Panofsky, to think of this as an allegory of the lower stages of the soul's ascent, and even without stopping to argue the rightness or wrongness of that interpretation, I know it isn't adequate. Something is missing from a Renaissance art history which can say of such a work no more than that it pertains to Renaissance Neo-Platonism.[140]

Michelangelo's ancestors on the Sistine vault strike me as among the most inexcusably overlooked of Renaissance works: inventive, reminiscent at once of life and of art, only vaguely if at all *all'antica*, they are more than anything else, modern, in sixteenth-century terms. They don't translate into worship of anything, not God, not Roman ancestry, not civic pride, not artistic genius. They are beautiful; they are not repetitious; of themselves or of anything before them; they reek neither of official function nor of personal revelation. They could fit integrally into a notion of the Renaissance that featured Ariosto's Angelica and Cranach's equally wry *Ages of Women* (Leipzig), but they have been overlookable in a Renaissance centered on Raphael's *Galatea* and Michelangelo's *David*, for they are not heroic.

Vital as Janson's Italian Renaissance was for American art history of the cold war era, now it is time for a fresh look. A good place to begin would be by considering the record of fifteenth- and sixteenth-century art left in printed imagery, the Renaissance version of our post cards, posters, and dvds. If—like Winckelmann with his dream journey to the stadium in Ellis, where he would see ranged before him the totality of the artistic production of the culture he aspired to understand—we thought of Renaissance art first as a totality, book illustration included, it would look very different to us and might provide ground on which to leverage our study of the Renaissance out of the rut made by modernism's rather arbitrary rejection (and vice versa). The printed imagery suggests that contemporaries looked at art and at literature more often with a wide-raging curiosity than in docile adulation. We should do the same. If we took Renaissance art, not only the print record but all the works, primarily as a record of the more or less communal imagination of a distant past, we could begin to ask more fundamental questions, questions about the importance of a variety of kinds of vision in Renaissance and later thought. We could include not only the innovations, but the false starts and clichés. The history of human imagination is something we can know only in the most fragmentary—and almost archaeologically cautious—way.

Prints point to the culture of love which was carnal without being either naughty or inspirational, the culture of love that was fun and whose artistic outlet was comedy in the broad sense. We have edited poetry out of the Renaissance, eliding it into epic hero worship, gender studies, or Neo-Platonism. Yet the poetical culture of love was one of the fastest evolving strands of Renaissance artistic endeavor. For Panofsky it was not particularly important; he was happy to fold Lorenzo's poetical efforts and their woodcut accompaniment into Ficino's philosophical musings, and he cared more about Latin and Greek literature (in the contexts of both the fifteenth and twentieth centuries) than he did about Italian lyric and burlesque. But not so the Florentines: Dante and Petrarch were their local sons. They, and other Italians, were not adverse to the *volgare* any more than they were to modernity, and there was some synergy between the two. We tend to emphasize their sense of decorum, sometimes forgetting that decorum needed such emphasis because so much of what was around was indecorous and daringly innovative. Although in the 1960s America professors of art history may not have wanted to champion license or poetry, thanks to Horace, poetic license was as vital a part of making Renaissance art as decorum. The *all'antica*, the decorous, the Neo-Platonic have served well in the art history of the past generation or so, but to the exclusion of the idea that the erotic impulse was neither sinful nor necessarily convertible into the stuff of salvation. A notion of poetic and irrational freedom was key to all in Renaissance culture that espoused modernity rather than retrospection. We have cheated ourselves of the modernity of the Renaissance during our own throes of modernism.

Titian we have recognized for some time now as fairly lusty; the growth of Venetian art history in general has remedied some of the old biases. Michelangelo has been tougher. Without doubt he was a more idealistic, and a more repressed, person. But he certainly understood that poetry was a realm of eroticism; he made drawings which visualized the cultural ideal of the beloved, which he learned from Dante and Petrarch if not from life; and he transferred the passion and license which was endemic to poetry into carving. What better surrogate for an obdurate beloved than obdurate stone? And what better way to escape the oppressiveness of the antique past, the broken works patrons were willing to pay more for than his modern ones, than through reconceptualizing his art as poetical? He could then be as free of Praxiteles as Ariosto had made himself of Virgil.

The Renaissance we have gotten used to studying was conceived of as an antidote to modernism's rebellion, and so was not even allowed license, except the shunned license described by Vasari, who was lobbying for academic art. At the same time we have followed Vasari in putting Michelangelo at the center of the Renaissance, as the greatest of artists, despite his being in so many ways an anomaly. Vasari did it because he had a problem. He needed a Florentine to cap his history of the greatness of Florentine art, and Michelangelo was a better bet than Raphael of Urbino, or Leonardo who had spent even more of his life elsewhere than Michelangelo. Although Michelangelo had refused, embarrassingly enough, to work for Duke Cosimo, at least he had worked for an astonishing number of impressively powerful patrons and had made a fortune, or enough to allow his relatives to live like gentlemen even if he chose not to himself. We have put Michelangelo in such prominence partly because we followed in the footsteps of Vasari, and partly because Romanticism taught us to expect anomaly of greatness. The problem comes when we study that anomaly called Michelangelo as though he were the epitome Vasari wanted him to be.

There were many things wrong with the twentieth century's view of the Renaissance, and there will be many things wrong with whatever view evolves out of that. But I think our general direction would be right if we understood the period as a little less Apollonian, and if we gave up the effort to slice up the artistic production according to a system of genre: the heroic, the feminist, the republican, the commercialistic, the popular—each with its key works of art according to the particular twentieth-century agenda. We are still struggling to see as a whole the vast, dynamic, and evolving whole of Renaissance arts (not only visual arts, but music, literature, early science, and history). The corresponding historical reality we need to allow to have been a good deal more chaotic and nasty than its more glowing reports, and despite that, not very much like our present. Instead of using the art to illustrate our notions of a Renaissance we narcissistically admire, our project now begins with allowing that even in the Renaissance, neither all the statues nor all the men were heroic, or exemplary. On the other hand, the arts could often be plain fun. As Aretino explained in Dolce's *Dialogo*, even children and unlettered people respond to painting's *dolcezza*.[141]

There has been a disciplinary tendency to shift some of the delight of art back onto the society out of which it came. Winckelmann credited the Greeks with "a joyousness of disposition;"[142] Pugin thought that "Catholic England was merry England, at least for the humbler classes."[143] Hippolyte Taine believed that "the Italians construe life as a delightful festivity."[144] All of this was very charming, but overly idealized. It led to a bland, not to say totally unreliable, conception of the history of art: happy people make beautiful art.

It remains for the twenty-first century to enjoy and to learn from Renaissance art without whitewashing the history of its production. We need to remember, for instance, that Renaissance paintings delighted people who, according to Sanudo, were feasting even while they ignored the starving peasants crying at the doors for food. The Renaissance was distinctly not a festival, not even for the upper classes. It is also our task to develop a more circumspect notion of the degree of freedom within which Renaissance artists worked than the post-Romantic scholars described, to trim some of the excesses of self-referentially the Freudian tradition left with us, and to repair the damages done by the combined forces of modernists' rejection of Renaissance art and Renaissance art historians' rejection of modernism. Twentieth-century modernism could now become what the middle ages was to Panofsky's Renaissance: the apparent break in tradition that makes possible a more focussed view of the past.

Joanna Woods-Marsden
Theorizing Renaissance Portraiture[*]

Somewhat ironically, portraiture and gender—the two areas of Renaissance art on which my own work has focused for some years—were hardly touched upon at the Art Seminar held in April 2006 in my native land. Gender, left undefined, was dismissed by several interlocutors as having "lost its cutting edge", and only Robert Williams mentioned portraiture. This brief essay was stimulated by his comment that portraiture in this period developed independently of theory.

The first mention of portraiture in an Italian theoretical context took place at the same chronological moment, the 1430s, as the re-invention of the independent likeness in Italy. Thus, so far as portraiture is concerned, theory and practice can be said to have coincided precisely. Basing himself on Plutarch and Pliny the Elder, Leon Battista Alberti set the stage in *De Pictura* for the subsequent development of both the theory and practice of this new genre. Among his key points, he outlined the *function* of the portrait; established *who* the sitters would be; and considered *how* they should be portrayed.

Alberti's declaration that the portraiture was primarily commemorative, based no doubt on his experience of Roman busts and relief portraits on Roman sarcophagi, did not have the same staying power as his other *dicta*.[145] The function of the earliest surviving Quattrocento portraits, given the lack of firmly identified sitters and established dates, will inevitably never be precisely established. By the 1440s, however, portraits were being painted of those who were not only alive but sufficiently youthful to anticipate many more years on this earth.[146] In this respect, therefore, practice can be said to have immediately diverged from theory. From having (theoretically) served the same function of glorifying ancestors that Pliny claimed for the Roman portrait bust, the Renaissance likeness rapidly took on the role of celebrating the breathing.[147]

Secondly, Alberti emphasized the social rank of potential sitters, by mentioning *only* portraits of the great, such as Pericles, Antigonus and Alexander the Great. Indeed, until at least the middle of the sixteenth century, only rulers, their close relatives, their *famiglia* of courtiers and humanists, and their most powerful governing officials, commissioned portraits. This phenomenon was peninsula-wide. Despite the different governmental systems of Florence and Venice, for instance, the upscale rank of Florentine and Venetian sitters was identical to those at Italian courts, such as Mantua or Naples: only the features of those in power were recorded. The elitism of this new, secular genre—as opposed to the democracy of, say, religious altarpieces in churches which were intended to be used by the entire community—was thus established from portraiture's very beginnings. How could it be otherwise, given the ideology of social hierarchy that prevailed in the period?

The humanists who subsequently wrote verse on works in this newly minted genre tended to focus on the sitters, the rulers, who were of course their own patrons. Thus the poems that the humanists, at mid-Quattrocento, wrote in praise of portraits were as intent on promoting the glory of the sitter as that of the artist or the created work. The theme was most succinctly stated by Ferrabos in 1466 when he claimed that it was the subject, Federico da Montefeltro, duke of Urbino, *not* the artist Piero della Francesca, who bestowed the soul on the former's portrait.[148] Thus, the expressive quality of the work was read as a function of the sitter's rank within the social and political hierarchy rather than the artist's skill of hand. It would not have served the writer's own best interests to acknowledge that the prince was dependent on the low-born artist's talent for fashioning visual signs evocative of his subject's elevated power. A hundred years later, for instance, the satirist Pietro Aretino would attribute the greatness of Titian's *Equestrian Portrait of Charles V*, 1548 (Madrid, Prado), which he never saw, to the grandeur of the Emperor himself.[149]

Aretino, himself from the lowest ranks of society, articulated what was obvious to his own culture, if not always to ours: the male portrait was intended to function as an image of the individual's power and heroic *virtù*. Indeed, in his sonnet on Titian's *Equestrian portrait* he stressed that the painting functioned as much as a representation of the role or position filled by the Emperor, and the qualities deemed essential for that role—clemency, justice, grandeur, grace, and so forth—as it did as a likeness of the particular Habsburg who currently embodied that position.[150]

This point—that Renaissance sitters were drawn only from the social elite—is confirmed by Aretino's famous comment in 1545 to the sculptor Leone Leoni: "It's your shame, oh century, to tolerate that tailors and butchers appear living in portraits."[151] Aretino, whose own father was a humble cobbler, was aping his patrons' aristocratic disdain for mechanical work. Aretino could have had in mind Girolamo Mazzola Bedoli's *Portrait of a Tailor* (Naples, Capodimonte), dated to the early 1540s, in the North Italian collection of the Sanvitale of Parma.[152] (Never mind the strange connection that Aretino should have made between butchers, who were at the very bottom of the social hierarchy, and tailors, who were not).

Gian Paolo Lomazzo's chapter devoted to portraiture in his 1584 *Trattato della Pittura* may be taken as codifying the theory of this genre as it had developed in the intervening 150 years since Alberti wrote his treatise. Like Aretino, Lomazzo lamented the degradation of contemporary portraits, so many of which were commissioned, he claimed, by plebians and the lower classes [*plebei e vili*], not to mention those he characterized as "charletans" [*ciurmatori*] and infamous [*infami*].[153] Artists needed, he insisted, to return to the principle that he correctly assumed underlay the genre in Antiquity: to depict only sitters of *qualità*, by which he meant those of high rank, whose lives were hence of interest to posterity. The equivalent English expression, people of quality, goes back to the seventeenth century.[154] Such portraits of the great were seen by conservative commentators as a means of political and social control. For instance, despite his disapproval of portraiture as promoting vanity, Gabriele Paleotti, the Counter Reformation bishop, nonetheless endorsed the dissemination of images of princes as a means, he stated, of encouraging the *popolo*'s obedience and respect.[155]

In sum, as theorized by the profoundly conservative society of Renaissance Italy, the prescriptive right to a portrait was *proibito* to all except those in power. Thus, at the risk of undermining my own work on Titian's court portraits, I have to acknowledge that the term "court portrait" is a misnomer.[156] For the first hundred years, at least, of the early modern portrait, *only* one type of likeness existed and that *was* the "court portrait." In effect, the label, "Renaissance court portrait," is redundant, the adjective being superfluous.

* * *

In 1435 Alberti further established *how* these up-scale sitters were meant to be represented by addressing the tension between the sitter's stated desire for verisimilitude as opposed to his or her actual need for idealization. The illusion of verisimilitude that the artist's skill gave to the Renaissance likeness often imparts the idea that it literally embodies the "truth." In addition, Renaissance comments on portraits, based on classical rhetoric, always focused on the image's resemblance to the sitter's somatic appearance. Typical of this rhetoric of naturalism was Isabella d'Este's condemnation of a lost 1493 portrait of her by Andrea Mantegna. She focused on its lack of verisimilitude: it was "so badly painted that it doesn't resemble us in the slightest" [*tanto mal facta che non ha alcuna de le nostre simiglie*].[157] It seems far more likely that this likeness, by an artist notorious for his lack of "grace" in portraiture [*nel retrare (Mantegna) poria havere più gratia e non fa cussì* bene] may have provided a resemblance that was all too accurate.[158]

"Plutarch tells how ancient painters, when painting kings who had some physical defect . . .," wrote Alberti, "corrected [the imperfection] as much as possible, while still maintaining the likeness."[159] The theorist sought to resolve this tension between, on the one hand, the need for sufficient verisimilitude to render the sitter recognizable, and, on the other, Italian cultural requirement for idealization, that is, for portraits that offered a flattering image of the subject. Given that most sitters had some kind of physical defect—however this was defined—Alberti encouraged the artist to compromise by "emending" or "dissimulating" those features that were contrary to "beauty," while nonetheless maintaining an adequate likeness. Indeed, as he saw it, it was only by "improving" on Nature that the artist could succeed. Thus, when Alberti reiterated the need for naturalism, he was referring to the face or figure with which Nature intended, but failed, to endow the sitter. In other words, to quote Cennino Cennini's beautiful phrase, even those painting portraits—or, perhaps, *especially* portraitists—required *fantasia* in order to discover things unseen [*di trovare cose non vedute*], hiding themselves under the shadow of natural objects [*cacciandosi sotto ombra di naturali*], demonstrating what does not actually exist [*dimostrando quello che nonne sia*].[160]

In 1435 Alberti theorized the genre of likeness so successfully that he profoundly influenced both the theory and practice of Italian portraiture for the foreseeable future. In 1557, for instance, Lodovico Dolce reiterated that it was essential for the artist to surpass Nature, not merely to "copy" her.[161] In the 1540s the Portuguese theorist, Francisco de Holanda, wrote a whole treatise on the subject, *Do tirar polo natural* [Of portraying from life]. In it he showed himself heir to Alberti's compromise between likeness and beauty: the young sitter must appear even younger; the old sitter, less old; the beautiful sitter, more beautiful; the ugly sitter, less ugly.[162]

Modern artists should, like those in Antiquity, reiterated Lomazzo in 1584, dissimulate and conceal Nature's inadequacies in order to amplify the "good parts" of the physical self and its *bellezze*, its pleasing features.[163] Like other kings and princes, portraits of the Holy Roman Emperor Charles V, for instance, needed to embody the majesty that corresponded to his rank, so that the sitter gave the impression of "breathing nobility and gravity"—especially if he was not naturally so [inclined] [*ancora che naturalmente non fosse tale*].[164] Such instructions recall Baldassare Castiglione's comment when discussing the importance of *mediocrità*, the tempered style, vis à vis the prince: the courtier needed to learn to accommodate himself to his ruler's wishes, "even when such behavior was contrary to his disposition" [. . . *si accomodi, se ben da natura sua vi fosse alieno*]. The courtier was obliged to "like that which he may perhaps be predisposed to dislike," [*farsi piacere quello che forse da natura gli dispiacesse*].[165] Thus, for Castiglione, demeanor, and for Lomazzo, portraiture, could and should dissemble for social purposes.

In 1567 Vincenzo Danti in his *Trattato delle perfette proporzioni* established a fundamental distinction between poetry and history that he applied to portraiture.[166] He used the term *ritrarre* to indicate "something exactly as another thing is seen to be," in other words, a faithful copy or literal duplication of reality, and *imitare* to signify a work "as it would have to be in order to be of complete perfection," in other words, reality "corrected" and idealized.[167] He instructed the artist to improve Nature [*imitare*] and to express the perfect form hidden behind the appearance of reality or, as Cennini put it, *cacciandosi sotto ombra di naturali.* Needless to say, the act of *imitare*, those cases where "the artist is capable of imitation," was considered infinitely superior to that of mere "replication" [*ritrarre*], in which artistic creativity was supposedly constrained by Nature.[168] Such duplication was condemned as an art that could be mastered even by an artist who possessed only "mediocre talent" [*mediocre ingegno*], as Giovanni Battista Armenini observed in 1587.[169]

The key term used by art theorists when discussing the issue of *imitare*—*dissimulazione*, "dissembling," "disguise," "counterfeit"— was frequently used in the Cinquecento in other contexts. In *The Prince* Niccolò Machiavelli wrote of the importance of learning how to disguise the self, stressing the necessity for the prince to be successful as a *simulatore* and *dissimulatore*, "pretender," "deceiver."[170] In *Book of the Courtier*, Castiglione specifically recommended that the courtier adopt demeanor consisting of *una certa avvertita dissimulazione*, "a certain circumspect deception."[171]

Torquato Accetto's treatise *Della Dissimulazione Onesta* [Of Honorable Dissimulation], written at the court of Naples in 1641, offers a number of definitions of *l'arte del fingere*, the art of pretense. Like *fingere, il dissimulare* was none other, he wrote, than a "veil composed of shadows" [*velo composto di tenebre*] that allowed truth to take a rest [*da qualche riposo al vero*].[172] Elsewhere, he explained that *dissimulazione* was an industry of not seeing things as they are. You simulate that which is not and dissimulate that which is.[173] Accetto's definition is akin to that of Francis Bacon in his essay on "Simulation and Dissimulation." He personified Simulation as "a man [who] expressly feigns and pretends to be that which he is not" and Dissimulation as a man who lets signs fall that he is not "what he is."[174] Bacon ended his essay by saying that, while it was best to be famed for one's openness, it was nonetheless important to be able to "feign and practice dissimulation" in life, should this become necessary.

Toward the end of the sixteenth century, some writers, rejecting such theories, expressed the view that portraits should be literal "copies" of Nature, that is, examples of *ritrarre*. They were, for the most part, ecclesiastics seeking to promote the ideology and values of the Counter-Reformation. Paleotti, bishop of Bologna, for instance, condemned portraits, especially of "silly women" [*donnicciole*] on moral grounds, as undesirable signs of vanity.[175] That of the prince, however, was exempt from these strictures, since he was one of God's anointed.[176] The prince's portrait focused on his Body public, which had to be respected and obeyed, wrote the bishop, since it embodied the power that God had given him. Even in this case, however, the portrait had to be exact, that is, of an historical [*ritrarre*], rather than poetic [*imitare*], nature. Insisting on "realism," which he identified with "truth," Paleotti declared that no feature should be altered nor any sitter rendered more beautiful.[177]

Despite these ecclesiastic concerns, however, the overall thrust of theoretical thinking about portraiture in the Cinquecento focused not on Paleotti's search for "the" truth but on Accetto's (later) proposal to give truth a rest. As to artistic practice, by adorning the truth in order "to make that, which is not, seem to be "[*far parere . . . quello che non é*], as Castiglione wrote of painting, most Italian artists presented the aristocratic world in art as it conceivably could have been in life, but almost certainly was not.[178]

In conclusion, from Alberti to Lomazzo and beyond, the new secular genre of "recording" the human face, and (later) body, was fully theorized. According to these writers, the functions of such works were commemorative and exemplary; its subjects were the great; and its means was dissimulation—that veil composed of shadows that allowed truth to rest. Theory and practice may be seen as having diverged with respect to the first criterion only. Indeed, when surviving Renaissance visual representations of wise and courageous aristocratic males and their beautiful, virtuous consorts are considered in tandem with the historical written record, their *res gestae* in life seldom live up to its adumbration in the artful fictions of their likenesses.[179]

Maria Ruvoldt

Responding to the Renaissance

We rewrite, reframe, revise and reimagine the Renaissance with remarkable frequency. This ongoing project of reassessment and review, if not unique to our chosen field of study, is nevertheless one of its key characteristics. Our preoccupation with defining the Renaissance testifies to the power of the label and its perceived centrality in narratives of Western history and art history. Almost thirty years ago, the historian William J. Bouwsma saw the state of Renaissance studies as symptomatic of nothing less than "the collapse of the traditional dramatic organization of Western history," noting with dismay that "Renaissance" was ceasing to be a meaningful designation, having become "little more than an administrative convenience, a kind of blanket under which we huddle together less out of mutual attraction than because, for certain purposes, we have nowhere else to go."[180] But when historians revisited Bouwsma's critique in the late 1990s, the results were more optimistic.[181] Recognizing a "new intersection between cultural and intellectual history" that promised new definitions of the Renaissance to ensure its continued relevance, Paula Findlen and Kenneth Gouwens called for a "conceptual *renovatio*."[182] The paradox of the Renaissance, it seems, is that its redefinition is necessary because of its importance, but its importance is contingent on its redefinition.

Any student of the Renaissance has to grapple with this problem, but as art historians, our relationship to the period is particularly fraught because the questions that shape our discipline emerged in the period we study. As the participants in the roundtable have already acknowledged, we travel on paths forged by our Renaissance predecessors, who struggled with the problem of using words to deal with images, with the relationship between form and meaning, with problems of interpretation, and with questions about what constitutes art. When we seek to redefine the Renaissance, we are thus also engaged in reflection on our own practice and on the meaning of art history. Remarking that "there is something systematic and rationalizing in Vasari that is carried on in what we now recognize as art history," James Elkins touches on part of the problem.[183] Vasari set the traditional parameters of the discipline, which have been challenged and recognized as problematic, but which nevertheless persist in forming the undercurrent of art-historical practice. Whether we embrace, reject, or modify his terms, we inherit from Vasari the narrative model, with its emphasis on individual biography and processes of artistic evolution, the traditional hierarchy of the arts favoring the "fine" arts of painting, sculpture and architecture over the "minor" or "decorative" arts, and also, though this is sometimes overlooked, an art history in the service of a political ideology.[184] We can even credit him with initiating the project of revision itself. Writing against an already established tradition of art criticism, Vasari changed the terms, treating the pressing questions of the day as if they had already been decided and introducing new questions in their place.[185] Stephen Campbell describes the chilling effect of Vasari's success as "a closing off of a rich array of other possibilities."[186] Attending to those "other possibilities," either by dealing with other strains of Renaissance art criticism or by introducing our own questions to the discourse, we enrich our view of the Renaissance and of the discipline itself.

Both the roundtable discussion and the essays contributed by its participants make clear what a complex undertaking it is to attempt the "best possible . . . account of Renaissance art."[187] The variety of approaches articulated here suggests that the idea of a perfect meta-narrative not yet achieved may be incompatible with the multifaceted nature of the Renaissance as we understand it. How might we even begin to write such a narrative? Should we focus on the tensions within Florence as a corrective to the dominance of Vasari's account, explore the political context that shaped his text, and attend to those oppositional voices that resisted his terms? Traditional narratives of the Renaissance tend, as Campbell points out, to deal with Grand-ducal Florence as an afterthought. Recovering Florence in the "forgotten centuries" allows us to see Vasari in context, not only as a critic and academician, but as a practicing artist.[188] It offers new perspectives on Mannerism, but also maintains the centrality of Florence in histories of Renaissance art. Should we instead go "Beyond Florence," as a recent collection of essays suggests, and look to other centers of artistic production, whether in Italy or else-where?[189] Should we focus on the influence of non-Western arts on European artists?[190] Should we follow Claire Farago's example, and leave the Italian peninsula behind to gain a clearer view of the meaning of the Renaissance for European and non-European centers alike?[191] Or should we abandon these traditional models of geographic and temporal boundaries altogether to focus on larger structural concerns, such as gender? Each of these strategies reveals a different aspect of the Renaissance. Feminist scholarship, to take just one example, has reshaped our view of Renaissance culture. Although it is true that a host of Renaissance *virtuose* have not displaced the canonical masters, the work of scholars like Joan Kelly and Fredrika Jacobs illuminates just why the role of female artist was so uncommon.[192] Feminist scholarship alerts us not only to female producers, but to the role that gender plays in the experience of both male and female viewers. It introduces objects like birth trays and domestic furnishings into analyses of Renaissance visual culture, offers new ways of thinking about such iconic works as the *Venus of Urbino*, and reminds us that "masculinity" is as socially- and culturally-constructed as "femininity."[193]

The picture that emerges is one of almost infinite avenues of inquiry, all testing the idea of a dominant narrative or paradigm for the history of Renaissance art. Yet the desire for such a narrative remains, despite the fact that the sheer variety of forms of visual expression and centers of production in the period frustrate attempts to create one. Greater attention to the decorative arts and other neglected forms of visual imagery, from high-end domestic and luxury goods to votive works and other "popular" images, suggests that among the more difficult questions we face is not simply how best to approach Renaissance art, but rather how open our definition of "art" should be. Painting, sculpture, and architecture retain pride of place as the objects of art-historical investigation, but the traditional hierarchy fails to reflect the reality of Renaissance visual culture—either from the point of view of artistic practice or from that of consumption. Raphael designed tapestries and, through his workshop, revived the ancient art of stucco decoration, Michelangelo designed daggers, candlesticks, and saltcellars, and artists such as Valerio Belli and Giovanni Bernardi, though absent today from conventional histories of Renaissance art, enjoyed renown and earned a place in Vasari's *Lives* for their work in crystal and gem-engraving.

The objects that we most often overlook were commonly the most expensive items in a household.[194] The social and economic value accorded to such things as engraved gems, tapestries, and other luxury goods was astronomical, and the sentimental value placed on objects like birth trays, which became prized family heirlooms, is also noteworthy, as several new studies and museum exhibitions have shown.[195] The "insatiable desire for all things antique" that has long defined Renaissance collecting practices was mirrored by an equally insatiable desire for the very latest and finest examples of luxury and decorative arts, and by a profound interest in the power of images as intercessors with the divine.[196]

In her discussion of cult and votive images, Fredrika Jacobs deals with works that have been relegated to the margins of art history because they are "popular" or "naïve," and have been "handed over to anthropologists and social historians."[197] They fail to fit the category of "high" art as defined by contemporary art-historical practice and also, arguably, by Renaissance standards as well. I want to approach Jacobs' provocative idea about "destabilizing what is historically taken as 'high' art" from a different angle by thinking about objects whose present marginality obscures their past significance as "high" art.[198] What happens when we recognize that entire categories of objects valued and appreciated by Renaissance artists and viewers alike have become mere footnotes in our histories of Renaissance art?[199] How is our perception of the period altered when we recover their significance?

The footnote I wish to recover here belongs to the history of perhaps the least marginal of Renaissance artists—Michelangelo— and relates to a well-known group of his works—the gift drawings for Tommaso de'Cavalieri. As Jacobs has already outlined in her contribution to this volume, in the mid-1530s, Michelangelo sent a series of drawings to Cavalieri, using the imagery of myth to com- municate complex messages of love, desire, and divine inspiration.[200] Much has been made of the intimate nature of these gifts, but the drawings quickly became objects of desire themselves, attracting the covetous attention of such exalted viewers as the Medici pope Clement VII and his nephew, Cardinal Ippolito de'Medici, and generating an astonishing number of copies.

Copies of Michelangelo's gift drawings appeared in prints, draw- ings, ceramics, plaquettes, and full-scale paintings.[201] They varied in their fidelity to the originals, ranging from careful replication to imaginative reworking. Disseminating Michelangelo's inventions across a wide spectrum of viewers, the copies allowed his supposedly private gifts for Cavalieri to pass into more public circulation. These second- and third-generation images represent the Renaissance commodification of an individual artist's "genius;" they are reproduced and valued in part because they are designs by Michelangelo. But with diffusion came the dilution of meaning. Primarily through prints, the drawings migrated into a variety of new contexts in which their original intention and meaning were obscured, including maiolica wares that misidentified the subject of one drawing, the *Dream*, and liturgical textiles that transformed another, the *Ganymede*, into a St. John.[202]

Despite the great range in medium and quality among the copies, they are generally treated, if at all, as a group, as part of an undifferentiated phenomenon of replication. But not all copies are created equal. Several versions of Michelangelo's drawings exist in what I would term "luxury" copies, works in media that were accorded considerable value by sixteenth-century viewers. These include high-end decorative art objects, such as a bedhead designed by Alessandro Allori, incorporating *Ganymede* and a Michelangesque *Leda*, paintings on supports of copper and slate, and gems, including cameos and rock crystal intaglios. Unlike relatively inexpensive prints produced for circulation to a wide and potentially unknown audience, copies like these represent considerable expense and the likely intervention of a patron who requested their production.

Perhaps the most remarkable of the luxury copies are in fact the very first copies made after the gift drawings. Almost as soon as he had received his gifts from Michelangelo, Cavalieri was compelled to relinquish them. On September 6, 1533, he wrote to Michelangelo to report that Clement VII, Cardinal Ippolito de'Medici and "everyone" had wanted to see the drawings and that the Cardinal had been so taken with them that "he wanted to have the Tityus and Ganymede made in crystal, and I didn't know how to speak well enough to prevent him from doing the Tityus and now maestro Giovanni is doing it."[203] "Maestro Giovanni" was the master gem-engraver Giovanni Bernardi da Castel Bolognese, an artist who enjoyed not only the patronage of Ippolito de'Medici, but also his great personal esteem.[204] At the cardinal's behest, Bernardi rendered Michelangelo's *Tityus, Ganymede*, and *Phaeton* in rock crystal intaglios.

We know a great deal about this initial act of copying. Cavalieri's letter to Michelangelo relates the genesis of the copies, names the patron who commissioned them and the artist who executed them. Two of the three original crystals are preserved today: the *Tityus* at the British Museum, London, and the *Phaeton* at the Walters Art Gallery, Baltimore. The lost *Ganymede* was last seen in the nineteenth century somewhere in Europe, when the Italian gem-engraver Tommaso Cades took an impression of it, recorded its dimensions and appearance, but failed to note its location.[205] Created in the prized and princely medium of rock crystal, Bernardi's gems generated copies of their own, in bronze and lead plaquettes that today are scattered throughout museum collections around the world. They have been hiding in plain sight for some time. Why have they been overlooked?

A significant factor in the neglect of these works is our modern prejudice about copies in general, which we tend to view as purely derivative works, of little interest beyond their usefulness as tools for understanding the originals from which they derive. At the most basic level, copies reveal how images circulated and how widely known they might have been. They also aid in the reconstruction of lost or altered works. Prints after Michelangelo's drawing, the *Dream*, for example, reproduce with great clarity details that are barely legible in the original, having been rubbed out by a later hand.[206] By maintaining focus on the original, these approaches to the copy reinforce notions of individual genius and the cult of originality, which were as much a part of the Renaissance experience of these images as our own.

But perceptions of the copy shift, as Richard Spear and others have noted, with changing attitudes about the value of originality and what constitutes authorship of a work of art.[207] It is not at all surprising therefore that we might find in the Renaissance—a period in which these very issues were of critical concern—different approaches to the copy. On the one hand, it is possible to see copies after Michelangelo's drawings functioning like the secular equivalents of icons, whose multiple iterations derive their significance and authenticity from their relationship to an original work, rather than from their author's inventive contribution. The reproductive print, a form that develops in this period in part from the collaboration between Raphael and Marcantonio Raimondi, offers a different way of conceptualizing the copy, acknowledging and identifying the roles of "inventor" and "sculptor" in its production, with the "inventor" taking precedence.[208] When the copy appears in the same medium as the original, as do several copies of Michelangelo's gift drawings, it raises the specter of "forgery," but other readings are equally plausible. Unable to distinguish Andrea del Sarto's copy of Raphael's *Leo X with Cardinals Giulio de'Medici and Luigi de'Rossi* from the original, for example, Giulio Romano claimed that he might value the copy *even more* than the original because of Andrea's extraordinary imitation of Raphael's style.[209] The copy in this instance becomes an occasion for the demonstration of exceptional skill, but it is the bravura performance of another artist's signature style, rather than originality, that is the test of Andrea's talent.

The luxury copies after Michelangelo's drawings suggest yet another way to think about the copy. Part of the value that Renaissance viewers found in them came from their difference from the originals. Cameos, intaglios, and paintings on metal and stone after Michelangelo's drawings were more than reiterations of Michelangelo's inventions, more than faithful recreations of style; they were elaborations on the originals by other masters, whose work enhanced the value of Michelangelo's design.[210] They were executed in media that outranked drawing in the hierarchy of the arts and in materials whose intrinsic and symbolic value outweighed those of chalk, ink, and paper. For the Renaissance viewers and collectors who avidly sought them, the luxury copies represented the fusion of two artists' skills, marrying Michelangelo's great strength in *disegno* to the technical virtuosity of Bernardi or to the refined *colore* of artists such as Marcello Venusti and Alessandro Allori.[211] For the eighteenth-century connoisseur Jonathan Richardson, who valued execution over invention, such works do not even count as "copies;" according to his standards, any work after another artist's design "cannot be said to be a copy: the thought indeed is partly borrowed, but the work is original."[212] For modern art historians, the distinction is not so clear. Not quite Michelangelo's, not quite someone else's, these works tend to slip from view in modern scholarship. The challenge is to find an appropriate place in the art-historical narrative for copying and collaboration as a model of work in which the contributions of both artists result in an object of equal or even greater value than the "original."

The luxury copies also fail to appeal to our aesthetic sensibilities or to current definitions of high art. Engraved gems and paintings on supports of metal and stone are not held in high esteem by contemporary scholars, curators, or collectors despite their significance for a Renaissance audience. Together with small bronzes, glass, and other objects that fall on the "decorative" end of the spectrum, they embodied the social and aesthetic aspirations of their owners. We recognize in such works the imitation of and rivalry with classical antiquity and the celebration of modern technological achievement that we identify as hallmarks of the period, and thus assimilate them into the traditional narrative of Renaissance art, but as "minor" expressions of its themes. At the same time, these works represent an aesthetic of luxury and excess that is not adequately contained in the terms we typically deploy, such as "magnificence" and "splendor," which imply classical values of virtuous display and mute the elements of the showy, the shiny, and even the garish that such objects seem to embrace.

Among the most significant consequences of our perception that the practice of art history emerged in the Renaissance is that it tends to naturalize our definitions of "Renaissance art," which are considerably more restricted than those a fifteenth- or sixteenth-century viewer would accept. The objects that attract our scholarly attention are determined by standards of art-historical practice and aesthetic judgment that owe more to contemporary systems of value than to Renaissance culture. Once again it seems necessary to invoke Vasari, in whose work we can trace this process of contraction. In the *Lives*, Vasari cites "*opere mirabili e divinissime*" in gem-engraving and devotes a chapter to the biographies of the premier practitioners of this art and their "*maravigliosi ingegni*."[213] But in his role as academician, he contributes directly to the installation of a hierarchy of media and artists that ultimately results in a narrowing of the definition of what counts as "art."[214]

The great contribution of the trend towards the study of "visual culture," in opening up new subjects for art-historical investigation, is that it elevates objects ordinarily overlooked to the status of meaningful cultural signifiers, which no doubt they were. But it leaves the category of "high art" relatively undisturbed. At the same time that we have admitted new types of objects into art-historical discussion, we have persisted in excluding from mainstream consideration works that belonged to the category of high art in the culture that produced them.

Made by the artist as gifts for an intimate friend, Michelangelo's gift drawings represent a moment in which we see—or imagine that we can see—the artist at work, if not purely for art's sake, at least for his own. By attending to the luxury copies, we complicate and expand our understanding of this crucial episode in Renaissance art. Ippolito de'Medici "borrowed" the drawings and had them rendered in rock crystal, appropriating Michelangelo's private inventions for his own ends. This transfer has many implications, but among the most important is the dynastic significance of the antique-inspired gem. Engraved gems and hardstone vessels had long featured in Medici collecting practices, lending the luster of nobility and antiquity to the upwardly mobile family of Florentine bankers.[215] By procuring Michelangelo's drawings and transferring them to a medium prized by, and closely identified with, his fifteenth-century forebears, Ippolito de'Medici may have been trying to wrestle the drawings back into the frame of the traditional artist/patron relationship. At the microscopic level, this is an important moment in the complicated relationship between Michelangelo and the Medici, but it has larger implications as well. This episode reveals a moment of transition, in which the shift towards greater artistic autonomy meets resistance by a great patron who recognizes that the model is changing.

This is not to suggest that the value of Michelangelo's original drawings was ever truly diminished in the face of the luxury copies, or to imply that the original works no longer require our attention. Those Renaissance collectors who actively sought copies after Michelangelo's drawings in rock crystal, cameos, and paintings also pursued the original drawings, just as we continue to pursue the meaning of the originals through the copies. Arguably among the most powerful men in Rome, and important patrons of Michelangelo at this time, the Medici and men like them could not compel gift drawings from the artist himself. The traditional artist/patron relationship failed them in the face of the private gift. Instead, they found other means to achieve ownership of Michelangelo's inventions. They brought their influence to bear on the owners of the drawings, forcing loans to facilitate the production of luxury copies, and eventually coercing the sale and even "gifts" of the originals.[216] And in so doing, they clearly wanted to rewrite, revise, reframe, and reimagine their own relationship to the master. We can hardly blame them.

Marzia Faietti
Mantegna's Line: Beyond Vasari's Terza Maniera

In the "Preface" to the Third Part of the *Lives*, Giorgio Vasari describes the transition to the modern *maniera* or style—literally "that third style that we want to call modern" (*quella terza maniera che noi vogliamo chiamare la moderna)*—of which Leonardo had been the initiator, while Raphael and, above all, Michelangelo were the principle exponents. Vasari mentions Andrea Mantegna among the artists who, because of "excessive study" (*soverchio studio*), could not eliminate "a certain dry, rough and sharp style" (*una certa maniera secca e cruda e tagliente).*[217] This notorious passage attracted the attention of Panofsky, who devoted a well-known study to Vasari's historiographic orientation and critical vocabulary.[218]

Stimulated by the kind invitation to participate in this "Renaissance Roundtable" and prompted by the observations on Mantegna offered by Stephen J. Campbell in his essay, "Vasari's Renaissance and its Renaissance Alternatives",[219] I would like to offer some ideas about the inadequacy of Vasari's text with respect to Mantegna. Owing to his notion of artistic progress, Vasari's account of history does not allow for different forms of artistic expression, nor does it attempt to explain them with reference to their cultural contexts. One result is to flatten out an innovative artist like Mantegna by lumping him together with colleagues from whom he is very different—and who, in turn, differ among themselves.

Mantegna's art simulates nature, rather than imitating or emulating it. If this critical insight has been articulated before (and the reference is once again to Campbell's work), then here I propose to confirm and reinforce it by presenting some of the first results of research in progress. I intend to do so by concentrating on technical investigation and stylistic observation in the field of drawing. More precisely, I want to focus on the act of drawing and on the strictly related field of printmaking, where Mantegna demonstrated a notable originality and a strong inclination to linguistic, as well as technical, experimentation. My methods and the thrust of my interpretation are in some respects similar those found in David Rosand's interesting volume *Drawing Acts. Studies in Graphic Expression and Representation*, released in 2002, in which the name of the great Paduan artist recurs repeatedly.[220] Yet Mantegna's contribution in the field of drawing, considered with respect to that of other individuals, among them Leonardo, Raphael and Michelangelo, has not been the object of a specific study. The re-evaluation of the artist in connection with the events of the 2006 "Mantegna Year" calls for such an addition to the existing research.

Leaving aside the age-old questions of attribution that have preoccupied scholars—and not always positively[221]—I intend to concentrate on Mantegna's line. The characteristic quality of his line seems to me to constitute a critical element essential for understanding, not only his stylistic objectives, but also and more especially, his most complex and profound artistic aims.

I refer primarily to the line drawn in pen in a set of drawings unanimously ascribed to the artist, but I do not mean to neglect the mark incised by the burin on a metal plate: I am thinking of seven engravings (Bartsch XIII, 229, 3; 231, 6; 232, 8; 238, 17; 239, 18; 240, 19; 240, 20) considered autograph by Kristeller,[222] about which opinions continue to be rather consistent, despite the recent discovery of new documents.[223] This new information has, in certain cases, tended to polarize the discussion negatively, rather than confirm what has basically been known for a long time, that Mantegna took advantage of professional engravers to render his complex compositions.

My objective is to establish groupings of lines that keep recurring in the same way, following them through their subsequent developments in relation to the chronology of the works involved. This approach relies on both the detailed study of the engraved line in prints, which has achieved notable results in recent years,[224] and on the valuable studies of underdrawing in paintings.[225] My objective, however, is to go a step further, to exceed the useful, acquired knowledge derived from technical investigations—admittedly fundamental to verify novelties of visual language and to evaluate, with greater depth, questions of attribution and connoisseurship—in an attempt to understand the relation of technical experimentation and innovation, of artistic intentions and stylistic results, to Mantegna's overall involvement in the cultural and social environment in which he was formed and found himself operating. The key to achieving such a broadly synthetic interpretation, I believe, is the observation that Mantegna's system for creating marks (his *tracciato segnico*) demonstrates the clear prevalence of parallel, perpendicular or oblique hatching, instead of cross-hatching, which appears only rather sporadically.

This observation is the point of departure for research that I intend to develop in several more phases, but whose first results I wish to bring together now in the form of some working hypotheses. To borrow a metaphor from the realm of drawing, I will limit myself on this occasion to presenting a sort of sketch or preliminary draft, rather than a *modello* or presentation drawing, finished in all of its parts. For this reason, I will avoid exhaustive bibliographic references—which, because of the vastness of the literature on Mantegna, would have required copious footnotes—and instead limit myself to indicating in summary fashion the most exemplary results of previous research.

A survey of Mantegna's line draws our attention to the following points:

1. Already by the second half of the 1450s, the Paduan artist shows that he has developed a kind of visual writing, both studiously meticulous and spontaneous. It is found principally in parallel hatching, a technique all the descriptive and expressive potential of which he explores, and with which, as a result, he achieves a strongly personal style that links the drawings and the engravings.

2. Elsewhere, beginning around the 1480s, the technique of cross-hatching achieves expressive maturity in central Italy, particularly in Florence, where it appears to be utilised most extensively in the workshop of Domenico Ghirlandaio,[226] and is reinforced by the experience of Northern graphic work, with Dürer serving as a fundamental point of reference and, at the same time, point of departure.

Even through Mantegna's hatching is more plastic than, for example, that of Pollaiuolo (I am thinking of the famous engraving of the *Battle of Ten Nude Men*, whose chronological position before of after the engravings of Mantegna has long been discussed), it remains a language capable of only strong two-dimensional projection. The cross-hatched line implies a three-dimensional vision of the object and achieves a more fully volumetric projection of it.

Among other things, this second vision leads to the rediscovery of the fundamental importance of statuary and the isolated monument. Vasari would, therefore, seem to be correct, when, in the "Preface" to the Third Age of the *Lives*, he affirms that it was really the discovery of certain "antiquities cited by Pliny as among the most famous"—the Laocoön, the Hercules and the Great Torso of the Belvedere and similarly the Venus, the Cleopatra, the Apollo—among others, that "were the reason for the abandonment [*furono cagione di levar via*] of that dry, rough and sharp style of which I spoke at the beginning". The fact that Mantegna dies in the same year in which the *Laocoön* was discovered might appear almost symbolic. But the situation is much more complex, and an indirect consequence of my project is to offer a critical analysis of Vasari's "Preface", one that might enable us to better grasp its meaning and so clear it of misinterpretation. To understand Vasari's passage as it concerns Mantegna, we must return to the Paduan's antiquarian cultural environment employing a method of investigation that, as I have said, considers technical and stylistic developments, and that is capable of relating artistic objectives to a vision of the antique, on the one hand, and to a sense of the communicative strategies of images, on the other.

If Mantegna's interest in the antique must have been stimulated and encouraged by painters close to him, from Squarcione to Jacopo Bellini, his own vision of the antique was primarily influenced by works of sculpture. In part, this explains why sculpture is an essential point of reference for his pictorial *simulatio*. I need only cite the well-known testimony of his friend Ulisse Aleotti, who in a poetic composition believed to date from 1448, in praise of a lost portrait by the artist, showed a particular appreciation of his capacity to sculpt in painting: "[Through] the industrious hand and the bright intellect/ the image, gathered in the mind/ was sculpted, properly alive and true, in the picture" (*La mano industriosa et l'alto ingegno/l'imagine, raccolta nel concepto/scolpì in pictura propria viva et vera*).[227] This point of view would seem to be diametrically opposed to that of Vasari. In a passage in the "Life of Mantegna", Vasari describes criticisms—supposedly made by Squarcione—of the frescoes in the Ovetari Chapel. Mantegna's figures were faulted "because he had imitated antique marbles in making them, from which one cannot learn the art of painting perfectly" (*perché aveva nel farle imitato le cose di marmo antiche, dalle quali non si può imparare la pittura perfettamente*)". Mantegna, Vasari says, took the criticism to heart; still, he would remain of the opinion "that the good antique statues were more perfect and have more beautiful parts than appear in nature" (*che le buone statue antiche fussino più perfette et avessino più belle parti che non mostra il naturale*). In fact, this opinion had been formulated prior to Vasari by the Paduan canon Bernardino Scardeone in his *De antiquitate urbis Patavii* (1560), but Vasari uses it to drive home his criticism of Mantegna when he adds: "And one recognizes by this opinion that he was very satisfied with his works, in which one does indeed sees a slightly sharp style that sometimes takes after stone more than living flesh" (*E si conosce di questa openione essersi molto compiaciuto nell'opere sue, nelle quali si vede invero la maniera un pochetto tagliente e che tira talvolta più alla pietra che alla carne viva*).[228]

On the other hand, the comparison of painting with sculpture—in anticipation of the *paragone* of the sixteenth century—seems to have been something of a tradition among the artists of Padua. Yet Mantegna drew in large part from sources in metal and inscribed stone rather than marble statuary: the particular antique world at his disposal thus encouraged a specific kind of *simulatio*. Among Paduan collectors of antiquities there were certainly plenty of statues and portrait busts in marble, recovered in the city, in the surrounding countryside and other parts of the Veneto, if not brought directly from Greek territory via Venice.[229] But there must also have been coins, Latin inscriptions, perhaps gems as well, which, together with works in bronze, had an even more inspirational effect on Mantegna's vision of the antique. Such an approach would also have been strongly reinforced by contemporary works. Donatello's Paduan bronzes, for example, mediate such a "metallic" vision of the antique: Andrea, who spent years in Padua during his youth, must always have retained a vivid memory of those works, as well as of the way in which they influenced subsequent sculptural production in the city.[230]

Another aspect of artistic interest in the antique, one which has received a good deal of scholarly attention, is its relationship to the world of epigraphers, antiquarians, humanists and manuscript copyists: outstanding, among others, are the scholars Giovanni Marcanova, Ludovico Trevisan, Bartolomero Sanvito, Biagio Saraceno and Felice Feliciano. The interwoven relations of such individuals are essential to the reconstruction of Mantegna's interests in the *maiuscola antiquaria*.[231] To my mind, however, the study of Mantegna's line might yield an even deeper, more illuminating set of relationships. Scholars have yet to consider, for example, the way in which his capacity for the creation and reinvention of images—from nature, history and mythology—follows a system of marks amounting to the letters of an artistic alphabet, drawing its own rigorous (and almost abstract) internal discipline from the severe and elegant vestiges of ancient script.

The first phase of the proposed research project involves investigating and interpreting the system of lines employed in Mantegna's ink drawings and correlate them to the style of the seven engravings ascribed to him. From his very first years in Padua, the artist's graphic strategy remained basically consistent, even as it also underwent a clear evolution over time. The analysis cannot but start with the *St James Lead to Martyrdom* in the British Museum (inv. 1976-6-16-1 recto),[232] a work that constitutes the most representative example of his Paduan period and is also the only study so far traced in relation to the cycle of the Ovetari chapel. This drawing contains, in highly-concentrated form, a vast sampling of marks and lines that are also found in later sheets. Though the lines are combined with great complexity, cross-hatching is almost entirely absent.

In the last years of the 1470s and through the '80s, however, Mantegna's drawings are constructed of finer and less dispersed lines, which seem to emulate the technique of niello work. The effect is enhanced by dark backgrounds out of which the figures emerge prominently. I refer, in particular, to two sheets in the British Museum that were exhibited at the 1992 Mantegna exhibition and have from then on been much discussed, sometimes in relation to the engravings: *Man Lying on a Stone Slab* (inv. 1860-6-16-63) and *Madonna and Child Enthroned with Angels* (inv. 1858-7-24-3), not to mention a third drawing, the *Risen Christ between SS Andrew and Longinus* from the Staatliche Graphische Sammlung in Munich (inv. 3065), last shown in the 2006 exhibition in Verona together with the engraving for which it acts as a preparatory study. The dark background of the first two sheets as been related to the concept of *circonscrizione*, or circumscription, theorized by Leon Battista Alberti,[233] but I do not mean to discuss that here: it is an issue that needs to be considered in relation to the overall effect of Alberti's theoretical prescriptions on Mantegna, and scholars who have addressed this complex problem have arrived at very different conclusions.[234]

By the 1490s, Mantegna realizes what is perhaps his graphic masterpiece, the engraving of the *Madonna with Child* (B. XIII, 232, 8), in which a new, more luminous style is evident. Here the dialogue between graphic techniques associated with drawings and those associated with engravings reaches its full maturity.

The advances made by the Bolognese Francesco Francia seem to derive from Mantegna's later drawings and engravings. Francia was described in Beroaldo's *Commentary* on Apuleius' *Golden Ass* (1500) as *inter pictores aurifex maximus. Inter Aurifices pictor absolutissimus.*[235] Indeed, Francia is traditionally assigned a fundamental role in the development of the Bolognese *niello*-prints.[236] Together with Perugino, he is credited by Vasari with helping to bring about the transition to the "modern style". In the work of these two artists is reflected "a spirit of readiness" (*uno spirito di prontezza*) and above all "a harmonious sweetness in the colours" (*una dolcezza ne' colori unita*), so that, as we are told by the Aretine, "people ran like madmen to see this new and more life-like beauty, since it seemed to them that nothing better could ever be done" (*i popoli nel vederla corsero come matti a questa bellezza nuova e più viva, parendo loro assolutamente che e' non si potesse già mai far meglio*).[237]

The same *Commentary* by Beroaldo on Apuleius just mentioned contains one of the most revealing passages about Francia by any contemporary Bolognese intellectual. In a gloss on the expression "art emulates nature" (*ars aemula naturae*), the humanist pauses to praise the painter's stupefying capacity to emulate nature in two paintings commissioned by the Bentivoglio family in the 1490s: the *Adoration of the Child*, ordered by Antongaleazzo Bentivoglio at the end of 1498, today in the Pinacoteca in Bologna, and the *Madonna with Saints*, executed a few years earlier for Giovanni I, destined for the family chapel in San Giacomo Maggiore in Bologna.[238] It is not difficult to see here an anticipation of Vasari's understanding of the transition from the "second" to the "third style" (*maniera*).[239]

It was in the very workshop of Francia that Marcantonio Raimondi learned the art of engraving: he would subsequently give thorough study to the work of Dürer and, in the end, systematically introduce cross-hatching into his engravings in a manner that would succeed in transforming engraving into the medium most appropriate for verisimilar narrative, and that would, in turn, contribute to making it the most suitable instrument in the dissemination of the stylistic language of Raphael.

These formal considerations represent only the first phase of my research into Mantegna's line. The second will involve an examination of the relationship between written and iconic marks, considering them in the context of antiquarian interests, particularly in Padua. In the third and final phase, I will look to clarify the technical and stylistic means adopted by artists who employed linear systems different from that of Mantegna, at times simultaneously using cross-hatching and curved parallel lines that follow the roundness of natural forms, as one sees, for example, in Leonardo's *Leda* (Chatsworth, Devonshire Collection, inv. 717). I will be especially concerned with those artists engaged in the development of that specific kind of *imitatio* and/or *emulatio* of nature which Vasari identified as definitive of the "third style", and particularly with a nexus central to the development of such an emulative strategy in graphic art, the link between Mantegna, Dürer, and Raphael provided by the engravings of Marcantonio Raimondi.

In summary, parallel- and cross-hatching represent to two options within a language of marks that correspond to two different artistic orientations (art that *simulates* nature as opposed to art that is *imitative* or *emulative* of nature). These orientations, in turn, involve two different visions of the antique, conditioned by local cultural context and by different types of ancient remains. Within an "ideal" history of line, I would place Mantegna among the most innovative and individual strategists: his work upends the unidirectional trajectory from a "second" to "third" age modelled by Vasari. Taking his initial inspiration from statuary, as in *A Saint Reading* in the British Museum (inv. 1895-9-15-780);[240] or in *Three Saints* held by The Morgan Library (Thaw Collection, inv. 1985.100),[241] he moves on to the delicate style reminiscent of niello, and thence to a more advanced, luminous technique that achieves subtle effects of chiaroscuro by transforming line itself into a marker of light.

For Andrea, an artist of distinctive vision, capable of such masterful manipulation of his medium, the burin is equal to the pen. Indeed, the greater spontaneity and fluidity of the drawn line can be transformed into the durable fixity of the engraved one; the fleeting trace of pen on paper transformed into a permanent incised mark on the plate parallels the transformation of painting into sculpture. In Mantegna's language of marks there is still something more, however: dwelling on the subtle relationship between icon and description, the artist opts for what might be called a "written icon" or an "iconic inscription", a strategy that makes his art of line and mark, an instrument for the expression of a simulated nature, into one of the most original and least understood in the history of art. Mantegna's linear vocabulary is thus calculated to have the same descriptive efficacy as carved inscriptions. His style is not "dry, rough, and sharp" through too much study; rather, his study brought to it a truly personal understanding of the relationship between visual imagery and language—*ut pictura poēsis*—and a vision entirely to the advantage of painting, or even better, to that of the line and stroke sculpted in the simulated hardness of a material that changes its nature. Marks set down on paper or incised on metal, like words sculpted in stone, become the rudimentary traces of an antiquity recognized as lost even as it is subjected to intensive investigation. The next issue which such an approach to Mantegna's line must address is precisely this *simulatio* of the antique.

October 2006

Caroline van Eck
Architectural Theory, Systematicity, and Living Presence

In last year's Cork round table about the state of art history Robert Williams made a very convincing case for systematicity of representation as the basis of a consistent account of Renaissance art, but his optimism was not shared by many of the participants in the round table discussion. One of the recurring grounds for their unease was what may be designated in conceptual short-hand as the work of art's perceived living presence, the phenomenon studied by Julius von Schlosser, David Freedberg, James Elkins and most recently by Frank Fehrenbach, Fredrike Jakobs and a research group on " 'Art, Agency and Living Presence" at Leiden University funded by the Dutch Organization for Scientific Research (NWO). Such response, in which paintings, statues or buildings appear to be alive, and to act on the viewer in ways similar to that of persons, disrupts traditional art-historical and aesthetic ways of reacting to works of art as the objects of disinterested aesthetic appreciation, in which the viewing subject enjoys the free play of its cognitive and sensual faculties. A work of art's living presence acts upon the viewer, makes him or her treat the painting, building or statue as a sentient or even active being, and thereby disrupts "normal" enjoyment of art safely located in a museum vitrine, where it is robbed of its agency. As was also noted in this round table, there were a few conspicuous absences: European art historians, and architectural history. Being European and an architectural historian I won't venture into the reasons why there were no participants from this part of the world, but I would like to offer a few thoughts on systematicity from the perspective of Renaissance architectural theory, and try to discern a connection between the highly systematic architectural treatises of Daniel Barbaro and Vincenzo Scamozzi, which represent the peak of Renaissance attempts at discursive rationality in the arts, and the irrational irruption of living presence response to paintings, statues or buildings.

Systematicity in Vasari's *Proemio delle Vite*

The founding moment of Renaissance systematiciy of representation, one might well argue, occurs in Vasari's *Proemio delle Vite*, where he tersely states that God is the supreme creator of Nature and man. Man imitates his creator, and art results from his imitating God's creation, that is nature.[242] As he put it in the Life of Masaccio: "la pittura è un contrafar tutte le cose della natura viva".[243] Hence the artist should imitate not only the visible aspects of the created world—colour, light and shape—but also its underlying characteristics. God made "la natura viva", that is not a collection of inanimate objects, but a living whole. As such, nature may be defined in the terms Aristotle had identified as the characteristics of living organisms: the most fundamental of these is teleological unity of purpose, which manifests itself by the phenomenon that in living organisms nothing may be added or taken away without disturbing that teleological unity.[244] In other words, the structure of organisms can only be understood as based on a concept of the whole that preceeds, if not in time than at least logically, the actual creation or coming into being of the organism—what Kant in the 1790s would describe as the systematic unity of organisms as opposed to the aggregates of dead matter.[245] Motion, metabolism, sentience and procreation are the other characteristics of living organisms.[246]

Vasari was an Aristotelian in many respects. In the preface to the 1568 edition of the *Vite*, probably written with the help of Vincenzo Borghini and other members of the Accademia Fiorentina, Vasari had defined *disegno* as "[. . .] having its origin in the intellect, [it] draws out from many single things a general judgement, it is like a form or idea of all the objects in nature [. . .]."[247] This is an almost literal adaptation of Aristotle's definition of knowledge as derived from the senses in the Prologue of the *Metaphysics*. It is also a conceptual sleight of hand, through which Vasari manages to present drawing as an intellectual, cognitive activity. It is made possible through the use of Aristotle's hylomorphism, according to which it is form which not only gives shape, but also visible and knowable reality to matter. *Disegno* becomes both knowledge of the form of things, the *idea*, and the actual drawing by which the hand gives visible form to the intellectual concept or form. *Disegno* became the key to Vasari's theory and historiography of the arts, "the medium of the painter's very thought as well as its concrete espression".[248] Vasari also drew on Aristotle's *Nicomachaean Ethics* when he used the latter's distinctions between knowing, making and doing, and between *epistèmè* versus *doxa* in the realm of scientific knowledge, and *technè*, the kind of knowledge used in making things on the basis of knowledge of principles, to establish his own category of nontheoretical knowledge to define the understanding and intellectual skills characteristic of art.[249] But although he never explicitly described how he conceived of nature, it is clear that his view of nature as a living whole created by the supreme *artifex*, consisting of matter given shape and substance by the form imposed on it by God, and subject to the laws of birth, growth, flowering and decay, is that of a Catholic profoundly influenced by Aristotle.[250]

Systematicity in Renaissance architectural theory: Barbaro and Scamozzi

The architectural theorists Daniel Barbaro and Vincenzo Scamozzi went much further than Vasari in their attempts to systematize both architectural design and the discursive statement of its principles, architectural theory.[251] Both Barbaro's extensive commentaries on Vitruvius of 1556 and 1567—practically treatises in their own right—and Scamozzi's *Idea dell'Architettura Universale*, published in 1615, attempted to apply Aristotelian concepts of systematicity to architecture on various levels.[252] They incorporated architecture into the Aristotelian classification of all human pursuits and knowledge by defining it as a productive art; they assimilated it to logic and rhetoric by stressing its general and useful character, dealing like these two disciplines with all aspects of human life; and in the ultimate conceptual strategy of appropriation, like Leon Battista Alberti they drew on the opening words of Aristotle's *Metaphysics* to claim for architectural design the same status as discursive rationality, capable of grasping the truth hidden by appearance.

Vincenzo Scamozzi took this Aristotelian analysis of architecture to its limits. Book I of Scamozzi's *Idea* consists of an analysis of architecture in Aristotelian terms.[253] It takes Barbaro's intellectualization even further in that architectural design is presented here as a *scienza* as well. The imitative or operative arts, painting or sculpture for instance, imitate nature; they do not operate "per via delle cause", and therefore cannot offer any certain knowledge. But architecture, like mathematics, is a speculative science. As such, it is concerned with the general principles of cause and effect ruling all natural phenomena and human artefacts, whereas experience is concerned with individual events.[254] Its principles are derived from mathematics, in particular geometry, and to a lesser degree from the other liberal arts astronomy and music. The subject matter of this science is architectural design conceived as applied geometry: the manipulation of geometrical shapes and bodies by means of a ruler and scales, and based on general knowledge of the mathematical structure God has given to the universe. This knowledge is both constituted and communicated by means of drawing.

With an appeal to Vitruvius' distinction of *ratiocinatio* and *opus* Scamozzi, like Barbaro, distinguishes between architecture as *artificium*, that is the activity of building or *opus* in Vitruvian terms, and *architettura* in the sense of *ratiocinatio*, that is its theory and method. *Opus* or the activity of building is specifically architectural, but *ratiocinatio* is the complex of knowledge through which it is linked to all other scientific disciplines.[255] Architecture is therefore both an activity—building—and a science, because it consists of two parts: method and exercise or practice. Its method is based on mathematics, its practice consists of drawing and the execution of designs. The science of architecture shows how to build well and in such a way as to be praised, and teaches the principles of architectural design. Design starts with an idea in the mind of the architect; the builders who execute the design based on such ideas are as the hands of the architect.[256] Like Barbaro Scamozzi considered architecture to be much closer to mathematics and natural philosophy because of its speculative character and the forms it uses taken from geometry or the human body.

Architectural design thus becomes *ratiocinatio*, rational, discursive disquisition, which can use both words and images as a means of exposition: in the case of classical architecture, the rational is not restricted to the discursive, but can use the visual as well, as long as the architect follows the Vitruvian representational techniques of groundplan, *orthographia*, and *scaenographia*, whose truthfulness and rationality are ultimately founded on their use of geometry. At the same time their exposition of the principles of architectural design draws on various classical varieties of systematicity, using methods of exposition developed by Aristotle, Galen and Quintilian, and applying Aristotelian classifications of arts and sciences to structure their books.[257]

Classical design was always defined by its systematicity: in its use of a restricted range of forms—the orders and a few building types such as the temple, the stoa, the villa or the triumphal arch—and above all in the use of proportion based on the consistent use of a module. Barbaro and Scamozzi incorporated this design system into a discursive, theoretical system—a *Lehrgebäude*—that derived its unity from an Aristotelian view of what we would now call the arts and sciences as bodies of rational knowledge about the principles underlying cause and effect. The difference between a *technè* or *ars* in the Aristotelian sense and a craft is that the practitioner of the first knows why things turn out the way they do, whereas for the craftsman it will always be a matter of hit-or-miss. Bodies of knowledge derive their scientific character from the unity of the principles underlying them, and ultimately from the rational structure of the universe. Classical architecture's use of proportion is one expression of the belief in this feature of the world, and would be greatly elaborated by Renaissance theorists who claimed that God had endowed the universe with the same mathematical structure as man, and that the architect should impose these same qualities on his designs. Looking at systematicity in Barbaro and Scamozzi helps to elucidate how Vasari and other sixteenth-century theorists may have conceived nature when they wrote that imitating her is the main task of the arts.

Presence in the representational systeem

But this sixteenth-century concept of representational systematicity is not as stable as it looks. Imitating nature is its foundation. But, as Vasari observed, the business of painting is "un contrafar la natura viva": not just any natural form, but *living* nature. Should the artist go so far as to equal God and nature, that is create works of art that actually live? Vasari often seems to think so, but at the same time he records how such works of art could make viewers very uneasy. The best-known case of this is the reaction of the Bolognese painter Francesco Francia, who, upon opening the case containing Raphael's *Saint Cecilia*, became half mad with terror at the sight of "la tavola di Raffaello divina, e non dipinta ma viva". Having realized as well that he would never equal the genius of Raphael, he took to his bed and died soon afterwards. It is a classic case of a work of art turning into a living presence. At the height of its power art ceases to look like art. It no longer inspires aesthetic delight in the artist's *disegno* or handling of colour, but terror, desire or even death itself, as the Latin epigram by Fiviziano illustrates that Vasari quoted to conclude his *Life of Francia*. By gazing too long at his image of death, the painter dies, but the painting of death continues to live:

> Dumque opere in facto defigit lumina pictor
> Intentus nimium palluit et moritur.
> Viva igitur sum mors non morta mortis imago
> Si fungor quo mors fungitur officio.[258]

> [While the painter fastens his eyes on his work
> too fixed in his gaze he becomes pale and dies.
> I am therefore living death, not a lifeless image of death
> If I perform death's task]

The same dialectic between inanimate works of art that appear to be alive and living and sentient viewers that are turned into lifeless stone is recorded in the early responses to the rediscovery of the Laocoön in 1506. In the Latin poem by Jacopo Sadoleto, for instance, the sculptors are praised because they were able to render rigid stone animate with living figures and endow the marble with living senses.[259] As a result the beholder sees movement, anger and grief, and almost hears the groans of Laocoön and his sons. This may be described as a typical, not very original example of the cliché of the work of art that seems to breathe, a recurrent motif in classical and Renaissance descriptions of art works. But many poems offer unexpected twists. The poem by Elio Lampridio Cervo opens by exclaiming that "the stone image lies true colours", in an interesting ungrammatical transitive use of the verb "to lie", which here takes an object, viz the true colours of the statue.[260]

In Evangelista Maddaleni de'Capodiferro's Latin poem it is not the poet, but Laocoön himself who speaks: "Laocoön I am". Then in the course of the poem the speaker is transformed from the person into the statue: "you will say, when you look at me, that the pains are real for the stone, and that death and fear are not fictive for my sons". But in a very clever twist at the end the poem plays on the phenomenon of the statue's silent cries that would receive so much attention in Lessing's essay on the *Laöcoon*: "If the sculptors who were able to give death and fear and living grief to stone could also endow it with a voice and soul, they would have refused, because it is more wondrous to struggle, suffer, beg, lament, fear and die without voice and without soul".[261]

Antonio Tebaldi also lets the statue speak: "I am Laocoön, so expressive and alive/that, if you are not made of the material/out of which I am made and my sons, I will make of your eyes a sorrowful river".[262] That is, this statue is so lifelike that it could transform a stone viewer into a living being overcome by pity. In some poems the poet plays on the theme of life and death in an almost Baroque or Metaphysical manner, recalling Fiviziano's epigram: death, or rather mortality, is presented as the supreme sign of life. Pushing the oscillation between marble and flesh, life and death even further, the poet Cerva describes the action of the serpent, wounding the father, strangling the son: "you could believe that the stones are bitten, strike, die": the vulnerability and mortality of the marble is the ultimate sign of life.[263] And in the most pre-Metaphysical twist of all, Giovanni Paolo Lancelotti addresses Laocoön, again identifying the person with the statue: "Cease, Laocoon, to lament in a sad voice/that the serpents kill you with their lethal tongues./For Death [. . .] forbids you ever to die."[264] The statue of the Laocoön is not only an extremely vivid and lifelike work of art; it was also capable of acting, like a person, on its viewers. Anton Francesco Doni observed that when a spectator sees it, he is so overcome by compassion that he feels compelled to adopt the pose of Laocoön.[265]

Now it could be argued that such extreme lifelikeness, bordering on what might be termed a magical presence of life, is restricted to the figurative arts. Buildings do not excite such response, and therefore architecture is not relevant when thinking about Vasari's foundation of the systematicity of representation in the imitation of *la natura viva*. But buildings did appear to share important characteristic with living persons to Renaissance viewers. In Filarete's *Trattato* their physicality is stressed. Buildings share with the living human body mortality and sickness, metabolism, the need to be nourished, and they come into being in a way that very much resembles human procreation, because the architect is the mother who for nine months carries around in him the design that ultimately will become a fully grown building.[266] Renaissance theorists thus attributed corporality to buildings, but in a very different manner from the analogy between the mathematical proportions shared by the universe, the human body and the building which Rudolf Wittkower saw as the defining characteristic of Renaissance religious architecture.

Renaissance builders, patrons and viewers also attributed the characteristics usually reserved for living persons to buildings. They credited *palazzi* with the personality traits of their owners, and hurt, wooed, or destroyed buildings with the aim of thereby acting on their inhabitants. Patrons sometimes had horoscopes cast to determine the right date to start building, just as they did when a child was born.[267] In literary accounts, such as Alberti's *Templum*, the foundations of a house rise up in anger at the immoral behaviour of the inhabitants.[268] These fictions of buildings that live have been very little investigated. They suggest connections with the sublime, which can be defined as an experience of extreme, disruptive rhetorical vividness or *enargeia*. They also bring to mind the architectural uncanny, which builds on the presence of life where there ought to be only inanimate matter, of which the vacant, staring eyes of the house of Usher in Edgar Allan

Poe are an early instance, and Gordon Matta Clark's haunted sectional elevations of houses a late descendant.

An excess of counterfeit

Practically all these cases of architectural living presence play in some way on an equation between the house and the family, that is, between the man-made and natural life. When statues or paintings become living beings to their viewers they suffer from what might be described as an excess of *hypotyposis*. As Vasari tells us, Raphael was unsurpassed in the imitation of nature because he was able to achieve an union of colour, in which there were no harsh contrasts, but all shadings were calibrated and connected as they are in living beings. But the moment a human being dies the colour of the skin becomes too harshly white, as can be seen in the contrast between the colour of Christ's dead arms and hands those of Mary and St John the Evangelist in Giovanni Bellini's *Brera Pietà*. When a painter becomes too successful in what might be described in rhetorical terms as *hypotyposis*, the detailed painting in words aiming at vivid presence or *enargeia, contrafar la natura viva* becomes too detailed, too refined and too sophisticated, and thereby destroys the representational character of art. At the height of systematic representation of nature, the very systematicity, that is discursive rationality, of art is destroyed and tilts back, one might say, into what such rationality has tried to replace: the fascination with living presence that borders on the magical, and is certainly not rational.

Looking at the way the sixteenth-century architectural theorists Barbaro and Scamozzi tried to articulate an account of architectural design as a systematic activity based on an equally systematic definition of nature, which would be the subject matter of an equally systematic architectural theory, may help to understand the Aristotelian underpinnings of many sixteenth-century concepts of nature, because Barbaro and Scamozzi were much more explicit about this than Vasari, his Florentine colleagues, or Lomazzo. At the same time, confronting these attempts at a system of representation with what happens when art is too successful in representing nature, shows why living presence response is such a worry to art history: it is a reaction to the Renaissance artistic systematicity at the height of its suggestive powers, but at the same time disrupts the discursive rationality on which these powers were based.

Robert Zwijnenberg

Mirroring the Renaissance: Reflections on a New Historical Approach to Leonardo

Introduction

Somewhere in the conversation among the seven art historians at the Art Seminar in Cork, Robert Williams dismissed the French philosopher and historian of art Georges Didi-Huberman with the following observation: "Didi-Huberman says some perceptive things about Vasari's concept of disegno, but in the end he uses it as a foil to set up his own post-rationalist, Freudian approach to images." And when later in the conversation James Elkins suggested that art historians run the risk of being "lost" in time (because "The sense of history that you are inside of is the one that is hardest to see") Williams declares emphatically: "Not 'lost' in time, perhaps just 'untimely.' If what I've said about the Renaissance is true, then I have succeeded as a historian whether I fit into current trends or not." To me, this exchange reveals an intriguing divide between two kinds of art historians: on the one hand, those who believe in at least the ideal possibility of an interpretative position outside the continuum of history, outside of time, an "untimely" position from which it is possible to make true statements about the Renaissance unaffected or untainted by "current trends". On the other hand, there are art historians who, as Claire Farago, another participant in the Cork conversation, remarks, "have been fundamentally concerned with the complexity of being faced with a work of art from another time. How do you understand it? There is always going to be a gap, and just thinking about that brings together a number of possible common points in contemporary approaches."

Farago points to an approach which involves reflection on the history of art, its theories and methods, and its relation to contemporary intellectual life. Since the origins of the discipline of art history in the nineteenth century, its borders have been fluid. Art history absorbed theories and methods from other fields such as philosophy, film and gender studies, and, of course, history; and in turn it influenced them. The history of art history itself reflects the intellectual history of the last two centuries. What counts as an art historical object and how it is to be approached and interpreted depends upon the intellectual and cultural background of the art historian involved. For this reason, a work of art is more than merely its reconstructed history, and the interpretation of a work of art must activate the self-reflexive capacity of art historical inquiry. Didi-Huberman is an art historian who makes his own position in time—and the reflection on this position—an explicit element of his historical writings, as, for instance, his book about Fra Angelico. Didi-Huberman "seeks to disrupt chronology, a radical reorganization of chronological art history"—as Elkins puts it—out of a strong conviction that art history as a discipline is always "in time", never untimely; he thereby acknowledges—on a fundamental, theoretical level—our own inescapable presence in our historical explorations.

The *fecundity of anachronism* became clear to me as I studied Leonardo da Vinci's manuscripts. I found it particularly difficult to understand the interconnectedness of Leonardo's thoughts and activities, or—to rephrase it in Farago's words quoted earlier—I experienced a gap between my historical position and that of Leonardo, one that hindered me in gaining intellectual access to this "interconnectedness", even though the experience of this gap was an important stimulus to my engagement with Leonardo in the first place. I could not agree more with Farago when she says that: "we're becoming more aware of ruptures that are always present. There is no other way to proceed to the Otherness. It is probably an important aspect of why people become historians: they become fascinated with the Otherness of past times."

What exactly was my problem in my historical understanding of Leonardo?

Leonardo left behind approximately 6500 sheets with text and drawings in notebooks or in loose-leaf collections, as well as a dozen paintings. Art historians from the nineteenth century onwards have approached Leonardo as *the* model Renaissance artist, producing paintings and drawings, which they interpreted with the help of their own era's art historical tool kit. Historians of science have shown in what ways Leonardo's thought as reflected in his notebooks links up with mediaeval philosophy of nature. A number of excellent studies published in recent decades not only illuminate and analyze his multifarious and original activities as an anatomist, engineer, architect, and inventor, but they also argue that the views of older Leonardo experts, who considered him a precursor of Galileo or one of the first modern scientists, have become untenable.[269] Although the apparent interconnectedness of Leonardo's thought and his various activities is considered in more or less elaborate ways by all historians writing on Leonardo, our contemporary notions of art and science as separate activities hamper an intellectual understanding of this interconnectedness. We simply lack the concepts to describe what it means to Leonardo that *Mona Lisa* is as much a painting affecting the spectator at the profoundest level of emotional response as it is the outcome of his anatomical and geological investigations.[270] We may describe the intellectual coincidence of Leonardo's artistic ideas and activities and his philosophy of nature from the outside, as visually reflected in, for instance, *Mona Lisa*, but it is far more difficult to penetrate this particular coincidence intellectually than to retrieve the meaning of his paintings by a purely art-historical study or, for that matter, to analyze his anatomical drawings from the perspective of the history of science, in order to see how much he did or did not move away from Galen.

In this essay, I want to begin to establish an intellectual understanding of Leonardo as someone for whom everything was connected to everything, every idea to all possible ideas, and every activity a non-hierarchical element of all the activities he performed in his life.[271] I want to do so without returning to the mythical concept of the unity of science and art, lost today but supposedly alive in Leonardo's time. And in response to the Cork conversation about the fate of Renaissance studies I seek an answer in which art history itself is also at stake, in the sense that I confess to the necessity of anachronism as an indispensable art-historical tool. I start with three observations that will set my story in motion.

In a book on Shakespeare's lives in which the author follows the historical quest for "Shakespeare the man" in the various lives of Shakespeare written since his death, Desmond McCarthy is quoted saying that "trying to work out Shakespeare's personality was like looking at a very dark glazed picture in the National Gallery: at first you see nothing, then you begin to see features, and then you realize that they are your own."[272] This claim of course testifies to the well-known fact that biography tends towards oblique self-portraiture or biographers' recurring self-identification with their subject.

Svetlana Alpers, in observing that the most penetrating analysis of *Las Meninas* is that of a philosopher (Foucault's introduction to *Les mots et les choses*, published in 1966), argues that this fact demonstrates the inadequacy of the standard interpretive methods of art history for analyzing a complex painting such as *Las Meninas*.[273]

Georges Didi-Huberman tells the story of how he was stopped in his tracks by a fresco in the convent of San Marco in Florence, painted around 1440 by Fra Angelico. This fresco is situated at eye level in the eastern corridor of the cloister, just below a *sacra conversazione*: "a blaze of colour which still bears the trace of its original spurt (the pigment was projected from a distance like rain in the fraction of a second) and which, since then, has assumed permanence as a constellation of fixed stars." After discussing that this non-mimetic fresco has hardly received any attention in art historical literature on Fra Angelico, Didi-Huberman argues that its emergence as historical object, as object of art-historical consideration, could not have been the result of a standard *historical approach*, but only of an almost aberrant *anachronistic moment*. He describes this moment as a kind of *displaced resemblance* between what he discovered in a Renaissance convent and the drippings of the American artist Pollock, which he discovered and admired many years before.[274] For Didi-Huberman the history of art is itself an anachronistic discipline, and that he is not alone in taking full advantage of the possibilities of an anachronistic approach becomes abundantly clear in Mieke Bal's *Quoting Caravaggio* (1999). To Bal the past does not determine the present, but the present determines the uniqueness of the past and its contemporary significance.[275]

What if we accept that our own presence in our historical explorations—a presence so disturbing to many art historians—cannot be avoided, that the past mirrors our own features and that we need more than the art-historical tool kit to discover the meaning of a work of art? What if we take advantage of the insights of McCarthy, Alpers, and Didi-Huberman in trying to come closer to an understanding of Leonardo's work, an understanding not motivated by the return to a kind of mythical, long lost unity of art and science? After all, such unity never existed in Leonardo's time, nor are there any signs that in our days such unity is bound to arise. And, finally, what if we take contemporary art forms to function as *displaced resemblances* in Didi-Huberman's sense, that is, art forms such as kinetic sculptures and body-art, as in the work of Stelarc, and so-called "sci-art"? The latter refers to the work of a growing number of contemporary artists who incorporate scientific objects and practices—such as tissue culture, brain imaging—into their works of art.[276]

Of course, Leonardo is in no way a precursor of these recent forms of art, nor, of course, can these contemporary art forms be used for an adequate interpretation of Leonardo's works. However, by taking the *displaced resemblances* between Leonardo's work and these contemporary forms of art seriously, Leonardo's work will perhaps emerge as a new kind of art-historical object—one that in fact invites an "anachronistic" approach and that accommodates the intellectual presence of the interpreter. Such an approach might allow us to come to a better understanding of the essential interconnectedness of Leonardo's thoughts and activities.

Leonardo's mirror room

Let us first look at a drawing by Leonardo. One of his notebooks (ms. B, folio 28r—circa 1487–90) contains a tiny sketch (measuring some 2 by 4.5 cm) of a device that is best described as a mirror room. Under the drawing Leonardo wrote: "If you have eight flat mirrors, each 2 braccia wide and 3 high, and have them placed in a circle so as to form eight sides of 16 braccia circumference and 5 of diameter, that man who will stand inside will be able to see each side of himself an infinite number of times."[277] The person standing inside this contraption is confronted very directly—through infinite reflections on all sides—with his or her self.

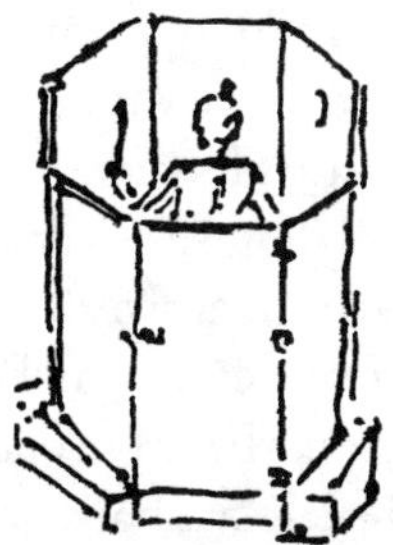

In all respects this is a sketch of a remarkable machine. First, it demonstrates Leonardo's indebtedness to scientific and technological knowledge from antiquity and the Middle Ages. In general, Leonardo's manuscripts show clear traces of his knowledge of medieval philosophy of nature, while also demonstrating he was well acquainted with ancient and medieval technology. Moreover, many of his drawings of technological inventions have their roots in older examples.[278]

The same is true of Leonardo's mirror room. The very notion of a room with mirroring walls, often consisting of polished marble, is very old indeed: Pliny already described one in his *Natural History*, XXXIII, 45.[279] Leonardo may have read about the concept of a mirror room in Herod of Alexandria's *De Speculis*, a text he knew. After the sixteenth century, when it became possible to produce glass mirrors of considerable size, the *cabinets de glace* were a well-known phenomenon especially in French houses and palaces: the *Salon des glaces* at Versailles is the best-known, but Catherine de Médicis had a famous *cabinet de miroirs* installed much earlier, following the death of Henri II.[280] Leonardo's drawing of a mirror room, then, can be considered as just another depiction of a familiar cultural idea or device that has a long tradition, one that even lives on into our own day and age, as evidenced, for instance, in the halls of mirrors one can find in luxurious department stores.

This small and seemingly insignificant drawing by Leonardo— insignificant in comparison to the beautiful and detailed drawings of machines and technological devices elsewhere in his notebooks— may still have been very important to him, especially when we consider the enormous cultural meaning of mirrors in the Renaissance.

At that time the mirror was all but a simple artifact. From antiquity onwards, mirrors have been replete with (cultural) meanings—meanings that also touched on a wide range of contexts. For one thing, mirrors were seen as stimulating self-reflection and passing on self-knowledge; they could represent wisdom and rational thinking, but they could also suggest deception. Epistemologically, mirrors revealed truth as well as error. Mirrors evoked the presence of an alter ego, but they also functioned as symbol of vanity.[281] The mirror was a popular theme in medieval and Renaissance painting, epitomizing the vice of Vanity but in some cases also the virtue of Prudence.[282] The metaphor of the eye as a mirror was also very popular in both the Middle Ages and the Renaissance, and it had various connotations. Furthermore, following a neo-platonic line of thought, mirrors provoked various magic practices, and occasionally they were seen as instruments of the devil. Leonardo was undoubtedly aware of this profusion of meanings, some of them being directly visible in fragments of his manuscripts. In designing his mirror room Leonardo perhaps reflected on these meanings.

Although it is not immediately clear from the drawing if Leonardo had mirrors of glass in mind, we know that he experimented with them.[283] This is why we have some reason to believe his room was intended to be constructed of glass mirrors. However, mirrors of the size suggested by the drawing and that allowed one to see one's entire body (*Specula totis paria corporibus*, as Seneca referred to them, and about which also Rabelais fantasized in *Gargantua*)[284] could not be made of glass yet in Leonardo's time: it became possible only by the end of the seventeenth century, while it was not until the nineteenth century that widespread diffusion of large, full-length mirrors took place. If this drawing has any meaning at all, then, apart from being a depiction of the well-known idea of a hall of mirrors, it has meaning as a thought experiment—one Leonardo proposed to himself.

As such the sketch is also a very special autobiographical document. Assuming that Leonardo intended the person standing in the machine not to be capable of looking upward and over the mirrors (as is clear from the sketch), and assuming that he designed this machine for his own use, we can conclude that Leonardo was no taller or slightly smaller than 3 brachia (which is about 1.74 m). The sketch, in other words, tells us something about his body height, something about which we have no information from other historical sources

At first sight it is difficult to tell whether this mirror room, even as a thought experiment, was intended for theoretical investigations and experimentation or that it was meant to serve other purposes. For example, Leonardo's interest in optics might account for his designing the device. In his optical studies, mirrors played an important role,[285] and this "machine" would allow him to experiment with the radiation of rays of light. It seems as if the person standing in the machine is holding a stick, which is possibly functioning as an instrument in his investigations.

Leonardo may also have invented this device to learn something about the human body, the structure and movements of which were intensely fascinating to him. We know that he performed a number of dissections with which he tried to understand, among other things, the body's mechanics: how it moves through the action of particular muscles and tendons.[286] The mirror room not only allows us to see parts of our body that are normally difficult or impossible to see—the back of our head, for example—but also offers us a much more dynamic spectacle than is available when standing before a single flat mirror or when having no mirror at all. It is as if in the mirror room we can capture in one glance and better understand the whole exterior of our body with all its movements. In this contraption, experiments become possible not only with movement, but also, and more generally, with appearance, with what the body looks like from all sides—experiments that are not possible in other conditions.

For Leonardo, this kind of knowledge about optical phenomena and bodily movements was crucial to the art of painting. Moreover, the knowledge conveyed by the mirror room could easily be applied. Even if we conceive of the mirror room primarily as a site for experimentation in the field of optics and anatomy, it would have been useful to Leonardo for painterly purposes as well.

Considering the uncertainty about Leonardo's intentions, I propose that we consider the mirror room as a thought experiment about a site of experimentation as such, since the experiment is about itself. Or, put differently: in his drawing of the mirror room Leonardo is reflecting on the interaction between experimenter and experimental device, on his own corporal position in relation to technological devices, and on how in this interaction his body is mediated by such a device. He thus capitalizes on the many cultural meanings of the mirror, especially its epistemological potential, its ability to engage the profoundly important values of self-reflection and self-knowledge. In what follows, I will elaborate this idea.

Mona Hatoum's *Corps étranger*

To understand the mirror room from the perspective of the interaction between man and machine, or rather, from the perspective of the mediation between body and image, I have to step inside. This means that I take Leonardo's drawing seriously as a thought experiment. My contention is that the drawing can only be understood properly if I somehow try to re-enact the thought experiment that the device provokes. To experience and understand a contraption by intellectually and physically entering it is something I know from my experience with twentieth-century installation art. Unlike any other art form, installation art has made the beholder acutely aware of the fact that beholding a work of art is an intellectual as well as bodily activity and experience. In installation art, intellectual detachment can never fully conceal or make us entirely forget that we have a body that interferes with or gets in the way of our intellectual perception. In installation art the body as active beholder is implied. I am capable of appreciating Leonardo's mirror room as a site of experimentation as such only because I, as a twenty-first-century art historian, have knowledge of and experience with installation art.

This is indeed what struck me when I encountered Mona Hatoum's remarkable video installation *Corps étranger* (1994), a work produced with the assistance of a surgeon. The video presents what might be called a self-portrait through the use of medical imaging techniques such as endoscopy, colonoscopy, and ultrasound. The installation consists of a cylindrical space the viewer must enter in order to see the show. The video is projected onto the floor and accompanied by the sound of the artist's heartbeat and other bodily noises. The video images show close-ups of the artist's skin and the inner cavities of her body. The camera circles around body orifices, enters and explores them, then moves on. One sees soft, glowing colors, shiny surfaces, and sensuous images of what at the same time remains abject. The ambience is made even more claustrophobic and disturbing by the sounds of the body, also recorded. The viewer must enter a space representing a body—a foreign body—in order to see the video, so that his or her entire body is inside the images of someone else's body. Standing in the installation, you experience a sense of the reversibility of inside and outside, as if your own body has been turned inside-out. The transgression of the inside/outside boundary is the work's primary concern. Hatoum challenges the notion of limits: limits between the inside and the outside of the body, between self and other, between permanence and decay, between present and past. In this installation, she evokes the feelings of intimacy and physical danger that characterize our understandings of the body.[287] As in Leonardo's mirror room, this work achieves the integration of performance and representation.

In *Corps étranger*, Hatoum reflects on our experience of our own inner, living body, made possible by medical visualization technology. Before 1895 a visual experience of your *own* body's interior was impossible. In that year, Wilhelm Röntgen developed a way of representing the inside of a living body without having to cut it open. Of course there had always been some knowledge of the inside of the body: by dissecting a dead body, for instance, one could see and gain knowledge of *someone else's* interior organs. Gaining direct knowledge or visual experience of the inside of one's *own* body, however, was usually—except under extreme conditions—beyond reach. A direct, visual confrontation with the inside of one's body in fact involves one of the oldest taboos known in human culture. Even modern surgeons are careful to shield any possible sight of what is beneath our skin when performing an operation on us.[288] Consequently, the ways in which we experience the inside of our body still differ greatly from our experience the exterior. We hardly have any direct knowledge of that what is most intimate, our inner body. We feel our heart beating, we hear our blood singing, we experience fresh oxygen being sucked into our lungs, and sometimes we even perceive the sounds of our digestive system, but we have no direct access to or exact knowledge of what is in the interior of our own body. This is why we often consider the inside of our body as abject and uncanny.

The development of X-ray technology and, more importantly, the recent development of medical visualization techniques such as ultrasound and various forms of scanning (CT, MRI and PET) have granted our eyes access to the interior body. For instance, in an endoscopic procedure a little video camera is inserted into the body either via one of its natural orifices or through a small incision in the skin. This technique provides live video images on a television screen; it allows us to see the inside of our body in full color and in real time. Anyone with personal experience of such a procedure as patient knows how difficult it is to establish a meaningful relationship between the image on the screen and your inner body as something lived and felt. Although you know you are watching your inner body, it is very difficult and most of the time impossible to experience the images as images of *your* inner body.

It is remarkable that in contemporary art so many artists make use of medical visualization techniques such as endoscopy. In some of these works, artists meditate on the new, direct and visual experience of their own bodily interior. In doing so, they add meaning—cultural meaning—to this new technological experience, a mediation of the body that did not exist until very recently. This suggests that art may help us to transform this new experience, rooted in medical practice and a scientific context, into an experience that has meaning in our daily life, in our experience of what we are as human beings. My assumption here is that this new visual experience of the inside of our body is mediated by art in ways that differ from how such experience is mediated in a hospital situation.

In Mona Hatoum's installation, the visitor is able to incorporate as a meaningful experience something that has always been unthinkable, ineffable, non-presentable and abject, and impossible to attain: the visual image of the interior of a living body. *Corps étranger* liberates, so to speak, the endoscopic technology from its instrumental function as a medical procedure. As a result, endoscopy is transformed from the realm of medico-scientific technology into a that of a technology with wider cultural meaning. Hatoum's installation inserts the endoscopic technology into our lived experience; it imbues medical images of our inner body with fresh meaning, so that we may incorporate these images into our existence and they can thus become part of our image of our own body. By representing parts of the body that artists could not have seen without the mediation of the video camera, Hatoum reconstitutes them as both culturally visible and meaningful.

Body and devices in Leonardo's work

Leonardo's manuscripts contain a number of drawings of a man inside a device or as part of a device, most involving some kind of flying machine. The interaction between man and machine varies between, on the one hand, the person involved as active and controlling the machine, and, on the other hand, the person being passive and subordinate, as in Leonardo's famous drawing of a man hanging under a parachute or in a drawing—found in his Codex *On the Flight of Birds*, f. 16r—of wine skins wrapped around a man to prevent him from injury when falling from a height of 6 braccia.[289]

These two ends of the spectrum of the interaction between man and machine are clearly visible in two drawings on one page of the Madrid Codex I, f. 64r. The upper drawing represents a *ventola*, perhaps one of Leonardo's finest and most intriguing inventions. It consists of three wooden rings with a diameter of about twelve meters that are set at right angles. In Leonardo's words, written under the drawing: "Let there be constructed a device like that drawn here, which is made of sendal [a thin silk fabric], ropes, canes, and shafts, and [that] has a diameter of 20 braccia or more. Place a perforated ball made from hoops of green elm in its middle. The ball shall be arranged like the box of the compass; and let a man be placed in its centre. If the instrument is exposed to the winds at the top of a hill, it will follow the course of the winds while the man will always remain upright."

In the most obvious sense, this apparatus is a vehicle, driven by the wind, in which a person can travel more or less comfortably—while standing upright—and gaze at the world around. The traveler in the *ventola* is the defenseless center of the construction; he is subject to natural forces that could easily destroy the vehicle with him in it. He surrenders to the *ventola* and to nature; blown forth by the wind he can do nothing but gaze at the landscape as it unfolds before him; he must passively undergo whatever happens. The *ventola* traveler will experience powerlessness physically; he will be acutely aware of his body as something controlled and acted upon by outside forces.[290] On the lower half of the same page is a drawing of a so-called glider. It depicts a device from which a person hangs while flying, blown forth by the wind. In this case, Leonardo took care to indicate how the operator can control it and even how one might make a landing. In contrast to the *ventola*, this device can be actively managed: it is an extension of the body, subject to the aviator's will as expressed in his bodily movements. The pilot does not find himself entirely at the mercy of nature but glides over it, asserting at least partial independence of it.

On this page of the Madrid Codex, Leonardo is thus meditating, among other things, on the two ends of the spectrum regarding the interaction between man and machine, active and passive. This same distinction is also fundamental to the drawing of the mirror room. Standing in the middle of this room would be a very dazzling experience. It would be difficult, at first, to get a handle on the infinite reflections of your body, which would change with every movement you made. It would be a challenge to focus on just one reflection or to understand the precise relationship between the reflections and your body. Partly because you would be having to deal for the first time with "impossible" views of your body, you might find it hard to distinguish between your body and its reflections. It might take some time before you are able to understand your body as the cause of the reflections. You would have to withdraw into yourself in order to recover some sense of yourself as a physical entity in the midst of an all-encompassing spectacle. The initial disorientation would thus bring about a heightened awareness of your self as center, as the midpoint of a centrifugal force that seems to change and penetrate the mirrors. At the same time, however, this awareness would probably be accompanied by a strong feeling of being imprisoned by your own reflections. This feeling would be strengthened by the fact that you would not be able to control your reflections completely. Every movement would be multiplied and exaggerated and the initial effect might well be frightening, as if the reflections had a life of their own.

To enter the mirror room would be to have your identity both challenged and consolidated. By extending the visual field of sight and revealing things that would be impossible to see any other way, the mirror room questions the relation between appearance and reality, and thus demands an exercise of critical faculties. If the mirror room is an instrument of reflection, it also offers itself as a *model* of reflection; standing in it would involve an experiment in reflective thought.

As a result of this complicated experience in the mirror room of Leonardo—an experience that in his case could only take place as a thought experiment—it becomes possible to reflect on the two most basic modes of experiencing your own body. To understand these two basic modes I use an old phenomenological distinction, elaborated by philosophers such as Maurice Merleau-Ponty and Helmut Plessner: the distinction between the body as subject of experience and the body as object of experience. We *have* a body and we *are* a body. Because of the body as subject of experience (our *being* a body) we are able to experience not only the world outside of us, but also our body *as* object (our *having* a body). When I act, I can use my body as a means to achieve what I was aiming to achieve. In this respect, I *have* my body in its instrumentality, as one *thing* among other things. I can see my body as a thing in the external world among all the other things that I can make use of. With the body I *have*, I occupy a certain place in the world. I *am* this body that allows me my place in the world. Above all, I will only be able to live *as* a body and *in* my body if I am actually capable of giving shape to the relationship between "having a body" and "being a body". In normal circumstances, in ordinary life, we somehow manage to bring about this relationship; normally, we do not experience a split between "having a body" and "being a body". In the mirror room as experimental site, the reflecting mirrors evoke this split, even though after a while a meaningful relationship between "having a body" and "being a body" can be restored by the experimenter, which results in a deeper insight in these two basic modes of experiencing one's body.

Being in the mirror room thus involves a double experience. On the one hand, I have to withdraw radically into my body as subject of experience in order to get a hold on the infinite, dynamic spectacle of reflections. On the other, I have all views of my body at my disposal in a single moment—I can even see myself looking at my body—and, as a consequence, I will intensely experience my body as object.

With his drawing of the mirror room Leonardo created space for a thought experiment that would allow him to isolate and understand the two basic modes of experiencing our body, modes that also under-lie the interaction between man and machine. These basic modes indeed constitute the basis for our bodily being and place in the world. I would conclude, therefore, that Leonardo's sketch is a depic-tion of his position in the world, on a corporeal, emotional, and intellectual level, and of the way in which a technological device might help him to relate to the world by mediating his body.

In a wonderful essay about the experience of his own body, Foucault seems to describe and explain the bodily and intellectual experience that Leonardo's mirror room evokes in a very succinct way: "Incomprehensible body, penetrable and opaque body, open and closed body, utopian body. Absolutely visible body, in one sense. . . . And yet this same body, which is so visible, is also withdrawn, cap-tured by a kind of invisibility from which I can never really detach it. This skull, the back of my skull, I can feel it, right there, with my fingers. But see it? Never. This back which I can feel leaning against the pressure of the mattress, against the couch when I am lying down, and which I might catch but only by the ruse of the mirror. And what is this shoulder, whose movements and positions I know with precision, but that I will never be able to see without dreadfully contorting myself? The body—phantom that only appears in the mirage of the mirror, and then only in fragmentary fashion."[291]

Conclusion

This text by Foucault and the artwork by Hatoum, both as *displaced resemblances*, project me right into the heart of Leonardo's mirror room. There my body is mediated by technology, and in this medi-ation I experience it in its two principal modes. This experience makes it possible for me to incorporate the impossible views of my body into the image I have of my own body, albeit in only fragmentary fashion.

After having experienced Mona Hatoum's installation, it has become possible for me, as a twenty-first-century art historian, to comprehend that the structure of Leonardo's installation is based on what could be called a psychological situation of "self-encapsulation" that turns the body and psyche into its own surround, cutting it off from any external object.[292] The mirror room is a feedback device that involves the viewer in a closed loop of vision. The optical illusion it creates is an unstable one, however: Leonardo must have known that a room designed to hold eight mirrors (as opposed to, say, six) would have an especially dramatic fragmenting effect on the reflected images of his body.[293] In other words, he fully intended the fragmentary and fragmenting space of the mirror room, i.e. the deconstruction of the image of wholeness of his body, including its impossible views. What the mirror room mediates is a dimension of our bodily experience that remains unavailable to us outside the installation—one that any other account of corporal "reality" fails to include.

Mirrors are associated with directness, immediacy, and presence. When I am standing in front of a mirror, the image is immediately there and there is a convincing and, even more importantly, inescapable synchronicity between the movements I know or feel I am making with my limbs and the movements I see in the mirror. Above all, my presence in front of the mirror is needed to produce an image; the mirror cannot produce an image of somebody or something that is not present in the optical vicinity of the mirror. In the mirror room this directness, immediacy, and presence is both confirmed and challenged. The mirror is a site of cultural articulation of the subject, a surface on which the body takes on a *meaningful* shape.

My consideration of Mona Hatoum's *Corps étranger* is not meant to support the conclusion that this installation can explain Leonardo's mirror room or that in any way Leonardo is a precursor of twentieth-century installation art. Rather, this detour served the purpose of creating a specific *anachronistic moment*, one that allowed me to conceive of the mirror room as an historical object in which the experience of the body, the body of Leonardo, is at the very center. All its meanings—anatomical, optical, artistic—are secondary to the way in which it enables him to experience his own body, to its relevance as a technological tool that helps him relate his body to the world by mediating and making visible what he cannot otherwise see or understand, even if only in fragmentary fashion. This conclusion opens up a new *historical* approach of Leonardo in which the experience of the human body in the world—that is, in nature, in society, in natural philosophy, in technology, in religion—needs to be considered as the starting point and driving force of Leonardo's studies of nature and man. We need to approach Leonardo's ideas and activities involving art and the philosophy of nature by looking at how he articulates the experience of his body in his texts, paintings, and drawings, in order to understand the interconnectedness of his various activities.

This brings me back to the Cork conversation and the dismissive responses to Didi-Huberman. James Elkins, concerned that Didi-Huberman's work is ignored by the art historical community and questioning the resistance to the principle of anachronism, says that: "It's true that there would have had to be a kind of naïveté to say, with Berenson, that Picasso is like Piero." Claire Farago immediately responded: "Maybe, or he was just trying to see what Piero was like. We start from what we know. [. . .] Why is it that certain things are appealing to us now? And why was Piero appealing at the end of the nineteenth century, and not before?" These are precisely this kind of questions I tried to answer in relation to Leonardo; precisely such questions are unavoidable for any historian of Renaissance art who is reflecting on the discipline and its future.

Elizabeth Alice Honig
The Place of Style and the Material of Culture

1. Style: the classical as other

> *And to saie trew all thes composed ornamentes the wch Proceed out of ye*
> *aboundance of dessignes and wear brought in by Mihill Angell and his*
> *followers in my oppignion do not well in sollid Architecture and ye*
> *facciati of houses, but in gardens loggis stucco or ornamentes of chimnie*

pieces or the innerparts of hoases thes composisiones are of necesety to be youced, for as outwardly euery wyse man carrieth a graviti in Publicke Places, whear ther is nothing els looked for, & yt inwardly hath his immaginacy set free, and sumtimes licenciously flying out, as nature hirsealf doeth often tymes stravagantly, to dellight, amase us sumtimes moufe us to laughter, sumtimes to contemplatio and horror, So in architecture ye outward ornamentes oft to be sollid, proporsionable according to the rulles, masculine and unaffected.

Inigo Jones, 1614

We are in Elysium. On the ceiling above our heads sprawl Ovid's gods and goddesses, naked and imperfect, earthy and pleasure-seeking. Even the chaste Diana lolls, heavily sensuous, beside a Bacchus who seems about to tumble downward to our level. Opening the room's single window, we find ourselves looking far down into a courtyard where the nude figure of Venus adorns a central fountain. Around her, naked women crouch and piss into the basin, all too evidently arousing the lust of the male creatures that accompany them. We are in a classical world—interpreted with a rather particular agenda, perhaps, but certainly classical in form and significance, style and iconography.

Venus's own view, however, would be rather different if she looked back at us. She would be looking at a distinctly medieval castle.[294] A small one, it's true, more an elaborate playhouse than a grand residence, but a medieval castle nonetheless, perched like its larger relatives on a high bluff overlooking rolling plains. Its construction does not predate to any great extent the execution of Elysium or the addition of Venus; and while we do not know the names of the artists who carried out the paintings or the sculpture, we do know that the renowned builder Robert Smythson was involved in the design of this crenellated fortress. Were Venus now to turn her head slightly and look away from us, over to the adjoining wing of this building complex, she would view a row of Dutch-style gables adorning the wing where state-rooms were located. What would Venus make of this, or what should we make of it? Are we in the Renaissance?

Bolsover Castle overlooks the plains of Derbyshire, not Tuscany. And since we are in England and not in Italy, our definition of the

Renaissance has to change somewhat. In this section of my response to the round table discussion, I will consider ways in which the Renaissance looks different from outside the Romano-Tuscan area championed by Vasari as the period's key center. His view has been adopted to no small degree by modern art history, which often addresses locations outside of Florence or Rome under the rubric of the "periphery," a notion I would like to avoid. For only from a place that has defined itself as the center does another place look peripheral.

Moreover, "center" is nearly always a term applicable only in one arena of human endeavor at any given time, with the result that its use sets that arena apart from all the others. In Vasari's lifetime, for instance, an argument could certainly be made that Central Italy held a key position in the development of a particular form and idea of visual art. But in the same period, the European economy was directed from Antwerp, clear across the continent. To natives of that city, and to economic historians, Antwerp was Europe's center in the age of Vasari. In Antwerp, a distinctive form of art was being produced as well: indeed, Flemish oil paintings, from Hugo Van der Goes's massive and unique *Portinari Altarpiece* to the gaudy standardized *Adoration of the Magi* altarpieces of the so-called Antwerp Mannerists, had been attracting the attention of Italian merchants for decades.[295] The art market was also becoming highly sophisticated in Antwerp, stimulating diversification, novelty, and the rise of genres of painting.[296] Thus the only way to set Antwerp at the periphery of Renaissance Europe is first to privilege one definition of art and then to isolate art from the economy, claiming that centrality is defined by the former, that Antwerp's status as the first world market is of a different order than Florence's revival of antiquity and glorification of the artist, and need not be considered alongside it. This division between developments in art and in the economy was indeed one that Vasari himself, along with other Italian art theorists, was concerned to maintain.[297] But that does not mean that we as historians are obligated to retain that division and the notion of center that it undergirds. Indeed, as I will argue in the second section of this essay, it is something we ought to be rejecting.

Viewed from outside of Italy, Italy's renaissance will also look different and its own self-declared priorities will be rearranged. To take some of the obvious criteria discussed at the round table and cited in most introductory texts on the subject: nowhere else was the status of the artist so fully revised as in Italy, nor with the same theoretical agenda. The entire idealizing philosophy behind renaissance painting, the place of the Idea in relation to the artwork, never gained full currency in most places. Naturalism had a different aesthetic meaning in other parts of Europe; both the philosophy and the technical practices by which is was supposed to be achieved were often so different as to be entirely contradictory to the norms of Italy. Key notions such as imitation, improvement, and tradition were all differently constructed in renaissances outside of Italy, had different values. To the extent that definitions of naturalism, the status of the artist, the originating (mental) site of the artwork or the notions of knowledge that art calls upon *are* shared among various locations in Europe, they tend to differ from the definitions usually attributed to the Renaissance.

We are often left with only one easily traceable, visible, constant factor to unite disparate renaissances and to maintain, if only by implication, Italy's position at the center of them, and that is a particular style: the classical style, revived in Italy from its ancient past, revised to meet the demands of a more modern moment, transmitted to all of Europe in varying degrees, instantly marking everywhere it emerges as touched by the Renaissance.[298] Lauded by Vasari, described, explained, and anatomized by Wölfflin, we certainly know Classic Art when we see it. Hence when art historians ask, "Did England (or some other peripheral spot) have a Renaissance?," one of the main things they will look for is the use of the classical style.[299] When it appears—earlier in some places, very late in others—it means that that culture has finally achieved Renaissance. Other artistic forms claiming ancient roots, notably the grotesque, can also be signs that a specific location is experiencing the Renaissance.

But again, viewed from outside of Central Italy, the way in which a classicizing stylistic ideal functions and what it signifies for the culture at large may be quite different from how that same style functioned in its original context. I will suggest a few important reasons why this is the case. First of all, in the model of style employed by writers from Vasari to Wölfflin and beyond, the classical is crucially the result of evolution, part of a fully organic process that can be traced through a succession of works over time until it reaches a certain culminating point. It can even be traced beyond that culminating point to something termed Baroque, a phenomenon that the great German founders of this discipline—among them Wölfflin, Panofsky, and Riegl—all struggled to explain.[300]

Renaissance art should thus be a hard-won cultural achievement, its success measurable by its relation to and distinction from other works within the same tradition. Whether an artwork can be read as revising and improving upon the work of a single prior master and moment (the most usual Vasarian model in earlier biographies), or as combining the achievements of numerous greats from within the tradition (the only real option once classical perfection had been achieved), style as embedded within the object is both part of a series and a unique individual achievement.

The more distant an artwork is from the essential series that produces style, the less its style can be measured and judged within this evolutionary framework. Even works we can easily label as renaissance or classical in, say, Flanders or England, are never part of an organic development. In organic terms, their style is inert. It has only been appropriated, whole and fully developed, from the study of immediately cognate artworks or from printed pattern-books. Entire mechanisms of judgment, relationality, and significance are therefore rendered inoperative. Instead of insisting that the public in these countries lacked the knowledge or the language with which to appreciate renaissance objects, art history needs to accept that those objects we identify as classical generally called for completely different means of appreciation in other contexts. Searching the discourses of judgment in these locations for Italianate structures of understanding is a self-defeating historical enterprise: no classicizing style would ever hold elsewhere the meaning it held in Central Italy.[301] The meanings it did hold could be extremely complex, but they would be localized and would relate to a different historical trajectory of formal concerns.

The localism of responses to renaissance style inflected its meanings in other ways as well. At the renaissance heart of the ancient Roman empire, the antique past was the subject of deliberate and self-conscious revival. The Classical represented the style of a glorious moment of its own culture–a local culture–that had risen, fallen, would rise again. To regain that culture was to repossess a past that belonged, inherently, to those whose ancestors had created it. But however vast Rome's empire had once been, all of Europe did not participate equally in its culture, and certainly lacked the vast bank of visual objects that Italy–and Rome in particular–contained from that past. Humanist texts travelled easily, while forms and artifacts were more embedded in and associated with place. No place outside of Italy really possessed the classical artistic past *as* past in the way it was possessed there.

Scholars of the Renaissance have long emphasized that what distinguished its relationship to the classical past from the relationship held in the Middle Ages, was a sense of historical distance. The middle ages, according to this model, felt itself to be entirely connected to antiquity, to still be a late part of that world. But in the historical mind of the renaissance, a chasm opened up between now and that past. There had been, once, the moment of antiquity; then there had been a rupture; and now there was a new moment in which the culture of the ancient past would be studied, understood, and brought back into proper usage. Rhetorical models of imitation and emulation depended on the new sense of difference created by history's faultline, for emulation necessitates difference. The renaissance, in Italy, thus consists of a dynamic interplay between that temporal difference, and a certain physical, geographical connectedness.

Elsewhere, however, there was no such easy sense of connectedness, and difference did not need to be constructed by a new sense of history. Even individual artists who felt most drawn to the forms linked by the renaissance to classical antiquity–Durer, Gossaert, Heemskerck, Jones–are more consistently aware of their own lack of a real organic connection with antiquity. If they reject familiar stylistic forms in order to imitate those of antiquity, they are rejecting on a geographical rather than a genealogical basis, and they are rejecting forms that are immediately present and available, not participating in what is conceived as a progressive movement toward higher cultural achievement. Rubens is unique as a non-Italian in constructing himself as the natural heir of antiquity, and his ability to truly emulate classical statuary stems from a remarkable assumption of personal connection that can then play off the sense of difference.[302]

Other sites in Europe lacked the formal genealogy by which the Classical was the great ancestor of the artistic present. But they had, instead, other genealogies, other great past moments with which other styles were associated. At Bolsover Castle, the glorious chivalric courts of the English middle ages are revived right alongside classical antiquity's nude figures and narratives of pleasure. Elizabethan chivalry, famous for its flamboyance, its performativity, its exquisite poetry, and its ability to carry charged political meanings, often seems more chivalric than did its medieval ancestor. In many senses it is a renaissance mode just as the classical is in Italy: a style, a rhetoric, a loaded means of cultural communication, that claims roots in a powerful moment of the local past and through those roots can exert a sense of idealism and domination over the present sociocultural scene.

If England (one could use other examples, even Venice) was able to import Italy's renaissance to stand beside its own as an effective artistic language, then it could import others as well. At Bolsover, and at other contemporary great houses like Knole, ranges of Dutch gables on exteriors and elaborate strapwork on interior walls and fireplaces testify to the popularity of Netherlandish patternbooks.[303] Builders did not apparently see any particular contradiction in combining these styles, as long as each was used in a location and with an intent that was, in some sense, true to its visual nature. Jones, in the quotation with which I began this section, proposes an analogy between the rational classical style and gentlemanly external self-restraint, while the grotesque (which he associates with Michelangelo but which, in his time, was more often derived in England from Flemish pattern books) is likened to the extravagant, irrational, humorous side of a gentleman that only his intimate friends will see. The assignment of significance and function to styles varies endlessly in cultures where style is seen as a choice, where styles are resolutely multiple, where the local competes freely with imports in contests of meaning. Even a fundamental form like linear perspective, a route to perfection and truth in Italy, is held to be the tool of perversion and falsehood in some places where it is just one alternative manner of visual making.

Artifacts like Bolsover are not what I would call hybrids, a term Claire Farago and others often use to explain the stylistic consequences of colonial encounters.[304] We might think of them more as multi-lingual, analogous to a multilingual child who keeps each language utterly apart from the other, never allows a word of one to intrude into conversations in another, doesn't even let a more predominant language accent one used less frequently. Likewise, styles in the wider European renaissance can exist alongside one another without any overlap, do not invade or accent one another but are each used and appreciated, separately, for what they can mean and how they can appear. From outside of Italy, this is precisely the hallmark of the Renaissance: like humanist scholars, artists and designers learn various (formal) languages, and appreciate them as new rhetorical tools with which new modes of communication and expression can be achieved.

In the peripheral renaissance, style becomes free, manipulable, and meaningful. Its meanings may be historical, national, biological, philosophical, religious, or locally political—in England, certain great families notoriously promoted classical forms, others as clearly did not; classicism was sometimes negatively associated with Roman Catholicism, sometimes positively; ornamentation—or its utter absence—could be of theological or social significance. Anyone who studies the art of the "periphery" could come up with endless examples of meaningful stylistic choices, decisions that are sometimes quite extreme, contrasts that would have been hideously jarring to the eye schooled at the "center." Van Mander can never really be the "Vasari of the North" because he has no master-narrative of development to tell us about his local renaissance.[305] There is no such narrative. There are only episodes of choice.

2. Art/image/artifact: theorizing process

. . . . On drawing nearer they spied, in one corner of the canvas, the tip of a foot emerging from this chaos of colors, tones, indecisive shadings, a kind of undefined mist; but a delectable foot, a living foot. They remained petrified with admiration before this fragment escaped from an incredible, slow, progressive, destruction. This foot appeared like the torso of a Venus of Parian marble rising amongst the ruins of a burnt city.

> *"There is a woman under there,"* cried Pourbus, calling Poussin's
> attention to the various layers of paint which the old painter had laid
> on, one after another, believing that he was perfecting his picture.
>   Balzac, *The Unknown Masterpiece*[306]

In Balzac's *Unknown Masterpiece*, the young Nicolas Poussin pays a visit to an elderly genius, Frenhofer, in the company of another painter named Pourbus. Frenhofer has been working for years on his masterpiece, a picture whose living subject in the end turns out to have been consumed by his obsessive attentions, a work in which process has destroyed product. Before that revelation, Frenhofer lectures the two younger artists on how to make pictures that are living and vital. At one point he hastily corrects a painting by Pourbus, bringing it to life with a few swift strokes of his brush. And then he turns to the two younger men and says, "Remember, my friends, it is only the final stroke of the brush that counts! No one will remember what was underneath." Yet at the tale's conclusion we learn that what was underneath may be all, that process is an act of making and of destroying, that the final stroke can be a killing gesture as well as one that brings life. Remembering always those things that were underneath is a vital aspect of making art, as it is a vital aspect of understanding it.

In this section of my response, I would like to make a plea for a history of renaissance art that attends to underneaths, on the one hand, and overlays on another; that sees the object, and not just its maker, as having a biography.[307] Art history has tended to view works of art as in some sense temporally static—sealed off as relics of their historical moment of making, and ready for competitions of modern interpretation to be held over them. The history of stylistic development, in the manner of Vasari or of Woelfflin, supposes every object to contain a particular style, mark of the moment of origin, that can be recognized, analyzed, and categorized. Renaissance art theory interpolates here the concept of the Idea, born within the mind of the maker and transferred into material form by some evidently rather transparent process. But even old master paintings have temporality as objects in the world. There is no simple moment of conception nor an absolute final product, but rather a process of physical making and physical change, creation and transition, ownership and viewership.

When we think about objects as having biographies, we may find ourselves losing some of the distinctions that troubled the discussants at the roundtable: those between Art, image, and artifact, for example. In the biographical narratives of objects, they will enter into contact with other created, collected, and interpreted things, be grouped and categorized, be altered and reframed and rethought in their series of contexts. Considering the physical genesis of an object allows distinctions such as "original," "workshop product," and "copy after" to stop being the bases of separation and exclusion and to instead become importantly meaningful descriptions of a dynamic system;[308] considering the circulation of objects after they leave the workshop or studio allows high and low, man-made and natural, painting and print and decorative art, to find their interest in relation to, rather than distinction from, one another.[309]

There is nothing ahistorical about considering works of art as being the result of a process. Vasari's inclination to focus on finished objects and their appearance may be the exception to a larger early modern habit of seeing artworks as the products of intriguing technical procedures. Van Mander, most obviously, is often more interested in describing processes of making than he is with analyzing the style of the final product. Other Italian artist/writers (Cellini) and patrons (Borromeo) were also concerned to understand artifacts as the results of technical ingenuity and experimentation, of manual gestures as much as mental ideas.[310]

Art history has never really lost sight of the process behind its objects. But studies of the activities occurring in the studio have been kept rather separate from studies dealing with what were implicitly taken to be more exalted, serious issues. Art historians who want to position their work as intellectually critical, who are savvy about current interdisciplinary methods or about the implications of historiography and theory, do not deal with technique except in the most general, even theoretical way.[311] This is not actually the case for some of the strongest art historians of this period—Svetlana Alpers, Michael Baxandall, Joseph Koerner. The round table participants certainly addressed their works, but not those dealing with the meaning of process. Other scholars who attend closely to the processes behind products would include many drawings specialists, museum conservators and scientists.[312] All of these voices were conspicuously absent from the round table discussion and their publications were not cited in the notes to the position papers.

Yet some of the most novel work in this field is now being done by those people, and the rest of us should accept the challenge of finding an intelligent way to integrate their findings into our own work. Museums have always been the primary site of this sort of research, beginning and continuing most notably with the National Gallery, London, and the Fogg Art Museum at Harvard University.[313] Yet despite the former's longstanding commitment to publishing the results of its technical research, and the latter's affiliation with a major American academic art history department, it has been surprisingly hard for technical research to be incorporated into other forms of art history writing.[314] Specific information, yes; larger implications, no. What seems particularly lacking is a modern effort to theorize process, as opposed to the theorization of hermeneutics, aesthetics, visualities.[315] Technical studies can seem arcane to those accustomed to different kinds of art-historical discourse, but we need to make more of an effort to absorb them as part of our way of understanding, not just of individual works but of alternative systems of renaissance painting. For instance, writing that tries to theorize systems of illusion and representation, that analyzes color and light, beholding and response, should be read beside writing that describes the physical process of producing those illusions.[316] Notions of value, merit, and worth, or originality and invention versus repetition and replication, all deserve to be examined at the intersection of physical praxis and theoretical constructs.

Of course, this is really a more complicated junction than I am describing, for another route that runs through it and needs to be integrated into our analysis is the study of the valuing, marketing, collecting and display of art. This represents the other side of what I've been terming the biography of the artwork, the afterlife of the made object. It is distinct from patronage studies, a well-established type of renaissance art history in which the interests of the one who commissioned a work substitute for or supplement the interests of the one who manufactured that work in what remains basically a narrative of intentions. Consumption studies, the larger rubric under which artworks' later biographies may be subsumed, is a type of analysis that largely avoids intention and that looks at larger social patterns rather than at the acts of individuals.[317] It sees fine paintings as one among many luxury goods in which persons of a given social group may choose to invest capital for a range of possible reasons. It positions those paintings firmly amongst other possible investments, other items of household decor, other social markers, other luxury commodities. Decisions made by artists themselves are measured in terms of profit margins and production efficiency. Consumption studies allow and indeed expect that the value of a given object will change greatly depending on its situation within larger social and market forces. There is no transcendence in the economics of art; indeed, the single work has little meaning here except as part of a system that includes many other comparably circulating objects.

Within the system of consumption, the art market and the phenomenon of collecting are two subjects that have received sustained attention in the past decade but were largely ignored in the roundtable discussion. For Renaissance Italy, the work of Richard Goldthwaite energized a generation of recent scholars to examine art markets, value, and habits of consumption.[318] Dutch art history has a longer tradition of attending to these issues. Hanns Floerke's fundamental work on Dutch art markets, studio practices, and collecting habits dates from over a century ago,[319] and the more recent writings of Michael Montias have inspired many scholars doing research today.[320]

The history of collecting—the theoretization of the "museum" and the search for its origins—has been a massive growth field on the edges of traditional art history, very much impacting our view of renaissance culture. The 1983 Ashmolean conference, published as *The Origins of Museums*, seems to have provided a major impetus for a great deal of further research and publication about forms of collecting all over Europe, about the circulation of exotica, the place of scientific research and thinking within early collections, the relationship between man's and nature's "artifice" and image-making, and the function of pictures and artistry in the context of collections.[321] The study of collections has given us a range of aesthetic notions, like "wonder" and "curiosity," that we can use in thinking about visuality between the late middle ages and the baroque period.[322] It has, more-over, allowed us to begin to imagine the *situation* of paintings, in particular, during the renaissance. We have always had ideas about the placement of altarpieces in sacred spaces, about the rituals that attended their beholding, about the devotional gaze elicited by pri-vate as well as public religious images. But the spaces of *kunstkammer* or of picture gallery had not been so easy to imagine, and we had no means to access the nature of the gaze within those spaces. Nor have we had the means of discussing how pictures increasingly competed for attention in the ordinary domestic environment, how they were positioned, examined, juxtaposed, discussed by relatively ordinary individuals as part of the surroundings of their daily lives. These are still open issues in the field of renaissance art history, but the publica-tion of inventories, the analysis of descriptive terms, the interweaving of multiple histories of collecting, is giving us the tools to answer them.[323]

Finally, the studies of production and consumption, the materials of making, the process of creation, the economics of acquisition and the recovery of socially situated viewing habits, offer perhaps new ways to conceptualize art history as social history. I was taken aback by the ease with which this rubric was dismissed by several of the round table participants, by the lack of argument against this pos-ition. During the past fifteen years many art historians have tried to distance themselves from any form of social history, as if it had been irredeemably tainted by marxism and feminism. But just because we need to update our social economics and our gender analysis from those of the heady 1970s should not mean that we jettison society and return to art theory and a self-referential image circuit. If art history is to have any hope of engaging with the big intellectual issues of the present and the future, it cannot simply retrench or become entirely introspective. A renaissance art history that theorizes pro-cess, narrates object-biographies, acknowledges the historical pres-sures of the market, and situates the gaze of the beholder within the material surroundings of different sorts of collection will help to write a new form of the social history of art as well.

Alice Jarrard
Of Authentic Performance

. . . l'Historia è il più vago teatro, che mai si possa immaginare.
Giovanni Botero (1598)

In our current culture that privileges the visual—where instantly recognized cultural icons are preferred to more complex approaches to understanding the past—the notions of history formulated in the Renaissance can appear increasingly strange. Yet thirty years since canonical conceptions of "Renaissance art" first came under fire during the so-called "culture wars," and fifteen-odd years into the era of identity politics, the edifice of Renaissance scholarship manifests a notable resilience and diversity. Today, whether questions originate from within the familiar boundaries of the discipline as defined by that Vasarian "evolutionary virus", are inspired by aesthetic principles, or are framed according to wider cultural criteria might be said to reflect personal avocation as much as a sense of driving responsibility about what constitutes the field.[324] In many different kinds of histories, notions of performance now frequently occupy centerstage.

A quick digression serves first to put these theoretical observations about Renaissance art history in a more pragmatic perspective. From a statistical point of view, as judged by the number of dissertations completed in the USA, the Renaissance field is about as healthy as it has been for the last quarter century: an average of 15% of the dissertations written still focus upon this relatively narrow temporal range.[325] Despite the fact that the total number of *dottorandi* in art history has tripled and competing areas of art historical focus have more than doubled in number, the Renaissance continues to be perceived as both interesting and important by students contemplating a career.

Numbers, of course, do not tell the whole story. The lists of dissertation topics, which were substantially redrawn in 2004 to be coherent across CAA's various professional endeavors and to better reflect the present-day discipline, reflect other shifts within the study of art history, shifts which indicate the way the Renaissance is conceptualized within the profession of art history.[326] In 2004, the field categories were increased from an initial ten to twenty-six, five of which, including "Architectural History" and "Decorative Arts", are now defined by medium alone. At the same time, "Renaissance" was recombined with its Wölfflinian companion "Baroque", the latter previously given a very different slant by its incorporation within the more neutral "Seventeenth and Eighteenth Century." The former additions would seem to reflect a continuing inability within the discipline to account for the deeper connections between art, architecture and objects in time. Rather than recognizing the cultural and conceptual links between buildings and objects in the age of polymaths such as Leonardo, Peruzzi and Michelangelo, the new categories have the effect of officially marginalizing these fields. The second change, that of expanding the "Renaissance" by pairing it with "Baroque", would seem to suggest an official return to the teleology of decline (Vasari and others) and cycle (Wölfflin). Given the fact that the seventeenth century remains one of the prime sources for "outlier" texts about art history in general, this reversion is surprising.[327] Contradicting the encouraging numbers and coming from within the discipline, such categorical regressions suggest an entrenched conservatism in how art history at large defines the Renaissance.

A focus upon performance has the potential to evade this return of the Renaissance to narrower confines. In 1636, while participating in the long current of historical reflection in which Vasari took part, the historian and political theorist Giovanni Botero penned the highly self-conscious words that preface this essay.[328] His words suggest a rhetorical structuring of history, and an awareness of its fundamental maleability, that is rarely attributed to early modern times. But from Aristotle's invocation to "tell what happened" up until the present day, concepts of theater and performance have animated Western ways of talking about the past. The present resurgence of the verb "perform" would seem in part, though, due to its apparent short-circuiting of historical time. Performance captures the dynamic essence of human activity, distilling the rich interplay between actors, audiences, settings, and events. In art history, where the primary actor is the enduring material object, the artwork, and where the experience of the object occurs both in the present moment and in many irrecoverable past ones, taking account of time is especially challenging.

Far from being a neutral term, the verb "performance" itself reverberates with meaning. Originating in the Old French *perfournil* and associated by the mid-fifteenth century with making, creation, and authorship in English, its most familiar connotation with stage acting seems to have arisen fairly late, only in Shakespeare's time.[329] In academic circles, the verb currently evokes an aspect of everyday action ("performative speech"), a means of describing subjectivity ("performative" identities), a specific kind of artistic practice ("performance art"), and a broad approach to studying the dramatic arts ("performance studies").[330] As the theater historian Marvin Carlson has perceptively put it while writing of the latter, the expansion of performance as an analytic tool in academe is "emblematic" of contemporary concerns: "with performance as a wedge, the metaphor of theatricality has moved out of the arts into almost every aspect of modern attempts to understand the human condition."[331]

The peculiarly contemporary drift of what is perhaps best called a theatrical metaphor creates specific problems for the historical interpretation of visual images.[332] Besides the problem of temporal experience alluded to above, in the context of art historical writing about the Renaissance, the metaphor's negative baggage in early Christian and Platonic ideas as the antithesis of the "authentic" is explicit, yet rarely acknowledged, in much writing: that modernism claimed the same view of theater as early Christians like Saint Augustine is instructive.[333] Shifting emphasis from the object to the action, the performative implicates the critical politics of the Situationists, of Fluxus, and of performance artists who—following Duchamp—probed the status of the art object in relation to its maker and its context.[334] By this standard it would seem particularly problematic for dealing with the problems of understanding the most singular invention of the Renaissance: the very idea of art. It seems obvious that precisely this kind of contemporary critique inspired (whether indirectly or not) a wave of art historians, from Belting onwards, to call attention to the particular role of humanist culture in defining the unique entity of "art".[335]

Within writings about Renaissance art history, two intertwined ways of looking at performance have emerged, one more philosophical and the other more anthropological. The first calls attention to language, and by contrast with a structuralist emphasis upon *parole* and *langue*, emphasizes the act of speech in a social context. The second, more concerned with culture at large, has entered mainstream histories of Renaissance art largely as a means of thinking about how works secure the social and political desires of artists, patrons, and audiences. Characterized by the fluidity of its disciplinary boundaries—consider, for example, that Greenblatt introduced his seminal notion of "self-fashioning" not through an analysis of English literature, but by examining a painting by Holbein—this approach reframes the traditional notion of "context" in a more dynamic way.[336]

Just as Alberti's interest in the ancient theater stemmed from his awareness of its potential as a means of fostering communal behaviour, a focus on performance can reinsert the art object in a wide range of social and physical spaces: the workshop, the church, and the street procession, as well as newer sites of interpretation such as the studiolo, the gallery, the theater, and the academy. An emphasis upon performance is inclusive, encompassing settings secular, spiritual, and in between. It proves particularly well-adapted to dealing with the Renaissance, since from the late fifteenth century in Italy and throughout Europe, as things multiplied and the category of "art" emerged, the sites for particular kinds of interpretation also multiplied.[337] Performance provides a means of integrating objects with meaningful ritual behaviours, and of enlivening texts by considering their actual usage. In the present resurgence of biographical studies, it remains a crucial concept even as authors search for an authenticity that appears elusive in the early twenty-first century. Beyond the tired metaphor of "theatrum mundi", the theater's very real physical reemergence in the late Quattrocento gives the concept special relevance for Renaissance studies.

Acknowledging the rhetorical dimension of historical writing as well as its contemporary motivation does not mean trading truth for relativism, or returning to an uncritical approach to the writing of history. Artworks can only be interpreted through present-day lenses. Just as methodologies are constructed around relevant problems, the interpretation of the archives, while providing a rich source of material for the analysis of past performances, will always be shaped by the questions we pose.[338] In the quest for analyses of art with future relevance, Renaissance art history still has a seminal role to play.

Pamela H. Smith

"Art" is to "Science" as "Renaissance" is to "Scientific Revolution"? The Problematic Algorithm of Writing a History of the Modern World

There are so many parallels between the questions raised in this roundtable about writing the history of "Renaissance Art" and the fraught historiography of "the Scientific Revolution" that it is difficult to know where to begin. These parallels are of course no coincidence, as both the concepts "Renaissance Art" and "Modern Science" were forged in the nineteenth century as part of a new narrative of modernity and Western progress that celebrated the Renaissance as giving birth to both Art and Science. Just as art historians debate whether we can trace a contemporary conception of art back to the Renaissance, or to the Enlightenment, or to Kant, so historians of science have also wrestled with the question of whether "modern science" can be traced back to the moment of the Renaissance or to the seventeenth-century Scientific Revolution, or to eighteenth-century positivism. The question of whether a break took place in the Renaissance (or whether it happened earlier or later) that brought about Art and Science (The Whether and When question)[339] leads immediately onto the question of what in fact is the Art or Science whereof we are speaking (The What question)? In the conversation, Robert Williams places the turning point at the articulation of a theory of art in the Renaissance because this theory "defines art as a form of knowledge." For Williams, this is not a disembodied theory, however, but rather it emerges out of debates over the question of representation which themselves are linked to social and intellectual developments. Others in the conversation disagreed with this, but placed the break at various other moments or with other figures: not so much with Vasari perhaps, but with the polemics of which he was a part, according to Steven Campbell, an achievement of several other writers who also worked to establish art as a form of knowledge. These two contributions, along with Matt Kavaler's, debate the first question of Whether and When a break took place, while

Claire Farago and Fredrika Jacobs ask the second question: what in fact are we talking about when we talk about Renaissance Art? In Farago's case, she asks whether the subject matter that historians have delimited as relevant to the history of Renaissance Art is actually useful, while in Jacobs's case, she asks the question "what are we talking about when we talk about Art in general?" Precisely the same two questions have been asked with respect to Science. Indeed, every position marked out in this debate has analogs in the history of science. David Freedberg's much remarked-upon opening line in the *Power of Images* that he is not writing the history of art might be placed alongside Steven Shapin's wonderful first line in his 1996 survey, *The Scientific Revolution*: "There was no such thing as the Scientific Revolution, and this is a book about it."

Such equivocation has its roots in the fact that art history and the history of science not only share a common originating discourse and moment, but also wrestle with the same problem of teleology: they seek to narrate the history of an entity that exists in a recognizable form and possesses great cultural significance in today's world, while at the same time trying to maintain their historical commitment to non-Whiggish history. The *telos* will never cease to exist for the historian, but the trick is not to let it determine the subject matter, the perspective, indeed the entire story. Art history and the history of science will always have this problem. It is not an easy balance to maintain.

Historians of science have tried to strike a balance in a variety of ways, not all of which can of course be covered here, but they are similar to efforts made by art historians. For example, with regard to the first question—was there a break during the period that we call the Renaissance (or the early modern period or the Scientific Revolution) roughly spanning the period 1400–1700?—we might answer that before 1400 people manipulated and investigated nature in various, completely un-unified ways, but after this point, such engagement with nature became a self-conscious endeavor and even came to have a name, the "new experimental philosophy." Obviously this is analogous to the art historical discussion that points out that a great deal of making—of images, of ornamentation, of a variety of human-made artifacts—went on before the period of the Renaissance, but, after this time (whenever its precise chronological location), there was a reflexive self-consciousness about making "art", perhaps denoted by the title by which individuals called themselves—perhaps "artist"—and certainly marked by a shift from the image as cult to the cult of images.

Other historians of science have tried to strike the balance by banning anachronistic words from their historical narratives. "Scientist," for example, was not coined until the early 1800s, thus it should not be employed to describe people of the sixteenth century.[340] Can the term "natural philosopher" be used? For some time, this was employed by historians of science, but then it became clear that "natural philosophy" had long been a subject long taught in medieval universities and did not describe the activity pursued by a diversity of people who began to make appeals to the authority of nature and to investigate nature in various ways during the period of the Renaissance. Historians of science began to investigate the meaning of the word *scientia* and how it may have changed during this period. They asked the question of whether it had anything to do with the activity that came to be known as "science." What they found is that "*scientia*" was used by individuals in this period as a term to give authority to an activity, and it most often implied a deductive structure that could be conveyed in propositional form (and it goes without saying in words), such as geometry. (This brings to mind Matt Kavaler's conclusion that "Geometric properties, critical to the design, guarantee its [the sixteenth-century Gothic artisans' architectural creations] truth and authority.")

Any examination of "*scientia*" leads directly on to an examination of the word "*ars*." And here we come to not just an analog between art history and history of science, but an intersection between the two fields. In the Renaissance, *ars* was used by scholars to denote a teachable discipline, i.e., teachable in words. Handwork might or might not be teachable in words, and that problem was part of what impelled humanist investigations of painting, sculpture, and other handwork in the period of the Renaissance. Much Renaissance "technical-writing" about image-making as well as about fortification-building and arms manufacture emerged out of such questions. But such examinations still leave us struggling with the same questions in both art history and the history of science: "What was art in the period of the Renaissance?" Was it representation? Was it image-making? Was it handwork in general? Can we reiterate Jacobs's quotation of David Morgan that "people use images to make and maintain their worlds,"[341] and conclude that this is the essence of "art"? Or was it the existence of a self-conscious art theoretical discourse? Likewise, what was science between 1400 and 1700? Was it studying and knowing nature? Manipulating nature? Employing nature for human use? Or was it forming theories about the deep structures of matter and nature? Or was it simply a rhetorical claim about possessing authority? Or perhaps it was the development of institutions (often aligned with the central state) in which a particular way of knowing nature was pursued?

Until recently, both art history and history of science have been dominated by narratives of theoretical change. In art history, some historians see the appearance of art theoretical treatises in the sixteenth century as bringing into being "Art." In the history of science, the shift from a geocentric Ptolemaic astronomy and Aristotelian cosmology to a heliocentric Newtonian universe is considered to have brought about "Modern Science." When in the 1980s, influenced by the new cultural history, historians of science began to examine the practices of science, or better said, the practices of engaging with nature, things began to look different. For there were many practices of engaging with nature, carried out by many different people, and most of them had little to do with the scholarly tradition of natural philosophy or astronomy. Thus the history of science was faced with the same quandary as art history. As Jacobs puts it, are the myriad practices of making images and the different significances with which they were invested by their makers and by the communities in which they were received really the stuff of art history? So with the history of science: are the practices of craftspeople who were the experts in the behavior of nature and of natural materials the stuff of the history of science, or does science commence with the declaration in the seventeenth century of new experimental philosophers that they are the sole experts in the behavior of nature?

The advent of "science studies" has brought about many new perspectives in the history of science, in particular from anthropology, from the sociology of knowledge, and from scholarship on material culture. A few examples of such new approaches seem relevant here. Helen Watson-Verran and David Turnbull, "Science and Other Indigenous Knowledge Systems," note that scientific knowledge is heterogeneous; there is no term that "captures the amalgam of place, bodies, voices, skills, practices, technical devices, theories, social strategies and collective work that together constitute technoscientific knowledge/practices."[342] So they use "assemblage." They argue that techno-scientific assemblages can make the transition from local to general knowledge if they possess a form of transmitting knowledge, as was the case, for example, in the templates that medieval cathedral masons used; in the calendars that the Anasazi built into their edifices; in the control of large amounts of information by means of the *ceque* and *quipa* by the Inca; in the memorized map of the heavens and the concepts embedded in navigational practices used by Polynesian navigators. All meld local practices into stable assemblages that connect local to general forms of knowledge, and thus form a "knowledge system." Such a conception of knowledge-making practices as part of a system of knowledge has ramifications for the history of science as well as for the history of art.

Second, from the perspective of the history of the book, that is, in considering intellectual objects as material culture, Roger Chartier, in "Culture as Appropriation: Popular Culture Uses in Early Modern France" examines readers, printers, and the contents of chapbooks, a cultural form that historians have usually viewed to be a marker and component of popular culture. Chartier argues that the idea of separate "cultural sets" that can be regarded as socially pure must be replaced with a "point of view that recognizes each cultural form as a mixture, whose constituent elements meld together indissolubly." Chartier demonstrates that there was not a single cultural boundary, but rather shifting boundaries that are redrawn by, in his analysis, publishing strategies of printers. One could argue that the self-conscious theorizing about image-making in the sixteenth century and the proclaiming of the new experimental philosophy in the seventeenth centuries were both moments at which cultural boundaries were redrawn.[343]

Finally, the work on "everyday technology" carried out by

Jean Lave brings us to reconsider the relationship of thinking and doing and of knowing and making.[344] As we all know, schemas of knowledge-making and knowledge-makers are hierarchical, and almost without exception have placed knowing above doing and making. Anthropologist Tim Ingold, in arguing for the primacy of doing over thinking, or experiential knowledge over propositional knowledge, as well as the embodied and situated nature of *all* knowledge, gives us a new starting point: "We do not have to think the world in order to live in it, but we do have to live in the world in order to think it."[345] If we follow the lead of these writers in not separating making and knowing, in not thinking in terms of pre-determined elite and popular, and in conceiving of practice and doing as primary, we might write a new history of science, in which phenomena that used to be seen as local can be integrated into an overarching narrative of the making of knowledge. Indeed, the history of science could be written as the history of material life and the human engagement with nature, the struggle with matter and nature in which all humans are engaged by virtue of being human. But this is a very broad prospect and brings to mind the same problems for the history of science that James Elkins pointed out with regard to visual studies: "you lose the ability to talk about fine art in the ways that have been developed for it." Despite this justifiable caveat, I believe that of the two questions broached at the beginning (the "Whether and When" question and the "What are we talking about" question), the question of "What are we talking about when we talk about the history of science?" more urgently demands an answer from historians of science.

And yet I cannot resist also considering how we might answer the "Whether and When" question! Was there a break? When was it? In my own work, I posit an extended process taking place in the period around 1400–1600 (whatever we call it—Renaissance, early modern, Scientific Revolution), in which both "science" and "art" recognizably emerge out of the same process by which handwork/practice/*ars* was theorized by humanist scholars at the same time that artisan/handworker/makers of all types began asserting a new kind of authority and making claims to higher intellectual and social status. New groups of people began to employ nature to claim authority about all kinds of things—from the proper way of attaining salvation to the best method of building beehives. People claimed authority through an appeal to their superior knowledge of nature and its processes. Artisans—*Handwerker, Künstler*—made this claim based on their knowledge of the behavior of natural materials, while others individuals such as the medical and religious reformer, Theophrastus von Hohenheim, called Paracelsus, made this claim on behalf of artisans. This was a powerful, and in most instances, a socially and intellectually subversive claim.

Moreover, from the late fourteenth century on, nature came to be employed in new ways, both substantively and rhetorically. In early modern Europe, the formal and discursive investigation of nature was carried out by natural philosophers—schoolmen—whom earlier historians of science used to call the "scientists" of their time. But this group's study of nature was probably far less visible than the increasing importance of natural knowledge to nobles, city fathers, reformers, collectors, and a diverse range of individuals. It appeared to them that nature was bound up with public good or the arts of war, or, according to some, with religious and intellectual reform, because the objects of nature and their analysis were perceived to allow an access to knowledge of God that eluded the warring religious sects. As natural knowledge became increasingly important in society in these various ways, it forged new connections among groups, helped create new identities, brought about new kinds of claims to authority and intellectual legitimacy, and gave rise to new ways of thinking about the senses, certainty, and epistemology. In the sixteenth and seventeenth centuries, nature began increasingly to function as a resource, both material and intellectual. It provided the matter for production and was the source of objects of desire and consumption, but, perhaps more importantly, it began to function as a new resource for individuals claiming social and intellectual authority.

At the same time, nature itself was under construction. New attitudes to nature emerged as very diverse individuals and communities began to question what was nature? How should it be understood, examined, probed, employed? What kind and quality of knowledge did the study of nature yield? I would argue that these attitudes to nature *are* new in the Renaissance and Scientific

Revolution. A new discourse about nature emerged that came to be part of the social and intellectual toolbox of all people from this time forward. This new discourse about "nature" could of course be compared to the new discourse about "art" that develops about the same time in Europe, and, as I have tried to indicate, these two discourses are in fact very much mixed up with each other.

As part of the development of this new discourse, a new relationship between making and knowing also emerged. The point of contact with the conversation here is Robert Williams's remark that

> Perhaps art is not a kind of object, but rather a kind of work, a particularly complex, highly-structured, demanding kind of work. In that case, Vasari's book might be seen as an attempt to describe how that work—the work of being an artist—had evolved over the three hundred years leading up to his own time. That's why the biographical format is so essential: it isn't a celebration of "genius"—which is how modernist critics always dismiss it—so much as an affirmation of the meaning of human productivity. His book is about a process of redefining art as a culturally significant kind of labor.

In the conversation, Michael Cole carries this point forward, noting that this provides a link between the two questions, "What happens in the Renaissance?" and "What is art?" I would agree that viewing art as one kind of labor, or handwork, could indeed constitute a bridge between artifact-making and art-making.

I would argue that one way of looking at science is as an engagement with nature, and this, too, can be viewed as a kind of labor, especially a labor of production, or "making," which employed natural materials and presupposed a knowledge of the behavior of nature. One marker of a new relationship between such making and the higher-status and more abstract activity of knowing in the period after 1400 is the greater intensity of technical writing among individuals of all social and intellectual ranks. I am using "technical writing" as a clumsy term to describe the accounts of handwork, of art, of engineering practices, of "how-to" books and of recipes that appear with increasing frequency from 1400 on. Such literature had of course not been entirely absent before this time—one need only think of Theophilus or Albertus Magnus—but from 1400 many more such writings ("treatises" is the wrong word, as is "manuals") appear. It represents a new attempt in the European world to put into writing processes that were non-verbal, tacit and involved embodied knowledge. The significant point about this development is that it took place on both sides of the handwork-mindwork divide. Humanist scholars visited workshops; artisans began to write poetry; vernacular and learned texts intersected. The new types of knowledge-making that came out of this process were the result of this dialectical and reciprocally influential relationship.

*   *   *

In the following example from my own work on sixteenth-century European metalworking, I attempt to ground my answers to both the "When and Whether" and the "What" questions. I also try to make explicit the balance I seek to strike between writing a history of the modern world and conveying the alien quality of the world around 1500.

Metalworking

An examination of metalworking techniques and practices in the period from 1400 to 1600 reveals that they can be related to the emergence of modern science in three principal ways. For a start, they involve a set of observational and empiricist practices, such as the precision measurements of assayers, that were incorporated into the methods of the new experimental philosophy by Francis Bacon and other individuals influential in shaping the practices, rhetorical and empirical, of the new "active" science of the seventeenth century. Second, sixteenth-century metalworking practices involved a systematic investigation of nature, as can be seen from numerous examples of technical writing from that time. It is clear from such manuals that artisans undertook constant experimentation, for example, in the first half of the sixteenth century, the writer on metalworking, Vanoccio Biringuccio, advised constant trial: "It is necessary to find the true method by doing it again and again, always varying the procedure and then stopping at the best."[346]

For this reason it is necessary to have a superabundance of tests, and to test and try enough to find the desired aid [to smelting], not only by using ordinary things but also by varying the quantities, adding now half the quantity of the ore and now an equal portion, now twice and now three times, so that the virtue that the ore contains may better defend itself from the fire and from the evilness of its companions.[347]

An anonymous sixteenth-century goldsmith's manuscript collection of recipes and account of his work also testifies to many experiments over the years, particularly with various types of sand for casting. To take one example from its numerous accounts of testing sands of differing compositions for casting: "I tried four kinds of sands for use with lead and tin: chalk, crushed glass, tripoly and burned cloth." At another point, he explicitly refers to the experimental nature of his work: "Since my last experiences, I moulded with burned bone, clinker and burned felt."[348] His manuscript also contains numerous observations on the behavior of animals he has caught and kept for life casting. For example,

> Keep your snake in a barrel full of bran, or, better, in a barrel full of earth in a cool place, or in a glass bottle. Give your snake some live frogs or other live animals, because snakes do not eat them dead. Also I've noticed that when snakes want to eat something or to bite, they do not strike straight on, on the contrary they attack sideways as do Satan and his henchmen. Snakes have small heads, but very large bodies, they can abstain from eating for 7 or 8 days, but they can swallow 3 or 4 frogs, one after the other. Snakes do not digest food all at once, but rather little by little. . . . If you worry and shake your snake, it will bring up digested and fresh food at the same time. Sometimes 2 or 3 hours after swallowing a frog, it can vomit it alive.[349]

A second goldsmith's manual from ca 1604 makes clear the first-hand observational and empirical underpinning of assayers' practices: In all, he wrote, assaying metals "asketh a good Judgment, gotten rather by years & experience, then by speculation & dispute." Besides a "grounded experience in this Science or mysterie," the goldsmith "should have a perfect Eye to vewe, & a stedye hand to waye [weigh] for other mens senses cannot serve him."[350] Such a statement could have been written by Francis Bacon.

Third, the activities of metalworking in many cases seem to have been informed by (or informed) particular theories of matter, such as the general theory that the principles of mercury and sulphur are the two elements of all metals.[351] Such a relationship between practice and theory is a familiar one to historians and philosophers of science, thus the knowledge and techniques of craftspeople have been viewed as contributing to greater knowledge about the behavior of metals that eventually led to theoretical change. In this way historians of science have incorporated the practices of early modern metalworking into a narrative about the rise of modern science. But this could never be the meaning that the making and matter of metalworking held for its early modern practitioners. In what follows, I attempt to map out a system of associations—the "vernacular science" that I believe underpinned the practices of pigment making and metalworking—a web of correspondences among vermilion, blood, gold, and lizards that can be teased out of artisanal recipes and practices.[352]

Red

The saturated red pigment vermilion may seem far removed from the practices of metalworking, however, pigment-making and metalworking overlapped in the process of making vermilion. The pigment vermilion was a red powder produced by heating together sulfur and mercury, in imitation of the naturally-occurring cinnabar (mercury sulphide). In medieval alchemical theory and in the work of color makers and metalworkers, sulfur and mercury were viewed as the basic principles of all metals, and central to metallic transformation.[353] The principles of sulfur and mercury were not identical with the familiar material forms of these two elements, but rather these "principles" drew upon the physical characteristics of material sulfur and mercury. In a pure form in nature, sulfur, on heating, turns a dark red color, and then, when cooled rapidly, forms a glassy red substance. Native mercury, on the other hand, is liquid at room temperature and possessed a silver glittering quality. In alchemical theory, these qualities were the basis of the principles of mercury and sulfur, and, as such, they accounted for the behavior of metals. Sulfur was viewed as the hot, fiery, male principle, representing the qualities of fire and air and giving metals their combustibility. It combined with the wet, cold, female principle of mercury that possessed the properties of earth and water. Mercury accounted for the liquidity of metals when heated. But mercury also possessed a solid state that gave way to its silvery, fluid state on heating, eventually vaporizing. These qualities could account for changes that metals underwent when subjected to fire as well as the transformation of base metals into noble ones.

The red powder of vermilion, produced by combining mercury and sulfur, thus manifested in material form a theory of metallic transformation, but, just as significant, the red color of vermilion possessed potent significance, being associated with generation and life, especially in relation to blood and gold. Blood was the carrier of life heat, and gold could stimulate heat and life when prepared as potable gold or even when worn on the body.[354] Red components, such as the pigment vermilion, were often added to processes that produced a gold pigment, even when they seem not to have had any practical effect on the chemical process.[355] This would indicate that red was seen as an essential ingredient in processes that sought to generate or transform.[356] The components of vermillion also often appear in recipes for gold pigments, such as that for mosaic gold (a pigment that imitated pure gold) by Cennino, which calls for "sal ammoniac, tin, sulphur, quicksilver, in equal parts; except less of the quicksilver."[357] Conservators have determined that the quicksilver (or mercury) is unnecessary to produce mosaic gold, but the underlying set of principles that informed this recipe seem to have held that sulfur and mercury, as the principles of all metals, were necessary for producing gold. It is of course also possible to understand the mosaic gold recipe as a transmutation of tin by means of the red powder of vermilion.[358]

Blood

Red was associated naturally with blood and in particular with the blood of Christ, which had purified mortals of their sins, just as gold purified their bodies and ores were purified by smelting and refining. A close relationship existed between religious devotion and metallurgical labor. For example, in indicating colors to be employed in illuminating manuscripts in the Middle Ages, scribes and illuminators often used a cross to indicate where the red pigment vermilion was to be used.[359] Cennino Cennini seems to have equated vermilion with blood and with the life force that blood carried. In "How to Paint Wounds," Cennino specified that a painter must "take straight vermilion; get it laid in wherever you want to do blood."[360] In a long passage, Cennino describes precisely how one is to lay in the flesh tones of living individuals in a fresco. He specifies that this flesh tone is never to be used on dead faces. Where this color in fresco is to be made from red ochre pigment, on panel, vermilion is used. Cennino called this color "incarnazione", and clearly regarded its use as akin to the incarnation of life in a body.[361] This giving life to (or "incarnating") a representation clearly represented to Cennino a straightforward artisanal technique by which the abstract principle and profound miracle of the incarnation of God and the Word in human flesh could be imitated.[362] No stronger link between the material and the spiritual and between devotion and making of materials could be found. This simultaneously material and spiritual understanding of the production of materials surely was an important component of the "theory" that underlay artisanal practices, although it was a *lived*, rather than *theorized* reality.

Blood was also regarded as an extremely powerful agent: it was often cited as the only way to soften or cut hard gemstones such as diamonds. Most such recipes called for goat's blood, but one recipe noted that human blood was also good for making gold and silver.[363] It is a feature of these recipes that they include details that would appear to indicate actual use:

If you want to carve a piece of rock crystal, take a two- or three-year-old goat and bind its feet together and cut a hole between its breast and stomach, in the place where the heart is, and put the crystal in there, so that it lies in its blood until it is hot. At once take it out and engrave whatever you want on it, while this heat lasts. When it begins to cool and become hard, put it back in the goat's blood, take it out again when it is hot, and engrave it. Keep on doing so until you finish the carving. Finally, heat it again, take it out and rub it with a woolen cloth so that you may render it brilliant with the same blood.[364]

The significance of blood itself for artisans can be seen in Benvenuto Cellini's (1500–71) account of casting his statue *Perseus Beheading Medusa* in 1545–1551, which Michael Cole has explored thoroughly.[365] Throughout Cellini's dramatic retelling of the casting, he equates his own life forces with those of the metal. As what Cellini called the "corpse" of the metal came back to life, he recovered from his fever. Thus, Cellini's own successful employment of a vivifying force that had sent life coursing back through the dead metal parallels his own recovery of life force.

A similar claim to control the life force was made in sculpture (in contrast to Cellini's words) by Adriaen de Vries (1556–1626) who displayed a similar understanding of the flow of metal and of blood. In his last statue, *Hercules Pomarius* (1626–27), de Vries left the sprues (concealed as vines) feeding directly into the figure's veins, thereby preserving, as Francesca Bewer has put it "the very channels through which the master metalsmith infuse[d] the figure with life."[366]

Red substances in general were associated with blood and regeneration, for example, coral was used against bleeding: "And it has been found by experience that it is good against any sort of bleeding. It is even said that, worn around the neck, it is good against epilepsy and the action of menstruation, and against storms, lightning, and hail. And if it is powdered and sprinkled with water on herbs and trees, it is reported to multiply their fruits. They also say that it speeds the beginning and end of any business."[367]

Lizards

This correspondence between blood, red, and gold is also of importance in a puzzling set of recipes such as that of the twelfth-century metalworker, Theophilus, for Spanish gold, concocted from "red copper, basilisk powder, human blood, and vinegar." In order to produce the basilisk powder, two 12–15-year-old cocks were put into a cage, walled in like in a dungeon with stones all around. These cocks are to be well-fed until they copulated and laid eggs, at which point toads then should replace the cocks to hatch the eggs, being fed bread throughout their confinement. Male chickens eventually emerged from the eggs, but after seven days they grew serpent tales. They were to be prevented from burrowing into the floor of their cage by the stones, and to further reduce the possibility of escape, they were to be put into brass vessels "of great size, perforated all over and with narrow mouths." These are closed up with copper lids and buried in the ground. The serpent-chickens, or basilisks, feed on the fine soil that falls through the perforations for six months, at which time, the vessels were to be uncovered and a fire lit under them to completely burn up the basilisks. Their ashes were finely ground and added to a third part of the dried and ground blood of a red-headed man which was then tempered with sharp vinegar. Red copper was to be repeatedly smeared with this composition, heated until red-hot then quenched in the same mixture until the composition eats through the copper. It thereby "acquire[d] the weight and color of gold" and was "suitable for all kinds of work."[368]

This recipe has excited much comment among historians, being viewed as a garbled set of instructions for making brass or for cementation.[369] The curator and conservator Arie Wallert has interpreted it as an alchemical recipe, with blood forming an alchemical "cover name" for sulfur and basilisk ash for mercury.[370] Sulphur and mercury were the essential components of the philosophers' stone to turn base metals—in this case copper—into gold. In his fascinating study of the relationship between red and yellow pigment recipes, conservator Spike Bucklow views this recipe as evidence for the centrality of the vermilion making process in providing the model for other processes of metallic transformation.[371]

Where Theophilus calls for basilisks, a later set of recipes calls for lizards. In a 1531 text that includes pigment-making and metal-working recipes, entitled the *Rechter Gebrauch der Alchimei*, there are several recipes for making noble metals through a process of catching, feeding, and burning lizards. Like in the instructions for softening hard stones by means of goat's blood, this recipe opens with quite precise instructions on how to catch these lizards. It instructs the reader to go very quietly in "felt slippers" and snatch the lizards very quickly before they give off their poison, then immediately plunge them into a pot of human blood. A recipe for making lizard-rib gold follows. It calls for two pounds of filed brass and a quart of goat's milk, and continues: In a pot wide at the bottom and narrow at the top, with a cover that has airholes in it, place nine lizards in the milk, put the cover on, and bury it in damp earth. Make sure the lizards have air so that they do not die. Let it stand until the seventh day in the afternoon. The lizards will have eaten the brass from hunger, and their strong poison will have compelled the brass to "transform itself to gold." Heat the pot at a low enough temperature to burn the lizards to ash but not to melt the brass. Cool the mixture, then pour the brass into a vessel, rinse it with water, then put it in a linen cloth and hang it in the smoke of sal ammoniac. Once it is washed and dried again, it will yield a "good calx solis," or powdered form of gold.[372] This recipe may employ lizard ash as a cover name for mercury, and the recipe may be to produce the painter's pigment mosaic gold.

The association of lizards with mercury occurs again in a book of secrets ascribed to Albertus Magnus, written no later than the fourteenth century. Among many secrets for lighting a house, one calls for cutting off the tail of a lizard and collecting the liquid that bleeds from it, "for it is like Quicksilver," and when it is put on a wick in a new lamp "the house shall seem bright and white, or gilded with silver."[373] In this recipe, lizards, mercury and the noble metal, silver, all were associated.

Lizards were associated with processes of putrefaction and generation more generally,[374] just as blood and mercury was associated with the generation of substances, both in pigments and metals. Animal and mineral generation might even be combined, as they are in a recipe that claims to yield a gold pigment that is produced by mixing mercury with a fresh hen's egg then putting it back under the hen for three weeks.[375] A similar identification of mercury with processes of generation appears in the 1540 *Pirotechnia* by the metalworker Vannoccio Biringuccio, who noted that the prospector for mercury should be on the lookout for verdant mountainsides, for all places where mercury is engendered "have abundant water and trees, and the grasses are very green, because it has a moist coolness in it and does not give off dry vapors as sulphur [does]."[376]

To conclude, then, the discussion of metalworkers' techniques and their practices of precision and experimentation have dominated historians' accounts of the relationship of metalworking to the development of modern chemistry. In contrast, I have attempted in this example to show how we might take account of these intersections between artisanal techniques and the development of modern ways of investigating nature, while at the same time delineating a less familiar worldview or "vernacular science" of materials and nature that appears to have underpinned and informed artisanal practices in pigment making and metalworking. Not surprisingly, this worldview does not overlap very neatly with a modern scientific understanding of the world. While I have done no more in this extended example than suggest the outlines of the web of correspondences, I think it is important to acknowledge that while the phrase "the working of metals" today conjures up the manipulation of inert matter with clear productive and economic meanings, in the early modern period, it had an entirely different meaning. Metalworking in the sixteenth century was part of a web that included vermilion, the color red, blood, mercury, gold, and lizards, and it gave access to the powers of nature, transformation, and generation. The manipulation of metals in early modern Europe was not simply about the handling and transformation of inert materials, but rather allowed the artisan to investigate and engage in life forces, in the relationship of matter to spirit, even the imitation of the most profound mysteries like the incarnation. On the one hand this was mundane and hard-headed practice that produced useful goods, but on the other, these artisanal techniques gave access to the greater powers of the universe. These practices, moreover, were neither rote, nor random, nor un-theorized, rather they were tied to a kind of lived theory, rather than one necessarily systematized and articulated in words, and they reveal an underlying set of principles. This is an assemblage of knowing and making, a means for struggling with matter; the broad prospect about which James Elkins was skeptical.

Global matters

Finally, I cannot help commenting on Claire Farago's challenge to the discipline of art history:

> The kind of art historical practice I would like to see in Renaissance studies goes all over the world, and deals with all kinds of practices, representational systems, cultural conditions; not at the level of social history, but at deeper epistemological levels, studying what happens when new identities are formed, when new communication occurs, when representational practices that have never been in contact before are suddenly in collision and contention, when the readability of the art changes because of contact, when people's ability to live changes because of their altered material culture. If those kinds of questions came to be of overriding importance in the field, if they were encouraged at the institutional level, we could have an entirely different kind of art history. It would look genuinely different. We would not just be looking at the canon of old masters in Europe. We would be looking at colonial productions. We would be looking at print culture. We would be looking at things made by artists without training. And we wouldn't be spending our time on taxonomies of that material. We would be examining the interesting processes that occur, maybe in terms of the Renaissance definition of art as work, as process: maybe that would be part of what we would be doing.

I cannot endorse strongly enough that this is what the history of science in the same period should also be about. The quickening of commerce and the advent of European expansion and colonialism were all important for the investigation of nature, but oddly, and similarly to art history, such large-scale phenomena have been almost completely neglected.[377] Historians of early modern science have considered the growth of science as part of the expansion of Europe in a relatively unsystematic manner. The entry of Europe into well-established trade routes in the eastern Mediterranean in the thirteenth through fifteenth centuries is a primary context for important developments in technical and textual knowledge of nature, and it marks an accelerated exchange of knowledge between different parts of the globe: Latin Christendom, Byzantium, the Ottoman Empire, Africa, China, and South Asia. A growing literature in art history examines the art objects and material goods that flowed into Europe from the East before and during the Renaissance. Art historians, especially those investigating material culture and commercial ties between Italy and the East, have begun to show how influential goods, commodities, and techniques from Byzantium and the Islamic world were in spurring the rapid changes in social and intellectual life beginning in fourteenth- and fifteenth-century Europe. We need analogous investigations in the history of science about trade routes and the manuscripts, instruments, and technological processes that followed them. Indeed, a history that integrates the flows of commodities and objects with the flow of knowledge—that is, that integrates material and intellectual culture—is sorely needed. This global commerce facilitated the accumulation and transformation of knowledge, but it also eventually shaped the growth of imperialism that came to employ science and ideas of progress as tools of empire.

We can think about knowledge and the objects of knowledge moving globally at this time, but as I tried to make clear in my answer to the "Whether and When" question, they also moved epistemically. The story of local modes of cognition and vernacular knowledge systems and the objects of knowledge, such as those of metalworkers, must be reconstructed by historians, but so must their connections to overarching developments like the emergence of modern science. How local ways of knowing became the purportedly transcendent, universal knowledge of science is a question that historians have only begun to research. But throughout all such research on both the local and the global, historians of science will continue to wrestle with the question of how to be a self-respecting historian and yet write a history of the modern world. Many more such stimulating conversations on this quandary remain to be convened among art historians and historians of science.

Adrian W. B. Randolph
Other Procrustations

The Cork conversation about the state of the field of Renaissance art history possessed a particular shape, for the transcript of the dialogue was structured by the familiar protruding figure of the bell curve.[378] The bell curve and the attendant term "outlier" were introduced by one of the seminar's conveners, James Elkins, and, despite some resistance from the panelists, it lodged the discussion within a potent set of visual forms. "One of my favorite metaphors for the idea of being 'inside' or 'outside' a field," said Elkins, "is what statisticians call an *outlier*: a point that is somewhere off on the thin tail of the bell curve, outside normative cut-off points. ('Standard distributions,' in statistics.)" At first blush, this textual image helped to sustain the binary with which Elkins had kicked off the conversation, pitting (good) "coherence" against (bad) "disarray". But it also complicated matters, for to Elkins it was clear that "outlier" status rather than contributing to the dissolution of the field was in fact a precondition of its coherence; creative "outliers" define the centre. Struggling to come to grips with this pattern, the participants found themselves, as it seems to me, set to the task of proving their status as "outliers" (that is, causes of creative "disarray"), while simultaneously engaged in a project of centre-formation (that is, trying to produce, or at least recognize, "coherence"). Could it be that the images suggested by, on the one hand, the words "coherence" and "disarray," and, on the other, by the guiding allusion to the bell curve distort?

Despite immediate challenges from the participants, especially Stephen Campbell and Fredrika Jakobs, the pattern of the bell curve, centres and outliers shaped the discussion in Cork. The conversation moved from one theme to another, considering issue by issue according to this vision of the field. Who occupies the centre? Who is an outlier? Is Vasari the centre against which all art historical practice is to be measured? Can humanism claim outlier status? Does the inclusion of women in the canon shift the centre? Can neo-aestheticist claims for the birth of art now fall on the fringes of the field's statistically arrayed methods? Is the field of Renaissance art history "centered" geographically, biographically, stylistically or politically? Are art historians who integrate modern methods and terminology in writing about Renaissance art "outliers"? The list could go on.

In addressing these and other questions, the participants adduced fascinating material; the intellectual vitality and variety of the field were amply demonstrated. The attention paid to intercultural studies that offer ways to address pre-modern internationalism and globalism, is, given broad trends in the humanities, appropriate. In different ways, Stephen Campbell and Claire Farago forwarded this agenda in their comments, the former, more obliquely, seeing in humanist culture and its dissonant framing of subjectivity a way out of (or beyond) tainted nationalistic agendas, and the latter promoting accounts of Renaissance art that trace the transmission of styles and motifs along the maritime trade routes of early modernity. Less fresh, but nonetheless still topical, were the tussles over Vasari; the status of the rational and irrational; and how the study of women artists alters views of the period. These, and other points of view, made reading the transcript for me a profitable experience. That said, the pattern of intellectual life suggested by the twinned metaphors of centre and "outlier" restricted the conversation. The imagery suggests data collected and plotted. It suggests that methodological choices and, indeed, authorship guarantee a form of stable academic identity, which can then be granted firm coordinates. Even if one admits that the writings that constitute the field can take on an ideal, plottable form, the figure that surely would result could never possess the centred, linear shape of a statistically-generated bell.

This is not to deny the transformative power, and therefore importance, of robust disciplinarity and of coherent intellectual movements and schools. These latter are, however, not singular centres, but rather distinct and dense clusters in an evolving environment. One may very well be an "outlier" in relation to another centre yet constitute a centre nonetheless. We live and work in a moment marked by intellectual diversity. The danger of incoherence posed by such *copia* is far less than that posed by narrowing projects of centre-production, prescriptions to follow, and the fear of different materials and methods. Rhizomatic lines of activity that traverse varied disciplinary territory, and in so doing cross and blur traditional boundaries, productively challenge monist models of intellectual life. They do not, as many seem to believe, necessarily lead to the dissolution of discipline and disciplinarity, or of fields and field-specific skills. A diffuse pattern of intellectual life can lead to increased metacritical sensitivity and to the development of more nodes and clusters in the intellectual environment. Such uncertainty at academic thresholds awakes considerable discomfort and it is understandable, emotionally if not intellectually, that projects like the Cork seminar should seek to reconstitute a singular charismatic core, for both field and discipline.

The alternative to such artificial order is not chaos. Other visual metaphors might have been more apt than centripetal coherence: George Kubler's constellations of objects might be adapted for productive historiographical ends; the internet and its webbed information offers an alternate, if already somewhat hackneyed, decentralizing model (although from a global perspective still very Western-centric); but I tend to think of academic life socially, as an urban environment marked by diversity, ragged neighbourhood precincts, political scuffles over public space, and the omnipresence of competing economic and social motivations. Rather than a complex environment, the tranquilizing order of the bell curve, which appeals to modes of knowledge inappropriate to humanistic understanding, simplifies matters.

The master metaphor of the Cork conversation of centre/outlier is not only empirically misleading. It also serves to reinforce disciplinary limits in a manner that corresponds to North American professional structures particularly. Within American academia art historians are, for the most part, rewarded by their declared identification not with the discipline but with their field. How many colleagues have told me how content they feel at RSA, and how dissatisfied by CAA? More often than not, we are hired to fulfil curricular time/spaces, not to work as art historians per se. For this reason alone, it would have been salutary to hear voices from scholars active in alternate systems.

I am sure that among those offering assessments of the Cork transcript, I shall not be alone in wondering how specifically European voices might have changed the course of the discussion. The presence of a scholar trained and working in Europe might have curtailed what I read as the sweeping, if not disdainful, characterization of

European scholars as period-bound and far less concerned with "theoretical debates" than their North American counterparts. It is indisputable that the history, present structures and tendencies of the discipline in Europe are quite different from those in North America; the European situation, however, cannot be summed up easily. The history of art in the UK, for example, should not be lumped together with the disciplinary practices in Austria, Belgium, Denmark, Finland, France, Germany, Ireland, Italy, the Netherlands, Poland, Russia, Spain, Sweden, or Switzerland (to name those countries that, to my knowledge, have a strong tradition in studying the Renaissance). It is true that the lower density of universities and research centres in Europe, in comparison to North America, means that despite much work possessing field-specific parameters, scholars also often tend to identify far more closely with the discipline than in North America. Thus many texts that appear to be rather local in their interests, may in fact play out within larger disciplinary debates. It is also only fair to point out that in certain countries the likelihood of scholars working in different periods is perhaps greater than in North America (the opposite was intimated at Cork). For example, the German system of having to publish one's *Habilitationsschrift*, which not only is meant to possess disciplinary and methodological range, but also has traditionally been particularly valued when written on a subject quite different than the author's Ph.D. dissertation. This system, although for various reasons now on the decline, actually encourages scholars to develop expertise in more than one field. My point is simply that the blanket characterizations offered at Cork do not do justice to the range of European art historical scholarship. And, that the admittance of a European voice might have made this clear. But, while we may bemoan the exclusion of European scholars from a discussion, pace Claire Farago, about European art (and I predict that other "assessors" will do so), I should like to point to another exclusion that, though perhaps less glaring, seems to me equally as troubling and determinant: the museum.

While I am sure that all the participants to one degree or another have worked in or with museums, there was no representative of what can only be understood as a major professional and methodological cluster in Renaissance art history. Lacking a representative, the museum ought to have at least figured in the discussions of the field of Renaissance art history. Why? For, at least, two reasons. Firstly, because so much necessary work is carried out by museum professionals, who produce fresh information and analyses. And secondly, because the museum and, especially, the exhibition define the field in a public and decisive manner. Ignoring the museum and its importance in framing the field is counter-productive. For in forming a picture of the discipline and field of the future, few areas are so badly in need of clarification. In North American Renaissance art history, there still exists a notable gap between progressive and curatorial art history. There are exceptions to this, but in their rarity they seem rather to prove than question the existence of the continuing breech. A legacy of the Cultural Wars, this division is lamentable for both sides. A lack of engagement with curatorial methods impoverishes much academic writing about art, and a concomitant ignorance or rejection of progressive art history weakens so much that passes through what is the major portal of communication between art history and the general public (leaving aside, of course, Dan Brown). The situation is not to be considered optimal. (Although I do not wish to present an overly optimistic view of Europe, it is helpful to consider the situation in the UK, France, or Germany where it is far more common to find major exhibitions curated by academic art historians, even progressive ones.)

Renaissance art historians can contribute to bridging the gap between the museum and academia. Indeed, in the diffuse wake of strong ideological criticism and poststructuralist scepticism, Renaissance art history possesses some formidable advantages, in general, over many other fields in the discipline. Having for the most part never jettisoned a belief in the productivity of the archive, nor in the essential utility of object-analysis, Renaissance art historians are not as unversed in the use of necessary disciplinary tools as practitioners in some other subfields. These tools should not be disdained as dull positivism; nor can I concur fully with Robert Williams's description of object-oriented scholarship at the end of his position paper as "largely a disguised form of bourgeois consumerism." Dealing with primary texts and especially objects, though perhaps not untainted ideologically, is nonetheless the essential task of the discipline of art history. It is unfortunate that students of the history of art seem often faced with a stark choice between connoisseurial fetishism and modes of analysis that seem destined to avoid the objects they purport to address. Renaissance art history, owing to its refusal to renounce certain commitments to object-analysis, can help demonstrate the falsity of such binaries.

Also, as Michael Cole quite rightly underlined, that the field of Renaissance art history possesses a particularly rich historiographical, even theoretical, tradition should be counted among one of its central strengths (although this should not be restricted to writings in German). This is perhaps worth emphasizing, because the most persuasive accounts of the nature of humanistic knowledge of which I am aware tend to stress the importance of complex and dynamic interpretative traditions. In Renaissance studies, we benefit not only from a relatively dense "archive" yielding positivistic data, but also a deep and (at least formerly) lively interpretative tradition. Maintaining a meaningful relation to this tradition is essential, if one wishes to avoid the sclerosis of thought that imperils so many humanistic disciplines. This hardening, to my thinking, often arises most dangerously from attempts to promote singular modes of understanding, usually imported from the sciences. This is not, at all, to denigrate scientific knowledge. Rather, it is only to acknowledge that if the humanities wish to play an active role in forming culture, the answer must reside not in a weak mimicry of dominant scientific methods, but rather in advancing strong modes of thinking appropriate to our disciplines and fields. As I see it, the historiographically lush field of Renaissance studies yields ample fodder for the development of humanistic approaches to understanding.

Given such advantages—enduring techniques and abilities to address primary sources, visual and textual, and a vibrant interpretative tradition—it is difficult for me to sympathize with the laments concerning Renaissance art history's lack of status. Anecdotal claims about historians of modern art not reading our texts should be dismissed for what they are, hearsay; this is not to contest their truth per se, so much as the status of such claims about assumed knowledge. Nonetheless, even if true, such a pattern may not only suggest Renaissance art history's fall from grace, but also certain deficiencies in the readership adduced. Rather than wringing our hands about the relative status of fields, we would be better served by exploring and affirming the forms of knowledge that Renaissance studies may sustain, and the disciplinary depth and interdisciplinary possibilities offered by the history of art.

Surely since William Bouwsma's AHA presidential address of 1979, it is common to state that the Renaissance does not represent a "natural" disciplinary centre, but only one that emerged from particular affective desires.[379] Bouwsma recognized the declining relevance of "Whig history" and the foundational accounts that pictured the Renaissance as the origin of modernity. His diagnosis could equally be seen to critique the supposedly transformative moments of the French Revolution, Benjamin's Paris, or Cold War New York. The history of art has lost much time seeking out modernity's seed in such time/places. Why? The Cork conversation helps answer. The division of the discipline into semi-autonomous fields tends to insulate art historians from broader concerns and to stimulate competition among fields. Thus, it is necessary to argue for the relevance of Renaissance art history, in reference to supposedly successful competitors (the art history addressing seventeenth-century Dutch art, or nineteenth-century Parisian). This is Neronian fiddling, since opinions hostile to the humanities burn close by. Instead of trying to formulate a priori specious claims for why the Renaissance deserves attention more than any other subfield, I would suggest we seek rather to invest in our disciplinary ties, reminding ourselves why the history of art is relevant today. In order to do so, we must possess a rudimentary sense of why Renaissance studies appeared to be so exemplary a field in the second-half of the twentieth century.

The erstwhile dominance of Renaissance studies in the United States developed, as it seems to me, from the thirst felt for European culture at the moment of its apparent disintegration in World War II and from its apparent "systematicity," which would seem to provide a reassuring prototype for American pragmatism.[380] A productive comparison may be drawn with the progressive strain of medieval studies that dominated the history of art's early development in North America. With the gradual eclipse of this school of thought, associated with Charles Haskins and Joseph Strayer, whose work tended to recognize in the Middle Ages modernity's roots, by what has been called "hard-edged alterity," the period has come to be understood less as a point of origin than as a defining "other". A similar process—as the portion of the Cork discussion devoted to the "irrational" in the Renaissance revealed—seems to be going on in Renaissance studies.[381]

In Cold War America, the Renaissance came to replace the Middle Ages in progressive historical accounts, especially owing to the work of expatriate German-speaking scholars, who advanced a modernizing image of the Italian Renaissance. This, of course, is most evident in the famous work of Hans Baron, but the anti-totalitarian ideology of the liberal individual (analogous to that described, in very different ways, by Karl Popper and Lionel Trilling) underpins the work of other expatriates like Paul Oskar Kristeller, Felix Gilbert, as well as Erwin Panofsky, to name but the most famous. Jettisoning the "irrational" view of the Renaissance, which emerged in the Weimar Republic and is now associated with Aby Warburg, the German-speaking émigrés offered a systematic account of a period marked by an integration of the intellectual, religious, cultural and political.[382] This system was held together by a pre-occupation with humanism, which held out the possibility of a logical order beneath the rag-tag reality of history, and by a commitment to methods with the promise of scientific disprovability. This combination proved to be very successful in securing Renaissance studies an enviable position within the North American academy.

But things have changed. Students of eighteenth- and nineteenth-century European culture have successfully linked their enterprises to a (predictable) cultural history that recognizes modernism's arrival in their periods. And, just as the modernizing view of the Middle Ages was upended by dutiful academic scions turned patricides (and the gender often does obtain), who toppled the totemic theories of their predecessors, so too in Renaissance studies, in the absence of a grand narrative, an altogether more varied picture of the period has emerged. The impulses of Annaliste historical methods, sociology and social history have led to far broader accounts of how cultural artefacts were commissioned, produced, circulated and used in the Renaissance. Perhaps even more telling is the struggle to decentre the assumed neutral subject at the core of most historical analysis. The movement toward history not written with the scientific ideal of comprehensive and universal truth, spearheaded, especially, by feminist historians and art historians, has altered decisively prevailing hermeneutic norms. It is more common in today's history and art history to hear not only autonomous, disembodied voices (past and present), but also the dialogic clash of historical opinions expressed by embodied subjects in action.[383]

This is a very positive development, with the only major peril I discern being complacency and conformity. At present it worries me that so many disciplines in the humanities seem to find closure in the religious, and especially in the cultic or mystical. Renaissance studies—historical and art historical—seems to be tending in a similar direction. In the history of art, neo-aestheticist (and, to my thinking, fundamentally anti-humanistic) claims gain sustenance from a very real frustration with predictable ideological critiques. This, rather than leading to probing analyses of objects, tends to be just another way of avoiding—through idealistic sublation—the objects at the heart of art historical analysis. And, the enduringly popular marionette-subjectivity of the now-old New Historicism often seems to mirror the preoccupations of the interpreter and too little those of the historical self summoned up. While I am gratified to see such divergent trends in the field, I would like to see developments of this kind discussed so that they do not harden into assumed orthodoxies. It is one of the positive contributions of the Cork dialogue that it opened up a forum for such discussion. It is my hope that the seminar will spur us all to frame further dialogues, not however with the goal of finding an allusive centre (that "exquisitely" sensitive political zone, as Elkins called it), but rather in a manner that recognizes the inherent pluralism and complexity of intellectual life—its many neighbourhoods, if you will. What is more, it is in my opinion desirable that humanistic disciplines like the history of art define more carefully the type of knowledge and understanding that they can forward. Instead of grafting our claims onto logical-positive appeals to scientific epistemological norms, or onto ethereal metaphysical ideals, the humanities should foster stronger and varied accounts of understanding appropriate to our data and interpretative traditions.

Historians of Renaissance art, owing to the historiographical and pedagogical tradition within which we operate, are well-positioned to participate actively in such an enterprise.

Notes

1. http://www.kum.dk/sw37439.asp (official home page of the Danish Ministry of Culture). The Cultural Canon proper: http://www.kulturkanon.kum.dk/.

2. Horst Appuhn, *Der Bordesholmer Altar und die anderen Werke von Hans Brüggemann* (Königstein i. T. 1983). Ingebord Kähler, *Der Bordesholmer Altar. Zeichen in einer Krise. Ein Kunstwerk zwischen kirchlicher Tradition und humanistischer Gedankenwelt am Ausgang des Mittelalters* (Neumünster 1981; Studien zur schleswig-holsteinischen Kunstgeschichte 14). Doris, Ottesen, *Bordesholmalteret i Slesvig Domkirke* (Copenhagen 2004). On the question of Brüggemann's place of birth: R. Doebner, "Des Bildschnitzers und Malers Hans Brüggemann Geburtsort," *Repertorium für Kunstwissenschaft* 24 (1901) 124–126; Friedrich Barenscheer, "Wurde der Schöpfer des Bordesholmer Altars in Husum oder Walsrode geboren?", *Nordelbingen* 30 (1961) 100–102.

3. Sculptor Hein Heinsen from the The Royal Danish Academy of Fine Arts quoted in Schleswig-Holsteinische Landeszeitung 26th of January, 2006.

4. Viggo Thorlacius-Ussing, "En Madonnafigur af Hans Brüggemann i det danske kongehus' eje," *Aarböger for Nordisk Oldkyndighed og Historie II*, 19 (1929) 263–282.

5. Nikolaus Pevsner, *The Englishness of English Art* (London 1956); Nikolaus Pevsner, *Ruskin and Viollet-le-Duc. Englishness and Frenchness in the Appreciation of Gothic Architecture* (London 1969); Paul Pieper, *Das Westfälische in Malerei und Plastik* (Münster 1964).

6. Michael Billig, *Banal Nationalism* (London 1995).

7. Horst Janson et al., *Janson's History of Art: The Western Tradition*, 7th ed. (2007); Marilyn Stokstad, *Art History*, 2nd ed. (2005); Helen Gardner et al., *Gardner's Art through the Ages*, 12th ed. (2005).

8. Georg Nordensvan, *Svensk konst och svenska konstnärer i nittonde århundradet* (Stockholm 1892); Georg Nordensvan, *Sveriges konst: från 1700-talets slut till 1900-talets början i dess hufvuddrag* (Stockholm 1904); Carl G. Laurin, *Konsthistoria* (Stockholm 1900); Carl G. Laurin, *Konsten i Sverige* (1915); *Svensk konsthistoria*, Axel L. Romdahl & Johnny Roosval, eds. (Stockholm 1913); Andreas Lindblom, *Sveriges konsthistoria: från forntid till nutid I–III* (Stockholm 1944–46); *Svensk konstkrönika under 100 år*, Ragnar Josephson, ed. (Stockholm 1944); Henrik Cornell, *Den svenska konstens historia I–II* (Stockholm 1944–1946); Andreas Lindblom, *Svensk konst: från stenåldern till rymdåldern* (Stockholm 1960); Gunnar Berefelt, *Svensk konsthistoria: en kort översikt* (Stockholm 1971); *Konsten i Sverige*, Sven Sandström, ed., 1–8 (Stockholm 1974–1981); *Svensk konsthistoria*, Mereth Lindgren, ed. (Lund 1986); *Svensk konsthandbok*, Lena Johannesson, ed. (Stockholm 2007). Another example is the current

work on a new Estonian many-volumed handbook, which replaces an older one, written during Soviet times: *Eesti kunsti ajalugu 2*, 1520–1770, Krista Kodres, ed. (Tallinn 2005).

9. Lena Johannesson, "Förord," *Svensk konsthandbok* (Stockholm 2007) 13.

10. Gunnar Danbolt, *Norsk kunsthistorie: bilde og skulptur frå vikingtida til i dag* (2nd ed., Oslo, 2001).

11. Jan Svanberg, *Saint George and the Dragon* (Stockholm, 1998).

12. Cf. The introduction "Om konst i allmänhet och den svenska i synnerhet" in Andreas Lindblom, *Sveriges konsthistoria fran frontid till nutid 1. Fran stenaldern till Gustav Vasa* (Stockholm 1944) vi ff.

13. Sw. *immigrantkonstnärer, passagekonstnärer.*

14. Brunkeberg is a ridge just north of the centre of Stockholm; in medieval times it was outside the city proper.

15. C. G. Styffe, *Bidrag till Skandinaviens historia ur utländska arkiver 4. Sverige i Sten Sture den äldres tid, 1470–1503* (Stockholm, 1875) xxvi.

16. S. U. Palme, *Sten Sture den äldre* (Stockholm, 1968; orig. ed. 1950) 7.

17. Jan Svanberg, *Sankt Göran och draken* (Stockholm, 1993); English translation of the same, *Saint George and the Dragon* (Stockholm, 1998). Gerhard Eimer, *Bernt Notke. Das Wirken eines niederdeutschen Künstlers im Ostseeraum* (Bonn, 1985).

18. D. Feldmann, "Zur Bedeutung von Notkes St. Georgs-Monument in Stockholm," *Konsthistorisk tidskrift* 65 (1976) 19–38; esp. p. 32 ff.

19. Jonny Roosval, *Nya Sankt Görans studier* (Stockholm, 1924) 93.

20. Eimer, *Bernt Notke*, 104.

21. This complicated reconstruction was done between 1914 and 1932: Johnny Roosval, *Riddar Sankt Göran i Stockholms Stora eller Sankt Nicolai kyrka* (Stockholm, 1919); also Roosval, *Nya Sankt Göran.*

22. The openings were later covered with thin painted boards. The style of painting seems to suggest that the boards were attached in late medieval times, that is, in the early sixteenth century.

23. Roosval, *Nya Sankt Göran*, 89, 117: "Mitt liik sattes tha i bykyrkone in/i sancti iörens altare [. . .]".

24. M.J. Liebmann, *Die deutsche Plastik 1350–1550* (Leipzig, 1982) 260. O.G. Oexle, "Memoria, Memorialüberlieferung", *Lexikon des Mittelalters* VI, 510 ff.

25. Feldmann, *Zur Bedeutung*, 31.

26. H. Hildebrand, "Hr Stens Sankt Jöran," *Antiqvarisk tidskrift för Sverige* 7:4 (1885), 1–76, 8. S. Anjou, *Sten Stures riksmounument. Bidrag till frågor angående rekonstruktion och uppställningsplats för S:t Göransgruppen i Stockholms Storkyrka* (Fornvännen, 1938), 343–359, esp. p. 343, Roosval, *Riddar Sankt Göran*, 13, 18.

27. Anjou, *Sten Stures*, 343.

28. "Darin zeigt sich der Dualismus von Notkes Werk, dass die Grenze zu einer humanistischen Weltauffassung berührt, aber nicht überschreitet". Liebmann, *Die deutsche Plastik*, 260.

29. Dan Brown, *The Da Vinci Code* (NY: Doubleday, 2003).

30. Leonardo da Vinci, *The Notebooks*, ed. and trans. Jean Paul Richter (NY: Dover, 1970), I: 301–303, 328.

31. Charles Hope, "Altarpieces and the Requirements of Patrons," in *Christianity and the Renaissance* (Syracuse, NY: Syracuse UP, 1990), 535–571.
32. Erwin Panofsky, *Studies in Iconology: Humanistic Themes in the Art of the Renaissance* (New York: Oxford UP, 1939), 3–31.
33. For disguised symbolism, see Erwin Panofsky, "Reality and Symbol in Early Flemish Painting: 'Spiritualia sub Metaphoris Corporalium,'" in *Early Netherlandish Painting: Its Origins and Character* (Cambridge, MA: Harvard UP, 1964), I: 131–148. Panofsky, 141–142, distinguishes between the type of symbolism in Trecento Italian painting as "having a definite and easily recognizable iconographic significance," and more densely symbolic Netherlandish paintings. Even in these works, however, most of the symbolic elements are repeated so often in many pictures, and expressed in popular hymns, that they would have been easily recognizable to a broad swathe of society in the Renaissance.
34. On the phenomenal success of Irving Stone's 1961 novel, see Paul Grendler, *The European Renaissance in American Life* (Westport, CT: Praeger, 2006), 204–212.
35. Hans Belting, *Likeness and Presence: A History of the Image before the Era of Art*, trans. Edmund Jephcott (Chicago: University of Chicago Press, 1994).
36. Belting's discussion of the Renaissance is complex. He states (p. 472) that the two types of images coexisted in the Renaissance and even that an image can have "two different faces." Nevertheless, his courageously broad account is a story of one type of image supplanting another.
37. David Freedberg, *The Power of Images: Studies in the History and Theory of Response* (Chicago: University of Chicago Press, 1989).
38. See John Shearman, *Only Connect . . . Art and the Spectator in the Italian Renaissance* (Princeton: Princeton UP, 1992).
39. For a discussion of these tropes of ekphrasis in Antiquity and the Renaissance, see Norman Land, *The Viewer as Poet: The Renaissance Response to Art* (University Park, PA: Pennsylvania State UP, 1994).
40. Shearman, *Only Connect*, 135–137.
41. Elizabeth Cropper, "On Beautiful Women, Parmigianino, *Petrarchismo*, and the Vernacular Style," *Art Bulletin* 57 (March 1976): 374–394.
42. See, for example, Vasari's *Justice*, which is an extraordinarily complex image of Astrea with, among other exotic attributes, an ostrich and a hippo scepter, discussed in Clare Robertson, *Il Gran Cardinale: Alessandro Farnese, Patron of the Arts* (New Haven: Yale UP, 1992), 55–57.
43. "rapir l'animo di meraviglia, & infiammarlo d'ardore," Gabriele Paleotti, *Discorso intorno alle imagini sacre et profane* (Bologna: Alessandro Benacci, 1582), 245. Paleotti is criticizing those who make allegorical images too easily understood.
44. Joan Kelly-Gadol, "Did Women Have a Renaissance?" in Renate Bridenthal and Claudia Koonz, eds., *Becoming Visible: Women in European History* (Boston, 1977) 137–164.
45. Denys Hays, *The Italian Renaissance in its Historical Background* (Cambridge, 1962) 2.
46. Williams, "Starting Points" essay.

47. "The Art Seminar" (JE).
48. Claire Farago, *Reframing the Renaissance: Visual Culture in Europe and Latin America 1450–1650* (New Haven & London, 1995). See also Norman Bryson, "Art in Context," in Mieke Bal and Inge Boer, ed. *The Point of Theory: Practices of Cultural Analysis* (New York, 1994); Jonathan Culler, *Framing the Sign: Criticism and Its Institutions* (Norman, Oklahoma, 1988).
49. Clifford Geertz, *The Interpretation of Culture*, (New York, 1973).
50. "The Art Seminar," n. 9.
51. " '*Fuori le mura*': Opening up the Period Eye on Florentine Renaissance Art," paper presented at the *Conference on Italian Art Art in Honor of Andrew Ladis*, Georgia Museum of Art, Athens, Georgia, September 7–9, 2006.
52. David Friedman, *Florentine New Towns: Urban Design in the Late Middle Ages* (Cambridge, MA, 1988), 167.
53. "A Document for Titian's *St. Roch*," a Shorter Notice in *Print Quarterly* 19 (2002) 275–277.
54. "The Art Seminar" (MK). See also my *Raphael, Dürer, and Marcantonio Raimondi: Copying and the Italian Renaissance Print* (London and New Haven, 2004) esp. 142–147.
55. Bruno Latour, "Drawing Things Together," in *Representation in Scientific Practice*, Michael Lynch and Steve Woolgar (eds.), MIT Press, Cambridge, MA, 1988, 19–68. See also my "Paint/Print/Public," in Peter Weibel and Bruno Latour, ed., *Making Things Public: Atmospheres of Democracy*, Cambridge, MA: MIT Press, 2005, 686–693.
56. Mikhail Bakhtin, *The Dialogic Imagination: Four Essays*, ed. Michael Holquist, trans. Caryl Emerson & Michael Holquist (Austin: University of Texas Press, 1981). See, with further bibliography, Dorothea Heitsch and Jean-François Vallée, eds., *Printed Voices: The Renaissance Culture of Dialogue* (Toronto, 2004).
57. Svetlana Alpers, *The Art of Describing: Dutch Art in the Seventeenth Century* (Chicago: Chicago University Press, 1983).
58. Erwin Panofsky, *Studies in Iconology: Humanistic Themes In the Art of the Renaissance* (New York: Harper & Row, 1962 [1st ed. 1939]), chap. V: "The Neoplatonic Movement in Florence and North Italy (Bandinelli and Titian)," 129–169, esp. 150–169.
59. Charles Hope, "Problems of Interpretation: Titian's Erotic Paintings," in *Tiziano e Venezia: Convegno internazionale di studi, Venezia 1978* (Vicenza: Editore Neri Pozza, 1980), 111–124. For other non-Neoplatonic, now mostly gendered approaches, see Carlo Ginzburg, Titian, Ovid, and Sixteenth-Century Codes for Erotic Illustration, *Clues, Myths and the Historical Method*, trans, by John and Anne Tedeschi (Baltimore: The Johns Hopkins University Press, 1989), 77–95 and 197–200; David Rosand, "So-And-So Reclining on Her Couch," in *Titian 500* (*Studies in the History of Art* 45, Center for Advanced Study in the Visual Arts, Symposium Papers XXV), ed Joseph Manca (Washington: National Gallery of Art, 1993), 101–119; Rona Goffen, *Titian's Women* (New Haven and London: Yale University Press, 1997); eadem, "Sex, Space, and Social History in Titian's *Venus of Urbino*," in *Titian's Venus of Urbino*, ed.

R. Goffen (Cambridge and New York: Cambridge University Press, 1997), 63–90; Daniel Arasse, "The Venus of Urbino, or the Archetype of a Glance," *ibidem*, 91–107; Daniela Bohde, *Haut, Fleisch und Farbe: Körperlichkeit und Materialität in den Gemälden Tizians* (Emsdetten and Berlin: Edition Imorde, 2002), esp. 127–200; François Quiviger, "Fleurs éparpillées dans deux tableaux du *Cinquecento* vénitien: Essai d'iconographie olfactive," in *Flore au paradis: Emblématique et vie religieuse aux XVI et XVII siècles*, ed. Paulettee Choné and Bénédicte Gaulard (Glasgow: Glasgow Emblem Studies, 2004), 153–167, esp. 162–166; Nicola Suthor, *Augenlust bei Tizian: Zur Konzeption sensueller Malerei in der Frühen Neuzeit* (Munich: Wilhelm Fink Verlag, 2004), esp. 51–74.

60. Christopher S. Wood, "Art History's Normative Renaissance," in *The Italian Renaissance in the Twentieth Century: Acts of an International Conference, Florence, Villa I Tatti, June 9–11, 1999*, ed. Allen J. Grieco, Michael Rocke and Fiorella Gioffredi Superbi (Florence: Leo S. Olschki Editore, 2002), 65–92, esp. 82. For another account of the demise of neoplatonic interpretations, see Horst Bredekamp, "Götterdämmerung des Neuplatonismus," *Kritische Berichte* 14. 4 (1986): 39–48 (reprinted in *Die Lesbarkeit der Kunst: Zur Geistes-Gegenwart der Ikonologie*, ed. Andreas Beyer [Berlin: Verlag Klaus Wagenbach, 1992], 75–83 and 102–106).

61. Panofsky, *Early Netherlandish Painting: Its Origins and Character* (Cambridge, Mass.: Harvard University Press, 1958). From the extensive literature in this area I will here mention only a few works that react critically to Panofsky's thesis on "disguised symbolism": James Marrow, "Symbol and Meaning in Northern Art of the Late Middle Ages and the Early Renaissance," *Simiolus* 16 (1986): 150–169; Craig Harbison, "Realism and Symbolism in Early Flemish Painting," *The Art Bulletin* 66 (1984): 588–602; idem, "Visions and Meditations in Early Flemish Painting," *Simiolus* 15 (1985): 87–118; and idem, "Iconography and Iconology," in *Early Netherlandish Paintings: Rediscovery, Reception and Research*, eds. Bernhard Ridderbos, Anne van Buren and Henk van Veen (Amsterdam: Amsterdam University Press, 2005), 378–406 and 436–438.

62. *Going for Baroque: 18 Contemporary Artists Fascinated with the Baroque and Rococo*, exh. cat. (Baltimore: The Contemporary and The Walters, 1995). Mieke Bal, "Auf die Haut / Unter die Haut: Barockes steigt an die Oberfläche," in *Barock: Neue Sichtweisen einer Epoche*, ed. Peter J. Burgard (Wien, Köln and Weimar: Böhlau Verlag, 2001), 17–51; "Ecstatic Aesthetics: Metaphoring Bernini," in *Compelling Visuality: The Work of Art in and out of History*, ed. Claire Farago and Robert Zwijnenberg (Minneapolis and London: University of Minnesota Press, 2003), 1–30.

63. Gilles Deleuze, *Le Pli: Leibniz et le baroque* (Paris: Les éditions de Minuit, 1988).

64. Bal, "Ecstatic Aesthetics," 5.

65. For two comprehensive surveys in English, see Jan Bialostocki, *The Art of the Renaissance in Eastern Europe: Hungary—Bohemia—Poland* (Oxford: Phaidon Press, 1976); and Thomas DaCosta Kaufmann, *Court, Cloister & City: The Art and Culture of Central Europe, 1450–1800* (Chicago: The University of Chicago Press, 1995). For more bibliography, see idem (in

collaboratopn with Heiner Borggrefe and Thomas Fusenig), *Art and architecture in central Europe, 1550–1620: An annotated bibliography* (new ed., Marburg: Jonas Verlag, 2003).

66. The concept of acculturation in regard to the relationship between Italian and Central European art was also advocated by DaCosta Kaufmann, "Italian sculptors and sculpture outside of Italy (chiefly in Central Europe): Problems of approach, possibilities of reception," in *Reframing the Renaissance: Visual Culture in Europe and Latin America, 1450–1650*, ed. Claire Farago (New Haven and London: Yale University Press, 1995), 46–66 and 306–308, esp. 57.
* I would like to thank Thomas DaCosta Kaufmann and Christopher Wood for their suggestions on the first version of this essay.

67. The subject has an enormous bibliography; important texts include: Werner Kaegi, *Jacob Burckhardt. Eine Biographie* (7 Bde., Basel- Stuttgart 1947–1982); Otto Kultermann, *Geschichte der Kunstgeschichte: der Weg einer Wissenschaft* (2nd ed., Frankfurt am Main and Vienna, 1981) 175–185; A.Buck, ed., *Renaissance und Renaissancismus von Jacob Burckhardt bis Thomas Mann* (Tübingen, 1990); Francis Haskell, *History and its Images: Art and the Interpretation of the Past* (New Haven: Yale University Press, 1993) 331–346; C.Farago, ed., *Reframing the Renaissance: Visual Culture in Europe and Latin America, 1450–1650* (New Haven and London, 1995); John Roderick Hinde, *Jacob Burckhardt and the Crisis of Modernity* (Montreal, Ithaca, 2000); Richard Sigurdson, *Jacob Burckhardt's Social and Political Thought* (Toronto, 2004).

68. Among the early reviews of the book are: Anthony Blunt, *The Burlington Magazine*, 119 (1977) 782–785; Rudolf Zeitler, *The Journal of the Society of Architectural Historians*, 36 (1977) 261–262; and Thomas DaCosta Kaufmann, *The Art Bulletin*, 60, (1978) 164–169. Among the later assessments of Bialostocki's importance are namely: Piotr Skubiszewski, "Jan Bialostocki," *The Burlington Magazine*, 131 (1989) 422; Ján Bakoš, "Peripherie und kunsthistorische Entwicklung," *Ars* (Journal of the Institute of Art History of the Slovak Academy of Sciences) (1991) 1–11; Lech Kalinowski, "Jan Bialostocki, jako historyk sztuki (Bialostocki as a Historian of Art)," *Folia historiae artium*, 28 (1992) 5–11: Sergiusz Michalski, "Jan Bialostocki a ewolucja historii sztuki po roku 1945 (Jan Bialostocki and the Evolution of Art History after 1945)," *Ars longa: prace dedykowane pamieci profesora Jana Bialostockiego (Ars Longa. Essays dedicated to the memory of Professor Jan Bialostocki)*; Materialy sesji Stowarzyszenia Historyków Sztuki,Warszawa (1999) 53–68; and Thomas DaCosta Kaufmann, *Toward a geography of art* (Chicago, 2004) esp. pp. 96–97.

69. Jacques Le Goff, *My Quest for the Middle Ages*, R. Veasey, trans. (New York, 2003) 28–29. (Originally published as Jacques Le Goff avec la collaboration de Jean-Maurice de Montremy, *À la Recherche du Moyen Âge*, Editions Louis Audibert, 2003, 45–47).

70. Claire Farago, " 'Vision Itself Has Its History': 'Race', Nation, and Renaissance Art History." In: *Reframing the Renaissance* (as in n. 1) 68–72.

71. Bruce Boucher, "Jacob Burckhardt and the 'Renaissance' North of the

Alps," *Time and Place. The Geohistory of Art*, Thomas DaCosta Kaufmann and Elizabeth Pilliod eds., (Aldershot, 2005) 21–35, esp. p. 22.

72. Michalski (as in n. 2) 57–58

73. Thomas DaCosta Kaufmann, (as in n.2) 168; Thomas DaCosta Kaufmann, "Will the Jagiellonias again have their day? The State of Scholarship on the Jagiellonians and Art in the Hungarian and Czech Lands," *Die Jagiellonen. Kunst und Kultur einer europäischen Dynastie an der Wende zur Neuzeit.* Dietmar Popp, Robert Suckale, eds. (Nürnberg : Germanisches Nationalmuseum, 2002) 207–213.

74. Ingrid Ciulisová, "Humanismus a renesancia. Mestá, umenie a idey Erazma Rotterdamského (Humanism and the Renaissance: Cities, Art, and the Ideas of Erasmus of Rotterdam)," *Problémy dejín výtvarného umenia Slovenska*, Ján Bakoš, ed. (Bratislava 2002) 120–145, esp. pp. 120–122.

75. Christopher Wood, "Art History's Normative Renaissance," *The Italian Renaissance in the Twentieth Century*, Allen J. Grieco, Michael Rocke, Fiorella Gioffredi Superbi, eds. (Florence 2002) 65–92, esp. p. 85

76. I would like to thank Stephen Campbell for his reading of my essay.

77. For the history of the art market, see Jean Wilson, "Marketing Paintings in the Late Medieval Belgium," in *Artistes, artisans et production artistique au Moyen Age: rapports provisoires* (Paris, 1986), 2, 1759–1766; Dan Ewing, "Marketing Art in Antwerp 1460–1560: Our Lady's Pand," *The Art Bulletin*, 72 (1990) 558–584; Filip Vermeylen, *Painting for the Market: Commercialization of Art in Antwerp's Golden Age* (Turnhout, 2003).

78. Ernst H. Gombrich, *Art and Illusion. A Study in the Psychology of Pictorial Representation* (Oxford, 1960); Victor I. Stoichita, *L'Instauration du tableau* (Paris, 1983).

79. "It is characteristic of the most dismal of minds always to use clichés and never their own inventions." See Jos Koldeweij, "Hieronymus Bosch and his city," in *Hieronymus Bosch. The Complete Paintings and Drawings* (Ghent-Rotterdam, 2001) 27.

80. On the connoisseurship, see Max J. Friedländer, *On Art and Connoisseurship* (London, 1942); *Berenson and the Connoisseurship* (London, 1942); *Berenson and the Connoisseurship of Italian Painting*, D. A. Brown, ed. (Washington, 1979).

81. Michel Hochmann, *Venise et Rome 1500–1600. Deux écoles de peinture et leurs échanges* (Geneva, 2004).

82. André Chastel, *La crise de la Renaissance* (Geneva, 1968) 65–68.

83. Ernst H. Gombrich, "Renaissance Artistic Theory and the Development of Landscape Painting," *Gazette des Beaux-Arts*, 41 (1953) 335–360.

84. We developed this idea in *La Naissance des genres* (Paris, 2005). See also Max J. Friedländer, *Über die Landschaftmalerei und andere Bildgattungen* (The Hague, 1949); Charles Sterling, *La Nature morte* (Paris, 1952).

85. Svetlana Alpers, *The Art of Describing* (Chicago, 1983).

86. Stephen J. Campbell, *The Cabinet of Eros: Renaissance Mythological Painting and the Studiolo of Isabella d'Este* (New Haven-London, 2006).

87. A survey of the different interpretations can be found in Salvatore Settis, *La "Tempesta" interpretata: Giorgione, i committenti, il soggetto* (Turin, 1978).

88. For the notion of "art," see Meyer Howard Abrams, "Art-as-such. The

Sociology of Modern Aesthetics" and "From Addison to Kant. Modern Aesthetics and the Exemplary Art," *in Doing Things with Texts. Essays in Criticism and Critical Theory*, Michael Fischer, ed. (New York-London, 1989) 135–187.

89. Developed during the 1960s, the reflection was enriched with the infra-category of "anticlassicism" which would define the Pontormo's generation. See Antonio Pinelli, *La Bella Maniera* (Turin, 1993).

90. The rediscovery of the "Antwerp Mannerists" is due to Max J. Friedländer, "Die Antwerpener Manieristen von 1520," *Jahrbuch der Königlich Preuszischen Kunstsammlungen*, 36 (1915) 65–91. The notion of "Gothic Mannerism" implicit in French and Belgian art historians such as Paul Philippot, *La peinture dans les anciens Pays-Bas. XVème-XVIème siècles* (Paris, 1994) 109–110. For the "Renaissance Gothic," see Ethan Matt Kavaler, "Renaissance Gothic in the Netherlands: the Uses of Ornament," *The Art Bulletin*, 82 (2000) 226–251; also the « Starting Points » essay in this volume. See also the discussion in "Architecture européenne: un gothique de la Renaissance autour de 1500?" *Perspective. La revue de l'INHA*, 2 (2006) 2, 280–288.

91. Erwin Panofsky, *Early Netherlandish Painting: its Origins and Character* (Cambridge, 1953) chap. 6. As the title of a collection in the Brepols Editions, the expression *"ars nova"* is frequently used by the contributors of the *Corpus des primitifs flamands* and the *Colloques du dessin sous-jacent*.

92. For example the exhibition of the Flemish Primitives in Bruges in 1902 or that of the French Primitives in Paris in 1904. See Francis Haskell, *The Ephemeral Museum. Old Masters Paintings and the Rise of the Art Exhibitions* (London-New Haven, 2000); *Primitifs français. Découvertes et redécouvertes*, Dominique Thiébaut, Philippe Lorentz and François-René Martin, eds. (Paris, 2004).

93. Enrico Castelnuovo and Carlo Ginzburg, "Centro e periferia," in *Storia dell'arte italiana. I. Questioni e metodi*, Giovanni Previtali, ed. (Turin, 1979) 285–352. See also Jan Bialostocki, "Some Values of Artistic Periphery," in *World Art. Themes of Unity in Diversity, Acts of the XXVIth International Congress of History of Art*, Irving Lavin, ed. (London, 1989) I, 49–58.

94. Developed by Fernand Braudel, the idea of a Mediterranean culture was illustrated by the *Exposicion de primitivos mediterraneos* (Barcelona, 1952) and more recently by the exhibitions *El Renacimiento Mediterraneo* (Madrid, 2001) and *The Age of Van Eyck: The Mediterranean World and Early Netherlandish Painting 1430–1530*, Till-Holger Borchert, ed. (London, 2002). Developed by Enrico Castelnuovo, the idea of an Alpine culture was exemplified by the recent exhibitions *Il Gotico nelle Alpi* (Trento, 2002) and *Corti e Città* (Turin, 2006).

95. For example the German identity was studied by Larry Silver, "Germanic Patriotism in the age of Dürer," in *Dürer and his culture*, Dagmar Eichberger and Charles Zika, eds. (Cambridge, 1998) 38–68.

96. For example, *Painting and Experience in Fifteenth Century Italy* (Oxford, 1972) or *The Limewood Sculptors of Renaissance Germany* (New Haven, 1980).

97. Erwin Panofsky, *Meaning in the Visual Arts: Papers in and on Art History* (New York, 1955).
    * I would like to acknowledge the helpful critiques of Sarah P. Pittock, Dana Leibsohn and Ann Jensen Adams on earlier drafts of this essay.

98. For one example, see Rogelio Ruiz Gomar, Unique Expressions: Painting in New Spain, In *Painting a New World*, eds. Donna Pierce et al. (Denver: Denver Art Museum, 2004), 47–77.

99. One of the initial studies on the impact of classical mythology is Francisco de la Maza's *La mitología clásica en el arte colonial de México* (México: Universidad Nacional Autonoma de México, 1968).

100. Max Harris, *The Dialogical Theater: Dramatizations of the Conquest of Mexico and the Question of the Other* (New York: St. Martin's Press, 1993), 13–14.

101. Serge Gruzinski, *The Mestizo Mind*, trans. by Deke Dersinberre (New York: Routledge, 2002), 82–84, 88–99.

102. Jeanette Favrot Peterson, *Paradise Garden Murals of Malinalco: Utopia and Empire in Sixteenth-century Mexico* (Austin: University of Texas Press, 1993).

103. A notable recent exception to this is Gruzinski's consistent use of "Renaissance Mexico" or "Amerindian Renaissance" for the second half of the sixteenth century, in *Mestizo Mind*, 79–80, 179, 193, and elsewhere.

104. Jonathan Brown, Spanish Painting and New Spanish Painting, 1550–1700, In *Painting a New World*, eds. Donna Pierce et al. (Denver: Denver Art Museum, 2004), 21.

105. Marcus B. Burke, On the Spanish Origins of Mexican Retablos, In *Art and Faith in Mexico*, eds. Elizabeth N. Celil Zarur and Charles M. Lovell (Albuquerque: University of New Mexico Press, 2001), 39–45.

106. As in Gauvin Alexander Bailey's organization of his *Art of Colonial Latin America* (New York & London: Phaidon Press, 2005). Andean colonial art poses even more of a challenge in its time lag with European stylistic designations, as painting and sculpture did not begin to emerge as independent art forms until 1600, and because the rugged topography and distinct ethnicities tended to form distinct regional schools around major population bases in Quito, Lima, Cuzco Potosí and others.

107. Charlene Villaseñor Black, "St. Anne Imagery and Maternal Archetypes in Spain and Mexico," In *Colonial Saints*, eds. Allan Greer & Jodi Bilinkoff (New York & London: Routlege, 2003) 3–29.

108. Diego Valadés, *Retórica Cristiana* [*Rhetorica Christiana* 1579], (México: Fondo de Cultura Económica, 2003), 479.

109. On the ambiguity and value-laden implications of the appellation "art" see Carolyn Dean, "The Trouble with (the Term) Art," *Art Journal* (Summer 2006), 25–32.

110. Andrés Pérez de Ribas, *History of the Triumphs of Our Holy Faith* [1645], trans. by Daniel Reff, Maureen Ahern, & Richard K. Danford (Tucson: University of Arizona Press 1999), 371.

111. *Ibid.*, 371. These responses conform to the Tridentine functions required of a sacred image where the sight of the Last Judgment triggers an educated, remembered recognition among the Yaquis and promotes a

heightened emotional and socially redeeming response, all very familiar Counter Reformation requisites for a Jesuit.

112. Samuel Y. Edgerton, *Theaters of Conversion* (Albuquerque: University of New Mexico Press, 2000), 141.

113. *Ibid*, 3.

114. Hal Foster, "Preface," In *Vision and Visuality*, ed. Hal Foster, (Seattle, Washington: Bay Press, 1988), x; and Michael Baxandall, *Painting and Experience in Fifteenth-century Italy* (Oxford: Oxford University Press, 1972), 29–40, 94–108.

115. Positive and powerful responses to the lifelike and emotive powers of European conventions by Asian converts to Christianity, however, do exist. See Bailey, *Art of Colonial Latin America*, 373–374.

116. Stephen Houston and Karl Taube, Archaeology of the Senses: perception and cultural expression in ancient Mesoamerica. *Cambridge Archaeological Journal*, (10 (2) 2000), 287–288.

117. *Ibid.*, 261, 263.

118. Jeanette Favrot Peterson, "Creating the Virgin of Guadalupe: The Cloth, Artist and Sources in Sixteenth-century New Spain," *The Americas* 61:4 (April 2005), 582.

119. Claire Farago, this volume. Also, among others, Gruzinski, *Mestizo Mind.*

120. Walter D. Mignolo, *Local Histories/Global Designs.* (Princeton, N.Y.: Princeton University Press, 2000), 21–22; Frederick Cooper, *Colonialism in Question: Theory, Knowledge, History.* (Berkeley: University of California Press, 2005), 91–112.

121. Mignolo, *Local Histories*, 21. See also Cooper, ". . . one can argue that the structures of power and exchange were not so global and not so systematic and that what was new was in the domain of political imagination . . .," *Colonialism in Question*, 101.

122. Cooper, *Colonialism in Question*, 101, 163.

123. On the multiple dimensions of global trade in precious goods, I would like to acknowledge several illuminating papers in the session "Locating the Global in the Art of the American Viceroyalties" (Organized by Kelly Donahue-Wallace & Michael Schreffler) at the 52nd International Congress of Americanists, in Sevilla, Spain (July of 2006), especially the papers of Dana Leibsohn and Sofia Sanabrais.

124. Such as the ivory figurine of St. Rose of Lima illustrated in Bailey, *Art of Colonial Latin America*, fig. 219, 364–367.

125. Just as Dipesh Chakrabarty has characterized European intellectual traditions and political thought for understanding nineteenth- and early twentieth-century India as contradictory, both "indispensable and inadequate." In his *Provincializing Europe: Postcolonial Thought and Historical Difference* (Princeton & Oxford: Princeton University Press, 2000), 5–6, 16.

126. Here Prof. Puttfarken intended to insert a brief discussion of the *disegno/ colorito* debate among Vasari's contemporaries and in subsequent academic art theory.

127. Here Prof. Puttfarken intended to say something about John Shearman's *Mannerism.*

128. *The Renaissance: Six Essays* (New York, 1962).

129. Cf. J.B. Bullen, *The Myth of the Renaissance in Nineteenth-Century Writing* (Oxford, 1994); P. Emison, *Creating the "Divine" Artist from Dante to Michelangelo* (Leiden, 2004) epilogue, 303–319.

130. Cf. P. Emison, *The Shaping of Art History: Meditations on a Discipline* (University Park, Pa., 2008) ch. IV.

131. J.J. Winckelmann, *History of Ancient Art*, tr. G.H. Lodge (Cambridge, Ma., 1880; orig. ed. 1764), I, 305.

132. Cf. Anne Hollander, *Moving Pictures* (New York, 1989); E. Panofsky, "Style and Medium in the Motion Pictures," in *Three Essays on Style*, ed. I. Lavin (Cambridge, Ma., 1995; orig. lectures 1936) 91–125.

133. Though cf. Paul Barolsky, *Infinite Jest: Wit and Humor in Italian Renaissance Art* (Columbia, MO, 1978).

134. In the commentary on the Criterion Collection dvd release, 1999.

135. Letters, *Art Bulletin* 29 (1947) 69.

136. Otto Brendel, "The Interpretation of the Holkham *Venus*," *Art Bulletin* 28 (1946) 68.

137. *Art Bulletin* (as in n. 135) 68.

138. E. Panofsky, *Problems in Titian, Mostly Iconographic* (New York, 1969) 137–138.

139. Cf. Anthony Molho, "The Italian Renaissance, Made in the USA," in *Imagined Histories: American Historians Interpret the Past*, eds. A. Molho and G. Wood (Princeton, 1998) 263–294.

140. See further, P. Emison, *The Simple Art: Works of Art on Paper in an Age of Magnificence*, exh. cat., University Art Gallery, University of New Hampshire (Durham, 2006) no. 24, 49–50.

141. Mark Roskill, *Dolce's "Aretino" and Venetian Art Theory of the Cinquecento* (New York, 1968) 114.

142. Winckelmann (as in n. 131) I, 286.

143. A. W. Pugin, *The True Principles of Pointed or Christian Architecture* (London, 1841) 70.

144. H. Taine, *Lectures on Art*, tr. J. Durand (New York, 1896) "The Philosophy of Art in Italy," 66.

*   I wish to thank the graduate students in UCLA Art History seminar 230 in Winter Quarter 2007, especially Daniel W. Maze, for their careful reading of this essay, and Shiela ffolliott for her help with internet bibliographic resources. The essay is for James Ackerman on his 88th birthday.

145. L.B. Alberti, *On Painting and On Sculpture. The Latin texts*, ed. C. Grayson (London, 1972) book 2, ch. 25.

146. See Joanna Woods-Marsden, "Portrait of the Lady, 1430–1520," *Virtue and Beauty: Leonardo's Ginevra de' Benci and Renaissance Portraits of Women*, ed. David Alan Brown (National Gallery of Art, Washington, DC, 2001) 64–87.

147. Pliny, *Natural History*, trans.. H. Rackham (Cambridge, MA, 1947–63) IX, book 35, ii, 6. See also the more idiomatic translation in Pliny, *Natural History: A Selection*, trans. John F. Healy (London, 1991) 324, para. 6.

148. David Rosand, "The Portrait, the Courtier, and Death," in *Castiglione: The*

Ideal and the Real in Renaissance Culture, eds. Robert W. Hanning and David Rosand (New Haven and London, 1983) 91–129, 95, 127n5.

149.   Pietro Aretino, *Lettere sull'arte*, eds. F. Pertile and E. Camesasca (Milan, 1957–60) II, 192–193, cclxxxv.

150.   Aretino, *Lettere sull'arte*, II, 192–193.

151.   "A tua infamia, secolo, che sopporti che sino i sarti e i beccai appaino là vivi in pittura." Aretino, *Lettere sull'arte*, I, 75, ccxxxvii.

152.   *Tiziano e il ritratto di corte da Raffaello ai Carracci* (Naples, 2006) cat. 264. The better known portrait of a tailor by Giovanni Battista Moroni (London, National Gallery) postdates Aretino's death.

153.   Gian Paolo Lomazzo, *Scritti sulle Arti*, ed. R.P. Ciardi (Florence, 1973) II, ch. 51.

154.   The Quattrocento architectural theorist Antonio Filarete had already used the term *qualità* in his Treatise on Architecture to designate the most honorable columns for positions requiring maximum elegance and minimum effort. John Onians, *Bearers of Meaning* (Princeton, 1988) 166 ff.

155.   "Servendo la statua al prencipe non solo per la sua propria insegna regale, che rappresenta la suprema maestà, ma ancor per essecuzione dell'ufficio regale, poiché produce effetto verso i sudditi simile a quello che fanno le imagini negli animi degli altri, rinovandoli la memoria dell'autorità regia e risvegliandoli l'affetto di onorare et obedire il suo prencipe." Gabriele Paleotti, *Discorso intorno alle imagini sacre e profane*, in Paola Barocchi, *Trattati d'Arte del Cinquecento fra Manierismo e Controriforma* (Bari, 1961) II, ch. 18, 327.

156.   The book is tentatively entitled *Visual Rhetoric of Power and Beauty: Gendered Identity in Titian's Court Portraits*.

157.   Alessandro Luzio, "Arte Retrospettiva: i ritratti di Isabella d'Este," *Emporium* 11 (1900): 432.

158.   Letter from Lodovico Gonzaga to Zaccaria Saggi, Mantua, November 30, 1475. See Joanna Woods-Marsden, "Ritratto al Naturale: Questions of Realism and Idealism in Early Renaissance Portraiture." *Art Journal* 46 (1987): 209–216, esp. 210.

159.   "Tum antiquos pictores refert Plutarchus solitos in pingendis regibus, si quid vitii aderat formae, non id praetermissum videri velle, sed quam maxime possent, servata similitudine, emendabant." Alberti, *On Painting*, Book II, ch. 40.

160.   Cennino Cennini, *The Craftsman's Handbook: Il Libro dell'Arte*, ed. Daniel V. Thompson, Jr. (New Haven, 1932) ch. 1.

161.   "Deve adunque il pittore procacciar non solo d'imitar ma di superar la Natura." Mark W. Roskill, *Dolce's Aretino and Venetian Art Theory of the Cinquecento* (New York, 2000) 130–131.

162.   ". . . e se for pessoa de pouca idade, pareça ainda de menos idade. E se for de muita idade? Pareça ainda, se quiserdes, de menos idade. E se for pessoa fremosa? Pareça ainda mais fremosa. E se for feia? Pareça que não é tão feia." Francisco D'Holanda, *Do Tirar Polo Natural*, ed. José Da Felicidade Alves (Lisbon, 1984) 39. The treatise was not published until the late nineteenth century.

163.   Lomazzo, *Scritti sulle arti*, II, ch. 51.

164. Lomazzo, *Scritti sulle arti*, II, ch. 51.

165. Baldassare Castiglione, *Book of the Courtier*, II, 18.

166. ". . . sia tanto differente il ritrarre all'imitare, quanto è differente lo scrivere istorie dal far poesie . . ." Vincenzo Danti, *Trattato delle perfette proporzioni* in Barocchi, *Trattati*, I, 266.

167. "l'una si è ritrarre le cose . . . come elle si veggiono . . .; e l'altra si è il ritrarre le cose che si veggiono essere di tutta perfezione." Danti, *Trattato*, in Barocchi, *Trattati*, I, 267. Translations are taken from David Summers, *Michelangelo and the Language of Art* (Princeton, 1981) 279–282.

168. ". . . né può essere buono un ritratto di mano di qual si voglia artefice, se non ha in sé qualche parte d'imitazione. . . . Quando colui che ritrae sarà capace della via dell'imitazione." Danti, *Trattato*, in Barocchi, *Trattati*, I, 266–267.

169. ". . . il che da quelli di mediocre ingegno con molto pazienza si conduce con osservar tutte le variazioni delle carni e le minutezza nel modo che in quello che essi imitan si scuopre." Giovanni Battista Armenini, *De Veri precetti della Pittura*, Ravenna, 1587, in Paola Barocchi, *Scritti d'arte del Cinquecento* (Milan-Naples, 1977) III, 2750.

170. Niccolò Machiavelli, *The Prince*, ch. xviii. The passage continues: "e sono tanto semplici li omeni e tanto obediscano alle necessità presente, che colui che inganna troverrà sempre chi si lascerà ingannare."

171. Castiglione, *Book of the Courtier*, II. 40.

172. "non essendo altro il dissimulare che un velo composto di tenebre oneste . . . [che] si dà qualche riposo al vero." Torquato Accetto, *Della Dissimulazione Onesta*, ed. G. Bellonci (Florence, 1943) 60.

173. "La dissimulazione è una industria di non far veder le cose come sono. Si simula quello che non è, si dissimula quello che è." Accetto, *Della Dissimulazione*, 71.

174. Francis Bacon, *The Essays*, ed. John Pitcher (London, 1985) 76–78.

175. ". . . massime di alcune donnicciole che ambiscono di essere ritratte con la faccia colorita e graziosa, credendosi pur troppo con questo mezzo di diventare più belle, che é cosa ridicola . . ." Paleotti, *Discorso*, in Barocchi, *Trattati*, II, ch. 22, 344.

176. ". . . considerando che i prencipi erano posti in questo mondo da Dio come luogotenenti suoi, per essequir le sue santissime leggi . . . per difendere et accrescere la religione, per introdurre la discipline . . . et imitare in somma . . . la divina providenza." Paleotti, *Discorso*, in Barocchi, *Trattati*, II, ch. 17, 319–320.

177. ". . . si dovria curare ancora che la faccia o altra parte del corpo non fosse fatta o più bella o più grave o punto alterata da quella che in natura in quella età gli ha conceduto, anzi, se vi fossero anco defetti, o naturali o accidentali, che molto la deformassero, né questi s'avriano da tralasciare. . . . Raccordiamo al pittore che egli, nel fare ritratti, non si scosti punto dalla verità, servando in questo la regola dell'istorico, che narra il fatto come é stato, e non dell'oratore, che spesso amplifica et estenua le cose . . ." Paleotti, *Discorso*, in Barocchi, *Trattati*, II, ch. 20, 340; ch. 21, 344.

178. Castiglione, *Book of the Courtier*, I, 1.

179. For other approaches to some of this material, see Luba Freedman, "The

Concept of Portraiture in Art Theory of the Cinquecento," *Zeitschrift für Ästhetik und allgemeine Kunstwissenschaft* 32 (1987): 63–82; Edouard Pommier, *Théories du Portrait de la Renaissance aux Lumières* (Paris, 1998).

180. William J. Bouwsma, "The Renaissance and the Drama of Western History," *American Historical Review* 84 (1979): 1–15.

181. See the "AHR Forum: The Persistence of the Renaissance," published in *American Historical Review* 103 (1998): 51–124, with an introduction and essays by Paula Findlen and Kenneth Gouwens followed by responses from William J. Bouwsma, Anthony Grafton, and Randolph Starn.

182. Paula Findlen and Kenneth Gouwens, "Introduction: The Persistence of the Renaissance," *American Historical Review* 103 (1998): 51–54.

183. "The Art Seminar" (JE).

184. Despite the (understandable) tendency to blame Burkhardt and his generation for co-opting the Renaissance to serve nineteenth-century nationalist agendas, the *Vite* and *Ragionamenti* were products of Medici Grand-ducal propaganda, designed to advance the cause of Florentine cultural supremacy. See Stephen Campbell, "Vasari's Renaissance and its Renaissance Alternatives" ("Starting Points" essay). Recent assessments of the larger context of Vasari's project include Patricia Lee Rubin, *Giorgio Vasari: Art and History* (New Haven: Yale University Press, 1995); Karen-edis Barzman, *The Florentine Academy and the Early Modern State: The Discipline of "Disegno"* (Cambridge: Cambridge University Press, 2000); and *Reading Vasari*, ed. Anne B. Barriault, Andrew Ladis, Norman E. Land and Jeryldene M. Wood (Athens, GA: Philip Wilson Publishers and Georgia Museum of Art, 2005).

185. Campbell (as in n. 5).

186. Campbell (as in n. 5).

187. Robert Williams, "Italian Renaissance Art and the Systematicity of Representation" ("Starting Points" essay) *Rinascimento* 43 (2002); 309–331.

188. I borrow the term from E.H. Cochrane, *Florence in the Forgotten Centuries, 1527–1800: A History of Florence and the Florentines in the Age of the Grand Dukes* (Chicago: University of Chicago Press, 1973).

189. *Beyond Florence: The Contours of Medieval and Early Modern Italy*, ed. Paula Findlen, Michelle M. Fontaine, and Duane J. Osheim (Stanford: Stanford University Press, 2003). See also Marina Belozerskaya, *Rethinking the Renaissance: Burgundian Arts Across Europe* (Cambridge: Cambridge University Press, 2002).

190. See, for example, Lisa Jardine and Jerry Brotton, *Global Interests: Renaissance Art Between East and West* (London: Reaktion, 2000); Rosamond Mack, *Bazaar to Piazza: Islamic Trade and Italian Art, 1300–1600* (Berkeley: University of California Press, 2002); *Bellini and the East*, ed. Caroline Campbell and Allan Chong, exh. cat. (London: National Gallery and Boston: Isabella Stewart Gardner Museum, distributed by Yale University Press, 2005); *Re-Orienting the Renaissance: Cultural Exchanges with the East*, ed. Gerald MacLean, foreword by William Dalrymple (New York: Palgrave Macmillan, 2005); *Venice and the Islamic World, 828–1797*, ed. Stefano Carboni, exh. cat. (New Haven: Yale University Press, 2007).

191. *Reframing the Renaissance: Visual Culture in Europe and Latin America, 1450–1650*, ed. and intro. Claire Farago (New Haven: Yale University Press, 2005). See also Gauvin A. Bailey, *Art of the Jesuit Missions in Asia and Latin America 1542–1773* (Toronto: University of Toronto Press, 1999).

192. Joan Kelly, "Did Women Have a Renaissance?" in *Woman, History & Theory: The Essays of Joan Kelly* (Chicago: University of Chicago Press, 1984), 19–50, originally published in *Becoming Visible: Women in European History*, ed. Renate Bridenthal and Claudia Koonz (Boston: Houghton Mifflin, 1977), 152–161; Fredrika H. Jacobs, *Defining the Renaissance "Virtuosa": Women Artists and the Language of Art History and Criticism* (Cambridge: Cambridge University Press, 1997).

193. See, for example, Rona Goffen, "Renaissance Dreams," *Renaissance Quarterly* 40 (1987): 683–706; *idem*, "Titian's *Sacred and Profane Love*: Individuality and Sexuality in a Renaissance Marriage Picture," *Titian 500*, ed. Joseph Manca, *Studies in the History of Art* 45 (1993): 121–144; Cristelle L. Baskins, *Cassone Painting, Humanism, and Gender in Early Modern Italy* (Cambridge: Cambridge University Press, 1998); Jacqueline M. Musacchio, *Art and Ritual of Childbirth in Renaissance Italy* (New Haven: Yale University Press, 1999).

194. See John Kent Lydecker, "The Domestic Setting of the Arts in Renaissance Florence," Ph.D. diss., The Johns Hopkins University, 1987; Richard A. Goldthwaite, *Wealth and the Demand for Art in Italy, 1300–1600* (Baltimore: Johns Hopkins University Press, 1993); and Luke Syson and Dora Thornton, *Objects of Virtue: Art in Renaissance Italy* (London: The British Museum Press, 2001).

195. Syson and Thornton, *Objects of Virtue*; Thomas P. Campbell, *Tapestry in the Renaissance: Art and Magnificence*, exh. cat. (New York: Metropolitan Museum of Art, 2002); Cristina Acidini Luchinat et al., *The Medici, Michelangelo, and the Art of Late Renaissance Florence*, exh. cat. (New Haven and London: Yale University Press, in association with The Detroit Institute of Arts, 2002); Marina Belozerskaya, *Luxury Arts of The Renaissance* (Los Angeles: Getty Publications, 2005); and *At Home in Renaissance Italy*, ed. Marta Ajmar and Flora Dennis, exh. cat. (London: Victoria and Albert Museum, 2006).

196. For Isabella d'Este's famous characterization of her desire for antiquities, see Clifford M. Brown, " 'Lo insaciabile desiderio nostro de cose antique:' New Documents on Isabella d'Este's Collection of Antiquities," in Cecil H. Clough, ed., *Cultural Aspects of the Italian Renaissance: Essays in Honour of Paul Oskar Kristeller* (Manchester: Manchester University Press, 1976), 324–353.

197. Fredrika Jacobs, "Rethinking the Divide: Cult Images and the Cult of Image" ("Starting Points" essay).

198. Jacobs (as in n. 18).

199. A case in point would be tapestry. Neglected at the high end of the spectrum because it falls too close to the decorative arts, overlooked in the decorative arts arena because it is perceived as "high art," this important art form was the focus of considerable expenditure, attracted artists such as

Mantegna, Raphael, and Bronzino, and marks a key place of artistic exchange between Northern and Southern Europe. See Campbell, *Tapestry in the Renaissance*, 9–10.

200. Jacobs, "Rethinking the Divide." "[E]t infinitamente amò più di tutti messer Tommaso de'Cavalieri, gentiluomo romano . . . [G]li disegnò un Ganimede rapito in cielo dall'uccel di Giove, un Tizio che l'avoltoio gli mangia il cuore, la cascata del carro del Sole con Fetonte nel Po, ed una baccanalia di putti . . ." Giorgio Vasari, *Le vite de'più eccellenti pittori, scultori, ed architettori, nelle redazioni del 1550 e 1568*, 6 vols., ed. Rosanna Bettarini and Paola Barocchi (Florence: Studio Per Edizioni Scelte, 1966–1987), 6: 109–110.

201. Copies after the gift drawings form the core of a larger study I am pursuing at present on copying and collaboration in Michelangelo's career. For the copies, see, among others, Mario Rotili, ed. *Fortuna di Michelangelo nell'incisione*, exh. cat., Benevento, Museo del Sannio (Benevento: Azienda Beneventana Tipografica, 1964) and Marcella Marongiu, ed., *Il Mito di Ganimede: Prima e Dopo Michelangelo*, exh. cat., Florence, Casa Buonarroti (Florence: Mandragora, 2002).

202. For the *Dream* copies see Maria Ruvoldt, *The Italian Renaissance Imagery of Inspiration: Metaphors of Sex, Sleep and Dreams* (Cambridge: Cambridge University Press, 2004), 211 n. 7. For the *Ganymede* textile, see Vilhelm Slomann, "Rock Crystals by Giovanni Bernardi," *Burlington Magazine* 48 (1926): 9–23.

203. Michelangelo Buonarroti, *Il carteggio di Michelangelo: Edizione postuma di Giovanni Poggi*, ed. Paola Barocchi and Renzo Ristori, 5 vols. (Florence: Sansoni, 1965–1983), 4: 932.

204. For Giovanni Bernardi da Castel Bolognese, see Slomann, "Rock Crystals," and Valentino Donati, *Pietre Dure e medaglie del Rinascimento: Giovanni da Castel Bolognese* (Ferrara: Belriguardo, 1989). Vasari reports that, on leaving for a diplomatic mission to France, Cardinal Ippolito de'Medici gave Bernardi the safekeeping of a cameo worth more than six hundred scudi, in recognition of his *virtù*. Vasari, *Vite*, 4: 621.

205. "Ganimede rapito da Giove in forma di Aquila, Opera di Giovanni da Castel Bolognese, ditto Giovanni dell Corniole, come si vide scritto a piedi della gemma sudetto . . . In Cristal di Monte." Tommaso Cades, *Descrizione di una collezione di no. 7069 impronte in stucco, posseduta in Roma da Tommaso Cades, incisore in gemme, cavate accuratamente dale più celebri gemme . . . che esistono nei principali musei e collezioni particolari di Europe*. University of Pennsylvania, Ms. Codex 452. [ca. 1822], 147v. For the impression of the lost *Ganymede*, see Slomann, "Rock-Crystals."

206. See Ruvoldt (as in n. 23) 182.

207. Richard E. Spear, "Notes on Renaissance and Baroque Originals and Originality," in *Retaining the Original: Multiple Originals, Copies, and Reproductions, Studies in the History of Art* 20 (1989): 97–99. See also Alexander Nagel, "The Copy and its Evil Twin: Thirteen Notes on Forgery," *Cabinet Magazine* 14 (2004): 102–105.

208. For the development of the reproductive print in Italy, see David Landau and Peter Parshall, *The Renaissance Print, 1470–1550* (New Haven: Yale

University Press, 1994), 103–168. For Raphael and Marcantonio, see Patricia Emison, "Raphael's Multiples," in *The Cambridge Companion to Raphael*, ed. Marcia B. Hall (Cambridge: Cambridge University Press, 2005), 186–206.

209. See Spear (as in n. 28): "Io non lo stimo meno che s'ella fusse di mano di Raffaello, anzi molto più, perché è cosa fuor di natura che un uomo eccellente imiti sì bene la maniera d'un altro e la faccia così simile," Vasari, *Vite*, 4: 380. For a case study in copying and workshop practice, see Megan Holmes, "Copying Practices and Marketing Strategies in a Fifteenth-Century Florentine Painter's Workshop," in *Artistic Exchange and Cultural Translation in the Italian Renaissance City*, ed. Stephen J. Campbell and Stephen J. Milner (Cambridge: Cambridge University Press, 2004), 38–74.

210. See William Wallace, "Michelangelo and Marcello Venusti: A Case of Multiple Authorship," in *Reactions to the Master: Michelangelo's Effect on Art and Artists in the Sixteenth Century*, ed. Francis Ames-Lewis and Paul Joannides (Aldershot: Ashgate, 2003), 137–156.

211. Ibid. In 1557, for example, agents for Guidobaldo II della Rovere, Duke of Urbino, compelled Cornelia Colonelli, the widow of Michelangelo's servant Urbino, to surrender two painted copies after drawings by Michelangelo. The paintings had come to the duke's attention after Colonelli resisted the efforts of a French cardinal to acquire them. See Michelangelo, *Carteggio*, 5: 1265. The subjects of the paintings are unknown.

212. Jonathan Richardson, *Two Discourses. I. An Essay on the Whole Art of Criticism as it relates to painting shewing how to judge I. Of the Goodness of a Picture; II. Of the Hand of the Master; and III. Whether 'tis an Original or a Copy. II. An Argument in Behalf of the Science of a Connoisseur; Wherein is Shewn the Dignity, Certainty, Pleasure, and Advantage of It* (1719), in Jonathan Richardson [senior], *The Works of Jonathan Richardson* (London, 1792), 157–158. As quoted by Jeffrey M. Muller, "Measures of Authenticity: The Detection of Copies in the Early Literature on Connoisseurship," in *Retaining the Original: Multiple Originals, Copies, and Reproductions, Studies in the History of Art* 20 (1989): 141–149, quote p. 147.

213. Vasari, *Vite*, 1: 106; 4: 620.

214. Vasari's estimation of goldsmithery undergoes a similar transformation between the 1550 and 1568 editions of the *Vite*. See Marco Collareta, "L'historien et la technique: Sur le role de l'orfèvriere dans les *Vites* de Vasari," *Histoire de l'histoire de l'art* (Paris: Klincksieck, Musée du Louvre, 1995), 165–176.

215. See Laurie Fusco and Gino Corti, *Lorenzo de'Medici: Collector and Antiquarian* (Cambridge: Cambridge University Press, 2006).

216. See Paul Joannides, *Michelangelo and His Influence: Drawings from Windsor Castle*, exh. cat., Washington, DC, National Gallery of Art, Washington; London, Queen's Gallery (Washington, DC: National Gallery of Art / London: Lund Humphries, 1996), 31–32.

217. Vasari, IV, 1550 and 1568; citation from the Giunti edition of 1568. G.

Vasari, *Le Vite de' più eccellenti pittori scultori e architettori nelle redazioni del 1550 e 1568*, R. Bettarini and P. Barocchi, eds. (Florence, 1966-) IV, 7.

218. E. Panofsky, *Renaissance and Renascences in Western Art* (Stockholm, 1960). For the collaboration of different authors in Vasari's *Vite*, especially in the *proemi*: C. Hope, "Le *Vite* vasariane: un esempio di autore multiplo", in A. Santoni, ed., *L'autore multiplo. Pisa, Scuola Normale Superiore 18 ottobre 2002* (Pisa 2005) 59–74.

219. See also S. J. Campbell, "Mantegna's Triumph. The Cultural Politics of Imitation 'all'antica,' 1490–1530", in *idem*. Ed., *Artists at Court. Image-Making and Identity 1300–1550* (Boston 2004) 91–106; and *idem, The Cabinet of Eros. Renaissance Mythological Painting and the "Studiolo" of Isabella d'Este* (New Haven and London, 2006) 117–168.

220. D. Rosand, *Drawing Acts: Studies in Graphic Expression and Representation* (Cambridge, 2002) esp. "*Invenzioni* and Invention" and Chapter II, "*Disegno*. The Invention of an Art."

221. The most recent bibliographic summary of the vast literature on the subject appears in the catalogues of the three exhibitions dedicated to Mantegna, opening in Padua, Verona and Mantua in the final months of 2006. In recent years, several monographic publications with extensive bibliographies have been released; these include: A. De Nicolò Salmazo, *Andrea Mantegna* (Geneva and Milan, 2004); P. Santucci, *Su Andrea Mantegna* (Naples 2004); G. Agosti, *Su Mantegna I* (Milan, 2005); and J. Manca, *Andrea Mantegna and the Italian Renaissance* (New York, 2006). The recent exhibition catalogues are: M. Lucco, *Mantegna a Mantova 1460–1506*, (ex. cat. Mantua, Fruttiere Palazzo Te, 16 September 2006–14 January 2007; Milan, 2006); D. Banzato, A. De Nicolò Salmazo and A. M. Spiazzi, *Mantegna e Padova 1445–1460*, (ex. cat. Padua, Musei Civici agli Eremitani, 16 September 2006–14 January 2007; Milan 2006); and S. Marinelli and P. Marini, *Mantegna e le Arti a Verona 1450–1500*, (ex. cat. Verona, Palazzo della Gran Guardia, 16 September 2006–14 January 2007; Venice, 2006).

222. P. Kristeller, *Andrea Mantegna* (London-New York-Bombay 1901).

223. A. Canova, "Gian Marco Cavalli incisore per Andrea Mantegna e altre notizie sull'oreficeria e la tipografia a Mantova nel XV secolo", *Italia medioevale e umanistica* 42 (2001) 149–179; A. Canova, "Mantegna ha davvero inciso? Nuovi documenti", *Grafica d'arte* 12, 47 (2001) 3–11; and A. Canova, "Andrea Mantegna e Gian Marco Cavalli: nuovi documenti mantovani," *Italia medioevale e umanistica* 43 (2002) 201–229.

224. S. Fletcher, "A Re-evaluation of Two Mantegna Prints," *Print Quarterly* 14 (1997) 67–77; S. Fletcher, "A Closer Look at Mantegna's Prints," *Print Quarterly* 18 (2001) 3–41; and S. R. Langdale, *Battle of the Nudes. Pollaiuolo's Renaissance Masterpiece*, (ex. cat. Cleveland, The Cleveland Museum of Art, 25 August–27 October 2002; Cleveland 2002).

225. K. Christiansen in J. Martineau, ed., *Andrea Mantegna* (ex.cat. London, Royal Academy of Arts and New York, The Metropolitan Museum of Art; London & New York, 1992) 68–78; Poldi and Villa, in Lucco (as in n. 221) 46–61; Limentani Virdis, in Marinelli and Marini (as in n. 221) 66–71; and Bertani, Consolandi, Gargano (as in n. 5) 72–75.

226. C. Fischer, "Ghirlandaio and the Origins of Cross-hatching," in *Il disegno al tempo di Lorenzo il Magnifico*, (Conference Proceedings, Villa Spelman, The Johns Hopkins University, July 1992; Bologna, 1994) 245–253; J. K. Cadogan, *Domenico Ghirlandaio. Artist and Artisan* (New Haven & London, 2000) R. G. Kecks, *Domenico Ghirlandaio und die Malerei der Florentiner Renaissance* (Munich & Berlin, 2000).

227. *Ulixes pro Andrea Mantegna pictore, dicto Squarzone, pro quadam moniali*, Modena, Biblioteca Estense, ms. III.D.22; cited in Santucci (as in n. 5) 60.

228. Vasari (as in n. 217) III, 549–550.

229. Favaretto-Bodon, in Banzato et al. (as in n. 221) 50–59.

230. So far there have been many remarkable contributions to our understanding of Mantegna the "antiquarian" since R. Eisler, "Mantegnas frühe Werke und die römische Antike," *Monatsberichte über Kunst und Kunstwissenschaft* 3 (1903) 159–169; and I. Blum, *Andrea Mantegna und die Antike* (Strassburg, 1936).

231. As continues to be emphasized, most recently by Lo Monaco, in Lucco (as in n. 221) 36–45; and Zamponi, "Le metamorfosi dell'antico: la tradizione antiquaria veneta," in C. Tristano, M. Calleri, and L. Magionami, eds., *I Luoghi dello scrivere da Francesco Petrarca agli albori dell'eta moderna. Atti del convegno internazionale, Arezzo, 8–11 ottobre 2003* (Spoleto, 2006) 37–67; *idem*, in Banzato et al. (as in n. 221) 72–79.

232. The most recent reproduction is in Banzato et al (as in n. 221) 201.

233. K. Christiansen, "The case for Mantegna as printmaker," *Burlington Magazine*, 135 (1993) 604–612.

234. For example, M. Muraro, "Mantegna e Alberti," in Arte, pensiero e cultura a Mantova nel primo Rinascimento in rapporto con la Toscana e con il Veneto. Atti del VI Convegno Internazionale di Studi sul Rinascimento (Florence, 1965) 103–132; J. Greenstein, Mantegna and Painting as Historical Narrative, (Chicago, 1992); K. Christiansen, "Rapporti presunti, probabili e (forse anche) effettivi fra Alberti e Mantegna," in J. Rykwert and A. Engel, Leon Battista Alberti, (ex. cat. Mantua, Palazzo Te, 10 September-11 December 1994; Mantua 1994) 336–357; L. Steinberg, "Leon Battista Alberti e Andrea Mantegna," in Rykwert and Engel, 330–335; Rosand (as in n. 220); Campbell (as in n. 219).

235. *Commentarii a Philippo Beroaldo conditi in Asinum Aureum Lucii Apuleii* [. . .] (Bononiae, 1500).

236. M. Faeitti and K. Oberhuber, *Bologna e l'Umanesimo 1490–1510* (ex. Cat. Bologna, Pinacoteca Nazionale and Vienna, Graphische Sammlung Albertina; Bologna, 1988) 323–340, and previously-listed bibliography.

237. Vasari (as in n. 217) IV, 8.

238. M. Baxandall and E. H. Gombrich, "Beroaldus on Francia," *Journal of the Warburg and Courtauld Institutes*, 25 (1962) 113–115.

239. M. Faietti, "Protoclassicismo e cultura umanistica nei disegni di Francesco Francia," in *Il Classicismo. Medioevo Rinascimento Barocco. Atti del Colloquio Cesare Gnudi (1986)*; Bologna, 1993) 171–192.

240. The most recent reproduction is in Marinelli and Marini (as in n. 221) 203.

241. This too is illustrated in Marinelli and Marini (as in n. 221) 202.

242. G. Vasari, *Le Vite de'più eccellenti pittori scultori ed architettori nelle redazioni*

del 1550 e 1568. Testo a cura di Rosanna Bettarini. Commento secolare a cura di Paola Barocchi, (Florence: Sansoni Editore, 1966) *Proemio delle vite*, vol. II, 3–4, 11.

243. Vasari, *Vita di Masaccio*, vol. III, 124 (G).

244. Aristotle, *Physics* II. 199a15–25 and 194b17–195b13, with the remarks by W. Charlton in Aristotle, *Physics I and II*. Translated with introduction and notes by W. Charlton (Oxford 1970) 126; *Metaphysics* A 983a23–32. See also D. Summers, *The Judgement of Sense* (Cambridge, 1986) 269.

245. I. Kant, *Kritik der Urteilskraft*, Introduction, p. xxviii, B32; cf K. Kuypers, *Kants Kunsttheorie und die Einheit der Kritik der Urteilskraft*. Verhandelingen der Koninklijke Nederlandse Academie van Wetenschappen, Nieuwe Reeks, 77, nr 3. (Amsterdam/London 1972) 23–27, and my *Organicism in Nineteenth-Century Architecture. An inquiry into its theoretical and philosophical background* (Amsterdam 1994) 41–43, and 114–125, for an overview of Aristotelian ideas of organic nature as a model for architecture.

246. Aristotle, *De anima* II.413ab.

247. Cf. T. Puttfarken, "The Dispute about *Colorito* and *Disegno* in Venice: Paolo Pino, Lodovico Dolce and Titian," in: P. Ganz et al. (eds.), *Kunst und Kunsttheorie 1400–1900* (Wiesbaden, 1991; (Wolfenbütteler Forschungen), 75–101, 175.

248. D. Rosand, *Painting in Sixteenth-Century Venice. Titian. Veronese. Tintoretto*. (Cambridge & New York, 1995) 11.

249. D. Cast, "Vasari on the Practical," in: Ph. Jacks (ed.), *Vasari's Florence* (Cambridge and New York 1998) 70–83, esp. p. 71.

250. Much has been written on the meaning of Vasari's *disegno*. See, among others, W. Kemp, "*Disegno*. Beiträge zur Geschichte eines Begriffes zwischen 1547 and 1607," *Marburger Jahrbuch für Kunstwissenschaft* 19 (1974) 219–43; D. Cast, "Reading Vasari, History and Philosophy," *Word and Image* 9 (1993), 29–38; B. Roggenkamp, *Vom Artifex zum Artista: Benedetto Varchis Auseinandersetzung mit dem Aristotelisch-scholastischen Kunstverständnis* (Berlin & New York, 1996); and R. Williams, *Art, Theory, and Culture in Sixteenth-Century Italy. From Techne to Metatechne* (Cambridge & New York, 1997) 29–73 esp. pp. 33–36.

251. *I Dieci Libri dell'Architettura di M. Vitruvio Tradotti e Commentati da Monsignor Barbaro Eletto Patriarca d'Aquileia*, published in 1556; *I Dieci Libri dell'Architettura di M. Vitruvio Tradotti e Commentati da Mons. Daniel Barbaro Eletto Patriarca d'Aquileia da Lui Riveduti et Ampliati*, published in 1567; *De architectura cum Commentariis*, published as well in 1567. Vincenzo Scamozzi, *L'Idea dell'Architettura Universale*, Venice 1615.

252. They had been preceded in presenting an Aristotelian, teleological view of nature as the basis of classical design by Cesariano, who quoted Aristotle's dictum that nature does everything according to order (*omne quod facit natura est secundem ordinem*) and adds that we have to observe the workings of nature if we want to contruct anything: Cesare Cesariano, *Dell'Architettura di L. Vitruvio Pollione*, reprinted in A. Bruschi et. al. (eds.), *Scritti Rinascimentali di Architettura* (Milan 1978) 440, 442.

253. On Scamozzi's relation to Barbaro, his debt to Aristotle (which is also

manifest in his highlighting of every passage in Barbaro's Vitruvius edition of 1567 that is indebted to Aristotle) see Alina Payne, *The Architectural Treatise in the Italian Renaissance* (Cambridge, 1999) 215–216 where she describes Scamozzi's manner of writing a treatise as printing his thought process.

254. See f.i. Scamozzi, *Idea*, I.xxiv (p. 71), with a characteristic reference to Aristotle, *Metaphysics* Book I.

255. Scamozzi, *Idea*, "Proemio," pp. 1–3 and 5.

256. Cf Alberti, *De Re Aedificatoria*, "Prologue," for a similar statement of the relation between the architect and his builders.

257. On the use of classical methods of scientific exposition, and their use by Alberti and Vitruvius see my "The Structure of Alberti's *De re aedificatoria* Reconsidered," *Journal of the Society of Architectural Historians* 56 (1998), 280–297.

258. Vasari, *Vite*, vol. III, 590–592.

259. J. Sadoleto, *De Laocoontis statua Jacobi Sadoleti Carmen*, in S. Settis, *Laocoonte. Fama e stile*. Con un apparato documentario a cura di Sonia Maffei su "La fama di Laocoonte nei testi del Cinquecento" (Rome: Donzelli Editore 1999), 120: "vos rigidum lapidem vivis animare figuris/eximii et vivos spiranti in marmori sensus/inserere."

260. Ibidem, p. 122: "Saxea quam veros mentitur imago colores/et simulat verum Laocoon lapis!"

261. Evangelista Maddaleni de'Capodiferro, *Laocoon in Titi imperatoris domo Julio II Pontifici Maximo repertus* (p. 126): "Laocoon ego sum. . . . Dices, me aspicias, veros lapidi esse dolores,/et natis haud fictum exitium atque metum./ . . . / Si mortem atque metum saxo vivumque dolorem/qui dederunt, possent vocem animamque dare,/abnuerent: mirum magis est sine voce animaque/niti, ferre, queri, flere, timere, mori."

262. Antonio Tebaldi, from his *Rime* (p. 132): "Laocoonte son, sì expresso e vivo/che, se de la materia tu non sei/onde son io formato e figli mei,/farai de gli occhi un doloroso rivo."

263. Elio Lampridio Cerva, *Opera latina* (p. 124): "Sibila mentiri, saniem manare cruentam/morderi credas saxa, ferire, mori."

264. Giovanni Paolo Lancellotti, *Io. Pauli Lancellotti Perusini i[uris] c[onsulti] de Lacoonte* (p. 146): "Quod te laetiferis morti dant orbibus angues/Laocoon, tristi desine voce queri./ Mors etenim—invideant licet (aspera numina) Parcae—/ te vetat haec ullo tempore posse mori."

265. A.F. Doni, *Il Disegno* (1549), quoted in S. Settis, *Laocoonte. Fama e stile* (Rome: Donazelli 1999) 118–120.

266. See for instance A. Averlino, detto Il Filarete, *Trattato di Architettura*. Testo a cura di A.M. Finoli e L. Grassi. Introduzione e note di L. Grassi (Milan 1972) 40–43, and for a more extended discussion of the physicality attributed to Renaissance buildings L. Devlieger, *The Birth of Artefacts. Architecture, Alchemy and Power in late-Renaissance Florence* (Unpublished PhD Thesis, Ghent University 2005) 249–275.

267. On the casting of horoscopes for Palazzo Strozzi and the Fortezza da Basso in Florence see N. Goldthwaite, *The Building of Renaissance Florence. An Economic and Social History* (Baltimore & London, 1980)

84–86; on the attribution of personality traits to buildings see the celebratory poem by Porcellio Pandoni reprinted in C.R. Mack, *Pienza. The Creation of a Renaissance City* (Ithaca & London, 1987) 170 and the poems by A. Avogadro da Vercelli and Niccolò Tignosi reprinted in R. Hatfield, "Some Unknown Descriptions of the Medici Palace in 1459," *Art Bulletin* 52 (1970) 232–249, esp. pp. 233–234. After the banishment of the Bentivoglio family from Bologna their palazzo was razed to the ground, and a poem was found attached to the ruins in which the building, in a reversal of the documents produced as part of the consecration rites of churches, explained why it had been destroyed (oral communication by dr Minou Schraven, Leiden University).

268. L.B. Alberti, "Templum," in: *Dinner Pieces. A Translation by D. Marsh* (Binghamton NY, 1987) 175–176.

269. Robert Zwijnenberg, *The Writings and Drawings of Leonardo da Vinci. Order and Chaos in Early Modern Thought*. Cambridge: Cambridge University Press, 1999, 4–7.

270. Martin Kemp, *Leonardo da Vinci. The Marvellous Works of Nature and Man*. London: J.M. Dent & Sons Ltd., 1981, 266–270.

271. This conclusion is based on Zwijnenberg (as in n. 269).

272. This statement of Desmond McCarthy is cited in Stephen Schoenbaum, *Shakespeare's Lives*, Oxford University Press, 1991, viii.

273. Svetlana Alpers, "Interpretation without Representation, or the Viewing of Las Meninas," *Representations*. No 1, 31–42.

274. Georges Didi-Huberman, "Before the Image. Before Time: The Sovereignty of Anachronism," *Compelling Visuality: the work of art in and out of History*, edited and introduction by Claire Farago and Robert Zwijnenberg, University of Minnesota Press, 2003, 31–34.

275. Mieke Bal, "An Aesthetics of Anachronism," *Art Out of Time*. Elizabeth Wesseling and Robert Zwijnenberg (ed. and introd.). Art, Science & Memory Series. Equinox Press (in preparation).

276. Siân Ede, *Art and Science*. London/New York: I.B.Tauris. 2005, 3.

277. Carlo Pedretti, The Literary Works of Leonardo da Vinci, compiled and edited from the original manuscripts by Jean Paul Richter. Commentary. 2 vols. Oxford: Phaidon, 1977, 136.

278. Zwijnenberg (as in n. 1) 1–9.

279. Sabine Melchior-Bonnet, *The Mirror: A History*. Translated by K.H. Jewett. London: Routledge. 2001, 11–12; the mirror room is also mentioned in an episode of Roman de Troie (1160) by Benoît de Sainte-Maure, and in Francesco Colonna's Hypnerotomachia Poliphili (1499). Cf. Melchior-Bonnet, 159–160.

280. *Ibid.*, 26–27.

281. J. Baltrusaitis, Der Spiegel: Entdeckungen, Täuschungen, Phantasien, Giessen: Anabas Verlag, 1996 (original: Essai sur une légende scientifique: le mirroir: rélévations, science-fiction et fallacies. Paris: Éditions du Seuil, 1978) 318.

282. J. Miller, *On Reflection*. London: National Gallery of Art/Yale U.P., 1998.

283. Pedretti (as in n. 277) 136.

284. Melchior-Bonnet (as in n. 279) 11, 163.

285. For instance, when Leonardo was in Rome, around 1515, he put much effort and time in constructing parabolic mirrors.

286. Zwijnenberg (as in n. 269) 147–174.

287. Mieke Bal, *Quoting Caravaggio. Contemporary Art, Preposterous History.* Chicago and London: The University of Chicago Press, 1999, 35, 142–144; and Renée Van de Vall, "Between battlefield and play: art and aesthetics in visual culture," *Contemporary Aesthetics* (www.contempaesthetics.org). Volume 1.

288. Jonathan Sawday, *The Body Emblazoned. Dissection and the human body in Renaissance Culture.* London and New York: Routledge. 1995, 6–15.

289. In other machine designs Leonardo invents devices intended to prevent injury to operators.

290. For a more detailed discussion of the Ventola and its cultural significance, see Zwijnenberg (as in n. 269) 176–181.

291. Michel Foucault, "Utopian Body," *Sensorium. Embodied experience, technology, and contemporary art.* Edited by Caroline A. Jones. Cambridge Mass.: The MIT Press, 229–234, esp. p. 231.

292. Ewa Lajer-Burcharth, "Real Bodies: Video in the 1990s," *Art History.* Vol 20, No. 2, 1997, 185–213.

293. I owe this observation to dr J.V. Field, in a personal conversation.

294. On Bolsover Castle see Mark Girouard, *Robert Smythson and the Elizabethan Country House* (New Haven, 1983) 205–245; Lucy Worsley, *Bolsover Castle* (London, 2000) with further bibliography; on the painted decoration see Timothy D. Raylor, " 'Pleasure Reconciled to Virtue': William Cavendish, Ben Jonson, and the Decorative Scheme of Bolsover Castle" *Renaissance Quarterly* 53 (1999) 402–439.

295. On art in Antwerp at the period of the High Renaissance, see most recently Peter Van den Brink, *ExtravagAnt! A Forgotten Chapter of Antwerp Painting, 1500–1530,* Exhibition catalogue (Antwerp/ Maastricht, 2005); a volume of essays is also forthcoming.

296. Much has been written in the past decade on the development of the Antwerp art market, but see especially Philip Vermeylen, *Painting for the Market: Commercialization of Art in Antwerp's Golden Age* (Turnhout, 2003) and the essays gathered in Neil De Marchi and Hans J. Van Miegroet eds., *Mapping Markets for Paintings in Europe, 1450–1750* (Turnhout, 2006).

297. See my "Art, Honor and Excellence in Early Modern Europe" in *Beyond Price: Value in Culture, Economics, and the Arts,* ed. Michael Hutter and David Throsby (Cambridge, forthcoming). Stephen Campbell notes in his paper in this volume that Vasari tried to keep the value of art separate from the mechanisms of the market, but in fact not all early writers (especially those outside of Italy) were so coy about the market.

298. The definition of style I am using: style is a set of formal properties, identified by the beholder, that enable one object to be compared with another, either in terms of similarity or difference. In other words, I believe that "style" is pretty much always comparative, if not evaluative. My definition expands upon that given by Meyer Schapiro in his classic article "Style" *Anthropology Today,* ed. A. L. Kroeber (Chicago, 1953) 287–312.

299. See for instance Alice Friedman's excellent article, "Did England Have a Renaissance? Classical and Anticlassical Themes in Elizabethan Culture" in Susan J. Barnes and Walter S. Melion eds., *Cultural Differentiation and Cultural Identity in the Visual Arts* (Washington, 1989) 95–110.

300. See Adolf Göller, "What is the Cause of Perpetual Style Change in Architecture?" (1887) in Harry Francis Mallgrave and Eleftherios Ikonomou, *Empathy, Form and Space* (Los Angeles, 1994) 193–225; Heinrich Wölfflin, *Renaissance and Baroque* (1888); *idem, Principles of Art History* (1915), especially 1–53; Alois Riegl, *L'Origine de l'art baroque à Rome* (1907), trans. Sibylle Muller (Paris 1993); Paul Frankl, *Principles of Architectural History* (Cambridge MA, 1968; orig. ed. 1914); Erwin Panofsky, "What is Baroque?" in *Three Essays on Style* (Cambridge MA, 1997; orig. lectures 1936) 17–88.

301. Lucy Gent, *Picture and Poetry 1560–1620* (Leamington Spa, 1981) is a fascinating but in some ways oddly self-defeating analysis of the lack of discursive tools available in England to describe or discuss artistic forms common in Italy at the time.

302. See Jeffrey Muller, "Rubens's Theory and Practice of the Imitation of Art" *The Art Bulletin* 64 (1982), 229–246. Rubens's ability to make this assumption stemmed in part from his unique social and educational background.

303. See Anthony Wells-Cole, *Art and Decoration in Elizabethan and Jacobean England: The Influence of Continental Prints, 1558–1625* (New Haven, 1997).

304. See Serge Gruzinski, *Images at War: Mexico from Columbus to* Blade Runner *(1492–2019)* (Duke, 2001).

305. This is not to dispute Walter Melion's contention that Karel van Mander's *Schilderboek* (1604) represents a conscious counterpoint to Vasari's account of Italian art, but only to reiterate his point that Van Mander's book does not present art as having genealogy and progression in the same way that Vasari's does. Walter S. Melion, *Shaping the Netherlandish Canon: Karel van Mander's Schilder-Boeck* (Chicago, 1992).

306. Honoré de Balzac, "Le Chef-d'oeuvre inconnu," 1832/1845, my translation. On this text see Hubert Damisch, "The Underneaths of Painting" *Word and Image* 1/2 (1985) 197–209.

307. On object-biographies, see Igor Kopytoff, "The Cultural Biography of Things: Commoditization as Process" in Arjun Appadurai ed., *The Social Life of Things: Commodities in Cultural Perspective* (Cambridge 1986) 64–91. Also very suggestive on this matter is Susan Stewart, *On Longing: Narratives of the Miniature, the Gigantic, the Souvenir, the Collection* (Baltimore, 1984).

308. Two relatively recent studies that have been exemplary in positioning works of art as moving, shifting products in circuits of production and consumption have explicitly dealt with copies, versions, and variants of "primary" masterworks: Pieter Van den Brink ed., *Brueghel Enterprises,* exhibition catalogue, Bonnefanten Museum (Maastricht, 2001), and Richard E. Spear, *The "Divine" Guido: Religion, Sex, Money and Art in the World of Guido Reni* (New Haven, 1997), especially chapters 12–14.

309. I am thinking of Alpers' *Rembrandt's Enterprise* (Chicago, 1988); her and
      Michael Baxandall's *Tiepolo and the Pictorial Intelligence* (New Haven,
      1994); Baxandall's *Limewood Sculptors of Renaissance Germany* (New
      Haven, 1980); and some elements of Koerner's work on Dürer in *The
      Moment of Self-Portraiture in German Renaissance Art* (Chicago, 1993).
310. On Borromeo's interest in technique see Lucy Cutler, "Virtue and
      Diligence: Jan Brueghel I and Federico Borromeo" in *Nederlands
      Kunsthistorisch Jaarboek* 54 (2003) 214.
311. A very useful exception is Mary Pardo and Michael W. Cole eds,
      Inventions of the Studio, Renaissance to Romanticism, (Chapel Hill NC,
      2005) especially the essay by Christopher S. Wood, "Indoor/Outdoor:
      The Studio Around 1500."
312. The museum-based studies listed in the following note are all examples,
      but there are also outstanding monographs such as Carmen Bambach,
      *Drawing and Painting in the Italian Renaissance Workshop: Theory and
      Practice 1300–1600* (Cambridge, 1999).
313. Now other museums are developing important programs that combine
      research with conservation studies. Ones that are already producing
      important work would include the National Gallery of Art in Washington,
      D.C., the Mauritshuis in The Hague, the Rijksmuseum in Amsterdam,
      the Prado in Madrid, and the Getty Museum in Los Angeles. For an
      introduction to current technical studies see Andrea Kirsh and Rustin S.
      Levenson, *Seeing through Paintings: Physical Examination in Art Historical
      Studies* (New Haven, 2000), and Molly Faries and Ron Spronk eds., *Recent
      Developments in the Technical Examination of Early Netherlandish Painting*
      (Cambridge MA & Turnhout, 2003) especially Faries' introductory article
      which gives an overview of recent developments, and Spronk's history of
      technical studies at the Fogg. For London see the publications by David
      Bomford, for instance *Art in the Making: Underdrawings in Renaissance
      Paintings* (London & New Haven, 2002). The classic introduction to the
      topic is J.R.J. van Asperen de Boer, "An Introduction to the Scientific
      Examination of Paintings" *Nederlands Kunsthistorisch Jaarboek* 26 (1975).
314. Even within museums it has sometimes seemed impossible for curators
      and conservators to talk meaningfully to one another. The London
      National Gallery has been an exception here: its publications give a sense
      of scientists, conservators and curators talking to one another, and this is
      why these works make the results of technical study particularly accessible
      to non-specialists. At other museums it has become standard practise for
      an exhibition catalogue to include a separate essay on conservation and
      technical issues, but the scientists' results are barely integrated into the
      catalogue's main essays. There have also been occasions when conservation
      and curatorial departments had notably unresolved conflicts: most
      notoriously, the Metropolitan Museum of Art's *Rembrandt/Not
      Rembrandt* exhibition in 1995, where the separate technical and curatorial
      catalogues were clearly at odds with one another, and the Rijksmuseum's
      1999 *Still Life* exhibition where the conservation department mounted an
      entire separate show with a separate catalogue, referred to not at all in the
      main show. The rare exhibitions that really integrate research on process

with their displays of artifacts should be taken as models for further creative thinking in both museum and academic praxis: see most recently Anne T. Woollett and Ariane van Suchtelen, *Rubens and Brueghel: A Working Friendship*, Los Angeles & The Hague, 2006).

315. See though the thoughtful introductory essay by Joseph Koerner in *Factura*, special issue of *Res: Anthropology and Aesthetics* 36 (Autumn 1999), 5–19. On the divide between curatorial and academic worlds see Charles W. Haxthausen, *The Two Art Histories: The Museum and the University* (Williamstown MA, 2003).

316. See Harry Berger Jr., "The System of Early Modern Painting" *Representations* 62 (Spring 1998) 31–57.

317. See the books written and edited in the mid-1990s by John Brewer: his *Early Modern Conceptions of Property* (London, 1994); edited with Roy Porter, *Consumption and the World of Goods* (London, 1993); and edited with Ann Bermingham, *The Consumption of Culture, 1600–1800: Image, Object, Text* London, 1995). An important recent contribution which includes useful methodological and historiographic material, is Linda Levy Peck, *Consuming Splendor: Society and Culture in Seventeenth-Century England* (Cambridge, 2005).

318. Richard Goldthwaite, *Wealth and the Demand for Art in Italy, 1300–1600* (Baltimore, 1993). Among more recent studies see the essays collected in Marcello Fantoni, Louisa C. Matthew, and Sara F. Matthews-Grieco eds., *The Art Market in Italy, 15th–17th Centuries* (Ferrara, 2003); and Evelyn Welch, *Shopping in the Renaissance* (New Haven, 2005).

319. Hanns Floerke, *Studien zur niederlaendischen Kunst- und Kulturgeschichte: Die Formen des Kunsthandels, das Atelier, und die Sammler in den Niederlanden vom 15.–18. Jahrhundert* (Munich & Leipzig, 1905). Major writers of more standard monographs at that period, like W. Martin, also tended to pay attention to questions of marketing and value.

320. Including John Michael Montias, *Artists and Artisans in Delft: A Socio-Economic Study of the Seventeenth Century* (Princeton, 1982); *idem*, "Cost and Value in Seventeenth-Century Dutch Art" *Art History* 10 (1995), 455–466; *idem, Le Marché de l'Art aux Pays-Bas (XVe–XVIIe siècles)* (Paris, 1996). See now the work by Marten Jan Bok, Filip Vermeylen, Maximiliaan Martens, and Neil de Marchi and Hans Van Miegroet, especially the latter's important co-edited *Mapping Markets for Paintings in Europe, 1450–1750* (Turnhout, 2006).

321. Oliver Impey and Arthur Macgregor, *The Origins of Museums: The Cabinet of Curiosities in Sixteenth- and Seventeenth-Century Europe* (London, 2001; orig. ed. 1985). The bibliography on these topics has, in the past twenty years, become too vast to give any overview of here; works by Ellinoor Bergvelt and Renée Kistemaker for the Netherlands, and Giuseppe Olmi and Paula Findlen for Italy, were foundational analytic models in those fields.

322. On curiosity see *Art and Curiosity*, a special issue of *Word And Image* 11/4 (December 1995); on wonder see Caroline Walker Bynum, "Wonder" *American Historical Review* 102/1 (February 1997), 1–26 and Philip

Fisher, *Wonder, the Rainbow, and the Aesthetics of Rare Experiences* (Cambridge MA, 1998).

323. In the field of Netherlandish art see recently Claudia Goldstein, "Artifacts of Domestic Life: Bruegel's Paintings in the Flemish Home" *Nederlands Kunsthistorisch Jaarboek* 51 (2000) 173–193. Michael Montias, John Loughman, C. Willemijn Fock and Julie Berger Hochstrasser have all been working on these issues in the seventeenth century.

324. The term is Campbell's; see his "Starting Points" essay.

325. A full gauge of vitality would include a look at job postings, course enrollments, and books published. Based on a survey of the *Art Bulletin*'s annual listings, begun in 1980, Renaissance dissertations have ranged from 18% of the total (1984; 1989) to as low as 7% (1996), averaging about 15%. In 2004, when the category was widened to include "Baroque," it included 24% of total dissertations.

326. According to Eve Siniako, present chair of the Publications committee of College Art Association, in personal communication with the author, the category changes, which confronted many landmines, began with a query of the membership, were overseen by several committees, and are meant to reflect to the categories frequently used for jobs and publications. For example, "Islamic," added only in 1992 but considered too broad, was dispersed in 2004 among chronological and geographic categories. See also the fragmenting of twentieth century (from "Nineteenth and Twentieth European" in 1980, to "Nineteenth" "Pre-1945" and "Post-1945" Modern American and European" (1997–8).

327. See the seminar discussion of these "outlier" texts, by northern European seventeenth-century specialists (by Alpers, 1983; Freedberg, 1989) as well as the frequent border crossings into the "Baroque" (not Renaissance) by modernists (Michael Fried, "Thoughts on Caravaggio," *Critical Inquiry* 24/1 (1997): 13–56; T.J. Clark, *The Sight of Death: An Experiment in Art Writing* (New Haven: Yale, 2006)). Vasari's formulation of decline finds echoes here in the seminar discussion of the falling off of humanist ideals, the turn to rationalism, and the absolutist political dominion on the seventeenth century. See Marshall Brown, "The Classic is the Baroque: on the Principle of Wölfflin's Art History," *Critical Inquiry* 9/2 (1982): 379–404. For the return of the "Baroque" as a contemporary term, see, for example, Christine Buci-Glucksman, *La raison baroque: de Baudelaire à Benjamin* (Paris: Galilée, 1984).

328. Botero, *Della ragion di stato* 2:23 (Venice: Giolitti, 1598): "History is the most pleasing theater, that one could ever imagine." For later debates about history, see E. Bellini, *Agostino Mascardi tra "ars poetica" e "ars historica"* (Milan: Vita e pensiero, 2002).

329. *OED*, (Oxford, Clarendon Press, 1991), 2nd edition, p. 1309. No single word with these multiple resonances exists in French, Italian, or German: the Italian "rappresentare" perhaps comes closest.

330. For the philosophy of language, see J. L. Austin, *How To Do Things With Words* (Cambridge: Harvard University Press, 1962) and J. Searles, *Speech Acts* (London: Cambridge, 1969); for an introduction to performance art, see Amelia Jones, *Body art/performing the subject* (Minneapolis: University

of Minnesota Press, 1998); for performance and identity, see Judith Butler, *Excitable Speech: a Politics of the Performative* (1997); for a genealogy of performance studies, see J.Reinelt and J. Roach, *Critical Theory and Performance* (Ann Arbor: University of Michigan Press, 1992), 9–15.

331. Marvin Carlson, *Performance: a Critical Introduction* (2nd. ed, New York: Routledge, 2004), 6, characterizes contemporary thought as "self consciousness, reflexive, obsessed with simulation and theatricalization in every aspect of its social awareness."

332. For allusions to artists as performers see Cole, Kavaler, and Campbell, as well as Farago's references to R.W. Nelson's analysis of Byzantine icons in her article, n. 22. The word appears as one of two critical binaries ("the situation of performance" versus that of "substitution") in C. Wood and A. Nagel, "A New Model of Renaissance Anachronism," *Art Bulletin* 83/3 (2005), 404, to designate a more traditional "relativist notion of style" of Renaissance approaches to antiquity; Dempsey links their use of the term to J.L. Austin's speech-act theory, loc. cit., 417. Also, by the present writer, *Architecture as Performance* (New York: Cambridge University Press, 2003).

333. See, for example, the account of Fra Angelico's use of *figura* and *locus* in the "long Middle Ages," in Didi-Hubermann, *Fra Angelico: Dissemblance et Figuration* (Paris: Flammarion, 1990) 32, which emphasizes authenticity of experience versus art viewed as "quelque chose comme une grande métaphore thêâtrale." For a broader view, Jonas A. Barish, *The Antitheatrical Prejudice* (Berkeley: UC Press, 1981).

334. A brief geneology appears in Catherine Soussloff and Mark Franko, "Visual and Performance Studies: A New History of Interdisciplinarity," *Social Text* 73/20 (2002), 29–46.

335. Belting, 1990; for his analysis of the relationship between contemporary art and art history, see Belting, *The End of the History of Art*, trans. C. Wood (Chicago: University of Chicago Press, 1987); for his own interests, *Szenen der Moderne* (2005). For an alternate approach to history, see the phenomenological emphases of Michael Fried, *Absorption and Theatricality* (Berkeley: University of California Press, 1980), founded in a broad critique of "theatricality" in eighteenth-century and minimalist art. See also Robert Williams, *Art Theory: an Historical Introduction* (Oxford: Blackwell, 2004).

336. For analysis of the "New History", see Lisa Jardine, "Strains of Renaissance Reading," *English Literary Renaissance* (Autumn, 1995), 289–306. In her alternate reading of Holbein's *Ambassadors*—the same painting which served as an emblem in Greenblatt's seminal *Renaissance Self-Fashioning* (1986)—Jardine notes the tension between "literary" and "historical" interests within the study of English literature; she does not elaborate on the primacy she too accords to images.

337. Richard Goldthwaite, *Wealth and the Demand for Art* (Baltimore: Johns Hopkins University Press, 1986).

338. By contrast with the disdain for the archives in some circles of art history, consider the ways in which contemporary artists have probed the archive's limitations and potential. For an introduction, see *Deep storage: collecting,*

storing, and archiving in art, ed. Ingrid Schaffner and Matthias Winzen (Munich and New York: Prestel, 1998).

339. For a recent comment on this debate from the purview of intellectual and social history, see John Monfasani, "The Renaissance as the Concluding Phase of the Middle Ages," *Bullettino dell'Instituto Storico Italiano per il Medio Evo, 108* (2006): 165–185.

340. It is important to note that "craft" is also an anachronistic word for this period, probably coming into use around the same time as "scientist." See Edward S. Cooke, unpublished lecture delivered at the conference "British Histories of Design: Where next?" Victoria & Albert Musuem, July 2006.

341. David Morgan, *Visual Piety: A History and Theory of Popular Religious Images* (Berkeley: University of California Press, 1998), xv.

342. Helen Watson-Verran and David Turnbull, "Science and Other Indigenous Knowledge Systems," *Handbook of Science and Technology Studies* (Sheila Jasanoff, Gerald E. Markle, James C. Peterson and Trevor Pinch, eds. (London: Sage Publications, 1995): 115–139, esp. p. 117. This view has been very helpfully developed in two special issues of *Perspectives on Science 13*, numbers 1 and 2 (2005).

343. Roger Chartier, "Culture as Appropriation: Popular Culture Uses in Early Modern France," *Understanding Popular Culture: Europe from the Middle Ages to the Nineteenth Century* ed. by Steven L. Kaplan (Berlin: Mouton, 1984): 230–253.

344. Jean Lave, *Cognition in Practice: Mind, mathematics and culture in everyday life* (Cambridge: Cambridge University Press, 1988). See also Edwin Hutchins, *Cognition in the Wild* (Cambridge: MIT Press, 1995).

345. Tim Ingold, *The Perception of the Environment: Essays in livelihood, dwelling and skill* (London and New York: Routledge, 2000), 418.

346. Vannoccio Biringuccio, *The Pirotechnia*, trans. by Cyril Stanley Smith and Martha Teach Gnudi (New York: Basic Books, 1943), xvi.

347. Biringuccio, *Pirotechnia*, 143–144. He goes on (144): this is a "treatment" for ore—the "ores must be so tormented that the obstinacy of their hardness is overcome."

348. Bibliotheque Nationale, Paris, Ms. Fr 640, f. 87r.

349. Ms. Fr 640, f. 109r.

350. Anonymous, "Goldsmith's Storehouse," f. 6v.

351. It seems likely that practices of pigment-making (in particular the process for producing vermilion out of sulphur and mercury) gave rise to the two-principle theory of metals. See Arie Wallert, "Alchemy and medieval art technology," in *Alchemy Revisited*, edited by Z.R.W.M. von Martels (Leiden: Brill, 1990): 154–161.

352. Some of the most successful efforts at getting at the parameters of an artisanal worldview are contained in Michael W. Cole, *Cellini and the Principles of Sculpture* (Cambridge: Cambridge University Press, 2002); and Spike Bucklow, "Paradigms and Pigment Recipes: Vermilion, Synthetic Yellows and the Nature of Egg," *Zeitschrift für Kunsttechnologie und Konservierung 13* (1999): 140–149.

353. See the work of Allen G. Debus, B. J. T. Dobbs, and, briefly, E.J. Holmyard, *Alchemy* (New York: Dover, 1990; reprint of 1957 ed.) and John

M. Stillman, *The Story of Alchemy and Early Chemistry* (New York: Dover, 1960; reprint of 1924 ed.).

354. Albertus Magnus, *Libellus de alchimia*, trans. by Virginia Heines, S.C. N. (Berkeley and Los Angeles, 1958), 19: gold stimulates heat/life.

355. For example, "Goldsmith's Storehouse," f. 55r: Ch. 25: To make salpeter with Vermilion for water that will part gold from silver as well as aquafortis. 4 oz of vermilion added to the lye, boil etc until it become salpeter.

356. Bucklow cites pigment recipes in which red and gold are associated, for example, Bucklow, "Paradigms and Pigment Recipes: Vermilion, Synthetic Yellows and the Nature of Egg," 145–147.

357. Cennini, *Il libro dell'Arte (The Craftsman's Handbook)*, 101–102: "Mosaic gold".

358. Bucklow, "Paradigms and Pigment Recipes: Vermilion, Synthetic Yellows, and the Nature of Egg," 146.

359. John Gage, "Colour Words in the High Middle Ages," in Erma Hermens, ed., *Looking through Paintings: The Study of Painting Techniques and Materials in Support of Art Historical Research (Leids Kunsthistorisch Jaarboek XI)* (Baarn, The Netherlands: Uitgeverij de Prom, 1998), 35–48, esp. p. 39.

360. Cennino D'Andrea Cennini, *Il libro dell'Arte*, translated by Daniel V. Thompson, Jr. (New York: Dover, 1960) 95.

361. Christiane Kruse, "Fleisch werden—Fleisch malen: Malerei als "incarnazione." Mediale Verfahren des bildwerdens in Libro dell'Arte von Cennino Cennini," *Zeitschrift für Kunstgeschichte*, 63 (2000): 305–325.

362. Through such a practice, Cennino acknowledged the transformative power of art and artisan.

363. Theophilus, *On Divers Arts*, trans. and intro. John G. Hawthorne and Cyril Stanley Smith (New York: Dover Publications, 1979), 189–190. Theophilus was in all probability the monk Roger of Helmarshausen. See also, *Rechter Gebrauch der Alchimei/ Mitt vil bisher verborgenen uund lustigen Künstien/ Nit allein den fürwitzigen Alchmisten/ sonder allen kunstbaren Werckleutten/ in und ausserhalb feurs. Auch sunst aller menglichen inn vil wege zugebrauchen* (1531), f. III v: to make precious stones capable of cutting and of casting. In Petrus Kärtzenmacher, *Alchimia. Wie mann alle farben/ wasser/ olea/ salia und alumina damit mann alle corpora/ spiritus und calces preparirt/ sublimirt und fixirt machen sol. Und wie mann diese ding nutze-auff das Sol und Luna werden mög. Auch von solviren uund schaidung aller metal/ Polirung aller handt edel gestain/ fürtrefflichen wassern zum etzen/ schaiden und solviren/ undt zletst wie die gifftige dämpf züverhüten ein kurtzer begrif* (Strassburg: Jacob Cammerlander, 1538), p. xxix verso: philosophers have hidden the fact that human blood is good for making silver and gold. All should know that menstrual blood or "sanguis rubei collerici" is the best for the work of transmutation.

364. Theophilus, *On Divers Arts*, 189–190. This recipe endured for at least four hundred years, which probably indicates its power in organizing an understanding of the world. Four hundred years after Theophilus's treatise, the anonymous German author of a printed treatise on metalworking offered a strikingly similar formula for cutting and

engraving crystal and precious stones: "Take goose and goat's blood and dry it until it is hard. Take crystal or any stone. Pound the blood to powder, pour ashes on it. Let it mix well in a container. Mix in strong vinegar, then lay the stone in it, warm it a little. And the stone allows you to cut or form it as you want. Throw it in cold water and it will become hard again in an hour." *Rechter Gebrauch der Alchimei*, p. III verso. The anonymous author of the "Goldsmith's Storehouse" (ca. 1604) writes, however: 62v: "some Aucthors doe wryte that the Dyamon cannot be broken, butt with the new warme bludd of a goate, but is is not soe, for Dyamon Cutters have dayly experience to the Contrary, who doe continually use the powlder of Dyamons."

365. Michael Cole, "Cellini's Blood," *Art Bulletin*, 81 (1999): 215–235.

366. Francesca G. Bewer, "The Sculpture of Adriaen de Vries: A Technical Study," *Small Bronzes in the Renaissance*, ed. Debra Pincus (Washington, D. C.: Center for Advanced Study in the Visual Arts, 2001), 159–193. Wheat, 180; Hercules, 182.

367. Albertus Magnus, *Book of Minerals*, trans. by Dorothy Wyckoff (Oxford: Clarendon Press, 1967): 81.

368. Theophilus, *On Divers Arts*, 119–120

369. Robert Halleux, "The reception of Arabic alchemy in the West," *Encyclopedia of the History of Arabic Science*, ed. by Roshdi Rashed, vol. 3 (London and New York: Routledge, 1996): 886–902; esp. pp. 887–888, argues that it is based on Arabic recipes, perhaps part of the Jabirian corpus.

370. Arie Wallert, "Alchemy and medieval art technology," in *Alchemy Revisited*, edited by Z.R.W.M. von Martels (Leiden: Brill, 1990): 154–161, p. 161.

371. Bucklow, "Paradigms and Pigment Recipes: Vermilion, Synthetic Yellows and the Nature of Egg," 145.

372. *Rechter Gebrauch der Alchimei* (1531), ff. XII–XIV.

373. Albertus Magnus, *The Book of Secrets of Albertus Magnus of the Virtues of Herbs, Stones and Certain Beasts. Also A Book of the Marvels of the World*, ed. by Michael R. Best and Frank H. Brightman (Oxford: Clarendon Press, 1973): 104.

374. See Pamela Smith, *The Body of the Artisan: Art and Experience in the Scientific Revolution* (University of Chicago Press, 2004), 117–123.

375. Anonymous, *Kunstbüchlein, Auff mancherley weyß Dinten und allerhandt farben zu bereiten. Auch Gold unnd Silver/ sampt allen Metallen auß der Federn zu schreiben/ Mit viel anderen nützlichen künstlin. Schreybfedern unnd Pergamen mit allerley Farben zu ferben. Auch wie man Schrifft und gemälde auff stähes lene/ Eysene Waffen/ und dergleichen etzen soll. Etliche zugesetzte Kunststüclin/ vormals im druck nye außgangen. Allen Schreybern/ Brieffmalern/ sampt andern solcher Künsten Liebhabern/ gantz lustig und fruchtbar zu wissen*, (Augsburg: Michael Manger, 1538), f. 19v.

376. Biringuccio, *The Pirotechnia*, 83.

377. I discuss why this neglect has occurred in the history of science in the Introduction to *Merchants and Marvels: Commerce, Science, and Art in Early Modern Europe*, with Paula Findlen (Routledge, 2002). A recent volume

that begins to fill this glaring gap is Londa Schiebinger and Claudia Swan, eds., *Colonial Botany: Science, Commerce, and Politics in the Early Modern World* (Philadelphia: University of Pennsylvania Press, 2005).
My title is adapted from Isaiah Berlin, "Some Procrustations," *Oxford Outlook* 10 (1930) 491–502.

378. My comments respond to the conversation and not to the position papers.

379. William J. Bouwsma, "The Renaissance and the drama of western history," *American Historical Review* 84 (February 1979) 1–15.

380. In order to grapple with such unwieldy terms as "systematicity," without collapsing the difference between order and logic, it is useful to consider the writings of Niklas Luhmann (and his protracted rewriting of Talcott Parsons's sociology).

381. For mediaeval studies, see Paul Freedman and Gabrielle M. Spiegel, "Medievalisms old and new: the rediscovery of alterity in North American medieval studies," *American Historical Review* (June 1998), 677–704. Also stimulating in this regard is Thomas Crow, "The practice of art history in America," *Daedelus* (Spring 2006), 70–90. My thanks to John Onians for drawing this article to my attention.

382. Christopher Wood, "Art history's normative Renaissance," in *The Italian Renaissance in the twentieth century*, ed. Allen J. Grieco, Michael Rocke, and Fiorella Gioffredi Superbi, I Tatti Studies 19 (Florence: Olschki, 2002) 65–85.

383. I was fascinated, but troubled by the different meanings granted to the "rational" and "irrational," especially in relation to humanism. Without delving into this rather complex binary, it seems to me useful to reconsider the poetic thinking at the core of Ernesto Grassi's account of humanism (and rereading of Heidegger's critique of humanism). More generally, what is called "irrational," it seems to me, is often simply that which individuals who do not study the humanities *from within* cannot comprehend.

5

AFTERWORDS

RENAISSANCE THEORY?[*]

Alessandro Nova

Forgive me if I begin my afterword with a sentence which might be perceived as a self-serving humility topos, but it is impossible to offer in a few pages a fair account of the quality, variety and complexity of the arguments so admirably discussed in the essays collected in this volume. The credit for all this most interesting reading goes to the authors as well as to James Elkins' and Robert Williams' brilliant *regia*. If I dare to add my opinion to this very distinguished chorus, it has to do with my own biography, which is characterized by prolonged professional experiences in four completely different geographical areas, namely Italy, the United Kingdom, California, a land with its own distinctive intellectual panorama, and Germany. This fact should not be misinterpreted as a claim to "objectivity"; it means only that I inevitably evaluate certain issues through the filter of my own prejudices and shortcomings, from multiple standpoints. Such a background can be both an asset and a liability. It is an asset in that it has given me a deep respect for different methodological traditions: for example, the great tradition of Italian scholarship devoted to the study of theoretical writing on the arts yet not especially engaged with modern critical theory. It is a liability in that the brilliant array of possibilities it offers me can be overwhelming: seeming to point to an inevitable and all-consuming relativism, it can induce a kind of aphasia or paralysis.

"Italy", time and space

To judge from the starting points and the speakers invited to the Cork seminar, the organizers have framed the "Renaissance" from an Italian point of view, even if Matt Kavaler and Claire Farago represented, respectively, a European and a global perspective. Many scholars who do research in other countries were later asked to respond to the original essays, but they were "compelled"—so to speak—to confront a body of data and opinion that had developed around the question of the state of Italian Renaissance art historical studies in North America. It makes sense, therefore, to begin my comments by asking what role Italian scholarship plays in this volume. Only one theoretical contribution made by Italian colleagues is mentioned repeatedly in the pages of the seminar, namely Enrico Castelnuovo's and Carlo Ginzburg's very influential essay on center and periphery, even if one encounters along the way and mostly in the footnotes the names of other well-known art historians.[1] Considering that Ginzburg is a scholar who has taught for many years at UCLA, it seems inescapable to conclude that Italian art history is somehow reluctant to address issues of critical theory, and if this is the case, one should try to explain why.

Of course, it all depends on how one defines critical theory in the first place, but it is probably fair to maintain, without running the risk of being contradicted, that Italian art history is more "object"-oriented than theoretical in scope, although Marzia Faietti's "assessment" in these pages combines the two approaches. The simplest explanation for this state of affairs is that in Italy art historians are confronted from the very beginning of their studies with the overwhelming presence of "objects"—I will return to this term—which shape, or should shape, their cultural memory and personal identity, as well as posing urgent problems of their own. Issues of classification and conservation, of cultural property and politics—which were hardly touched upon at the seminar yet are potentially of theoretical concern—therefore take centre stage, even if they tend to be dealt with in a matter-of-fact way. This is the "view from within", which has its own *raison d'être* but is often myopic and sometimes self-centered.

The authors of the Cork seminar may be interested in knowing that their concerns are instead shared by their German speaking colleagues. The same debate about the lost centrality of Renaissance studies, and of Italian Renaissance studies in particular, is going on in Germany. In this "view from outside"—if this inaccurate and not entirely felicitous expression is permitted—there is a sense of loss which is compensated for by an increasing investment in theoretical issues. It is evident that scholars working in Berlin, Bonn, Munich or in North America, where there is a long tradition of teaching art history in global or at least European terms, have a much broader perspective than their Italian colleagues, almost overwhelmed, as they are, by their obligation to defend a material-cultural heritage constantly under physical threat. Yet, if this fact can help to explain the divergence of orientation and approach, it does not excuse the indifference toward larger methodological issues that one notices in Italy (I am referring to scholars working on Italian soil irrespective of their origins or nationality). The risk of the proliferation of parallel discourses—with the consequent danger of paralysis—is real, but one should not therefore avoid the task of confronting the issues and trying to develop useful proposals. As I will argue at the end of this paper, this difficult intellectual environment does not necessarily represent a deficit; it could also be an added value.

There is no reason to be nostalgic for a past grandeur, and for that matter I am not at all certain that the paradigm "Italian Renaissance" was ever really so overwhelmingly dominant as it is often assumed. Ruskin was interested in Gothic forms and modern painters like Turner, Viollet-le-Duc reconstructed medieval churches and walls, Riegl investigated the *Spätrömische Kunstindustrie* as well as the group portraiture of the Golden Age in Holland, even Saxl and Panofsky built many of their most influential publications in a diachronic way. Be that as it may, we should all greet with enthusiasm a trend which expands the geographical as well as the temporal limits of our core-subject. It is wonderful that an American institution of higher education is cooperating with the universities of Cordova and

Messina; this reminds me of the project on the exchanges between Mediterranean cultures, in medieval as well as early modern times, fostered by my colleague Gerhard Wolf at the Kunsthistorisches Institut in Florence. Cultural interactions are at the center of these enterprises, and we should not be afraid of the possible tensions between the local and the global. The history of collecting has already shown what is to be gained from such broadly planned research projects, and one should pursue this goal also in a European context.

As far as time is concerned, it is difficult, on the one hand, to avoid disagreement about the chronological limits of the "Renaissance", but on the other hand I am increasingly interested, like Claire Farago, in diachronic work. The book I have just finished deals with the problem of the representation of the wind in the visual arts from Antiquity to the present day. The question is: How can I represent an invisible natural phenomenon, namely air's transparency and movement? This problem posed a challenge to the mimetic qualities and aspirations of Western art, as was well understood by Turner: "One word is sufficient to establish what is the greatest difficulty of the painter's art: to produce wavy air, as some call the wind. [. . .] To give that wind we must give the cause as well as the effect [. . .] with mechanical hints of the strength of nature perpetually trammeled with mechanical shackles".[2] Leonardo and Poussin were also greatly interested in this phenomenon. Originally, therefore, I wanted to concentrate my research on the early modern period, but it soon became clear that such a project would make sense only if treated globally and diachronically: only from such a perspective can the innovations of Alberti and Leonardo be properly appreciated; it thus works to reclaim a central place for "Renaissance" contributions.

The method is not new. As I said before, Saxl and Panofsky—whose scholarship, incidentally, seems to me to be misrepresented in some of the comments made at the Cork seminar—had already conceived their work diachronically, the great book on *Saturn and Melancholy* being only the most venerable example of their highly sophisticated interdisciplinary approach. This does not imply that so-called micro-histories should not be pursued: indeed, Warburg used to say that God hides in details. But this truth should not discourage us from expanding the geographical and chronological limits of our vision; after all, it did not discourage Warburg from doing so.

One point, however, should be forcefully made: it is not enough to invoke the names of the fathers, Riegl and Warburg; one should also follow their example. This plea should not be interpreted as an invitation to "mimic" their unrivalled scholarship a century later; rather, art history should try to regain a central position in the humanities through the investment in new methods and questions. If I may be allowed to sound a note of dissent, one of the limitations of the Cork seminar was its concentration on "pure" art history: the presence of philosophers, historians, and experts on literature would have been very beneficial. Indeed, it is not enough to discuss the apparent decline of Italian Renaissance studies in art history; one should also reexamine the general premises and goals of our discipline. If art history wants to regain its cutting edge, one should argue in favor of the centrality of the "object" *and* of the "image", a terminology which refers to all artifacts, architecture included, without discarding but instead taking advantage of the valuable insights developed by critical theory over the last few decades.

Begriffe—systematicity

Of course, one cannot avoid invoking Burckhardt's name, as many authors do, when one opens up a debate on the "Renaissance". However, one should not forget that it is a French word, which circulated in that land well before Michelet and which derived from the Italian *rinascita*, a term already used by Giorgio Vasari. One can well sympathize with the organizers of the seminar, if they were reluctant to re-open admittedly worn-out files, but it is unwise to write about a topic or any historical period without doing first an archeology of its concepts. Exemplary in this respect remains the analysis of the word *maniera*, scrutinized by John Shearman in 1961.[3]

The Cork seminar had other, greater ambitions. It was not the place to rehearse well-known historiographical debates. Yet scholars have the duty to define the concepts (*Begriffe*) used in their analyses: What is the meaning of "rationalism" and "irrationalism", if we mention them in sweeping statements without any theoretical specification? Philosophers would shake their heads in disappointment. And what does "modern" mean? Is it a tautologically "good" thing? Is it good to be "modern"? If we do not define these concepts, they remain vague and meaningless. It is therefore exemplary that Elizabeth Honig tells us very clearly what her definition of style is. Equally commendable is the fact that the most important and innovative concept of the entire seminar, namely *systematicity*, is amply illustrated, explained and discussed in Williams' provocative as well as brilliant essay. "Renaissance theory defines art as a form of knowledge", he writes, adding: "The new conception of art that emerges in the Renaissance is directly related to [a] new sense of the significance of representation; art is redefined as a principle that superintends representation, both as a mental faculty and a social practice. [. . .] Italian Renaissance art is structured by the assumption that *what is properly artistic is a concern with the specifically systematic features of representation* [Williams' emphasis]".

I feel challenged by this very sophisticated analysis because I am not certain that I can do justice to all its important implications. There is no question that art is a form of knowledge in Renaissance theory and practice: Leonardo's anatomical drawings, for example, are not simply illustrations of "scientific" texts, but autonomous cognitive instruments as well as products, and this observation can be extended to other forms of this period's artistic output. The very complex issue of representation needs instead to be further explored and defined in a contextualized form, i.e. in concrete and not generic theoretical terms. Williams' short essay originally published in the journal *Rinascimento* is inevitably assertive and without the cumbersome but necessary evidence which will be surely supplied in his forthcoming book on Raphael. I look forward to its publication because it will not be the traditional descriptive biography of a great master. Michael Cole and Alexander Nagel have already written excellent critical monographs on Cellini and Michelangelo, but the book on Raphael will be equally if not more embedded in theory.

Two points need to be clarified, however. First: Why should

systematicity be an exclusive product of the Italian Renaissance? Is there any reason why Dürer's *Self-portrait* in Munich or Holbein's *Ambassadors* in London should show less "systematicity" than, say, Raphael's *Transfiguration*? Williams is rightly irritated by some claims made by Northern European art-scholarship, which often places the emergence of pictorial "self-awareness" in the works produced by that great cultural tradition, and he points out, therefore, that Masaccio's *Trinity*, Leonardo's *Last Supper* and Raphael's *School of Athens* are also potently self-aware images. His criticism is well justified because it is a healthy reaction against intellectual oversimplifications, but why then follow the same path? Are we positive— and this is the second point—that the ancient world and the Middle Ages did not have their own *systematicity*? Our interpretations should not be tainted by the accidents of survival. Vitruvius' text, for instance, enjoys a status which goes well beyond its real merit because its success was determined by the loss of much more important treatises on architecture. Could it be that such lacunae are the cause of the perceived lack of systematic features of representation in periods preceding the "Renaissance"? It is indeed odd that the Middle Ages were completely erased from the Cork seminar's narrative.

To pursue this line of thought, I would like to challenge the idea that a source must be a written text. Not all visual traditions without texts lack theory: *Gemalte Theorie* is a concept which has been successfully employed by Matthias Winner and Rudolf Preimesberger, among others; a useful category which is echoed in Stephen Campbell's "Starting Points" essay, when he alludes to "practiced theory" [Campbells' inverted commas].[4] I ask myself, therefore, whether Italian Renaissance art was really the first to be concerned with the specifically systematic features of representation. This is not to say that I find Williams' cleverly argued proposal unconvincing: my response is only a *caveat*, an encouragement to persevere, to make the argument even more compelling in his forthcoming book; I would be the first to congratulate him heartily if my present skepticism could be proved wrong.

The open criticism of the "object" and of a social history of art, instead, seems to me untenable. It may be that from a North American perspective the collection and classification of objects can be interpreted as "a disguised form of bourgeois consumerism", but even if this were true, one should not abandon a necessary and highly difficult *kunstimmanente* analysis of the artifacts. Such a merciless condemnation of the "object" does not take into account the notions of cultural heritage and social memory. Our colleagues who are working with a great spirit of dedication, often at sacrifice to themselves, and for very low salaries in the Soprintendenze, in small provincial museums, and in laboratories di restauro to keep alive and transmit our cultural heritage deal with objects on a daily basis. I cannot imagine an art history without objects.

As far as the social history of art is concerned, it has now become modish to denigrate it, but many colleagues are practicing it even when they seem to dismiss it. For example, the critique of the academy and of other institutional structures—like the seminar at Cork— as well as the history of collecting are forms of a social history of art. One of the greatest books of the twentieth century, Baxandall's *Painting and Experience in Fifteenth Century Italy*, carries the undertitle *A primer in the social history of pictorial style*, and the characterization of patronage studies as an opportunistic shift of attention from the artist to the commissioner, a shift which does not really put into question the traditional narrative of the grand masters, is unfair and certainly inaccurate: there are not only studies on the patronage of bankers, popes, and cardinals, but also of social groups and religious orders; they are stories of complex networks which interact with issues of production, reception and theory. It is indeed a great relief that Williams himself takes into account social practices in his definition of representation quoted above.

Desiderata

A good friend of mine, the late Stefan Germer, told me once, in 1997, that all apocalypses are reactionary or at least conservative. Even if I do not completely share his opinion, I have since become a little wary of institutionalized lament. Is Renaissance scholarship "sunken into a kind of fourth-rate status", as Elkins argues? Can one speak of neglect and oblivion? Does the study of Italian Renaissance art find itself "in something of a backwater within the discipline of art history", as

William maintains? I happen to agree more with Adrian Randolph's "assessment", above all when he praises the intellectual vitality and diversity of the field documented in this book. Ironically, it is the excellent *niveau* of the papers discussed at Cork and of the responses they have triggered that demonstrate the good health enjoyed by Italian Renaissance studies in North America. To be self-critical is always a very positive sign, and the sophisticated level of self-reflexivity reached by the authors is reassuring for the future of the discipline. It can be presumptuous, therefore, to end this short note with three desiderata; yet since they echo important issues raised by the seminar's participants, it seems to me that I am simply summarizing their own conclusions.

To begin with, I hope that James Elkins will write his abandoned book because it is a diachronic project. His planned table of contents shows that he is interested in fundamental art historical issues, but on a more elementary, prosaic level one could add that the artists of the twentieth century have been deeply concerned with (not influenced by!) the art of the Renaissance, and that this exchange is still going on in the twenty-first century. For instance, one cannot understand the work of Duchamp, Beuys, Pasolini, Warhol, Viola, Sugimoto or even Kentridge without referring to Leonardo, Rosso Fiorentino, Pontormo, the *Sacro Monte* in Varallo, Raphael, Holbein and Dürer. Influential contemporary artists seem to be more attracted by Renaissance art than by the monk Maius' or Jacques-Louis David's aesthetically equally ambitious works. The problems implicit in the pairs constructed in Elkins' summary of his abandoned book go, of course, well beyond the superficial issue of direct quotation, appropriation and manipulation of "old works". Nonetheless, the link between modern art and Renaissance models is also a viable way of reinterpreting the latter, of adding a new dimension to the constant process of semiosis which revolves around them.

Second, let us remain unconventional. The multiple points of view presented at the Cork seminar produced a marvelous polyphony which is a good metaphor for the richness of the texture of Renaissance studies in the field of art history. The plea for an even higher argumentative level is certainly worthy of praise, but what is wrong with plurality? Recently a friend of mine rebuked me by saying that plurality is not a program. I must admit that there is some truth to his statement, and yet we should be proud of our variegated intellectual landscape: "theory" cannot be done without the "objects" and vice versa. We do not need prescriptions; we need flexible instruments to deal successfully with the *iconic turn*.[5]

A last desideratum: To improve the quality of our writing, and of course I speak of myself in the first place. It is perhaps odd to make this point because the level of the narratives presented at the seminar is truly magnificent, and yet it is not representative of the average texts produced by the discipline. One is therefore pleased, amused and at the same time surprised to note how many colleagues have mentioned critically as well as positively the name of Vasari. Like Williams, I also think that his was the most influential book ever written in our field. There are many reasons to explain its importance and success, but one of them is certainly its extraordinary literary value. As many participants have pointed out, one should not be afraid of the disarray in Renaissance art historical studies, but if we are serious when we claim that one of our goals should be the "re-appropriation" of a supposedly lost leadership, one of the ways to reach it passes through the pleasure of writing and reading.

Notes

* I am deeply grateful to Robert Williams for his improvements to my English text and to both editors for their kind invitation to comment on the outstanding results of the Cork seminar.

1. Enrico Castelnuovo and Carlo Ginzburg, "Centro e periferia", in *Storia dell'arte italiana. Parte prima*, vol. I, *Questioni e metodi*, ed. Giovanni Previtali (Turin: Giulio Einaudi Editore, 1979), 283–352.

2. Quoted from Monika Wagner, "Luft sichtbar machen. Neue Konzepte für ein altes künstlerisches Problem", in *Luft*, ed. Bern Busch (Köln: Wienand Verlag & Medien GmbH), p. 85. [pp. 85–94]

3. John Shearman, "*Maniera* as an Aesthetic Ideal", in *The Renaissance and Mannerism* (Princeton: Princeton University Press, 1963), 200–221. Acts of the Twentieth International Congress of the History of Art, held in New York City September 7–12, 1961.

4. Matthias Winner, "Gemalte Kunsttheorie. Zu Gustave Courbets <<Allégorie réelle>> und der Tradition", in *Jahrbuch der Berliner Museen* 4 (1962), 151–185. Of course, nineteenth-century France is a cultural panorama with a strong theoretical tradition, but in this case the author is

referring to the fact that Courbet's painting is a "text". For the reconstruction of the theory of the Flemish masters of the Quattrocento through their painted works, see e.g. Rudolf Preimesberger, "Zu Jan van Eycks Diptychon der Sammlung Thyssen-Bornemisza", in *Zeitschrift für Kunstgeschichte* 54 (1991), 459–489.

5. W.J.T. Mitchell, *Picture Theory. Essays on Verbal and Visual Representation* (Chicago and London: The University of Chicago Press, 1994).

HUGGING THE SHORE

James Elkins and Robert Williams

August 21, 2007

Dear Bob,

Let's start where Alessandro Nova left off: with the question of writing. It is such a central question, and so often relegated to the end of a discussion. It's as if people say: writing is crucial to what we do, but it's a matter of individual initiative and talent, and it can't really be fruitfully discussed. I'm on holiday at the moment, in Villefranche-sur-Mer, and I've been occupying my time with books that have nothing to do with Renaissance studies or even art history. I've just finished Leonid Tsypkin's amazing *Summer in Baden-Baden*.[1] It's a novel about Dostoyevsky, but wholly unlike J.M. Coetzee's *Master of Petersburg*.[2] Tsypkin's book is irreproachably well-researched, even though it's a novel. (It's about Dostoyevsky's disastrous summer in Baden-Baden, where he nearly gambled his way into debtor's prison.) The author keeps rigorously to facts, and yet it is written in an intense, stream-of-consciousness way, ventriloquizing Dostoyevsky's monomaniacal, injured, petulant, desperate, aggressive state of mind. This book is, among many other things, an absolutely brilliant piece of literary criticism. It is more intensely felt, far better expressed, more fluid and capacious, and even more scholarly, than most books of literary criticism.

When art historians talk about writing, I don't think we often mean Tsypkin's kind of experiment. I think we picture something more domestic, more bourgeois—I'll get to that word in a moment—we intend to spruce up our prose, find better adjectives, write more persuasively. From a scholar's point of view, Tsypkin's book should be genuinely disturbing, because it raises the possibility that we might write something that is *not recognized* as art history, and yet outdoes art history at its own game. Another example of a wild text that is entirely incredible *as* art history, but outdoes art historical writing on many fronts, is Salvador Dalí's book on Millet's *Angelus*.[3] Dalí does better research than any art historians have: he looks at children's books and scientific journals; he supervises new X-Rays of the painting; he actually helps write the psychoanalytic theory he uses, in personal collaboration with Jacques Lacan. But at the same time he openly and happily admits his book is a paranoid fantasy, not at all intended to prove something about a nineteenth-century painting—and in that fashion he slams the door on art history as he knew it. Even Georges Didi-Huberman does not do that. Georges's ideas, as I am fond of repeating, could potentially disrupt art history, but his texts have always been available to be read *as* art history. Dalí's book isn't credible *as* art history, and it isn't useful *for* art history.[4] Dalí and Tsypkin are, in my mind, really writers. The rest of us hug the shore.

Calls for changes in the rhetoric or quality of art historical writing, for instance Nova's and Alice Jarrard's, are normally meant to be heard *within* art history. Among writers on the Renaissance, there are few who have crossed the border from expository, dramatic, or epistolary prose (like this, like your *Art Bulletin* dialogue) into the broader field of writing—meaning writing that needs to be read as fiction, and not merely as a fictionalized setting for real-world exposition.[5] Who has crossed that border? I don't count Dan Brown, because as Una Roman D'Elia implies, he didn't so much cross a border as blithely ignore it. Among writers who have addressed the Renaissance there is the inimitable Jean-Louis Schefer, and some passages in Roberto Longhi . . . all in all, very little. If Tsypkin had written a book like *Summer in Baden-Baden*, but on an art historical subject, he would not have been able to get a job in a university—in fact he probably wouldn't even have gotten an interview. And Dalí's book would have been a good way to get kicked out of a university. No: I think what we have in mind in calling for renewed attention to writing has little to do with crossing genre boundaries (or risking our jobs!): it's more a matter of writing better expository, non-fiction historical accounts. And since that's the case, what I wonder is: What *kinds* of writing would count as "better"? I'm asking this partly as a lead-in to your claim—which I notice provokes some resistance among the Assessors, for example Charlotte Houghton!—that the object-oriented aspect of our discipline is a bourgeois pastime. I'd like to extend that to our writing in general.

Bourgeois writing has its rules, and entails, I'll say, a certain care in articulation, a certain elegance of diction: exactly the kinds of carefully combed, well-behaved, toothless styles that writers like Martin Amis love to savage. In art history, people often point to Panofsky as an example of a confident, emotionally cool, impeccably balanced authorial voice that seems especially inadvisable, or literally unbelievable, in the twenty-first century. And yet many people write in ways that aren't so distant from Panofsky's English-language style.[6] What would be "better writing" for Renaissance art historians, or for art historians in general? Because there isn't any such thing as neutrally, historically unaffiliated "good writing," we must be thinking of something. But what?

I'd like to know if your idea of art history as a partly bourgeois enterprise can help open a discussion about what might count as interesting writing in art history, and in Renaissance studies in particular. Can we identify *appropriately* bourgeois ways of writing, and if not—if we'd rather not—then what, exactly, should count as interesting writing? And how far outside our habits are we really willing to go?

Of course we have any number of pressing things to talk about. But I wanted to let writing have the first word instead of the last.

Best,

Jim

23 August

Dear Jim,

When I use the word "bourgeois" to characterize contemporary art history, it's not so much the writing as the thinking I'm complaining about: more than our writing, it's our thinking that "hugs the shore." I'm suspicious of the assumption that good writing makes good scholarship: when I was young I studied with Leo Steinberg—a spectacular writer—but soon decided that there were serious problems with his approach to the Renaissance, and I went to work with John Shearman instead. I happen to think that Shearman is a great writer, too, but in an obviously more limited way; still, I harbor a certain affection for the self-effacing academic prose that you find "carefully-combed, well-mannered, and toothless." I don't see such writing as bourgeois so much as an extension of scholarly— "scientific"—discipline. I don't believe that it's necessarily an obstacle to thinking original thoughts, and it tends to favor the virtues of clarity and rigor, which are in short supply. I'm not in principle opposed to a more transgressive kind of writing, but I often find that such writing masks conceptual weaknesses and content that is in fact very conventional.

That said, it will amuse you to know that I actually wrote a screenplay a couple of years ago. It was about the Carracci: Annibale, his brother Agostino, and their cousin Ludovico. I've told almost none of our colleagues about it, of course, mindful of the very resistances you describe, yet I thought of it as a serious extension of my scholarship and teaching. I was intrigued by the possibility of using drama as a way to say something urgent and important about Renaissance art, and of using the Carracci to say something subtler than could likely be said in yet another movie about Caravaggio. It even seemed to me that drama might be the best possible vehicle to convey the specifically *historical* kind of insight I pursue my work. If the historicity of art lies in its being produced and consumed in time, in the daily wear and tear of human life, then drama, which is about that wear and tear, ought to allow for the emergence of just such truth about art as the history of art also aims to reveal.

When I finished the script I gave it to some friends of mine with

Hollywood experience. They thought the idea had great potential but that to make it marketable I would have to embellish the story in rather predictable ways: create a romantic interest of some kind, perhaps have the two brothers actually come to blows in the course of one of their arguments! I was never so eager to sell it that I was willing to load it up in that way: it's not that I'd rule out any fictional embellishments, just that any such embellishments would have to justify themselves by revealing a deeper, otherwise inaccessible aspect of the historical truth. I haven't gotten very far with the revisions, but I continue to think about how I might make the story both dramatically compelling and historically illuminating, and I haven't given up on the belief that if I were somehow to succeed at doing so, I would also be achieving something essential to my aims as a scholar.

So the question that you pose, the question of what kind of writing we want—the question of literary mode or genre—comes down to the kind of *knowledge* we want. For me it has to be an irreducibly *historical* kind of knowledge, which means that, whatever sense of nearness underlies our relation to the objects we study, some sense of their distance must also be preserved. Such distancing is what makes art history *critical*; it works against the ready absorption of things into our own conceptual regimes, our tendency to use the past to justify ourselves. This is why I am so adamant—to the chagrin of so many of my colleagues—about the way in which our preoccupation with objects feeds into bourgeois consumerism.

Here's an example. I recently got around to reading a relatively new book about the decorative arts in Renaissance Italy. It's highly-regarded by many of my colleagues and is an admirable book in many ways. In the introduction, the authors explain why, though the kinds of objects they are going to discuss have generally been neglected by art historians—perceived to be lacking in the qualities that distinguish "art" from "craft"—their book is nonetheless about the history of *art*:

> As such, this is unashamedly a book about art and its contemporary understanding. More than that, it concerns objects of high quality purchased and commissioned by the most educated and wealthy men and women of Italy, those who could afford to

discriminate and to parade their discrimination. We are therefore dealing with the material culture of the elite.[7]

These three sentences begin by invoking the concept of "art" but end by reducing it to the "material culture of the elite." The authors claim to be performing a critical operation, distancing us from our old, limited conception of what art is, yet they actually simply reinforce and offer legitimation to our tendency to engage the objects as commodities. It isn't just simpleminded and methodologically inadequate; it isn't just politically repulsive; it's actively, aggressively dishonest. Yet such posturing is common in art-historical writing today, particularly in the kind that offers itself as progressive: masquerading as critique, it actually functions as an apology for our own unreflexive disposition toward the world, a justification for our deeper intellectual laziness. To me it indicates the much more disturbing way in which we "hug the shore."

It's not that all engagement with objects is of this crass kind, of course, and I feel chastened by Alessandro Nova's gentle reminder of all the modest, hardworking, underpaid people at the *Soprintendenze* —and elsewhere—many of whom are quite traditional in their methods, yet whose work often demonstrates genuine critical objectivity. But my feeling is that those of us who pride ourselves on our methodological self-consciousness must be especially diligent, particularly about keeping the way we think and write about objects from slipping back into the cesspool of consumerism. It's certainly not the only challenge facing contemporary art history, but I think it may be the most conspicuous and therefore the most urgent.

So you see, it is not as easy to answer your question about what kind of writing we want as to identify the kinds of writing we don't want.

Best,
Bob

24 August

Bob,

Let's leave writing aside, then, for the moment. I want be sure we address questions specific to the subject of this book.

I think this book is different from the other seven in the *Art Seminar* series, for a couple of reasons. The idea of the series is to ask questions about unresolved subjects, and observe the degree of conceptual coherence in the resulting discussions without imposing an order derived from some pre-existing set of interests or theories. The seven volumes vary widely in the degree of the divergence of opinions. Some are amazingly wild. Volume two, *Photography Theory*, is partly a concerted disagreement between Rosalind Krauss and Joel Snyder, but most of the contributors don't care or even see the points those two argue.[8] Volume four, *States of Art Criticism*, shows that critics fail to agree even on the most basic concepts of criticism, such as whether or not criticism entails judgment of any kind.[9]

This volume is different from the other six in two ways: first, this is the only one on a *specialty* or a *period*.[10] The reason for including a book on a specialty or period, for me, is that the Renaissance is a different *kind* of specialty, a different kind of period, than some others. It is the hinge between religious objects and aesthetic objects, or it is the moment when art history became available as a subject, or it is the inception of the idea of history—you know the entangled claims, any one of which would be enough to make the case that considering the Renaissance as a specialty, as it is in job descriptions and departmental politics, is an interesting distortion, an elision of its actual functions in the discourse of the discipline. That's why I was comparing it, in the Art Seminar, to other specialties or periods like nineteenth-century French and seventeenth-century Dutch: I am curious to see the effect on the discipline of the misidentification of Renaissance as a specialty or a period analogous to others.

Second, the Assessments in this volume are remarkable because so many of them contribute by adding knowledge and new subjects, rather than by directly debating the issues. In all the other volumes, the great majority of Assessments are argumentative, philosophic, polemic, or otherwise conceptually engaged. Few writers in *Photography Theory*, for example, chose to add examples of photographs we hadn't considered. (Maybe three out of twenty-five or so did that.) In volume 1, *Art History versus Aesthetics*, only one or two people decided to contribute new examples. But here, a number of

Assessments work by changing the subject, adding new material. I'm thinking for example of Joanna Woods-Marsden's, Pamela Smith's, Marzia Faietti's, Ingrid Ciulisová's, and Jan von Bonsdorff's Assessments. This is not to say evidence isn't argument: it is to note a kind of intervention by example, rather than by logic. Some of the Assessments, which argue more directly, are more typical of what you'll find in other volumes in the series—I am thinking for example of Elizabeth Honig's oblique, systematic challenges; Adrian Randolph's very lucid and pertinent objections; and Robert Zwijnenberg's and Lubomir Konečný's perspectival challenges. Now it would be easy to read the un-argumentative Assessments as signs of conservatism in the field, and I don't want to undervalue that: but I want to ask, instead, what qualities of the critical discourse within the field nourish these kinds of responses?

For both these reasons I'm glad I chose the Renaissance as a topic for the series, because it introduces a new *kind* of conceptual disarray that isn't present in the other six volumes. I'd like to know your take on this, since I have drifted away from Renaissance studies, and now I only observe it from the outside.

Best,

Jim

26 August

Dear Jim,

I'm not surprised that this volume is so unlike the others, and in just the ways you describe. I'm also struck by your claim that the common understanding of the Renaissance as a field of specialization like any other is a "distortion" or "elision" of its real significance within the discipline. You seem to be saying that our sense of its being a specialty has led to our losing touch with its specialness. It's an important point, and I think that Alessandro Nova is saying much the same thing when he advocates a diachronic approach.

The pressures of specialization, the need to present oneself as an expert, have certainly tended to inhibit the kind of speculative exchange we've tried to generate here: experts can't afford to be wrong, so they avoid taking risks. Not only will they tend to fall back, when challenged, onto what they know best—hence the "argument by example"—they will try to reframe any discussion in such a way that its resolution becomes a matter of "proof" by appeal to specialized knowledge. Such are the rules of the game as it has evolved over time; it isn't the worst thing in the world, and even some of our "argument by example" Assessments are excellent essays. Yet the aversion to risk has had the effect of preventing Renaissance studies from redefining itself more robustly, from rounding upon and confronting its most urgent challenges. In thus losing touch with its specialness it has settled for being a substitute, a stand-in, a place-holder for itself.

As regards the aversion to risk, it's worth mentioning that while many people accepted our invitation to participate in this project, a good many did not. In most cases it was simply a matter of timing—we were asking for a fairly quick turn-around with the Assessments, and Renaissance scholars are not used to writing quickly—but in at least a few conspicuous cases there was a reluctance to get involved in what might prove to be an uncomfortable situation. Adrian Randolph criticizes us for not having had a museum scholar on the panel, but we *did* invite one, someone whose work I admire very much: he declined politely enough, yet suggested that he didn't feel that he would have much to contribute to the kind of discussion we were planning. A couple of other scholars, asked contribute Assessments, seemed to feel that the conversation at Cork did not offer the right kind of platform for the articulation of their positions. Such reactions point to yet another level of the "conceptual disarray."

Perhaps the traditions and conventions specific to the field are partly to blame, but I also think we've been bullied into this position of submissiveness and frustration by forces beyond our control, by the development of the discipline of art history as a whole. The shape and character of Renaissance studies is very significantly determined from the outside, and not just by the kinds of institutional pressures alluded to in the discussion. If the discipline of art history needs the Renaissance to be both a reassuring place, a refuge, and something to set up in contrast to our own time, that is at least partly because our culture needs the art of the past to be a refuge—a place where beauty, meaning, and all the most rarified qualities of the spirit still count for something—a place we visit on our days off but then put behind us, so that we can get on with real life. The way in which the general public engages with art—which is to say, the way in which mass culture has redefined what it means to engage with art—exerts a direct effect on the function art history is expected to perform in society and the way art historians define their work.

This situation, which I likened to a "choke hold" in my essay on systematicity, lends a pathological dynamic to the whole field: Renaissance art must serve as an antidote to modern life but also as something through which we try to assert our own values. I find it analogous to what Horkheimer and Adorno describe when, in their account of the pathological dynamic of modern culture, they observe how the forms of leisure have become "afterimages" of the processes of labor and production. So where you may see a distinctive kind of conceptual disarray, I see a more general condition. That's why I resist the idea that the way to make Renaissance studies more interesting is to borrow concepts from other fields: it's not that we don't have a great deal to learn from other disciplines, but that we shouldn't allow them to determine our thematics or set our agenda. To do so seems to me to be a good way to guarantee further loss of specialness.

Your interest in the conceptual disarray of the field is clearly related to the idea, expressed in several of your books, that what remains resistant to articulation in art historical writing is potentially an object of the greatest interest. I doubt that what might be called the "unconscious" of Renaissance studies is all that different from the unconscious of art history as a whole, and perhaps even you suspect that Renaissance studies may be symptomatic of something deeper and more pervasive. Maybe, on some level, art history wants *to keep art from being understood*, to defer and frustrate the attainment of its ostensible aims, and Renaissance studies happens to be one field in which that obscure desire is easiest to glimpse just beneath the surface.

Best,
Bob

August 27

Dear Bob,

I can think of four ways that art history—and in particular Renaissance studies—wants to keep art from being understood.

1. Some art historians have a complex about their specialization, a toxic mixture of tremendous security (they know the relevant languages, the scripts, the cities, the archives, the dates and documents) and deep insecurity. In my experience, some of the stubbornest insecurity comes from the fact that so many art historians do not have first-hand experience in making objects similar to the ones they study. This is partly a matter of not knowing how to paint or draw. I don't mean we need transcendent skills, but that art history can be more fluent and capacious when it is written by people who feel confident and capable in making the kinds of art they study. This is one of my principal concerns with art history as a whole, and I find it is relevant to art history's interpretive methods (which are often tailored for people who do not make objects), and to art history's relation to disciplines such as art practice, music, and literary criticism. There is a lot to be said, but this isn't the place. Here I just want to note one of the effects of the slight but pervasive unease caused by our lack of hands-on familiarity with the methods used by the artists we study. That unease makes it necessary to *substitute* other kinds of knowledge that are *similar* to studio knowledge. Several of the Assessments in this book, including Elizabeth Honig's and Frédéric Elsig's, call for greater engagement with museums, conservation, and art making—but I have to say that for me, those calls always sound like workable substitutes for what is really missing, what is causing the appearance of a lack to begin with: a relaxed, first-hand knowledge of production. When Elizabeth Honig calls for an "effort to theorize process" and says "writing that tries to theorize systems of illusion and representation, that analyzes color and light . . . should be read beside writing that describes the physical processes of producing those illusions," I completely agree, but it's not enough: in the end it's not *writing* that needs to be put beside writing, but *practice*. Schematic theories of color and perspective can be read alongside schematic accounts of how color and perspective are perceived,

but both are schematic and both are theories. Many accounts, for instance Michael Baxandall's description of Chardin in *Patterns of Intention*, show the limits of the approach: Chardin's practice, as it can be reconstructed, is much more unwieldy and challenging than intellectual schemata *about* the practice. (I'm glad to be able to put in something critical of Baxandall: he seems to me to be the most consistently praised and seldom critiqued of all art historians, and even though I usually find myself agreeing with the praise, I tend to wonder when someone seems so wholly without faults.)

Renaissance art is especially prone to the anxiety provoked by lack of engagement with studio production, because it is the exemplary moment for the exposition of so many skills. To take just a single example, but a pointed one: I don't know any art historian except Sam Edgerton who can actually construct the perspectives in paintings like the *Città ideali*. Damisch definitely could not; his analyses show that at every point. Calls for revisions of perspective are colored by that ignorance, which goes hand in hand with the assumption that the methods involved are, after all, matters of manual skill, and therefore ultimately uninteresting.

2. Then there is the realization, which we all share but often choose to ignore, that we really aren't as interesting or creative as the artists we study. We represent those artists, and their art, but we know we must be missing something. Leo Steinberg was excellent on this subject—I remember a pointed review he wrote of the psychoanalytic critic Robert Liebert, who had "shrunk" Michelangelo so that he could be understood.[11] In some fashion, we all need to imagine we have interpretive power over our subjects, who course actually outstrip us in imagination, skill, rhetorical power, and nearly every other conceivable category. (This is where writing, for me, would come back into the picture. What is writing in art history? Writing is really nothing less than what we have chosen to do with our lives: we all work our entire careers to produce writing in response to images. There doesn't need to be any other reason to think writing should be our pre-eminent concern: we should each work as hard as possible to produce the best possible writing.[12])

The Renaissance is a specialty, or a period, which shows our inadequacy in relation to artists very acutely. As Robert Zwijnenberg notes, Leonardo's practice, and his sense of the relations between part of that practice, are elusive. *Daunting* would be another word. I think a fairly high percentage of what we write, and the way we write it, can be laid at the door of an anxiety about the astonishing stature of the artists we study. We know, in some unpleasant, dim way, that we don't amount to much in relation to them, and therefore that we must be missing things, and I think we form our writing to cover that wound. We are hyper-articulate in relation to many of the artists we study: but is that appropriate when the artist isn't hyper-intellectual? In a studio art critique, when a student artist comes out with an elaborate speech about how her work is dependent on recent texts by Hélène Cixous, Alain Badiou, or Niklas Luhmann, an instructor's first reaction is likely to be: What truths about the art are these theories hiding? Or, in art historical terms: What are we managing to ignore by insisting that the objects we study are intellectual puzzles?[13]

3. Another reason we may want the art *not* to be understood is that we need to continue to own the work intellectually. Derrida's meditation on Meyer Schapiro is a great text in this regard: Derrida thinks that painting is a peculiar kind of gift, an unasked-for gift, and one that we can't ever repay.[14] That imbalance creates all sorts of desires, which play out in different professions: curators get to move paintings, art historians get to own their meanings, millionaires get to put them in their houses, conservationists get to alter them. As art historians, we can't relinquish our interpretive power by letting the art be understood once and for all. This is why it is relevant when Una Roman d'Elia and others mention *The Da Vinci Code*. That book claims to tell everything, in a way everyone can understand. Its electric effect on the non-academic public is exactly parallel to the astonishing effect of David Hockney's *Secret Knowledge*. At the NYU conference on *Secret Knowledge*, lines went halfway around Washington Square, and ninety seats were set aside for journalists.[15] That stupendous degree of interest came directly from the promise that untrained people could finally understand the old masters. And once again, I think this condition pertains more to the Renaissance than to other specialties. You—Renaissance specialists—work with a "lush historiography," in Adrian Randolph's phrase, and a tremendous mass of accumulated knowledge. It may not be greater than the

knowledge involved in some other specialties, and it is certainly not more arcane or difficult in any objective sense, but it occupies a privileged position in the structure of our understanding of Western art. That knowledge, concentrated in the Renaissance, is a stronghold of Westernness, and it is the property of Renaissance scholars.

4. And then there's the reason you articulate so accurately: the Renaissance needs to be a "refuge," a "place where beauty, meaning, and all the most rarefied qualities of the spirit still count." It needs to be embalmed, not only to support our idea of Western culture in general, but to support our ideas of particular nation-states. Most Western countries have a stake in the Renaissance—they invented it, or else they nurtured it, or nurtured its study, or developed its consequences. And I agree that Adorno is an apposite source here, because we—those of us who participate in contemporary culture, and identify ourselves with one of the nations that have a stake in the Renaissance—we need the Renaissance as an "antidote to modern life." In all this, the Renaissance is once again the exemplary period or specialty that bears the greatest burden.

Renaissance art historians may argue about what it is, exactly, that is being embalmed, but the main thing is that they are its custodians. I find the Assessments by Thomas Puttfarken, Ingrid Ciulisová, and Patricia Emison especially enlightening in that regard. A theme in this volume is the performative or "living" aspects of Renaissance art, which is proposed in different ways by Rebecca Zorach, Caroline van Eck, and Una Roman D'Elia. But no matter how it is described at any given time, the Renaissance needs to be cared for and preserved. For me, the conservatism of some Renaissance scholarship is not something that should be shaken out: conservatism shows something needs to be conserved; it is a sign of the heavy burden of the past. It's as if Renaissance scholars worked on Jupiter, and had to struggle to take even a single step in the oppressive gravity. (People who study contemporary art are sometimes like explorers on the Moon, happily bounding over the landscape.)

So, to return one last time to writing: there is more than a trace of Panofsky's Olympian calm in some Renaissance scholarship, more than a trace of the overwhelming scholarship of a Theodor Mommsen or the high games of an A.E. Houseman. There are tones and styles of Renaissance scholarship. I don't think we recognize these qualities in ourselves, but only in other people. It's a tricky subject, but there is gravitas, Victorian polish, Edwardian *preciosité*, emotional distance, a ponderous manner mingled with a refined delicacy (I always think of George Steiner in this regard), and many more. They are a loose but identifiable set. Few styles of scholarship should be thought of as belated, and none should be excised. When they appear in our writing, they show how much we need the Renaissance to remain where it is.[16]

That is why, even though I am extremely sympathetic to calls for new approaches (I am thinking of Robert Zwijnenberg's and Adrian Randolph's excellent Assessments, full of provocations and doubt), we also need to pay attention to what refuses to move. And it is why I think that Renaissance studies is symptomatic of something deep and pervasive in the discipline, and wholly appropriate for the *Art Seminar*.

Best,

Jim

29 August

Dear Jim,

That seems like a good place to end, yet I'm a little bothered by what you say, and feel as though I can't let it go entirely unchallenged. Not everything that "refuses to move" should be left in place. George Bush refuses to move, for example, and among some people his intransigence passes for integrity: a great deal—everything, in fact—depends on our being able to make the case that intransigence is *not* the same as integrity, that it is just a cheap substitute, a stand-in. Among the things that refuse to move we must distinguish clearly between those that should be left alone and those that must not be; once we have made that critical determination, we must be prepared to do the difficult work, which also means—in this case, I think, it *primarily* means—overcoming our *internal* resistances. While we should certainly listen to our internal resistances in the process of critical determination—we have to, if we're going to persuade ourselves we're doing the right thing—we must also decide which of those resistances are worth attending to and which should be rejected. We must, in other words, be critical of ourselves as well: the critical process must be made to work in both directions at once; only then, it seems to me, are we practicing history at the requisite level of intellectual sophistication and moral engagement. Above all, we mustn't go around moving things that are easy to move in order to compensate for our inability to move the really tough ones, then claim we've accomplished something important: it's then that our innovations become just so many tokens of our failure to innovate.

When you say that the rest of art history needs the Renaissance to "stay where it is", you seem to be agreeing with what I said in my last letter, yet you seem untroubled by what I think is a very big problem. You seem to be referring primarily to the literary qualities associated with the best Renaissance scholarship of the past: you present that tradition in optimal terms as constituting a kind of treasury of literary riches—of stylistic devices, but also subject positions and modes of engagement—upon which we are free to draw and that can serve to remind us, both of what once was and what may yet be possible. And so it is. Yet the fact that elements from older writers continue to turn up in today's writing can be taken in two ways: either as an indication of the richness of our intellectual heritage or as a sign of inertia, of our failure to have worked through that heritage completely. A skillful writer can deploy the kinds of literary touches you describe with great virtuosity, scattering them over his or her work like a great chef might season a dish. Yet isn't what distinguishes our pleasure in writing of this kind from the feeling that the author is simply retailing old-fashioned forms and attitudes the sense we have as we read that we're learning something even by the way references are deployed? In the hands of such a writer their juxtaposition may offer us fresh perspectives on the different traditions they come from, new insights into the history of the discipline: we don't just see a work of art or an issue in a new light, but we see different ways of seeing them in a new light. In other words, such references do significant work, the work of historical synthesis. All good writing could probably be said to do some kind of work; good historical writing does specifically historical work.

On the other hand, the old literary elements we position like precious *spolia* in our texts may function as fetishes, compensation for a lack of solid argument or sufficient empirical evidence. Insofar as it is an object in which significant psychic energy is invested, any fetish deserves the sympathetic regard of the historian—especially the art historian!—but a fetish is also a sign of failure, an object onto which psychic energy has been *displaced*. It is, ultimately, a stand-in for something else. I think art history is already much too fetishistic in the way it engages objects, too prone to devolve into a ritualized game of displacements, and thus into simple intellectual dishonesty and charlatanry, so I suppose I think we should try to avoid fetishism in our writing.

The necessity of distinguishing critically between good and bad—in art, in art-historical writing, in ourselves—prompts me to suggest my own variation on the metaphor that got such a work-out in the discussions at Cork, that of the baby and the bathwater: we must take care not to throw out the baby with the bathwater, but in the end we do have to throw out the bathwater.

Best,
Bob

30 August

Dear Bob,

What does it mean for the Renaissance to "stay where it is"? Not that it remains immobile. Rethinking the Renaissance is foundational to our perception of it *as* the Renaissance. Revisions aren't optional, they are constitutive. Writing, on the other hand, does remain obdurate as long as we're focusing on history.

For me the Renaissance is the hinge of our conception of Western art, and therefore also the hinge of our sense of art history's project and coherence. If I over-emphasize what is static, it's because I think the sheer weight of the old and the uninteresting needs to be taken as seriously as what can be moved. (As you say, it's tempting to move only what is easily moved: theories, which seem heavy, are actually the lightest things art history owns.)

I am very glad we produced this book: it is a wonderful mixture of unsolved problems, insoluble problems, problems that appear solved, and refusals to recognize problems—a telling mixture of weight and weightlessness.

Jim

Notes

1. Tsypkin, *Summer in Baden-Baden*, translated by Roger and Angela Keys, with an introduction by Susan Sontag (New York: New Directions, 2001).
2. Susan Sontag calls Coetzee's book a "fantasy" in her introduction. *Summer in Baden-Baden*, xv.
3. I discuss Dalí's book in the final chapter of *Why are Our Pictures Puzzles? On the Modern Origins of Pictorial Complexity* (New York: Routledge, 1999).
4. It is useful to distinguish three kinds of writing: art history, texts that are of use *for* art history (sources, contemporaneous criticism, archival materials), and texts that are of no use for art history. This *for/as* distinction is one I've pursued in several venues. In relation to Chinese art history: see the "Afterword" to *Discovering Chinese Painting: Dialogues With Art Historians*, edited by Jason Kuo, second edition (Dubuque, IO: Kendall/Hunt Publishing, 2006), 249–56. In relation to Didi-Huberman's work in particular: see "Über die Unmöglichkeit des *close reading*," in *Was aus dem Bild fällt: figuren des Details in Kunst und Literatur, Friedrich Teja Bach zum 60. Geburtstag*, edited by Edith Futcher, Stefan Neuner, Wolfram Pichler, and Ralph Ubl (Munich: Wilhelm Fink, 2007), 107–40. In relation to contemporary global art history and art criticism, in discussion with Fredric Jameson, Susan Buck-Morss, and others: see *Globalization and Art*, vol. 1 of the *Stone Summer Theory Institutes*, forthcoming.
5. Robert Williams and Christopher Wood, "A Newer Protagoras," *Art Bulletin* 88 (2006) 567–82.
6. All these questions of style and writing are explored in my *Our Beautiful, Dry, and Distant Texts: Art History as Writing*, paperback edition, with new preface (New York: Routledge, 2000 [1997]). I have experimented with writing that is not usable as art history, for example in a work in progress that is framed as a response to Roland Barthes's *Camera Lucida*, which is itself a book that is deliberately not ordinary expository prose, philosophy, or history. An excerpt is published as "Camera Dolorosa," *History of Photography* 31 no. 1 (2007): 22–30.
7. L. Syson and D. Thornton, *Objects of Virtue: Art In Renaissance Italy* (Los Angeles: Getty, 2001), 8.
8. *Photography Theory*, vol. 2 of *The Art Seminar* (New York: Routledge, 2006). See also the post-mortem, "Is Anyone Listening?" *Photofile* 80 (winter 2007): 80.
9. The only other Afterword that is co-written by the co-editors is in *States of Art Criticism*: it is an analysis of what it means when a field can't even agree on what its most basic concepts *are*, let along agree on what might be said *about* them. *States of Art Criticism*, edited by James Elkins and Michael Newman, vol. 4 of *The Art Seminar* (New York: Routledge, 2008).
10. The others: Art History versus Aesthetics, Is Art History Global?,

Photography Theory, States of Art Criticism, Landscape Theory, Re-Enchantment (New York: Routledge, 2005–2008).

11. Steinberg, "Shrinking Michelangelo," *New York Review of Books* (28 June, 1984), 41–45, discussed in my "The Failed and the Inadvertent: The Theory of the Unconscious in the History of Art" *International Journal of Psycho-Analysis* 75 part 1 (1994): 119–32.

12. I don't have anything to add to what I say in the Preface to the Routledge edition of *Our Beautiful, Dry, and Distant Texts: Art History as Writing* (New York: Routledge, 2000 [1997]).

13. The many ways in which art works are *not* like puzzles, and art history's aptitude for picturing art as puzzles, are the subjects of my *Why are Our Pictures Puzzles? On the Modern Origins of Pictorial Complexity* (New York: Routledge, 1999), which contains a section on the contemporary fascination with mirrors, doors, and other metaphors, which I think is anachronistic (pace Zwijnenberg's Assessment).

14. Derrida, "Restitutions de la vérité en pointure," in *La Vérité en peinture* (Paris, 1978), in English as *Truth in Painting*, translated by Geoffrey Bennington and Ian McLeod (Chicago: University of Chicago Press, 1987). An earlier translation of "Restitutions de la vérité en pointure" appeared in *Research in Phenomenology* VII (1978), 1–44. A different French version appeared as part of "Martin Heidegger et les souliers de Van Gogh," *Macula* 3/4 (1978), pp. 3–47; and an earlier translation, now often ignored, is "Restitutions of Truth to Size, *De la vérité en pointure*," translated by J. P. Leavey, Jr., *Research in Phenomenology* 8 (1978): 14.

15. The conference was December 1–2, 2001. The book is Hockney and Charles Falco, *Secret Knowledge: Rediscovering the Lost Techniques of the Old Masters* (London: Thames and Hudson, 2006 [2001]). Several people who attended the conference, especially Falco and David Stork, have continued to research and lecture on the subject. One of my reviews is in *Circa* 99 (spring 2002): 38–39, online at recirca.com/backissues/c99/elkins.shtml; my original conference paper and papers by some others are online at http://webexhibits.org/hockneyoptics/post/elkins.html.

16. *Our Beautiful, Dry, and Distant Texts* is an exploration of this theme.

NOTES ON CONTRIBUTORS

Jan von Bonsdorff is Professor in the Department of Art History at Uppsala University. His publications include *Kunstproduktion und Kunstverbreitung im Ostseeraum des Spätmittelalters* (Helsinki, 1993); "Art Transfer in the Baltic Sea Area", *Künstlerischer Austausch/ Artistic Exchange* (Proceedings of the XXVIIIth International Congress of the History of Art, Berlin, July 15–21, 1992 [vol. 2], Berlin 1993, 39–50); "Die Rolle Münchens für skandinavische Malerinnen und Maler am Ende des 19. Jahrhunderts? ein Blick von außen", *Nationale Identitäten/ Internationale Avantgarden zeitenblicke* 5:2, 2006 (http:// www.zeitenblicke.de/2006/2/Bonsdorff); and "Innovation och individuation: Några betraktelser över senmedeltida konstnärer i Nordeuropa", *Kunst og kultur* 2007:1, 92–101. (Department of Art History, Box 630, SE-751 26 Uppsala, Sweden; jan.von.bonsdorff@konstvet.uu.se)

Stephen J. Campbell is Professor and Chair of History of Art at The Johns Hopkins University. He is the author of *The Cabinet of Eros: Renaissance Mythological Painting and the Studiolo of Isabella d'Este* (Yale, 2006) and *Cosmè Tura of Ferrara. Style, Politics and the Renaissance City 1450–1495* (Yale, 1997), as well as articles on Michelangelo, Mantegna, Giorgione, Bronzino and the Carracci. He is also the editor of *Artists at Court. Image Making and Identity in Europe 1300–1550* (Boston, Isabella Stewart Gardner Museum, 2005) and, with Stephen J. Milner, of *Artistic Exchange and Cultural Translation in the Italian Renaissance* (Cambridge, 2004).

Ingrid Ciulisová works at the Institute of Art History of the Slovak Academy of Sciences in Bratislava. Her recent publications include *Paintings of the 16th Century Netherlandish Masters. Slovak Art Collections* (Bratislava, 2006); *Art Collecting of Central-European Aristocracy in Nineteenth Century: The Case of Count Pálffy* in *Journal of the History of Collections*, Vol. 18 (2006), no. 2, 201–209 and "Mestá, umenie a idey Erazma Rotterdamskeho (Cities, art and the ideas of Erasmus of Rotterdam)" in *Problémy dejín výtvarného umenia Slovenska*. Edited by Ján Bakoš. (Bratislava 2002) 120–144, 263–267. She was awarded a Fellowship of the American Academy in Rome for the academic year 2007/2008. (Michalská 06, SR-811 01 Bratislava, Slovak Republic, dejuciul@savba.sk).

Michael Cole is Associate Professor of the History of Art at the University of Pennsylvania. He is the author of *Cellini and the Principles of Sculpture* (Cambridge and New York, 2002) and the editor of *The Early Modern Painter-Etcher* (University Park, 2006), the catalogue to an exhibition he co-curated with Madeleine Viljoen. With Mary Pardo, he edited *Inventions of the Studio, Renaissance to Romanticism* (Chapel Hill, 2004), and with Rebecca Zorach, *Idols in the Age of Art: Objects and Devotions in the Early Modern World* (London, in press). Currently he is completing a book on sculpture and architecture in early modern Florence.

Caroline van Eck is Professor of Architectural History and Theory at the University of Leiden, where she directs a VICI program on art, agency and living presence in the Italian Renaissance, funded by the Dutch Foundation for Scientific Research (NWO). Recent publications include *Dealing with the Visual. Aesthetics, Art History and Visual Culture* (Aldershot: Ashgate, 2005), edited together with Edward Winters, and *Classical Rhetoric and the Arts in Early Modern Europe* (Cambridge and New York: Cambridge University Press, 2007).

Una Roman D'Elia is Assistant Professor in the Department of Art at Queen's University, Kingston, Ontario. Her publications include *The Poetics of Titian's Religious Paintings* (Cambridge, 2005); "Tintoretto, Aretino, and the Speed of Creation," *Word & Image* 20 (2004): 206–18; "The Decorum of a Defecating Dog," *Print*

Quarterly 22 (2005): 119–32; "Drawing Christ's Blood: Michelangelo, Vittoria Colonna, and the Aesthetics of Reform," *Renaissance Quarterly* 59 (2006): 90–129; and "Niccolò Liburnio on the Boundaries of Portraiture in the Early Cinquecento," *The Sixteenth Century Journal* 37 (2006): 323–50. (Department of Art, Ontario Hall, Queen's University, Kingston, Ontario K7L 3N6, Canada; deliau@post.queensu.ca)

James Elkins teaches at the School of the Art Institute of Chicago. His most recent books are *On The Strange Place of Religion in Contemporary Art* (New York, 2004), *Master Narratives and Their Discontents* (New York, 2005), and *Visual Practices Across the University* (ed.) (Munich: Wilhelm Fink, 2007).

Frédéric Elsig works at the Department of Art History at the University of Geneva. His publications include *La Renaissance en Savoie* (Geneva, 2002); *Painting in France in the 15th century* (Milan, 2004); *Jheronimus Bosch: la question de la chronologie* (Geneva, 2004); *La Naissance des genres* (Paris, 2005). (Route de Malagnou 36A, 1208 Geneva, Switzerland; elsig.f@bluewin.ch)

Patricia Emison, Professor of Art History at the University of New Hampshire, has recently published *The Simple Art: Printed Works on Paper in an Age of Magnificence* (Durham, NH, 2006); "The Arts of Replication", *Renaissance Florence: A Social History*, edited by John Paoletti and Roger Crum (Cambridge, 2006) 431–53, 606–13; "Raphael's Multiples", *The Cambridge Companion to Raphael*, edited by Marcia Hall (Cambridge, 2005) 185–206; "Dürer's *Rider*", *Renaissance Studies* 19 (2005) 511–22; "Rembrandt's Allegory of the Phoenix", *Zeitschrift fur Kunstgeschichte* 68 (2005) 554–56; and *Creating the "Divine" Artist from Dante to Michelangelo* (Leiden, 2004). Forthcoming is *The Shaping of Art History: Meditations on a Discipline* (University Park, 2008). (Dept. of Art and Art History, University of New Hampshire, Durham NH 03824, USA; patricia.emison@unh.edu).

Marzia Faietti directs the Gabinetto Disegni e Stampe of the Uffizi and teaches the history of graphic arts at the University of Bologna. Her publications include *Bologna e l'Umanesimo 1490–1510; Un siècle de dessin à Bologne 1480–1580* (Bologna, Vienna 1988); *Amico*

Aspertini (Modena, 1995); *I grandi disegni italiani della Pinacoteca Nazionale di Bologna* (Milano, 2002); and "Amico's friends: Aspertini and the Confraternita del Buon Gesù in Bologna" in *Drawing Relationships in Northern Italian Renaissance Art Patronage and Theories of Invention*, edited by Giancarla Periti (London, 2004), 51–74. (Gabinetto Disegni e Stampe degli Uffizi via della Ninna 5, 50122 Firenze, Italia; faietti@polomuseale.firenze.it)

Claire Farago is Professor of Renaissance Art, Theory, and Criticism at the University of Colorado at Boulder. Her publications include *Leonardo da Vinci's Paragone: A Critical Interpretation* (Leiden-Cologne-Sydney, 1992); *Reframing the Renaissance: Visual Culture in Europe and Latin America 1450 to 1650* (London-New Haven, 1995); *Compelling Visuality: The Work of Art in and out of History*, co-edited with Robert Zwijnenberg (Minneapolis, 2003); *Grasping the World: The Idea of the Museum*, co-edited with Donald Preziosi (London, 2004); *Transforming Images: New Mexican Santos in-between Worlds* (University Park, Pennsylvania, 2006), co-authored with Donna Pierce and additional contributors; and *Leonardo da Vinci and the Ethics of Style* (Manchester, UK, 2008). (Department of Art and Art History, University of Colorado. UCB 318, Boulder, CO 80309, USA; farago@colorado.edu)

Charlotte M. Houghton is Associate Professor of early modern art ("Northern Renaissance and Baroque" in course listings) at The Pennsylvania State University. She has been the recipient of a Fulbright Fellowship to Belgium, a Roy Buck Award for best peer-reviewed publication in her college, and Penn State's university-wide Fellowship for Excellence in Teaching. Her publications include "This Was Tomorrow: Pieter Aertsen's *Meat Stall* as Contemporary Art," *Art Bulletin*, 86, no. 2 (2004), 276–299, and "A Topical Reference to Urban Controversy in Pieter Aertsen's 'Meat Stall,' " *Burlington Magazine*, 143, no. 1176 (2001), 158–60. Her current project investigates playfulness in Netherlandish art.

Elizabeth Alice Honig is Associate Professor of the History of Art at the University of California, Berkeley. She is the author of *Painting and the Market in Early Modern Antwerp* (Yale, 1998). Her articles on Dutch, Flemish, and British art have been published in *Art Bulletin*,

RES, the *Nederlands Kunsthistorisch Jaarboek*, the *Yale Journal of Criticism*, and other journals and collections. (416 Doe Library, Berkeley CA, 94720–6020; eahonig@berkeley.edu)

Fredrika Jacobs is Professor of Art History at Virginia Commonwealth University. Her publications include *Defining the Renaissance Virtuosa: Women Artists and the Language of Art History and Criticism* (Cambridge, 1997) and *The Living Image in the Renaissance* (Cambridge, 2005). She has published in *The Art Bulletin, Renaissance Quarterly, Artibus et historiae* and *Word & Image* as well as contributed essays to various volumes including *Reading Vasari*, ed. A. Barriault and A. Ladis (Athens, GA., 2005) *Leonardo and the Ethics of Style*, ed. C. Farago (forth-coming Manchester, 2008) and *The History of Sexuality: The Renaissance*, ed. B. Talvacchia (forthcoming London, 2009). (Dept. of Art History, Box 843046, Virginia Commonwealth University, Richmond, VA 23284; fjacobs@vcu.edu).

Alice Jarrard is an independent scholar who teaches at Harvard Extension School and the Harvard Graduate School of Design. Besides her book, *Architecture as Performance in Seventeenth-century Europe* (Cambridge, 2003), recent publications include "Perspectives on Piranesi and Theater," in *Piranesi as Designer*, ed. Sarah Lawrence and John Wilton-Ely (New York, 2008). Her articles explore the practices of artists including Bernini and Pietro da Cortona, as well as the effects of ritual, notably in "The Escalation of Ceremony and Ducal Staircases in Italy, 1560–1680," *Annali di architettura* 8 (1996): 159–178. She is completing a book, *Baroque Theater: Architecture and the Technology of Marvel*. (ajarrard@gmail.com)

Ethan Matt Kavaler works at the Graduate Department of the History of Art at the University of Toronto. His publications include *Pieter Bruegel, Parables of Order and Enterprise* (Cambridge, 1999) and numerous articles on the art and architecture of the Northern Renaissance. He is now completing a book on Gothic architecture at the turn of the sixteenth century. (Dept. of Art, 100 St. George Street, Toronto Ontario M5S 3G3, Canada; matt.kavaler@ utoronto.ca)

Lubomír Konečný is Director of the Institute of Art History,

Academy of Sciences of the Czech Republic, and Professor at the Institute for Art History at Charles University in Prague. In addition to numerous articles on Renaissance and Baroque art and architecture, iconography, and on the history and theory of art history, he recently published two books: *Between Text and Image: Miscellaneous Studies on the History of Emblematics* (Prague, 2002), and *Beyond the Mountains You Will Find a Valley: A Study of the Iconography of the Flight into Egypt in the Art of the Late Middle-Ages and the Early Renaissance* (Prague, 2005). (Institute of Art History, ASCR, Husova 4, CZ-110 00 Praha, Czech Republic; konecny@udu.cas.cz).

Alessandro Nova is Co-Director of the Kunsthistorisches Institut in Florence (Max-Planck-Institut). He was previously Assistant Professor of Art History at Stanford and Professor of Italian Renaissance Art at the Goethe-Universität, Frankfurt am Main. He has published extensively in the most important international art historical journals. His books include *The Artistic Patronage of Pope Julius III (1550–1555). Profane Imagery and Buildings for the De Monte Family in Rome* (New York and London, 1988), *Girolamo Romanino* (Turin, 1996), *Imagination und Wirklichkeit. Zum Verhältnis von mentalen und realen Bildern in der Kunst der frühen Neuzeit*, ed. with Klaus Krüger (Mainz, 2000), *Benvenuto Cellini. Kunst und Kunsttheorie im 16. Jahrhundert*, ed. with Anna Schreurs (Cologne, Weimar and Vienna 2003), *Il libro del vento: rappresentare l'invisibile* (Milan, 2007) also published as *Das Buch des Windes. Das Unsichtbare sichtbar machen* (Berlin, 2007). (Kunsthistorisches Institut in Florenz, via Giuseppe Giusti 44, I-50121 Firenze, Italy; nova@khi.fi.it)

Jeanette Favrot Peterson is an Associate Professor at the University of California, Santa Barbara, where she teaches Precolumbian and Colonial American art. Her recent publications include "Crafting the Self: Identity and the Mimetic Tradition in the *Florentine Codex*", in *Sahagún at 500*, edited by John F. Schwaller (Berkeley 2003), 223–53; "Creating the Virgin of Guadalupe: The Cloth, Artist and Sources in 16th- century New Spain" (*The Americas*, 2005) 571–610; "The Reproducibility of the Sacred: Simulacra of the Virgin of Guadalupe", in *Exploring New World Imagery*, edited by Donna Pierce (Denver, 2005) 41–78; and "Canonizing a Cult", in *Religion in New*

Spain, edited by Susan Schroeder and Stafford Poole (New Mexico, 2007), 125–156. (PO Box 983, Rancho Santa Fe, California; jeanette@arthistory.ucsb.edu)

Lisa Pon is Assistant Professor of Art History at Southern Methodist University, and exhibition reviews editor of *SHARP News*. She is co-editor of special issues of *Word & Image*" (with Graham Larkin), "Printing Matters: The Materiality of Print in Early Modern Europe," vol. 17 (January-June 2001); and *Miscellanea Marciana* (with Craig Kallendorf and Marino Zorzi), "Il Libro Veneziano/The Books of Venice," forthcoming. Her other publications include *Raphael, Dürer, and Marcantonio Raimondi: Copying and the Italian Renaissance Print* (London and New Haven, 2004); "Paint/Print/Public," in *Making Things Public: Atmospheres of Democracy*, edited by Peter Weibel and Bruno Latour (Cambridge, MA, 2005), 686–93; and essays and reviews in *Art Bulletin, Sixteenth Century Journal*, and the *Journal of the Warburg and Courtauld Institutes*. (SMU Meadows School of the Arts, PO Box 750356, Dallas, TX 75275 USA; lpon@smu.edu)

Thomas Puttfarken was Professor and Head of the Department of Art History and Theory at the University of Essex until his untimely death on 5 October 2006. His publications include *Roger de Piles' Theory of Art* (London, 1986); *The Discovery of Pictorial Composition: Theories of Visual Order in Painting, 1400–1800* (London, 2000) and *Titian and Tragic Painting: Aristotle's "Poetics" and the Rise of the Modern Artist* (London, 2005). At the time of his death he was directing a research project, funded by the Arts and Humanities Research Council, on "The Moral Nature of the Image in the Renaissance".

Adrian W. B. Randolph is Leon E. Williams Professor of Art History and Director of the Leslie Center for the Humanities at Dartmouth College. His publications include *Engaging Symbols: Gender, Politics, and Public Art in Fifteenth-Century Florence* (New Haven and London, 2002); "The Bust's Gesture," in *Kopf—Bild: Die Büste in Mittelalter und Früher Neuzeit*, edited by Jeanette Kohl and Rebecca Müller (Munich and Berlin, forthcoming); "Republican

Florence, 1400–1434," in *Renaissance Florence*, edited by Francis Ames-Lewis for the series *Artistic Centers of the Renaissance* (Cambridge and New York, forthcoming); "Renaissance Genderscapes," in *Attending to Early Modern Women: Structures and Subjectivities*, edited by Joan Hartman and Adele Seeff (Newark and London, 2006), 21–49; "Gendering the Period Eye: *deschi da parto* and Renaissance Visual Culture," *Art History* 27, no. 4 (2005), 538–62; and "Der homosoziale Blick in der Renaissance: Kunst, Geschlecht, Macht," in *Männlichkeit im Blick: Visuelle Inszenierungen in der Kunst seit der Frühen Neuzeit*, edited by Mechtild Fend and Marianne Koos (Cologne and Weimar, 2004), 35–52. He is also co-editor, with Mark J. Williams, of the book series *Interfaces: Studies in Visual Culture*, published by UPNE (6033 Dartmouth College, Hanover, NH 03755 USA; awbr@dartmouth.edu)

Maria Ruvoldt is Assistant Professor in the Department of Art History and Music at Fordham University. Her publications include *The Italian Renaissance Imagery of Inspiration: Metaphors of Sex, Sleep, and Dreams* (Cambridge, 2004); "Michelangelo's Dream," *Art Bulletin* 85 (2003), 86–113; and "Sacred to Secular, East to West: The Renaissance *Studiolo* and Strategies of Display," *Renaissance Studies* 20 (2006), 640–657.

Pamela H. Smith is Professor of History at Columbia University and the author of *The Business of Alchemy: Science and Culture in the Holy Roman Empire* (Princeton 1994) and *The Body of the Artisan: Art and Experience in the Scientific Revolution* (Chicago 2004). She co-edited with Paula Findlen *Merchants and Marvels: Commerce, Science, and Art in Early Modern Europe* (Routledge 2002). In her present research, she attempts to reconstruct the vernacular knowledge of early modern European metalworkers from a variety of disciplinary perspectives. (Department of History, Columbia University, MC 2516, 1180 Amsterdam Ave., New York, NY 10027; ps2270@columbia.edu)

Robert Williams is Professor of the History of Art at the University of California, Santa Barbara. He is the author of *Art, Theory, and Culture in Sixteenth-Century Italy: From Techne to Metatechne*

(Cambridge, 1997) and *Art Theory: An Historical Introduction* (Blackwell, 2004). Together with Thomas Frangenberg (University of Leicester) he has translated Francesco Bocchi's *Le Bellezze della città di Fiorenza* (*The Beauties of the City of Florence: A Guidebook of 1591*; Harvey Miller, 2006) and edited the volume *The Beholder: The Experience of Art in Early Modern Europe* (Ashgate, 2006). His recent articles include "The Artist as Worker in Sixteenth-Century Italy" in *Taddeo and Federico Zuccaro: Artist-Brothers in Renaissance Rome* (Julian Brooks. ed., Getty Museum, 2007). (Dept. of the History of Art & Architecture, University of California, Santa Barbara, Santa Barbara, CA 93109; robertw@arthistory.ucsb.edu).

Joanna Woods-Marsden got her B.A. and M.A from Trinity College, Dublin University, and her Ph.D from Harvard University. After working at the National Gallery of Canada and teaching at the University of British Columbia, she joined the faculty at UCLA in 1984, where she is Professor of Italian Renaissance art. Her research interests include the social context for and the function of art, as well as issues of identity in portraiture; *Renaissance Self-Portraiture: The Visual Construction of Identity and the Social Status of the Artist* was published by Yale in 1998. Her current book project also involves portraiture: *The Visual Rhetoric of Male Power and Female Beauty: Gendered Identity in Titian's Court Portraits*. She has long focused on feminist critical issues, and published "Portrait of the Lady, 1430–1520" in the exhibition catalog *Virtue and Beauty*, National Gallery of Art, 2001. She has also published widely on issues of patronage, court art and artists (*The Gonzaga of Mantua and Pisanello's Arthurian Frescoes*, Princeton, 1988, and many articles).

Rebecca Zorach is Associate Professor of Art History at the University of Chicago. Her publications include *Blood, Milk, Ink, Gold: Abundance and Excess in the French Renaissance* (Chicago, 2005) and "Desiring Things," Art History v. 24, no. 2 (April 2001), 195–212. Forthcoming work includes an essay on Louis XIV and the letter of the King of Siam. (Department of Art History, 5540 S. Greenwood Ave., Chicago, IL 60637; rezorach@uchicago.edu)

Robert Zwijnenberg is Professor of art history in relation to the development of science and technology at the Universities of Leiden and Maastricht. He is the author of *The Writings and Drawings of Leonardo da Vinci. Order and Chaos in Early Modern Thought* (Cambridge University Press, 1999), contributing co-editor (with Claire Farago) of *Compelling Visuality. Works of art in and out history* (University of Minnesota Press, 2003), and contributing co-editor (with Florike Egmond) of *Bodily Extremities. Preoccupations with the Human Body in Early Modern European Culture* (Ashgate Press, 2003). (R.Zwijnenberg@let.leidenuniv.nl).

Volume 5 in The Art Seminar series, *Renaissance Theory* presents an animated conversation among art historians about the optimal ways of conceptualizing Renaissance art, and the links between Renaissance art and contemporary art and theory. This is the first discussion of its kind, involving not only questions within Renaissance scholarship, but issues of concern to art historians and critics in all fields. Organized as a virtual roundtable discussion, the contributors discuss rifts and disagreements about how to understand the Renaissance and debate the principal texts and authors of the last 30 years who have sought to reconceptualize the period. They then turn to the issue of the relation between modern art and the Renaissance: why do modern art historians and critics so seldom refer to the Renaissance? Is the Renaissance our indispensable heritage, or are we cut off from it by the revolution of modernism?

The volume includes an introduction by Rebecca Zorach and two final, synoptic essays, as well as contributions from some of the most prominent thinkers on Renaissance art, including Stephen J. Campbell, Michael Cole, Frederika Jacobs, Claire Farago, and Ethan Matt Kavaler.

JAMES ELKINS is E.C. Chadbourne Chair in the Department of Art History, Theory, and Criticism at the School of the Art Institute of Chicago, and Head of History of Art at the University College Cork, Ireland. His many books include *Pictures and Tears*, *How to Use Your Eyes*, and *What Painting Is*, all published by Routledge.

ROBERT WILLIAMS is Professor of Art History at the University of California, Santa Barbara. His fields of specialty are Italian Renaissance art and the history of art theory. He is the author of *Art, Theory, and Culture in Sixteenth-Century Italy* (Cambridge, 1997) and *Art Theor___ ___ ___ ___al Introduction* (Blackwell, 2004).

THE AR___
Volume Fi___

Cover design: ___
Cover image: ___

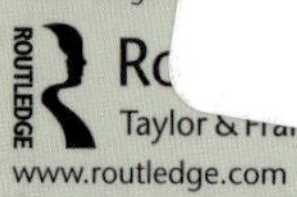

9780415960465

76523813–34

Taylor & Fra___
www.routledge.com